LATTER-DAY
Commentary
ON THE BOOK OF MORMON

compiled by

K. DOUGLAS BASSETT

Covenant Communications, Inc.

Published by Covenant Communications, Inc.
American Fork, Utah

Printed in the United States of America
First Printing: August 1999

06 05 04 03 02 01 00   10 9 8 7 6 5 4

ISBN 1-57734-534-7

Introduction

This Book of Mormon commentary has come about more by accident than by design on my part. Let me explain this confession.

As a missionary in England in 1971, I discovered the power of the Book of Mormon in my own life. I began saving and filing any supplementary materials I could get on the Book of Mormon. As the years passed, this resource material increased in volume and proved very helpful to me when I later became a full-time seminary teacher. I studied talks by the Brethren and read commentaries. Then I edited the quotes down to a useable format for my teaching. Rather than file these materials by topic, I placed them under the chapters and verses in the Book of Mormon where they most applied.

In 1989 I began teaching Book of Mormon at Brigham Young University. At first it was a little frustrating because I seemed to be spending so much of my time responding to the requests of students for copies of the quotes I was using in class. After a few weeks of this, I promised to give them a handout each class period with all the quotes that I would be using in our study for that day. This continued over the course of the six years I taught at BYU.

When I went back into the seminary classroom, I found that using the quotes really helped. I have continued using this same basic format for the past three years at the Orem Institute of Religion, near Utah Valley State College. Each summer for the past 10 years, I have sat down at my computer and typed all the quotes that I had found that could be helpful to my students. While this has been a wonderful help in the classroom, it has turned into something I could not control outside of the classroom. I have received literally hundreds of calls and letters from all over the world requesting my research. I am honored that so many people have requested it; however, I was simply not in a position to serve them as I would have liked. It is for this reason that I handed it over to the good people at Covenant.

The format of the text is simple. Like all Book of Mormon commentaries, it travels chronologically through the text. I have tried to stay with the Brethren on all points of doctrine. In addition, I include the insights of scholars to illustrate doctrinal background topics, or to support the doctrinal ideas previously stated by the Brethren. It is my responsibility as a teacher to quote the Brethren regarding the doctrines, and when I depart from that I may be treading on ground where I have no authority.

The power of this commentary comes from the words of the prophets. I have found in my teaching that if I stay with the Brethren in explaining the scriptures, I can invite the Spirit into the classroom and gain the trust of my students to a greater degree. I hope that this commentary reflects such an approach.

I have compiled the quotes and cross references in an effort to support both Gospel teachers and serious students in their studies. If this book is used in any way to replace or 'short-cut' the Book of Mormon, it is being used incorrectly. Read the Book of Mormon first, then use this commentary only to enhance the study of the scriptural text.

Because I do not comment directly in this book, the reader may have questions about certain items in the commentary that reflect my classroom methods. Feel free to contact me personally for any explanation or insights I can share. I accept full responsibility for any mistakes in the text.

I love the Book of Mormon. I know the text is of divine authenticity. My desire is that this commentary may be of help to those who seriously want to increase their understanding of the truths of the Book of Mormon.

1 Nephi 1~2

"I read the Book of Mormon as a young man and fell in love with Nephi more than any other character in profane or sacred history that I have ever read, except the Savior of the world. No other individual has made such a strong impression upon me as did Nephi. He has been one of the guiding stars in my life."

Heber J. Grant (Improvement Era, Sept. 1941, p. 524)

"Young men who hold the priesthood of Aaron, may I offer an 'I will' for your serious consideration? It is *I will* become very well acquainted with the noble prophet Nephi through studying, pondering, and feasting upon the first two books of the Book of Mormon. My young friends, I promise that when you come to really know Nephi, you will be so impressed with his determination, courage, and desire to be obedient to the 'things the Lord commands' that you will have a strong desire to incorporate his attributes into your own lives. Then when you are tempted by the adversary, as you may be nearly every day, to deviate from the counsel of the prophets, the wishes of your parents, or what 'the Lord commands,' you can immediately have the words of stalwart Nephi automatically come to your mind: 'I will go and do the things which the Lord hath commanded' (1 Ne. 3:7). And when someone with whom you associate suggests you participate in something that is not as 'the Lord commands,' you can think of the courageous plea Nephi made to his elder brothers: 'Let us be faithful in keeping the commandments of the Lord' (v. 16). I am aware of a group of courageous young men who followed the example of Nephi. After winning a baseball state championship for their age group, their team, made up mostly of Aaronic Priesthood holders, was invited to represent their state in a tournament to be held in a distant location. Upon arriving at the tournament site, they learned that some of the games were scheduled to be played on the Sabbath day. Each of these young men had to make a difficult personal decision: would he support the team, including several non-member team members; or if scheduled on Sunday, would he follow what 'the Lord commands' in keeping the Sabbath day holy? Their honoring the Sabbath day could mean the team would forfeit their chances of winning the tournament. One by one they quietly approached the coaches, and following the example of Nephi, they independently chose to decline participation on the Sabbath day. . . . I have had occasion to closely follow these young men over the years. They have continued to pattern their lives after the sterling example of Nephi. They have gone on missions; and they continue to strive to do and say what the Lord has commanded."

H. David Burton (Ensign, Nov. 1995, p. 44)

1 Ne. 1:1

GOODLY PARENTS
(Ancient American Setting of the Book of Mormon, pp. 52-53; *Doctrinal Commentary on the Book of Mormon*, Millet & McConkie, 1:19; 2:96; Enos 1:1)

"After all, to do well those things which God ordained to be the common lot of all man-kind, is the truest greatness. To be a successful father or a successful mother is greater than to be a successful general or a successful statesman. One is universal and eternal greatness, the other is ephemeral. . . . Let us not be trying to substitute an artificial life for the true one."

Joseph F. Smith (Gospel Doctrine, pp. 285-286)

"The newspapers give front page to ever increasing acts of violence, and magazines devote pages to the growing menace. . . . Can it be arrested? . . . . The answer is yes . . . The Lord has given us a plan so simple, so costless. It requires a change of attitudes and a transformation of lives. But the answer has always been here though ignored by the masses because it requires that sacrifice and dedication which men are reluctant to give . . . . But the Lord . . . gives promise to return the world to sane living, to true family life, to family interdependence. It is to return the father to his rightful place at the head of the family, to bring mother home from social life and employment, the children from near total fun and frolic. . . . An early American prophet said: [1 Nephi 1:1]."

Spencer W. Kimball (Conference Report, Apr. 1965, pp. 60-61)

1 Ne. 1:2

WHY NOT HEBREW?
(1 Ne. 3:19; Morm. 9:32-34; Mosiah 1:4; *Lehi in the Desert*, Nibley, pp. 13, 26; *Companion to Your Study of the Book of Mormon*, Ludlow, p. 173; refer to 1 Ne. 3:19)

". . . reformed Egyptian was a type of shorthand. . . . It must have required less space to write reformed Egyptian than to write Hebrew. . . . The Hebrew language is very compact when compared to English and many other western languages. A typical English sentence of fifteen words will often translate into seven to ten Hebrew words."

Book of Mormon 121-122 Student Manual, p. 4

"Hebrew is a completely alphabetic language, whereas in Egyptian a symbol can represent an entire concept."

R. Millet & J. F. McConkie (Doctrinal Commentary on the Book of Mormon, 1:20)

"We now realize that the ancient Jews could write quickly and boldly, in an artistic flowing hand, with the loving penmanship of those who enjoy writing. And the Nephites got rid of this to learn in its place the most awkward, difficult, and impractical system of writing ever devised by man! *Why all the trouble? Simply to save space. What space? Space on valuable plates.* . . . People who were not crowded for space would not have continued to write Hebrew in the difficult Egyptian characters for hundreds of years, when all the time they might just as well have been writing in the twenty-two simple and practical characters of the Hebrew alphabet."

Hugh Nibley (Lehi in the Desert, p. 16)

1 Ne. 1:1-3   **EGYPTIAN COLOPHON**
(1 Ne. 22:30-31; Jacob 1:2; 7:27; Jarom 1-2; Omni 1:3-4; Words of Mormon 9; Mosiah 1:4; 9:1; Hel. 16:25; *Since Cumorah*, Nibley, pp. 170-171, *Rediscovering the Book of Mormon*, ed. by Sorenson and Thorne, pp. 32-37; *Lehi in the Desert*, Nibley, pp. 17-18)

1 Ne. 1:4   **IT CAME TO PASS**
(The Messiah in Ancient America, Warren & Ferguson, pp. 62-64; *Ensign*, Dec. 1992, p. 29)

"Instead of punctuation the original manuscript of the Book of Mormon divides up its phrases by introducing each by an 'and,' 'behold,' 'now,' or 'It came to pass.' Simply outrageous—as English historical texts. . . . Dramatic texts are held together by the constant repetition of . . . 'It came to pass.' In Egyptian these expressions were not merely adornments, . . . they are a grammatical necessity and may not be omitted."

Hugh Nibley (Since Cumorah, p. 169)

1 Ne. 1:4   **THE REIGN OF ZEDEKIAH**
(2 Kings 24-25; 2 Chron. 36; Josephus, pp. 216-220; *Companion to Your Study of the Book of Mormon*, Ludlow, pp. 62-63, 90-91; *It Begins With a Family*, Deseret, pp. 17-21; *The Messiah in Ancient America*, Warren & Ferguson, pp. 51-52)

1 Ne. 1:4   **LEHI DWELT AT JERUSALEM**
(Alma 10:3; Alma 7:10; *Lehi in the Desert*, Nibley, pp. 4-6; *An Approach to the Book of Mormon*, Nibley, 1957 edition, pp. 85-86; *Ensign*, Aug. 1984, pp. 51-52)

"Lehi and his family were living *at* Jerusalem. (See 1 Ne. 1:4,7 and 2 Ne. 25:6). The preposition 'at' in this case could mean on, in, within, close by, or near. Lehi could have lived several miles away and still lived at Jerusalem. It is recorded at least 33 times throughout the Book of Mormon that Lehi and Nephi went out from "the land of Jerusalem." Any satellite towns or villages that surrounded larger population or political centers were regarded in ancient times as belonging to those larger centers. That Lehi and his family lived outside of Jerusalem proper is also evidenced in the account of the sons' attempt to obtain the plates with their abandoned wealth: 'We went down to the land of our inheritance, and we did gather together our gold, and our silver, and our precious things. And after we gathered these things together, we went up again unto the house of Laban' (1 Ne. 3:22-23)."

Kelly Ogden (Studies in Scripture, ed by K. Jackson, 7:19-20)

"Lehi was of the house of Joseph through his son Manasseh (Alma 10:3). The land apportioned by the prophet Joshua to the sons of Joseph (Manasseh and Ephraim) was north of Jerusalem and south of the Sea of Galilee in the area generally known as Samaria at the time of Christ. . . . [Lehi] was also a wealthy man. He may have had property in Jerusalem (see 1 Nephi 1:4), but he definitely owned some outside of Jerusalem in the land of his inheritance (1 Nephi 3:16). . . . When his four sons collected their father's gold, silver, and precious things in an attempt to purchase the plates of brass from Laban, they got it outside of Jerusalem (1 Nephi 3:16, 25)."

Donl Peterson (First Nephi, The Doctrinal Foundation, BYU Religious Studies Center, p. 56)

1 Ne. 1:4   **MANY PROPHETS**
(First Nephi, The Doctrinal Foundation, BYU Religious Studies Center, pp. 37-38)

1 Ne. 1:6   **PILLAR OF FIRE**
(Isa. 33:14; JS-H 1:16; JST Ex. 3:2; Ezek. 1:4; *Teachings of the Prophet Joseph Smith*, pp. 325, 347; *First Nephi, The Doctrinal Foundation*, BYU Religious Studies Center, p. 39; *Doctrinal Commentary on the Book of Mormon*, Millet and McConkie, 1:25-26)

1 Ne. 1:7   **OVERCOME BY THE SPIRIT**
(D&C 324-325 Student Manual, pp. 158-159; JS-H 1:20; 1 Ne. 17:47; 19:20; Alma 18:42; 19:6,13-17; 22:18; 27:17-19; Dan. 10:8; refer to Alma 18:42)

1 Ne. 1:8   **HEAVENLY COUNCIL**
                     (*Since Cumorah*, Nibley, pp. 212-213; *First Nephi, The Doctrinal Foundation*,
                     BYU Religious Studies Center, pp.39-41)

1 Ne. 1:9   **HE SAW ONE**
                     (*Conference Report*, Oct. 1970, p. 28)

1 Ne. 1:18   **LEHI THE MISSIONARY**
                     (Jer. 26:20-24; 2 Chron. 36:15-16)

"Only a few years earlier, for example, the prophet Urijah had been persecuted, had fled to Egypt, was extradited, convicted, and ignominiously executed for preaching the same message that the prophets were again preaching in the first year of the reign of Zedekiah (Jeremiah 26:20-23). . . . The fact that he [Lehi] was willing to deliver that very message entrusted to him by God, knowing full well that precisely the same thing would undoubtedly happen to him as had already happened to others delivering that identical message only a few months or years before, marks Lehi as a man of extraordinary courage, commitment, and devotion to the Lord and to his people, one of the hallmarks of a true prophet of the Lord."

John W. Welch (First Nephi, The Doctrinal Foundation, BYU Religious Studies Center, p. 38)

1 Ne. 1:20; 2:20   **NEPHI'S FREEDOM THESIS**
                     (1 Ne. 4:14; Jarom 1:9-10; Omni 1:6; Mosiah 1:7; 2:22,31; Alma 36:1,30; 37:13; 38:1; 48:15,25; 50:19-22; 3 Ne. 5:22; Prov. 14:34; Lev. 26:3-6; Deut. 8:11-14,17; D&C 71:9; 124:45-46; 2 Chron. 20:12-20; Isa. 54:17; *Doctrines of Salvation*, Smith, 3:73-74; *Conference Report*, Oct. 1965, p. 146; *Conference Report*, Oct. 1961, p. 30; *This Nation Shall Endure*, Benson, p. 145; *Discourses of Brigham Young*, p. 342; refer to 2 Ne. 1:7,20, 30-32; Ether 2:7-9,12,15; Alma 48:15)

"All we have to do is to live up to the commandments of God, and we can destroy all the munitions. And there is no nation under the sun, today, or yesterday, or tomorrow that can touch us. Is that fanciful? Is that wishful thinking? Not if you believe in God. If you know that God lives, and that Jesus is Christ, and that they have the world and everything within their power, it is not fanciful."

Teachings of Spencer W. Kimball, p. 159

"O foolish men who think to protect the world with armaments, battleships, and space equipment, when only righteousness is needed! . . . Perhaps it is too simple for us to see. We look to foreign programs, summit conferences, land bases. We depend on fortifications, or gods of stone; upon ships and planes and projectiles, our gods of iron—gods which have no ears, no eyes, no hearts. We pray to them for deliverance and depend upon them for protection . . . like the gods of Baal."

Teachings of Spencer W. Kimball, p. 416

[Lincoln's remarks following the victory of Gettysburg] "In the stress and pinch of the campaign there, I went to my room, and got down on my knees and prayed God Almighty for victory at Gettysburg. I told Him that this was His country, and the war was His war, but that we really couldn't stand another Fredericksburg or Chancellorsville. And then and there I made a solemn vow with my Maker that if He would stand by you, boys, at Gettysburg, I would stand by Him. And He did, and I will! And after this I felt that God Almighty had taken the whole thing into His hands."

Abraham Lincoln (Lincoln's Life - Stories and Speeches, Selby, p.222)

"This land is a land choice above all other lands, and God has blessed the people upon this land. He has fulfilled the words recorded in this book time and time again, that those who should come up to fight against the people of this land should not prosper."

Heber J. Grant (Conference Report, Oct. 1899, p. 18)

"This America is no ordinary country. It is a choice land, 'choice above all other lands' (1 Ne. 2:20). It has a tragic and bloody past, but a glorious and peaceful future if its inhabitants really learn to serve their God. It was consecrated as a land of promise to the people of the Americas, to whom God gave these great promises:
    'It will be a land of liberty to its people' (2 Nephi 1:7).
    'They shall never be brought down into captivity' (2 Nephi 1:7).
    'And there shall be none to molest them' (2 Nephi 1:9).
    'It is a land of promise' (1 Nephi 2:20).
    'It shall be free from all nations under heaven.'
    'There shall be no enemies come into this land.'
    'It shall be free from bondage' (Ether 2:12).
    'There shall be no kings upon the land' (2 Nephi 10:11).
    'I will fortify this land against all other nations.' (2 Nephi 10:11).
    'He that fighteth against Zion shall perish' (2 Nephi 10:13).
"But these promises, glorious though they be, desirable as they are, can come

only '. . . if they will but serve the God of this land who is Jesus Christ. . . .' (Ether 2:12). There is only one way. That infallible cure is simply righteousness, obedience, Godliness, honor, and integrity. There is no other cure. Mountains of arms and ammunitions will not guarantee safety, for enemies can also build fortifications and missiles and bomb shelters. If we would but believe the prophets! For they have warned that if the 'inhabitants of this land are ever brought down into captivity and enslaved, it shall be because of iniquity; for if iniquity shall abound cursed shall be the land' (See 2 Nephi 1:7)."

Spencer W. Kimball (Conference Report, Oct. 1961, pp. 30-31)

1 Ne. 2:4   **HE LEFT HIS PRECIOUS THINGS**
(Mosiah 22:12; 24:17-20; Ether 1:39-42; Jacob 7:26)

"Nephi and all the others were called upon to make a great sacrifice, to leave behind practically all they had known; but the Lord promised, despite the sacrifice of the moment, that they would eventually possess more and greater blessings. We of modern times struggle with that principle also. One of the most dangerous problems we face is wanting immediate gratification. Few people, it seems, believe in postponement—if we want something, we want it now. . . . There seems to be a follow-up principle to sacrificing: Whenever we give something up or go without, we find ourselves in possession of *more* and *greater.*"

Kelly Ogden (Studies in Scripture, ed. by K. Jackson, 7:25)

1 Ne. 2:6   **RIVER OF WATER**
(*In Search of Lehi's Trail*, Hilton & Hilton, pp. 64-65; *Lehi in the Desert*, Nibley, p. 91; *Studies in Scripture*, ed. by Jackson, 7:23)

"Although the term 'river of water' probably seemed foreign to Joseph Smith, . . . the use of the term in the Book of Mormon is consistent with both modern and ancient Hebrew and with other Semitic languages of the Middle East. Different words are used in these languages to differentiate between (1) a riverbed that has water flowing in it and (2) a dry riverbed. This is one of many examples that prove the Book of Mormon is translation literature. It was not written by Joseph Smith; rather it was translated by him from ancient records."

Daniel H. Ludlow (Companion to Your Study of the Book of Mormon, pp. 92-93)

1 Ne. 2:7   **AN OFFERING UNTO THE LORD**
(*Teachings of the Prophet Joseph Smith*, pp. 172-173, 180-181; refer to 2 Ne. 5:26)

"As a prophet, Lehi held the Melchizedek Priesthood and by that authority offered sacrifice *(Teachings of the Prophet Joseph Smith*, p. 181). . . . The Aaronic Priesthood was the province of the tribe of Levi, and thus was not taken by the Nephites to America. It would appear, therefore, that the sacrifices performed by the Lehite colony were carried out under the direction of the higher priesthood, which comprehends all the duties and authorities of the lesser."

R. Millet and J. F. McConkie (Doctrinal Commentary on the Book of Mormon, 1:31)

"All the prophets held the higher priesthood, having been ordained by the hand of God (see *Teachings of the Prophet Joseph Smith*, pp. 180-81). It was by right of this higher priesthood that the Old Testament prophets performed their labors in the name of the God of Israel and could officiate in the ordinances of the Aaronic Priesthood, just as today bishops in the Church officiate in an Aaronic Priesthood office by right of the Melchizedek Priesthood. . . . Though the Book of Mormon does not explicitly state so, Lehi, like all other prophets in Old Testament times, held the Melchizedek Priesthood. . . . The Nephites administered the ordinances and blessings of the law of Moses before the coming of Christ and the law of the gospel after the coming of Christ by the authority of the Melchizedek Priesthood."

Paul Y. Hoskisson (Ensign, Mar. 1994, p. 54)

1 Ne. 2:8-10   NAMING LOCATIONS
(Amos 5:24)

"By what right do these people rename streams and valleys to suit themselves? No Westerner would tolerate such arrogance. But Lehi is not interested in western taste; he is following a good old Oriental custom. . . . Any water you may discover, either in your own territory or in the territory of another tribe, is named after you. . . . One and the same place may have several names, and the *wadi* running close to the same, or the mountain connected with it, will naturally be called differently by members of different clans. . . ."

Hugh Nibley (Lehi in the Desert, pp. 85-86)

"The ancient Hebrew people loved imagery and figures of speech. The most powerful way to illustrate a truth was to find something in human nature or conduct that corresponded to something in nature."

Kelly Ogden (Studies in Scripture, ed. by K. Jackson, 7:24)

1 Ne. 2:9   **THE FOUNTAIN OF THE RED SEA**
(footnote 9a; *Lehi in the Desert*, Nibley, pp. 88-89; *In Search of Lehi's Trail*, Hilton & Hilton, p. 68)

1 Ne. 2:10   **A FIRM AND STEADFAST VALLEY?**
(contrast with LDS *Hymns,* no. 255)

"As if to prove that no Westerner could possibly have dreamed up Nephi's account, we are challenged by the remarkable expression, 'like unto this valley, firm and steadfast, and immovable . . .' Who west of Suez would ever think of such an image? . . . The Arabs, to be sure. For them the valley, and not the mountain, is the symbol of permanence. It is not the mountain of refuge to which they flee, but the valley of refuge. The great depressions that run for hundreds of miles across the Arabian peninsula pass for the most part through plains devoid of mountains. It is in these ancient riverbeds alone that water, vegetation, and animal life are to be found when all else is desolation. They alone offer men and animals escape from their enemies and deliverance from death by hunger and thirst. The qualities of firmness and steadfastness, of reliable protection, refreshment, and sure refuge when all else fails, which other nations attribute naturally to mountains, the Arabs attribute to valleys."

Hugh Nibley (Lehi in the Desert, pp.105-106)

1 Ne. 2:13   **HIS SONS SOUGHT TO KILL LEHI**
(1 Ne. 16:35-39)

"How was it possible that sons could seek to take the life of their father? What must have happened for family members to seek the overthrow and death of their own flesh and blood? Simply stated, the wicked take the truth to be hard (1 Nephi 16:1-2), too hard to handle. Wickedness and corruption know no family. When iniquity abounds, the love of men waxes cold (D&C 45:27; Joseph Smith-Matthew 1:10, 30). Laman and Lemuel, like their spiritual counterparts in Jerusalem, would not receive the message, even if the messenger was their own father."

R. Millet & J. F. McConkie (Doctrinal Commentary on the Book of Mormon, 1:32)

1 Ne. 2:21   **CUT OFF FROM THE PRESENCE OF THE LORD**
(Alma 12:16; 40:26; 42:9; Hel. 14:18; refer in this text to 2 Ne. 5:21-23 under "Three Elements of the Lamanite Curse")

1 Ne. 2:22   **THE INHERITANCE OF THE ELDEST SON**
(1 Ne. 18:10; 16:37; 2 Ne. 5:3,19; Alma 54:17-18; Deut. 21:17; refer to Mosiah 10:15)

1 Ne. 2:23-24   **LAMANITES NOT THE REAL ENEMY TO THE NEPHITES**
(2 Ne. 5:25)

"[The Lamanites] were not the Nephite problem. They were merely kept there to remind the Nephites of their real problem, which was to walk uprightly before the Lord."

Hugh Nibley (Since Cumorah, p. 376)

1 Nephi 3~7

1 Ne. 3:3, 12 **CONTENTS OF THE BRASS PLATES**
(Alma 10; 1 Ne. 5:11-16; 3 Ne. 10:16; *Messiah in Ancient America*, Warren & Ferguson, pp. 124-127, 231-237; *Lehi in the Desert*, Nibley, p. 26)

"The brass plates obtained from Laban contained . . . a record of the Jews from the beginning down to Zedekiah, and the prophecies of the prophets from the beginning down to Jeremiah. (1 Nephi 3:3-20, 5:11-13.) This would explain how the biblical stories were known by the American Indian groups even before the arrival of the Catholic fathers and their Bibles after the time of Columbus. Historians have concluded the American Indians knew of the story of the creation, the flood, etc., before the time of Columbus, although they have not been able to explain how the Indians came into possession of this knowledge."

Daniel H. Ludlow (Companion to Your Study of the Book of Mormon, pp. 98-99)

1 Ne. 3:5-6, 31 **THOU HAST NOT MURMURED**
(refer in this text to 1 Ne. 18:16; Alma 58:9-11, 34-35)

1 Ne. 3:7 **I WILL DO WHAT THE LORD COMMANDS**
(1 Ne. 17:3; D&C 5:34; Heb. 13:17; D&C 21: 4-5; 132:7; 1:38; refer in this text to 1 Ne. 17:50; Ether 13:13-15, 20-22; Hel. 16:2)

"I believe with all my heart, for example, that if our young people could come out of our homes thoroughly acquainted with the life of Nephi, imbued with the spirit of his courage and love of truth, they would choose the right when a choice is placed before them. How marvelous it would be if, when they must make a decision, there would flash into their minds, from long and intimate association with them, the words of Nephi: 'I will go and do the things which the Lord hath commanded. . . .'"

Marion G. Romney (Conference Report, Apr. 1960, p. 112)

"But in rendering that strict obedience, are we made slaves? No, it is the only way on the face of the earth for you and me to become free, and we shall become the slaves of our own passions, and of the wicked one, and servants to the devil, if we take any other course. . . ."

Brigham Young (Journal of Discourses 18:246)

"That is the kind of faith to have. Let us be faithful in keeping the commandments of God and then we know that we can win the battle, though we may be opposed by a man with his tens of thousands. The final result was that Nephi got the plates."

Heber J. Grant (Conference Report, Oct. 1899, p. 18)

"When my feeling of incompetence wholly overwhelmed me, I remembered the words of Nephi when he said: [1 Nephi 3:7]. I want to tell you that I lean heavily on these promises, that the Lord will strengthen and give me growth and fit and qualify me for this great work. I have seen the Lord qualify men. In my Church experience I have helped to . . . [call] many bishops. I have seen them grow and prosper and become great and mighty men in the Church; men who were weak and men who were foolish, and they became strong and confounded the wise, and so I rely upon that promise of the Lord that he will strengthen and empower me that I may be able to do this work to which I have been called."

Spencer W. Kimball (Conference Report, Oct. 1943, p. 18)

"We don't need a prophet—we have one; we need a listening ear. And if we do not listen and heed, then 'the day cometh that they who will not hear the voice of the Lord, neither the voice of his servants, neither give heed to the words of the prophets and apostles, shall be cut off from among the people.'"

Ezra Taft Benson (God, Family, Country, pp. 348-349)

"There are some people who seem to have the idea that rebellion and disobedience are evidences of independence and of manhood. Well, I am glad to know that, so far as I am concerned, I never took that view. I always felt that I was just as independent in being obedient, and I know I felt much better than I could possibly feel if I were disobedient. It is not necessary to be disobedient to show independence. . . . I suppose each one of us is fond of having his own way. I know I am. I am willing to confess that I like to have my own way. But I do not like my own way well enough to want it in opposition to [the leaders of the Church]."

George Q. Cannon (Gospel Truths, pp. 162-163)

". . . as my life consisted of activity and unyielding exertions, I made this my rule: When the Lord commands, do it."

Joseph Smith (History of the Church, 2:170)

"To obey! To hearken! What a difficult requirement! Often we hear: 'Nobody can tell me what clothes to wear, what I shall eat or drink. No one can outline my Sabbaths, appropriate my earnings, nor in any way limit my personal freedoms! I do as I please! I give no blind obedience!' Blind obedience! How little they understand! The Lord said through Joseph Smith: 'Whatever God requires is right, no matter what it is, although we may not see the reason thereof until long after the events transpire.'"

Teachings of Spencer W. Kimball, p. 59

"It is in the way we answer the call that we show the measure of our devotion. . . . Avoid being critical of those serving in responsible priesthood callings. Show yourself to be loyal. Cultivate the disposition to sustain and to bless. Pray. Pray continually for your leaders. Never say 'No' to an opportunity to serve in the Church. If you are called to an assignment by one who has authority, there is but one answer. It is, of course, expected that you set forth clearly what your circumstances are, but any assignment that comes under call from your bishop or your stake president is a call that comes from the Lord. An article of our faith [#5] defines it so, and I bear witness that it is so. Once called to such positions, do not presume to set your own date of release. A release is in effect another call. Men do not call themselves to offices in the Church. Why must we presume that we have the authority to release ourselves? A release should come by the same authority from whence came the call. Act in the office to which you are called with all diligence. Do not be a slothful servant. Be punctual and dependable and faithful."

Boyd K. Packer (BYU Devotional, Mar. 23, 1965)

"We haven't yet had a prophet who earned a doctorate in any subject, but as someone said, 'A prophet may not have his Ph.D. but he certainly has his LDS.' . . . If there is ever a conflict between earthly knowledge and the words of the prophet, you stand with the prophet, and you'll be blessed and time will vindicate you."

Ezra Taft Benson (BYU Speeches of the Year, pp. 26-30)

"One day when President Grant was living, I sat in my office across the street following a general conference. A man came over to see me, an elderly man. He was very upset about what had been said in this conference by some of the Brethren, including myself. I could tell from his speech that he came from a foreign land. After I had quieted him enough so he would listen, I said, 'Why did you come to America?' 'I am here because a prophet of God told me to come.' Who was the prophet?' I continued. 'Wilford Woodruff.' 'Do you believe Wilford Woodruff was a prophet of God?' 'Yes, I do.' 'Do you believe that President Joseph F. Smith was a prophet of God?' 'Yes, sir.' Then came the sixty-four dollar question. 'Do you believe that Heber J. Grant is a prophet of God?' His answer, 'I think he ought to keep his mouth shut about old age assistance.' Now I tell you that a man in his position is on the way to apostasy. He is forfeiting his chances for eternal life. So is everyone who cannot follow the living Prophet of God."

Marion G. Romney (Conference Report, Apr. 1953, p. 125)

1 Ne. 3:9,10,16,   **DIRECTION BY ELEVATION**
22, 23, 29;   *(Lehi in the Desert, Nibley, p. 6; refer in this text to Omni 1:13)*
4:1, 5-6,
33; 5:5-6;   "The brothers set out with their tents to *go up* to the land of Jerusalem.
7:2-5,   Approaching Jerusalem from any wilderness requires an ascent in elevation. All
15, 22   the locative adverbs in the next pages of scripture accurately depict the topography of Judah and the deserts to the south."

Kelly Ogden (Studies in Scriptures, ed. by K. Jackson, 7:27)

1 Ne. 3:15   **OATH TAKING**
(refer in this text to 1 Ne. 4:32, 37; Alma 44:8)

"This matter of swearing with an oath in ancient days was far more significant than many of us have realized. For instance: Nephi and his brethren were seeking to obtain the brass plates from Laban. Their lives were in peril. Yet Nephi swore this oath: 'As the Lord liveth, and as we live, we will not go down unto our father in the wilderness until we have accomplished the thing which the Lord hath commanded us' (1 Nephi 3:15). Thus Nephi made God his partner. If he failed to get the plates, it meant God had failed. And because God does not fail, it was incumbent upon Nephi to get the plates or lay down his life in the attempt."

Bruce R. McConkie (Conference Report, Apr. 1982, pp. 49-50)

1 Ne. 3:19   **THE LANGUAGE OF OUR FATHERS**
(Mosiah 1:4; 1 Ne. 1:2)

"Lehi's forefathers were *not* natives of Jerusalem. We learn in Mosiah 1:4 that certain plates were written 'in the language of the Egyptians.' Nephi informs us (1 Nephi 3:19) that these same plates were in 'the language of our fathers,' and that the possession of them was necessary if a knowledge of that language was to be preserved among his people. . . . The language of Lehi's forefathers was a foreign language; and when Nephi tells us it was the language of the Egyptians he means what he says."

Hugh Nibley (Lehi in the Desert, p. 26)

"The statement that 'Lehi, . . . having been taught in the language of the Egyptians therefore he could read' the engravings on the brass plates of Laban quite clearly indicates these plates were written in the Egyptian language."

Daniel H. Ludlow (Companion to Your Study of the Book of Mormon, p. 173)

1 Ne. 3:27   **HID OURSELVES IN THE CAVITY OF A ROCK**
(*Commentary on the Book of Mormon*, Reynolds & Sjodahl, 1:34; *The Firm Foundation of Mormonism*, Vestal & Wallace, pp. 106-109)

1 Ne. 3:28-29 **SMOTE US WITH A ROD**
(*Lehi in the Desert,* , pp. 79-80; *An Approach to the Book of Mormon*, Nibley, p. 213)

1 Ne. 3:29-30 **AN ANGEL STOOD BEFORE THEM**
(D&C 5:1, 5, 7; Jacob 7:17; Alma 8:14-18; 12:28-30; Mosiah 3:2-3; 27:11-17; Hel. 13:1-7; 2 Ne. 6:8-11; 3 Ne. 17:24)

"Many men say: 'If I could only see an angel, if I could only hear an angel proclaim something, that would cause me to be faithful all the days of my life!' It had no effect upon these men [Laman and Lemuel] that were not serving the Lord, and it would have no effect today."

Heber J. Grant (Conference Report, Apr. 1924, p. 159)

"But Christ has himself declared that the manifestations . . . from a visitation of an angel . . . would not leave the impression . . . which we receive through a manifestation of the Holy Ghost (Luke 16:27-31; D&C 5:7-10). Personal visitations might become dim as time goes on, but this guidance of the Holy Ghost is renewed and continued, day after day, year after year, if we live to be worthy of it."

Joseph Fielding Smith (Doctrines of Salvation, 1:44)

1 Ne. 3:31; 4:1   **LABAN'S FIFTY**
(Lehi in the Desert, Nibley, pp. 111-112)

1 Ne. 4:6   **LED BY THE SPIRIT**
(D&C 112:10; 124:97; 100:6; 84:85; 28:15-16; Moses 6:32; Alma 21:16; 22:1,4)

"More than ever before, I understand what the ancient prophet Nephi felt when he had been given the seemingly insurmountable task by his father, Lehi, to gain possession of the brass plates. . . . I must go on many occasions, as did Nephi of old, being 'led by the Spirit, not knowing beforehand the things which I should do.' Yes, though the night be dark, 'I do not ask to see the distant scene—one step [is] enough for me.'"

Harold B. Lee (Conference Report, Apr. 1970, pp. 125-126)

"Without knowing what he would do, Nephi began moving forward while his brothers sulked outside the city walls. . . . He was moving by faith—confidence in the unknown, hope in things unseen. . . . Notice that faith and trust in the Lord came first. Then came action. He had no plan except confidence in the Lord. It was really a 'ready, fire, aim' approach, the opposite of conventional wisdom. Laman and Lemuel thought it foolhardy. Then the Lord's plan unfolded with Nephi being guided by unseen hands."

John K. Carmack (Ensign, May 1993, p.42)

"President Harold B. Lee gave some marvelous advice for modern pioneers: 'Walk to the edge of the light, and perhaps a few steps into the darkness, and you will find that the light will appear and move ahead of you' (as quoted by Boyd K. Packer, in Lucile C. Tate, *Boyd K. Packer: A Watchman on the Tower* [1995], 138). We must walk by faith. That means stepping into the dark unknowns because we believe that Heavenly Father is awaiting us. . . ."

Bonnie D. Parkin (Ensign, May 1997, p. 85)

1 Ne. 4:7-19   NEPHI SLAYS LABAN
(Lehi in the Desert, Nibley, pp. 113-115; D&C 98:23-33; 132:36; Jacob 4:5; Deut. 13:6-10)

"That which is wrong under any circumstance may be and often is, right under another . . . Whatever God requires is right, no matter what it is, although we may not see the reason thereof till long after the events transpire."

Teachings of the Prophet Joseph Smith, pp. 255-256

"The Lord is merciful, always merciful, and do you not think it is a merciful act, if people become so filled with disease and corruption through sin, and when they have turned away from God, and they are teaching their posterity all the evil which they themselves know, for the Lord to remove them from the face of the earth so they will not contaminate the generations yet to come and lead them to eternal destruction?"

Joseph Fielding Smith (Signs of the Times, pp. 95-96)

1 Ne. 4:12-13   THE IMPORTANCE OF THE SCRIPTURES
(1 Ne. 3:19; refer in this text to Omni 1:17)

"People as well as nations perish without scriptures. The scriptures are spiritual food for our spirit, which is just as important as physical food for our body. It was so important for Lehi to have the scriptures and records which were engraven on the brass plates that the Lord commanded Nephi to slay Laban in order to obtain them. The Lord knew of their importance for the spiritual nourishment of Lehi and his descendants. He explained: 'It is better that one man should perish than that a nation should dwindle and perish in unbelief.'"

L. Lionel Kendrick (Ensign, May 1993, p. 14)

1 Ne. 4:18   VOICE OF THE SPIRIT
(refer in this text to Enos 1:5,10)

"I have a believing heart because of a simple testimony that came when I was a child, I think maybe I was around ten—maybe eleven—years of age. I was with my father out on a farm away from our home, trying to spend the day busying myself until father was ready to go home. Over the fence from our place were some tumbledown sheds which had attracted a curious boy, adventurous as I was. I started to climb through the fence and I heard a voice as clearly as you are hearing mine—'Don't go over there!' calling me by name. I turned to look at father to see if he were talking to me, but he was way up at the other end of the field. There was no person in sight. I realized then, as a child, that there were persons beyond my sight and I had heard a voice. And when I had heard and read these stories of the Prophet Joseph Smith, I, too, know what it means to hear a voice because I've heard from an unseen speaker."

Harold B. Lee (BYU Devotional, Oct. 15, 1952)

1 Ne. 4:22, 26   **THE ELDERS, LABAN, AND THE BRETHREN OF THE CHURCH**
(refer in this text to 2 Ne. 5:26)

"Was there a Church anciently, and if so, how was it organized and regulated? There was not so much as the twinkling of an eye during the whole so-called pre-Christian Era when the Church of Jesus Christ was not upon the earth, organized basically in the same way it now is. Melchizedek belonged to the Church; *Laban was a member;* so also was Lehi, long before he left Jerusalem. There was always apostolic power. The Melchizedek Priesthood always directed the course of the Aaronic Priesthood. All of the prophets held a position in the hierarchy of the day."

Bruce R. McConkie (Symposium on the New Testament, BYU, 1984, p. 6)

"We know very little about the city government of the Jews, save that the 'elders' played the principal role. By 'elders' has been understood the heads of the most influential families of a city."

Hugh Nibley (Lehi in the Desert, p. 6)

"The elders of the Jews were undoubtedly the leading citizens of the community, the wise men of the synagogue or local church. The heads of several influential families may have formed a body which served in an advisory capacity to the king in civil and religious matters."

R. Millet and J. F. McConkie (Doctrinal Commentary on the Book of Mormon, 1:46)

1 Ne. 4:32,37   **OATH TAKING**
(JST Gen. 14:25-40; D&C 84:33-44; 3 Ne. 12:33-37; *Companion to Your Study of the Book of Mormon*, Ludlow, pp. 96-97; *Symposium on the Old Testament*, Aug. 1983, Ricks College, pp. 139-142; refer in this text to Alma 44:8 & 1 Ne. 3:15)

"In such a situation there was only one thing Nephi could possibly have done, both to spare Zoram and to avoid giving alarm—and no westerner could have guessed what it was. Nephi, a powerful fellow, held the terrified Zoram in a vice-like grip long enough to swear a solemn oath in his ear. . . . But not every oath will do: to be most binding and solemn an oath should be by the life of something. . . . Today it is glibly employed by the city riffraff, but anciently it was an awful thing. . . . So we see that the one and only way that Nephi could have pacified the struggling Zoram in an instant was to utter the one oath that no man would dream of breaking, the most solemn of all oaths to the Semite: 'as the Lord liveth, and as I live . . .' (4:32)."

Hugh Nibley (Lehi in the Desert, pp. 117-118)

1 Ne. 5:2-7   **A LESSON IN MARRIAGE**
(Eph. 5:25, 28-29, 33; Col. 3:19; *Conference Report,* Hinckley, Apr. 1991; *An Approach to the Book of Mormon*, Nibley, 1957 ed., p. 214; *Ensign*, Nov. 1993, p. 17)

"I learned respect for womanhood from my father's tender caring for my mother, my sister, and his sisters. Father was the first to arise from dinner to clear the table. . . . In later years, after Mother had a stroke, father faithfully cared for her every need. The last two years of her life required 24-hour care, he being called by Mother every few minutes, day or night. I shall never forget his example of loving care for his cherished companion. He told me it was small payment for over fifty years of my mother's loving devotion to him. . . . . Selfishness is so frequently at the core of family relationship problems. When individuals focus on their own selfish interests, they miss opportunities to listen, to understand, or to consider the other person's feelings or needs."

Robert D. Hales (Ensign, Nov. 1993, pp. 9-10)

"No tender hand of the sister gives a gentle touch of healing and encouragement which the hand of a man, however well intentioned, can ever quite duplicate. . . . However much priesthood power and authority the men may possess—however much wisdom and experience they may accumulate—the safety of the family, the integrity of the doctrine, the ordinances, the covenants, indeed the future of the Church, rests equally upon the women. . . . No man receives the fulness of the priesthood without a woman at his side. For no man, the Prophet said, can obtain the fulness of the priesthood outside the temple of the Lord. (See D&C 131:1-3). No man achieves the supernal exalting status of worthy fatherhood except as a gift from his wife."

Boyd K. Packer (Ensign, May 1998, pp. 72-73)

"Brethren, please remember: The highest degree of glory is available to you only through that order of the priesthood linked to the new and everlasting covenant of marriage (See D&C 131:1-4). Therefore, your first priority in honoring the priesthood is to honor your eternal companion."

Russell M. Nelson (Ensign, May 1993, p. 40)

"Those who enter into marriage should be fully prepared to establish their marriage as the first priority in their lives. . . . domestic harmony results from forgiving and forgetting, essential elements of a maturing marriage relationship. Someone has said that we should keep our eyes wide open before marriage and half shut afterward. True charity ought to begin in marriage, for it is a relationship that must be rebuilt every day. . . . Either partner who diminishes the divine role of the other in the presence of the children demeans the budding femininity within the daughters and the emerging manhood of the sons. I suppose there are always some honest differences between husband and wife, but let them be settled in private."

James E. Faust (Ensign, May 1993, p. 36)

"The greatest joys of life are experienced in happy family relationships. . . . We have many failures in the world, but the greatest of these, in my judgment, is that failure which is found in broken homes. . . . The root of most of this lies in selfishness. The cure for most of it can be found in repentance on the part of the offender and forgiveness on the part of the offended. . . . The cultivation of such a home requires effort and energy, forgiveness and patience, love and endurance and sacrifice; but it is worth all of these and more. I have learned that the real essence of happiness in marriage lies not so much in romance as in an anxious concern for the comfort and well-being of one's companion. Thinking of self alone and of the gratification of personal desires will build neither trust, love, nor happiness. Only when there is unselfishness will love, with its concomitant qualities, flourish and blossom. Marriage, in its truest sense, is a partnership of equals, with neither exercising dominion over the other, but, rather, with each encouraging and assisting the other in whatever responsibilities and aspirations he or she might have."

Gordon B. Hinckley (Ensign, Aug. 1992, p. 6)

"The sensible couple or family who start on a trip in an automobile, whether on business or pleasure, with a promise of something valuable or worthwhile at the end of the journey, will not be deterred or thrown into panic if something goes wrong with the car. They stop and fix it or take it to a garage. If a new part is needed, which cannot be obtained at the service station or small town en route, and a layover is required while the garage man obtains and installs a new part, they, if they are wise and well adjusted, will make good use of the enforced rest. Without recriminations or worry, they will see the sights of the area, get acquainted with some of the people, go to a show, and, in various ways, turn what might have been a tragedy into a holiday and enrich the trip for all. They continue on and win the reward. [Likewise], if something goes wrong in the home, or if there is a storm of quarreling, caused by tensions and triggered by temper, why not be as wise and sane here as on an automobile trip. Why not relax, go for a walk, chop some wood, whip up a cake, get some recreation, and let the storm blow over as all storms do? Unfortunately, some couples, in such situations, figuratively set fire to the car and walk off in opposite directions into the desert, without regard for the welfare of other members of the family, and convert what was a minor matter to an irreparable tragedy. Oh, that married people would grow up and act their age!"

Hugh B. Brown (You and Your Marriage, pp. 53-54)

"Many years ago I had the opportunity to deliver a commencement address to a graduating class. I had gone to the home of President Hugh B. Brown that we might drive together to the university where he was to conduct the exercises and I was to speak. As President Brown entered my car, he said, 'Wait a moment.' He looked toward the large bay window of his lovely home, and then I realized what he was looking for. The curtain parted, and I saw Sister Zina Brown, his beloved companion of well over fifty years, at the window, propped up in a wheelchair, waving a little white handkerchief. President Brown took from his inside coat pocket a white handkerchief, which he waved to her in return. Then, with a smile, he said to me, 'Let's go.' As we drove, I asked President Brown to tell me about the sign of the white handkerchiefs. He related to me the following incident: 'The first day after Sister Brown and I were married, as I went to work I heard a tap at the window, and there was Zina, waving a white handkerchief. I found mine and waved in reply. From that day until this I have never left my home without that little exchange between my wife and me. It is a symbol of our love one for another. It is an indication to one another that all will be well until we are joined together at eventide.'"

Thomas S. Monson (Ensign, Nov. 1992, p. 98)

"Personal ego and pride—both are enemies to the full enjoyment of the Spirit of God and walking humbly before him. The ego interferes with husbands and wives asking each other for forgiveness. It prevents the enjoyment of the full sweetness of a higher love. The ego often prevents parents and children from fully understanding each other. The ego enlarges our feelings of self-importance and worth. It blinds us to reality."

James E. Faust (Ensign, May 1994, p.6)

"Don't be too critical of each other's faults. Recognize that none of us is perfect. We all have a long way to go. . . . Generally, each of us is painfully aware of our weaknesses, and we don't need frequent reminders. Few people have ever changed for the better as a result of constant criticism or nagging. If we are not careful, some of what we offer as *constructive* criticism is actually *destructive*.

As a newlywed, Sister Lola Walters read in a magazine that in order to strengthen a marriage a couple should have regular, candid sharing sessions in which they would list any mannerisms they found to be annoying. She wrote: . . . 'I told him that I didn't like the way he ate grapefruit. He peeled it and ate it like an orange! Nobody else I knew ate grapefruit like that. Could a girl be expected to spend a lifetime, and even eternity, watching her husband eat grapefruit like an orange? . . . After I finished, it was his turn to tell the things he disliked about me. . . . [He] said, 'Well, to tell the truth, I can't think of anything I don't like about you, Honey.' . . . I quickly turned my back, because I didn't know how to explain the tears that had filled my eyes and were running down my face. Sister Walters concluded: Whenever I hear of married couples being incompatible, I always wonder if they are suffering from what I now call the Grapefruit Syndrome' *(Ensign*, Apr. 1993, p. 13).

Be swift to say, 'I apologize, and please forgive me,' even though you are not the one who is totally at fault. True love is developed by those who are willing to readily admit personal mistakes and offenses. When differences do arise, being able to discuss and resolve them is important, but there are instances when it is best to take a time-out. Biting your tongue and counting to ten or even a hundred is important. And occasionally, even letting the sun go down on your wrath can help bring you back to the problem in the morning more rested, calm, and with a better chance for resolution. . . . Any intelligent couple will have differences of opinion. Our challenge is to be sure that we know how to resolve them."

Joe J. Christensen (Ensign, May 1995, pp. 64-65)

1 Ne. 5:10   **SEARCH THE SCRIPTURES**
(refer in this text to 1 Ne. 8:19, 24, 30; 1 Ne. 19:23; Alma 17:2)

1 Ne. 5:18-19   **PROPHECY CONCERNING BRASS PLATES**
(Alma 37:1-5; refer in this text to 1 Ne. 3:3,12)

"Since many of the precious truths of the brass plates were known and record-ed by Book of Mormon prophet-writers, and since the Book of Mormon will eventually go to all the world as a witness of Jesus Christ and also of the great latter-day work, this particular prophetic utterance is being and will yet be ful-filled. In addition, undoubtedly at some future day the brass plates themselves will be brought forth and their contents thereafter will be available for study to all those with pure hearts and with ears to hear."

R. Millet and J. F. McConkie (Doctrinal Commentary on the Book of Mormon, 1:50)

1 Ne. 6   **NEPHI'S WRITINGS**
(refer in this text to 1 Ne. 9)

"Approximately ten years after Lehi and his family left Jerusalem, Nephi was commanded to begin a record of his proceedings, the record we have come to know as the large plates [the historical record] . . . (See 1 Nephi 9; 19:1-6). About twenty years later Nephi was given an additional writing assignment: he was to begin a record which would concentrate upon spiritual matters, the dealings and revelations of God with the Lehites (2 Nephi 5:29-33). This record, known to us as the small plates, covers the material in the Book of Mormon from 1 Nephi through the book of Omni, approximately 475 years of Nephite history. At the time of King Benjamin (Mosiah 1), the small plates came to a close, and the large plates were thereafter used to record both secular and spiritual doings. Nephi was writing upon (and we are now reading from) the small plates, a record which, incidentally, was written in retrospect, thirty years after the fact."

R. Millet and J. F. McConkie (Doctrinal Commentary on the Book of Mormon, 1:51)

1 Ne. 7:1, 6   **ARRANGED MARRIAGE**
(2 Ne. 5:6; *Companion to Your Study of the Book of Mormon*, Ludlow, pp. 99-100)

"The Prophet Joseph informed us that the record of Lehi was contained on the 116 pages that were first translated and subsequently stolen, and of which an abridgment is given us in the first Book of Nephi, which is the record of Nephi individually, he himself being of the lineage of Manasseh; but that Ishmael was of the lineage of Ephraim, and that his sons married into Lehi's family, and Lehi's sons married Ishmael's daughters. . . ."

Erastus Snow (Journal of Discourses 23:184-185)

1 Ne. 7:13-14   **SPIRIT WITHDRAWAL AND DESTRUCTION**
(Refer in this text to 2 Ne. 26:11; Mormon 1:14-17)

1 Ne. 7:19   **WOMEN PLEAD**
(Mosiah 19:13; *An Approach to the Book of Mormon*, Nibley, 1957 ed., p. 215; *Lehi in the Desert*, Nibley, p. 80)

1 Ne. 7:20-21   **FRANKLY FORGIVE**
(D&C 64:9-11; Matt. 6:14-15; 7:1-5; 18:21-35; 2 Tim. 4:14,16; Rom. 12:19-20; *Companion to Your Study of the Book of Mormon*, Ludlow, p. 269; *Gospel Standards*, Grant, p. 32; *Teachings of Spencer W. Kimball*, pp. 240-243; refer in this text to Mosiah 26:30-31 & 3 Ne. 13:14-15)

"I consider it is a disgrace to the community, and in the eyes of the Lord, and of Angels, and in the eyes of all the Prophets and Revelators that have ever lived upon the earth, when a community will descend to the low, degraded state of contention with each other; this little bickering, jarring, fault-finding, somebody's abused me. . . . Suppose every heart should say, if my neighbor does wrong to me. I will not complain, the Lord will take care of him. Let every heart be firm, and every one say, I will never contend any more with a man for property, I will not be cruel to my fellow-creature, but I will do all the good I can, and as little evil as possible. Now, where would be the wrong of taking this course? This is the way to approximate toward a celestial state."

Brigham Young (Journal of Discourses 1:32)

"How are we supposed to act when we are offended, misunderstood, unfairly or unkindly treated, or sinned against? What are we supposed to do if we are hurt by those we love, or passed over for promotion, or are falsely accused, or have our motives unfairly assailed? Do we fight back? . . . Do we revert to an eye for an eye and a tooth for a tooth, or as Tevye says in *Fiddler on the Roof,* do we come to the realization that this finally leaves us blind and toothless? . . . We can all be a little more forgiving."

Howard W. Hunter (Ensign, Nov. 1992, p. 18)

"After his father became ill, Vern Crowley took responsibility for running the family wrecking yard although he was only fifteen years of age. Some customers occasionally took unfair advantage of the young man, and parts were disappearing from the lot overnight. Vern was angry and vowed to catch someone and make an example of him. . . . Just after his father had started to recover from his illness, Vern was making his rounds of the yard one night at closing time. . . . In a distant corner of the property, he caught sight of someone carrying a large piece of machinery toward the back fence. . . . His first thought was to take out his frustrations with his fists and then drag the boy to the front office and call the police. . . . He had caught his thief, and he intended to get his just dues. Out of nowhere, Vern's father came along, put his weak and infirm hand on his son's shoulder, and said, 'I see you're a bit upset, Vern. Can I handle this?' He then walked over to the young would-be thief and put his arm around his shoulder, looked him in the eye for a moment, and said, 'Son, tell me, why are you doing this? Why were you trying to steal that transmission?' Then Mr. Crowley started walking toward the office with his arm around the boy, asking questions about the young man's car problems as they walked. By the time they had arrived at the office, the father said, 'Well, I think your clutch is gone and that's causing your problem.' In the meantime, Vern was fuming. 'Who cares about his clutch?' he thought. 'Let's call the police and get this over with.' But his father just kept talking. 'Vern, get him a clutch. Get him a throwout bearing, too. And get him a pressure plate. That should take care of it.' The father handed all of the parts to the young man who had attempted robbery and said, 'Take these. And here's the transmission, too. You don't have to steal, young man. Just ask for it. . . .' The young man came back to the lot often. Voluntarily, month by month, he paid for all of the parts Vic Crowley had given him, including the transmission. During those visits, he asked Vern why his dad was the way he was and why he did what he did. Vern told him something of their Latter-day Saint beliefs and how much his father loved the Lord and loved people. Eventually the would-be thief was baptized. Vern later said, 'It's hard now to describe the feelings I had and what I went through in that experience. I, too, was young. I had caught my crook. I was going to extract the utmost penalty. But my father taught me a different way.'"

Howard W. Hunter (Ensign, May 1992, p. 62)

"When anguish comes from evil acts of others, there should be punishment and corrective action taken, but the offended is not the one to initiate that action. Leave it to others who have that responsibility. Learn to forgive; though terribly hard, it will release you and open the way to a newness of life. Time devoted by one injured to ensure the offender is punished is time wasted in the healing process."

Richard G. Scott (Ensign, May 1994, p. 9)

"In the listening audience today are Jeff and Joyce Underwood of Pocatello, Idaho. . . . Their daughter Jeralee, age eleven, was going door to door collecting money for her newspaper route. Jeralee never returned home. . . . It was learned that Jeralee had been abducted and brutally murdered by an evil man. When her body was found, the whole city was horrified and shocked. Some became angry and wanted to take vengeance. After Jeralee's body was found, Jeff and Joyce appeared with great composure before the television cameras and other media . . . Joyce said, . . .' I have learned a lot about love this week, and I also know there is a lot of hate. I have looked at the love and want to feel that love, and not the hate. We can forgive.' . . . President Kert W. Howard, Jeralee's stake president, wrote, 'The Underwoods have received letters from people both in and out of the Church stating that they prayed for Jeralee, and they hadn't prayed in years, and because of this, they had a renewed desire to return to the Church.' President Howard continued, 'We will never know the extent of activation and rededication this single event has caused. Who knows the far-reaching effects Jeralee's life will have for generations untold.' Many have come into the Church because they wanted to know what kind of a religion could give the Underwoods their spiritual strength."

James E. Faust (Ensign, May 1994, pp. 6-7)

"[Refusing to forgive others is] to hold hostage those whom the Lord would wish to set free."

Neal A. Maxwell (Conference Report, Oct. 1991)

"We must speak no ill of anyone. We must see the good in each other and speak well of each other whenever we can. . . . We must forgive and bear no malice toward those who offend us. The Savior set the example from the cross: 'Father, forgive them; for they know not what they do' (Luke 23:34). We do not know the hearts of those who offend us. Nor do we know all the sources of our own anger and hurt."

Henry B. Eyring (Ensign, May 1998, p. 68)

1 Nephi 8~10

1 Ne. 8 *(History of Joseph Smith by His Mother*, p. 47-48; The *Messiah in Ancient America*, Ferguson, p. 71; *Lehi in the Desert*, Nibley, p. 47-51; *Conference Report*, Bangerter, Apr., 1984)

Symbols in Lehi's Dream	Interpretation of the Symbols
1 Ne. 8:10-12	1 Ne. 11:9-23; Alma 5:34; Heb.3:14
1 Ne. 8:13	1 Ne. 15:26-29
1 Ne. 8:19	1 Ne. 15:23-24; Hel. 13:29
1 Ne. 8:20	2 Ne. 31:17-20
1 Ne. 8:23	1 Ne. 12:17
1 Ne. 8:26	1 Ne. 11:36; 12:18

Five Groups of People (Matt. 13:3-8, 18-23)

1 Ne. 8:26, 27

1 Ne. 8:22, 23

1 Ne. 8:24, 25, 28

1 Ne. 8:30

1 Ne. 8:31-32

1 Ne. 8:2, 36 **I HAVE DREAMED A DREAM**
(1 Ne. 1:16; 2:1-2; 3:2; 10:2; 15:21; Gen. 15, 20, 28, 31, 37, 40, 41; Judges 7; 1 Kings 3; Dan. 2; Matt. 1, 2, 27; *Conference Report*, Apr. 1974, pp. 173-174; *Mormon Doctrine*, McConkie, p. 208; *Ensign*, Mar. 1993, p. 64; *BYU Studies*, v. 23, No. 3, pp. 52-53; *Articles of Faith*, Talmage, p. 229)

"Oh, I'm not here to tell you that every dream you have is a direct revelation from the Lord—it may be fried liver and onions that may have been responsible for an upset nervous disorder. But I fear that in this age of sophistication there are those of us who are prone to rule out all dreams as of no purpose, and of no moment. . . . Let me read you what Parley P. Pratt said about this matter. 'In all ages and dispensations God has revealed many important instructions and warnings to men by means of dreams. When the outward organs of thought and perception are released from their activity, the nerves unstrung, the whole of mortal humanity lies hushed in quiet slumbers in order to renew its strength and vigor, it is then that the spiritual organs are at liberty in a certain degree to assume their wanted functions. . . . Their kindred spirits, their guardian angels, then hover about them with the fondest affection, the most anxious solicitude. Spirit communes with spirit, thought meets thought, soul blends with soul, in all the raptures of mutual pure and eternal love. In this situation the spiritual organs . . . our spirit body has eyes to see, ears to hear, tongue to speak, and so on . . . the spiritual organs are susceptible of converse with Deity, or of communion with angels, and the spirits of just men made perfect. In this situation we frequently hold communion with our departed father, mother, brother, sister, son or daughter, or with the former husband or wife of our bosom whose affections for us, being rooted and grounded in the eternal elements, issuing from under the sanctuary of love's eternal fountain, can never be lessened or diminished by death, distance of space, or length of years.' When we begin to understand that, beyond sight, as Brigham Young said, is the spirit world right here round about us. If our spiritual eyes could be open, we could see others visiting with us, directing us. And if we will learn not to be so sophisticated that we rule out that possibility of impressions from those who are beyond sight, then we too may have a dream that may direct us as a revelation."

Harold B. Lee (BYU Devotional, Oct. 15, 1952)

"I believe in dreams. . . . The Lord has given me dreams which to me are just as real and as much from God as was the dream of . . . Lehi who through a dream led his colony out of the old country across the mighty deep to this promised land. . . . I had a dream which I am sure was from the Lord. In this dream I was in the presence of my Savior as he stood in mid-air. He spoke no word to me, but my love for him was such that I have not words to explain. I know that no mortal man can love the Lord as I experienced that love for the Savior unless God reveals it to him. I would have remained in his presence, but there was a power drawing me away from him. As a result of that dream, I had this feeling that no matter what might be required of my hands, what the gospel might entail unto me, I would do what I should be asked to do even to the laying down of my life."

George F. Richards (Conference Report, Apr. 1974, pp. 173-174)

"I did have a dream one time. To me it was a literal thing; it was a reality. I was very much oppressed, once, on a mission. I was almost naked and entirely friendless. . . . While in that condition I dreamed that I was on a journey, and I was impressed that I ought to hurry—hurry with all my might, for fear I might be too late. . . . Finally I came to a wonderful mansion. . . . As I passed towards it, as fast as I could, I saw a notice, 'Bath.' I turned aside quickly and went into the bath and washed myself clean. I opened up this little bundle that I had, and there was a pair of white, clean garments, a thing I had not seen for a long time. . . . I put them on. Then I rushed to what appeared to be a great opening, or door. I knocked and the door opened, and the man who stood there was the Prophet Joseph Smith. He looked at me a little reprovingly, and the first words he said: 'Joseph, you are late.' Yet I took confidence and said: 'Yes, but I am clean—I am clean!' He clasped my hand and drew me in, then closed the great door. I felt his hand just as tangible as I ever felt the hand of man. . . . I was determined to test whether this was a dream or a reality. . . . So I purposely thrust myself up against the Prophet. I felt the warmth of his stomach. He smiled at me, as if he comprehended my purpose. . . . When I awoke that morning I was a man, although only a boy [of fifteen years old]. There was not anything in the world that I feared. I could meet any man or woman or child and look them in the face, feeling in my soul that I was a man every whit. . . . I felt the hand of Joseph Smith. I felt the warmth of his stomach, when I put my hand against him. I saw the smile upon his face. I did my duty as he required me to do it, and when I woke up I felt as if I had been lifted out of a slum, out of a despair. . . ."

Joseph F. Smith (Gospel Doctrine, pp. 541-543)

1 Ne. 8:2-4;   **THE FOREKNOWLEDGE OF GOD**
9:5-6   (refer in this text to Alma 13:3-5)

"Respecting the foreknowledge of God, let it not be said that divine omniscience is of itself a determining cause whereby events are inevitably brought to pass. A mortal father, who knows the weaknesses and frailties of his son, may by reason of that knowledge sorrowfully predict the calamities and sufferings awaiting his son. Can it be said that the father's foreknowledge is a cause of the son's sinful life? . . . Our Heavenly Father has a full knowledge of the nature and disposition of each of His children, a knowledge gained by long observation and experience in the past eternity of our primeval childhood . . . He foresees the future as a state which naturally and surely will be; not as one which must be because He has arbitrarily willed that it shall be."

James E. Talmage (Jesus the Christ, pp. 28-29)

1 Ne. 8:10-12   **THE FRUIT OF THE TREE OF LIFE**
(1 Ne. 11:21-23; 15:36; Rev. 2:7; 2 Ne. 31:20; *First Nephi, The Doctrinal Foundation,* BYU Religious Studies Center, p. 123)

"Figuratively, the tree from which the faithful pick the fruit of eternal life. To eat thereof is to inherit eternal life in the kingdom of God."

Bruce R. McConkie (Doctrinal New Testament Commentary, 3:447)

1 Ne. 8:19,   **ROD OF IRON**
24, 30   (Hel. 3:29-30; D&C 18:34-36; John 4:14; 5:38; 3 Ne. 23:1; refer in this text to Alma 17:2)

"A casual, infrequent exposure to the scriptures will generally not open the door to the whisperings of the Spirit or provide insights . . . There are certain blessings obtained when one searches the scriptures. As a person studies the words of the Lord and obeys them, he or she draws closer to the Savior and obtains a greater desire to live a righteous life. The power to resist temptation increases, and spiritual weaknesses are overcome. Spiritual wounds are healed. . . . In the dream Lehi saw a tree which produced a fruit which was exceedingly white, very sweet to the taste, and desirable above all other fruit. . . . According to the vision, the only way to reach the tree and become a permanent partaker of the fruit was to 'continually [hold] fast' to the iron rod (1 Ne. 8:30). What was the rod of iron? Nephi defined it as the 'word of God'—the words of the living prophets and the scriptures which point people to Christ. Nephi further stated that those who hearkened and held fast to the word of God would never perish (See 1 Ne. 15:24). . . . Holding fast to the iron rod builds faith in Christ and his work. . . . President Benson, in the April 1986 general conference, expressed these thoughts: 'However diligent we may be in other areas, certain blessings are to be found only in the scriptures, only in coming to the word of the Lord and holding fast to it as we make our way through the mists of darkness to the tree of life.' (*Ensign,* May 1986, p. 82.)

Merrill J. Bateman (Ensign, Nov. 1992, pp. 27-28)

"We must engage in activities that bring spiritual power. I speak of such activities as immersing ourselves in the scriptures. There is a power that flows into our lives when we read and study the scriptures on a daily basis that cannot be found in any other way."

Ezra Taft Benson (1987-1988 BYU Devotional and Fireside Speeches, pp. 53-54)

"The greatest achievement mankind can make in this world is to familiarize themselves with divine truth, so thoroughly, so perfectly, that the example or conduct of no creature living in the world can ever turn them away from the knowledge that they have obtained. . . . From my boyhood I have desired to learn the principles of the gospel in such a way . . . that it would matter not to me who might fall from the truth. . . . My foundation would be certain in the truths . . . I have learned."

Joseph F. Smith (Gospel Doctrine, pp. 3-4)

"Our children practice musical instruments, and I encourage them to do this in the morning when there are fewer distractions. But sometimes they would go to bed late and get up late. On those days they would not have enough time to finish practicing, dress, eat, and read the scriptures before going out the door. The activity usually slighted was scripture study. Sometimes we would read a verse or two, and sometimes we'd say we'd get to it after school, but our efforts were inconsistent. This year I realized that my priorities were wrong. It occurred to me that I might be conveying to the children that the study of music was more important than the study of the gospel. I decided that on those mornings when time was short, we would study the scriptures and postpone music practice. I want to bear you my testimony that I have felt a great peace as we have followed the counsel of the prophet in this matter."

Jeanne Inouye (Ensign, Nov. 1993, p. 97)

1 Ne. 8:20   **THE STRAIT AND NARROW PATH**
(2 Ne. 9:41; 3 Ne. 14:13-14; D&C 22:4; 132:22, 25; Matt. 7:13-14; *Teachings of the Prophet Joseph Smith*, pp. 197-198)

"To enter the straight gate implies obedience to gospel requirements, and the narrow way that leads to life connotes additional requirements, rites, and ordinances for all who desire salvation and exaltation. . . . I should like to ask, 'What is the straight gate spoken of by the Savior by which we should enter?' All who have repented and then been baptized and received the Holy Ghost by authorized servants of God have entered in by the strait gate. The narrow way can only be followed by obedience and faithfulness to all the sacred ordinances and requirements of the higher gospel plan, obtained in the holy temples of God."

Delbert L. Stapley (Conference Report, Apr. 1955, pp. 66-68)

"The strait and narrow path, though clearly marked, is a path, not a freeway nor an escalator. Indeed, there are times when the only way the strait and narrow path can be followed is on one's knees! And we are to help each other along the path."

Neal A. Maxwell (Ensign, May 1982, p.38)

"Mark you, this word *strait* is spelled s-t-r-a-i-t and not s-t-r-a-i-g-h-t. While no doubt, that path which leads into the presence of God is *straight*, it is also *strait*, which means that those who enter into it will find it restricted; it is narrow; they cannot take with them that which does not apply, or which does not belong to the kingdom of God. All such things must be left behind when we enter into this narrow way which leads into the presence of God, where we can receive life eternal. 'Few there be that find it.'"

Joseph Fielding Smith (Doctrines of Salvation, 2:13-14)

1 Ne. 8:25   **ASHAMED-POPULARITY**
(1 Ne. 6:5; Heb. 6:4-6; Alma 46:21; Morm. 8:38; Rom. 1:16; 2 Tim. 1:8; Prov. 23:17; Mal. 3:14-15; 1 Cor. 7:31; D&C 60:2; 121:33-36; refer in this text to Mosiah 17:11-13; Alma 39:4)

"What young musician, after years of agonizing rehearsal was finally scheduled to debut in a capacity concert hall, would, while en route to the performance, stop to join a long line forming at the latest hit movie, forgetting the thousands of people waiting to hear her? What world-class runner, after training for well over a decade, would find himself in the Olympic finals, only to stop running halfway through his race to watch the high-jump finals taking place on the other side of the field? These examples may seem preposterous—but how much more tragic for someone who, equipped with a testimony of the truth and a knowledge of the purpose of life, becomes more absorbed in life today than in life forever. Who's just a little more concerned about his or her status and standing in mortality than in eternity. Whose focus is not directed to God the Father and his Son, Jesus Christ."

Marvin J. Ashton (Ensign, Nov. 1992, p. 23)

"So let us have patience and faith as did Lehi who saw pointing fingers of scorn directed at those who grasped the iron rod, which rod, ironically, some of those same fingers once grasped. But, said Lehi, 'we heeded them not.' So it should be with us! Brothers and sisters, being pointed in the right direction, we do not need to worry about being pointed at!"

Neal A. Maxwell (Ensign, Nov. 1993, p. 20)

"I do not want 'Mormonism' to become popular. . . . I would rather pass through all the misery and sorrow, the troubles and trials of the Saints, than to have the religion of Christ become popular with the world. . . . Take a straight-forward course, and meet the jeers and frowns of the wicked."

Brigham Young (Journal of Discourses 10:297)

"Being popular can become narcotic. We can come to crave it and to need the frequent 'fixes' brought by the world's praise and caresses of recognition. A turned head bows much less easily. Popularity is dangerous especially because it focuses us on ourselves rather than keeping us attentive to the needs of others. We become preoccupied with self and with being noticed, letting those in real need 'pass by' us, and we 'notice them not' (Morm. 8:39). . . . To like being liked for its own sake is unhealthy. Similarly, overmuch concern with public image can cause us to rearrange priorities rather than striving to have Jesus' image in our countenance (see Alma 5:14,19). . . . The narrow and straight way that leads to salvation, alas, is the path less traveled by. Hence, there is no way we can both move with the herd and also move toward Jesus. Nevertheless, there are some who try to serve the Lord without offending the devil. . . . Firm followers of Jesus, therefore, will not be mere chameleons—adapting their colors to match the ever-changing circumstances by simply blending in."

Neal A. Maxwell (Ensign, Mar. 1995, p. 15)

"You have fears about being accepted. You worry about being popular in your age-group. It is natural to want to belong. Recently I heard of a good man who, after being married in the temple and having four children, fell away from the Church. His physical appearance became shabby and his demeanor sad as he became a drug addict, an alcoholic, and then a chain-smoker. He continued in this destructive lifestyle for many years. However, in time, . . . he eventually started on the long road back. One of the proudest days in his life came when he once again qualified for a temple recommend. Looking back on those bad years, he later admitted, 'All I ever wanted was to belong.' Seeking acceptance from the wrong source brought untold misery and pain."

James E. Faust (Ensign, Nov. 1997, p. 43)

1 Ne. 8:26-27   **THE GREAT AND SPACIOUS BUILDING**
(1 Ne. 11:36; 12:18; 22:23; refer in this text to 2 Ne. 9:28-30 & Jacob 2:13-17; 3 Ne. 6:10-16)

"A few members of the Church, alas, desert the cause; they are like one who abandons an oasis to search for water in the desert. Some of these few will doubtless become critics, and they will be welcomed into the 'great and spacious building.' Henceforth, however, so far as their theological accommodations are concerned, they are in a spacious but third-rate hotel. All dressed up, as the Book of Mormon says, 'exceedingly fine' (1 Nephi 8:27), they have no place to go except—one day, hopefully, home."

Neal A. Maxwell (First Nephi, The Doctrinal Foundation, BYU Religious Studies Center, p. 11)

"The current cries we hear coming from the great and spacious building tempt us to compete for ownership in the things of this world. We think we need a larger home, with a three-car garage, a recreational vehicle parked next to it. We long for designer clothes, extra TV sets, all with VCRs, the latest model computers, and the newest car. Often these items are purchased with borrowed money, without giving any thought to providing for our future needs. The result of all this instant gratification is overloaded bankruptcy courts and families that are far too preoccupied with their financial burdens."

L. Tom Perry (Ensign, Nov. 1995, p. 35)

"Unfortunately, some are among us who claim to be Church members but are somewhat like the scoffers in Lehi's vision—standing aloof and seemingly inclined to hold in derision the faithful who choose to accept Church authorities as God's special witnesses of the gospel and his agents in directing the affairs of the Church."

Harold B. Lee (Conference Report, Apr. 1971, p. 91)

1 Ne. 9   **NEPHI - AUTHOR & EDITOR**
                     (refer in this text to 1 Ne. 6)

                     "1 Nephi chapters 1-8 are apparently an abridgment of the book of Lehi; from
                     that point on Nephi became an author rather than an editor."

                                         R. Millet and J. F. McConkie (Doctrinal Commentary on the Book of Mormon, 1:27)

1 Ne. 9:5   **FOR A WISE PURPOSE**
                     (1 Ne. 6; D&C 10; refer in this text to Words of Mormon 1:5-7)

                     "He stated that he had been commanded to keep the small plates for 'a wise pur-
                     pose' in the Lord. That purpose would not be fully realized until the year 1828,
                     when Joseph Smith would be involved (with Martin Harris) in the loss of the first
                     116 manuscript pages of the Book of Mormon, pages translated from the large
                     plates. At that point the Lord commanded Joseph Smith to turn to the small
                     plates and undertake a translation of material which would cover approximately
                     the same time period as that which had been lost."

                                         R. Millet and J. F. McConkie (Doctrinal Commentary on the Book of Mormon, 1:62)

1 Ne. 9:59:6   **AND THUS IT IS**
                     (1 Ne. 14:30; 22:31; *Lehi in the Desert*, Nibley, p. 18; *The Messiah in Ancient
                     America*, Warren and Ferguson, p. 234)

1 Ne. 10:14   **GATHERING OF ISRAEL**
                     (2 Ne. 30:7; 1 Ne. 19:15-17; refer in this text to 2 Ne. 6:10-11; 3 Ne. 20:13,
                     29-33)

1 Ne. 10:16   **MY FATHER DWELT IN A TENT**
                     (*Lehi in the Desert*, Nibley, pp. 57-58; *In Search of Lehi's Trail*, Hilton & Hilton,
                     pp. 52, 68-70; 1 Ne. 2:15; 9:1; 16:6)

1 Ne. 10:17, 19 **SEEK**
                     (1 Ne. 2:19; 2 Ne. 1:25; Jacob 2:18-19; 3 Ne. 13:33; 14:7-8; Ether 12:41; Matt.
                     7:7-8; Deut. 4:29; John 5:39)

1 Nephi 11~15

The angel instructing Nephi uses world history (prophecy) to amplify the meaning of the vision of the tree of life.

1 Ne. 11:11

THE HOLY GHOST AS A PERSON
(John 16:7; *Answers to Book of Mormon Questions*, Sperry, pp. 27-30; *Book of Mormon Compendium*, Sperry, pp. 116-118; *Conference Report*, Apr., 1974, p. 131; *Teachings of the Prophet Joseph Smith*, p. 77)

"That the Spirit of the Lord is capable of manifesting Himself in the form and figure of man, is indicated by the wonderful interview between the Spirit and Nephi, in which He revealed Himself to the prophet, questioned him concerning his desires and belief, instructed him in the things of God, speaking face to face with the man [1 Nephi 11:11]. However, the Holy Ghost does not possess a body of flesh and bones, as do both the Father and the Son, but is a personage of spirit. Much of the confusion existing in human conceptions concerning the nature of the Holy Ghost arises from the common failure to segregate His person and powers. Plainly, such expressions as being filled with the Holy Ghost, and His falling upon persons, have reference to the powers and influences that emanate from God, and which are characteristic of Him; for the Holy Ghost may in this way operate simultaneously upon many persons even though they be widely separated, whereas the actual person of the Holy ghost cannot be in more than one place at a time."

James E. Talmage (Articles of Faith, p. 42)

"The Holy Ghost is a male personage. Note how often Jesus refers to the Holy Ghost as 'he' and 'him.'"

LeGrand Richards (A Marvelous Work and a Wonder, p. 115)

1 Ne. 11:16-23   **THE CONDESCENSION OF THE FATHER**
(*Behold the Lamb*, Clark, p. 97; *Crusader For Righteousness*, Ballard, p. 144; *Mormon Doctrine*, McConkie, pp. 155, 741-742; *BYU Speeches of the Year*, Dec. 1969, p. 4; *Come Unto Christ*, Benson, pp. 2-4; refer in this text to Alma 7:10 under the heading "Conceived by Power of Holy Ghost")

1 Ne. 11:24-36   **THE CONDESCENSION OF THE SON**
(2 Ne. 4:26; Mosiah 3:5-9)

"He showed condescension in his patience and restraint when brought before men for judgment. . . . (1 Nephi 19:9.) The God who created everything was judged to be nothing! And yet he endured it with complete patience. Imagine the Being whose power, whose light, whose glory holds the universe in order, the Being who speaks and solar systems, galaxies, and stars come into existence—standing before wicked men and being judged by them as being of no worth or value! When we think of what he could have done to these men who took him to judgment, we have a new and different sense of his condescension. When Judas led the soldiers and the high priests to the Garden of Gethsemane and betrayed him with a kiss, Jesus could have spoken a single word and leveled the entire city of Jerusalem. When the servant of the high priest stepped forward and slapped his face, Jesus could have lifted a finger and sent that man back to his original elements. When another man stepped forward and spit in his face, Jesus had only to blink and our entire solar system could have been annihilated. But he stood there, he endured, he suffered, he condescended."

Gerald N. Lund (Doctrines of the Book of Mormon, 1991 Sperry Symposium, pp. 85-86)

"The condescension of God (meaning the Son) consists in the fact that though he himself is the Lord Omnipotent, the very Being who created the earth and all things in it, yet being born of mortal woman, he submitted to all the Trials of mortality, suffering temptations, and pain of body, hunger, thirst, and fatigue, even more than man can suffer, except it be unto death' (Mosiah 3:5-8), finally being put to death in a most ignominious manner."

Bruce R. McConkie (Mormon Doctrine, p. 155)

"The condescension of God the Son thus consists in the fact that the Eternal One would 'descend from his throne divine' (*Hymns*, 1985, no. 193), be born in the most humble of circumstances, become among the most helpless of all creation—a human infant—and submit to the refining influences of mortal life."

Robert Millet (First Nephi, The Doctrinal Foundation, BYU Religious Studies Center, p. 169)

1 Ne. 11:21-23   **THE LOVE OF GOD**
                      (John 3:16-17; *Kisses at the Window*, Bassett, pp. 37-42)

"The tree laden with fruit was a representation of the love of God which he sheds forth among all the children of men. The Master himself, later in his earthly ministry, explained to Nicodemus how that great love was manifested. Said he: 'For God so loved the world, that he gave his only begotten Son, that whosoever believeth in him should not perish, but have everlasting life'; and then the Master added: 'For God sent not his Son into the world to condemn the world; but that the world through him might be saved' (John 3:16-17)."

Harold B. Lee (Conference Report, Apr. 1971, p. 90)

1 Ne. 11:25   **THE FOUNTAIN OF LIVING WATERS**
                      (Jer. 2:13; John 4:10,14)

1 Ne. 11:27   **THE FORM OF A DOVE**
                      (2 Ne. 31:8)

"The sign of the dove was instituted before the creation of the world, a witness for the Holy Ghost. . . . The Holy Ghost is a personage, and is in the form of a personage. It does not confine itself to the form of the dove, but in sign of the dove. The Holy Ghost cannot be transformed into a dove; but the sign of a dove was given to John to signify the truth of the deed, [Christ's baptism] as the dove is an emblem or token of truth and innocence."

Joseph Smith (History of the Church, 5:260-261)

1 Ne. 11:36   **THE PRIDE OF THE WORLD**
                      (refer in this text to Jacob 2:13-17; 2 Ne. 9:28-30; Alma 1:6; 3 Ne. 6:10-16)

1 Ne. 12:15,19   **KNOWING THIS, WHY DIDN'T NEPHI GIVE UP?**
                      (1 Ne. 13:35; 15:5; 2 Ne. 26:7, 10; Alma 45:10-14; Morm. 5:1-2; Moro. 9:6; Jacob 1:19)

1 Ne. 12:17   **TEMPTATIONS, BLIND EYES, HARD HEARTS, BROAD ROADS**
                      (1 Ne. 8:23)

"To blind the eyes is not to see or acknowledge the consequence of our actions. To harden the heart is to ignore or not be willing to accept counsel. To be led into the broad roads is to give in to worldly enticements and lose the influence of the Holy Spirit in our lives. . . . Temptation is like a magnetic force which holds a metal object in its power. It loses its magnetic force and power when you turn away from it. So we must turn away from temptation; then it will lose its power. . . . Temptation can be a compassionate way of warning us of possible dangers. It acts like a caution sign. It warns us of possible danger ahead. Temptation can alert the mind to turn away from an improper thought or act. As eternal beings living this earthly experience, we will not be free from temptation. Temptation implies an inner struggle to do that which is right. . . . We should expect temptation, for without temptations there would be little education and little character improvement."

Rulon G. Craven (Ensign, May 1996, pp. 76-77)

"Unless . . . [individuals] were exposed to temptation they never could know themselves, their own powers, their own weaknesses nor the power of God. If Satan had no power to tempt mankind, they would be in a state where they could neither know good nor evil; they could not know happiness nor misery. All their powers would lie dormant, for they would be destitute of that experience which prepares men to become like God, their Eternal Father."

George Q. Cannon (Gospel Truths, 1:109)

1 Ne. 13:3   **THE NATIONS AND KINGDOMS OF THE GENTILES**
(Mormon Doctrine, McConkie, pp. 310-311; *Book of Mormon Prophecies,* Warner, pp. 83-86)

"For the Nephites, 'Jews' are nationals, persons from the kingdom of Judah. (2 Nephi 30:4; 33:8). 'Gentiles' are persons from elsewhere. In this sense, the Latter-day Saints are called Gentiles (D&C 109:60). In this vision the 'nations and kingdoms of the Gentiles' are the European nations."

R. Millet and J. F. McConkie (Doctrinal Commentary on the Book of Mormon, 1:89)

1 Ne. 13:4-6,26,   **THE GREAT AND ABOMINABLE CHURCH**
28;14:10   (2 Ne. 10:16; 2 Ne. 26:21; Rev. 17-18; D&C 86:1-4; *Doctrinal New Testament Commentary,* McConkie, 3:548-552; *Mormon Doctrine,* McConkie, p. 137-139; *Book of Mormon Prophecies,* Warner, pp. 183-188; *First Nephi. The Doctrinal Foundation,* BYU Religious Studies Center, pp.177-191; *New Witness for God,* Roberts, 3:263-265; *Defense of the Faith and the Saints,* Roberts, 1:30-31)

"We should emphasize at this point that The Church of Jesus Christ of Latter-day Saints has not officially identified the great and abominable church. We are left to our own supposition and conclusion. If a person identifies it as one church in Europe, that is his personal opinion. And if another wishes to define it as all organizations in Europe, Asia Minor, and the Middle East through which the devil operated, that is his opinion. The scriptures are before us to study, but in the absence of an official declaration from the Church, our conclusions remain our private views and should not be taught as Church doctrine. As one studies chapter 13, one should be more concerned with what the great and abominable church did than with who or what the great and abominable church was."

Robert E. Parsons (Studies in Scripture, ed. by K. Jackson, 7:47)

"[Nephi] witnessed the great and abominable church in two separate time periods: the period following the New Testament era, [1 Ne.13] wherein the mother of harlots would essentially be apostate Christianity; and its rise in the last days to global status (1 Ne.14). After the restoration of the gospel in its fulness, Lucifer's forces—social, economic, political, fraternal, and religious—would become rampant in defiance of the church of the Lamb of God."

R. Millet and J. F. McConkie (Doctrinal Commentary on the Book of Mormon, 1:111)

"Individual orientation to the Church of the Lamb or to the great and abominable church is not only by membership but by loyalty. Just as there are those on the records of The Church of Jesus Christ of Latter-day Saints who belong to the great and abominable church by virtue of their loyalty to Satan and his life-style (2 Nephi 10:16), so there are members of other churches who will eventually belong to the Lamb by virtue of their loyalty to him and to his life-style, which will lead to their accepting the saving ordinances. The distinction is based on who has your heart, not on who has your records."

Stephen E. Robinson (First Nephi, The Doctrinal Foundation, BYU Religious Studies Center, p. 184)

CHARACTERISTICS OF THE GREAT & ABOMINABLE CHURCH
(1 Ne. 13:5, 1 Ne. 13:7, 1 Ne. 13:7, 1 Ne. 13:26-29, 1 Ne. 14:11, 1 Ne. 22:13-14, 1 Ne. 22:23)

1 Ne. 13:12   **A MAN AMONG THE GENTILES**
(Gospel Truths, Cannon, pp. 530-531; *Christopher Columbus*, Garr)

"Those who heard of my emprise called it foolish, mocked me, and laughed. But who can doubt but that the Holy Ghost inspired me?" (Columbus)

(Columbus—Don Quixote of the Seas, Wasserman, p. 18)

"[Referring to Moroni] This same angel was with Columbus, and gave him deep impressions, by dreams and by visions, respecting this New World. Tramelled by poverty and by an unpopular cause, yet his persevering and unyielding heart would not allow an obstacle in his way too great for him to overcome; and the angel of God helped him—was with him on the stormy deep, calmed the troubled elements, and guided his frail vessel to the desired haven."

Orson Hyde (Journal of Discourses 6:368)

"We interpret [1 Ne. 13:12] to refer to Columbus. It is interesting to note that the Spirit of God wrought upon him. . . . I recognize that in this anniversary year a host of critics has spoken out against him. I do not dispute that there were others who came to this Western Hemisphere before him. But it was he who in faith lighted a lamp to look for a new way to China and who in the process discovered America. His was an awesome undertaking—to sail west across the unknown seas faster than any before him of his generation. He it was who, in spite of the terror of the unknown and the complaints and near mutiny of his crew, sailed on with frequent prayers to the Almighty for guidance. In his reports to the sovereigns of Spain, Columbus repeatedly asserted that his voyage was for the glory of God and the spread of the Christian faith. Properly do we honor him for his unyielding strength in the face of uncertainty and danger."

Gordon B. Hinckley (Ensign, Nov. 1992, p. 52)

1 Ne. 13:13   **OTHER GENTILES**
(Conference Report, Oct. 1950, p. 64)

"It was the Lord that inspired that little band of people [Pilgrims] who crossed the mighty ocean and landed at Plymouth rock, because they desired to worship him according to the dictates of their own conscience. He watched over them and safeguarded their descendants and those who followed them to America, and in due time, there came an opportunity to establish liberty such as humankind had not known before."

George Albert Smith (Conference Report, Oct. 1922, pp. 95-96)

1 Ne. 13:14-15   LAMANITES SCATTERED & SMITTEN BY THE GENTILES
(2 Ne. 1:10-11; 10:19; 26:15,19; 3 Ne. 20:27-28; *Gospel Doctrine*, Smith, p. 409; *Companion to Your Study of the Book of Mormon*, Ludlow, pp. 280-281; *Bury My Heart at Wounded Knee*, Brown, pp. 6, 8; refer in this text to 3 Ne. 16:8-9)

". . . you will shine brightly, fired by the strength of the God who brought you to this Land and for some special purpose gave you dominion over this Land and over the red man. That destiny is a mystery to us, for we do not understand when the buffalo are all slaughtered, the wild horses are tamed, the secret corners of the forest heavy with scent of many men, and the view of the ripe hills blotted by talking wires. Where is the thicket? Gone. Where is the eagle? Gone. The end of living and the beginning of survival."

Chief Seattle's reply to the President's request for a large area of Indian land in 1854

1 Ne. 13:16   GENTILES - HUMBLED THEMSELVES BEFORE GOD
(*Conference Report*, Apr. 1952, p. 52)

[President Benson quoting Wilford Woodruff] "'I am going to bear my testimony to this assembly, if I never do it again in my life, that those men who laid the foundation of this American Government . . . were the best spirits the God of Heaven could find on the face of the earth. They were choice spirits, not wicked men. General Washington and all the men that labored for the purpose were inspired of the Lord' (*Journal of Discourses*, Sept. 16, 1898, p. 89). [Pres. Benson then added his own testimony] Yes, our nation's foundation is spiritual. Without spirituality, we are no better than any of the other nations which have sunk into oblivion."

Ezra Taft Benson (Righteousness Exalteth a Nation, p. 4)

1 Ne. 13:17-19   BATTLE WITH THEIR MOTHER GENTILES - DELIVERED BY GOD
(*Book of Mormon Authorship*, BYU Religious Studies Center, p. 189-211; *Cowley & Whitney on Doctrine*, pp. 314-315)

"It was not Satan who caused the heroic struggle of the American colonies, giving them power to win their freedom and independence, to the end that a nation might arise upon this chosen soil with a mission to foster and protect the infant and growing Church of Christ. That was a righteous war, and the divine inspiration for it rested upon the Patriot Fathers . . ."

Cowley & Whitney on Doctrine, p. 391

"It is an interesting thing that Washington, during the progress of the Revolutionary War and more particularly at the close of the Revolutionary War, expressed himself repeatedly to the effect that the American armies by themselves were altogether too weak to bring about this independence they now had achieved—but that independence came as a gift of God to these American colonies."

Mark E. Petersen (BYU Speeches of the Year, Feb. 20, 1968)

"From the standpoint of numbers, equipment, training, and resources, the ragtag army of the Colonists should never have won the war for independence. But America's destiny was not to be determined by overwhelming numbers, or better military weapons or strategy. As Adams declared: 'There's a divinity which shapes our ends.' God took a direct hand in the events that led to the defeat of the British. When the war was over, here is how Washington ascribed the victory; 'The success, which has hitherto attended our united efforts, we owe to the gracious interposition of heaven, and to that interposition let us gratefully ascribe the praise of victory, and the blessings of peace.' *(To the Executives of New Hampshire,* Nov. 3, 1789) It seems fashionable today for historians to 'secularize' our history. Many modern scholars seem uncomfortable with the idea that a Divine Power had a hand in the beginnings of our nation. They seek to explain away what the colonists themselves saw as divine intervention in their behalf."

Ezra Taft Benson (Righteousness Exalteth a Nation, p. 3)

1 Ne. 13:20-29   PLAIN AND PRECIOUS THINGS TAKEN FROM THE BIBLE
(Teachings of the Prophet Joseph Smith, pp. 9,10, 327; *A New Witness for the Articles of Faith,* McConkie, pp. 403, 405-406; preface to D&C 76)

"I believe the Bible as it read when it came from the pen of the original writers. Ignorant translators, careless transcribers, or designing and corrupt priests have committed many errors."

Teachings of the Prophet Joseph Smith, p. 327

"Surely the most plain and precious of all truths lost from the Bible, particularly the Old Testament, are the clear, unequivocal, and extensive declarations regarding the coming of Christ and the eternal, essential covenantal elements of his gospel which have been taught beginning with Adam and continuing on down in each dispensation of time. Thus the highest and most revered purpose of the Book of Mormon is to restore to Abraham's seed that crucial message declaring Christ's divinity, convincing all who read its pages with 'a sincere heart and real intent' that Jesus is the Christ (see Moroni 10:4)."

Jeffrey R. Holland (Nurturing Faith Through the Book of Mormon;
24th Annual Sperry Symposium, p. 4)

1 Ne. 13:34-38;   GENTILES PREACH TO LAMANITES
15:13-17;   (refer in this text to 3 Ne. 21:4; *Book of Mormon Prophecies*, Warner, pp. 126-141)
22:7-8;
2 Ne. 10:   "The Gentiles who administer spiritual blessings will be collectively part of the
18; 30:3-6   house of Israel, or Church members who have been gathered out from the Gentile nations but are still identified with the Gentiles culturally (see D&C 109:60)."

Monte Nyman (Ensign, Aug. 1994, p. 62; compare Bro. Nyman's words to
the quote by R. Millet and J. F. McConkie under 1 Ne. 13:3)

"If the Indians had all that was rightfully theirs they would not be where they are and we would not be where we are. Remember that. We are here through the grace of God, and do not forget it. The Lord gave us to share an inheritance with the Indians in this glorious land which is choice above all other lands in all the world. But it is ours only on the condition, as I see it, that we do our part in seeing that these people come into the Church."

Teachings of Spencer W. Kimball, p. 237

1 Ne. 13:37   MISSIONARIES TO HAVE POWER OF HOLY GHOST
(Journal of Discourses 7:128; New Witness for God, Roberts, pp. 244-245)

1 Ne. 14:13   MULTITUDES FIGHT AGAINST THE LAMB
(Journal of Discourses 7:184-185; 25:127-128)

1 Ne. 14:13-14   POWER OF GOD UPON SAINTS IN THE LAST DAYS
(HC, 2:381; 1 Ne. 22:16-17, 19; Hel. 5:20-52)

1 Ne. 14:14   COVENANT PEOPLE SCATTERED UPON ALL THE FACE OF THE EARTH
(Neal A. Maxwell, CES Fireside, BYU, Apr. 4, 1995)

1 Ne. 14:26   THE SEALED PORTION OF GOLD PLATES
(Ether 4:4-6; 2 Ne. 30:17-18; refer in this text to 2 Ne. 27:6-7, 11)

1 Ne. 15:3-4,   **HARD HEARTS**
10-11   (2 Ne. 33:2,5; Alma 9:31; 3 Ne. 2:1; Morm. 1:14,17; Ether 15:19; Moro. 8:28, 36-39; 9:4-5; refer in this text to 2 Ne. 9:28-30; 3 Ne. 6:10-16)

"One of Satan's greatest tools is pride: to cause a man or a woman to center so much attention on self that he or she becomes insensitive to his Creator or fellow beings. It is a cause for discontent, divorce, teenage rebellion, family indebtedness, and most other problems we face."

Ezra Taft Benson (Ensign, May 1979, p. 34)

1 Ne. 15:3, 8-9   **HAVE YE INQUIRED OF THE LORD**
(Ether 2:14; James 5:16; *Improvement Era,* Aug. 1961, p. 587; refer in this text to Alma 17:3)

"Let us all revive our individual and family prayers. Prayer is an armor of protection against temptation and I promise you that if you will teach your children to pray, fervently and full of faith, many of your problems are solved before they begin."

Teachings of Spencer W. Kimball, p. 117

1 Ne. 15:25   **HEED**
(Alma 45:23-24; 37:43-44; 12:9; D&C 11:2)

"'Heed,' as it is used in the Book of Mormon, has a certain permanency about it that is opposite to temporary obedience or alternating 'on again—off again' obedience. It is understood that as you continue to heed the Lord, you will not waver, vacillate, or complain, but rather, you will weather the storm and persevere no matter what you may be called upon to endure: [1 Nephi 16:3]. Sometimes *heed* can mean to be careful. In King Benjamin's great sermon, at the temple, he tells us that we must take upon ourselves the name of Christ and then be careful to avoid transgression:
    "[Mosiah 5:11 and Moroni 7:14]. . . . The Prophet Joseph used the word *heed* in telling the brethren that their mind, or intellect, could learn more than they thought. Contrary to the 'Fixed I.Q. Theory,' he taught: 'God has created man capable of instruction, with a faculty which may be enlarged in proportion to the heed and diligence given to the light communicated from heaven to the intellect.' *(Teachings of the Prophet Joseph Smith, p. 51.)* Could not this same principle apply to the Spirit?"

Robert E. Wells (Doctrines of the Book of Mormon, 1991 Sperry Symposium, pp. 12-13)

1 Ne. 15:33   **DIE IN WICKEDNESS & BE CAST OUT**
(Miracle of Forgiveness, Kimball, pp. 145-146; refer in this text to Alma 34:33)

1 Nephi 16~18

1 Ne. 16:2-3 **THE GUILTY TAKE THE TRUTH TO BE HARD**
(2 Ne. 9:40; Mosiah 13:4; Moro. 9:4-5; Mark 4:17)

"The prophet tells us what we need to know, not always what we want to know.
. . . 'The guilty taketh the truth to be hard, for it cutteth them to the very center'
(1 Ne. 16:1,3). Or, to put it in another prophet's words, 'Hit pigeons flutter.'
. . . The world prefers that prophets either be dead or mind their own business.
Some so-called experts of political science want the prophet to keep still on politics. Some would-be authorities on evolution want the prophet to keep still on
evolution. And so the list goes on and on. How we respond to the words of a
living prophet when he tells what we need to know, but would rather not hear,
is a test of our faithfulness."

Ezra Taft Benson (BYU Speeches of the Year, pp. 26-30)

1 Ne. 16:10, **LIAHONA**
26-29 (1 Ne. 18:12,21; Mosiah 1:16; Alma 37:38-47; D&C 17:1; *Since Cumorah,*
Nibley, pp. 283-296; *Messiah in Ancient America,* Warren & Ferguson, p. 116;
Commentary on the Book of Mormon, Reynolds and Sjodahl, 4:178-179;
Improvement Era, Feb. 1961, pp. 104-110)

"Wouldn't you like to have that kind of a ball—each one of you—so that
whenever you were in error it would point the right way and write messages to
you? . . . The Lord gave to . . . every person, a conscience which tells him every time
he starts to go on the wrong path. He is always told if he is listening; but people
can, of course, become so used to hearing the messages that they ignore them
until finally they do not register anymore. You must realize that you have something like the compass, like the Liahona, in your own system. Every child is
given it. When he is eight years of age, he knows good from evil, if his parents

have been teaching him well. If he ignores the Liahona that he has in his own makeup, he eventually may not have it whispering to him. But if we will remember that everyone of us has the thing that will direct him aright, our ship will not get on the wrong course . . . if we listen to the dictates of our own Liahona, which we call the conscience."

Spencer W. Kimball (Conference Report, Oct. 1976, pp. 116-117)

"The same Lord who provided a Liahona for Lehi provides for you and for me today a rare and valuable gift to give direction to our lives, to mark the hazards to our safety, and to chart the way, even safe passage—not to a promised land, but to our heavenly home. The gift to which I refer is known as your *patriarchal blessing.*"

Thomas S. Monson (Ensign, Nov. 1986, p. 65)

"One fascinating peculiarity of the Liahona was that not only did its pointers guide them in the wilderness but 'a new writing, which was plain to be read' appeared on the pointers to give them 'understanding concerning the ways of the Lord; and it was written and changed from time to time, according to their faith, diligence' and heed (1 Nephi 16:29). Very little is said about this phenomenon. In fact, I can find no further reference to this changeable writing. As I read the Book of Mormon, however, something strange seems to happen to me. Passages of scriptures that I have read many times in one light seem to change—and suddenly there is a new meaning to that old and familiar scripture. I like to think that the Book of Mormon is truly like the Liahona of old. Not only does it point us in the way of the Lord and to the Lord according to the faith, diligence, and heed we give it, but if we are interested enough to read it again and again, from cover to cover, there are times when a 'new writing'—plain to be read—seems to appear."

Robert E. Wells (Doctrines of the Book of Mormon, 1991 Sperry Symposium, p. 13)

1 Ne. 16:18,21   BROKEN BOW (location)
(Since Cumorah, Nibley, p. 254)

"This would locate the incident roughly in the vicinity of Jiddah, Saudi Arabia, where the weather is a merciless combination of heat, humidity, sand, and salt— a force strong enough to destroy steel. We were stunned to see holes rusted through car fenders in a few months' time. Between March and November the heat is pitiless. Even in late January the temperature hovers around 85 degrees. Humidity averages about 60 percent year round, and in the more moist part of a fifteen-year cycle the humidity rises to a yearly average of 92 percent.

Unpainted metal simply cannot survive such conditions. We saw little metal used in either local building or the shipyards. Might this have also happened to Nephi's bow? Weakened by rust, it could have snapped in his hands when he drew it to its limits. The climate would also explain why his brothers' bows lost their springs at or around the same time. If they were wooden bows, they would have remained tensile and strong in the dry area around Jerusalem; but several years in the humid climate along the Red Sea's coastal plain, and even a short time in the vicinity of Jiddah, would inevitably have caused them to absorb moisture until they became as limber as saplings. In fact, acquaintances of ours often reported similar experiences with some of their wood possessions."

Lynn M. and Hope Hilton (In Search of Lehi's Trail, pp.81-82)

"According to the ancient Arab writers, the only bow-wood obtainable in all Arabia was the nab' wood that grew only amid the inaccessible and overhanging crags of Mount Jasum and Mount Azd, which are situated in the very region where, if we follow the Book of Mormon, the broken bow incident occurred."

Hugh Nibley (Lehi in the Desert, pp. 66-68)

1 Ne. 16:20,23   SUPPORTING OUR LEADERS DURING TOUGH TIMES
(1 Ne. 5:2-7; 7:19-21; D&C 28:6,12; 43:3-4; Acts 23:5,10-11; Eph. 6:1; *History of the Church* 2:177; refer in this text to Alma 61:9,19)

"The bishop may be a humble man. Some of you may think you are superior to him, and you may be, but he is given authority direct from our father in heaven. You recognize it. Seek his advice. . . . Recognition of authority is an important principle."

David O. McKay (Conference Report, Oct. 1965, p. 105)

"No man possessing a correct understanding of the spirit of the gospel and of the authority and law of the Holy Priesthood will attempt for a moment to run before his file leader or to do anything that is not strictly in harmony with his wish and the authority that belongs to him. The moment a man in a subordinate position begins to usurp the authority of his leader, that moment he is out of his place, and proves by his conduct that he does not comprehend his duty, that he is not acting in the line of his calling, and is a dangerous character. . . . He is in error the moment he acts contrary to and independent of the direction of his presiding officer; and if he continues in that course he will go astray entirely, and those who follow him will follow him astray."

Joseph F. Smith (Gospel Doctrine, pp. 185-186)

"The Prophet Joseph Smith taught that 'it is contrary to the economy of God for any member of the Church, or any one, to receive instruction for those in authority, higher than themselves' *(Teachings of the Prophet Joseph Smith, p. 21).* That same principle precludes receiving revelation for anyone outside one's defined circle of responsibility."

Russell M. Nelson (Ensign, May 1993, p. 39)

"Years ago my great-grandfather, while an investigator, attended a Mormon meeting during which a member had a quarrel with the branch president. When the service was over, Mrs. Benson turned to Ezra T. and asked him what he thought of the Mormons now. I'll always be grateful for his answer. He said he thought the actions of its members in no way altered the truth of Mormonism. That conviction saved him from many a tragedy."

Ezra Taft Benson (God, Family, Country, p. 335)

"I say again, *FOLLOW THE BRETHREN.* In a few days there opens another general conference of the Church. The servants of the Lord will counsel us. You may listen with anxious ears and hearts, or you may turn that counsel aside. As in these devotionals, what you shall gain will depend not so much upon their preparation *of* the messages as upon your preparation *for* them. . . . On one occasion [Karl G. Maeser], was leading a party of young missionaries across the Alps. As they slowly ascended the steep slope, he looked back and saw a row of sticks thrust into the glacial snow to mark the one safe path across the otherwise treacherous mountains. Something about those sticks impressed him, and halting the company of missionaries he gestured toward them and said, 'Brethren, there stands the priesthood. They are just common sticks like the rest of us—some of them may even seem to be a little . . . [less than perfect], but the position they hold makes them what they are. If we step aside from the path they mark, we are lost.'"

Boyd K. Packer (BYU Devotional, Mar. 23, 1965)

"Nephi broke his bow when they were in the wilderness. . . . Laman and Lemuel complained, of course. . . . But for the first and only time the book tells us about, that I know of, even wonderful old father Lehi complained. He to whom God had revealed his will, this Lehi, when it came to facing starvation, even he complained. . . . Lehi was the prophet, but he was old. Nephi had already been designated to succeed. He had seen angels and had talked with the spirit of the Lord. He had had marvelous experiences. The time was here, now, for him to take over—his dad was wavering. The old man had lost it. What to do? Nephi says he made a bow and an arrow out of some available wood, got a sling and stones and, 'I said unto my Father, 'Whither shall I go to obtain food?' It is a simple thing, isn't it? This is what Goethe meant when he said, 'If you treat an individual as he is, he will stay as he is. But if you treat him as if he were what he could be and ought to be, he will become what he ought to be.' This means that Nephi went to his father and said, 'Dad, the Lord has blessed you. You are his servant. I need to know where to go to get food. Dad, you ask him, will you?' Oh, he could have gone to his own knees. He could have taken over. I count this one of the really significant lessons of life in the book. . . . A son who had strength enough, and humility enough, and manliness enough to go to his wavering superior and say, 'You ask God, will you?' Because somehow he knew this is how you make men strong, that wise confidence in men builds them. Lehi asked God and God told him, and Lehi's leadership was restored."

Marion D. Hanks (BYU Speeches of the Year, May 4, 1960)

"Individual members of the Church may receive revelation for their own callings and areas of responsibility and for their own families. They may not receive spiritual instruction for those higher in authority. . . . Those who claim direct revelation from God for the Church outside the established order and channel of the priesthood are misguided."

James E. Faust (Ensign, May 1996, p. 7)

1 Ne. 16:23 **I DID MAKE A BOW**
(refer in this text to Mosiah 24:14-15)

"Obedient as Nephi was, his obedience did not shield him from afflictions. The Book of Mormon teaches that opposition is a necessary part of life's test. Nephi's bow broke in the wilderness, even though his family needed food. Today righteous Saints lose their jobs even though they have paid their tithing and magnified their Church callings. The test of the 'broken bow' is not only for the one who breaks the bow but also for those affected by the break. . . . Yet Nephi found a solution to his dilemma in one simple act: 'I, Nephi, did make out of wood a bow, and out of a straight stick, an arrow' (1 Nephi 16:23). Instead of murmuring, Nephi simply went to work and made another bow. Murmuring wastes time, lengthens one's journey, and hardens one's heart. . . . God may not always stop bows from breaking, but he does help in the construction of new ones."

Dennis L. Largey (Doctrines of the Book of Mormon, 1991 Sperry Symposium, p. 61)

1 Ne. 16:24,   **THEY DID REPENT**
32, 39;   (refer in this text to 1 Ne. 3:29-30; 1 Ne. 18:20)
17:53-55;
18:15, 20

1 Ne. 16:34-35   **WOMEN MOURN**
                         (Lehi in the Desert, Nibley, pp. 90-91; *An Approach to the Book of Mormon*, 1957
                         ed., Nibley, pp. 214-215; *In Search of Lehi's Trail*, Hilton & Hilton, p. 95)

1 Ne. 17:1,6   **TRAVEL EASTWARD TO BOUNTIFUL**
                         (In Search of Lehi's Trail, Hilton & Hilton, pp. 40-41)

"The best guide [American text] to Arabia at the time of the writing of the Book
of Mormon imagined forests and lakes in the center of the peninsula, while
insisting that the whole coastline was 'a rocky wall as dismal and barren as can
be: not a blade of grass or a green thing,' to be found. The Book of Mormon
reverses the picture and has Lehi avoid the heart of the continent to discover
smiling woodlands on the south coast."

Hugh Nibley (Lehi in the Desert, p. 127)

1 Ne. 17:2,   **EAT RAW MEAT - NO FIRE**
12-13   *(In Search of Lehi's Trail*, Hilton & Hilton, pp. 101-102)

"All this bears out the conviction, supported both by modern experience and the
evidence of archaeology, that Lehi was moving through a dangerous world. In
ancient times Jewish merchants traveling through the desert fell so often into
the hands of Bedouin raiders that by the beginning of the Christian era their
word for 'captor' normally meant simply 'Arab'!

Hugh Nibley (Lehi in the Desert, pp. 73-74)

"On the probable trail which Lehi traveled there are today 118 waterholes,
spaced (on the average) eighteen miles apart. It was the custom of experienced
travelers in Arabia that they never built a fire, as it could attract the attention of
a prowling, raiding party. As a result, they ate much of their food raw, as recorded in the Book of Mormon. Attacking and plundering camps still seems to be
the chief object of some Arab tribes."

Paul Cheesman (First Nephi, The Doctrinal Foundation, BYU Religious Studies Center, p. 245)

1 Ne. 17:8-11, **NEPHI'S WORK ETHIC**
16 (refer in this text to 2 Ne. 5:24; *Conference Report,* L. Tom Perry, Oct. 1991)

1 Ne. 17:19 **THEY DID REJOICE OVER ME**
(refer in this text to 1 Ne. 7:20-21)

1 Ne. 17:20-22 **HORIZONTAL vs. VERTICAL THINKING**
(Since Cumorah, Nibley, pp. 270-273)

1 Ne. 17:35,40 **RIGHTEOUS ARE FAVORED OF GOD**
(D&C 95:12; Matt. 5:45; 1 Sam. 2:30; John 14:21; 15:10; Rom. 2:11; Col. 3:25; refer in this text to 2 Ne. 26:24-28, 33)

"It is common in our day to hear reference made to the unconditional love of God. If such an expression is intended to convey the idea that all will enjoy the love of God to the same degree, irrespective of what they do or how they live, such is incompatible with the testimony of the scriptures and the voice of the Lord himself (see D&C 95:12)."

R. Millet and J. F. McConkie (Doctrinal Commentary on the Book of Mormon, 1:136)

1 Ne. 17:41 **FIERY FLYING SERPENTS**
(Hel. 8:14-15; Alma 33:20; Num. 21; John 3:14-17; 2 Kings 5:8-14; *Messiah in Ancient America,* Ferguson, pp. 138-144; *Conference Report,* Oct. 1968, pp. 75-76)

1 Ne. 17:41 **THE SIMPLENESS OF THE WAY**
(D&C 64:33; 2 Kings 5:1-14)

"Brothers and sisters, we must not fail to do the simple and easy things that the gospel requires and thereby deny ourselves and our families the great blessings that the Lord has promised. . . . Charles Francis Adams, the grandson the second president of the United States, was a successful lawyer, a member of the U.S. ambassador to Britain. Amidst his responsibilities, he had little time to spare. He did, however, keep a diary. One day he wrote, 'Went fishing with my son today—a day wasted!' On that same date, Charles's son, Brooks Adams, had printed in his own diary, 'Went fishing with my father today—the most wonderful day of my life' *(Daily Guideposts,* 1994). President Hunter has said, 'Frequently it is the commonplace tasks that have the greatest positive effect on the lives of others' *(BYU 1986-87 Devotional and Fireside Speeches,* p. 115). I pray that we will heed the counsel of our prophet and have the faith to follow the Savior by doing the simple things His gospel requires."

Rex D. Pinegar (Ensign, Nov. 1994, p. 82)

1 Ne. 17:45   **PAST FEELING**
(Heb. 5:11; *Ensign*, May 1991, p. 13; refer in this text to Moro. 9:20)

1 Ne. 17:47;   **MY FRAME HAS NO STRENGTH**
19:20   (JS-H. 1:20; 1 Ne. 1:7; Dan. 8:27; Moses 1:10; D&C 324-325 Student Manual, pp. 158-159; *Teachings of the Prophet Joseph Smith*, pp. 280-281)

1 Ne. 17:47-48   **FULL OF THE SPIRIT OF GOD**
(Mosiah 13:2-3,5; John 7:30; Acts 6:15; Doctrinal *Commentary on the Book of Mormon*, Millet & McConkie, 1:139)

1 Ne. 17:50   **IF GOD COMMANDS - I CAN DO IT**
(refer in this text to 1 Ne. 3:7; *Manchester Conference Report*, Aug. 1971, pp. 101-103)

"God revealed to Nephi the necessity of building a ship. The means were not within his reach, but he felt it was right to build, and with that knowledge he proceeded to find the way to make the tools and to build the ship. Did he make mistakes? Did he falter? No doubt,—else why did his murmuring brothers say: 'We told you you could not build a ship; we knew you did not have the wisdom.' But he knew he was right, and he knew that God would strengthen him in building. That thought held him; it supported him; and he succeeded in the task before him. So it is with us; when we are asked to do a thing, the question in our minds should be: Is that necessary; is that right? If so, then it shall be done, and God will open the way."

David O. McKay (Conference Report, Apr. 1909, p. 68)

"Half obedience will be rejected as readily as full violation, and maybe quicker, for half rejection and half acceptance is but a sham, an admission of lack of character, a lack of love for Him. It is actually an effort to live on both sides of the line."

Mark E. Petersen (Ensign, May 1982, p. 16)

1 Ne. 17:55   **HONOR THY FATHER AND MOTHER**
(Ex. 20:12; Mosiah 13:20)

"The fifth commandment's laudable emphasis upon honoring parents, unless checked by the first commandment, could result in unconditional loyalty to errant parents rather than to God."

Neal A. Maxwell (Ensign, May 1993, p.78)

"Let us also learn to be forgiving of our parents, who, perhaps having made mistakes as they reared us, almost always did the best they knew how. May we ever forgive them as we would likewise wish to be forgiven by our own children for mistakes we make."

Ezra Taft Benson (Ensign, Nov. 1989, pp. 6-7)

"Be true to your parents and your heritage. Regrettably there are a few parents who act in a way that does serious injustice to their children. But these cases are relatively few. No one has a greater interest in your welfare, in your happiness, in your future than do your mothers and fathers. They are of a prior generation. That is true. But they were once the age that you are now. Your problems are not substantially different from what theirs were. If they occasionally place restrictions on you, it is because they see danger down the road. Listen to them. What they ask you to do may not be to your liking. But you will be much happier if you do it."

Gordon B. Hinckley (Ensign, May 1996, pp. 92-93)

"I have frequently walked by a rest home that provides excellent care. But it is heart-rending to see so many parents and grandparents in that good care facility so forgotten, so bereft of dignity, so starved for love. To honor parents certainly means to take care of physical needs. But it means much, much more. It means to show love, kindness, thoughtfulness, and concern for them all of the days of their lives. It means to help them preserve their dignity and self-respect in their declining years. It means to honor their wishes and desires and their teachings both before and after they are dead. . . . Besides being one of God's commandments, the kind, thoughtful consideration of parents is a matter of common decency and self-respect. On their part, parents need to live so as to be worthy of the respect of their children. I cannot help wondering about parents who adopt the attitude with their children, 'do as I say, not as I do.' . . . Children often take license from their parents' behavior and go beyond the values the parents wish to establish."

James E. Faust (Ensign, Nov. 1986, pp. 9-10)

1 Ne. 18:5-6,10   **LAW OF PRIMOGENITURE**
(2 Ne. 5:3; Mosiah 10:11-15; *Companion to Your Study of the Book of Mormon*, Ludlow, p. 116)

1 Ne. 18:9   **MUSIC**
(3 Ne. 4:31; Moro. 7:16-17; D&C 88:121; 25:12; 50:23; Eph. 5:19; Psalm 114:1-4; 1 Sam. 16:23; Mark 14:26; *Companion to Your Study of the Book of Mormon*, Ludlow, pp. 115-116; *Kisses at the Window*, Bassett, pp. 75-76; Benson, *Ensign*, May 1986, p. 45; refer in this text to Ether 6:9)

"In our day music itself has been corrupted. Music can, by its tempo, by its beat, by its intensity, dull the spiritual sensitivity of [people]. . . . Our youth have been brought up on a diet of music that is loud and fast, more intended to agitate than to pacify, more intended to excite than to calm. . . . Be selective in what you consume and what you produce. It becomes a part of you. . . . Young people, you cannot afford to fill your mind with the unworthy hard music of our day. It is *not* harmless.'"

Boyd K. Packer (Ensign, Jan. 1974, pp. 25-28)

"And so we urge parents in the Church to show as much interest in the records and tapes their children purchase as they would the books and magazines they bring into the home. There are many parents who would not for one moment tolerate a pornographic magazine in their homes who unwittingly provide money for music, some of which in its influence can be quite as damaging. . . . Keep that in mind when you have a problem with young people and their music. To change it may take some time and require inspiration. . . . Our people ought to be surrounded by good music of all kinds. Parents ought to foster good music in the home and cultivate a desire to have their children learn the hymns of inspiration. . . . We encourage parents to include musical training in the lives of their children. . . . How wonderful is the music instructor who will teach children and youth to play and will acquaint them with good music in their formative years, including the music of worship."

Boyd K. Packer (Ensign, Jan 1974, pp. 25-28)

"It was pleasing unto Satan when Lehi's children and the 'Sons of Ishmael and also their wives began to make themselves merry, insomuch that they began to dance, and to sing, and to speak with much rudeness."

Ezra Taft Benson (God, Family, Country, pp. 248-249)

"Should you have any reservations whether . . . a style of dancing or tempo of music is in accord with Church standards, may I suggest this guide: Does it uplift and inspire one to higher ideals? Does it develop wholesome relationships between young men and women, or appeal to and arouse their baser instincts? Will it cause one to be a better Latter-day Saint and lead one closer to the Savior?"

Ezra Taft Benson (Finglas Ireland Branch Dedication, Sept. 10, 1980)

"A loving stake presidency helped their youth have a better understanding of the pitfalls of being continually bombarded by the degrading lyrics of many of today's popular songs and the indecent images portrayed in some movies and videos. They were taught these mediums can produce much that is positive, inspiring, uplifting, and attractive; or they can also desensitize the mind and make what is wrong and evil look normal, exciting, and acceptable. Many of the young people hearkened to their stake presidency and courageously destroyed their tapes, discs, and videos which were not 'virtuous, lovely, or of good report or praiseworthy' (A of F 1:13) Young people, please don't listen to music that contains ideas that contradict principles of the gospel. 'Don't listen to music that promotes Satanism or other evil practices, encourages immorality, uses foul and offensive language, or drives away the Spirit" (*For the Strength of Youth,* Salt Lake City: The Church of Jesus Christ of Latter-day Saints, 1990, p. 14).

H. David Burton (Ensign, May 1994, p. 68)

"The Pied Piper of Hamelin? You will recall that he entered Hamelin and offered, for a specified sum of money, to rid the town of the vermin with which it was plagued. When the contract was agreed upon, he played his pipe and the rats came swarming from the buildings and followed him to the river, where they drowned. When the town leaders refused to pay him for his services, he returned to play his pipe and led the precious children away from the safety of their families and their homes, never to return. Are there Pied Pipers even today? Are they playing alluring music to lead, to their own destruction, those who listen and follow?"

Thomas S. Monson (Ensign, May 1995, p. 49)

1 Ne. 18:16   **MURMURING**
(1 Ne. 16:3, 20, 25, 35-36; 17:2,17, 22, 49; 2 Ne. 27:35; Maxwell, *Ensign* Nov. 1989, p. 83; *Conference Report*, Ballard, Oct. 1991; refer in this text to Alma 58: 9-11, 34-35)

"Murmuring against priesthood and auxiliary leaders is one of the most poisonous things that can be introduced into the home of a Latter-day Saint."

David O. McKay (Improvement Era, Mar. 1969, p. 3)

"We find here a man of faith; a man who submits to affliction without murmuring. In all his history we find that he followed the commandments of the Lord. The Lord said to him in the beginning that if he followed His commandments he should be prospered in the land, and he was prospered. I wish to bear my testimony to the Latter-day Saints that all of us who will obey the commandments of God will be prospered in the land. Sacrifice doth bring forth the blessings of heaven."

Heber J. Grant (Conference Report, Oct. 1899, p. 19)

"Apostasy often begins with criticism of current leaders. Apostasy usually begins with question and doubt and criticism. . . . They allege love for the gospel and the Church but charge that leaders are a little 'off the beam'! He generally wants all the blessings of the Church: membership, its priesthood, its temple privileges, and expects them from the leaders of the Church, though at the same time claiming that those same leaders have departed from the path. He now . . . adopts a martyr complex. . . ."

Teachings of Spencer W. Kimball, p. 462

"In both the Old Testament and the Book of Mormon, *murmur* is used primarily for the exoduses. Forms of the Hebrew root l*wn* (translated "to murmur" in the King James version) occur eighteen times in the Old Testament. All but one of them are connected with the Exodus. How is the English word *murmur* used in the Book of Mormon? It appears thirty-three times; of these, nineteen describe events in the Old World wilderness."

Terrence L. Szink (Rediscovering the Book of Mormon, F.A.R.M.S., p. 40)

1 Ne. 18:20   **WORLDLY SORROW**
(1 Ne. 7:20; 2 Cor. 7:9-10; refer in this text to Morm. 2:13; Alma 34:33; Alma 42:29)

"Very frequently people think they have repented and are worthy of forgiveness when all they have done is to express sorrow or regret at the unfortunate happening, but their repentance is barely started. Until they have begun to make changes in their lives, transformation in their habits, and to add new thoughts to their minds, to be sorry is only a bare beginning."

Teachings of Spencer W. Kimball, p. 87

"In August 1899, the steamship *City of Rome* collided with an iceberg just off the coast of Newfoundland. There was panic aboard the vessel, and for a time passengers wondered whether they would have to take to the lifeboats. Among those passengers was one who professed belief in God and in the restored gospel but had actually not conformed to his belief. He would not participate in worship; he violated the Word of Wisdom and assumed generally a careless attitude toward things religious. Every morning from the time that boat left Glasgow harbor until the morning of the collision this gentleman had taken his coffee at breakfast. At the moment of the collision he was at the bar. Strange as it may seem, in the hour of imminent danger he was the first of his group to suggest that they retire for prayer and seek God's protection. The vessel made no progress that night, a sleepless one for this particular passenger. Next morning he ordered neither tea nor coffee, and, seeing this, one of his companions said: 'What's the matter, Doctor? Aren't you going to have your coffee this morning?'

'No, sir,' came the prompt reply. And then seemingly in all earnestness he added: 'I am not going to taste another drop of tea or coffee until we get to New York!'

No self-denial, no outward act, no pretense can conceal from the Lord an insincere heart."

David O. McKay (Gospel Ideals, p. 508)

1 Ne. 18:23   **WHERE DID THEY LAND?**
(Teachings of the Prophet Joseph Smith, p. 267; *History of the Church*, Smith, 6:318-319; *New Witness for God*, Roberts, 3:501-503; *Treasures from the Book of Mormon*, Skousen, 1:1157-1158)

1 Ne. 18:25   **HORSES**
(Enos 1:21; *Companion to Your Study of the Book of Mormon*, Ludlow, p.117; *Messages and Evidences of the Book of Mormon*, Harris, pp. 85-90)

1 Nephi 19

1 Ne. 19:1-7 **THESE PLATES**
(refer in this text to 1 Ne. 6; 1 Ne. 9; Words of Mormon 1:5-7)

"When the family of Lehi reached the western hemisphere, Nephi was commanded of God to make a set of plates upon which the history of his people was
to be kept. He did so, recounting their journey in the wilderness and prophecies
he and his father had made. This record is known to us as the large plates, which
apparently contained the book of Lehi. Some twenty years later (ca. 570 B.C).
Nephi was commanded to make another set of plates known to us as the small
plates or book of Nephi (see 2 Nephi 5:28-31), in which he recorded only that
which was sacred. Thus the book of Lehi became primarily a temporal history,
while the book of Nephi became a record of prophecies and a collection of sacred
events."

R. Millet and J. F. McConkie (Doctrinal Commentary on the Book of Mormon, 1:145)

1 Ne. 19:8-10 **PRE-MORTAL DECISIONS**
(Acts 17:26; Deut. 32:7-9; D&C 122:9; 138:53-56; Job 14:5; *But for a Small
Moment*, Maxwell; *Kisses at the Window*, Bassett, pp. 33-36; refer in this text to
Alma 13:3-5; Ether 12:26-27)

"I believe the Savior possessed a fore-knowledge of all the vicissitudes through
which He would have to pass in the mortal tabernacle. If Christ knew beforehand, so did we. But in coming here, we forgot all, that our agency might be
free indeed, to choose good or evil."

Joseph F. Smith (Gospel Doctrine, p. 13)

"God does nothing by chance but always by design as a loving Father. The manner of our coming into the world, our parents, the time, and other circumstances of our birth and condition, are all according to eternal purposes, direction, and appointment of divine Providence."

Spencer W. Kimball (Ensign, Dec. 1974, p. 5)

". . . we had our own free agency in our pre-mortal existence, and whatever we are today is likely the result of that which we willed to be heretofore. We unquestionably knew before we elected to come to this earth the conditions under which we would here exist. . . . I have a conviction deep down in my heart that we are exactly what we should be, each one of us, except as we may have altered that pattern by deviating from the laws of God here in mortality."

Henry D. Moyle (Conference Report, Oct. 1952, pp. 71-72)

"When in situations of stress we wonder if there is any more in us to give. We can be comforted to know that God, who knows our capacity perfectly, placed us here to succeed. No one was foreordained to fail or to be wicked. Let us remember that we were measured before and were found equal to our tasks; therefore, let us continue, but with a more determined discipleship. When we feel overwhelmed, let us recall the assurance that God will not over-program us; he will not press upon us more than we can bear."

Neal A. Maxwell (BYU Speeches of the Year, 1978, p. 156)

"It was my father who taught me about the premortal life. He explained that long ago you and I were born as daughters in our Heavenly Father's family. We made sacred decisions there that have influenced what we are doing now. When I was younger, my grandfather gave me a blessing. He blessed me that I would 'continue my ministry here that I had so nobly performed there.' Now, if I had a ministry in the premortal existence, then so did you. It is not by chance that you were born now, in this season of the world's history. . . . We all come from many different kinds of families. Some of you are doing hard things. . . . Some of you may worry about your relationships with your mother or father as you learn together how to live in families. You are learning that sometimes the Savior calms the storm. Sometimes He lets the storm rage and calms you. . . . In every young woman's heart is a deep yearning to someday be a wife and a mother. These feelings were nurtured in your soul long before you came to this earth."

Carol B. Thomas (Ensign, May 1998, pp. 91-92)

"Before we were born, . . . we made certain commitments and we agreed to come to this earth with great, rich, but different gifts. . . . Hold your soul very still, and listen to the whisperings of the Holy Spirit. Follow the noble, intuitive feelings planted deep within your souls by Deity in the previous world."

James E. Faust (Ensign, May 1998, pp. 95,97)

1 Ne. 19:10   **ZENOCK AND ZENOS**
(Answers to Gospel Questions, Smith, 4:138-139)

1 Ne. 19:10   **HOW IS CHRIST THE FATHER?**
(2 Ne. 31:21; Mosiah 16:15; Morm. 3:21; 9:12; *Man: His Origin and Destiny*, Smith, pp. 117-129; *Articles of Faith*, Talmage, pp. 465-473; *A Marvelous Work and a Wonder*, Richards, pp. 296-297; *Doctrines of Salvation*, Smith, 1:26-27)

1. *Doctrinal New Testament Commentary*, McConkie, 1:73-74; *Promised Messiah*, McConkie, p. 363; *Articles of Faith*, Talmage, pp. 468, 470; Mosiah 5:7; 15:10-12; 27:25-26; Ether 3:14; D&C 25:1; 34:1-4; 39:4; Heb. 5:9

2. Ether 3:14-15; D&C 38:1-3; 2 Ne. 9:5; 11:7; 25:12; Mosiah 3:8; Alma 11:39; 3 Ne. 9:15; Hel. 16:18

3. *Lectures on Faith* 5:2; *Doctrines of Salvation*, Smith, 1:27-30; *Promised Messiah*, McConkie, p. 371; Mosiah 15:1-5; 3 Ne. 11:14; D&C 29:1, 42; 19:16-19; 45:5, 28; 49:5, 28; John 5:43; 7:16; Moses 4:6, 32-33; refer in this text to 3 Ne.1:12-14

"Jesus is even described as the Father, because he is the Father-Creator of this and other worlds. Furthermore, he is the Father of all who are born again spiritually. When we take upon ourselves his name and covenant to keep his commandments, we then become his sons and daughters, "the children of Christ." Additionally, since he and the Father are one in attributes and in purpose, Jesus acts for the Father through divine investiture, sometimes speaking as the Father."

Neal A. Maxwell (Mosiah, Salvation Only Through Christ, ed. by Nyman and Tate, pp. 5-6)

1 Ne. 19:13-14   **A HISS AND A BYWORD**
(1 Ne. 22:5; 3 Ne. 29:8; Matt. 27:24-25; *Israel! Do You Know*, Richards, pp. 237-238; *The Way to Perfection*, Smith, pp. 133-134)

1 Ne. 19:15-17   **THE GATHERING OF ISRAEL**
(Teachings of Spencer W. Kimball, pp. 438-439; *Rediscovering the Book of Mormon,* F.A.R.M.S., pp. 186-196; McKay, *Conference Report,* Oct. 1918, pp. 44-46; *Doctrines of Salvation,* Smith, 3:9; refer in this text to 2 Ne. 6:10-11; 30:7; 3 Ne. 20:13,29-33)

1 Ne. 19:23   **LIKEN SCRIPTURES TO YOURSELF**
(Alma 13:20; 33:14; 3 Ne. 27:24-26; *Journal of Discourses* 7:333; *Church News,* Jan. 24, 1976, p. 4; refer in this text to Alma 17:2)

"Do you read the Scriptures, my brethren and sisters, as though you were writing them, a thousand, two thousand, or five thousand years ago? Do you read them as though you stood in the place of the men who wrote them? If you do not feel thus, it is your privilege to do so, that you may be as familiar with the spirit and meaning of the written word of God as you are with your daily walk and conversation, or as you are with your workmen or with you households."

Discourses of Brigham Young, p. 128

"The Book of Mormon was written for us today. . . . God who knows the end from the beginning, told (Mormon) what to include in his abridgement that we would need for our day. . . ."

Ezra Taft Benson (Conference Report, Apr. 1975, pp. 96-97)

"The Nephites never had the book; neither did the Lamanites of ancient times. It was meant for us. Mormon wrote near the end of the Nephite civilization. Under the inspiration of God, who sees all things from the beginning, he abridged centuries of records, choosing the stories, speeches, and events that would be most helpful to us. Each of the major writers of the Book of Mormon testified that he wrote for future generations (see 2 Nephi 25:21; 2 Nephi 26:14; Jacob 1:3; Enos 1:15-16; Jarom 1:2; Mormon 7:1; Mormon 8:34-35; 9:30). . . . If they saw our day and chose those things which would be of greatest worth to us, is not that how we should study the Book of Mormon? We should constantly ask ourselves, 'Why did the Lord inspire Mormon (or Moroni or Alma) to include that in his record? What lesson can I learn from that to help me live in this day and age?'"

Ezra Taft Benson (Conference Report, Oct. 1986, p.5)

"The type of apostates in the Book of Mormon are similar to the type we have today. God, with his infinite foreknowledge, so molded the Book of Mormon that we might see the error and know how to combat false educational, political, religious and philosophical concepts of our time."

Ezra Taft Benson (Ensign, May 1975, p. 64)

1 Nephi 20~22

1 Ne. 20:1	**WATERS OF JUDAH - WATERS OF BAPTISM**

(Since Cumorah, Nibley, pp. 7, 151; Companion to Your Study of the Book of Mormon, Ludlow, p. 120)

"This clause first appeared in the 1840 and 1842 editions of the Book of Mormon. It did not appear again until the 1920 edition, and it has been in all editions since that time. It appears to be a prophetic commentary by Joseph Smith to explain the meaning of the phrase 'out of the waters of Judah.' . . . If this phrase were a restoration of the original text, as found in the more pure version on the brass plates from which it comes, it would have appeared in the 1830 edition of the Book of Mormon. . . . Through the use of this phrase, Joseph Smith is calling our attention to the fact that the ordinance of baptism was as common to the people of the Old Testament as it was to the people of the Book of Mormon."

R. Millet and J. F. McConkie (Doctrinal Commentary of the Book of Mormon, 1:151-152)

1 Ne. 20:3-8	**THE LORD FORETOLD ISRAEL'S DESTINY FROM THE BEGINNING**

1 Ne. 20:9-11	**THE LORD WILL DEFER HIS ANGER & NOT CUT ISRAEL OFF**

1 Ne. 20:12	**MY CALLED**

(Abr. 2:9-11; Deut. 32:7-9; Doctrinal Commentary on the Book of Mormon, Millet & McConkie, 1:155)

1 Ne. 20:12-22	**ISRAEL INVITED TO HEARKEN UNTO GOD WHO IS THE FIRST AND THE LAST**

1 Ne. 20:13   **RIGHT HAND**
(Answers to Gospel Questions, Smith, 1:156; *Doctrinal Commentary on the Book of Mormon*, Millet and McConkie, 1:178)

1 Ne. 20:14-15   **THE LORD HATH LOVED HIM**
(Isa. 48:14-15)

"Sidney Sperry suggests the servant is Cyrus, king of Persia, through whom the Lord will accomplish His work. *(Book of Mormon Compendium*, 130). This is consistent with the footnote reference in the LDS edition of the Bible. Monte Nyman believes the referent of "him" is Israel *(Great Are the Words Of Isaiah*, 171), while Victor Ludlow believes the description best fits the Lord Jesus Christ Himself *(Isaiah: Prophet, Seer, and Poet*, 405). In the latter instance, Jesus could be delivering a prophecy about Himself as a Spokesman for the Father. In any event, the work to be done by this servant, whoever he may be, has the divine approbation of Deity."

Hoyt W. Brewster, Jr. (Isaiah Plain and Simple, pp. 181-182)

1 Ne. 20:14, 20   **BABYLON**
(D&C 133:5, 7,14; *Doctrines of Salvation*, Smith, 3:305)

Chapter 21—Foretells the Mission of Latter-Day Saints & the Destiny of the Land of America in Connection with the House of Israel.

". . . the patriarchs and prophets who saw by vision and revelation the last dispensation & fulness of times plainly tell us what is to come to pass. The 49th chapter of Isaiah (1 Nephi 21) is having its fulfillment."

Wilford Woodruff (as quoted in Isaiah: Prophet, Seer, & Poet, Ludlow, p. 407)

1 Ne. 21:1-6   **O YE HOUSE OF ISRAEL**
(Isaiah: Prophet, Seer, and Poet, Ludlow, pp. 408-409; Jer. 23:1-2)

1 Ne. 21:2   **HID ME**
(Isa. 49:2; D&C 86:9; Col. 3:3)

"The Prophet Joseph Smith gave an interpretation to this phrase. Placing his hands upon one of the faithful members of the Church, he said: 'Your life is hid with Christ in God, and so are many others. Nothing but the unpardonable sin can prevent you from inheriting eternal life for you are sealed up by the power of the priesthood unto eternal life, having taken the step necessary for that purpose.'"

Joseph Smith (as quoted by Hoyt W. Brewster, Jr., Doctrine and Covenants Encyclopedia, p. 241-242)

1 Ne. 21:2   **A POLISHED SHAFT**
(Teachings of the Prophet Joseph Smith, p. 304)

1 Ne. 21:3   **MY SERVANT**
(Isaiah: Prophet, Seer, and Poet, Ludlow, pp. 408-410; *Great Are the Words of Isaiah*, Nyman, pp. 175-176; *Doctrinal Commentary on the Book of Mormon*, McConkie & Millet, 1:157-158; *Isaiah Plain and Simple*, Brewster, p. 186; D&C 90:3-4; 133:30-34)

1 Ne. 21:6   **A LIGHT TO THE GENTILES**
(Isa. 42:6; D&C 86:11)

1 Ne. 21:9   **PRISONERS GO FORTH**
(Doctrinal Commentary on the Book of Mormon, Millet & McConkie, 1:162-163)

1 Ne. 21:14   **ZION**
(Teachings of the Prophet Joseph Smith, p. 362)

1 Ne. 21:16   **GRAVEN UPON THE PALMS**
(Zech. 13:6)

"The clause is an allusion to the ancient practice of tattooing the palm with a symbol of the temple or some other sacred emblem to show devotion so that it might serve as a reminder of one's commitment. This is an idiomatic and graphic way for the Lord to say: 'You are constantly before me; I have not forgotten my covenant with you.'"

R. Millet and J. F. McConkie (Doctrinal Commentary on the Book of Mormon, 1:165)

1 Ne. 21:17   **MAKE HASTE AGAINST THY DESTROYERS**
(3 Ne. 21:12-13)

1 Ne. 21:22;   **SET UP MY STANDARD**
22:6-9   *(Teachings of the Prophet Joseph Smith, p. 147; Conference Report*, Romney, Apr. 1961, p. 119; D&C 45:9; 115:3-5; 2 Ne. 6:6; 29:2; 1 Ne. 22:6-9)

1 Ne. 21:23;   **KINGS AND QUEENS: NURSING PARENTS**
22:6   (2 Ne. 10:9; Ezra 1:1-4; Isa. 49:23; *Conference Report*, Oct. 1918, pp. 46-47)

"Kings and queens are representative of the Gentiles among whom the house of Israel was scattered. . . . The role the 'Gentile nations,' particularly the United States and Great Britain, have played in that gathering is significant."

Monte Nyman (Ensign, Aug. 1994, pp. 61-62)

"Only through us, the 'nursing fathers and mothers,' may they [the Lamanites] eventually enjoy a fulfillment of the many promises made to them."

Teachings of Spencer W. Kimball , p. 606

"Since the Church was restored in 1830, the Jewish population in the Holy Land has grown from seven thousand to over three million people. Whereas in 1830 only one out of five hundred Jews resided in Palestine, one out of five now live in the modern state of Israel. . . . Britain assisted in the establishment of a Jewish homeland in Palestine after World War I; Holland and Denmark helped protect many Jews from the holocaust; the United States, Russia, and others in the United Nations voted for the creation of a Jewish free state in 1947; the United States and France assisted Israel with military equipment in the first decades of her existence after 1948; and German reparation payments and large contributions from the United States and other nations have helped Israel financially."

Daniel H. Ludlow (Isaiah: Prophet, Seer, and Poet, p. 414)

"The Jews are now being gathered back to their own land. . . . The Jews have commenced to rebuild their cities and waste places—the nations and wealth of the Gentiles are greatly assisting them."

LeGrand Richards (Israel! Do You Know?, p. 209)

1 Ne. 21:23   **THEY SHALL NOT BE ASHAMED THAT WAIT FOR ME**
(Isa. 49:23; 2 Ne. 6:7; 1 John 2:28)

"The word *wait* in Hebrew means hope for or anticipate. . . . Thus, one who waits upon the Lord places his trust in Him and lives in accordance with His will as he or she anticipates His coming. Such persons will have their 'confidence wax strong in the presence of God' (D&C 121:45), for they will have no unresolved sins to cause them to be ashamed."

Hoyt W. Brewster, Jr. (Isaiah Plain and Simple, pp. 203-204)

1 Ne. 21:26;   **FEED WITH THEIR OWN FLESH, DRUNKEN WITH THEIR OWN**
22:13-14   **BLOOD**
                     (Isa. 49:26; 2 Ne. 6:18)

"Perhaps the depraved condition of the ancient Nephites is descriptive of those wicked ones of the future who will 'be drunken with their own blood': 'They have lost their love, one towards another; and they thirst after blood and revenge continually.' (Moroni 9:5). The carnage among the wicked may be such that they resort to cannibalism both to satisfy their physical hunger and to demonstrate their depravity. Once again we look to the past for a prototype of this abominable behavior: 'They did murder them in a most cruel manner . . . and after they have done this, they devour their flesh like unto wild beasts, because of the hardness of their hearts; and they do it for a token of bravery.' (Moroni 9:10.)"

                                         Hoyt W. Brewster, Jr. (Isaiah Plain and Simple, pp. 203-204)

1 Ne. 22:4   Interprets 1 Ne. 21:1

1 Ne. 22:4-5   **LOST & SCATTERED**
                     (Book of Mormon Prophecies, Warner, pp. 151-153; *New Witness for the Articles of Faith*, McConkie, pp. 515, 599)

"The lost tribes are not lost in the sense that we do not know where they are. The scriptures plainly tell us they have been scattered among every nation, kindred, tongue, and people. How then are they lost? They are lost temporally in the sense that they are in many instances lost to the lands of their inheritance. Of greater importance, they are lost in a spiritual sense: they are lost to the gospel and its saving ordinances, they are lost to the priesthood and all the blessings that flow from it. . . . They are so intermingled with the Gentiles of the world that they can only be identified by revelation—this revelation must come through ordained patriarchs, declaring to them their lineage and promised blessings as the chosen seed, but this only after they have found their way back to the fold of God. . . . Our Israelite forebears were scattered because they rejected the gospel. . . . They were scattered because they turned from the Lord. . . ."

                         R. Millet and J. F. McConkie (Doctrinal Commentary on the Book of Mormon, 1:10)

1 Ne. 22:6-9   Interprets 1 Ne. 21:22-23

1 Ne. 22:7   **A MIGHTY NATION AMONG THE GENTILES**
                     (Book of Mormon Prophecies, Warner, pp. 86-88)

"Whatever may be said of the persecutions suffered by the Latter-day Saints in various States of the Union—persecutions inflicted, not because of the Constitution, nor the genius of American Government, but in spite of them—persecutions inflicted by lawless force, by mob violence, ever to be execrated and condemned by every true patriot—whatever may be said of such deplorable happenings, still must our noble Nation be credited with what it has done in the direction of fulfilling its God-given mission. It is extremely doubtful that in any other land, or in any other nation upon this land, would the Lord's people have been treated with the same degree of consideration. In no other country on earth, without special divine interposition in its behalf, would this marvelous work and wonder have been permitted to come forth."

Orson F. Whitney (Cowley & Whitney on Doctrine, p. 227)

1 Ne. 22:8   **LAMANITES NOURISHED BY THE GENTILES**
                     (refer in this text to 1 Ne. 13:14-15; 1 Ne. 13:34-38)

"A loving father does not despise his children. These [Lamanites] are a chosen people, and this Church has an important part in restoring them to their rightful inheritance. The chasm between what they are and what they will be is opportunity. The gospel furnishes that opportunity; it is ours to give."

Spencer W. Kimball (Ensign, Dec. 1975, p. 7)

"Relatively little progress had been made since Columbus discovered America until recent years. Hundreds of thousands of Indians were killed by the invading gentiles from Europe, 128,000 in New England, according to historians. The rest were pushed back, scattered, and finally placed on reservations. The battle of America continued for hundreds of years, the red people fighting for their families, their homes, their hunting grounds, and their very existence. Finally the scriptures are being fulfilled. 'Nursing fathers and mothers' are being raised up to bring the blessings . . . to the sons of Lehi. It is said that 'The darkest hour is just before dawn.' But their day is dawning. There has perhaps been more constructive consideration given to the Indian people in the last decade than in the entire century before."

Spencer W. Kimball (Conference Report, Oct. 1956, pp. 52-53)

"[Speaking to the Indians] You had a rugged history with many tribulations, but you have a brilliant future. You are a chosen people; your destiny is in your own hands, your friends', and the Lord's. You were scattered in the great dispersion six centuries before Christ, and again on this continent in the pre and post-Christian eras, and your more complete dispersion came since Columbus, and the explorers and the colonists. . . . Like the Israelites released from Egyptian bondage, you have been promised deliverance from your foes of superstition, fear, illiteracy, and from the curses of want and disease and suffering. . . . Today you are arising from your long sleep and are stretching, yawning, and reaching. . . . My Lamanite brothers and sisters, we love you. Our bringing the gospel to you is 'likened unto their being nourished by the gentiles and being carried in their arms and upon their shoulders' (1 Nephi 22:8). . . . You have been preserved to this epochal day, and the gospel is available to you now. Wash your souls in the blood of the Lamb. Cleanse your lives, study the scriptures, accept the gospel and ordinances. These predictions can be fulfilled and come to you through one channel only, the path of righteousness and faith; else all these promises are but empty unfulfilled dreams. May God bless you that you may accept the truths now revealed to you. . . ."

Spencer W. Kimball (Conference Report, Oct. 1959, pp. 59,61-62)

1 Ne. 22:12   Interprets 1Ne. 21:12-13

1 Ne. 22:13-16 Interprets 1 Ne. 21:17, 25-26

1 Ne. 22:14   **ALL THAT FIGHT AGAINST ZION SHALL BE DESTROYED**
(JS-H 1:37; *Book of Mormon Prophecies*, Warner, pp. 196-198; *New Witness for the Articles of Faith*, McConkie, pp. 562-563; *Mormon Doctrine*, McConkie, p. 494)

"It is one of the sad heresies of our time that peace will be gained by weary diplomats as they prepare treaties of compromise, or that the Millennium will be ushered in because men will learn to live in peace and to keep the commandments, or that the predicted plagues and promised desolations of latter days can in some way be avoided. We must do all we can to proclaim peace, to avoid war, to heal disease, to prepare for natural disasters—but with it all, that which is to be shall be."

Bruce R. McConkie (Conference Report, Apr. 1979, pp. 131-132)

1 Ne. 22:15   **THE PROPHET**
(Mal. 4:1-2; *Doctrinal Commentary on the Book of Mormon*, Millet & McConkie, 1:175; *New Witness for the Articles of Faith*, McConkie, p. 563; *Great Are the Words of Isaiah*, Nyman, p. 185)

1 Ne. 22:16-17,   **SAVED, EVEN IF IT SO BE AS BY FIRE**
19   (D&C 71:7-10; 2 Kings 6:16-17; 2 Ne. 30:10; Jacob 3:1; Alma 19:22-23; 3 Ne. 17:23-25; 19:13-15; JS-M 1:30; Moses 7:61; *Life of a Pioneer*, Brown, pp. 245-251; *Journal of Discourses* 21:177-178; *Teachings of the Prophet Joseph Smith*, p.162; *Powerful Stories from Lives of Latter-day Saint Men*, Hartshorn, pp. 18-22; *Journal of Discourses* 15:362-363; refer in this text to Hel. 5:20-52)

"In the mist of all these tribulations God will send fire from heaven, if necessary, to destroy our enemies while we carry forward our work until it fills the whole earth! . . . You do not need to fear about anybody. Just serve the Lord and keep his commandments and build the kingdom, and as you do so you will be protected in these last days. God will have his hand over you, and you can plan your lives in confidence."

Mark E. Petersen (Conference Report, Oct. 1960, pp. 81-83)

"Yes, it was here under a free government and a strong nation that protection was provided for His restored Church. Now God will not permit his base of operations—America—to be destroyed. He has promised protection to this land if we will but serve the God of the land. He has also promised protection to the righteous even, if necessary, to send fire from heaven to destroy their enemies (1 Nephi 22:17). No, God's base of operations will not be destroyed. But it may be weakened and made less effective. One of the first rules of war strategy—and we are at war with the adversary and his agents—is to protect the base of operations. This we must do if we are to build up the kingdom throughout the world and safeguard our God-given freedom. How will we protect this base of operations? We must protect this base of operations from every threat—from sin, from unrighteousness, immorality, from desecration of the Sabbath day, from lawlessness, from parental and juvenile delinquency. We must protect it from dirty movies, filthy advertising, from salacious and suggestive TV programs, magazines, and books. We must protect this base from idleness, subsidies, doles, and soft governmental paternalism which weakens the initiative, discourages industry, destroys character, and demoralizes people. We must protect this base from complacency—from the dangerous feeling that all is well—from being lulled away into a false security. We must protect this American base from the brainwashing, increasingly administered to our youth in many educational institutions across the land, by some misinformed instructors and some wolves in sheep's clothing. Their false indoctrination, often perpetrated behind the front of so-called academic freedom, is leaving behind many faithless students, socialist-oriented, who are easy subject for state tyranny."

Ezra Taft Benson (Conference Report, Apr. 1962, pp. 104-105)

"During my life I have had many experiences of being guided in what I should do and in being protected from injury and also from evil. The Lord's protecting care has shielded me from the evil acts of others and has also protected me from surrendering to my own worst impulses. I enjoyed that protection one warm summer night on the streets of Chicago. . . . My wife, June, had attended a ward officers' meeting. When I came to drive her home, she was accompanied by a sister we would take home on our way. She lived in the nearby Woodlawn area, which was the territory of a gang called the Blackstone Rangers. I parked at the curb outside this sister's apartment house and accompanied her into the lobby and up the stairs to her door. June remained in the car on 61st Street. . . . Before stepping out into the street, I looked carefully in each direction. By the light of a nearby streetlight, I could see that the street was deserted except for three young men walking by. As I came to the driver's side and paused for June to unlock the door, I saw one of these young men running back toward me. He had something in his right hand, and I knew what it would be. There was no time to get into the car and drive away before he came within range. . . . The young man pushed the gun against my stomach and said, 'Give me your money.' I took the wallet out of my pocket and showed him it was empty. . . . I offered him some coins I had in my pocket, but he growled a rejection. 'Give me your car keys,' he demanded. 'Tell her to open the car,' he replied. For a moment I considered the new possibilities that would present, and then refused. He was furious. He jabbed me in the stomach with his gun and said, 'Do it, or I'll kill you.' . . . When I refused, the young robber repeated his demands, this time emphasizing them with an angrier tone and more motion with his gun. . . . 'Give me your money.' 'I don't have any.' 'Give me your car keys.' 'They're in the car.' 'Tell her to open the car.' 'I won't do it.' 'I'll kill you if you don't.' ' Won't do it.' . . . His gun wavered from my stomach until its barrel pointed slightly to my left. My arm was already partly raised, and with a quick motion I could seize the gun and struggle with him without the likelihood of being shot. I was taller and heavier than this young man, and at that time of my life was somewhat athletic. I had no doubt that I could prevail in a quick wrestling match if I could get his gun out of the contest. Just as I was about to make my move, I had a unique experience. I did not see anything or hear anything, but I knew something. I knew what would happen if I grabbed that gun. We would struggle, and I would turn the gun into that young man's chest. It would fire, and he would die. I also understood that I must not have the blood of that young man on my conscience for the rest of my life. I relaxed. . . . I followed an impulse to put my right hand on his shoulder and give him a lecture. June and I had some teenage children at that time, and giving lectures came naturally. 'Look here,' I said. 'This isn't right. What you're doing just isn't right. . . . You could get killed or sent to jail for this.' With the gun back in my stomach, the young robber replied to my lecture by going through his demands for the third time. But this time his voice was subdued.

When he offered the final threat to kill me, he didn't sound persuasive. When I refused again, he hesitated for a moment and then stuck the gun in his pocket and ran away. June unlocked the door, and we drove off, uttering a prayer of thanks. . . . I am grateful that the Lord gave me the vision and strength to refrain from trusting in the arm of flesh and to put my trust in the protecting care of our Heavenly Father. I am grateful for the Book of Mormon promise to us of the last days that 'the righteous need not fear,' for the Lord 'will preserve the righteous by his power' (1 Ne. 22:17)."

Dallin H. Oaks (Ensign, Nov. 1992, pp. 39-40)

"God has been and is our helper, and is on our right and left, and round about us like a wall of fire to defend this people, if they serve him with an undivided heart."

Brigham Young (Journal of Discourses 8:172)

"Can you tell me where the people are who will be shielded and protected from these great calamities and judgments which are even now at our doors? . . . The priesthood of God who honor their priesthood, and who are worthy of their blessings are the only ones who shall have this safety and protection. . . . No other people have a right to be shielded from these judgments. They are at our very doors; not even this people will escape them entirely. . . . And none but the priesthood will be safe from their fury."

Wilford Woodruff (The Young Woman's Journal, Aug. 1894, p. 512)

"The calamities that have been promised will be poured out upon the peoples of the earth, and we shall escape them, yea, they shall pass us by. But remember the Lord says if we fail to keep his word, if we walk in the ways of the world, they will not pass us by, but we shall be visited with floods and with fire, with sword and with plague and destruction. We may escape these things through faithfulness. Israel of old might have escaped through faithfulness."

Joseph Fielding Smith (Doctrines of Salvation, 3:34)

"Do not think for a moment that the days of trial are over. They are not. If we keep the commandments of the Lord, we shall prosper, we shall be blessed; the plagues, the calamities that have been promised will be poured out upon the peoples of the earth, and we shall escape them, yea, they shall pass us by. But remember the Lord says if we fail to keep his word, if we walk in the ways of the world, they will not pass us by, but we shall be visited with floods and with fire, with sword and with plague and destruction. We may escape these things through faithfulness."

Joseph Fielding Smith (Doctrines of Salvation, 3:34)

"It is a false idea that the Saints will escape all the judgments, whilst the wicked suffer; for all flesh is subject to suffer, and 'the righteous shall hardly escape;' still many of the Saints will escape, for the just shall live by faith; yet many of the righteous shall fall a prey to disease, to pestilence, etc., by reason of the weakness of the flesh, and yet be saved in the Kingdom of God. So that it is an unhallowed principle to say that such and such have transgressed because they have been preyed upon by disease or death. . . ."

Joseph Smith (History of the Church, 4:11)

"Of course, Satan will slay some of the righteous that their blood—with the blood of all the martyrs of all the ages—may cry from the ground as a witness against those who fight against God. Yet, as a people the true saints shall prevail. The Lord 'will preserve the righteous by his power, even if it so be that the fulness of his wrath must come, and the righteous be preserved, even unto the destruction of their enemies by fire.' This refers to the day of burning that shall attend the Second Coming. 'Wherefore, the righteous need not fear; for thus saith the prophet, they shall be saved, even if it so be as by fire.'"

Bruce R. McConkie (Millennial Messiah, p. 313)

1 Ne. 22:18   **VAPOR OF SMOKE**
"It may be, for instance, that nothing except the power of faith and the authority of the priesthood can save individuals and congregations from the atomic holocausts that surely shall be."

Bruce R. McConkie (Conference Report, Apr. 1979, p. 133)

1 Ne. 22:22-23   **THOSE WHO MUST BE BROUGHT LOW IN THE DUST**
"These marvelous declarations that the day would come, in the history of the world, when everything that was set up by man, that was not in harmony with God's will and purpose, would be shaken and destroyed, indicates a new epoch in the history of the world. . . . Everything to be tested, to be tried and to be shaken, and only that which is the truth and that which was set up by the Lord shall survive."

Melvin J. Ballard (Conference Report, Apr. 1932, p. 57)

1 Ne. 22:23

QUALITIES OF THOSE IN THE GREAT AND ABOMINABLE CHURCH
(1 Ne. 8:26; 3 Ne. 6:15; JS-H 1:46; refer in this text to Mosiah 17:11-13; Alma 39:4-6; 3 Ne. 13:19-24,33; Ether 8:18-25)

"Unrestrained passion, ungoverned appetite, envy, hatred, wealth, and power used to govern men and to crush them—these are the enemies of peace. They bring misery to the individual. They bring unhappiness in the home. They bring war and contention in the world, discontent, misery and death. They are the opposite of the peace which Christ came to give the world."

David O. McKay (as quoted by Henry D. Moyle, BYU Fireside, Jan. 6, 1963)

"Now, nearly every temptation that comes to you and me comes in one of those forms. Classify them, and you will find that under one of those three nearly every given temptation . . . comes to us as (1) a temptation of the appetite; (2) a yielding to the pride and fashion and vanity of those alienated from the things of God; or (3) a gratifying of the passion, or a desire for the riches of the world, or power among men."

David O. McKay (Conference Report, Oct. 1911, p. 59)

1 Ne. 22:26

THE HOLY ONE REIGNETH
"Christ and the resurrected Saints will reign over the earth during the thousand years. They will not probably dwell upon the earth, but will visit it when they please, or when it is necessary to govern it."

Joseph Smith, Jr. (Teachings of the Prophet Joseph Smith, p. 268)

1 Ne. 22:31

ENDURE TO THE END
(1 Ne. 8:30; 13:37; 2 Ne. 31:15-16, 19-20; 33:4, 9; Omni 1:26; Mosiah 4:6-7; 18:9; 23:22; Alma 13:29; 36:3; 37:37; 38:5; 3 Ne. 15:9; 21:22; 27:16; Ether 4:19; Moro. 3:3; 6:3; D&C 5:35; 9:14; 14:7; 17:8; 18:22; 20:29; 24:8; 75:16; Matt. 24:13; Mark 13:13; James 5:11)

"So, we are talking about durable discipleship! Not the kind that stays in place only for a season and then disappears. In fact, it could be truly said of each one of us here tonight that how much we will have to give later on, in some respects, will depend on how much we can take now. Learning to 'endure well' is, among many other things, being able to lose face without losing heart. It is also being able to pass through seeming or real injustice, as did Job, without, as the scriptures say, '[charging] God foolishly' (Job 1:22). A friend of mine who passed through a most severe trial, when I discussed it with him, said simply, 'If it's fair, it isn't a trial.' He passed through it most gracefully. I know a widow of a General Authority who waited patiently for over forty years to rejoin her husband. I doubt she ever murmured; she merely went on quietly doing as Nephi urged: 'Following the example of the Son of the Living God."

Neal A. Maxwell (BYU Fireside, Dec. 2, 1984)

"I testify that it is not sufficient to be baptized and then live an acceptable life avoiding major transgressions. The Lord has decreed that . . . additional ordinances and covenants . . . must be received for exaltation and eternal life. Being worthy of temple ordinances means that you will choose to do what many in the world are not willing to do. You will keep the Sabbath day holy, exercise faith through the payment of tithing and fast offerings, consistently participate in Church worship, give service, and show love and appreciation for your family by helping each member of it. After you have received all of the temple ordinances, you will continue to grow by keeping the covenants made and faithfully 'endur[ing] to the end' (Omni 1:26)."

Richard G. Scott (Ensign, May 1997, p. 54)

"Early in our married life Sister Nelson and I . . . decided to enjoy a free afternoon with our two-year-old daughter. We went to one of Minnesota's many beautiful lakes and rented a small boat. After rowing far from shore, we stopped to relax and enjoy the tranquil scene. Suddenly, our little toddler lifted one leg out of the boat and started to go overboard, exclaiming, 'Time to get out, Daddy!'

Quickly we caught her and explained: 'No, dear, it's not time to get out; we must stay in the boat until it brings us safely back to land.' Only with considerable persuasion did we succeed in convincing her that leaving the boat early would have led to disaster.

Children are prone to do such dangerous things simply because they have not acquired the wisdom their parents have. Similarly, we as children of our Heavenly Father may foolishly want to get 'out of the boat' before we arrive at destinations He would like us to reach. . . .

Applied to my analogy, we are first to get 'in the boat' with Him. Then we are to *stay* with Him. And if we don't get 'out of the boat' before we should, we shall reach His kingdom, where we will be lifted up to eternal life.

Whenever an undertaking is begun, both the energy and the will to endure are essential. The winner of a five-kilometer race is declared at the end of *five* kilometers, not at one or two. If you board a bus to Boston, you don't get off at Burlington. If you want to gain an education, you don't drop out along the way—just as you don't pay to dine at an elegant restaurant only to walk away after sampling the salad.

Whatever your work may be, endure at the beginning, endure through opposing forces along the way, and endure to the end. Any job must be completed before you can enjoy the result for which you are working. So wrote the poet:

Stick to your task till it sticks to you;
Beginners are many, but enders are few.
Honor, power, place, and praise
Will always come to the one who stays.

Stick to your task till it sticks to you;
Bend at it, sweat at it, smile at it too;
For out of the bend and the sweat and the smile
Will come life's victories, after awhile."

Russell M. Nelson (Ensign, May 1997, pp. 70-71)

"The doctrine of endurance to the end is taught twenty-two times in the Book of Mormon . . . The requirement of endurance to the end appears consistently in context with the first principles and ordinances of the gospel. One could easily make the case that the Book of Mormon teaches that there are five first principles and ordinances of the gospel, the fifth being enduring to the end. . . . Many who enter through the gates of baptism and begin their walk on the path to eternal life fail to continue. Sin, apathy, boredom, burnout, discouragement, and pride all take their toll. For this reason, the concept of enduring is critical to all of us."

Dennis L. Largey (Doctrines of the Book of Mormon, 1991 Sperry Symposium, pp. 59-60)

"Endure to the end. What does that mean? I believe it means basically three things. One: We must continue to repent for the rest of our lives because we will still make mistakes, and we must go home clean or we can't dwell with the Father and the Son (see D&C 84:74). Two: We must continue to forgive others. If we do not forgive others, we cannot obtain forgiveness ourselves (see D&C 64:9-10). And three: Yes we must be nice. If we're not nice, I don't think we're going to make it. In other words, we must have charity, which is really love plus sacrifice."

Hartmon Rector Jr. (Ensign, Nov. 1994, p. 26)

"In 1968 a marathon runner by the name of John Stephen Akhwari represented Tanzania in an international competition. 'A little over an hour after [the winner] had crossed the finish line, John Stephen Akhwari . . . approached the stadium, the last man to complete the journey. [Though he was suffering from fatigue, leg cramps, dehydration, and disorientation,] a voice called from within to go on, and so he went on. Afterwards, it was written, 'Today we have seen a young African runner who symbolizes the finest in human spirit, a performance that gives meaning to the word courage. For some, the only reward is a personal one. [There are no medals, only] the knowledge that they finished what they set out to do' *(The Last African Runner,* Olympiad Series, Bud Greenspan, Cappy Productions, 1976, videocassette). When asked why he would complete a race he could never win, Akhwari replied, 'My country did not send me 5,000 miles to start the race; my country sent me to finish the race.' He knew who he was—an athlete representing the country of Tanzania. He knew his purpose—to finish the race. He knew that he had to endure to the finish, so that he could honorably return home to Tanzania. Our mission in life is much the same. We were not sent by Father in Heaven just to be born. We were sent to endure and return to Him with honor. . . . We learn to endure to the end by learning to finish our current responsibilities, and we simply continue doing it all of our lives. We cannot expect to learn endurance in our later years if we have developed the habit of quitting when things get difficult now."

Robert D. Hales (Ensign, May 1998, pp. 76-77)

2 Nephi 1~2

2 Ne. 1:5   **THIS PROMISED LAND**
(2 Ne. 10:19; 3 Ne. 15:13; 16:16; 20:14, 22; 21:22; D&C 38:17-20; 49:24; *Journal of Discourses* 1:332-333; *Since Cumorah*, Nibley, pp. 420-421; refer in this text to 3 Ne. 15:13)

"Different portions of the earth have been pointed out by the Almighty, from time to time, to His children, as their everlasting inheritance. As instances—Abraham and his posterity, that were worthy, were promised Palestine, Moab and Ammon—the children of righteous Lot—were promised a portion not far from the boundaries of the twelve tribes. The meek among the Jaredites, together with a remnant of the tribe of Joseph, were promised the great western continent. . . . In the resurrection, the meek of all ages and nations will be restored to that portion of the earth previously promised to them. And thus, all the different portions of the earth have been and will be disposed of to the lawful heirs. . . ."

Orson Pratt (Journal of Discourses 1:332-333)

2 Ne. 1:6   **BROUGHT BY THE HAND OF THE LORD**
(*Doctrinal Book of Mormon Commentary*, Millet & McConkie, 1:184; *Conference Report*, Oct. 1932, p. 108)

". . . they have come and are coming and shall come, led hither by the hand of the Lord. What, you say, these undesirable elements? Well, they are permitted to be here that the people may be tried and tested and given the experience which is so necessary to make them what the Lord intends that they shall be. And so let us not fear that our nation is going to lose its identity, or is going to lose its sovereignty or is going to be overwhelmed or overpowered by other nations. It cannot be so save through iniquity? Well, you may say, are not the people of this nation iniquitous? It is true that sin befouls and defiles the land; but in spite of it, I know not where you will find a nation with higher ideals or with plainer purposes to uphold the institutions that God has established for the government and freedom of men."

James E. Talmage (Conference Report, Oct. 1919, pp. 97-98)

2 Ne. 1:7, 20,
30-32

CONDITIONAL FREEDOM IN THE PROMISED LAND
1. Ether 2:12 (refer in this text to 1 Ne. 1:20; Ether 2:7-15)
2. Mosiah 29:25 27 (refer in this text to Hel. 5:2)
3. Hel.2:13; 3 Ne. 9:9; Ether 8:21-22 (refer in this text to Ether 8:18-25)
4. 2 Ne. 26:11; Hel. 13:8-10 (refer in this text to Morm. 1:14-17)

"It is also my firm conviction that His protective hand is still over the United States of America. I know, too, that if we will keep the commandments of God—live as He has directed and does now direct, through His prophets—we will continue to have His protecting hand over us. But we must be true to the eternal verities, the great Christian virtues that God has revealed. Then, and only then, will we be safe as a nation and as individuals."

Ezra Taft Benson (This Nation Shall Endure, p. 145)

". . . we Americans must learn that [our nation] can continue to exist only as it aligns itself with the powers of heaven. If we turn our back upon the Almighty, even by ignoring him, we jeopardize our national future. If we deliberately oppose his purposes, we place ourselves in danger of destruction. These stern facts have been taught to Americans from the beginning of our national history, starting with our first President, George Washington. He realized and he publicly announced that we obtained our independence through an act of Providence, since we were far too weak to gain it by ourselves. Knowing this, he warned that if we are to survive as a free and independent nation, we must obey the Almighty God who brought us into being. Abraham Lincoln, another inspired President, said virtually the same thing, warning that if we fail to obey the commandments of God, we shall go down to ruin. . . . It is no imaginary ruin that faces our nation if we reject Jesus Christ, as Lincoln pointed out so dramatically. And it is possible that our greatness can be buried in profound obscurity if we refuse to turn to God. . . ."

Mark E. Petersen (Conference Report, Apr. 1968, pp. 59,61,62)

"Since 1960, the U.S. population has increased 41%. . . . But during the same . . . period there has been a 560% increase in violent crime; a 419% increase in illegitimate births; a quadrupling in divorce rates; a tripling of the percentage of children living in single-parent homes. . . . The health of any society, the happiness of its people, their prosperity, and their peace all find their roots in the teaching of children by fathers and mothers."

Gordon B. Hinckley (Ensign, Nov. 1993, pp. 54,59-60)

2 Ne. 1:7   **CURSED SHALL BE THE LAND FOR THEIR SAKES**
(Jacob 2:29; Alma 45:15-16; Hel. 13:17-19, 23, 30, 35; Morm. 1:17-18; Ether 14:1; *Conference Report*, Oct. 1961, pp. 30-31)

2 Ne. 1:8-9   **PROMISED LAND HIDDEN FOR A TIME**
". . .God deliberately kept the American continent hidden until after the Holy Roman Empire had been broken up and the various nations had established themselves as independent kingdoms. Keeping America hidden until this time was no accident."

Ezra Taft Benson (God, Family, Country, p. 343)

"The claim is made that the Norsemen at a very early day visited the American continent; that they established colonies here and took back reports of their discoveries. Out of this, however, nothing has come, if it be true. There is a good and sufficient reason why nothing came of such discoveries. The Lord, as here declared by Lehi, promised to keep this western world from the knowledge of other nations until the time should come for that knowledge to be made known."

Joseph Fielding Smith (The Progress of Man, p. 253)

2 Ne. 1:10-11   **LAMANITES SCATTERED & SMITTEN**
(1 Ne. 22:7-8; 3 Ne. 16:8-9; 3 Ne. 20:27-28; refer in this text to 1 Ne. 13:14; 1 Ne.13:34-38)

"The fulfillment of this prophecy turned out to be rather fantastic. In the 1500's Hernando Cortez (with only 11 ships, 400 Europeans, 200 natives, 16 horses and 14 guns) attacked, plundered and massacred into subjugation the whole Aztec empire of several million natives. Francisco Pizarro's experience in South America was equally amazing. With a starved and desperate band of 168 Spaniards, he subverted and conquered the entire domain of several million Incas. The conquest of both the Aztecs and Incas was largely the result of their confusion in thinking that the Spaniards might be the returning Fair God who had visited their ancestors in ancient times, established a golden age of prosperity and peace, and then said he would come again at a later time. The expectation of a coming Messiah who would be fair-skinned and have a beard was one of the most universal cultural characteristics to be found among the millions of Indians whom the Spanish conquered. Unfortunately, these benighted descendants of Lehi had lost the records which we are now reading, so they did not know that before their Fair God returned to earth, the Gentiles would come and scatter them to the four winds. They also did not know that after they were conquered it would be another group of GENTILES who would bring them the Gospel and prepare them for the return of the Fair God, Jesus Christ. All this the descendants of Lehi were going to have to find out the hard way."

Cleon Skousen (Treasures From The Book Of Mormon, 1:1186-1187)

2 Ne. 1:13, 23   **SATAN'S CHAINS**
(2 Ne. 8:25; 9:45; 26:22; Alma 5:7; 12:6; 3 Ne. 20:37; Isa. 5:20; Moses 7:26; refer in this text to 2 Ne. 28:19-22)

"*Shake off the awful chains by which ye are bound* indicates the need to overcome bad habits, even the seemingly little habits that grow into strong 'chains of hell.'"

Carlos E. Asay (Ensign, May 1992, p. 41)

"When I was a little boy, somebody gave me a cucumber in a bottle. The neck of the bottle was small, the cucumber large. I wondered how it got there. Then, out in the garden one day, I came upon a bottle slipped over a little green *fellow*. Then I understood. The cucumber had grown in the bottle. Often I see men with habits I wonder how any strong, sensible man could form. Then I reflect that likely they grew into them when young, and cannot now slip out of them. They are like the cucumber in the bottle."

Anonymous (Jewels of Thought, p. 85)

"Who among us hasn't felt the chains of bad habits? These habits may have impeded our progress, may have made us forget who we are, may have destroyed our self-image, may have put our family life in jeopardy, and may have hindered our ability to serve our fellow men and our God. So many of us tend to say. 'This is the way I am. I can't change. . . .' Lehi warned his sons to 'shake off the chains' because he knew that chains restrict our mobility, growth, and happiness. They cause us to become confused and less able to be guided by God's Spirit. . . . Samuel Johnson wisely shared, 'The chains of habit are too small to be felt until they are too strong to be broken' (*International Dictionary of Thoughts*, p. 348). . . . Living a life of righteousness is a chainbreaker. Many of us today are shackled by the restrictive chains of poor habits. We are bound by inferior self-images created by misconduct and indifference. We are chained by an unwillingness to change for the better. . . . Shaking off restrictive chains requires action. . . . It requires commitment, self-discipline, and work. Chains weigh heavily on troubled hearts and souls. They relegate us to lives of no purpose or light. They cause us to become confused and lose the spirit. . . . These chains cannot be broken by those who live in lust and self-deceit. They can only be broken by people who are willing to change. We must face up to the hard reality of life that damaging chains are broken only by people of courage and commitment who are willing to struggle and weather the pain. . . . To change or break some of our chains even in a small way means to give up some behavior of habits that have been very important to us in the past. . . . Even if our present way of life is painful and self-destructive, some of us . . . become comfortable with it. Those who are committed to improvement break chains by having the courage to try."

Marvin J. Ashton (Ensign, Nov. 1985, pp. 13-15)

"There is so much of the good and the beautiful and the uplifting in literature and art and life that there should be no time for any man who holds the priesthood of God to patronize, to watch, to buy that which only carefully leads him down to hell."

Gordon B. Hinckley (Conference Report, Oct. 1983, pp. 67-68)

"Vice is a monster of so frightful mien,
As, to be hated, needs but to be seen;
Yet seen too oft, familiar with her face,
We first endure, then pity, then embrace."

Alexander Pope (as quoted by Neal A. Maxwell, Ensign, May 1993, p. 76)

"Some foolishly try and justify conduct they know is wrong with, 'It's such a little sin; it won't matter.' While it may be true that the particular conduct is not at the top of the scale, the more dangerous part is the road that it puts you on. 'Little wrongs' just seem to have a way of leading into 'bigger wrongs.' The words of the American clergyman Harry Emerson Fosdick provide further instruction here: 'The tragic evils of our life are so commonly unintentional. We did not start out for that poor, cheap goal. That aim was not in our minds at all. . . . Look to the road you are walking on! He who picks up one end of [a] stick picks up the other. He who chooses the beginning of a road chooses the place it leads to' *(Living Under Tension, 1941, pp. 110-111)*."

W. Eugene Hansen (Ensign, May 1996, p. 39)

2 Ne. 1:21, 23 **ARISE . . . AWAKE . . . COME FORTH**

"The challenge to '*Arise from the dust*' means to overcome evil behaviors that destroy character and ruin lives. Physical appetites must be controlled. '*Awake from a deep sleep . . . even from the sleep of hell*' suggests a process of learning and becoming aware of God's holy purposes. No sleep is deeper or more deadly than the sleep of ignorance. . . . '*Come forth out of obscurity*' instructs one to model goodness and serve as a light to others. True men are living light fountains which are pleasant to be near. (See D&C 103:9-10.)"

Carlos E. Asay (Ensign, May 1992, p. 41)

2 Ne. 2:3-4 **THOU HAST BEHELD CHRIST**

(2 Ne. 11:2-3; *Autobiography of Parley P. Pratt*, p. 123)

2 Ne. 2:10 **ATONEMENT**

(2 Ne. 9:7, 26; 10:25; Jacob 4:11; 7:12; Mosiah 3:11,15; 4:6-7; 13:28; 22:14; 24:13; 30:17; 34:8,11; 42:15; 23; Hel. 5:9; Moro. 7:41; 8:20; refer in this text to 2 Ne. 9:7-9)

"In the English language, the components are *at-one-ment*, suggesting that a person is at one with another. Other languages employ words that connote either *expiation* or *reconciliation*. *Expiation* means 'to atone for.' *Reconciliation* comes from Latin roots *re*, meaning 'again'; *con*, meaning 'with'; and *sella*, meaning 'seat.' *Reconciliation*, therefore, literally means 'to sit again with.' . . . In Hebrew, the basic word for atonement is *kaphar*, a verb that means 'to cover' or 'to forgive.' Closely related is the Aramaic and Arabic word *kafat*, meaning 'a close embrace' —no doubt related to the Egyptian ritual embrace. . . . While the words *atone* or *atonement*, in any of their forms, appear only once in the King James translation of the New Testament, they appear 35 times in the Book of Mormon. As another testament of Jesus Christ, it sheds precious light on His Atonement."

Russell M. Nelson (Ensign, Nov. 1996, pp. 34-35)

2 Ne. 2:11, **OPPOSITION - AGENCY**
15-16, 27 (2 Ne. 10:23; D&C 29:35, 39; 130:18-21; 132:5; Moses 5:33; 6:55-56; Hel. 14:30-31; *Conference Report*, Oct. 1965, p. 8; *Conference Report*, Apr. 1950, p. 32; *Journal of Discourses* 10:2-3; *Teachings of the Prophet Joseph Smith*, p. 49; Hymn, no. 240)

"We are free to choose, but we are not free to alter the consequences of those choices."

Ezra Taft Benson (Come Unto Christ, p. 40)

"Because free agency is a God-given precondition to the purpose of mortal life, no person or organization can take away our free agency in mortality. . . . What can be taken away or reduced by the conditions of mortality is our freedom, the power to act upon our choices. Free agency is absolute, but in the circumstances of mortality freedom is always qualified. . . . If I should hang from the cat-walk here in the Marriott Center and release my grip, I would not be free to will myself into a soft landing. And I cannot choose to run through a brick wall. A loss of freedom reduces the extent to which we can act upon our choices, but it does not deprive us of our God-given free agency."

Dallin H. Oaks (1987-88 BYU Devotional & Fireside Speeches, p. 43)

"Difficulty comes when agency is used to make choices that are inconsistent with . . . covenants. Study the things you do in your discretionary time, that time that you are free to control. Do you find that it is centered in those things that are of highest priority and of greatest importance? Or do you unconsciously, consistently fill it with trivia and activities that are not of enduring value nor help you accomplish the purpose for which you came to earth? Think of the long view of life, not just what's going to happen today or tomorrow. *Don't give up what you most want in life for something you think you want now.*"

Richard G. Scott (Ensign, May 1997, p. 54)

"Sadness, disappointment, severe challenge are events in life, not life itself. . . . A pebble held close to the eye appears to be a gigantic obstacle. Cast on the ground, it is seen in perspective. Likewise, problems or trials in our lives need to be viewed in the perspective of scriptural doctrine. . . . Some people are like rocks thrown into a sea of problems. They are drowned by them. Be a cork. When submerged in a problem, fight to be free to bob up to serve again with happiness. . . . When you trust in the Lord, when you are willing to let your heart and your mind be centered in His will, when you ask to be led by the Spirit to do His will, you are assured of the greatest happiness along the way and the most fulfilling attainment from this mortal experience. If you question everything you are asked to do, or dig in your heels at every unpleasant challenge, you make it harder for the Lord to bless you."

Richard G. Scott (Ensign, May 1996, pp. 24-25)

"Our destiny is not based on *chance*. It is based on *choice* !"

Boyd K. Packer (CES Religious Educators Symposium, Aug. 10, 1993, p. 9)

"We who lived in concentration camps can remember the men who walked through the huts comforting others, giving away their last piece of bread. They may have been few in number, but they offer sufficient proof that everything can be taken from a man but one thing: the *last of human freedoms*—to choose one's attitude in any given set of circumstances, to choose one's own way."

Viktor Frankl (Man's Search For Meaning, p. 104)

". . . the Father's plan, which required that all people obtain mortal bodies, be tried and proven in all things, and have opportunity to choose of their own free will. . . . Lucifer—a personage of prominence—sought to amend the plan, while Jehovah sustained the plan. The central issue in that council, then, was: Shall the children of God have untrammeled agency to choose the course they should follow, whether good or evil, or shall they be coerced and forced to be obedient? Christ and all who followed Him stood for the former proposition— freedom of choice; Satan stood for the latter—coercion and force. Because Satan and those who stood with him would not accept the vote of the council, but rose up in rebellion, they were cast down to the earth, where they have continued to foster the same plan. The war that began in heaven is not yet over. The conflict continues on the battlefield of mortality. And one of Lucifer's primary strategies has been to restrict our agency through the power of earthly governments. Proof of this is found in the long history of humanity (see *Teachings of the Prophet Joseph Smith*, p. 357)."

Ezra Taft Benson (The Constitution: A Heavenly Banner, pp. 2-3)

"Sydney Harris wrote, in the *Chicago Daily News*:
   I walked with my friend, a Quaker, to the newsstand the other night, and he bought a paper, thanking the newsie politely. The newsie didn't even acknowledge it.
   'A sullen fellow, isn't he?' I commented.
   'Oh, he's that way every night,' shrugged my friend.
   'Then why do you continue to be so polite to him?' I asked.
   'Why not?' inquired my friend. 'Why should I let him decide how I'm going to act?'"

Boyd K. Packer (1966-67 BYU Speeches of the Year, Oct. 4, 1966, p. 9)

"I was down in Old Mexico a few years ago at Telacapaca where they feature the molding of clay into various kinds of pottery. There I saw them take lumps of clay which had been molded, usually by crude, primitive methods, the molder wading in the mud to mix it properly. Then it was put upon a potter's wheel, and there the potter began to fashion the intricate bits of pottery which he was to place on the market. And as we watched, we saw occasionally, because of some defect in the mixing, the necessity for pulling the whole lump of clay apart and throwing it back in to be mixed over again, and sometimes the process had to be done several times before the proper kind of mud was mixed for the potter. With that in mind, I thought I began to see the meaning of this scripture: 'We are as clay in the hands of the potter, and we are all the work of His hands.' Yes, we too, have to be tried and tested by poverty, by sickness, by the death of loved ones, by temptation, sometimes by the betrayal of supposed friends, by affluence and riches, by ease and luxury, by false educational ideas, and by the flattery of the world. A father, explaining this matter to his son, said, [2 Ne. 2:15]."

Harold B. Lee (BYU Speeches, Oct. 1956, pp. 2-3)

"We can choose our reactions to difficulties and challenges. . . . Self-pity and discouragement do not come from the teachings of the gospel of Jesus Christ. But life can be both bitter and sweet. It is up to us to choose whether we want to reflect the voices of gloom or gladness."

Marvin J. Ashton (Conference Report, Apr., 1991, p. 24)

"We give up our agency when we examine our circumstances as if we were trapped by them. We lose our agency and make ourselves victims by the use of phrases like these:

"You make me mad."
"I could be happy if it weren't for . . ."
"I'll change if you do."
"He did it to me first."
"I could be a good parent if it weren't for my children."
"Everybody's doing it."

Terry Olson (BYU Religious Educators Summer Conference, 1991)

"We are . . . the sum of all the choices we make. We should always remember that our choices do not begin with the act, but in the mind with the idea. As a poet stated, 'Sow a thought, and you reap an act; sow an act, and you reap a habit; sow a habit, and you reap a character; sow a character, and you reap a destiny' [Anonymous]. Given our agency, we are therefore individually responsible for our ideas, acts, habits, character, and, yes, even our destiny."

Richard B. Wirthlin (Ensign, Nov. 1997, p. 10)

"To you adults who repeat the pattern of neglect and abuse you endured as little children, believing that you are entrapped in a cycle of behavior from which there is no escape, I say: It is contrary to the order of heaven for any soul to be locked into compulsive, immoral behavior with no way out! It is consistent with the workings of the adversary to deceive you into believing that you are."

Boyd K. Packer (Ensign, Nov. 1986, p. 18)

"Sometimes the solution is not to change our circumstance, but to change our attitude about that circumstance and its difficulties so that we see more clearly. . . . There are those today who say that man is the result of his environment and cannot rise above it. Those who justify mediocrity, failure, immorality of all kinds, and even weakness and criminality are certainly misguided. Surely the environmental conditions found in childhood and youth are an influence of power. But the fact remains that every normal soul has its free agency and the power to row against the current and to lift itself to new planes of activity and thought and development. Man can transform himself. Man must transform himself. . . . Man has in himself the seeds of godhood, which can germinate and grow and develop. As the acorn become the oak, the mortal man becomes a god. It is within his power to lift himself by his very bootstraps from the plane on which he finds himself to the plane on which he should be. It may be a long, hard lift with many obstacles, but it is a real possibility. In other words, environment need not be our limit. Circumstance may not need to be our ruler. . . ."

Spencer W. Kimball (Ensign, July 1978, pp. 3-7)

2 Ne. 2:13   **IF NO LAW, THERE IS NO SIN**
(Rom. 5:13; Heb. 10:26; 1 John 3:4; 2 Ne. 9:25; Alma 42:17-18; Packer, *The Book of Mormon: Jacob Through Words of Mormon, To Learn with Joy,* BYU Religious Studies Center, ed. by Nyman & Tate, pp. 4-6)

2 Ne. 2:18   **DEVIL - FATHER OF LIES**
(refer in this text to 2 Ne. 28)

"The Hebrew translation for *devil* is the 'spoiler' *(Bible Dictionary,* s.v. 'devil.' See also Robert Young, *Analytical Concordance to the Bible* (1972), p. 252). Satan is the spoiler because he would confound our moral compass and spoil our journey back to a loving Father in Heaven. Satan, 'the Father of lies' (2 Ne. 2:18), increasingly uses various devices, ancient and modern, to confuse us. He would convince us that joy is not where it is. And contrarily, he would have us believe that joy is where it is not. One of Satan's most spiritually damaging lies

which undermines our sense of self-worth and hope is that we cannot be forgiven of our sins."

Richard B. Wirthlin (Ensign, Nov. 1997, pp. 9-10)

2 Ne. 2:26   **NOT TO BE ACTED UPON**
"Being acted upon means somebody else is pulling the strings. . . . Many of you
worry about your future. . . . After a lifetime of dealing with human affairs, I
am persuaded that your future will be beyond your dreams if you observe the
following:
1. Do not live on the edge.
2. Avoid not only evil, but even the appearance of evil
3. Follow the counsel of Nephi to act for yourselves and not be acted upon.
4. Seek first the kingdom of God and receive the great promise that all else will
be added upon you.
5. Follow the counsel of Church leaders.

James E. Faust (Ensign, Nov. 1995, pp. 46-47)

2 Ne. 2:18-25   **THE FALL OF ADAM**
(Moses 5:10-11; Mormon 9:12-13; *Answers to Gospel Questions*, Smith, 3:100-
101; *Doctrines of Salvation*, Smith, 1:76-77, 91,107-108; *Man: His Origin &
Destiny*, Smith, pp. 278-280; *Conference Report*, Apr. 1953, pp. 123-124; *The
Broken Heart*, Hafen; *Conference Report*, Apr. 1967, p. 122; "Eve and the Fall,"
Woman, McConkie, pp. 67-68; *The Words of Joseph Smith*, Ehat and Cook, p.
63; *Journal of Discourses* 13:145; *Alpha to Omega,* Kimball, pp. 46-47)

"No, we do not believe, with Calvin, in the moral depravity of men and women.
No, we do not believe, with Luther, that man does not even have the power to
choose good over evil. And we do not believe that children inherit the so-called
sin of Adam through either sexual union or by birth. Rather, children are born
into a *world* of sin; conception is simply the vehicle by which the effects of the
Fall (not original guilt) are transmitted to Adam's posterity. Lehi taught Jacob
that in the beginning God 'Gave commandment that all men must repent; for
he showed unto all men that they were lost, because of the transgression of their
parents (2 Ne. 2:21).'"

Robert Millet (Ensign, June 1992, p. 8)

"It is easier for me to understand the word fall in the scriptures if I think both in
terms of location and condition. The word fall means to descend to a lower place.

. . . The fall of man was a move from the presence of God to mortal life on earth. . . . Fall may also describe a change in condition. . . . The word fall describes well what transpired when Adam and Eve were driven from the garden. . . . The bodies formed for mankind became temporal or physical bodies. The scriptures say 'the life of all flesh is in the blood thereof' (Lev. 17:11-13; Deut. 12:23; *Teachings of the Prophet Joseph Smith*, pp. 199-200). After the transformation caused by the Fall, bodies of flesh and bone and blood (unlike our spirit bodies), would not endure forever. Somehow the ingredient blood carried with it a limit to life. It was as though a clock were set and a time given. There-after, all living things moved inexorably toward mortal or temporal death. Temporal . . . means temporary. . . . Had man evolved from animals, there could have been no fall, no law broken, no penalty, no need for a mediator. . . . Many who perceive organic evolution to be law rather than theory do not realize they forsake the Atonement in the process."

Boyd K. Packer (The Book of Mormon: Jacob Through Words of Mormon, To Learn with Joy, BYU Religious Studies Center, ed. by Nyman & Tate).

"Adam had a spiritual body until mortality came upon him through the violation of the law under which he was living, but he also had a physical body of flesh and bones. Now what is a spiritual body? It is one that is quickened by spirit and not by blood. Our Father in heaven and our Savior and all those who have passed through the resurrection have physical bodies of flesh and bones, but their bodies are quickened by spirit and not by blood, hence they are spiritual bodies and not blood bodies. The immortal body is quickened by spirit, but the mortal body is quickened by blood. . . . Now when Adam was in the Garden of Eden, he was not subject to death. There was no blood in his body and he could have remained there forever. This is true of all the other creations."

Joseph Fielding Smith (Doctrines of Salvation, 1:76-77)

COMMANDMENTS IN THE GARDEN
(Moses 2:28, 3:16-17, Moses 4:18)

"Adam did not commit sin in eating the fruits, for God had decreed that he should eat and fall."

Joseph Smith (The Words of Joseph Smith, p. 63)

"What did Adam do? The very thing the Lord wanted him to do; And I hate to hear anybody call it a sin, for it wasn't a sin. Now this is the way I interpret that: [Moses 3:16-17]. The Lord said to Adam, here is the tree of the knowledge of good and evil. If you want to stay here, then I forbid you to eat it. But you may act for yourself, and you may eat of it if you want to. And if you eat it, you will die."

Joseph Fielding Smith (Charge to Religious Educators, p. 124)

"Adam and Eve therefore did the very thing that the Lord intended them to do. . . . The Lord said to Adam that if he wished to remain in the garden, then he was not to eat the fruit, but if he desired to eat it and partake of death he was at liberty to do so. So really it was not in the true sense a transgression of a divine commandment. . . . It was the divine plan from the very beginning that man should be placed on the earth and be subject to mortal conditions and pass through a probationary state as explained in the Book of Mormon. . . ."

Joseph Fielding Smith (Answers to Gospel Questions, 4:79-82)

"God issued to Adam and Eve the first commandment ever given to mankind. It was a commandment to beget children. A law was explained to them. Should they eat from 'the tree of the knowledge of good and evil' (Gen. 2:17), their bodies would change; mortality and eventual death would come upon them. But partaking of that fruit was prerequisite to their parenthood. . . . Their bodies did change; blood began to circulate in their bodies. Adam and Eve thereby became mortal. Happily for us, they could also beget children and fulfill the purposes for which the world was created. . . . We and all mankind are forever blessed because of Eve's great courage and wisdom. By partaking of the fruit first, she did what needed to be done. Adam was wise enough to do likewise. Accordingly, we could speak of the fall of Adam in terms of a mortal creation, because 'Adam fell that men might be' (2 Ne. 2:25). Other blessings came to us through the Fall. It activated two closely coupled additional gifts from God, nearly as precious as life itself—agency and accountability. We became 'free to choose liberty and eternal life . . . or to choose captivity and death' (2 Ne. 2:27)."

Russell M. Nelson (Ensign, Nov. 1993, p. 34)

"When Adam and Eve received the first commandment, they were in a transitional state, no longer in the spirit world but with physical bodies not yet subject to death and not yet capable of procreation. They could not fulfill the Father's first commandment without transgressing. . . . For reasons that have not been revealed, this transition, or 'fall,' could not happen without a transgression

. . . It was Eve who first transgressed the limits of Eden in order to initiate the conditions of mortality. . . . Adam showed his wisdom by doing the same. And thus Eve and 'Adam fell that men might be' (v. 25). Some Christians condemn Eve for her act, concluding that she and her daughters are somehow flawed by it. Not the Latter-day Saints! Informed by revelation, we celebrate Eve's act and honor her wisdom and courage in the great episode called the Fall. . . . Modern revelation shows that our first parents understood the necessity of the Fall."

Dallin H. Oaks (Ensign, Nov. 1993, pp. 72-73)

"I do not look upon Adam's action as sin. I think it was a deliberate act of free agency."

Marion G. Romney (Conference Report, Apr. 1953, p. 124)

"Adam and Eve . . . were ordained of God to do what they did, and it was therefore expected that they would eat of the forbidden fruit in order that man might know both good and evil by passing through this school of experience which this life affords us."

Wilford Woodruff (Journal of Discourses 23:125)

"President Smith also gave an enlightening definition and application to the idea of the 'forbidden fruit.' He indicated that the 'forbidden' aspect was not in the partaking, but instead had reference to Adam and Eve's not being able to remain in the garden if they partook. This explanation suggests that the Lord wanted the Fall to occur."

(Unpublished address given by Joseph Fielding Smith at the LDS Institute of Religion, SLC, Utah, Jan. 14, 1961. Transcript approved by President Smith)

"Lehi explains that if Adam had not fallen, he and Eve would have remained endlessly in the Garden of Eden and that all things that had been created would have 'remained in the same state in which they were after they were created.' There would have been an endless state in which there was no change: no aging, no separation of the body and spirit in death, no reunion of the same in resurrection, no rewards for righteousness, no punishments for wickedness, no future kingdom of glory, no eternal life. Nor is this all, for Adam and Eve would have remained incapable of having seed of their own. Thus, as Lehi so eloquently stated it, 'Adam fell that men might be; and men are that they might have joy.' (2 Nephi 2:22-25)."

R. Millet and J. F. McConkie (Doctrinal Commentary on the Book of Mormon, 1:11-12)

2 Nephi 3~5

2 Ne. 3   **THE FOUR JOSEPHS**
(Compare to JST Gen. 50: [1] 2 Ne. 3:4-22; [2] 2 Ne. 3:1-3, 22-25; [3] 2 Ne. 3:15; [4] 2 Ne. 3:7-9, 11, 13-15, 17-19)

2 Ne. 3:7   **A CHOICE SEER WILL I RAISE UP**
(Mosiah 8:13-17; *Book of Mormon Prophecies*, Warner, pp. 52-53)

"In a December 1834 blessing, Father Smith confirmed to his son that ancient Joseph in Egypt 'Looked after his posterity in the last days . . . [and] sought diligently to know . . . who should bring forth the word of the Lord [to them] and his eyes beheld thee, my son [Joseph Smith, Jr.]: [and] his heart rejoiced and his soul was satisfied.'"

Neal A. Maxwell (Ensign, May 1992, p. 39; quoting from Patriarchal Blessings, 1:3)

"It was decreed in the counsels of eternity, long before the foundations of the earth were laid, that he, Joseph Smith, should be the man, in the last dispensation of this world, to bring forth the word of God to the people, and receive the fulness of the keys and power of the Priesthood of the Son of God. The Lord had his eyes upon him, and upon his father, and upon his father's father, and upon their progenitors clear back to Abraham, and from Abraham to the flood, from the flood to Enoch, and from Enoch to Adam. He has watched that family and that blood as it has circulated from its fountain to the birth of that man. He was fore-ordained in eternity to preside over this last dispensation."

Discourses of Brigham Young, p. 108

"We as a people have long been distressed and oppressed. We have been driven from our lands many times. We have been wasted away by wars, until there are but few of us left. The white man has hated us and shed our blood, until it has appeared as though there would soon be no Indians left. We have talked with the Great Spirit to save us and let us live; and the Great Spirit has told us that he had raised up a great Prophet, chief, and friend, who would do us great good and tell us what to do; and the Great Spirit has told us that you are the man (pointing to the Prophet Joseph). We have now come a great way to see you, and hear your words, and to have you to tell us what to do. Our horses have become poor traveling, and we are hungry. We will now wait and hear your word."

Interview with Pottawattamie Chiefs (from Wilford Woodruff's Journal as quoted in
History of the Church 5:479-480)

2 Ne. 3:8

NONE OTHER WORK
(Book of Mormon Prophecies, Warner, pp. 53-55; D&C 135:3)

"Joseph Smith was martyred in Carthage, Illinois, on the 27th of June, 1844— 14 years after the organization of the Church. What did he accomplish in these 14 years? He opened up communication with the heavens in his youth. He brought forth the Book of Mormon, which contains the fullness of the Gospel; and the revelations contained in the Book of Doctrine and Covenants; restored the holy Priesthood unto man; established and organized the Church of Jesus Christ of Latter-day Saints, an organization which has no parallel in all the world, and which all the cunning and wisdom of men for ages has failed to discover or produce and never could have done. He founded colonies in the States of New York, Ohio, Missouri and Illinois, and pointed the way for the gathering of the Saints into the Rocky Mountains; sent the Gospel into Europe and to the Islands of the sea; founded the town of Kirtland, Ohio, and there built a temple that cost about a quarter of a million of dollars; he founded the city of Nauvoo in the midst of persecution; gathered into Nauvoo and vicinity some 20,000 people, and commenced the building of the temple there, which when completed cost one million dollars; and in doing all this he had to contend against the prejudices of the age, against relentless persecution, mobocracy and vile calumny and slander, that were heaped upon him from all quarters without stint or measure. In a word, he did more in 14 to 20 years for the salvation of man than any other man save Jesus only, that ever lived. . . ."

Joseph F. Smith (Journal of Discourses 24:14-15)

2 Ne. 3:9

GREAT LIKE UNTO MOSES
(Moses 1:41)

"The Prophet Joseph Smith is here compared to Moses. The comparison is striking. (1) Both saw and spoke with Jehovah. (2) Both were liberators who led multitudes in exodus for the sake of liberty from oppression. (3) Both were law-givers by divine inspiration. (4) Both were prophets and seers. (5) Both performed mighty miracles. (6) Both encountered opposition, from 'friends' and enemies. (7) Both depended largely on a brother for success: Moses on Aaron; Joseph on Hyrum."

G. Reynolds and J. Sjodahl (Commentary on the Book of Mormon, 1:253)

2 Ne. 3:12

WRITINGS OF JUDAH & THE SEED OF JOSEPH
(Ezek. 37:15-17)

"The stick or record of Judah—the Old Testament and the New Testament—and the stick or record of Ephraim—are now woven together in such a way that as you pore over one you are drawn to the other; as you learn from one you are enlightened by the other. They are indeed one in our hands."

Boyd K. Packer (Conference Report, Oct. 1882, p. 75)

2 Ne. 3:13

OUT OF WEAKNESS HE SHALL BE MADE STRONG
(Ether 12:27; D&C 1:19-23; 35:13; 124:1; 1 Cor. 1:26-29; *Journal of Discourses* 18:118)

"Joseph Smith (as a young man) . . . could neither write nor dictate a coherent and well-worded letter, let alone dictate a book like the Book of Mormon, and though I was an active participant in the scenes that transpired, was present during the translation of the plates, and had cognizance of things as they transpired, it is marvelous to me—a marvel and a wonder—as much as to anyone else. . . . My belief is that the Book of Mormon is of divine authenticity—I have not the slightest doubt of it . . . when acting as his scribe, your father (she was being interrogated by her son) would dictate to me hour after hour; and when returning after meals, or interruptions, he would at once begin where he had left off, without either seeing the manuscript or having any portion of it read to him. This was an unusual thing for him to do. It would have been improbable that a learned man could do this and for one so ignorant and unlearned as he was, it was simply impossible."

Emma Smith (The Witnesses of the Book of Mormon, Preston Nibley, pp. 28-29)

2 Ne. 3:17-18   **I WILL MAKE FOR HIM A SPOKESMAN**
(D&C124:104; *New Witness for the Articles of Faith*, McConkie, pp. 426-427)

"Joseph was told that the seer of the latter days would also have a spokesman appointed for him. Although he, himself, would have the responsibility of bringing forth the writings of Joseph's descendants (The Book of Mormon), the spokesman would have the responsibility of going forth to declare it. This turned out to be Oliver Cowdery whom the Lord designated as 'The first preacher of this church unto the church, and before the world, yea, before the Gentiles; yea, and thus saith the Lord God, lo! to the Jew also' (D&C 21:12). Later, the Lord specifically said that Oliver Cowdery had a calling 'even as Aaron (the spokesman of Moses), to declare faithfully the commandments and the revelations, with power and authority unto the church' (D&C 28:3). After Oliver Cowdery fell, Sidney Rigdon was designated the 'spokesman' (D&C 100:89)."

Cleon Skousen (Treasures of the Book of Mormon, 1:1204)

"God afterwards revealed that this man, [Sidney Rigdon] was to be a spokesman, and he became the spokesman to this people and to the world for the prophet Joseph. Those who knew Sidney Rigdon, know how wonderfully God inspired him, and with what wonderful eloquence he declared the word of God to the people. He was a mighty man in the hands of God, as a spokesman, as long as the prophet lived, or up to a short time before his death. Thus you see that even this . . . was predicted about 1,700 years before the birth of the Savior, and was quoted by Lehi 600 years before the same event, and about 2,400 years before its fulfillment, and was translated by the power of God through his servant Joseph, as was predicted. . . ."

George Q. Cannon (Journal of Discourses 25:126)

2 Ne. 3:24   **THERE SHALL RISE UP ONE MIGHTY AMONG THE LAMANITES**
(Doctrines of Salvation, Smith, 2:251)

"The Lamanites must rise in majesty and power. . . . And in the day when their prophet shall come, one shall rise . . . mighty among them . . . being an instrument in the hands of God, with exceeding faith, to work mighty wonders. . . . (2 Nephi 3:24)."

Spencer W. Kimball (Conference Report, Oct. 1947, p. 22)

2 Ne. 4:2   **THE PROPHECIES OF JOSEPH**
(Companion to Your Study of the Book of Mormon, Ludlow, pp. 130-131)

2 Ne. 4:4   **NEPHI'S FREEDOM THESIS**
(refer in this text to 1 Ne. 1:20; Ether 2:12)

2 Ne. 4:5-6   **ANSWERED UPON THE HEADS OF YOUR PARENTS**
(D&C 68:25; 83:4; 93:40-42; Jacob 3:10; Moses 7:37; Prov. 22:6; *Ensign*, Nov. 1988, pp. 73-75; refer in this text to Jacob 1:19; Mosiah 25:12)

"There are parents who say: 'We will let our children grow to manhood and womanhood and choose for themselves.' In taking this attitude, parents fail the discharging of a parental responsibility. . . . It is the responsibility of parents to teach religion to their children."

David O. McKay (Treasures of Life, pp. 71-75)

"Not long after we were married, we built our first home. . . . The first of many trees that I planted was a thornless honey locust. . . . It was so supple that I could bend it with ease in any direction. I paid little attention to it as the years passed. Then one winter day, . . . I chanced to look out the window at it. I noticed that it was leaning to the west, misshapen and out of balance. . . . I went out and braced myself against it as if to push it upright. But the trunk was now nearly a foot in diameter. . . . It seemed to say, 'You can't straighten me. It's too late. I've grown this way because of your neglect, and I will not bend.' Finally in desperation I took my saw and cut off the great heavy branch on the west side. The saw left an ugly scar, more than eight inches across. . . . I had cut off the major part of the tree, leaving one branch growing skyward. More than half a century has passed since I planted that tree. . . . The other day I looked again at the tree. It is large. Its shape is better. . . . But how serious was the trauma of its youth and how brutal the treatment I used to straighten it. . . . When it was first planted, a piece of string would have held it in place against the forces of the wind. . . . I have seen a similar thing, many times, in children whose lives I have observed. The parents who brought them into the world seem almost to have abdicated their responsibility. The results have been tragic. A few simple anchors would have given them the strength to withstand the forces that have shaped their lives. Now it appears it is too late."

Gordon B. Hinckley (Ensign, Nov. 1993, p. 59)

"Parents haven't measured up to their responsibilities. It is evident. A nation will rise no higher than the strength of its homes. If you want to reform a nation, you begin with families, with parents who teach their children principles and values that are positive and affirmative and will lead them to worthwhile endeavors. That is the basic failure that has taken place in America. . . . Parents have no greater responsibility in this world than the bringing up of their children in the right way. . . ."

Gordon B. Hinckley (Ensign, Nov. 1996, pp. 48-49)

"Though the parents are not always charged with the failures of their children, we are sure that many times the failures of the children could be charged to the parents. . . . We realize that there are times when belligerent sons and daughters may draw upon themselves the condemnation, having totally ignored and failed all the teachings that have been given them. But we the parents cannot escape the responsibility that is ours of training our children. . . . As we think of these young people who rebel against their parents and society, we wonder, have you held your family prayers with regularity? Do you have your family home evenings regularly? Are your children taught to be faithful and true? Most parents protect their children with shelter for their comfort, tender care and medicine for their illnesses, clothes for their looks and comfort, and food for their taste and growth, but what do they do for their souls?"

Spencer W. Kimball (Tokyo Area Conference Report, Aug. 1975, pp. 38-39)

"The Lord has given us the answer. It is so simple that many people cannot see it. Let every family fortify itself against the tough and corrupt and godless world by methodically and determinedly teaching the children in regular, devout family prayers—night and morning every day—and in all Church programs and loyalties, and in the home evenings where fathers and mothers teach and train their children in all the ways of the Lord. Most people are largely the result of their home environment, good or bad. As Lehi said, on the brink of the grave, to his children, 'I know that if ye are brought up in the way ye should go, ye will not depart from it' (2 Ne. 4:5). Our conclusions must therefore be taking life at its best and life at its worst; the difference seems to be the catalyst of love and family solidarity."

Spencer W. Kimball (Manchester Area Conference Report, Aug. 1971, p. 82)

"If we do not take the pains to train our children, to teach and instruct them concerning these revealed truths, the condemnation will be upon us, as parents, or at least in a measure."

Discourses of Brigham Young, p. 207

"This teaching is to be done before a child reaches the age of accountability, and while innocent and sin-free. This is protected time for parents to teach the principles and ordinances of salvation to their children without interference from Satan. It is a time to dress them in armor in preparation for the battle against sin. When this preparation time is neglected, they are left vulnerable to the enemy. To permit a child to enter into that period of his life when he will be buffeted and tempted by the evil one, without faith in the Lord Jesus Christ and an understanding of the basic principles of the gospel, is to set him adrift in a world of wickedness. During these formative, innocent years, a child may learn wrong behavior; but such is not the result of Satan's temptations, but comes from the wrong teachings and the bad example of others. In this context, the Savior's harsh judgment of adults who offend children is better understood, wherein he said, 'It were better for him that a millstone were hanged about his neck, and he cast into the sea, than that he should offend one of these little ones' (Luke 17:2). We offend a child by any teaching or example which leads a little one to violate a moral law; causes him to stumble, go astray; excites him to anger; creates resentment; or perhaps even leads him to become displeasing and disagreeable."

Merlin R. Lybbert (Ensign, May 1994, pp. 31-32)

"Recent research on the development of a child's brain has revealed new insights into how and when a child learns. I quote from a recent study: 'From birth, a baby's brain cells proliferate wildly, making connections that may shape a lifetime of experience. The first three years are critical' (J. Madeleine Nash, *Time*, Feb. 3, 1997, 49). . . . The years from birth to age 10 are the peak years for acquiring the language that will become the foundation for understanding future knowledge and truth. . . . It is an ideal time for parents to read to their children from the scriptures. They will begin to learn the language of the scriptures. . . . One Primary leader shared . . . that she and her husband read the scriptures to their children—ages 2, 3, and 4—every night before they go to bed. . . . I must admit I questioned that children so young could understand the language of the scriptures. . . . She said after the first week the language was not an issue. The children love reading together and feeling the Spirit, and it's amazing how much they understand. A very young child's potential for learning and understanding is far greater than we tend to believe. The exciting possibility is that while children are learning new words daily, they can learn the language of the scriptures. In time, through the guidance of parents and teachers, they will grow in their understanding that Heavenly Father is speaking to them through the scriptures, that the scriptures can help them find answers to their problems."

Anne G. Wirthlin (Ensign, May 1998, pp. 9-10)

2 Ne. 4:7, 9   **IN THE END THY SEED (LAMANITES) SHALL BE BLESSED**

"I saw it in South America as I looked into the faces of missionaries. Hundreds of them passed by me shaking my hand and looking deeply into my eyes. I was nearly overwhelmed with the confirmation that these children of Father Lehi and of Sariah were there in the Lord's service because our Heavenly Father honors his promises to families. To nearly his last breath, Lehi taught and testified and tried to bless his children. Terrible tragedy came among his descendants when they rejected his testimony, the testimonies of other prophets, and of the scriptures. But in the eyes and faces of those missionaries I felt confirmation that God has kept his promises to reach out to Lehi's covenant children. . . ."

Henry B. Eyring (Ensign, May 1996, p. 64)

2 Ne. 4:15-16   **MY SOUL DELIGHTETH IN THE SCRIPTURES**
(refer in this text to 1 Ne. 8:19; 19:23; Alma 17:2)

"During the war in Vietnam, some of our men were taken prisoner and kept in nearly total isolation. Permitted no access to the scripture, they later told how they hungered for the words of truth, more than for food, more than for freedom itself. What they would have given for a mere fragment of the Bible or Book of Mormon that lay so idly on our shelves! They learned by hard experience something of Nephi's feelings when he said: [2 Ne. 4:15-16]."

Spencer W. Kimball (Ensign, Sept. 1976, p. 4)

2 Ne. 4:15-35   **PSALM OF NEPHI**
(Romans 3:23; 7:18-19; James 5:17; Acts 14:15)

"Nephi's references to personal sins should not be taken to imply any serious moral transgression on his part. No man could have seen and known God as did who was not pure in heart. Rather, he is almost surely alluding to the negative emotions of anger, impatience, and frustration he must have felt at times in dealing with his enemies, his own family, and others who lacked his singleness of purpose."

Rodney Turner (First Nephi, The Doctrinal Foundation, BYU Religious Studies Center, p. 93)

2 Ne. 4:31   **SHAKE AT THE APPEARANCE OF SIN**
(Alma 13:10-12)

2 Ne. 4:34   **THE ARM OF FLESH**
(D&C 1:19; refer in this text to Mosiah 11:9; Alma 39:2; Morm. 3:9)

"Ah, the arrogant arm of flesh, like the quarterback whose arm was so strong it was boasted that he could throw a football through a car wash and it would come out dry on the other side! Such naivete, such triviality symbolize not only the arm, but also the mind of flesh, which misses 'things as they really are, and . . . things as they really will be' (Jacob 4:13)."

Neal A. Maxwell (Ensign, May 1997, p. 16)

2 Ne. 5:3,19   **THE BIRTHRIGHT**
(1 Ne. 2:21-22; refer in this text to Mosiah 10:15)

2 Ne. 5:17   **INDUSTRY AND LABOR**
(Alma 1:3; 1:26; 23:17-18; 24:18; Enos 1:20-21; D&C 60:13; 75:3, 29; 88:124; 2 Thes. 3:10; Gen. 3:19; Prov. 6:6; Haggai 2:4; Neh. 4:6; Ezek.14:49; Ezek. 16:42; *Teachings of Spencer W. Kimball*, pp. 360-361)

"There is no substitute under the heavens for productive labor. . . . Most of us are inherently lazy. We would rather loaf than work. . . . But it is work that spells the difference in the life of a man or woman."

Gordon B. Hinckley (Ensign, Aug. 1992, p. 4)

"My father had a horse and buggy when I was a boy. Then one summer day in 1916, a wonderful thing happened. It was an unforgettable thing. When he came home that evening he arrived in a shining black brand-new Model T Ford. . . . The most interesting thing was the lights. The car had no storage battery. The only electricity came from what was called a magneto. The output of the magneto was determined by the speed of the engine. If the engine was running fast, the lights were bright. If the engine slowed, the lights became a sickly yellow. I learned that if you wanted to see ahead as you were going down the road, you had to keep the engine running at a fast clip. So, just as I'd discovered, it is with our lives. Industry, enthusiasm, and hard work lead to enlightened progress. You have to stay on your feet and keep moving if you are going to have light in your life."

Gordon B. Hinckley (Ensign, May 1993, pp.53-54)

"When President N. Eldon Tanner presided over the West European Mission some years ago, his slogan was 'Have a good time.' One day he said to a group of missionaries in Germany, 'I would like you all to have a good time.' After the meeting, one of the missionaries came up to him and said: 'President

Tanner, I don't think that it is quite fair for you to tell the missionaries to have a good time. You know, the only way they can have a good time is to do their work.' President Tanner said, 'Well, go have a good time.'"

James E. Faust (Ensign, May 1996, p. 40)

"There is divine security in learning the value and dignity of honest work. The right to work is inherent in man's divine nature. Work is a blessing and a privilege, not a penalty."

Bernard P. Brockbank (BYU Speeches of the Year, July 6, 1971)

"The spirit of the Gospel of the Lord Jesus Christ is opposed to idleness. We do not believe that a man who has the spirit can rest content if he is not busily employed."

George Q. Cannon (Gospel Truths, p. 520)

"We must protect . . . [America] from idleness, subsidies, doles and soft governmental paternalism which weakens initiative, discourages industry, destroys character and demoralizes people."

Ezra Taft Benson (A Nation Asleep, p. 12)

"If we want to keep the Spirit, we must work. There is no greater exhilaration or satisfaction than to know, after a hard day of work, that we have done our best."

Ezra Taft Benson (Come Unto Christ, p. 96)

"Cutting trees is more important than thinking about cutting trees or planning to cut trees. We are becoming the world experts in meeting, thinking, planning, and organizing about working the work, but we need to *do* it. We need to *work*. While many are sitting and saying and even shouting great swelling words of marginal effectiveness, hard-working Latter-day Saints will always be found diligently doing and delivering potatoes to their neighbors. Contrary to the belief of many, 'Say' and 'Sit' will never replace 'Diligently Do.' . . . My young friends of the Aaronic Priesthood, say less and do more. Get it done."

F. David Stanley (Ensign, May 1993, p. 45)

[Speaking of his youth] "Back then . . . we were all poor together, and we didn't know it. Work was a given. Today, for some receiving is a given. . . . I certainly did not always put my shoulder to the wheel with a 'heart full of song,' but I did learn about shoulders and wheels, which helped later in life, when the wheels grew larger. Some of today's otherwise good young men mistakenly think that putting their shoulders to the wheel is the same thing as putting their hands on a steering wheel! . . . I remind you that the gospel of work is part of 'the fulness of the gospel' . . . Alas, a few of our underwhelmed youth work all right, but mostly at trying to please themselves. . . . The hardest work you and I will ever do is to put off our selfishness. It is heavy lifting! . . . How blessed we would be if more sons could work alongside their fathers. . . . Fathers and sons, if such teaming up is not already happening at all, please, in the next three months, select just one, stretching chore to do together. . . . Knowing how to work will give you an edge in life. . . . The capacity to work and work wisely will never become obsolete. . . . I have not seen any perspiration free shortcuts to the celestial kingdom; there is no easy escalator to take us there."

Neal A. Maxwell (Ensign, May 1998, pp. 37-39)

2 Ne. 5:24   **SEEK FOR BEASTS OF PREY**
(D&C 49:18-19, 21; 89:12; JST Gen. 9:10-11; *Life of Joseph Smith*, Cannon, pp. 174-175; *Journal of Discourses* 15:227)

"Nephi's denunciation of the Lamanites does not focus on hunting 'wild animals' (D&C 89:14) from which they would obtain both meat and clothing. Rather his attention is centered on their hunting 'beasts of prey.' Apparently they killed for sport, a practice strongly condemned in the scriptures (see JST, Genesis 9:10-11)."

R. Millet & J. F. McConkie (Doctrinal Commentary on the Book of Mormon, 1:225)

"In pitching my tent we found three massasaugas or prairie rattlesnakes, which the brethren were about to kill, but I said, 'Let them alone — don't hurt them! How will the serpent ever lose his venom, while the servants of God possess the same disposition and continue to make war upon it? Men must become harmless, before the brute creation: and when men lose their vicious dispositions and cease to destroy the animal race, the lion and the lamb can dwell together, and the sucking child can play with the serpent in safety.' The brethren took the serpents carefully on sticks and carried them across the creek. I exhorted the brethren not to kill a serpent, bird, or an animal of any kind during our journey unless it became necessary in order to preserve ourselves from hunger."

Joseph Smith (History of the Church, 2:71-72)

"There is no statement in the scriptures indicating that the flesh of animals and birds and other living creatures was used as food before the days of Noah. It was after the landing of the ark that the Lord gave his commandment concerning the eating of flesh. 'And surely, blood shall not be shed, only for meat, to save your lives; and the blood of every beast will I require at your hands.' (JST Gen. 9:11.) . . . There is no inference in the scriptures that it is the privilege of men to slay birds or beasts or to catch fish wantonly. . . . It was intended that all creatures should be happy in their several elements. Therefore to take the life of these creatures wantonly is a sin before the Lord. . . . Man should be more the friend and never an enemy to any living creature. The Lord placed them here."

Joseph Fielding Smith (Improvement Era, Aug. 1961, p. 568)

"Cease hostility with the serpents and lay aside all enmity and treat all animals kindly."

Brigham Young (Brigham Young Manuscript History 1846-1847, Watson, pp. 142-143)

"It is a good thing to teach our boys to be kind [to animals]. A man who was working for me once on the farm came home about sundown, and said, 'I have just killed a porcupine over there.' I said, 'Why did you kill it?' 'Oh,' he said, 'just for fun.' And I said, 'Did you kill it or is it over there suffering?' 'Oh, I killed it.' Well, I wondered, so I just took time to cross those two creeks and go over to the little hill. He had not killed it. The poor creature was just stunned; its head was beaten, and it was struggling. What fun can there be in treating dumb animals in that cruel way?"

David O. McKay (Conference Report, Oct. 1951, pp. 180-181)

"I found many young boys around my age who, with their flippers and their slings, destroyed many birds. In Primary and Sunday School we sang the song:

"Don't kill the little birds
That sing on bush and tree,
All thro' the summer days,
Their sweetest melody.'
(Deseret Song Book, 1909, no. 163).

. . . It is not only wicked to destroy [wildlife], . . . it is a shame, in my opinion. I think that this principle should extend not only to the bird life but to the life of all animals. . . . It is quite a different matter when a pioneer crossing the plains would kill a buffalo to bring food to his children and his family."

Spencer W. Kimball (Ensign, Nov. 1978, pp. 44-45)

"With reference to the killing of our innocent birds. . . . It is not only wicked to destroy them, it is abominable, in my opinion. I think that this principle should extend, not only to the bird life, but to the life of all animals. When I visited, a few years ago, the Yellowstone National Park, and saw in the streams and the beautiful lakes, birds swimming quite fearless of man, allowing passers-by to approach them as closely almost as tame birds, and apprehending no fear of them, and when I saw droves of beautiful deer herding along the side of the road, as fearless of the presence of men as any domestic animal it filled my heart with a degree of peace and joy that seemed to be almost a foretaste of that period hoped for when there shall be none to hurt and none to molest in all the land. . . . These same birds, if they were to visit other regions, inhabited by man, would, on account of their tameness, doubtless become more easily a prey to the gunner. The same may be said of those beautiful creatures—the deer and antelope. . . . I never could see why a man should be imbued with a blood-thirsty desire to kill and destroy animal life. I have known men—and they still exist among us—who enjoy what is, to them, the 'sport' of hunting birds and slaying them . . . and who will come in after a day's sport, boasting of how many harmless birds they have had the skill to slaughter. . . . I do not believe any man should kill animals or birds unless he needs them for food, and then he should not kill innocent little birds that are not intended for food for man. I think it is wicked for men to thirst in their souls to kill almost everything which possesses animal life. It is wrong, and I have been surprised at prominent men whom I have seen whose very souls seemed to be athirst for the shedding of animal blood. They go off hunting deer, antelope, elk, anything they can find, and what for? 'Just for the fun of it!' Not that they are hungry and need the flesh of their prey, but just because they love to shoot and to destroy life."

Joseph F. Smith (Gospel Doctrine, pp. 265-266)

[A hunting experience of Lorenzo Snow at age 24] "Up until now, it had never seemed to him that shooting turkeys, squirrels and other animal life was sinful. . . . 'While moving slowly forward in pursuit of something to kill,' said Lorenzo, 'my mind was arrested with the reflection on the nature of my pursuit—that of amusing myself by giving pain and death to harmless, innocent creatures that perhaps had as much right to life and enjoyment as myself. I realized that such indulgence was without any justification, and feeling condemned, I laid my gun on my shoulder, returned home, and from that time to this have felt no inclination for that murderous amusement.'"

Thomas C. Romney, The Life of Lorenzo Snow, p. 23

"The Lord will not judge a single animal for its treatment of man, but He will adjudge the souls of men towards their beasts in this world, for men have a special place. Familiar early Jewish and Christian teaching was that the animals will appear at the bar of God's judgment to accuse those humans who have wronged them. . . . Animals do possess real rights, 'for all things have an *equal* right to live (!)' as President Joseph F. Smith would say *(Gospel Doctrine*, 2 vols. 1:372)."

Hugh Nibley (Brother Brigham Challenges The Saints, pp. 10,12)

"No man can be considered to be a child of Abraham who is cruel to any creature."

Hugh Nibley (CES Lecture, Utah Valley State College Institute, June 14, 1995)

2 Ne. 5:26   **PRIESTHOOD AMONG THE NEPHITES**
(2 Ne. 6:2; Alma 5:44; 13:1-5; 43:1-2; *New Witness for the Articles of Faith*, McConkie, p. 348; *Answers to Gospel Questions*, Smith, 1:124-126; *Doctrines of Salvation*, Smith, 3:87; refer in this text to 1 Ne. 4:22, 26)

"Among the Nephites, brethren holding the Melchizedek Priesthood were selected, consecrated *teachers*, and given teaching and administrative powers and responsibilities. (1 Ne. 2:22; 2 Ne. 5:19; Mosiah 23:17; 25:19; 26:7; Alma 4:7). They had jurisdiction over the churches and, along with the *priests*, were 'to preach and to teach the word of God.' (Alma 23:4.) They had power to baptize (Alma 15:13), a privilege not enjoyed by teachers in the Aaronic Priesthood (D&C 20:58). It should be noted that those consecrated *priests and teachers* among the Nephites were not receiving offices in the lesser priesthood, for there was no Aaronic Priesthood among the Nephites from the time Lehi left Jerusalem down to the ministry of Christ among them. From the time of Aaron to the coming of our Lord, the Aaronic Priesthood was an hereditary priesthood; it was conferred only upon the Levites, none of whom journeyed with father Lehi and his colony."

Bruce R. McConkie (Mormon Doctrine, p. 776)

2 Ne. 5:21-23   **THREE ELEMENTS OF THE LAMANITE CURSE**
(2 Ne. 30:3-6; 3 Ne. 2:14-16; Alma 3:6-16; 1 Kings 11:2)

"This is the only reference in the entire Book of Mormon where a definite color adjective is used to refer to this mark. All other references call it a 'skin of darkness' or a 'dark skin.' It is of interest to note that the terms 'blackness' and 'darkness' are interchangeable in the Hebrew. Even in modern Hebrew it is not unusual for some skilled translator to render a word black whereas other equally skilled translators select *dark* as the best translation."

Daniel H. Ludlow (Companion to Your Study of the Book of Mormon, p. 132)

"The dark skin was placed upon the Lamanites so that they could be distinguished from the Nephites and to keep the two peoples from mixing. The dark skin was a sign of the curse. The curse was the withdrawal of the Spirit of the Lord. The dark skin . . . is no longer considered a sign of the curse. Many of these converts are delightsome and have the Spirit of the Lord."

Joseph Fielding Smith (Answers to Gospel Questions, 1:123-124)

"Because of their iniquity the Lamanite peoples were cursed with 'a skin of blackness.' Our text tells us that they were so cursed in order that they would not be enticing to the Nephites. The Old Testament contains ample evidence that when the children of Israel married outside the covenant they were dissuaded from the worship of the true and living God and quickly embraced the idolatry and whoredoms of the Canaanites."

R. Millet and J. F. McConkie (Doctrinal Commentary on the Book of Mormon, 1:224)

2 Ne. 5:24   (Refer in this text to 1 Ne. 2:21; 2 Ne. 5:17.)

"One can hardly suffer a greater loss in mortality than to lose the Spirit of the Lord (see Alma 28:14; D&C 84:45-46). . . . *Such was the real curse that came upon the Lamanites.* There is no warrant for assuming that being dark-skinned inevitably disposed the early Lamanites to idleness . . ."

Rodney Turner (Second Nephi. The Doctrinal Structure, BYU Religious Studies Center, p. 140)

"The wickedness of this people caused the Spirit of the Lord to be withdrawn, bringing upon themselves a curse. . . . All who live in a state of rebellion are heirs to such a curse. A mark of that curse among the Lamanites was a dark skin."

R. Millet and J. F. McConkie (Doctrinal Commentary on the Book of Mormon, 1:224).

2 Ne. 5:25   (1 Ne. 2:23-24; refer in this text to Alma 53:8-9)

"So it was a blessing to the Nephites after all to have the Lamanites on their doorstep to stir them up to remembrance. . . . No matter how wicked and ferocious and depraved the Lamanites might be (and they were that!), no matter by how much they outnumbered the Nephites, . . . they were not the Nephite problem. They were merely kept there to remind the Nephites of their real problem, which was to walk uprightly before the Lord."

Hugh Nibley (Since Cumorah, p. 376)

2 Nephi 6~10

2 Ne. 6:2   **HIS HOLY ORDER**
(D&C107:1-4; JST Gen. 14:27-29)

2 Ne. 6:6   **STANDARD TO MY PEOPLE**
(refer in this text to 1 Ne. 21:22; *Commentary on the Book of Mormon*, Reynolds & Sjodahl, 1:281)

"As the newly formed nation of Israel journeyed from Egypt to Palestine, each tribe was assigned its position in the order of march and in the place of encampment. As ranks were formed, a representative of each tribe would raise a standard or banner on a pole around which the tribes could rally and quickly find their places. (Numbers 2.) This standard or ensign which was the ancient rallying point for Israel provides an excellent symbol for the gospel to which the lost and disordered tribes of Israel will return in the latter days. The promise that the Lord would again set up his standard among the people is the promise that the gospel will be restored and that Israel will rally to it (see D&C 45:9)."

R. Millet and J. F. McConkie (Doctrinal Commentary on the Book of Mormon, 1:229)

2 Ne. 6:10-11   **GATHERING IS FIRST TO CHRIST**
(2 Ne. 9:2; 10:7-8; 25:16-17; 30:7; 3 Ne. 5:26; refer in this text to 3 Ne. 20:13, 29-33; *Mormon Doctrine*, McConkie, pp. 722-723; *Book of Mormon Prophecies*, Warner, pp. 156-167; *Signs of the Times*, Smith, pp. 58-71; *Conference Report*, Apr. 1973, pp. 6-7; *Doctrines of Salvation*, Smith, 3:9; *Church News*, Oct. 25, 1952, pp. 2-3)

"The return of the Jews to the ancient land of Palestine and the creation of the state of Israel in 1948 constituted a marvelous foreshadowing of the fulfillment of prophecy. This did not match the vision of Book of Mormon prophets, however, who were insistent that *the Jews must first return to Christ and accept the Holy One of Israel before they would have claim upon the covenants made with their ancient fathers.*"

R. Millet and J. F. McConkie (Doctrinal Commentary on the Book of Mormon, 1:230)

2 Ne. 7:1   **BILL OF DIVORCEMENT**
(Isa. 50:1; refer in this text to 3 Ne. 12:31-32)

"The question posed to Israel about her divorced status is a metaphorical reference to the law of divorce given in Deuteronomy 24:1-4. Under this law, if a wife was found unfaithful (unclean) her husband could dissolve the marriage by giving her a 'bill of divorcement.' Even though Israel had been unfaithful to her husband—the Lord—He had never given her such a document; she was never officially divorced. . . . The Lord further states that neither has Israel been sold into bondage to relieve a debt, for He has no creditors. (At that time, one in debt could sell his children into servitude to pay the debt. See Exodus 21:7; Nehemiah 5:1-5. . . . In speaking to latter-day Israel, who is to be redeemed, reference is made to her 'mother' who was 'put away' (separated) because of her 'transgressions.' Some have suggested this implies ancient Israel (the mother) was divorced (put away) but that the bill of divorcement does not apply to modern Israel. However, it appears that ancient 'mother Israel' left her Husband (put herself away)."

Hoyt W. Brewster, Jr. (Isaiah Plain and Simple, pp. 206, 208)

2 Ne. 7:4-9   **SERVANT'S SONG**
(Isa. 50:4-9; *Isaiah: Prophet, Seer, and Poet*, Ludlow, pp. 358-360)

"These verses are known among biblical scholars as a 'servant's song.' This is a major poetic passage wherein a servant of the Lord is described, although not specifically identified. There are differences of opinion among commentaries regarding the identity of this Servant. While there may be dual meaning to these verses, . . . the song in Isaiah 50 refers primarily to the Messiah. He will be treated despicably, but the power of God will be manifest in Him. Those who oppose Him will be destroyed."

Hoyt W. Brewster, Jr. (Isaiah Plain and Simple, p. 209)

2 Ne. 8:19-20   **TWO SONS**
(Isa. 51:19-20; Zech. 4:11-14; D&C 77:15; Rev. 11:1-14; *Behold, I Come Quickly*, Brewster, pp. 100-104)

"These two prophets were also spoken of by John the Revelator (Revelation 11:1-14), Zechariah (Zechariah 4:11-14), and Joseph Smith (D&C 77:15). The two will 'have power to shut heaven, that it rain not in the days of their prophecy: and have power over waters to turn them to blood, and to smite the earth with all plagues, as often as they will (Revelation 11:6).'"

Hoyt W. Brewster, Jr. (Isaiah Plain and Simple, p. 225)

"These two shall be followers of that humble man, Joseph Smith. . . . No doubt they will be members of the Council of the Twelve or of the First Presidency of the Church. Their prophetic ministry to rebellious Jewry shall be the same in length as was our Lord's personal ministry among their rebellious forebears."

Bruce R. McConkie (Doctrinal New Testament Commentary, 3:509-510)

"At the end of their designated ministry, the two prophets will be slain. Their dead bodies will lie in the streets of Jerusalem for three and one-half days while the wicked of the world rejoice. However, their victory will be short-lived, for the two martyrs will arise as resurrected beings. A great earthquake, of a magnitude never before known, will follow and the Savior will shortly appear. The wicked will be destroyed and the earth prepared for the millennial reign."

Hoyt W. Brewster, Jr. (Isaiah Plain and Simple, p. 226)

2 Ne. 8:24   **BEAUTIFUL GARMENTS**
(Isa. 52:1; refer in this text to 2 Ne. 9:14)

"What comes about as a result of exercising the Priesthood is equivalent to putting on 'her beautiful garments. . . .'"

Hyrum M. Smith (as quoted in Doctrine & Covenants Encyclopedia, Brewster, p. 40)

Chapter 9 is Jacob's Commentary of Isaiah in 2 Nephi 7-8

"One of the most enlightening discourses ever delivered in regard to the atonement is found in the ninth chapter of 2 Nephi in the Book of Mormon. It is the counsel given by Jacob, brother of Nephi. It should be carefully read by every person seeking salvation. We have been taught that the greatest gift of God is eternal life, and eternal life comes through obedience to all of the commandments and covenants given to man by our Heavenly Father."

Joseph Fielding Smith (Answers to Gospel Questions, 4:57)

2 Ne. 9:6   **DEATH FULFILLS THE MERCIFUL PLAN OF THE CREATOR**
(D&C 42:8; 93:33-34; *Answers to Gospel Questions*, Smith, 4:59)

"But who would like to live forever in this mundane world, filled with pain, decay, sorrow, and tribulation, and grow old and infirm and yet have to remain with all the vicissitudes of mortality? I think all of us would come to the conclusion, if that proposition were placed before us, that we would not like to have it. We would reject it. We would not want life of that nature. Life here in this world is short of necessity, and yet all that is required may be accomplished, but death is just as important in the plan of salvation as birth is. We have to die—it is essential—and death comes into the world 'to fulfill the merciful plan of the great Creator.'"

Joseph Fielding Smith (Doctrines of Salvation, 1:116)

2 Ne. 9:6,13   **PLAN**
(Jacob 6:8; Alma 12:25, 30-33; 34:9, 16; 41:2; 42:5, 8, 11, 15; Jarom 1:2; Moses 6:62; Abr. 4:21)

"No less than fifteen times, the Book of Mormon uses the word plan in connection with the plan of salvation or its components. The very use of the word plan is itself striking. In bringing back this particular 'plain and precious' truth—namely, God not only lives but does have a plan for mankind—the Book of Mormon is unusually relevant for our age and time. Phrases about God's planning from the 'foundation of the world' appear not at all in the Old Testament. . . ."

Neal A. Maxwell (First Nephi, The Doctrinal Foundation, BYU Religious Studies Center, p. 5)

2 Ne. 9:7-9   **INFINITE ATONEMENT**
(D&C 76:20-24, 41-42; Moses 1:33-35; 7:30; Alma 34:10-12; Heb. 1:1-2; John 1:10; *Answers to Gospel Questions*, Smith, 4:123-125; *Journal of Discourses* 17:332; *Doctrinal Commentary on the Book of Mormon*, Millet & McConkie, 1:236-238; 3:247-249; *Doctrines of the Book of Mormon*, 1991 Sperry Symposium, pp. 82-84)

"When the prophets speak of an infinite atonement, they mean just that. Its effects cover all men, the earth itself and all forms of life thereon, and reach out into the endless expanses of eternity. . . . Now our Lord's jurisdiction and power extend far beyond the limits of this one small earth on which we dwell. He is, under the Father, the Creator of worlds without number (Moses 1:33). And through the power of his atonement the inhabitants of these worlds, the revelation says, 'are begotten sons and daughters unto God' (D&C 76:24), which means that the atonement of Christ, being literally and truly infinite, applies to an infinite number of earths."

Bruce R. McConkie (Mormon Doctrine, pp. 64-65)

"Jesus Christ, in the sense of being its Creator and Redeemer, is the Lord of the whole universe. Except for his mortal ministry accomplished on this earth, his service and relationship to other worlds and their inhabitants are the same as his service and relationship to this earth and its inhabitants."

Marion G. Romney (Ensign, Apr. 1976, p. 32)

"His Atonement is infinite—without an end. It was also infinite in that all humankind would be saved from never-ending death (see 2 Ne. 9:7; 25:16; Alma 34:10,12,14). It was infinite in terms of His immense suffering. It was infinite in time, putting an end to the preceding prototype of animal sacrifice. It was infinite in scope—it was to be done once for all (see Heb. 10:10). And the mercy of the Atonement extends not only to an infinite number of people, but also to an infinite number of worlds created by Him (see D&C 76:24; Moses 1:33). It was infinite beyond any human scale of measurement or mortal comprehension. Jesus was the only one who could offer such an infinite atonement, since He was born of a mortal mother and an immortal Father. Because of that unique birthright, Jesus was an infinite Being."

Russell M. Nelson (Ensign, Nov. 1996, p. 35)

[Speaking of Christ's Infinite Atonement] "Yet, to help us begin to grasp with our finite, mortal minds the enormous price required, consider a few rough indicators of how much sin there is in our world. If you look at the United States alone, there are now more than fifty murders committed every day (that's nearly nineteen thousand per year). There are more than twenty-one thousand thefts reported every day, and more than fifty-five hundred reported cases of child neglect and abuse. . . . Think of how many times on a single day adultery or some other violation of the law of chastity is committed somewhere in the world. How many cases of incest, child abuse, pornography, burglary, robbery? How many times in any one day is the name of God taken in vain? How many times are sacred things profaned? Then multiply these over the span of human history. And that takes into consideration only our world. We know that the Atonement extended to other worlds as well."

Gerald Lund (Doctrines of the Book of Mormon, 1991 Sperry Symposium, p. 86)

"The effect of the infinite, atoning sacrifice was twofold: First, resurrection and immortality for all, unconditionally granted. Second, eternal life for each one who fulfills the prescribed conditions, which are faith in Jesus Christ as Savior and Redeemer, followed by repentance. Then we must qualify for and receive the saving and exalting ordinances of the gospel with their associated covenants, continuously striving to keep those covenants and obey the commandments of God."

Ronald E. Poelman (Ensign, Nov. 1993, p. 85)

2 Ne. 9:10 **THAT AWFUL MONSTER**
(Eccl. 12:1-7)

2 Ne. 9: 10 **DEATH OF THE SPIRIT**
(Alma 12:16; Hel. 14:16; refer in this text to Alma 40:26; *Doctrines of Salvation*, Smith, 2:222)

"One definition of the word spiritual is 'of or pertaining to the spirit or things of the spirit'; the definition of death includes the idea of separation. Thus spiritual death rightfully refers to a state of spiritual separation from God; it may or may not have anything to do with a physical separation from God."

Daniel H. Ludlow (Companion to Your Study of the Book of Mormon, p. 136)

". . . all the world today, I am sorry to say, with the exception of a handful of people who have obeyed the new and everlasting covenant, are suffering this spiritual death. They are cast out from the presence of God. They are without God, without Gospel truth, and without the power of redemption; for they know not God nor His Gospel. In order that they may be redeemed and saved from the spiritual death which has spread over the world like a pall, they must repent of their sins, and be baptized by one having authority, for the remission of their sins, that they may be born of God. That is why we want these young men to go out into the world to preach the Gospel. While they themselves understand but little perhaps, the germ of life is in them."

Joseph F. Smith (Conference Report, Oct. 1899, p. 72)

2 Ne. 9:10-12 **HELL**
(Rev. 20:13; Psalm 16:10; Acts 2:27; D&C 76:81, 84, 106; refer in this text to Alma 40:13-14)

". . . many other great truths not known before, have been declared to the people, and one of the greatest is that to hell there is an exit as well as an entrance. Hell is no place to which a vindictive judge sends prisoners to suffer and to be punished principally for his glory; But it is a place prepared for the teaching, the disciplining of those who failed to learn here upon the earth what they should have learned. . . . No man will be kept in hell longer than is necessary to bring him to a fitness for something better. When he reaches that stage the prison doors will open and there will be rejoicing among the hosts who welcome him into a better state."

James E. Talmage (Conference Report, Apr. 1930, p. 97)

"What is Hell? It is another modern term, and is taken from Hades. Hades, the Greek, or Sheol the Hebrew, these two significations mean a world of spirits. Hades, Sheol, paradise, spirits in prison, are all one: It is a world of spirits. The righteous and the wicked all go to the same world of spirits until the resurrection."

Teachings of the Prophet Joseph Smith, p. 310

2 Ne. 9:13

PARADISE
(D&C 138:22, 30, 57; *Life Beyond*, Millet, p. 18; *Gospel Doctrine*, Smith, p. 448; refer in this text to Alma 40:12)

SPIRIT PRISON INCLUDES PARADISE AND HELL
(Moses 7:55-57; D&C 138:50; *Teachings of the Prophet Joseph Smith*, pp. 310-311; *Journal of Discourses* 1:289-290)

"I know it is a startling idea to say that the Prophet and the persecutor of the Prophet, all go to prison together. What is the condition of the righteous? . . . They have a privilege of seeing and understanding more than you or I have, in the flesh; but they have not got their bodies yet, consequently they are in prison."

Brigham Young (Journal of Discourses 3:95)

"The designation *spirit prison* may be said to have two meanings—*hell*, which is the prison proper; and the *whole spirit world*, in the sense that all who are therein are restricted and cannot gain a fulness of joy until after their resurrection (D&C 93:33-34)."

Bruce R. McConkie (Doctrinal New Testament Commentary, 3:309)

WHERE IS THE SPIRIT WORLD?
(Journal of Discourses 1:9)

"Where is the spirit world? It is right here. . . . Can you see it with your natural eyes? No. Can you see spirits in this room? No. Suppose the Lord should touch your eyes that you might see, could you then see the spirits? Yes, as plainly as you now see bodies. . . ."

Discourses of Brigham Young, pp. 376-77

2 Ne. 9:14   **NAKED OR ROBES OF RIGHTEOUSNESS**
(Morm. 9:5; D&C 29:12; 109:76; Alma 7:25; Rev. 19:7-8)

2 Ne. 9:14, 33   **PERFECT KNOWLEDGE OF OUR GUILT**
(Alma 5:18; refer in this text to Alma 11:43; *Companion to Your Study of the Book of Mormon*, Ludlow, pp. 203-204: *Psycho-Cybernetics*, Maltz, p. 19; *Journal of Discourses* 11:78-79)

"This verse has no reference to gaining a fulness of knowledge in and after the resurrection. We will not know all things at the time of our resurrection, but will come to know things as God knows them 'in due time' (D&C 93:19). In the words of Joseph Smith, omniscience is not to be had immediately at death or even at the time of our rise from death. 'It is not all to be comprehended in this world; it will be a great work to learn our salvation and exaltation even beyond the grave' *(Teachings,* p. 348). This verse refers instead to knowledge of what a person has done with his mortal life, how he has lived in relation to commandments of God. Each person's knowledge of his life—good or bad—will be perfect at the time he is raised from the dead. Facades or cover-ups or denials will be no more: we will see as we are seen. . . ."

R. Millet and J. F. McConkie (Doctrinal Commentary on the Book of Mormon, 1:243)

2 Ne. 9:15   **RESURRECTION—JUDGMENT**
"The resurrection precedes the final judgment. In a sense, this judgment is a formality so far as concerns assigning persons to their respective kingdoms of glory."

R. Millet and J. F. McConkie (Doctrinal Commentary on the Book of Mormon, 1: 243)

2 Ne. 9:16   **FIRE IN HELL**
(Jacob 6:10; Mosiah 2:38-39; 3:27; Alma 12:17; 36:12-16; Morm. 9:5; *Teachings of the Prophet Joseph Smith*, pp. 310-311, 357; *Answers to Gospel Questions*, Smith, 2:210; *Life Beyond*, Millet, pp. 21-22)

"This fire and brimstone, we are informed, is a representation of the torment which shall be suffered by the wicked. It is not actual fire, but it is the torment of the mind."

Joseph Fielding Smith (Doctrines of Salvation, 2:224)

"A man is his own tormenter and his own condemner. Hence the saying, They shall go into the lake that burns with fire and brimstone. The torment of disappointment in the mind of man is as exquisite as a lake burning with fire and brimstone. I say, so is the torment of man."

Teachings of the Prophet Joseph Smith, p. 357

2 Ne. 9:20   **GOD KNOWETH ALL THINGS**
(2 Ne. 2:24; Moro. 7:22; Psalm 147:5; D&C 38:1-2; 88:41; Alma 13:7; 26:35; Isa. 66:18; *History of the Church*, Smith 4:597; 6:30; *Lectures on Faith*, p. 43; *Doctrines of Salvation*, Smith, 1:5-10)

"Without the knowledge of all things God would not be able to save any portion of his creatures; for it is by reason of the knowledge which he has of all things, from the beginning to the end, that enables him to give that understanding to his creatures by which they are made partakers of eternal life; and if it were not for the idea existing in the minds of men that God had all knowledge it would be impossible for them to exercise faith in him."

Joseph Smith (Lectures on Faith, 4:11)

"The notion that our God is still progressing in knowledge—that he is gaining new truths—seems to have come from . . . a misunderstanding of what is meant by eternal progression. God progresses in the sense that his kingdoms expand and his dominions multiply (see D&C 132:31; 63; Moses 1:39)."

R. Millet & J. F. McConkie (Doctrinal Commentary on the Book of Mormon, 1:247)

"God is Omniscient—By Him matter has been organized and energy directed. He is therefore the Creator of all things that are created; and 'Known unto God are all his works from the beginning of the world.' His power and His wisdom are alike incomprehensible to man, for they are infinite. Being Himself eternal and perfect, His knowledge cannot be otherwise than infinite. To comprehend Himself, an infinite Being, He must possess an infinite mind. Through the agency of angels and ministering servants He is in continuous communication with all parts of creation, and may personally visit as He may determine."

James E. Talmage (Articles of Faith, pp. 43-44)

2 Ne. 9:24 **DAMNED**
(*Mormon Doctrine*, McConkie, pp. 176-177; *Teachings of the Prophet Joseph Smith*, p. 198)

2 Ne. 9:25-27 **WHERE THERE IS NO LAW GIVEN THERE IS NO PUNISHMENT—BUT WO UNTO HIM THAT HAS THE LAW**
(D&C 29:50; 82:3; 137:7-9; Mosiah 3:11; Alma 9:15, 19-24; 34:32-34; Luke 12:48; *Journal of Discourses* 3:206; Hel. 7:23-24; refer in this text to Moro. 8:22; Mosiah 15:24)

"What is Sin? Sin is the transgression of divine law. A man sins when he violates his conscience, going contrary to light and knowledge—not the light and knowledge that comes from his neighbor, but that which has come to himself. He sins when he does the opposite of what he knows to be right. Up to that point he only blunders. One may suffer painful consequences for only blundering, but he cannot commit sin unless he knows better than to do the thing in which the sin consists."

Orson F. Whitney (Cowley & Whitney on Doctrine, pp. 435-436)

"No person will be condemned for not observing a commandment or participating in an ordinance of which he or she was ignorant."

Robert Millet (Studies in Scriptures, ed. by K. Jackson, 7:124)

2 Ne. 9:28-30, **EDUCATIONAL PRIDE**
42-43, (2 Ne. 27:20; 28:15; Alma 32:23; D&C 6:7; 23:21; 88:118; 130:18-19; 2 Cor.
50-51 2:14; 2 Tim. 3:9; Prov. 16:18; Col. 2:8; *Conference Report*, Apr. 1901, p. 72; *Doctrines of Salvation*, Smith, 3:275-276; refer in this text to Jacob 2:13-17; 3 Ne. 6:10-16)

"It is easy to see why a proud man fails; he is content to rely on himself only."

Howard W. Hunter (Conference Report, Apr. 1984, p. 89)

"There is almost a universal tendency for men and women who are specialists in an academic discipline to judge the Church against the principles of their profession. There is a great need in my mind for us, as students and as teachers, to consciously and continually subjugate this tendency and relegate our professional training to a position secondary to the principles of the gospel of Jesus Christ. In other words, rather than to judge the Church and its program against the principles of our profession, we would do well to set the Church and its accepted program as the rule, then judge our academic training against this rule."

Boyd K. Packer (BYU Speeches of the Year, 1969, p. 6)

"Knowledge of the physical universe and of the laws which govern it is cumulative. Thus each generation builds upon and expands the knowledge gained from discoveries of the past. . . . Unlike knowledge of the physical universe, the moral knowledge of each generation begins where the previous began rather than where they left off. For example, the remedy for an infection in the physical body has changed dramatically over the centuries; the remedy for infidelity, not at all. . . . This apparent imbalance in accumulating knowledge can easily contribute to a spirit of arrogance in students of the physical world, especially in so-called intellectuals."

Boyd K. Packer (The Book of Mormon: Jacob Through Words of Mormon, To Learn with Joy, BYU Religious Studies Center, ed. by Nyman & Tate, pp. 8-9)

"Self-sufficiency, often through financial success, high educational attainment, fame, and honor among men, can keep us from having faith."

John K. Carmack (Ensign, May 1993, p. 43)

"When men are humble they acknowledge an intelligence far superior to their own and they seek guidance and wisdom from that source."

Stephen L. Richards (Conference Report, Apr. 1935, p. 30)

"To the proud, the applause of the world rings in their ears; to the humble the applause of heaven warms their hearts."

Ezra Taft Benson (Conference Report, Apr. 1986, pp. 3-7)

"The two groups who have the greatest difficulty in following the prophet are the proud who are learned and proud who are rich. The learned may feel the prophet is only inspired when he agrees with them; otherwise, the prophet is just giving his opinion—speaking as a man. The rich may feel they have no need to take counsel of a lowly prophet."

Ezra Taft Benson (1980 BYU Speeches of the Year, p. 29)

"Increasingly the Latter-day Saints must choose between the reasoning of men and the revelations of God. This is a crucial choice, for we have those within the Church today who, with their worldly wisdom, are leading some of our members astray. President J. Reuben Clark, Jr., warned that the 'ravening wolves amongst us from our own membership and they, more than any others, are clothed in sheep's clothing, because they wear the habiliments of the Priesthood. . . . We should be careful of them.'"

Ezra Taft Benson (Conference Report, Oct. 1967, p. 34)

"A university education, I believe, would be desirable for every intelligent man and woman. . . . A little learning is a dangerous thing, and too many men and too many women who have become experts in a tiny field of learning think that because they are trained in that field of learning, they are experts in all fields of learning. Many men who are well-trained in one limited field feel that this equally qualifies them to express learned opinions in the field of faith and religion. . . . Now, brothers and sisters, in our Church in this day and age, when education is becoming more and more popular and more and more necessary, there is grave danger of intellectual apostasy . . . (2 Nephi 9:28-29). What causes intellectual apostasy? . . . Principally out of vanity and pride. They want to impress others with their learning. To put it indelicately, it is the problem of the swelled head, because that is exactly what the Prophet said" [2 Nephi 9:42].

Theodore M. Burton (Conference Report, Apr. 1961, pp. 128-129)

"If there is any one group in the Church for whom I feel sorriest, it is those who brand themselves as intellectuals. I believe that class of people can go to apostasy along a broader road and through a wider gate than any other group. . . . And so this Church, which believed at the very outset that the glory of God is intelligence and has done more to encourage its membership to become intellectual than any other church upon the face of the earth, in any era, does not look upon intellect as its God. That is what these intellectual apostates do, and they are not sufficiently intelligent to know when they have apostatized. . . . I want to tell you that I think the humblest elder in the Church who knows what he knows and has the courage and the conviction to testify to the world what he knows is just as intellectual as a man can be. Under the inspiration of the Spirit of the Lord, that man's mind will develop, it will reach its maximum capacity, and he will accomplish more in mortality than the man without the Holy Spirit who strives, along man-made lines, to accomplish a mortal goal. . . . Any man who does not have the courage of his convictions, who is willing to the slightest degree to compromise [his testimony] with anyone, anywhere, and under any circumstance in this world is, to that extent, unworthy of the priesthood he holds."

Henry D. Moyle (Address to Seminary & Institute Instructors, BYU, June 27, 1962)

"Now then, speaking of this matter of revelation as it pertains to our studies here [at BYU], President [Joseph F.] Smith again gave us some wonderful counsel about our studies in philosophy and science. . . . This is what he said, 'Our young people are diligent students. They reach out after truth and knowledge with commendable zeal and in so doing they must necessarily adopt for temporary use many theories of men. As long, however, as they recognize them as scaffolding, useful for research purposes, there can be no special harm in them. It is when these theories are settled upon as basic truth that trouble appears and the searcher then stands in grave danger of being led hopelessly from the right way.' And then he said this: 'Philosophic theories of life have their place and use, but they are out of their place in Church schools or anywhere else when they seek to supplant the revelations of God.' Now if we'll just remember that. The revelations of God are our standards, the things by which we measure all learning. And if these things square not with the revelations, then we may be certain that they are not the truth."

Harold B. Lee (BYU Devotional, Oct. 15, 1952)

"Pride is concerned with *who* is right. Humility is concerned with *what* is right."

Ezra Taft Benson (quoted in Ensign, Nov. 1993, p. 16)

"A problem occurs on occasion when, in the pursuit of higher degrees, one becomes so imbued with the terminology and methodology of a secular discipline that, almost without realizing it, he compromises the gospel message. . . . We encourage you to get your higher degrees and further your education; but let us not forget that disaffection from the gospel and the Lord's church was brought about in the past by the attempts to reconcile the pure gospel with secular philosophies of men."

Ezra Taft Benson (address given to Religious Educators at the Assembly Hall, Sept. 17, 1976)

"Do some teachers and students create the impression . . . that salvation is unimportant or that salvation is to be found in academic disciplines? Salvation is in Christ, not in most of the things we do on the BYU campus or anywhere else. . . . All of our important and interesting debates about politics, academic subjects, and educational policy are insignificant by comparison with this."

Dallin H. Oaks (Ensign, Mar. 1994, p. 65)

2 Ne. 9:38   **BEHOLD HIS FACE**
(2 Ne. 33:11)

"Nothing is going to startle us more when we pass through the veil to the other side than to realize how well we know our father and how familiar his face is to us."

Ezra Taft Benson (1974 BYU Speeches of the Year, p. 313)

2 Ne. 9:41   **HE CANNOT BE DECEIVED**
(refer in this text to 4 Ne. 1:2)

"We all need to know what it means to be honest. Honesty is more than not lying. It is truth telling, truth speaking, truth living, and truth loving. . . . Honesty is a moral compass to guide us in our lives. You young . . . [people] are under great pressure to learn the technology that is expanding and will continue to expand so rapidly. However, the tremendous push to excel in secular learning sometimes tempts people to compromise that which is more important— their honesty and integrity. Cheating in school is a form of self-deception. We go to school to learn. We cheat ourselves when we coast on the efforts and scholarship of someone else. . . . In reality, we are only in competition with ourselves. Others can challenge and motivate us, but we must reach down deep into our souls and call forth our God-given intelligence and capabilities. We cannot do this when we depend on the efforts of someone else. Honesty is a principle, and we have our moral agency to determine how we will apply this principle. We have the agency to make choices, but ultimately we will be accountable for each choice we make. We may deceive others, but there is One we will never deceive (2 Nephi 9:41). . . . No one has ever gained anything of value by theft. . . . There are different shades of truth telling. When we tell little white lies, we become progressively color-blind. . . . The degree to which each of us tells the whole truth and nothing but the truth depends on our conscience."

James E. Faust (Ensign, Nov. 1996, pp. 41-43)

2 Ne. 9:51   **FEAST . . . LET YOUR SOUL DELIGHT IN FATNESS**
(refer in this text to 1 Ne. 19:23; Alma 17:2)

"And did you know that the Lord doesn't expect us to diet? Trust me! Turn to 2 Nephi 9:51. Now look at the very last line. It says, 'Let your soul delight in fatness.' But feast on what? Chocolate? Look closely: Feast on his *word*. . . . Did you know that feasting could be so guilt-free? . . . Why not gain some spiritual weight? It's not always easy [to read the scriptures], and there are things I still don't understand. But . . . craving the Lord's companionship, the scriptures infuse my spirit with *the* Spirit. They will do the same for you."

Bonnie D. Parkin (Ensign, May 1995, p. 90)

2 Ne. 10:3   **THEY SHALL CRUCIFY HIM**
(Moses 7:55; 1 Ne. 19:10; Gal. 3:13; Deut. 21:22-23)

"The prophecy was the more remarkable because crucifixion was unknown to Hebrew law. The Mosaic code prescribed the penalty of death in four forms: stoning, burning, beheading, and strangling."

R. Millet & J. F. McConkie (Doctrinal Commentary on the Book of Mormon, 1:266)

2 Ne. 10:3-4   **NONE OTHER NATION WOULD CRUCIFY THEIR GOD**
(Moses 7:36)

2 Ne. 10:3   **CHRIST**
(2 Ne. 25:19; Mosiah 3:8; *Commentary on the Book of Mormon*, 1:313, Reynolds & Sjodahl)

"Critics of the Book of Mormon have raised two objections to this verse: first, since *Christ* is understood to be a title, meaning the 'anointed one,' we are told that it would not have been given by an angel as a proper name; and second, because *Christ* is the anglicized form of the Greek *Christos*, it could not have appeared in an ancient record purportedly found in the Americas. Neither objection is well founded. To the first it ought be observed that though *Christ* is properly a title, it has in common usage become a proper name. Indeed, dictionaries list it as a proper noun, and many Christians would be surprised to learn that it was a title rather than a proper name. A great many words descriptive of status have in like manner come to be used as names; examples are King, Bishop, Hunter, Taylor, Cooper, Baker, etc. Even among his contemporaries Jesus was known as *Christ*. For instance, Mark refers to him as '*Christ* the King of Israel' (Mark 15:32). As to the Greek *Christos* being found on the gold plates from which the Book of Mormon came, it of course was not. What the ancient Nephite equivalent was we do not know. Since the Book of Mormon was translated into the English equivalent of the Nephite word, which is *Christ*."

R. Millet and J. F. McConkie (Doctrinal Commentary on the Book of Mormon, 1:265-266)

2 Ne. 10:7-8 **GATHERING IS FIRST TO CHRIST**
(refer in this text to 2 Ne. 6:10-11)

2 Ne. 10:9 **NURSING FATHERS TO ISRAEL**
(Signs of the Times, Smith, pp. 57-60; refer in this text to 1 Ne. 21:23)

2 Ne. 10:11 **NO KINGS UPON THE LAND**
(Mosiah 29:25-40; Deut. 17:14-17; 1 Sam. 9:17; *Book of Mormon Prophecies,* Warner, pp. 76-80;

"It is remarkable that so few attempts have been made to establish thrones in America. Perhaps the most substantial barrier has been the Monroe Doctrine, although, there has, for the most part, been so little real force behind that 'doctrine' that its very weakness has invited more than one European monarch to attempt to 'smash it.' It defied all the world to attempt to set up any authority of their own, or to interfere with any of the independent governments then existing in North or South America. . . . In a word the real meaning of the Monroe Doctrine is, 'Hands off' and that too, to all the world. . . . One could imagine that the Book of Mormon prophet might have been standing at the elbow of President Monroe when he signed the document as it was handed to him by the Secretary of State, John Quincy Adams. For the Monroe Doctrine is nothing more than the Book of Mormon prophecy put in the form of a state paper. It has been tested and tried. It has been called the 'most magnificent bluff in history, and so far the most successful.' At any rate, it has stood. It has been affirmed and re-affirmed by President after President until it is now upheld and proclaimed as with the voice of a hundred millions of people."

Nephi Lowell Morris (Prophecies of Joseph Smith and Their Fulfillment, pp. 136-138)

2 Ne. 10:16 **THE WHORE OF ALL THE EARTH**
(Rev. 17:5; refer in this text to 1 Ne. 13:4-6, 26, 28)

2 Ne. 10:18   **AFFLICT THY SEED BY THE HAND OF THE GENTILES**
(refer in this text to 1 Ne. 13:14-15)

2 Ne. 10:19   **THE INHERITANCE OF THE LAMANITES**
(refer in this text to 2 Ne. 1:5)

2 Nephi 11–24

"If our eternal salvation depends upon our ability to understand the writings of Isaiah as fully and truly as Nephi understood them—and who shall say such is not the case!—how shall we fare in that great day when with Nephi we shall stand before the pleasing bar of Him who said: 'Great are the words of Isaiah'? (3 Ne. 23:1) . . . It just may be that my salvation (and yours also!) does in fact depend upon our ability to understand the writings of Isaiah as fully and truly as Nephi understood them."

Bruce R. McConkie (Ensign, Oct. 1973, p. 78)

HELPS IN UNDERSTANDING ISAIAH
(Studies in Scripture, Jackson, 7:131-139; *Doctrinal Commentary on the Book of Mormon*, Millet & McConkie, 1:273-277; *Rediscovering the Book of Mormon*, Sorenson & Thorne, pp. 197-206; *The Living Message of Isaiah*, Adams, pp. 29-64; *Isaiah Plain and Simple*, Brewster)

2 Ne. 11:2-3

THE LAW OF WITNESSES
(2 Ne. 27:12-13; 2 Cor. 13:21)

"I am suggesting here that Nephi, Jacob, and Isaiah are three early types and shadows of Oliver Cowdery, David Whitmer, and Martin Harris, if you will—witnesses positioned right at the front of the book where Oliver, David, and Martin would be positioned—that Nephi, Jacob, and Isaiah are the three great ancient witnesses of the Book of Mormon—or more particularly, the first three great witnesses in the Book of Mormon testifying to the divinity of Jesus Christ, the Son of God, he who will be the central, commanding, presiding figure throughout the Book of Mormon. Nephi stresses this idea himself when he writes in the eleventh chapter of 2 Nephi: [verses 2-3]."

Jeffrey R. Holland (CES Symposium, BYU, Aug. 9, 1994, pp. 13-14)

2 Ne. 11:7   **THERE IS A GOD AND HE IS CHRIST**
(refer in this text to 1 Ne. 19:10)

2 Ne. 12:1-4   **MOUNTAIN OF THE LORD'S HOUSE**
(Psalms 65:4; D&C 133:10-13; 2 Ne.30:15; Micah 4:1-2; Zech.6:12-15; *Conference Report*, Oct. 1975, p. 77)

"The expression 'the mountain of the Lord's house,' as here indicated, was undoubtedly to be referred to as a place as well as a definition of a righteous people. . . . And then the ancient prophet said, 'And many nations shall come, and say, Come, and let us go up to the mountain of the Lord, to the house of the God of Jacob; and he will teach us of his ways, and we will walk in his paths; for the law shall go forth of Zion, and the word of the Lord from Jerusalem.' (2 Nephi 12:3). With the coming of the pioneers to establish the Church in the tops of the mountains, our early leaders declared this to be the beginning of the fulfillment of that prophecy. . . . Years ago I went with the brethren to the Idaho Falls Temple [dedication], and I heard in that inspired prayer of the First Presidency a definition of the meaning of that term 'out of Zion shall go forth the law.' Note what they said; 'We thank thee that thou hast revealed to us that those who gave us our constitutional form of government were men wise in thy sight and that thou didst raise them up for the very purpose of putting forth that sacred document. . . . We pray that kings and rulers and the peoples of all nations under heaven may be persuaded of the blessings enjoyed by the people of this land by reason of their freedom and under thy guidance and be constrained to adopt similar governmental systems, thus to fulfill the ancient prophecy of Isaiah and Micah that '. . . out of Zion shall go forth the law and the word of the Lord from Jerusalem.' (*Improvement Era*, Oct. 1945, p. 564)."

Harold B. Lee (Ensign, Nov. 1971, p. 15}

"All of the holy temples of our God in the latter days shall be built in the mountains of the Lord, for his mountains—whether the land itself is a hill, a valley, or a plain—are the places where he comes, personally and by the power of his Spirit, to commune with his people."

Bruce R. McConkie (Millennial Messiah, p. 275)

"This has specific reference to the Salt Lake Temple and to the other temples built in the top of the Rocky Mountains, and it has a general reference to temple yet to be built in the New Jerusalem in Jackson County, Missouri. Those in all nations, be it noted, shall flow to the houses of the Lord in the tops of the mountains, there to make the covenants out of which eternal life comes."

Bruce R. McConkie (Another Witness For The Articles of Faith, p. 539)

"Traditionally the world has supposed that Isaiah's reference to the law going forth from Zion and the word of the Lord going forth from Jerusalem was a Hebrew parallelism and that both references pointed to the Old World. That such was not Isaiah's intent is illustrated in a revelation given to Joseph Smith wherein it was announced that the Gentiles (meaning non-Jewish nations) were to flee to Zion of the New World while those who are of Judah were to flee to Jerusalem 'unto the mountains of the Lord's house (D&C 133:12-13)."

R. Millet and J. F. McConkie, Doct. Commentary on the Book of Mormon, 1:278

"The word *mountain* is used in the scriptures in different allegorical or figurative senses. In 2 Nephi 12:1-4 the word *mountain* refers to a high place of God, a place of revelation, even the temple of the Lord."

G. Reynolds and J. Sjodahl (Book of Mormon Commentary, 1:323)

"It will be noted that the words of the above verses from the Book of Mormon are identical with the King James translation of Isaiah 2:1-4 except for the change of one word. In the second verse the word 'that' (an italicized word) in the King James translation is changed to 'when.' . . . If the word 'when' is used, time is indicated and not place. Thus the Book of Mormon supplies a key to understanding these passages by saying that *when* the mountain of the Lord's house is established in the top of the mountains, then certain events will follow."

Ross Warner (The Fulfillment of Book of Mormon Prophecies, p. 175)

[The dedicatory prayer of the Salt Lake Temple, Apr. 6, 1893] "In past ages Thou didst inspire with Thy Holy Spirit Thy servants, the prophets, to speak of the time in the latter days *when the mountain of the Lord's house should be established in the tops of the mountains, and should be exalted above the hills. We thank Thee that we have had the glorious opportunity of contributing to the fulfillment of these visions of Thine ancient seers. . . .*"

Discourses of Wilford Woodruff, p. 337

2 Ne. 12:3

THE LAW FROM ZION—THE WORD FROM JERUSALEM
(Why the Religious Life?, Petersen, pp. 200-201, 305-307)

[Part of the dedicatory prayer at the Idaho Falls Temple] "We thank thee that thou hast revealed to us that those who gave us our constitutional form of government were men wise in thy sight and that thou didst raise them up for the very purpose of putting forth that sacred document. . . . We pray that kings and rulers and the peoples of all nations under heaven may be persuaded . . . to adopt similar governmental systems, thus to fulfill the ancient prophecy of Isaiah [and Micah] that 'out of Zion shall go forth the law.'"

George Albert Smith (Improvement Era, Oct. 1945, p. 564)

"He [God] will assemble the Natives, the remnants of Joseph in America; and make of them a great, and strong, and powerful nation: and he will civilize and enlighten them, and will establish a holy city, and temple, and seat of government among them, which shall be called Zion. And there shall be his tabernacle, his sanctuary, his throne, and seat of government for the whole continent of North and South America forever. In short, it will be to the western hemisphere what Jerusalem will be to the eastern. And there the Messiah will visit them in person; and the old Saints, who will then have been raised from the dead will be with him. And he will establish his kingdom and laws over all the land. . . . The city of Zion, with its sanctuary and priesthood, and the glorious fulness of the gospel, will constitute a *standard* which will put an end to jarring creeds and political wranglings, by uniting the republics, states, provinces, territories, nations, tribes, kindred, tongues, people, and sects of North and South America in one great and common bond of brotherhood. . . . Americans! This mighty and strange work has been commenced in your midst, and must roll on in fulfillment."

[originally published Apr. 6, 1845] (Messages of the 1st Presidency 1:259-261)

2 Ne. 12:4

NEITHER SHALL THEY LEARN WAR
"Obviously Isaiah is describing a condition in the world that shall come at or after the Second Advent of the Lord."

Sidney Sperry (Book of Mormon Compendium, p. 175)

2 Ne. 12:6

REPLENISHED FROM THE EAST
(Psalm 106:35)

2 Ne. 12:6   **SOOTHSAYERS LIKE THE PHILISTINES**
(2 Kings 1)

2 Ne. 12:7-18   **SYMBOLS OF PRIDE BROUGHT DOWN BY THE SAVIOR'S COMING**
(Book of Mormon Commentary, Reynolds and Sjodahl, 1:325-326)

2 Ne. 12:13   **CEDARS OF LEBANON AND OAKS OF BASHAN**
(Isa. 2:13)

"One of the ways in which the proud will 'be brought low' (vs. 12) is the destruction of, or the taking away of, those material possessions they hold so dear. Among these are the 'cedars of Lebanon,' which provided beautiful, fragrant wood for buildings of status. . . . Bashan was the area east of Jordan and the Sea of Galilee and north of Gilead. Its wooded areas provided highly prized but scarce hardwood. It too will be taken from the proud."

Hoyt W. Brewster, Jr. (Isaiah Plain and Simple, p. 19)

2 Ne. 12:16   **SHIPS OF THE SEA AND . . . THE SHIPS OF TARSHISH**
(Isa. 2:16)

[The ships of the sea] "The added phrase from the Book of Mormon is also found in the ancient Greek (Septuagint) text. 'All the ships of the sea,' represent the commercial enterprises of the proud and lofty. Tarshish is believed to be a location in Spain. Her ships were renowned for their strength, size, and ability to successfully complete long voyages. These too will be stripped from the wicked when the Lord returns."

Hoyt W. Brewster, Jr. (Isaiah Plain and Simple, p. 20)

2 Ne. 12:16   **PLEASANT PICTURES**
(Book of Mormon Compendium, Sperry, p. 178; *Isaiah: Prophet, Seer, and Poet*, Ludlow, p. 91; *The One Volume Bible Commentary*, Dummelow, p. 415)

2 Ne. 12:20   **CAST IDOLS TO THE MOLES AND BATS**
(refer in this text to 3 Ne. 13:19-24, 33)

"The imagery of verse 20 is striking: the people will throw their gold and silver idols to moles and bats, animals who are blind from living so long in darkness. The irony of this is that people who understood the material value of the precious metals, and should also have seen the spiritual impotence of the idols, will throw these precious items to animals who will not be able to see them at all."

Victor Ludlow (Isaiah: Prophet, Seer, and Poet, p. 92)

2 Ne. 12:21   **HE ARISETH TO SHAKE TERRIBLY THE EARTH**
(Rev. 11:11-13; 16:18, 20; Ezek. 38:20; Isa. 62:4; Haggai 2:6-7; D&C 45:48; 133:23)

2 Ne. 13   "Isaiah's vision of the effects of wickedness continued from the preceding chapter. For Nephi and his people this would have been a prophetic confirmation of the suffering and degradation they were spared by fleeing Jerusalem. . . . Given that Nephi included these chapters of Isaiah in his record for the benefit of those of our day, we properly see in this description of Judah's haughtiness, pride, and intoxication with fashion a pattern and warning for the last days."

R. Millet and J. F. McConkie (Doctrinal Commentary on the Book of Mormon, 1: 278-279)

2 Ne. 13:9, 11   **THE REWARD OF THEIR HANDS SHALL BE UPON THEM**
"Isaiah foresaw that Judah and Jerusalem would be punished by the Lord as a result of their wickedness. In 587 B. C. the city of Jerusalem was destroyed, and Judah was taken into captivity by Nebuchadnezzar, king of Babylon. In A.D. 70, 657 years later, the Romans destroyed Jerusalem and scattered the Jews to various portions of the world. Surely they had, as Isaiah said, 'rewarded evil unto themselves' (2 Nephi 13:9)."

Book of Mormon 121-122 Student Manual, p. 31

2 Ne. 13:12   **THEY WHO LEAD THEE CAUSE THEE TO ERR**
"And so today, the undermining of the home and family is on the increase, with the devil anxiously working to displace the father as the head of the home and create rebellion among the children. The Book of Mormon describes this condition when it states, 'And my people, children are their oppressors, and women rule over them.' And then these words follow—and consider these words seriously when you think of those political leaders who are promoting birth control and abortion: 'O my people, they who lead thee cause thee to err and destroy the way of they paths.' (2 Ne. 13:12)."

Ezra Taft Benson (Conference Report, Oct. 1970, p. 21)

2 Ne. 13:16-24   **DAUGHTERS OF ZION**
(2 Ne. 8:25; Amos 4:1-4; *Book of Mormon Compendium*, Sperry, pp. 182-183)

"If, indeed, Isaiah's words refer to the last days, we must look for a time when even some of the 'daughters of Zion or the children of Israel are haughty, and walk with stretched-forth necks and wanton eyes.' . . . Sometimes the phrase 'daughters of Zion' refers to the cities of Judah."

Book of Mormon 121-122 Student Manual (1981 edition), p.91

"Isaiah, one of the great prophets of early times, saw our day, and he described the conditions that would prevail among the 'daughters of Zion' in these latter days [Nephi 13:16-24]. As I sit on the stand in a stake conference and look down over the congregation, I see some of the conditions existing of which Isaiah spoke. . . . The standards expressed by the General Authorities of the Church are that women, as well as men, should dress modestly. They are taught proper deportment and modesty at all times. It is, in my judgment, a sad reflection on the 'daughters of Zion' when they dress immodestly. Moreover, this remark pertains to the men as well as to the women."

Joseph Fielding Smith (Answers to Gospel Questions, 5:172-174)

2 Ne. 14   "In the preceding chapter we read of the bitter winter seasons of apostate darkness. Now we read of darkness and wickedness giving way to light and righteousness; we read of the glorious spring of restoration with its heaven-sent cleansing rains, followed in turn by the pleasant summer of millennial splendor. It is a day when Zion's daughters have abandoned worldly fashions and have adorned themselves with robes of righteousness, while Jacob's faithful sons have, in the language of Isaiah, put on their beautiful garments—the authority and power of the holy priesthood (see Isaiah 52:1; D&C 113:7-8)."

R. Millet and J. F. McConkie (Doctrinal Commentary on the Book of Mormon, 1:279)

2 Ne. 14:1   **SEVEN WOMEN SHALL TAKE HOLD OF ONE MAN**
(*Book of Mormon Commentary*, Reynolds & Sjodahl, 1:330,332)

"'In that day,' (14:1) when the judgments will have removed so many men that there is a great scarcity of them, 'seven women' (meaning simply a lot of women) will request a man's hand in marriage. Economic problems will be such that these women will be willing to provide their own food and clothing, contrary to the usual marriage customs. According to the Hebrew scriptures (Ex. 21:10), a man was required to provide a wife with food and clothing; but in this case Isaiah observes that the women are willing to waive that right. Having a good knowledge of the importance of marriage, they request a man to take away their reproach. In Isaiah's day and, indeed, in many parts of the Near East today, it was and is a disgrace to remain unmarried."

Sidney Sperry (Book of Mormon Compendium, pp.183-184)

"Many years ago I attended a large gathering of Church members in the city of Berlin, Germany. . . . The majority of those who sat on crowded benches were women about middle age—and alone. Suddenly it dawned on me that perhaps these were widows, having lost their husbands during World War II. . . . So I asked the conducting officer to take a sort of standing roll call. When he asked all those who were widows to please arise, it seemed that half the vast throng stood. Their faces reflected the grim effect of war's cruelty. Their hopes had been shattered, their lives altered, and their future had in a way been taken from them."

Thomas S. Monson (Ensign, Nov. 1994, p. 68)

2 Ne. 14:2   **BRANCH**
(Commentary on the Book of Mormon, Reynolds & Sjodahl, 1:330)

"The word 'branch' in Hebrew was symbolic of the Messiah. *The* Branch is the Messiah even Jesus Christ, He whose 'glory def[ies] all description.' (JS-H 1:17; see also Jeremiah 23:5-6). In another sense, the 'branch' could represent dispersed remnants of the house of Israel who have been redeemed and brought back to the glory of the Lord (See Isaiah 4:2; 60:21; 61:3; 2 Ne. 3:5; Jacob 2:25)."

Hoyt W. Brewster, Jr. (Isaiah Plain and Simple, p. 37)

2 Ne. 14:5-6   **ZION—A PLACE OF REFUGE**
(D&C 45:64-75; 115:6; 124:36)

"The time is soon coming, when no man will have any peace but in Zion and her stakes. I saw men hunting the lives of their own sons, and brother murdering brother, women killing their own daughters, and daughters seeking the lives of their mothers. I saw armies arrayed against armies. I saw blood, desolation, fires. The Son of Man has said that the mother shall be against the daughter, and the daughter against the mother. These things are at our doors. They will follow the Saints of God from city to city. Satan will rage, and the spirit of the devil is now enraged. I know not how soon these things will take place . . ."

Teachings of the Prophet Joseph Smith, p. 161

2 Ne. 15:1-7   **SONG OF THE VINEYARD**
(Jacob 5)
"The Israelites had a yearly festival, at the end of their year, called the feast of ingathering (Ex. 23:16; 34:22), because on that occasion the people were required to give thanks especially for the harvest of fields and vineyards. It has been suggested that this song, or poem, was composed and recited on such an occasion. It contains a parable in which Israel is represented as a vineyard (as in Is.3:14), and the consequences of the neglect of unfaithful keepers (Matt. 21:33-41)."

G. Reynolds and J. Sjodahl (Commentary on the Book of Mormon, 1:333)

2 Ne. 15:8-25   **THE SIX WOES UPON THE WICKED**

2 Ne. 15:8   **WO UNTO THEM WHO JOIN HOUSE TO HOUSE**
(3 Ne. 24:5; Gal. 6:17; D&C 19:26; Micah 2:1-2; *Journal of Discourses* 1:248-256)

"This woe is pronounced on the wealthy landowners who covet and buy up property, thus depriving the poor of their heritage. (See Micah 2:1-2). The law of ancient Israel prescribed that land could not 'be sold for ever.' (Leviticus 25:23; see also 1 Kings 21). It was to remain within families as a heritage for posterity. When economical circumstances necessitated the sale of land, it was to be returned to the original owners in the year of jubilee, which occurred every fifty years. *(LDS Bible Dictionary*, 'Jubilee, Year of,' p. 718)."

Hoyt W. Brewster, Jr. (Isaiah Plain and Simple, p. 46)

"Property acquired for selfish purposes is not a blessing. Greed is never satisfied. Ownership of property is not condemned. The only question is, how did the owner get it, and to what use does he put it?"

G. Reynolds and J. Sjodahl (Commentary on the Book of Mormon, 1:334)

"We are gathering to this beautiful land, to build up 'Zion.' . . . But since I have been here I perceive the spirit of selfishness. Covetousness exists in the hearts of the Saints. . . . Here are those who begin to spread out buying up all the land they are able to do, to the exclusion of the poorer ones who are not so much blessed with this worlds goods, thinking to lay foundations for themselves only, looking to their own individual families, and those who are to follow them."

Brigham Young (quoted in Brother Brigham Challenges the Saints, Nibley, p. 47)

"The surplus property of this community, as poor as we are, has done more real mischief than everything else besides. . . . A man has no right with property, . . . [when the property doesn't] do good to himself and his fellow-man."

Brigham Young (Journal of Discourses 1:252)

"I was a newlywed and my husband was in medical school. [My landlady] lowered our rent when we had our first baby. When my husband later owned apartments in Provo, I reminded him often of that landlady, especially as he rented to young marrieds."

Janette C. Hales (BYU Devotional, Mar. 16, 1993)

"It is frequently astounding to see the dereliction of people in keeping the standards of ordinary fairness and justice. . . . It is sometimes evident in commercial transactions, as well as in private contacts. . . . This unfairness and injustice results principally from one person seeking an advantage or an edge over another. Those who follow such a practice demean themselves greatly. How can those of us who do not practice ordinary fairness and justice have serious claim on the blessings of a just and a fair God? Do some of us seek to justify our taking of shortcuts and advantage of others by indulging in the twin sophistries, 'There isn't any justice' and 'Everybody does it'"?

James E. Faust (Ensign, Nov. 1986, p. 10)

2 Ne. 15:10   **10 ACRES, 1 BATH, A HOMER, AN EPHAH**
(Isa. 5:10)

"The lands of the wealthy will become extremely unproductive. *Ten acres* represents the amount of land that ten yoke of oxen can plow in a day, or the equivalent of five acres of land by our modern measurement. From this acreage, the yield will be only one bath (four to eight gallons of wine). One homer of seed (about six bushels) will yield only an ephah of produce (four to six gallons of dry measure)."

Hoyt W. Brewster, Jr. (Isaiah Plain and Simple, p. 47)

2 Ne. 15:11-12,   **DRUNKENNESS**
22   *(Teachings of Spencer W. Kimball, pp. 203-207)*

2 Ne. 15:14-15,   **PRIDE**
21   (refer in this text to Jacob 2:13-17; 2 Ne. 9:28-30; 3 Ne. 6:10-16)

2 Ne. 15:20   **EVIL GOOD AND GOOD EVIL**
(Isa. 5:20; D&C 121:16-17; *Behold I Come Quickly*, Brewster, pp. 38-51; refer
in this text to Alma 30:12-28)

"The fact that some governments and some churches and numerous corrupted
individuals have tried to reduce such behavior from criminal offense to personal privilege does not change the nature nor the seriousness of the practice."

Spencer W. Kimball (Ensign, Nov. 1980, p. 97)

2 Ne. 15:26-30   **AN ENSIGN TO THE NATIONS**
(D&C 115:5-6)

"In the last days the Lord 'will lift up an ensign to the nations from far.' Those
who gather to this ensign will come quickly and with power. They will do so
amidst contrasting conditions of light and darkness or good and evil. A secondary interpretation of these verses focuses on the Assyrian invasion of Israel
in 722-721 B.C. Commentators who subscribe to this belief identify the speed
with which the Assyrian soldiers invaded the land and the quick destruction
they brought about. Nevertheless, the major focus of these verses appears to
align itself more closely with events of the last days."

Hoyt W. Brewster, Jr. (Isaiah Plain and Simple, p. 51)

"This Church is the standard which Isaiah said the Lord would set up for the
people in the latter days. . . . This Church is the ensign on the mountain spoken of by the Old Testament prophets."

Marion G. Romney (Conference Report, Apr. 1961, p. 119)

"We see that an ensign in the last days can refer to Zion, the gospel, missionary
work, the gathering, and the Book of Mormon. . . . In short, the term *ensign*
encompasses the Lord's whole work, and all aspects of his Church serve as his
'standard' to the world."

Victor Ludlow (Isaiah: Prophet, Seer, and Poet, pp. 122-123)

2 Ne. 15:26-30   **LATTER DAY TRANSPORTATION**
(Book of Mormon Compendium, Sperry, p. 191)

"In fixing the time of the great gathering, Isaiah seemed to indicate that it would
take place in the day of the railroad train and the airplane: [Isaiah 5:26-29].

Since there were neither trains nor airplanes in that day, Isaiah could hardly have mentioned them by name. However, he seems to have described them in unmistakable words. How better could 'their horses' hoofs be counted like flint, and 'their wheels like a whirlwind' than in the modern train? How better could 'their roaring . . . be like a lion' than in the roar of the airplane? Trains and airplanes do not stop for night. Therefore, was not Isaiah justified in saying: 'none shall slumber nor sleep; neither shall the girdle of their loins be loosed, nor the latchet of their shoes be broken'? With this manner of transportation the Lord can really 'hiss unto them from the end of the earth,' that 'they shall come with speed swiftly.' Indicating that Isaiah must have foreseen the airplane, he stated: 'Who are these that fly as a cloud, and as the doves to their windows?'"

LeGrand Richards (Israel! Do You Know?, p. 182)

2 Ne. 16

ISAIAH'S CALL TO SERVE

"Isaiah, writing in imagery difficult to the modern mind, describes his call to the prophetic office. Caught up in vision to the heavenly council, Isaiah is purged of his sins and granted his mission and commission as the Lord's anointed, with an accompanying admonition that a wayward people would be more than slow to hearken to his words. The chapter is consistent with what we know about prophetic calls generally, the pattern having been established with the Savior and others in the Grand Council of Heaven (Abraham 3:27; *Teachings of the Prophet Joseph Smith*, p. 365)."

R. Millet and J. F. McConkie (Doctrinal Commentary on the Book of Mormon, 1:279-280)

2 Ne. 17

ISAIAH AND KING AHAZ

(*Book of Mormon Compendium*, Sperry, pp. 196-201; Book of Mormon 121-122 Student Manual [1981 edition], pp. 92-93)

"At this time, the southern kingdom of Judah was threatened by an alliance of the northern kingdom of Israel with Syria. The kings of these two countries wanted Ahaz to join them in an alliance against the Assyrians, but the king of Judah decided to cast his lot with the Assyrians. In verse 3, the Lord sends Isaiah to counsel Ahaz against entering any alliances; instead, he is to depend on the protection of the God of Israel. Isaiah prophesies that the threat from the northern kingdom and from Syria will come to naught and that these two countries will be the ones that will be destroyed. The Lord offers to give the disbelieving Ahaz a sign of the verity of His words, but the king refuses to ask for confirmation of the prophecy. The Lord gives the king a sign anyway: a sign involving the future birth of the Messiah through the house of David. Because of rejecting divine counsel, Judah suffers consequences that could have been avoided. The people are oppressed, scattered, and taken into slavery. The once-fertile lands are left barren of crops and become useful only for wandering animals."

Hoyt W. Brewster, Jr. (Isaiah Plain and Simple, p. 62)

2 Ne. 17:14-16   **A VIRGIN SHALL CONCEIVE**
(Isaiah 7:14-16; *Isaiah: Prophet, Seer, and Poet*, Ludlow, pp. 143-145; *Great Are The Words of Isaiah*, Nyman, pp. 56-59)

"Now if Immanuel of verse 14 is the Messiah, the Savior, what is his connection with the 'child' of verses 15 and 16? Many Jewish commentators, not to mention some non-Jewish ones, think that the 'virgin' or 'young woman' of verse 14 may be a woman of the royal family, or any other young woman of Judah, and that her son, a boy whom she called Immanuel, does not refer to the Christ. Personally, I am inclined to accept Immanuel as a reference to the Savior, and especially in the light of [Isaiah 8:8], where Judah is referred to as Immanuel's land. The allusion to Immanuel suggests that the land of Judah (about which Ahaz was concerned) had a great destiny to fulfill, and hence that it was not about to be destroyed by Syria and Ephraim. Verses 15 and 16 of [Isaiah 7] simply make our Lord's infancy a symbolical representation of the short-lived nature of the threat to Judah."

Sidney B. Sperry (Book of Mormon Compendium, p. 199)

"Isaiah, then, declared that the Lord would, nevertheless, give him a sign: Behold, a virgin—a young wife, possibly the wife of the Prophet—would become the mother of a son, whom she would call Immanuel, meaning, 'God is with us.' Syria and the land of Ephraim. Both would be overrun by the Assyrians before the child would be old enough to discern between evil and good. This prophecy was literally fulfilled in the days of Ahaz, but it had another fulfillment in the person of our Lord. According to Matthew 1:20-24, Joseph, when thinking of leaving Mary secretly, without causing a public scandal, had a dream, in which an angel appeared to him and explained that he had no cause against Mary. The evangelist adds that, all this was done, that it might be fulfilled which was spoken of the Lord by the Prophet, saying: 'Behold, a virgin shall be with child, and shall bring forth a son, and they shall call his name Emmanuel.' A most notable instance of the double application of a prophetic utterance!"

G. Reynolds and J. Sjodahl (Book of Mormon Commentary, 1:342)

2 Ne. 17:17-25 RESULTS OF KING AHAZ REJECTING ISAIAH'S WORDS
(Isa. 7:17-25)

"With King Ahaz having rejected the word of the Lord, the prophet now proceeds to pronounce the penalties that would befall the king and the people of Judah. Instead of becoming a partner with the Assyrians, Ahaz and his people would become their prey. They would experience a devastation such as they had not seen since the days the northern tribes broke away from the united kingdom of the twelve tribes. Flies and bees would infest the land, and thorns and briers would take over the once-productive land. The people would be taken into captivity, and those who remain would have to forage for food."

Hoyt W. Brewster, Jr. (Isaiah Plain and Simple, p. 70)

2 Ne. 18 We have seen, in Chapter 17, Isaiah's failure to influence King Ahaz of Judah. Now the prophet turns to the people, and in prophecies that parallel those in Chapter 17 he assures them that their present enemies, Israel and Syria, will fall before Assyria. But since they refuse to believe, like their king in this respect, he prophesies disaster, the coming of Assyrian forces to overrun their land like a flood. . . . Despite Assyria's success in overrunning Judah, Isaiah makes clear that God will not permit the entire destruction of His people. On the contrary, the peoples (the reference is to Assyria) will be overthrown and a remnant of Israel will survive, 'for God is with us,' a play on the name Immanuel. The Lord's plan, not Assyria's will prevail."

Sidney Sperry (Book of Mormon Compendium, pp. 201-203)

2 Ne. 18:1-12, 18 SYMBOLIC NAMES
"Isaiah was the father of two sons, Maher-shalal-hash-baz (see 2 Nephi 18:3) and Shear-jashub (see 2 Nephi 17:3). Both names are symbolic of the Lord's intentions for the northern kingdom of Israel. Maher-shalal-hash-baz is a Hebrew term meaning 'to speed to the spoil, he hasteneth the prey' (Isaiah 8:1d; see also 2 Nephi 18:1b). This name describes the events spoken of in 2 Nephi 18:4. The ten tribes were overrun and despoiled by the Assyrians when Samaria, the capital of the northern kingdom, was besieged. Shear-jashub is a Hebrew term meaning 'the remnant shall return' (Isaiah 7:3a). This is a reference to the day when Israel will be gathered from her scattered condition. Thus Isaiah could report: 'Behold, I and the children whom the Lord hath given me are for signs and for wonders in Israel from the Lord of Hosts' (2 Nephi 18:18)."

Book of Mormon 121-122 Student Manual, p. 33

2 Ne. 18:3   **PROPHETESS**
(Isa. 8:3; *Journal of Discourses* 13:165; Ex. 15:20; Judges 4:4-5; Luke 2:36-38)

2 Ne. 18:19   **PEEP**
(Deut. 18:10-12; Isa. 8:19)

"To 'peep' is to chirp as a bird. According to J.R. Dummelow, chirping refers 'to the thin and feeble voice of ghosts from Sheol' [hell] *(The One Volume Bible Commentary*, p. 420)."

Hoyt W. Brewster, Jr. (Isaiah Plain and Simple, p. 82)

2 Ne. 19:3-7   **A CHILD IS BORN**
(Isa. 9:3-7)

"If Isaiah is prophesying about Hezekiah [the king of Judah who helped deliver Israel from the Assyrians], then verse 3 describes the Israelites' joy at their deliverance; verse 4 portrays how the Assyrians were defeated in spite of their greater numbers, just as the many Midianites were by Gideon and his 300 men (Judg. 7); verse 5 describes the Assyrian casualties; and verses 6 and 7 tell us about Hezekiah's titles and righteous, peaceful rule as king. If the verses describe a righteous people fighting against wickedness, then verse 3 describes their joy at success, verses 4 and 5 portray the defeat of the enemy, and verses 6 and 7 describe a new age of millennial peace that may be assisted or ushered in by a messianic figure. Finally, the identification of the ruler in verses 3-7 with Jesus Christ has a number of possibilities, as verse 3 talks about his many followers who rejoice at the spiritual blessings he has provided; verse 4 describes how he was able to overcome the temptations of Satan, break the yoke of sin, and maintain power over the legions of Satan's devils; verse 5 symbolizes his atonement and the cleansing powers of baptism and the Holy Ghost ; verse 6 presents some of his titles and roles; and verse 7 describes his eternal position as the Lord and King of this earth."

Victor L. Ludlow (Isaiah: Prophet, Seer, and Poet, p. 154)

2 Ne. 19:12,17, 21; 20:4   **HIS HAND IS STRETCHED OUT STILL**
2 Ne. 19:8 through 20:4 comprises a prophetic poem. (2 Ne. 7:2; 15:25; 28:32; Jacob 6:4-5; Alma 19:36; Mosiah 16:12; 29:20; 3 Ne. 9:13-14; D&C 35:8)

"Before we leave this prophetic poem (19:8-20:4) it should be pointed out that the last clause of the four refrains (19:12, 17, 21, 20:4), 'but his hand is stretched out still,' is usually interpreted to mean that God's wrath against his people is unappeasable, that Isaiah has no word of hope for his people, still unrepentant. Some commentators express the meaning of the clause in this manner: 'But his hand is stretched out still to strike.' I may be wrong, but I feel that Isaiah was by no means completely a prophet of doom, that he still held out to his people a note of encouragement intended to bring about their repentance (cf. Isa. 1:16-20). Let me express it this way: 'But his hand is stretched out still if only you but change your ways.'"

Sidney Sperry (Book of Mormon Compendium, p. 213)

"His arm is galactic."

Neal A. Maxwell (Conference Report, Apr. 1976, p. 9)

"Our merciful and long-suffering Lord is ever ready to help. His 'arm is lengthened out all the day long' (2 Ne. 28:32), and even if His arm goes ungrasped, it was unarguably there! In the same redemptive reaching out, our desiring to improve our human relationships usually requires some long-suffering. Sometimes reaching out is like trying to pat a porcupine. Even so, the accumulated quill marks are evidence that our hands of fellowship have been stretched out, too."

Neal A. Maxwell (Ensign, Nov. 1996, p. 22)

2 Ne. 20   **CHIASMUS**
             (refer in this text to Alma 36)

"A. The wicked will bow down (vs. 1-4)
   B. Assyria raised by the Lord (5)
      C. The Assyrian king speaks against Jerusalem (6-11)
         D. The Lord will punish proud Assyria (12-14)
            E. An ax is used as a tool (15)
               F. The Lord is a burning fire in the land (16-17)
                  G. Out of all the [multitudes]—only a remnant returns (18-19)
                     H. A remnant of Israel shall return to the Lord (20-21)
                  G. Out of the 'sands of the sea'—only a remnant returns (22)
               F. A divine consumption is in the land (23)
            E. A rod is used as an instrument (24-26)
         D. Assyria's yoke will be lifted (27)
      C. Assyrian army approaches Jerusalem (28-32)
   B. Assyria humbled by the Lord (33)
A. The haughty will be cut down (34)"

Victor L. Ludlow (Isaiah: Prophet, Seer, and Poet, p. 161)

2 Ne. 20:1-19   **BOASTING AGAINST THE LORD**
(refer in this text to Alma 39:2)

"The Lord said that Israel's wickedness would cause him to send Assyria, 'the rod of [his] anger' (2 Nephi 20:5), against his people 'to take the spoil, and to take the prey, and to tread them down like the mire of the streets' (v.6). This prophecy was literally fulfilled when Assyria captured the northern kingdom of Israel and took the people captive to Assyria. This prophecy further revealed that when Assyria became lifted up in pride the Lord would 'punish the fruit of the stout heart of the king of Assyria, and the glory of his high looks' (v. 12). The Lord made it clear that even though Assyria accomplished his purposes against Israel, they had no reason to be proud. As the ax cannot boast of itself against the one who uses it, so the Assyrians could not think of themselves as being higher than the Lord (see v. 15). Assyria was but an instrument in the hand of the Lord in fulfilling his purposes."

Book of Mormon 121-122 Student Manual, p. 33

2 Ne. 20:12,   **ASSYRIAN INVASION AND EVENTUAL DESTRUCTION**
28-34   (Isa. 10:12; *Book of Mormon Compendium*, Sperry, pp. 219-221; *Commentary on the Book of Mormon*, Reynolds & Sjodahl, 1:355-356)

"The Assyrians will attack Mount Zion, the hill upon which Solomon built his temple. (1 Kings 8:1). (This attack occurred in 701 B.C., under the Assyrian king Sennacherib). Yet the Lord will punish the king of Assyria for his 'stout heart' and 'high looks' (arrogance, pride, and boasting). This prophecy was fulfilled when a desolating sickness was sent into the Assyrian camps, causing many deaths, and the king was later slain by his own sons (2 Kings 19:32-37; Isaiah 37:33-38)."

Hoyt W. Brewster, Jr. (Isaiah Plain and Simple, p. 100)

2 Ne. 21   **ISAIAH VIEWS LATTER DAYS & MILLENNIAL CONDITIONS**
(Isa. 11)

"In addition to the Old Testament and Book of Mormon accounts, portions of these writings are found in the New Testament (Revelation 2:16; 5:5; 19:15; and Romans 15:12) and the Doctrine & Covenants (19:15; 113:1-6; and 133:26-29); and in Joseph Smith's history as found in the Pearl of Great Price, he tells us that the entire chapter of Isaiah 11 was quoted to him by the Angel Moroni (JS-H 1:40). Additionally, on several occasions the Prophet provided commentary on verses in this chapter. (See *Teachings of the Prophet Joseph Smith*, pp. 14-15, 71, 93, 316)."

Hoyt W. Brewster, Jr. (Isaiah Plain and Simple, p. 107)

2 Ne. 21:1,10   **STEM, ROD, & ROOT**
(D&C 113:1-6; JS-H 1:40; *Book of Mormon Compendium*, Sperry, pp. 223, 226-227)

"Isaiah testifies of Christ as both the 'stem of Jesse' (mortal Messiah) and the righteous judge (millennial Messiah). He further testifies of a rod and root of Jesse (Joseph Smith), 'a servant in the hands of Christ, who is partly a descendant of Jesse as well as of Ephraim, or of the house of Joseph, on whom there is laid much power,' a man 'unto whom rightly belongs the priesthood, and the keys of the kingdom, for an ensign, and for the gathering of [the Lord's people in the last days]' (D&C 113:1-2,4-6; cf. Joseph Smith—History 1:40)."

R. Millet and J. F. McConkie (Doctrinal Commentary on the Book of Mormon, 1:281)

" '*Root of Jesse*.' The Doctrine and Covenants identifies this individual as 'a descendant of Jesse, as well as of Joseph, unto whom rightly belongs the priesthood, and the keys of the kingdom, for an ensign, and for the gathering of my people in the last days' (D&C 113:5-6). The apostle Paul mistakenly identified the 'root' as Christ. (Romans 15:12). Dr. Sidney B. Sperry explained the reason for this mistake:

'Examination of Romans 15:12 demonstrates that Paul was closely following the Septuagint (LXX, Greek translation) text of Isaiah 11:10 rather than the Hebrew. As a matter of fact, the LXX version is only a paraphrase of the original Hebrew. We notice that the Greek version of Isaiah 11:1 translates the Hebrew text, 'stem of Jesse,' as the 'root of Jesse' and uses the same phrase in Isaiah 11:10. Of interest is the fact that the Greek word *riza* (root) is used in both verses to translate different Hebrew words. Paul would be quick to discern that the 'root of Jesse' of the LXX text of Isaiah 11:1-5 was the Christ. And when he observed that the phrase 'root of Jesse' was used again in verse 10, he would naturally assume that it, too, had reference to the Christ. Hence the reason for his quotation in Romans 15:12.' (*Book of Mormon Compendium*, p. 227).

Who, then, is the 'root of Jesse'? It appears that the Prophet Joseph Smith is both the 'rod' and the 'root' that will come from Jesse. (See *Book of Mormon Compendium*, Sperry, p. 223; *Great Are The Words of Isaiah*, Nyman, pp. 73-74). . . . However, Victor Ludlow suggested that:

'Joseph Smith might not be the only 'root of Jesse' in these last days. Many presidents of the Church have been related to him by blood, and all have held the priesthood and the keys of the kingdom that he held. . . . The 'root of Jesse' could also be that particular prophet who will hold the keys when Christ returns to preside personally over his kingdom. The term could even represent the office of the president of the Church. In any case, the 'root of Jesse' designates a great leader in the Church of Jesus Christ in this dispensation' *(Isaiah: Prophet, Seer, and Poet*, p. 174)."

Hoyt W. Brewster, Jr. (Isaiah Plain and Simple, pp. 112-113)

2 Ne. 21:10-12   TWO GATHERINGS

"From this scripture we learn that the events described were to be in the future: 'The Lord shall set his hand again the second time to recover the remnant of his people.' There could not be a 'second time' unless there had been a first time as when the Lord led Israel out of Egyptian bondage and captivity."

LeGrand Richards (A Marvelous Work and a Wonder, p. 202)

"The time has at last arrived when the God of Abraham, of Isaac, and of Jacob, has sct His hand again the second time to recover the remnants of his people, which have been left from Assyria, and from Egypt, and from Pathros, and from Cush, and from Elam, and from Shinar, and from Hamath, and from the islands of the sea, and with them to bring in the fulness of the Gentiles, and establish that covenant with them, which was promised when their sins should be taken away. . . . This covenant has never been established with the house of Israel, nor with the house of Judah. . . . Christ, in the days of His flesh, proposed to make a covenant with them, but they rejected Him and His proposals, and in consequence thereof, they were broken off, and no covenant was made with them at that time. . . . Thus after this chosen family had rejected Christ and His proposals, the heralds of salvation said to them, 'Lo, we turn unto the Gentiles;' and the Gentiles received the covenant, and were grafted in from whence the chosen family were broken off."

Joseph Smith (History of the Church, 1:313)

2 Ne. 21:12   AN ENSIGN
(D&C 45:9; *Conference Report*, Apr. 1911, p. 124)

"What the Statue of Liberty has symbolized to the oppressed and downtrodden of Europe, the gospel of Jesus Christ is to the world. The restored gospel, the Church, has reared an ensign to the nations. . . ."

David O. McKay (Conference Report, Apr. 1963, p. 97)

"This Church is the standard which Isaiah said the Lord would set up for the people in the latter days. . . . This Church is the ensign on the mountain spoken of by the Old Testament prophets."

Marion G. Romney (Conference Report, Apr. 1961, p. 119)

2 Ne. 21:12   **GATHER ISRAEL & JUDAH**
(refer in this text to 2 Ne. 6:10-11; 2 Ne. 30:7; 3 Ne. 20:13,29-33)

2 Ne. 21:14   **THE SHOULDERS OF PHILISTINES**
(Book of Mormon Compendium, Sperry, p. 228)

"'They shall fly upon the shoulders of the Philistines toward the West.' We recognize the fulfillment of that prophecy in the founding of this Church by Joseph Smith, a lineal descendant of Abraham, Isaac and Jacob, who thus lifted the Ensign for the gathering of their descendants from their long dispersion among the nations. But a part of the fulfillment rests with the Gentiles. Their steamships, their railroads, their means of rapid transit and communication—these are 'the shoulders of the Philistines,' upon which the children of Ephraim have been and are being brought to the West, to the land of Zion, where the New Jerusalem is to rise, where the pure in heart will assemble, and the necessary preparation be made for the coming of the Lord in his glory. God works outside as well as inside his Church, and uses big things and little things for the accomplishment of his purposes."

Orson F. Whitney (Conference Report, Oct. 1919, p. 69)

2 Ne. 21:15   **THE TONGUE OF THE EGYPTIAN SEA**
(Commentary of the Book of Mormon, Reynolds & Sjodahl, 1:359)

"The large inland sea created late each spring as the Nile overflows its banks and floods a large part of the valley, like a tongue sticking far inland. Isaiah 19:5-10 describes the destruction of the Nile River in greater detail. If the Nile River is the 'tongue of the Egyptian Sea,' then this prophecy might have been fulfilled since the building of the Aswan Dam and the destruction of the traditional way of life along the Nile."

Victor Ludlow (Isaiah: Prophet, Seer, and Poet, p. 176)

2 Ne. 22   This chapter is a hymn consisting of two short psalms. It is uncertain if verse 3 is the end of the first psalm (a thanks psalm) or the beginning of the second psalm (a praise hymn).

2 Ne. 22:2   **JEHOVAH**
(Isa. 12:2; 26:4; Exodus 6:3; Psalm 83:18; Moro. 10:34; D&C 109:34, 42, 56, 68; 110:3; 128:9; Abr. 1:16)

"The covenant or proper name of the God of the Old Testament was so highly reverenced that it was rarely spoken. In fact, the original pronunciation of the name may be unknown to mortal man. When reading orally, the Israelites substituted the name *Adonai*, meaning literally, *my Lord*. Elder James E. Talmage tells us that '*Jehovah* is the Anglicized rendering of the Hebrew, *Yahveh* or *Jahveh*, signifying the *Self-existent One*, or *The Eternal*. This name is generally rendered in our English version of the Old Testament as LORD, printed in [small] capitals.' (*Jesus the Christ*, p. 36). Of the four times the sacred name appears unchanged in the Old Testament, Isaiah uses it twice. Latter-day Saints affirm that this holy name is the premortal name of Jesus Christ and has been used in behalf of the Savior in sacred places during His postmortal ministry."

Hoyt W. Brewster, Jr. (Isaiah Plain and Simple, p. 121)

2 Ne. 23-24   **DESTRUCTION OF BABYLON—DESTRUCTION AT SECOND COMING**
(*Commentary on the Book of Mormon*, Reynolds and Sjodahl, 1:364)

"As the Medes conquered the Babylonians in 538 B.C., so shall the conquest of the wicked by the destroying angels be accomplished at the coming of the great and dreadful day of the Lord. As ancient Israel was left to marvel at the once mighty but now deposed and displaced king of Babylon, so latter-day Israel will marvel at the dethronement of Lucifer, the despot of darkness and king of evil. . . . Thus the past becomes the key that unlocks the future. As history has its cycles, so prophecies have multiple fulfillments and repeated applications. Isaiah's prophecies of events now past foretell events yet future. The past is the stage upon which the future is portrayed."

R. Millet and J. F. McConkie (Doctrinal Commentary on the Book of Mormon, p. 282)

2 Ne. 23:14-22   **DESTRUCTION OF BABYLON**
(Isa. 13:19-22)

"[Babylon] was the greatest city in all the world. . . . Yet Isaiah announced that that city would be destroyed; he said that it would never be rebuilt, that it would never be inhabited from generation to generation, that it would become the abode of reptiles and wild animals and that the Arabs would no more pitch their tents there. That was a declaration that the greatest city in the world would not only be destroyed, but it would also never be rebuilt."

LeGrand Richards (Conference Report, Apr. 1954, p. 54)

2 Ne. 23:17   **THE MEDES**
(Isa. 13:17)

"[They] came from Persia and easily conquered Babylon in 538 B.C. The walls were destroyed twenty years later, after which the city never again became the capital of an independent, strong Mesopotamian power. Two centuries later, after Alexander the Great and his Greek armies conquered the Persians, Babylon rapidly declined in commercial and cultural importance; Seleucia became the major city in the area. By the time of Christ, only a few astronomers and mathematicians continued to live in the ancient, sparsely populated city. After they left, Babylon became a deserted *tell* (mound), gradually covered by sand and brush until it became a hill used only by wild animals and as grazing land for nomadic flocks."

Victor Ludlow (Isaiah: Prophet, Seer, and Poet, p. 185)

2 Ne. 24:4-21   **TAUNT-SONG**
(Isa. 14:4-8; D&C 88:110)

"These verses begin the *taunt-song* aimed at the once-powerful king of Babylon. Even the trees rejoice in the demise of this once-powerful king. Although the historical context of these verses is couched in ancient Babylon, the application extends to the latter days as well. It could apply to the ultimate removal of any wicked leader, particularly Satan. He will be bound at the commencement of the Millennium, reducing him to the role of a powerless prisoner for one thousand years (see D&C 88:110)."

Hoyt W. Brewster, Jr. (Isaiah Plain and Simple, pp. 136-137)

2 Ne. 24:12-17   **LUCIFER**
(Conference Report, Apr. 1971, p. 23)

"The only places in the Bible and the Book of Mormon where the title Lucifer is used are Isaiah 14:12 and 2 Nephi 24:12. In D&C 76:25-28 we learn that Lucifer (which means 'lightbearer') was the premortal name of Satan. Because of his rebellion against God he fell from his position of 'authority in the presence of God' (v. 25) and 'was called Perdition' (v. 26), which means 'destruction.'"

Book of Mormon 121-122 Student Manual, p. 34

2 Ne. 24:25   BRING THE ASSYRIANS IN MY LAND
(Isa. 14:25; *The One Volume Bible Commentary*, Dummelow, p. 426)

"It is difficult to determine whether Isaiah is prophesying about the destruction of
Sennacherib's Assyrian army in 701 B.C. or the defeat of the army of the nations
led by King Gog in the last days. (Compare Isaiah 36-37 with Ezek. 38-39.) In
both cases, the Lord's punishment is felt by the wicked nations of the earth."

Victor Ludlow (Isaiah: Prophet, Seer, and Poet, p. 189)

2 Ne. 24:28-31   PALESTINA
(Isa. 14:28-31; *Book of Mormon Commentary*, Reynolds & Sjodahl, 1:369)

"The country of Philistia consisted essentially of five city-states, each governed by
its own lord. The nation was home of the Philistines, detested enemies of Judah
and the Israelites. This country was at the height of its power at the time of King
Saul's death, but declined during the reign of King David. The Philistines were
conquered by the Assyrians in 734 B.C., later they became part of the Persian
Empire, and finally the land was annexed to Syria by the Romans."

Hoyt W. Brewster, Jr. (Isaiah Plain and Simple, p. 148)

"A number of thorny, unresolved historical problems prevent the giving of a
reasonably exact interpretation of some parts of the prophecy. But Isaiah seems
to be telling Philistia not to rejoice over his predictions of the ruin and downfall of Judah, her traditional enemy. For whereas the kingdom of Judah will fall,
there will come a glorious day when the people of Israel will rise above their
troubles. . . . On the other hand, Philistia is to be ruined and to fall without
having any prospects of recovery."

Sidney Sperry (Book of Mormon Compendium, pp. 244-245)

2 Ne. 24:29   SERPENT'S ROOT—COCATRICE—FIERY SERPENT
(Isa. 14:29)

"Sidney Sperry points out the serpent's root, cockatrice (venomous viper), and
fiery flying serpent are 'all symbolic of evil to come upon her [Philistia].' *(Book
of Mormon Compendium*, p. 245). Each of these represents a more deadly threat
than the previous one mentioned. J.R. Dummelow identified Sargon (Assyrian
king from 722 to 705 B.C.) and Sennacherib (Assyrian king from 705 to 681
B.C.) as the cockatrice and fiery serpent, 'each one proving more terrible and

formidable to the nations of Western Asia than his predecessor.' *(The One Volume Bible Commentary, p. 426)."*

Hoyt W. Brewster, Jr. (Isaiah Plain and Simple, p. 149)

2 Ne. 25:16-17   **GATHERING OF ISRAEL**
(2 Ne. 6:11; 9:2; 10:7-8; 30:7; 3 Ne. 5:26; 16:4-5; D&C 101:20-21; Jer. 16:14-21; *Millennial Messiah*, McConkie, pp. 351-352; refer in this text to 3 Ne. 20:13, 29-33; 3 Ne. 21:28-29)

"The gathering of Israel is first *spiritual* and second *temporal*. It is spiritual in that the lost sheep of Israel are first 'restored to the true church and fold of God,' meaning that they come to a true knowledge of the God of Israel, accept the gospel which he has restored in latter-days, and join the Church of Jesus Christ of Latter-day Saints. It is temporal in that these converts are then 'gathered home to the lands of their inheritance, and . . . established in all their lands of promise.' (2 Ne. 9:2; 25:15-18; Jer. 16:14-21), meaning that the house of Joseph will be established in America, the house of Judah in Palestine, and that the Lost Tribes will come to Ephraim in America to receive their blessings in due course (D&C 133)."

Bruce R. McConkie (Mormon Doctrine, p. 280)

"In that day when Israel remembers their God—that is, accepts Jesus as the Christ—then he will remember them and the covenants which he made with their fathers. This spiritual gathering must precede the temporal gathering."

R. Millet and J. F. McConkie (Doctrinal Commentary on the Book of Mormon, 1:148)

2 Ne. 25:18, 22,   **JUDGED BY THE WORDS WRITTEN IN THIS BOOK**
28; 29:11;   (D&C 20:8-15; 84:57-58; Ether 5:4, 6; Moro. 10:27; refer in this text to 2 Ne.
33:14   33:4,14)

"No member of this Church can stand approved in the presence of God who has not seriously and carefully read the Book of Mormon. . . ."

Joseph Fielding Smith (Conference Report, Oct. 1961, p. 18)

"Do eternal consequences rest upon our response to this book? Yes, either to our blessing or our condemnation. Every Latter-day Saint should make the study of this book a lifetime pursuit. Otherwise he is placing his soul in jeopardy and neglecting that which could give spiritual and intellectual unity to his whole life. There is a difference between a convert who is built on the rock of Christ through the Book of Mormon and stays hold of that iron rod, and one who is not."

Ezra Taft Benson (A Witness and a Warning, pp. 7-8)

"For me there could be no more impelling reason for reading the Book of Mormon than this statement of the Lord that we shall be judged by what is written in it."

Marion G. Romney (Conference Report, Apr. 1960, pp. 110-111)

"If the early Saints were rebuked for treating the Book of Mormon lightly, [D&C 84:54-57] are we under any less condemnation if we do the same?"

Ezra Taft Benson (Ensign, Nov. 1986, pp. 4-5)

"It [the history of the church] is the most important to us because that history contains the hand dealings of God direct to us through revelation as it has come in the *Doctrine and Covenants,* in the *Book of Mormon,* and in any revelation that comes to us through the servants of the Lord for our guidance. Do you know that the time is coming when we are going to be judged out of the books that are written."

Joseph Fielding Smith (Doctrines of Salvation, 2:199-200)

2 Ne. 25:23 **SAVED BY GRACE AND WORKS**
(2 Ne. 10:24; Jacob 4:7; Hel. 12:21-24; Ether 12:27; Moro.10:32-33; D&C 93:20; Heb. 4:16; *Doctrines of Salvation,* Smith 2:309-311; *Articles of Faith,* Talmage, pp. 107-108, 480-481; Eph. 2:8-10; 2 Tim. 1:9; James 2:14-26; Matt. 5:16; 16:27; Rev. 20:12; John 1:17; Acts 15:11; *BYU Devotional,* May 1990; *Ensign,* May 1993, pp. 79-81; *BYU Devotional,* Jan. 10, 1984; *Promised Messiah,* McConkie, pp. 346-7)

"The Savior's blood, His atonement, will save us, but only after we have done all we can to save ourselves by keeping His commandments."

Harold B. Lee (Ye Are the Light of the World, p. 245)

"All mortals have been saved from the permanence of death through the Resurrection of Jesus Christ (1 Cor. 15:22). As to salvation from sin and the consequences of sin, our answer to the question of whether or not we have been saved is 'yes, but with conditions.' Our third article of faith declares our belief: 'We believe that through the Atonement of Christ, all mankind may be saved, by obedience to the laws and ordinances of the Gospel' (*Articles of Faith* 1:3) . . . . The New Testament frequently refers to the grace of God and to salvation by grace (e.g., John 1:17; Acts 15:11; Eph. 2:8). But it also has many specific commandments on personal behavior, and many references to the importance of works (e.g., Matt. 5:16; Eph. 2:10; James 2:14-17). In addition, the Savior taught that we must endure to the end in order to be saved (see Matt. 10:22; Mark 13:13)."

Dallin H. Oaks (Ensign, May 1998, p. 55)

"There are those who contend that man is saved by grace alone, and that no works of any kind are of value. Such persons might reconstruct Nephi's language as follows: 'We are saved by grace; after all, what can we do?' . . . On the other hand, there are those who become so obsessed with their own 'works-righteousness,' with their own goodness, that they do not look to Christ. . . . It is only after a person has so performed a lifetime of works and faithfulness—only after he has come to deny himself of all ungodliness and every worldly lust—that the grace of God, that spiritual increment of power, is efficacious."

R. Millet & J. F. McConkie (Doctrinal Commentary on the Book of Mormon, 1:294-5)

2 Ne. 25:24-30   WE KEEP THE LAW OF MOSES
(2 Ne. 5:10; Jarom 1:5; Alma 25:15; 30:3; 34:14; Jacob 4:5-6; Hel. 13:1; 4 Ne. 1:12; *The Promised Messiah*, McConkie, p. 427)

"The Nephites lived the Law of Moses in the sense that they obeyed the endless ethical laws and abided by the myriad moral restrictions. They kept the Ten Commandments. They observed the law of animal sacrifice. But theirs was not a Levitical life-style; they had the higher priesthood and the everlasting gospel. Their vision was more keen than that of their Old World kinsmen—they were able to recognize the person and powers and religion of Christ the Lord behind the ritual of the preparatory gospel. . . . Inasmuch as the Nephites had the spiritual maturity to see beyond the type—to look beyond the Law the Lawgiver, to penetrate the myriad means to the great end—it was with them as if there was no Law of Moses, no lesser or preparatory gospel. Life was and is and forever will be in Christ."

R. Millet and J. F. McConkie (Doctrinal Commentary on the Book of Mormon, 1:296)

2 Ne. 26:2, 7, 10   (refer in this text to 1 Ne. 12:15-19)

2 Ne. 26:11   **WITHDRAWAL OF THE SPIRIT—RIPE FOR DESTRUCTION**
(1 Ne. 7:13-14; Mosiah 2:36-37; Morm. 1:14-16; Ether 2:15; Moses 8:17; D&C 1:33; Moro. 8:27-28; 9:4-5; 1 Cor. 3:16-17; *Teachings of the Prophet Joseph Smith*, p. 328; *Journal of Discourses* 21:317-318; *Ensign* Nov. 1996, pp. 60-61; refer in this text to Hel. 13:8; Morm. 1:14-17)

"This [the Spirit], when withdrawn, will make it difficult for you to pray, difficult for you to have direction and guidance, difficult for you to withstand evil. . . . I hope you haven't come to that state, but if you are not careful and this experience is repeated again, with each repetition there comes a diminishing of that spirit until you, like they, will have lost, not only the power of the Holy Ghost, but also the light of the Christ. . . ."

Harold B. Lee (BYU Speeches, Oct. 1956, pp. 6-7)

2 Ne. 26:12   **CHRIST—THE ETERNAL GOD**
(refer in this text to 1 Ne. 19:10)

2 Ne. 26:24   **HE LOVETH THIS WORLD**
(Moses 1:33, 37-39; Isa. 45:18)

2 Ne. 26:24-28, 33   **THE LORD IS NOT PREJUDICED**
(D&C 1:35; 38:16, 24-27; 1 Sam. 16:7; 1 Ne. 17:35, 40; D&C 38:24-27; 1 Tim. 2:4; Acts 10:34-35; Gal. 3:26-29; *Teachings of the Prophet Joseph Smith*, p. 189; *Doctrines of Salvation*, Smith, 1:61; refer in this text to 1 Ne. 17:35, 40)

"Our Father in Heaven loves all of His children equally, perfectly, and infinitely. His love is no different for His daughters than for His sons. Our Savior, the Lord Jesus Christ, also loves men and women equally. His atonement and His gospel are for all of God's children. During His earthly ministry Jesus served men and women alike: He healed both men and women and He taught both men and women. . . . For example, faith, repentance, baptism and the gift of the Holy Ghost are requirements for all of God's children, regardless of gender. The same is true of temple covenants and blessings. Our Father's work and glory is to bring to pass the immortality and eternal life of His children (see Moses 1:39). He loves us all equally, and His greatest gift, the gift of eternal life, is available to all."

M. Russell Ballard (Ensign, Nov. 1993, p. 89)

"I hope we can all overcome any differences of culture, [and] race. . . . In my experience, no race or class seems superior to any other in spirituality and faithfulness. . . . Spiritual peace is not to be found in race or culture or nationality, but rather through our commitment to God and to the covenants and ordinances of the gospel."

James E. Faust (Ensign, May 1995, pp. 61,63)

2 Ne. 26:29-31 **PRIESTCRAFT**
(refer in this text to Alma 1:3-5,16; *Conference Report*, D. Oaks, Apr. 1989, pp. 34-39)

2 Ne. 26:32 **ENVY**
(Ex. 20:17; Matt. 6:19-24; D&C 6:6-7; 88:123; Mark 19:21-22; *Ensign*, Dec. 1994, pp. 22-26)

2 Ne. 27 *(Church News*, July 17, Aug. 21, 1983)

2 Ne. 27:1-2 **THE LAST DAYS—THE DAYS OF THE GENTILES**
(D&C 45:28-33; *Doctrines of Salvation*, Smith, 3:259,278; *Conference Report*, Oct. 1960, pp. 103-105; *Book of Mormon Prophecies*, Warner, pp. 96-98, 106-108; refer in this text to 3 Ne. 16:10-16)

"We are living in the days of the Gentiles when this prediction was to be fulfilled. . . . If we are living the religion which the Lord has revealed and which we have received, we do not belong to the world. We should have no part in all its foolishness. . . . If I sometimes, and once in a while I do, go to a football game or a baseball game or some other place of amusement, invariably I will be surrounded by men and women who are puffing on cigarettes or cigars or dirty pipes. It gets very annoying, and I get a little disturbed. I will turn to Sister Smith, and I will say something to her, and she will say, 'Well, now, you know what you have taught me. You are in their world. This is their world.' And that sort of brings me back to my senses. Yes, we are in their world, but we do not have to be of it. So, as this is their world we are living in, they prosper, but, my good brethren and sisters, their world is coming to its end."

Joseph Fielding Smith (Conference Report, Apr. 1952, pp. 27-28)

2 Ne. 27:6-7, 11   SEALED PORTION OF THE PLATES
(Ether 4:4-6; 3 Ne. 26:9-10; *Doctrines of Salvation*, Smith, 3:224-225; *Millennial Messiah*, McConkie, pp. 114, 149-150; *History of the Church*, Smith, 4:537)

"Now the Lord has placed us on probation as members of the Church. He has given us the Book of Mormon, which is the lesser part, to build up our faith through our obedience to the counsels which it contains, and when we ourselves, members of the Church, are willing to keep the commandments as they have been given to us and show our faith as the Nephites did for a short period of time, then the Lord is ready to bring forth the other record and give it to us, but we are not ready to receive it. Why? Because we have not lived up to the requirements in this probationary state in the reading of the record which had been given to us and in following its counsels."

Joseph Fielding Smith (Conference Report, Oct. 1961, pp. 19-20)

"When, during the Millennium, the sealed portion of the Book of Mormon is translated, it will give an account of life in the premortal existence; of the creation of all things; of the fall and the Atonement and the Second Coming; of temple ordinances, in their fulness; of the ministry and mission of translated beings; of life in the spirit world, in both paradise and hell; of the kingdoms of glory to be inhabited by resurrected beings; and many such like things."

Bruce R. McConkie (CES Symposium, Aug. 1984, p. 1)

2 Ne. 27:12   THE THREE WITNESSES
(2 Cor. 13:1; Deut. 19:15; Ether 5:2-3; D&C 17:1-3; *History of Joseph Smith by His Mother, Lucy M. Smith*, pp. 151-153; *History of the Church*, Smith, 1:52-57)

2 Ne. 27:15-19   CHARLES ANTHON
(Isa. 29:11-12; JS-H 1:61-65; *Treasures of the Book of Mormon*, Skousen, 1:54-57; *History of the Church*, Smith, 1:20; *Doctrines of Salvation*, Smith, 3:213)

2 Ne. 27:20   THEY HAVE REJECTED THEM
(refer in this text to 2 Ne. 9:28-30)

"This is not solely a reference to professor Anthon, since the plural pronoun *they* is used. The reference suggests a mind-set of most of the learned of the world, who, by and large, do not take the Book of Mormon seriously. Even when they read it, they do not *really* read it, except with a mind-set which excludes miracles, including the miracle of the book's coming forth by the 'gift and power of God.'"

Neal A. Maxwell (First Nephi, The Doctrinal Foundation, BYU Religious Studies Center, p. 9)

2 Ne. 27:26   **A MARVELOUS WORK AND A WONDER**
(D&C 4:1; 6:1; 11:1; 12:1; 14:1; 18:44; Isa. 29:14)

"More than seven hundred years before the birth of Jesus Christ the Lord spoke through Isaiah of the coming forth of the Book of Mormon and the restoration of the Gospel. Isaiah, by prophecy, spoke of the restoration of the new and everlasting covenant, and the Lord performing a 'marvelous work and a wonder,' which should cause 'the wisdom of their wise men' to be hid. . . . This marvelous work is the restoration of the Church and the Gospel with all the power and authority, keys and blessings which pertain to this great work for the salvation of the children of men."

Joseph Fielding Smith (as quoted in Isaiah Plain and Simple, Brewster, p. 168)

2 Ne. 27:28   **LEBANON**
(Isa. 29:17; Deut. 1:6-7; Josh. 11:1-4)

"Lebanon was the northernmost portion of Palestine. It was part of the land promised to the Israelites when they crossed into Canaan. Isaiah's prophecy has been interpreted to include the entire land of Canaan. President Joseph Fielding Smith wrote of the 'deplorable condition' of this land prior to its redemption in recent years, which redemption was in fulfillment of prophecy. *(Doctrines of Salvation*, 3:260-261). Elder Orson Pratt noted that this changed condition would occur only following the publication of the book which Isaiah saw; at which time Lebanon and all the land of Canaan is again to be blessed, while the fruitful field occupied by the nations of the Gentiles, 'will be esteemed as a forest:' the multitude of the nations of the Gentiles are to perish, and their lands which are now like a fruitful field, are to be left desolate of inhabitants and become as Lebanon has been for many generations past: while Lebanon shall again be occupied by Israel, and be turned into a fruitful field. These great events could not take place until the Lord should first bring forth a book out of the ground *(Orson Pratt's Works*, pp. 276-277)."

Hoyt W. Brewster, Jr. (Isaiah Plain and Simple, pp. 171-172)

2 Ne. 27:32   **LAY A SNARE . . . TURN ASIDE THE JUST**
(Isa. 29:21; D&C 121:16-17; refer in this text to Hel. 16:2; Ether 13:13-15, 20-22)

"By one means or another, the swiftest method of rejection of the holy prophets has been to find a pretext, however false or absurd, to dismiss the man so that his message could also be dismissed."

Spencer W. Kimball (Conference Report, Apr. 1978, p. 115)

2 Ne. 27:33   **JACOB . . . WAX PALE**
(Isa. 29:22)

"The house of Jacob has been made ashamed, and his face has waxed pale, ever since he was driven away from Lebanon or Canaan, but the Lord has now brought forth out of the ground a book which shall, accompanied by His power, restore the tribes of Jacob from the four quarters of the globe, and establish them in the land of Palestine and Lebanon forever."

Orson Pratt's Works, p. 278

2 Ne. 28   *(Ensign*, Largey, Dec. 1989, pp. 7-11)

2 Ne. 28:7-8   **EAT, DRINK, & BE MERRY**
(D&C 1:31)

"The idea that one is better off after one has sinned and repented is a devilish lie of the adversary. Does anyone here think that it is better to learn first-hand that a certain blow will break a bone, or a certain mixture of chemicals will explode and sear off our skin? Are we better off after we have sustained and then been healed from such injuries? I believe we all can see that it is better to heed the warnings of wise persons who know the effects on our bodies . . . [as well as our spirits]."

Dallin H. Oaks (BYU Fireside, 8-5-90)

2 Ne. 28:8   **LIE A LITTLE**
(2 Ne. 9:34; D&C 63:17-18; Articles of Faith, 1:13)

2 Ne. 28:19-22 **THE CAREFUL CHAINS OF SATAN**
(refer in this text to 2 Ne. 1:13, 23)

"We live in a day of slick, quiet and clever sins."

Ezra Taft Benson (A Nation Asleep, p. 44)

"I like that word 'carefully.' In other words, don't shake them, you might awake them."

Ezra Taft Benson (Conference Report, Apr. 1965, pp. 124-125)

"An influence is in the world today trying to make people believe that by their own intelligence and by their own power they can gain eternal life. . . . He does not come and grab you bodily and take you into his territory, but he whispers, 'Do this little evil,' and when he succeeds in that, another little evil and another. . . . He makes you believe that you are gaining something when you are losing . . . . that is the condition of the world today. Nephi could not have stated it plainer if he had been right here in the world now."

George Albert Smith (Conference Report, Apr. 1918, pp. 39-41)

"The safest road to Hell is the gradual one—the gentle slope, soft underfoot, without sudden turnings, without milestones, without signposts."

C.S. Lewis (Screwtape Letters, p. 56) as quoted by James E. Faust (Ensign, Nov. 1987, p. 35)

"Every transgression, regardless of how minor, makes us more susceptible to Satan's influence the next time he tempts us. Satan takes us an inch at a time, deceiving us as to the consequences of so-called minor sins until he captures us in major transgressions. Nephi describes this technique as one of pacifying, lulling, and flattering us away until Satan 'grasps [us] with his awful chains, from whence there is no deliverance.'"

Richard C. Edgley (Ensign, Nov. 1994, p. 40)

"Unfortunately the people of this land have not been willing to do this thing, [keep the commandments]. They have turned from righteous ways and the keeping of their bodies clean to ways of evil. Immorality rages, drunkenness prevails from sea to sea, the filthiness of tobacco has debased both men and women, and the stench thereof has ascended to high heaven. By the practice of these evils humanity is binding itself by the chains of hell."

Joseph Fielding Smith (Doctrines of Salvation, 3:277)

2 Ne. 28:20

THE DEVIL STIRS THEM UP TO ANGER
(D&C 10:24, 32; 63:27-28: Hel. 16:22)

"It should come as no surprise that one of the adversary's tactics in the latter days is stirring up hatred among the children of men. He loves to see us criticize each other, make fun or take advantage of our neighbor's known flaws, and generally pick on each other. The Book of Mormon is clear from where all anger, malice, greed, and hate come [2 Ne. 28:20]. By the looks of what we constantly see depicted in the news media, it appears that Satan is doing a pretty good job. In the name of reporting the news, we are besieged with sometimes graphic depictions—too often in living color—of greed, extortion, violent sexual crimes, and insults between business, athletic, or political opponents."

Marvin J. Ashton (Ensign, May 1992, p. 19)

2 Ne. 28:21,
24-25

ALL IS WELL IN ZION
(D&C 27:15; 82:14)

"We have discussed elsewhere that other class of people who are basically unrepentant because they are not doing the commandments. They are Church members who are steeped in lethargy. They neither drink nor commit the sexual sins. They do not gamble nor rob nor kill. They are good citizens and splendid neighbors, but spiritually speaking they seem to be in a long, deep sleep. They are doing nothing seriously wrong except in their failures to do the right things to earn their exaltation."

Spencer W. Kimball (Miracle of Forgiveness, pp. 211-212)

"It is not possible, as some of us have supposed, for us to slip along easily through this life, keeping the commandments of the Lord indifferently— accepting some of the doctrines and not others, and indulging our appetites or desires, and, because we consider them little things, failing to understand and comprehend our duty to them—and then expect to receive a fulness of glory in the kingdom of God."

Joseph Fielding Smith (Doctrines of Salvation, 2:14-15)

"Never have the forces of evil been so insidious, widespread, and enticing. Everywhere there seems to be a cheapening, weakening, downgrading of all that is fine, good, and uplifting—all aimed at our youth, while many of their parents are lulled away into a false security as they enjoy their comfortable complacency. All is not well in Zion. The inspired Book of Mormon prophets saw this day and, as watchmen on the towers, issued grave warnings. . . ."

Ezra Taft Benson (God, Family, Country, p.245)

2 Ne. 28:3-6,22   NO GOD TODAY AND NO DEVIL
(Book of Mormon Prophecy, Warner, pp. 198-203; The Screwtape Letters, Lewis, p. 3)

"Several years ago in a seminary recognized as perhaps the greatest in this country, a doctor of divinity, who had a string of honorary doctoral degrees and who is on the board of directors of one of the largest Protestant churches in America, in lecturing to a large group of students, most of whom already had bachelor of divinity degrees, said sympathetically: 'I know that it is difficult for you men to teach creeds which you, yourselves do not believe, but you have the social obligation to do it.' Another man in the same institution, having about the same academic credentials, declared: 'Who knows but what in the year 2004 or some other year, there will live a man who will love more perfectly than did Jesus. Then we will worship him as the Son of God, rather than Jesus. The reason we worship Jesus as the Son of God is because he lived the most perfect life of any man of whom we have knowledge.'"

A. Theodore Tuttle (Conference Report, Oct. 1960, p. 54)

"I doubt if there was a Christian minister in all the world who would have said there was no devil at the time the Book of Mormon was published in 1830, and yet when a questionnaire was sent out by the Northwestern University School of Religion in 1934 to five hundred Christian ministers, of the five hundred, fifty-four percent, or two hundred and ninety-five, said there would be no judgment day. . . . Twenty-six percent or 130 of the five hundred ministers were opposed to the Deity of Jesus. What in the world could the devil, the enemy of all righteousness, desire more than to make our young people think that chastity is outmoded? To accomplish this, he must make them believe there is no devil, and that there is not hell or judgment day. Thus 'he whispereth in their ears, until he grasps them with his awful chains, from whence there is no deliverance.' I read an article in the newspaper at the close of the war [WWII] indicating that in Germany there were thirteen thousand illegitimate babies whose fathers were American boys!"

LeGrand Richards (Conference Report, Oct. 1949, pp. 51-54)

2 Ne. 28:19   **KINGDOM OF DEVIL . . . STIRRED UP**
"During this time when nations are in distress, with perplexity, there will actually be some redemptive turbulence: 'For the kingdom of the devil must shake, and they which belong to it must needs be stirred up unto repentance' (2 Ne. 28:19). Being so 'stirred up' will be a real thing, though we can only speculate as to how it will be achieved."

Neal A. Maxwell (Ensign, Nov. 1998, p. 62)

2 Ne. 28:20   **THE DEVIL WHISPERETH IN THEIR EARS**
"Some of Satan's most appealing lines are 'Everyone does it'; 'If it doesn't hurt anybody else, it's all right'; 'If you feel all right about it, it's OK'; or 'It's the *in* thing to do.' These subtle . . .[whisperings] make Satan the . . . master deceiver. . . . Nephi has given to us the pattern or formula by which Satan operates."

James E. Faust (Ensign, Nov. 1987, p. 34)

2 Ne. 28:30   **LINE UPON LINE**
(Isa. 28:10; D&C 98:12; 128:21; refer in this text to Mosiah 4:27)

"A testimony is not thrust upon you; a testimony grows. We become taller in testimony like we grow taller in physical stature; we hardly know it happens because it comes by growth. . . . You cannot force spiritual things. . . . You can no more force the Spirit to respond than you can force a bean to sprout, or an egg to hatch before its time. You can create a climate to foster growth, nourish, and protect; but you cannot force or compel: you must await the growth. Do not be impatient to gain great spiritual knowledge. Let it grow, help it grow, but do not force it or you will open the way to be misled."

Boyd K. Packer (Ensign, Jan. 1983, p. 53)

"Joseph's vision of the Father and the Son opened this dispensation. Then came the Restoration of the fulness of the gospel of Jesus Christ with the same organization that existed in the primitive Church, built upon the foundation of apostles and prophets. (see Article of Faith 1:6; Eph. 2:20). Some suppose that the organization was handed to the Prophet Joseph Smith like a set of plans and specifications for a building, with all of the details known at the beginning. But it did not come that way. Rather, it came a piece at a time as the Brethren were ready and as they inquired of God. . . . It took a generation of asking and receiving before the order of things as we know it today was firmly in place. Each move to perfect that order has come about in response to a need and in answer to prayer. And that process continues in our day."

Boyd K. Packer (Ensign, Nov. 1996, p. 6)

2 Ne. 29:3-11   A BIBLE! A BIBLE!
(Journal of Discourses 25:121-122)

"Does God love us less than those led by the ancient prophets? Do we need his guidance and instruction less? Reason suggests that this cannot be. Does he not care? Has he lost his voice? Has he gone on a permanent vacation? Does he sleep? The unreasonableness of each of these proposals is self-evident."

James E. Faust (Conference Report, Apr. 1980, p. 16)

2 Ne. 29:12-14   OTHER NATIONS SHALL WRITE
(3 Ne. 17:4; *Companion to Your Study of the Book of Mormon*, Ludlow, p. 271; *Conference Report*, Apr. 1916, p. 130; *Conference Report*, Oct. 1916, p. 76; refer in this text to 3 Ne. 21:28-29)

"The splendid Book of Mormon advises that a third scriptural witness is yet to come from the lost tribes (see 2 Nephi 29:12-14). . . . We do not know when and how this will occur, but we are safe in assuming that the third book will have the same fundamental focus as the Book of Mormon—'that . . . their seed [too] . . . may be brought to a knowledge of me, their Redeemer' (3 Nephi 16:4). If there is a title page in that third set of sacred records, it is not likely to differ in purpose from the title page in the Book of Mormon, except for its focus on still other peoples who likewise received a personal visit from the resurrected Jesus (see 3 Nephi 15:20-24; 16:1-4)."

Neal A. Maxwell (First Nephi, The Doctrinal Foundation, BYU Religious Studies Center, p. 15)

"Lost books are among the treasures yet to come forth. Over twenty of these are mentioned in the existing scriptures. Perhaps most startling and voluminous will be the records of the lost tribes of Israel (see 2 Nephi 29:13). We would not even know of the impending third witness for Christ except through the precious Book of Mormon, the second witness for Christ! This third set of sacred records will thus complete a triad of truth. Then, just as the Perfect Shepherd has said, 'My word also shall be gathered in one' (v. 14). There will be 'one fold and one shepherd' (1 Nephi 22:25) in a welding together of all the Christian dispensations of human history (see D&C 128:18)."

Neal A. Maxwell (Ensign, Nov. 1986, p. 52)

2 Nephi 30–33

2 Ne. 30:1-2 **THE COVENANT PEOPLE OF THE LORD**
(Rom. 4:13; 8:14; 9:6-7; 10:12)

2 Ne. 30:4; 33:8 **NEPHI DESCENDED FROM THE JEWS**
(Book of Mormon 121-122 Student Manual, p. 41; Omni 1:15; refer in this text to Alma 10:3)

"It is true that Lehi and his family were descendants of Joseph through the lineage of Manasseh (Alma 10:3), and Ishmael was a descendant of Ephraim, according to the statement of the Prophet Joseph Smith. That the Nephites were descendants of Joseph is in fulfillment of the blessings given to Joseph by his father Israel. The Nephites were of the Jews, not so much by descent as by citizenship, although in the long descent from Jacob, it could be possible of some mixing of the tribes by intermarriage."

Joseph Fielding Smith (Answers to Gospel Questions, 1:142-143)

2 Ne. 30:6 **PURE—WHITE**
(Doctrinal Commentary on the Book of Mormon, Millet and McConkie, 1:355-356)

"Except the 1840 edition of the Book of Mormon, in all editions prior to 1981 this verse read 'a white and delightsome people.' The 1981 change was made in conformity with the 1840 edition (the only one personally revised by Joseph Smith) where the word 'pure' rather than 'white' is found. Commenting on this point, Robert J. Matthews wrote: 'The decision to use 'pure' in this passage was made not on the basis of the original manuscripts (as were most other cases) but on the 1840 revision by the Prophet Joseph Smith and the judgment of the [current] living prophets. This correction does not negate the concept that future generations of Lamanites will become white, but it removes the concept that one has to be white to be delightsome to the Lord.'"

Rodney Turner (Second Nephi, The Doctrinal Structure, ed. by Nyman and Tate, p. 156)

"We were recently with the Navajo Nation at Window Rock in Arizona. . . . It was difficult to hold back the tears as we mingled with these sons and daughters of Father Lehi. In my imagination I have seen him weeping for his progeny who for so long have walked in poverty and pain. But the shackles of darkness are falling. Some of them now are men and women of achievement. They have partaken of the fruits of education. They have come to know and love the gospel. They have become pure and delightsome. But there is so much more to do among them. Alcohol and drugs literally destroy many of them. We must do more to help. As I look to the future, I envision the Spirit of the Lord being poured out upon these people. Education will unlock the door of opportunity, and the gospel will bring new light and understanding into their lives."

Gordon B. Hinckley (Ensign, Nov. 1997, p. 67)

2 Ne. 30:7   **GATHERING IS FIRST TO CHRIST**
(1 Ne. 22:25; *Book of Mormon Prophecies*, Warner, pp. 167-174; refer in this text to 3 Ne. 20:13, 29-31)

"The work of gathering that will *commence* in the Millennium will be of such a magnitude that the extent of the gathering previously will hardly constitute a beginning by comparison."

R. Millet and J. F. McConkie (Doctrinal Commentary on the Book of Mormon, 1:357)

2 Ne. 30:10   **SAVED BY FIRE**
(refer in this text to 1 Ne. 22:16-17, 19; Hel. 5:20-52)

2 Ne. 30:11   **GIRDLE—LOINS—REINS**
(Psalm 7:9; Jer. 17:10; Rev. 2:23)

"*Girdle.* The Orientals, when walking fast, or working, found it convenient to gather up their long, flowing robes by means of a girdle. . . . *Loins.* Were supposed to be the seat of strength. To gird up the loins was, in prophetic parlance, to make ready for work, or for traveling untrammeled. *Reins.* The same as kidneys. Supposed to be the symbols of desire; also of knowledge, joy, pleasure. Sometimes coupled with the heart."

G. Reynolds and J. Sjodahl (Book of Mormon Commentary, 1:421)

2 Ne. 30:17   **NOTHING IS SECRET SAVE IT SHALL BE REVEALED**
(D&C 1:3)

2 Ne. 31:5-9   **BAPTISM OF CHRIST**
(Moro. 4:3; *Companion to Your Study of the Book of Mormon*, Ludlow, pp. 139,153-154)

2 Ne. 31:8   **FORM OF A DOVE**
(refer in this text to 1 Ne. 11:27)

2 Ne. 31:8-11,   **THE GATE TO THE STRAIT & NARROW PATH**
17-18;   (D&C 22:2, 4; 43:7; 2 Ne. 9:41; Alma 5:62; 3 Ne. 14:13-14; 27:33; Jacob
33:9   6:11; D&C 22:2, 4; refer in this text to 1 Ne. 8:20)

2 Ne. 31:11-15   **CONVERSATION WITH THE FATHER & THE SON**
"2 Nephi 31 is a most distinctive scriptural text. In verse 11 Nephi records the words of the Father to him. In verse 12 the voice of the Son comes to him. The pattern repeats itself in reverse order in verses 14 and 15: in verse 14 we have a record of that spoken by the voice of the Son, verse 15 the voice of the Father. Apparently Nephi finds himself in conversation with both members of the Godhead. If such is the case, this is a singular occasion, inasmuch as revelation since the Fall has normally come by and through Jehovah, who is Jesus Christ. The prophet Enoch seems to have had an experience similar to Nephi's (see Moses 7:50, 53, 59). Those instances wherein Elohim has appeared or spoken have been for the purpose of introducing Jesus Christ as his Son. In compliance with the principle of divine investiture of authority, there are also numerous instances wherein the Son has spoken for and in behalf of the Father."

R. Millet and J. F. McConkie (Doctrinal Commentary on The Book of Mormon, 1:364)

2 Ne. 31:13,17   **BAPTISM—HOLY GHOST—REMISSION OF SINS**
(Alma 13:12; 3 Ne. 12:2; John 3:3-5; Luke 3:16; Moses 6:66; *Teachings of the Book of Mormon*, Barrett, p. 93; refer in this text to 3 Ne. 27:20)

"You might as well baptize a bag of sand as a man, if not done in view of the remission of sins and getting of the Holy Ghost. Baptism by water is but half a baptism, and is good for nothing without the other half—that is, the baptism of the Holy Ghost."

Teachings of the Prophet Joseph Smith, p. 366)

"The Holy Ghost is a sanctifier (Alma 13:12; 3 Nephi 27:19-20). The ordinance of baptism consists of two parts: the baptism of water and the baptism of fire or the Holy Ghost (see John 3:3-5). The Holy Ghost is the sanctifying medium by which one's sins—after the outward ordinances—may be purged, as though by fire."

R. Millet and J. F. McConkie (Doctrinal Commentary on The Book of Mormon, 1:366)

"Sins are remitted not in the waters of baptism, as we say in speaking figuratively, but when we receive the Holy Ghost. . . . The baptism of the Holy Ghost is the baptism of fire. . . . After baptism in water, legal administrators lay their hands upon a repentant person and say: 'Receive the Holy Ghost.' This gives him the gift of the Holy Ghost, which is the right to the constant companionship of that member of the Godhead based on faithfulness. Either then or later, depending upon the individual's personal worthiness, the Holy Ghost comes. The baptized person becomes a new creature. He is baptized with fire, sin and evil are burned out of his soul, and he is born again."

Bruce R. McConkie (A New Witness for the Articles of Faith, pp. 290-291)

"Water baptism is only a preparatory cleansing of the believing penitent . . . whereas, the baptism of fire and the Holy Ghost cleanses more thoroughly, by renewing the inner man, and by purifying the affections, desires, and thoughts which have long been habituated in the impure ways of sin."

Orson Pratt (The Holy Spirit, pp. 56-57)

2 Ne. 32:2-3;   **HOLY GHOST & THE TONGUE OF ANGELS**
33:1   (D&C 88:63-65)

"No man can receive the Holy Ghost without receiving revelations. The Holy Ghost is a revelator."

Teachings of the Prophet Joseph Smith, p. 328

"Three manifestations of the gift of 'speaking in tongues' are evident in God's dealings with his children: (1) speaking the pure Adamic language (Moses 6:6, 46; Orson Pratt, *Journal of Discourses* 3:99-103; HC 1:297); (2) speaking a foreign but known tongue (Acts 2:2, 4-6; and (3) speaking by the power of the Holy Ghost."

R. Millet and J. McConkie (Doctrinal Commentary on The Book of Mormon, 1:369-370)

2 Ne. 32:6-7   **NO MORE DOCTRINE**
(Doctrines of Salvation, Smith, 1:283)

[Why no more doctrine?] "Because the people had refused to pray. Because they had hardened their hearts, even in his [Nephi's] day. Therefore the Lord closed his mouth, and said, there shall be no more doctrine till Christ comes, so far as you are concerned, and I cannot say more, because the Lord won't permit it. . . . Now that applies in our day. We have members of the Church to whom this ought to be read (2 Ne. 32:6-7)."

Joseph Fielding Smith (Conference Report, Oct. 1919, pp. 145-146)

2 Ne. 32:7   **THE SPIRIT STOPPETH MINE UTTERANCE**
(Moses 4:32; Matt. 7:6; 13:11-12; 2 Ne. 28:30; D&C 71:1; refer in this text to Alma 12:9)

"The revelation that restrains is one of the most common forms of revelation. It often comes by surprise, when we have not asked for revelation or guidance on a particular subject. But if we are keeping the commandments of God and living in tune with his Spirit, a restraining force will steer us away from things we should not do. One of my first experiences in being restrained by the Spirit came soon after I was called as a counselor in a stake presidency in Chicago. . . . Our stake president made a proposal that our new stake center be built in a particular location. . . . When asked for my counsel, I opposed the proposal. . . . The stake president wisely proposed that each of us consider the matter prayerfully for another week. . . . I prayed about the subject and immediately received a strong impression that I was wrong. . . . Needless to say, I was restrained and promptly gave my approval . . . My reasons to the contrary turned out to be shortsighted, and I was soon grateful to have been restrained from relying on them. . . . Several years ago I picked up the desk pen in my office at BYU to sign a paper that had been prepared for my signature. . . . As I went to sign the document, I was filled with such negative thoughts and forebodings that I put it to one side and asked for the entire matter to be reviewed again. It was, and within a few days additional facts came to light which showed that the proposed course of action would have caused the university serious problems in the future."

Dallin H. Oaks (BYU Devotional & Fireside Speeches, 1981-1982, pp. 20-26)

2 Ne. 32:8-9   **PRAY ALWAYS AND NOT FAINT**
(Alma 34:18-27; Jacob 4:10; *Ensign,* Feb. 1990, pp. 2-5)

"Have we any right as Latter-day Saints who profess to keep the commandments of the Lord, to open our dances without prayer, or other amusements, and to close them in improper hours and without prayer? Have we that right, professing to be Latter-day Saints, keeping the commandments of the Lord? I say unto you, No. It makes no difference whether it is pleasure, whether it is our daily labor, whether it is the service of the Lord in teaching the gospel and trying to save mankind. Whatever it may be, that thing should be consecrated by prayer, and every performance, for the welfare of our souls."

Joseph Fielding Smith (Conference Report, Oct. 1919, p. 145)

"A business associate of mine asked me to go with him to make the acquaintance of and visit and talk with eight wonderful young Latter-day Saint practicing physicians. He wanted me to go to see these doctors and meet them, wishing that I would agree to write a letter of recommending consideration for these doctors so they could successfully get a loan to build a medical clinic. . . . We left Salt Lake City very early. . . . Soon their individual cars appeared at the office. I was then made acquainted with these wonderful, fine doctors, and we were invited into their office. After all had assembled, and we were comfortably seated, the oldest of these eight doctors . . . walked over and shut the door. Then he said, 'Would you mind joining us in morning prayer before we discuss our business with you?' . . . I was somewhat astounded at this procedure, but I confess I was humbly grateful and proud of these young doctors. The presiding doctor called on one of the other doctors to offer the morning prayer, and he offered a very beautiful, appropriate petition to the Lord and asked for his guidance. To my recollection, I have never had that experience with professional or businessmen before. I asked the doctors before I left, 'Is this your common practice?' 'Oh, yes, every morning, six days a week, we meet here between 6:30 and 7, where we lock our door, and before starting our duties of the day, call on God our Eternal Father for his divine guidance. If for any reason one of the doctors has important or urgent surgery or an urgent patient call, we go ahead without him, and each takes his turn offering the morning prayer.' Of course these doctors were successful! I thought they were wonderful. How many teachers, how many bankers, how many business or professional men, how many of us follow that kind of procedure every morning? These doctors are seeking the divine guidance of God their Eternal Father, and mainly they are men skilled in science, trained in their profession, but not sufficiently so that they can rely upon their own training and their own natural abilities."

Thorpe B. Isaacson (Conference Report, Apr. 1957, pp. 68-69)

"My friends and I went to a fireside where the speaker taught us about our Savior's love. . . . The speaker suggested that to help us remember to think about the Savior, we could listen to the school bell that rang often during the day. Each time we heard the bell, we were to say a silent prayer, even with our eyes open, even walking down the hall. We could thank our Heavenly Father for our blessings, especially for our Savior. We could tell Him of our love and ask for His help. He taught us that in just a few seconds, many times during the day, we could practice thinking about our Heavenly Father and Savior. . . . The speaker suggested that almost immediately we move from praying about ourselves to praying for someone else—a friend, a teacher, a stranger—and asking Heavenly Father to bless that person. . . . It was awkward at first, but soon I found myself thinking about my Heavenly Father and Savior, not only when the bell rang but many times during the day. I remember walking across a muddy field one morning and seeing a tiny yellow flower. It was probably a weed, but to me it was beautiful, and I felt that He had created it just for me. I loved Him so much. My faith had increased, and I was happy."

Patricia P. Pinegar (Ensign, May 1994, p. 94)

"Follow the directions of the Book of Mormon, and . . . ask the blessing of God upon all your labors, and everything that you engage in."

Teachings of the Prophet Joseph Smith, p. 247

2 Ne. 33:4, 14   BOOK OF MORMON PROMISES
(1 Ne. 15:24; 2 Ne. 25:22; 29:11; Morm. 8:12; refer in this text to Moro.10:3-5)

"The Book of Mormon (is) the most correct of any book on earth, and the keystone of our religion, and a man would get nearer to God by abiding by its precepts, than by any other book."

Joseph Smith (History of Church 4:461)

"The Prophet's expression that 'the Book of Mormon is the keystone of our religion' means precisely what it says. The keystone is the central stone in the tip of the arch. If that stone is removed, then the arch crumbles, which, in effect, means that Mormonism . . . stands or falls with the truth or the falsity of the Book of Mormon. . . . If the Book of Mormon is true, our message to the world is truth; the truth of this message is established in and through this book."

Bruce R. McConkie (Conference Report, Apr. 1961, p. 39)

"What is the major purpose of the Book of Mormon? To bring men to Christ and to be reconciled to him. . . . [It] helps us draw nearer to God. Is there not something deep in our hearts that longs to draw nearer to God, to be more like Him in our daily walk, to feel His presence with us constantly? If so, then the Book of Mormon will help us do so more than any other book. It is not just that the Book of Mormon teaches us truth, though it indeed does that. It is not just that the Book of Mormon bears testimony of Christ, though it indeed does that, too. But there is something more. There is a power in the book which will begin to flow into your lives the moment you begin a serious study of the book. You will find greater power to resist temptation. You will find the power to avoid deception. You will find the power to stay on the strait and narrow path. . . . When you begin to hunger and thirst after those words, you will find life in greater and greater abundance."

Ezra Taft Benson (Ensign, Nov. 1984, pp. 6-7)

"May I admonish you to participate in a program of daily reading and pondering of the scriptures. . . . The Book of Mormon will change your life. It will fortify you against the evils of our day. It will bring a spirituality into your life that no other book will."

Ezra Taft Benson (Ensign, May 1986, p. 43)

"It is the book that will save the world and prepare the sons of men for joy and peace here and now and everlasting life in eternity."

Bruce R. McConkie (Conference Report, Oct. 1983, p. 107)

"I feel certain that if, in our homes, parents will read from the Book of Mormon prayerfully and regularly, both by themselves and with their children the spirit of that great book will come to permeate our homes and all who dwell therein. The spirit of reverence will increase; mutual respect and consideration for each other will grow. The spirit of contention will depart. Parents will counsel their children in greater love and wisdom. Children will be more responsive and submissive to that counsel."

Ezra Taft Benson (Ensign, Nov. 1986, p. 7)

"Success in righteousness, the power to avoid deception and resist temptation, guidance in our daily lives, healing of the soul—these are but a few of the promises the Lord has given to those who will come to his word."

Ezra Taft Benson (Ensign, May 1986, p. 82)

"Now, in our day, the Lord has revealed the need to reemphasize the Book of Mormon to get the church and all the children of Zion out from under the condemnation—the scourge and judgement (see D&C 84:54-58). . . . I bless you with increased understanding of the Book of Mormon. I promise you that from this moment forward, if we will daily sup from its pages and abide by its precepts, God will pour out upon each child of Zion and the Church a blessing hitherto unknown."

Ezra Taft Benson (Conference Report, Apr. 1986)

"He [Pres. Benson] has spoken prophetically and wonderfully on many things, but his most oft-repeated message to the people of the Church has been, 'Read the Book of Mormon.' Why? Because he knows that the reading of this sacred testament will bring us closer to God and that there is no greater need among us than this. Could there be a call from a prophet more timely than this call? One need only look at the filth and rot that are sweeping over the world in the form of pornographic movies, pornographic videocassettes, pornographic television, to see the need for a great and powerful and moving counter-force for righteousness."

Gordon B. Hinckley (Ensign, May 1992, p. 53)

Jacob 1~3

Jacob 1:7	**ENTER INTO HIS REST**

(D&C 84:24; refer in this text to Alma 37:34; Moro. 7:3)

PROVOCATION IN THE DAYS OF TEMPTATION
(Jacob 1:7 JST Deut. 10:1-2; JST Ex. 34:1; Psalm 95:10-11; Heb. 3-4; D&C 84:19-26)

Jacob 1:8   **SUFFER HIS CROSS**
(JST Matt. 16:25-26; Matt. 10:38; 2 Ne. 9:18; 3 Ne. 12:30)

Jacob 1:13-14   **NEPHITES—LAMANITES**
(Alma 3:10-11; refer in this text to Hel. 11:24)

"The Book of Mormon is careful to specify that the terms Lamanite and Nephite are used in a loose and general sense to designate not racial but political (Moroni 1:9), military (Alma 43:4), religious (4 Nephi 38), and cultural (Alma 53:10,15; 3:10-11) divisions and groupings of people. The Lamanite and Nephite division was tribal rather than racial, each of the main groups representing an amalgamation of tribes that retained their identity (Alma 43:13; 4 Nephi 36)."

Hugh Nibley (Since Cumorah, p. 246)

"Plainly it [Book of Mormon] is meant for us, as it reminds us many times; it is the story of what happened to the Nephites—and we are the Nephites."

Hugh Nibley (Since Cumorah, pp. 390-391)

Jacob 1:18   **PRIESTHOOD AMONG THE NEPHITES**
(Doctrines of Salvation, Smith, 2:236-237; refer in this text to 2 Ne. 5:26;

Promised Messiah, McConkie, p. 412; *New Witness for the Articles of Faith*, McConkie, p. 348)

Jacob 1:19; 2:2; 3:10

THEIR SINS UPON OUR HEADS IF WE DON'T TEACH
(Mosiah 2:27-29; *Journal of Discourses* 20:23; D&C 88:81-82; 93:39; 1 Tim. 5:8; Ezek. 33:6; 3:17-19; Ether 12:37; *Ensign*, Apr. 1992, pp. 60-61; refer in this text to 2 Ne. 4:5-6)

"If you do not magnify your calling, God will hold you responsible for those whom you might have saved had you done your duty. And who of us can afford to be responsible for the delay of eternal life of a human soul? If great joy is the reward of saving one soul, then how terrible must be the remorse of those whose timid efforts have allowed a child of God to go unwarned or unaided . . ."

John Taylor (quoted by Thomas S. Monson, Ensign, May 1992, p. 48)

"President John Taylor said on one occasion, speaking to the brethren of the priesthood: 'If you do not magnify your callings, God will hold you responsible for those you might have saved, had you done your duty.' This is a challenging statement. If I by reason of sins of commission or omission lose what I might have had in the hereafter, I myself must suffer and, doubtless, my loved ones with me. But if I fail in my assignment as a bishop, a stake president, a mission president, or one of the General Authorities of the Church—if any of us fail to teach, lead, direct, and help to save those under our direction and within our jurisdiction, then the Lord will hold us responsible if they are lost as the result of our failure."

Hugh B. Brown (Conference Report, Oct. 1962, p. 84)

"Our youth are not children spiritually; they are well on towards the normal spiritual maturity . . . You do not need to disguise religious truths with a cloak of worldly things; you can bring these truths to them openly, in their natural guise. . . . There is no need for gradual approaches, for 'bed-time' stories, for coddling, for patronizing, or for any of the other childish devices used in efforts to reach those spiritually inexperienced and all but spiritually dead."

J. Reuben Clark, Jr. (The Charted Course of the Church in Education)

Jacob 2:5

I CAN TELL YOU CONCERNING YOUR THOUGHTS
(Luke 9:47; 18:18-24; D&C 6:16; refer in this text to Alma 12:3, 7)

Jacob 2:13-17

PRIDE—RICHES
(D&C 49:20; 52:40; 56:14-16; 104:15-18; Mosiah 4:17-19; Alma 4:6-12; 35:9; 3 Ne. 27:27-32; 4 Ne.1:24-26; Prov. 16:18; 1 Tim. 6:9-10; Rev. 3:15-21;

Luke 12:15-21; *Teachings of the Book of Mormon*, Berrett, pp. 150-154; *Discourses of Brigham Young*, pp. 305-318; refer in this text to 2 Ne. 9:28-30; Alma 1:6; 3 Ne. 6:10-16)

"Pride is the great stumbling block of Zion. . . . Pride is ugly; it says if you succeed I am a failure. . . . Pride is basically competitive in nature, when competition ends, pride ends."

Ezra Taft Benson (Conference Report, Apr. 1989)

"The two groups who seem to have the greatest problem with pride are the learned and the rich."

Ezra Taft Benson (Conference Report, Apr. 1986, p. 6)

"There will come a time, however, in the history of the Saints when they will be tried with peace, prosperity, popularity and riches."

Daniel H. Wells (Journal of Discourses 19:367)

"Continuing with the words of Paul, 'For the love of money is the root of all evil' (1 Tim. 6:10). It is the love of money and the love of those things which money can buy which destroys us. We all need money to supply our needs. But it is the love of it which hurts us, which warps our values, which leads us away from spiritual things and fosters selfishness and greed."

Gordon B. Hinckley (Ensign, May 1997, p. 49)

"Today we are basking in the lap of luxury, in the like of which we have never seen in the history of the world. It would seem that probably this is the most severe test of any we have ever had in the history of the Church."

Harold B. Lee (Address to Church Employees, Dec. 13, 1973)

"The worst fear I have about this people is that they will get rich in this country, forget God and His people, wax fat, and kick themselves out of the Church and go to hell. This people will stand mobbing, robbing, poverty, and all manner of persecution, and be true. But my greater fear . . . is that they cannot stand wealth."

Brigham Young (Life of a Pioneer, James S. Brown, pp. 122-123)

"I have been in homes of rich people. I have never seen any tears of joy shed because of anything they could purchase with their money, but I have been in groups of missionaries and groups of Saints, when for hours at a time there was not a dry eye there; just because the spirit of God was there."

LeGrand Richards (Conference Report, Apr. 1952, pp. 113-114)

"Plato says the honest man is a man who will do right even with the 'ring of Gyges.' Gyges was one of the tyrants, and he had a ring that made you invisible. Now, if you had the ring of Gyges, you could do anything you wanted to because you would be invisible. [Plato warned] That [the ring] shouldn't change your behavior at all. You should do the right thing because it is the right thing—not because it will make you money, bring you financial success, or in the long run dollars and cents."

Hugh Nibley (Semester 3 Transcript, F.A.R.M.S).

"I remember reading the results some time ago of a national survey which attempted to summarize the responses as to what brings happiness. . . . Most people felt money was a significant part of happiness. The author's research, however, indicated that money alone seldom, if ever, resulted in true happiness. . . . It's important to have sufficient money for our needs, but beyond that, money has little to do with true happiness."

W. Eugene Hansen (Ensign, Nov. 1993, p. 81)

Jacob 2:18-19   **THE LORD'S PROGRAM FOR WEALTH**
(3 Ne.13:33; 14:12; D&C 49:20; 52:40; 104:17-18; Matt. 22:39; JST Mark 10:19-26; JST Matt. 6:38; *Lectures on Faith* 6:7)

"Gold does not corrupt man; it is in the motive of acquiring that gold that corruption lies."

David O. McKay (Treasures of Life, pp. 174-175)

Jacob 2:23-28   **PLURAL MARRIAGE**
"I hold the keys of this power in the last days; for there is never but one on earth at a time on whom the power and its keys are conferred; and I have constantly said no man shall have but one wife at a time, unless the Lord directs otherwise."

Teachings of the Prophet Joseph Smith, p. 324

"The most common of these conjectures is that the Church, through plural marriage, sought to provide husbands for its surplus of female members. The implied assumption in this theory, that there have been more female than male members in the Church, is not supported by existing evidence. On the contrary, there seems always to have been more males than females in the Church. . . ."

John A. Widtsoe (Evidences and Reconciliations, pp. 307-309)

"Plural marriage is not essential to salvation or exaltation. Nephi and his people were denied the power to have more than one wife and yet they could gain every blessing in eternity that the Lord ever offered to any people. In our day, the Lord summarized by revelation the whole doctrine of exaltation and predicated it upon the marriage of one man to one woman (D&C 132:1-28). . . . All who pretend or assume to engage in plural marriage in this day, when the one holding the keys has withdrawn the power by which they are performed, are guilty of gross wickedness."

Bruce R. McConkie (Mormon Doctrine, pp.578-579)

Jacob 2:24, 27; 3:5

CONCUBINES
(D&C 132:34-43; Mosiah 11:2, 4)

"In modern times a concubine is a woman who cohabits with a man without being his wife. But from the beginning of creation, all down through the history of God's dealings with his people, including those with the house of Israel, concubines were legal wives married to their husbands in the new and everlasting covenant of marriage (D&C 132:1, 37-39, 65). Anciently they were considered to be secondary wives, that is, wives who did not have the same standing in the caste system then prevailing as did those wives who were not called concubines. There were no concubines connected with the practice of plural marriage in this dispensation, because the caste system which caused some wives to be so designated did not exist."

Bruce R. McConkie (Mormon Doctrine, p. 154)

"By definition, a concubine would be either a woman kept for lewd purposes or a lawful wife of a lower social standing than her husband's other wife or wives (see also Mosiah 11:2). Hagar, plural wife of Abraham, would be an example of the latter, inasmuch as Abraham did only that which he was commanded (D&C 132:37). The offense to which Jacob made reference was the Nephites' consorting either with paramours or with wives improperly taken."

Robert Millet and Joseph McConkie (Doctrinal Commentary on the Book of Mormon, 2:20)

HOW DID THE BRETHREN FEEL TOWARD PLURAL MARRIAGE ?

"(Joseph Smith) . . . knew the commandment of the Almighty to him was to go forward—to set the example, and establish Celestial plural marriage. He knew that he had not only his own prejudices and prepossessions to combat and overcome, but those of the whole Christian world stared him in the face; but God, who is above all, had given the commandment, and he must be obeyed, yet the Prophet hesitated and deferred from time to time, until an angel of God stood by him with a drawn sword, and told him that, unless he moved forward and established plural marriage, his Priesthood would be taken from him and he should be destroyed."

Eliza R. Snow (Biography and Family Record of Lorenzo Snow, pp. 69-70)

"If any man had asked me what was my choice when Joseph Smith revealed the doctrine, . . . I would have said, 'let me have but one wife.' . . . It was the first time in my life that I desired the grave, and I could hardly get over it for a long time."

Brigham Young (Comprehensive History of the Church, ed. by B. H. Roberts, 2:201-203)

"I had always entertained the strict ideas of virtue, and I felt as a married man that this was to me, outside of this principle, an appalling thing to do. The idea of going and asking a young lady to be married to me when I had already a wife! I had always entertained the strictest regard of chastity. . . . With the feelings I had entertained, nothing but a knowledge of God, and the revelations of God, and the truth of them, could have induced me to embrace such a principle as this."

John Taylor (The Life of John Taylor, Roberts, p.100)

BACKGROUND READING CONCERNING PLURAL MARRIAGE

Answers to Gospel Questions, Smith, 4:213-214
A Comprehensive History of the Church, Roberts, 2:93-110
A Companion to Your Study of the Doctrine & Covenants, Ludlow, 1:659-669
D&C Official Declaration #1, p.291-293
Mormon Doctrine, McConkie, p.577-579
Life of Heber C. Kimball, Whitney, p. 323-328
Mary Fielding Smith, Corbett, pp. 152-154

Jacob 3:4   **PROPHESY OF ANOTHER NEPHITE SPLIT**
(Omni 1:12-19)

Jacob 3:5,7   **LAMANITES MORE RIGHTEOUS THAN NEPHITES**
(2 Ne. 4:5; Hel. 6:36; 7:24; 15:7-11)

Jacob 3:10   **NEGATIVE EXAMPLE OF THE FATHERS**
(Jacob 2:31, 35; D&C 93:40-50; 1 Sam. 3:13; Col. 3:20; Eph. 6:4; Prov. 15:18; Mosiah 25:12; Moses 7:37)

"Consider this sobering forecast: 'About 40 percent of U.S. children will go to sleep in homes in which their fathers do not live' (David Blankenhorn). Some estimate this will rise to 60 percent. This same commentator has written, 'Fatherlessness is the engine driving our most urgent social problems, from crime to adolescent pregnancy to domestic violence' (ibid.). Such outcomes, brothers and sisters, unfortunately, constitute America's grossest national product, produced in the slums of the spirit created by spreading secularism!"

Neal A. Maxwell (Ensign, May 1995, p. 67)

Jacob 4~7

Jacob 4:1   **DIFFICULTY OF ENGRAVING UPON PLATES**
(Morm. 9:33-34; 3 Ne. 5:18; 1 Ne. 1:2; *Book of Mormon Authorship*, BYU
Religious Studies Center, p. 106)

Jacob 4:5   **THE LAW OF MOSES—POINTING OUR SOULS TO CHRIST**
(Mosiah 13:29-30; Alma 25:15-16; 34:13-14)

Jacob 4:6-7   **OUR WEAKNESS & THE POWER OF THE LORD**
(refer in this text to Ether 12:26-27)

Jacob 4:12   **WHY NOT SPEAK OF THE ATONEMENT OF CHRIST?**
(Mosiah 13:33-35; Ether 13:2-14; Alma 12:30-33; 18:36-39, 22:12-14)

"'Why not speak of the atonement of Christ?' (Jacob 4:12). Brothers and sisters,
given man's true self-interest, why should we really speak much of anything else?"

Neal A. Maxwell (Ensign, Nov. 1986, pp. 52-54, 59)

Jacob 4:13   **THE SPIRIT SPEAKETH TRUTH AND LIETH NOT**

"When President Elaine Jack was called in 1990, and Chieko Okazaki and I
became her counselors, we humbly sought to be instruments . . . for our sisters
throughout the world. We were well aware that their circumstances vary greatly. . . . We centered on Jacob chapter 4, verse 13. . . . We knew that women
struggling to clarify their identities could best do that not by comparing themselves to other women but by understanding their important place as full and
equal partners with men in receiving, in righteousness, the saving ordinances
established by Christ. We saw that men and women are baptized, are offered
the gift of the Holy Ghost, partake of the sacrament, and make sacred

covenants in the temples of the Church in exactly the same ways. We would not try to describe an ideal Mormon woman. We would seek instead to teach that Christ is our model and that as we are filled with his love, we are his disciples."

Aileen H. Clyde (Ensign, Nov. 1993, p. 92)

Jacob 4:13   **THINGS AS THEY REALLY ARE . . . AS THEY REALLY WILL BE**
"The temple is the matchless setting for receiving priesthood blessings. . . . Priesthood authority assures that the covenants we make in the temple are everlasting. . . . When we attend the temple, we are blessed with knowledge of 'things as they really are and of things as they really will be' (Jacob 4:13)."

Elaine L. Jack (Ensign, Nov. 1996, pp. 77-78)

Jacob 4:14   **LOOKING BEYOND THE MARK**
(Titus 3:9; 2 Tim. 4:2-4; 1 Tim. 1:4)

"They were apparently afflicted with a pseudosophistication and a snobbishness that gave them a false sense of superiority over those who came among them with the Lord's words of plainness. . . . They must have reveled in speculative and theoretical matters that obscured for them the fundamental spiritual truths. . . . There are other ways in which many of us often look beyond the mark. Sometimes we focus too much of our attention and energy upon our temporal wants, not only to entertain ourselves and gratify our physical appetites, but also to gain recognition, position, and power. We can become so consumed by the pursuit of these things that we sacrifice the sweetness and enduring peace of mind that are found in spiritual well-being, in well-nurtured family relationships, and in the love and respect of friends and associates."

Dean L. Larsen (Conference Report, Oct. 1987, pp. 12-13)

"We are 'looking beyond the mark' (Jacob 4:14), therefore, when, figuratively speaking, we are more interested in the physical dimensions of the cross than what was achieved thereon by Jesus. Or, when we neglect Alma's words of faith because we are too fascinated by the light-shielding hat reportedly used by Joseph Smith during some of the translating of the Book of Mormon."

Neal A. Maxwell (First Nephi, The Doctrinal Foundation, BYU Religious Studies Center, p. 5)

"So many times young people are enticed to go to the very edge or even beyond it. With only a precarious toehold, it is easy to be seriously injured or even die.

Life is too precious to throw away in the name of excitement, or, as Jacob said in the Book of Mormon, 'looking beyond the mark.' You young people may think that you are indestructible and that you are going to live forever. In a few years you will learn that this is not so. . . . Of even more danger is to put your souls at risk by dabbling in drugs or other mind-abusing substances to 'get a buzz.' Some of you may think that you will discover your strengths and abilities by living on the edge. . . . Your strengths and identity will come from honoring your priesthood, developing your talents, and serving the Lord."

James E. Faust (Ensign, Nov. 1995, pp. 45-46)

Jacob 4:18   **ANXIETY**
(D&C10:4; 101:16; Heb. 12:1; refer in this text to Mosiah 4:27; 3 Ne. 11:3-5; *Psycho-Cybernetics*, Maltz, p. 143)

"You absolutely cannot feel angry, fearful, anxious, insecure, unsafe as long as your muscles remain perfectly relaxed."

Maxwell Maltz (Psycho-Cybernetics, p. 176)

"In today's overloaded society, some of the healing agents that our parents enjoyed seem not to be at work in our lives. Fewer and fewer are able to relieve stress by working with their hands and by tilling the soil. The increasing demands, the diversity of voices, the entreating sales pitches, the piercing noises, the entanglement of many personal relationships can rob our soul of the peace they need to function and survive. Our hurry to meet the relentless demands of the clock tears away at our inner peace. The pressures to compete and survive are great. Our appetite for personal possessions seems enormous. The increasing forces that destroy the individual and family bring great sadness and heartbreak."

James E. Faust (Ensign, May 1992, p. 6)

"Only as we seek to be purged of selfishness and of concern for recognition and wealth can we find some sweet relief from the anxieties, hurts, pains, miseries, and concerns of this world."

James E. Faust (Ensign, May 1995, p. 63)

"In this school environment, you are not immune from pressures which relate to schoolwork—tensions and problems—and the long list of attendant emotionally-oriented difficulties and disorders—insecurity, worry, stress, confusion, dependency, suspicion, withdrawal, fear . . . If you happen to hit a good sorry mood once in a while, relax and enjoy it—it is a good sign that you are normal. It is all right to worry about things now and again, I suppose, but when you get worried about being worried, that is when you are getting off the track."

Boyd K. Packer (BYU Devotional, Oct. 4, 1966, pp. 3, 6)

CHAPTER 5   **JACOB'S ATTEMPT TO ANSWER THE QUESTION HE POSES IN 4:17**
"I have a key by which I understand the scriptures. I enquire, what was the question which drew out the answer. . . ."

Teachings of the Prophet Joseph Smith, p. 276

Jacob 5   **THE ALLEGORY OF ZENOS**
(Book of Mormon Symposium 1986, Fowles, pp. 29-36; *Messiah in Ancient America,* Warren and Ferguson, p. 285-293;   Book of Mormon 121-122 Student Manual, pp. 47-49; *Answers to Gospel Questions,* Smith, 4:138-142; *To Learn with Joy,* ed. by Nyman & Tate, pp. 87-102)

"Olive trees do have to be pruned and cultivated diligently; the top branches are indeed the first to wither, and the new shoots do come right out of the trunk; the olive is indeed the most plastic of trees, surpassing even the willow in its power to survive the most drastic whacking and burning; a good olive tree is greatly cherished, and no end of pains are taken to preserve it even through many centuries, for really superior fruit is very rare and difficult to obtain and perpetuate; the ancient way of strengthening the old tree (especially in Greece) was to graft in the shoots of the oleaster or wild olive; also, shoots from valuable old trees were transplanted to keep the stock alive after the parent tree should perish; to a surprising degree the olive prefers poor and rocky ground, whereas rich soil produces inferior fruit; too much grafting produces a nondescript and cluttered yield of fruit; the top branches if allowed to grow as in Spain and France, while producing a good shade tree, will indeed sap the strength of the tree and give a poor crop; fertilizing with dung is very important, in spite of the preference for rocky ground, and has been practised since ancient times; the thing to be most guarded against is bitterness in the fruit. All these points . . . are duly, though quite casually, noted in Zenos's Parable of the Olive Tree."

Hugh Nibley (Since Cumorah, pp. 269-270)

"But we have something in the Book of Mormon that, if we did not have any other truth expressed in it, would be sufficient evidence of the divinity of this book. I have reference to the fifth chapter of Jacob. . . . I think that as many as ninety-nine out of every hundred who read the Book of Mormon, read this parable through without grasping the fulness and meaning of it. And I think this is one of the greatest passages in the Book of Mormon. . . . No matter how many times you have read the Book of Mormon, . . . take a few minutes at some convenient time and sit down and just read carefully every word in the fifth chapter of the Book of Jacob. . . . No greater parable was ever recorded. . . . I tell you, my brothers and sisters, Joseph Smith did not write it. That was written by the inspiration of the Almighty. . . .When you read that chapter through if you cannot say in your soul, 'this is absolutely a revelation from God,' then there is something wrong with you."

Joseph Fielding Smith (Answers to Gospel Questions, 4:203-207)

". . . Israel is a tame olive tree. It is an olive tree that begins to decay. The branches that are dying are cut off. But the gardener takes certain of those branches off that tree that seem to be decaying and plants them in all parts of the Lord's vineyard. And the Lord says, 'I will take these branches and plant them in the distant parts of my vineyard. Have my servants attend to them. The old tree seems to be dying and we shall see if we can't take these severed branches and raise fruit.' Not only that, but they took some of the branches and grafted them in to all the wild olive trees. Who were the wild olive trees? The Gentiles. And so the Lord sent his servants to all parts of this vineyard, which is the world, and planted these branches of the tree. As they grew, they bore fruit. In the course of time, some of these branches began to wither and decay. And the Lord nurtured them. He had his servants dig around them, cultivate them, care for them the best they knew how, and yet some of them practically died. Others bore fruit. Then comes the time of the harvest. The Lord says, 'I will cultivate my field for the last time. These branches that I have taken to various parts of the world are dying. I'll gather the fruit and do the best I can with them.' . . . the House of Israel, . . . in its native land . . . began to die. So the Lord took branches like the Nephites, like the lost tribes, and like others that the Lord led off that we do not know anything about, to other parts of the earth. He planted them all over his vineyard, which is the world. No doubt he sent some of these branches into Japan, into Korea, into China. No question about it, because he sent them to all parts of the world. . . . What's the use of going out among the Chinese, the Japanese, the Koreans, and the people of the Far East to preach the gospel to them? The answer: because they are branches of the tree, they are of the house of Israel. The Lord took the branches of the tree, grafted them into the wild olives, the Gentiles, and is bringing the Gentiles into the gospel of Jesus Christ. . . . Are we going to preach the gospel in Korea, in Japan, in China? Yes, we are. Why? Because the blood of Israel is there. . . . [The Lord] scattered [Israel] over the whole face of the earth. So now the Gentiles are sanctified by the blood of Abraham."

Joseph Fielding Smith (Answers to Gospel Questions, 4:203-207)

JACOB	SYMBOLS	EXPLANATION
5:3	Vineyard	(Jacob 6:3)
5:3	Tame Olive Tree	(Jacob 5:3)
5:4	Master of the Vineyard	(D&C 104:86)
5:6	Main Top	(Footnote 6a)
5:7	Wild Olive Tree	(Roman 11:13, 17, 19)
5:7	Servant	(Amos 3:7; D&C 1:38)

JACOB	EVENTS	EXPLANATION
5:3	Decay of tame olive tree	(Footnote 3d)
5:8	Take away many of these young and tender branches	(Footnote 8a)
5:9	Graft in the branches of wild olive tree	(1 Ne.10:14;15:13; 2 Ne. 30:2)
5:14	Hid branches of tame olive tree in nethermost parts of the vineyard.	(Hosea 8:8; 1 Ne. 10:12; 15:12; 22:3-4)
5:17	Fruit born following the grafting of the wild olive branches	(Gal. 3:7-9, 29)
5:24-25	Planted natural branches in a good spot of ground	(Footnote 25a; Alma 26:36)
5:25	Part of the tree hath brought forth tame fruit	(Jacob 5:45; Hel.15:3)
5:25	Part of the tree hath brought forth wild fruit	(Jacob 5:45; Hel. 15:4)
5:29	A long time passed . . . the Lord . . . said unto his servant	(D&C: 103:21)

JACOB	EVENTS	EXPLANATION
5:32	The wild branches have produced fruit, "there is none of it which is good."	(JS-H. 1:19)
5:43	This last that "I did plant in a good spot of ground."	(Jacob 5:25)
5:44	"Cut down that which cumbered this spot of ground."	(Footnote 44a)
5:45	"They have overcome the good branch"	(Morm. 8:2)
5:48	How could the branches have overcome the roots?	(Footnote 48a)
5:52	Graft branches back into tame olive-tree	(1 Ne. 10:14)
5:61-62; 6:2	"Call servants that we might labor"	(D&C 24:19; 88:84; Larsen, Conf. Report, Apr. 1983, p. 33)
5:72, 74-75	What makes missionaries successful?	(Jacob 6:3)
5:77	"Evil fruit shall again come into my vineyard"	(*Answers to Gospel Questions*, Smith, 4:206; *"That means there will be some apostasy."*)

JACOB 6

JACOB'S COMMENTARY CONCERNING THE ALLEGORY OF ZENOS

Jacob 6:10

FIRE AND BRIMSTONE
(refer in this text to 2 Ne. 9:16)

Jacob 6:11

THE STRAIT GATE
(refer in this text to 2 Ne. 31:17-18; 1 Ne. 8:20)

Jacob 6:12

BE WISE
"I carry in my daily date book a few brief memo sheets. . . . One sheet almost worn out now has nothing more on it than Jacob 6, verse 12: 'O be wise; what can I say more?' Be wise enough to accept appropriate discipline and guidelines. Be wise enough to say the right words at the right time to the right person. . . . Ever bear in mind that Jesus was the wisest of the wise, even brilliant, in his relationships with people. . . . President Spencer W. Kimball, on one occasion a few years ago asked me to accompany him to the Utah State Prison. . . . I learned much from a prophet who

was wise. . . . We were greeted by the warden and taken to his office. . . . Two inmates were invited to come in and meet with us. They were in their prison garb and looked hard. I felt very uneasy when the steel door closed behind them and we were left with the two of them. . . . President Kimball shook their hands before we all sat down. This was followed by a brief period of intense silence. The prisoners were looking at the floor. President Kimball was looking at them, and I was looking at him. After this awkward period of silence was over, President Kimball started off with what seemed to me to an unusual approach. The thought crossed my mind that he could say: 'What are you in here for? Why did you do it? When do you get out? You ought to be ashamed of yourselves,' or 'What is your previous record?' . . . He looked at the one, and said to my surprise: 'Tell me about your mother.' The prisoner responded and told President Kimball and others of us assembled about his mother. . . . President Kimball finally looked at the other prisoner and said: 'What does your father do for a living?' He too responded with comments, and the Prophet gave complete attention and listened intently. . . . They looked at him, responded, and looked in his face while he gently listened. . . . Word had spread that President Spencer W. Kimball was at the prison visiting, and some of the media were outside the doors waiting for pictures and conversation with President Kimball. [He] . . . invited some of the press into the room with a cameraman. One reporter said, 'President Kimball, we'd like to have a picture of you talking to these two inmates.' President Kimball granted the interview by standing up promptly and getting between the two prisoners as the picture was taken. I recall as though it were yesterday what he said after the picture was taken. He shook one hand and then the other and said, 'Thank you, boys, for letting me have my picture taken with you.' One of these hardened prisoners was in for murder and the other one for grand larceny. To say they were touched and responsive is an understatement. I will never forget the impact of this visit upon me and my future. A wise, gentle prophet conducted his interview without embarrassment, without ridicule, and without condemnation . . . interviewing, counseling, instructing, and touching lives with wisdom."

Marvin J. Ashton (BYU University Conference, Aug. 24-25, 1992)

Jacob 7	**SHEREM: AN ANTI-CHRIST** (*Studies in Scripture*, Jackson, 7:180-182; refer to Korihor lesson in this text Alma 30)
Jacob 7:19	**THE UNPARDONABLE SIN** (*Companion to Your Study of the Book of Mormon*, Ludlow, pp. 162-163; refer to "Deny the Holy Ghost" in this text Alma 39:5-6)
Jacob 7:27	**ADIEU** (*Companion to Your Study of the Book of Mormon*, Ludlow, p. 163)

Enos ~ Words of Mormon

Enos 1:1-3

PARENTAL RESPONSIBILITY
(1 Ne. 1:1; 2:16; 11:1-5; Mosiah 1:2; Alma 36:16-19; Hel. 5:5; Eph. 6:4; *Conference Report*, Apr. 1965, p. 60-61; *Conference Report*, Apr. 1929, p. 110; *Doctrines of Salvation*, Smith, 2:90-91; *Ensign*, July 1973, p. 98; *Eternal Families*, ed. by Brinley & Judd, pp. 90-101; refer in this text to 2 Ne. 4:5-6; Mosiah 25:12; Alma 56:47-48)

"Sometimes as I go throughout the Church, I think I am seeing a man who is using his church work as a kind of escape from family responsibility. And sometimes when we've talked about whether or not he's giving attention to his family, his children and his wife, he says something like this: 'Well I'm so busy taking care of the Lord's work that I really don't have time.' And I say to him, 'My dear brother, the greatest of the Lord's work that you and I will ever do is the work that we do within the walls of our own home.' Now don't you get any misconception about where the Lord's work starts. That's the most important of all the Lord's work. And you wives may have to remind your husbands of that occasionally. That here in the home—family home night—you must see to it that all the principles are involved so that father takes his place and doesn't neglect the children."

Harold B. Lee (Address to Seminary and Institute Personnel, BYU, July 8, 1966)

"In the divine scheme every soul has been given a father whose responsibility is not only to sire and provide the necessities of life, but also to train for mortality and life eternal. Undoubtedly Sariah cooperated with Lehi, but it was the father who called his family together to teach them righteousness. The teaching of the children by the fathers is basic from the beginning. The Lord ordained it so. Though Enos had strayed for a time, the teachings of his father prevailed, and he returned to worthiness."

Spencer W. Kimball (Conference Report, Apr. 1965, pp. 61-62)

"No other success can compensate for failure in the home."

David O. McKay (Improvement Era, June 1964, p. 445)

"We emphasize that the greatest work you will do will be within the walls of your home. . . . It is not uncommon for responsible parents to lose one of their children, for a time, to influences over which they have no control. They agonize over rebellious sons or daughters. They are puzzled over why they are so helpless when they have tried so hard to do what they should. It is my conviction that those wicked influences one day will be overruled. 'The Prophet Joseph Smith declared—and he never taught a more comforting doctrine—that the eternal sealings of faithful parents and the divine promises made to them for valiant service in the Cause of Truth, would save not only themselves, but likewise their posterity. Though some of the sheep may wander, the eye of the Shepherd is upon them, and sooner or later they will feel the tentacles of Divine Providence reaching out after them and drawing them back to the fold. Either in this life or the life to come, they will return. They will have to pay their debt to justice; they will suffer for their sins; and may tread a thorny path; but if it leads them at last, like the penitent Prodigal, to a loving and forgiving father's heart and home, the painful experience will not have been in vain. Pray for your careless and disobedient children; hold on to them with your faith. Hope on, trust on, till you see the salvation of God.' (Orson F. Whitney, *Conference Report,* April 1929, p. 110) . . .When parents keep the covenants they have made at the altar of the temple, their children will be forever bound to them. President Brigham Young said [Discourses of Brigham Young, p. 208]: 'Let the father and mother, who are members of this Church and Kingdom, take a righteous course, and strive with all their might never to do a wrong, but to do good all their lives; if they have one child or one hundred children go, they are bound up to their parents by an everlasting tie, and no power of earth or hell can separate them from their parents in eternity; they will return again to the fountain from whence they sprang.'"

Boyd K. Packer (Ensign, May 1992, p. 68)

"An ancient grandmother lived with her daughter and grandson. As she grew frail and feeble, instead of being a help around the house, she became a constant trial. She broke plates and cups, lost knives, spilled water. One day, exasperated because the old woman had broken another precious plate, the daughter sent the grandson to buy his grandmother a wooden plate. The boy hesitated because he knew a wooden plate would humiliate his grandmother. But his mother insisted, so off he went. He returned bringing not one, but two wooden plates.

'I only asked you to buy one,' his mother said. 'Didn't you hear me?' 'Yes,' said the boy. 'But I bought the second one so there would be one for you when you get old.'"

Thomas S. Monson (Ensign, May 1993, p. 62)

"God has placed within us a will, and we should be satisfied to have it controlled by the will of the Almighty. . . . It has been the custom of parents to break the will until it is weakened, and the noble, God-like powers of the child are reduced to a comparative state of imbecility and cowardice. Let that heaven-born property of human agents be properly tempered and wisely directed, instead of pursuing the opposite course, and it will conquer in the cause of right. Break not the spirit of any person, . . . until God shall reign within us to will and do his good pleasure."

Discourses of Brigham Young, p. 264

Enos 1:4

PRAYER—HUNGER—REAL INTENT
(Moro. 7:9; 10:4; *Miracle of Forgiveness*, Kimball, p. 211)

"I have been driven many times to my knees by the overwhelming conviction that I had nowhere else to go."

Abraham Lincoln (as quoted in A Nation Asleep, Benson, p. 42)

"To those of us who would pay pennies toward our unfathomable debt, we remember Enos, who, like many of us, had great need. Like many sons of good families he strayed. How heinous were his sins I do not know, but they must have been grievous. . . . Here is no casual prayer; here no trite, worn phrases; here no momentary appeal. All the day long, with seconds turning into minutes, and minutes into hours, and hours into an 'all day long.' But when the sun had set, relief had still not come, for repentance is not a single act nor forgiveness an unearned gift. So precious to him was communication with, and approval of, his Redeemer that his determined soul pressed on without ceasing. . . . Could the Redeemer resist such determined imploring? How many of you have thus persisted? How many of you, with or without serious transgressions, have ever prayed all day and into the night? Have you ever wept and prayed for many hours? How many of you have prayed for five hours? for one? for thirty minutes? for ten?"

Spencer W. Kimball (BYU Speeches of the Year, Oct. 11, 1961, pp. 8-9)

"In answer to my first prayer, no answer came. The faith was there, I felt, to the extent that I could exert it. The need was there, I felt certainly no doubt about that, but was the worthiness? I could always think of something, as I prayed night after night without an answer, . . . and so I continued to pray, feeling that when I could make myself worthy of an answer, I would get it. It was after I had been praying nightly for five years that the whole family . . . attended a Sunday School entertainment. My class rendered its number, followed by another that sang, and I remember some of the words of that song: 'Keep on asking, God will answer by and by.' To me that was a revelation. I kept on praying. Some four years later, in the latter part of the month of August, 1887, in my nineteenth year, after I had been praying nightly for nine long years with all the earnestness of my soul for this special blessing, I was alone in the bedroom, and I said, half aloud, 'O Father, wilt thou not hear me?' I was beginning to get discouraged. Then, brethren, something happened. the most glorious experience that I have received came. In answer to my question I heard as distinctly as anything I ever heard in my life the short, simple word: 'Yes.' Simultaneously my whole being, from the crown of my head to the soles of my feet, was filled with the most joyous feeling of elation, of peace and certainty that I could imagine a human being could experience. I sprang from my knees, and jumped as high as I could, and shouted: 'O Father, I thank thee.' At last an answer had come. I knew it."

Joseph F. Merrill (Conference Report, Apr. 1944, pp. 151-152)

"I have a longtime friend. . . . Occasionally, to find relief from the stress of his responsibilities, he would partake of substances forbidden by the Word of Wisdom. As the stress in his life increased, so did his consumption of alcohol. Indeed, he was becoming a prisoner to alcohol. One afternoon he felt the enticing of the Spirit prompting him to overcome this addiction. . . . He . . . drove to a very secluded spot far removed from the city. There he knelt in humble prayer and pled with the Lord with all the energy of his heart for added strength to overcome this addiction, which robbed his spirituality and threatened to destroy his very soul. He remained on his knees for a very long time, and eventually a sweet, purifying spirit began to distill upon his soul, cleansing him from any desire to drink and fortifying him with a firm resolve to keep the commandments. A spiritually sensitive bishop noticed a change in my friend and extended a call for him to work with the young Aaronic Priesthood brethren of the ward. He was a natural, enthusiastic leader of youth, and about a year later he was called to be the new bishop, dearly loved by all . . ."

Spencer H. Condie (Ensign, Nov. 1993, p. 16)

Enos 1:5, 10   **THE VOICE OF THE LORD CAME INTO MY MIND**
(1 Ne. 17:45; 3 Ne. 11:3-5; Hel. 5:29-33; 1 Kings 19:12-13; D&C 6:23; 8:2-3; 88:1, 66:97:1; *Teachings of the Prophet Joseph Smith*, p. 151)

"We do not have the words (even the scriptures do not have words) which perfectly describe the Spirit. The scriptures generally use the word voice, which does not exactly fit. These delicate, refined spiritual communications are not seen with our eyes, nor heard with our ears. And even though it is described as a voice, it is a voice that one feels, more than one hears."

Boyd K. Packer (Ensign, Jan. 1983, p. 52)

"Thus the Lord, by revelation, brings into our mind as though a voice were speaking. May I bear humble testimony, if I may be pardoned, to that fact? I was once in a situation where I needed help. The Lord knew I needed help and I was on an important mission. I was awakened in the hours of the morning as though someone had wakened me to straighten me out on something that I had planned to do in a contrary course, and there was clearly mapped out before me as I lay there that morning, just as surely as though someone had sat on the edge of my bed and told me what to do. Yes, the voice of the Lord comes into our minds and we are directed thereby."

Harold B. Lee (BYU Speeches of the Year, Oct. 15, 1952)

"Sometimes the Lord puts thoughts in our minds in answer to prayers. . . . [He] gives us peace in our minds."

Marion G. Romney (Taiwan Area Conference, 1975, p. 7)

Enos 1:10   **I WILL VISIT ACCORDING TO THEIR KEEPING THE COMMANDMENTS**
(D&C 82:10; 130:20-21)

"'I will visit thy brethren according to their diligence in keeping my commandments. . . .' There you have, in simple language, a great principle: It isn't the Lord who withholds himself from us. It is we who withhold ourselves from him because of our failure to keep his commandments."

Harold B. Lee (Conference Report, Oct. 1966, p. 117)

"When you received your confirmation, you were commanded to receive the Holy Ghost. He was not obligated to seek you out. . . . If our lives are responsive and clean, if we are reaching and cultivating, the Holy Ghost will come, and we may retain him and have the peace his presence thus affords."

Spencer W. Kimball (BYU Speeches of the Year, Oct. 1961, p. 7)

Enos 1:2, 9, 13   **THE PROGRESSIVE DIMENSIONS OF PRAYER**
(The Ten Most Wanted Men, Dunn, pp. 13-15)

"Very often the Twelve and the First Presidency pray together. When President Kimball takes his turn to be voice, he generally includes this phrase in his prayers: 'Bless our enemies. Help us to understand them, and them to understand us.' He doesn't ask for vengeance or retaliation, just for understanding so differences can be resolved. Perhaps, family differences and neighborhood problems could be resolved if we would follow our prophet's example and pray for patience and forgiveness."

Marvin J. Ashton (Conference Report, Apr. 1985, p. 59)

Enos 1:13-18   **THE IMPORTANCE OF SCRIPTURE**
(D&C 3:19-20; 10:46-51; 1 Ne. 4:12-13, 17; Omni 1:14, 17)

Enos 1:21   **A SOCIETY IN TRANSITION**
(contrast with Jarom 1:8)

Enos 1:27   **IN CHRIST I WILL FIND REST**
(Matt. 11:28-30)

"Peace in this world always comes after the receiver has done the works of righteousness. . . . This is the way peace comes in this world. It can be obtained no other way. The promised peace . . . emanates from Christ. He is the source of it. His spirit is the essence of it."

Marion G. Romney (Conference Report, Apr. 1967, pp. 80-82)

Jarom 1:5   **SABBATH DAY**
(Mosiah 13:16-19; 18:23; Ex. 20:8-11; D&C 59:9-13; Neh. 10:31; Isa. 58:13-14; Moses 3:3; Gen. 2:2-3)

"We have become a nation of pleasure-seeking Sabbath breakers."

Ezra Taft Benson (A Nation Asleep, p. 44)

"There isn't anybody in this Church who has to buy furniture on Sunday. . . . There isn't anybody in this Church who has to buy a new automobile on Sunday. . . . There isn't anybody in this Church who, with a little care and planning, has to buy groceries on Sunday. . . . I don't think we need to patronize the ordinary business merchants on the Sabbath day. Why do they stay open? To get customers. Who are those customers? Well, they are not all nonmembers of this Church."

Gordon B. Hinckley (Heber City/Springville, Utah, Regional Conference, Priesthood Leadership Meeting, May 13, 1995)

"The Sabbath of the Lord is becoming the play day of the people. It is a day of golf and football on television, of buying and selling in our stores and markets. Are we moving to mainstream America as some observers believe? In this I fear we are. What a telling thing it is to see the parking lots of the markets filled on Sunday in communities that are predominantly LDS. Our strength for the future, our resolution to grow the Church across the world, will be weakened if we violate the will of the Lord in this important matter."

Gordon B. Hinckley (Ensign, Nov. 1997, p. 69)

"What fits the purpose of the Sabbath? Here are a few suggestions: Activities that contribute to greater spirituality; essential Church meetings in the house of prayer; acquisition of spiritual knowledge—reading the scriptures, Church history and biographies, and the inspired words of the Brethren; resting physically, getting acquainted with the family, relating scriptural stories to children, bearing testimonies, building family unity; visiting the sick and aged shut-ins; singing the songs of Zion and listening to inspired music; paying devotions to the Most High—personal and family prayer; fasting, administrations, father's blessings; preparing food with singleness of heart—simple meals prepared largely on Saturday. . . . I don't believe that it is possible to keep our spirituality on a high plane by spending our Sabbaths on the beach, on the golf course, . . . or in our own homes . . . looking at television."

Teachings of Ezra Taft Benson, p. 439

"The Lord said: 'Remember the Sabbath day, to keep it holy' (Ex. 20:8) and made Sabbath day observance a sign between Him and the people to indicate their obedience. (See Ex. 31:13-17). That commandment and sign have never been rescinded. In our day, standards for keeping the Sabbath day holy are lowered a little at a time by some individuals until practically anything seems to become acceptable. The sign between the Lord and His covenant people is

trampled underfoot as Church members skip Sunday meetings to seek recreation at lakes and beaches, in the mountains, at sports arenas, and at theaters.
Parking lots at supermarkets and discount stores often are full on Sundays.
Many store owners feel compelled to open their doors on Sundays because of
the demand for the merchandise and services. The people who misuse the
Sabbath lose the blessings of spiritual food and growth promised to those who
keep this commandment."

Joseph B. Wirthlin (Ensign, Mar. 1993, p. 71)

"In Hebrews the term Sabbath means 'rest.' . . . The Sabbath day is given
throughout the generations of man for a perpetual covenant. It is a sign between
the Lord and his children forever. . . . It is a day not for lavish banqueting but
a day of simple meals and spiritual feasting; . . . a day when maid and mistress
might be relieved from the preparation. . . . A day when employer and employee, master and servant may be free from plowing, digging, toiling. It is a day
when the office may be locked and business postponed, and troubles forgotten.
. . . A day to study the scriptures, . . . a day to nap and rest and relax, a day to
visit the sick, a day to preach the gospel, a day to proselyte, a day to visit quietly
with the family and get acquainted with our children, a day for proper courting, a day to do good. . . . The Savior . . . recognized also that the ox might get
into the mire or the ass fall into the pit; but neither in the letter nor in the spirit did he ever approve the use of the Sabbath for ordinary and regular work or
for amusements and play."

Teachings of Spencer W. Kimball, pp. 215-216

"Members of The Church of Jesus Christ of Latter-day Saints recognize Sunday
as the Sabbath in commemoration of the fact that Christ came forth from the
grave on Sunday, and the Apostles commenced meeting thereafter on the first
day of the week (see John 20:1-6; Luke 24:1; Mark 16:1; Matt. 28:1; Acts 20:7).
. . . Let's not shop on Sunday. One way we avoid this is by planning ahead. Fill
up the gas tank on Saturday. Acquire the needed groceries for the weekend on
Saturday. Don't you be the means of causing someone to work on Sunday
because you patronize their establishment. . . . The justification for and reason
often cited by the owners and operators of such businesses is to be competitive,
to conform to corporate policy, and so on. I well remember an interview
President Spencer W. Kimball once had with a faithful Church member. It went
like this: 'What is your occupation?' And [the man] said, 'I operate a service station.' And I asked, 'Do you operate on the Sabbath?' His answer was, 'No, I do
not.' 'Well, how can you get along? Most service station operators seem to think

they must open on the Sabbath.' 'I get along well,' he said. 'The Lord is good to me.' 'Do you not have stiff competition?' I asked. 'Yes, indeed,' he replied. 'Across the street is a man who keeps open all day Sunday.' 'And you never open?' I asked. 'No, sir,' he said, 'and I am grateful, and the Lord is kind, and I have sufficient for my needs' *(Teachings of Spencer W. Kimball*, p. 227). What are the promises and blessings of the Lord to those who honor the Sabbath day . . . ? The fulness of the earth is yours, the land will be blessed with rain and will yield its increase, there will be peace in the land, and God will magnify His faithful people, have respect for them, and establish His covenant with them (see D&C 59:16-19; Lev. 26:2-6, 9)."

Earl C. Tingey (Ensign, May 1996, p. 10-12)

Jarom 1:9-12   **NEPHI'S FREEDOM THESIS**
(Omni 1:6; Mosiah 1:7; 2:22; refer in this text to 1 Ne. 2:20)

Omni 1:1-3   **I AM A WICKED MAN**
(Ether 10:11)

"All he did was lay his life on the line so that others would be free to make decisions he didn't make."

Marion D. Hanks

Omni 1:12-19   **ANOTHER SPLIT IN THE FAMILY**
(Jacob 3:4)

Omni 1:13,   **NEPHITE DIRECTIONS**
27, 28   (Words of Mormon 1:13; refer in this text to 1 Ne. 3:9)

"The concept of going 'up' when you go north and of going 'down' when you go south is of relatively recent origin, and thus was not used by the Nephites. When the Nephites stated they went from Nephi down to Zarahemla, they were referring to elevation and not to direction. Zarahemla was definitely lower in elevation than Nephi because the river Sidon had its head in the land of Nephi but flowed down through the center of the land of Zarahemla (Alma 16:6-7; 22:27-29)."

Daniel H. Ludlow (Companion to Your Study of the Book of Mormon, p. 169)

Omni 1:17   **THEY BROUGHT NO RECORDS WITH THEM**
(Mosiah 1:3; refer in this text to 1 Ne. 4:12-13)

"The Mulekites, who migrated to the American continent shortly after Lehi and his family left Jerusalem, failed to bring with them any sacred scriptures or records. Omni recorded the condition of a nation without scriptures: [Omni 1:17]. Even more serious than their continuous contentions and wars and the corruption of their language was the tragedy that they did not know the Savior. The pattern is the same for individuals as it is for nations. Without searching the scriptures, they cease to know the Savior."

L. Lionel Kendrick (Ensign, May 1993, p. 14)

WORDS OF MORMON

"The Words of Mormon were apparently written near the end of Mormon's life for the purpose of connecting two major records [large & small plates of Nephi.] . . . So that a gap would not occur in the history of the Nephites, Mormon included the major events of the lifetime of King Benjamin in The Words of Mormon, thus connecting the account on the small plates of Nephi with Mormon's abridgment of the book of Mosiah."

Daniel H. Ludlow (Companion to Your Study of the Book of Mormon, p. 170)

W. of M. 1:3   **I SEARCHED AMONG THE RECORDS**
(Journal of Discourses 19:38)

W. of M. 1:5-7   **FOR A WISE PURPOSE . . . I DO NOT KNOW**
(A New Witness for God, Roberts, 2:384-385)

"At the beginning of the Book of Mormon history, Nephi had been commanded to make two separate sets of plates. After starting what would be known as the large plates of Nephi, he was later commanded to make a set of more religious records, known as the small plates of Nephi. (1 Ne. 9:2,4 and 1:17). After Nephi's death, the large plates remained with the kings down to the time of Mormon, while the small plates went to Jacob and his posterity until the time of Amaleki, who gave them to King Benjamin. Thus the two set of plates were back into the possession of one person. After Mormon had completed his abridgment of five hundred years of Nephite history, he may have been somewhat surprised to find the small plates of Nephi, which largely duplicated his efforts. Instead of keeping only one of the sets of records, Mormon was prompted to include the small plates with his abridgment, without really knowing why.

(See verse 7). He apparently did not know what would happen to his records after they would come into the hands of Joseph Smith. After Joseph Smith received the plates of Mormon, he had completed the translation of 116 pages of manuscript, which comprised Mormon's abridgment from the time of Lehi down to King Benjamin. After the loss of these pages by Martin Harris, the Lord commanded the Prophet to translate further in the plates of Mormon without retranslating the first portion. However, since the small plates contained a more spiritual account of the same time period, the teachings of greatest value were not lost for the readers of the Book of Mormon. In order for this more spiritual record to be available, Nephi first had to start the small plates, and Mormon had to include them with his abridgment. We can be thankful today that Mormon had the courage to follow his spiritual promptings so that these valuable teachings are now part of our contemporary scripture."

Victor L. Ludlow (Studies in Scriptures, ed. by K. Jackson, 7:203)

"At least six times in the Book of Mormon the phrase 'for a wise purpose' is used in reference to the making, writing, and preserving of the small plates of Nephi (see 1 Nephi 9:5; Words of Mormon 1:7; Alma 37:2,12,14,18). We know one such wise purpose—the most obvious one—was to compensate for the loss of the earlier mentioned 116 pages of manuscript. But it strikes me that there is a 'wiser purpose' than that. . . . The key to such a suggestion is in verse 45 of Section 10. . . . He says, 'Behold, there are many things engraven upon the [small] plates of Nephi which do throw *greater views* upon my gospel.' So clearly . . . it was not tit for tat, this for that—you give me 116 pages of manuscript and I'll give you 142 pages of printed text. Not so. We got back more than we lost. And it was known from the beginning that it would be so. We do not know exactly what we missed in the 116 pages, but we do know that what we received on the small plates was the personal declarations of three great witnesses, [Nephi, Jacob, and Isaiah], . . . testifying that Jesus is the Christ. . . . I think you could make a pretty obvious case that the *sole* purpose of the small plates was to give a platform for these three witnesses. After all, their writing constitutes a full 135 pages of what is only a 145-page record."

Jeffrey R. Holland (CES Symposium, BYU, Aug. 9, 1994)

Mosiah 1~8

Mos. 1:1-2   **THIRD PERSON AUTHORSHIP**
"Note that the main story in the book of Mosiah is told in the third person rather than in the first person as was the custom in the earlier books of the Book of Mormon. The reason for this is that someone else is now telling the story and that 'someone else' is Mormon. With the beginning of the book of Mosiah we start our study of Mormon's abridgment of various books that had been written on the large plates of Nephi (3 Nephi 5:8-12). The book of Mosiah and the five books that follow—Alma, Helaman, 3 Nephi, 4 Nephi, and Mormon—were all abridged or condensed by Mormon from the large plates of Nephi, and these abridged versions were written by Mormon on the plates that bear his name, the plates of Mormon. These are the same plates that were given to Joseph Smith by the angel Moroni on September 22, 1827."

Daniel H. Ludlow (Companion to Your Study of the Book of Mormon, p. 173)

Mos. 1:4   **BRASS PLATES—EGYPTIAN**
(1 Ne. 1:2; 3:19; Morm. 9:32-34; *Lehi in the Desert*, Nibley, pp. 13, 26; *Companion to Your Study of the Book of Mormon*, Ludlow, p. 173-174; *Doctrinal Commentary on the Book of Mormon*, Millet and McConkie, 2:130; refer in this text to 1 Ne. 3:19)

Mos. 1:6-7   **PLATES OF NEPHI**
(Words of Mormon 1:5-7)

"It appears the large plates of Nephi were kept and expanded by the kings, but the small plates of Nephi were kept by the prophets, and were not expanded. . . . The first important change that took place at the time of King Benjamin was that the small plates of Nephi became full, and this separate spiritual record was given to King Benjamin for safe keeping (Omni 1:25). . . . A second important change during the time of King Benjamin was that the large plates of Nephi were now used to record both secular and spiritual events. There was no longer a separate spiritual record being kept; therefore preachings, visions, and prophecies, etc., were included in the large plates."

Rex C. Reeve, Jr. (First Nephi, The Doctrinal Foundation, BYU Religious Studies Center, p. 106)

Mos. 1:11-12;   **A NAME GIVEN**
5:8-12   (Hel. 5:6; *Doctrines of Salvation*, Smith, 2:28-29; *Answers to Gospel Questions*, Smith, 3:2-4)

"As his followers, we cannot do a mean or shoddy or ungracious thing without tarnishing his image. Nor can we do a good and gracious and generous act without burnishing more brightly the symbol of him whose name we have taken upon ourselves."

Gordon B. Hinckley (Be Thou An Example, p. 90)

Mos. 1:18   **TEMPLE**
(2 Ne. 5:16; Jacob 1:17; 3 Ne. 11:1,10)

Mos. 2:14   **TAXATION**
"Burdensome, unjust taxation is a form of theft. King Benjamin realized that a government has no more right to steal from its citizens than the citizens have to steal from one another."

Rodney Turner (Studies in Scriptures, ed. by K. Jackson, 7:211)

Mos. 2:16-17   **SERVICE**
(John 13:13-14; 21:15-17; Mark 10:42-44; Matt. 18:12; 20:26-27; 23:12; 25:40; 3 Ne. 12:1; D&C 24:7; 50:26; 81:4-6; Luke 15:4; Ezek. 34:1-10; Prov. 3:27-29; 1 Kings 12:7; 2 Tim. 2:24; *Discourses of Wilford Woodruff*, pp. 123-124; *Conference Report*, Oct. 1948, pp. 47-48; *Conference Report*, Apr. 1985, pp. 56-60; refer in this text to Alma 17:18)

"Continue to seek opportunities for service. Don't be overly concerned with status. Do you recall the counsel of the Savior regarding those who seek the 'chief seats' or the 'uppermost rooms'? 'He that is greatest among you shall be your servant' (Matt. 23:6, 11). It is important to be appreciated. But our focus should be on righteousness, not recognition; on service, not status. The faithful visiting teacher, who quietly goes about her work month after month, is just as important to the work of the Lord as those who occupy what some see as more prominent positions in the Church. Visibility does not equate to value."

Howard W. Hunter (Ensign, Nov. 1992, pp. 96-97)

"When we understand why we serve we will not worry about where we serve."

Howard W. Hunter (BYU Devotional, Sept. 2, 1990)

"People serve one another for different reasons. . . . [1] Some serve for hope of earthly reward. Such a man or woman may serve in a Church position or in private acts of mercy in an effort to achieve prominence or cultivate contacts that will increase income or aid in acquiring wealth. Others may serve in order to obtain worldly honors, prominence, or power. . . . The scriptural word for gospel service 'for the sake of riches and honor' is *priestcraft* (Alma 1:16). . . . [2] Another reason for service . . . is that which is motivated by a desire to obtain good companionship. We surely have good associations in our Church service, but is that an acceptable motive for service? . . . Persons who serve only to obtain good companionship are more selective in choosing their friends than the Master was in choosing his servants. [3] Some serve out of fear of punishment. The scriptures abound with descriptions of the miserable state of those who fail to follow the commandments of God. . . . [4] Other persons serve out of a sense of duty or out of loyalty to family, friends, or traditions. I would call such persons 'good soldiers.' They instinctively do what they are asked, without question. . . . Such persons . . . do much good. We have all benefited from their good works. . . . Service of this character is worthy of praise and will surely qualify for blessings, especially if it is done willingly and joyfully. . . . [5] One such higher reason for service is the hope of an eternal reward. This hope . . . is one of our most powerful motivations. . . .

The above five motives for service have a common deficiency. In varying degrees each focuses on the actor's personal advantage, either on earth or in the judgment to follow. Each is self-centered. There is something deficient about any service that is conscious of self. A few months after my calling to the Council of the Twelve, I expressed my feelings of inadequacy to one of the senior members of my quorum. He responded with this mild reproof and challenging insight: 'I suppose your feelings are understandable. But you should work for a condition where you will not be preoccupied with yourself and your own feelings and can give your entire concern to others, to the work of the Lord in all the world.' Those who seek to follow [the Savior's] . . . example must lose themselves in their service to others. . . . [6] If our service is to be most efficacious, it must be unconcerned with self and heedless of personal advantage. It must be accomplished for the love of God and the love of his children. . . . Here we learn that it is not enough to serve God with all of our *might* and *strength*. He who looks into our hearts and knows our minds demand more than this. In order to stand blameless before God at the last day, we must also serve him with all our *heart* and *mind*."

Dallin H. Oaks (Pure in Heart, pp. 38-49)

"Service to others deepens and sweetens this life while we are preparing to live in a better world. It is by serving that we learn how to serve. When we are engaged in the service of our fellow men, not only do our deeds assist them, but we put our own problems in a fresher perspective. When we concern ourselves more with others, there is less time to be concerned with ourselves! In the midst of the miracle of serving, there is the promise of Jesus that by losing ourselves, we find ourselves!"

Spencer W. Kimball (Ensign, July 1978, pp. 3-7)

"Sometimes, because of the pressures of the world around us, our service projects become self service projects rather than selfless service projects. . . . Of all influences that cause men to choose wrong, selfishness is undoubtedly the strongest. Where it is the Spirit is not."

William R. Bradford (Conference Report, Oct. 1987, pp. 80-83)

"Those who stand at the head must set the example. They must walk in the right path, and invite the people to follow them. They should not seek to drive the people; they should not seek to become rulers; but they should be brethren and leaders of the people."

Joseph F. Smith (Conference Report, Apr. 1901, p. 72)

 "Rings and other jewels are not gifts, but apologies for gifts. The only gift is a portion of thyself."

Ralph Waldo Emerson

"I speak of that service which is given without expectation of monetary reward. Most of the troubles of the world come because of human greed. What a therapeutic and wonderful thing it is for a man or woman to set aside all consideration of personal gain and reach out with strength and energy and purpose to help the unfortunate, to improve the community, to clean up the environment and beautify our surroundings."

Gordon B. Hinckley (Ensign, Aug. 1992, p. 5)

"Service . . . is the golden key which unlocks the doors to celestial halls. . . . Wise undershepherds, in helping others to partake of the bread of life and the living water, seek neither acclaim nor accolade. The honors of men are of no consequence to them."

Alexander B. Morrison (Ensign, May 1992, p. 14)

"Many great people I know work for much less money than they are worth because service is a greater value to them than money. Whatever career or profession you pursue, consider the value of service."

Janette C. Hales (BYU Devotional, Mar. 16, 1993)

"Love is a potent healer. Realizing that, Satan would separate you from the power of the love of God, kindred, and friends. . . . He would lead you to feel that the walls are pressing in around you and there is no escape or relief. He wants you to believe you lack the capacity to help yourself and that no one else is really interested. . . . His strategy is to have you think you are not appreciated, loved, or wanted so that you in despair will turn to self-criticism, and in the extreme to even despising yourself and feeling evil when you are not. . . . If you have such thoughts, break through those helpless feelings by reaching out in love to another in need. That may sound cruel and unfeeling when you long so much for healing, but it is based upon truth. Paul taught, 'Bear ye one another's burdens, and so fulfil the law of Christ.' (Gal. 6:2). Love comes by learning how to give it to another in a spirit of trust. If you feel deprived of love, that is difficult. Yet sustained concern and support of others will engender their interest and love. You will feel needed. You become an instrument through which the Lord can bless another."

Richard G. Scott (Ensign, May 1994, pp. 8-9)

"Position in the Church does not exalt anyone, but faithfulness does. On the other hand, aspiring to a visible position—striving to become a master rather than a servant—can destroy the spirit of the worker and the work. Occasionally confusion exists regarding servants and masters. The Bible reports that a group of men 'had disputed among themselves, who should be the greatest' among them. Jesus said, 'If any man desire to be first, the same shall be last of all, and servant of all' (Mark 9:34-35). . . . The word servant comes from the Greek noun diakonos, which means 'one who executes the commands of another, especially of a master,' Diakonos is the Greek word from which the English word deacon is derived."

Russell M. Nelson (Ensign, May 1996, pp. 15-16)

Mos. 2:24   **SIN OF INGRATITUDE**
(Discourses of Brigham Young, p. 176-177; *Doctrines of Salvation*, Smith, 1:15)

"I believe that one of the greatest sins of which the inhabitants of the earth are guilty today is the sin of ingratitude. . . . We see a man raised up with extraordinary gifts, or with great intelligence, and he is instrumental in developing some great principle. He and the world ascribe his great genius and wisdom to himself. He attributes his success to his own energies, labor and mental capacity. He does not acknowledge the hand of God in anything connected with his success, but ignores him altogether and takes the honor to himself; this will apply to almost all the world. In all the great modern discoveries in science, in the arts, in mechanics, and in all material advancement of the age, the world says, 'We have done it.' The individual says, 'I have done it,' and he gives no honor or credit to God. Now, I read in the revelations through Joseph Smith, the prophet, that because of this, God is not pleased with the inhabitants of the earth but is angry with them because they will not acknowledge his hand in all things (D&C 59:21)."

Joseph F. Smith (Gospel Doctrine, p. 270)

Mos. 2:25-26;   **LESS THAN THE DUST**
4:2, 5, 11   (Jacob 2:21; Alma 26:12; Moses 1:10; 6:59; refer in this text to Hel. 12:7; *Conference Report*, Apr. 1973, pp. 177-178; *An Approach to the Book of Mormon*, 1957 edition, Nibley, p. 264)

"[Regarding man] science tells us that without the spirit about all that is left is a quantity of water, fat enough to make about seven bars of soap, sulphur enough to rid one dog of fleas, iron enough for a large nail, magnesium for one dose, lime enough to whitewash a chicken coop, phosphorous sufficient to tip some 2200 matches, potassium enough to explode a toy cannon, sugar to fill a shaker, and little more. But with a spirit directing mental processes and physical maneuvers man is 'little lower than the angels' and is 'crowned . . . with glory and honour' (Psalm 8:5). And yet man in his vanity and impudence has taken unto himself the glory of all his accomplishments, set himself up as God and, as has been said, has even 'created God in his (man's) own image.' It is as if the Boulder Dam should say: 'I am powerful. I hold back great quantities of water. Parched land becomes fertile and productive because of me. There were no builders. I am the great cause and responsible to no power.'"

Teachings of Spencer W. Kimball, p. 27

"The animal, vegetable, and mineral kingdoms abide the law of their Creator; the whole earth and all things pertaining to it, except man, abide the law of their creation. . . . We tame the animals and make them do our drudgery and administer to our wants in many ways, yet man alone is not tamed—he is not subject to his Great Creator. Our ignorant animals are faithful to us, and will do our bidding as long as they have any strength; yet man who is the offspring of the Gods, will not become subject to the most reasonable and self-exalting principles. How often have we witnessed a faithful animal conveying his master home so drunk that he could not see his way or sit up; yet his faithful animal will plod through mud, shun stumps, trees, and bad places, and land him safely at home."

Brigham Young (Journal of Discourses 9:246-247)

Mos. 2:32   **AVOID CONTENTION**
(refer in this text to 3 Ne. 11:28-30)

Mos. 3:7   **CHRIST'S SUFFERING**
(2 Ne. 9:20-21; Mosiah 14:4; JST Luke 22:43-44; D&C 19:17-18; *Jesus the Christ,* Talmage, p. 613; *Doctrines of Salvation,* Smith, 1:130-131; 2:274-275; *The Mortal Messiah,* McConkie, 4:125).

"The Father withdrew His spirit from His Son, at the time he was to be crucified. . . . at the very moment, at the hour when the crisis came for him to offer up his life, the Father withdrew Himself, withdrew His Spirit, and cast a veil over him. That is what made him sweat blood [in Gethsemane]. If he had had the power of God upon him he would not have sweat blood. . . ."

Brigham Young (Journal of Discourses 3:206)

"We know that an angel came from the courts of glory to strengthen him in his [Christ's] ordeal, and we suppose it was mighty Michael, [Adam] who foremost fell that mortal man might be. As near as we can judge, these infinite agonies— this suffering beyond compare—continued for some three or four hours."

Bruce R. McConkie (Conference Report, Apr. 1985, p. 10)

"All of the anguish, all of the sorrow, and all of the suffering of Gethsemane recurred during the final three hours on the cross, the hours when darkness covered the land."

Bruce R. McConkie (The Mortal Messiah, Vol. 4, footnotes, p. 232)

"This sacrifice . . . took place in Gethsemane when he sweat great gouts of blood from every pore . . . And it also took place as he hung on the cruel cross of Calvary. During the last three hours of that agonizing ordeal, while darkness overspread the land, all the pains and suffering of Gethsemane returned."

Bruce R. McConkie (A New Witness for the Articles of Faith, p. 109)

Mos. 3:11, 16-18   CHILDREN & THOSE WHO DIED WITHOUT THE GOSPEL

(Companion to Your Study of the Book of Mormon, Ludlow, p. 175-176; refer in this text to Moro. 8:8-22)

Mos. 3:19   THE NATURAL MAN

(Mosiah 24:15; 1 Cor. 2:14; D&C 20:20; Moses 5:13; Book of Mormon 121-122 Student Manual, p. 55; *Conference Report*, Neal A. Maxwell, Oct. 1990, pp. 16-17)

"The natural man is the earthy man who has allowed rude animal passions to overshadow his spiritual inclinations."

Spencer W. Kimball (Conference Report, Oct. 1974, pp. 160-161)

"At the one end of the spectrum, the natural man may be a person bent on lasciviousness; he may be one who loves Satan more than God and thereby is carnal, sensual, and devilish. . . . At the other end of the spectrum, the natural man may well be a 'nice man,' a moral and upright person bent upon benevolence. Such a person, acclimated to the present fallen world, still does not enjoy the enlivening powers of the Holy Ghost and does not enjoy the sanctifying power of Christ's covenants and ordinances. Even though the light of Christ is making an impact on him, he has not followed it into the Lord's full gospel truths. . . . And what of members of the Church of Jesus Christ of Latter-day Saints? Are any of us 'natural' beings? We can answer that question, perhaps, by examining some broad characteristics of the natural man: **1.** *The natural man is unable or unwilling to perceive spiritual realities* (1 Cor. 2:14; Alma 26:21; *Journal of Discourses* 1:2). **2.** *The natural man is proud.* President Benson explained. 'We pit our will against God's. When we direct our pride toward God, it is in the spirit of my will and not thine be done. . . . The proud wish God would agree with them' *(Ensign*, May 1989, p. 4). **3.** *The natural man is overly competitive and externally driven.* 'Such people are tempted daily to elevate [themselves] above others and diminish them.' There is no pleasure in 'having something,' only in 'having more of it than the next man' *(Ensign*, Benson, May 1989, p. 4). **4.** *The natural man yields himself to the harsh and the crude.*"

Robert Millet (Ensign, June 1992, pp. 8-9)

"Men have become carnal. They have become enemies to God. They are seeking for their own advancement and not for the advancement of the kingdom of God."

Joseph Fielding Smith (Conference Report, Apr. 1952, p. 27)

Mos. 3:19   **BECOMETH A SAINT**

"The word *saint* is tied to the Hebrew root *Kadosh*, which means to separate, to be apart from, and to become sacred and holy *(Hebrew, and English Lexicon*, Brown, Driver, Briggs, p 872). In all dispensations of time the Lord's people have been called Saints, thus emphasizing that they are a people who have separated themselves from that which is worldly and are seeking through obedience to the laws and ordinances of the gospel to become a holy people."

R. Millet and J. F. McConkie (Doctrinal Commentary on the Book of Mormon, 2:153)

Mos. 3:19   **BECOMETH AS A CHILD**
(3 Ne. 9:22; 11:37-38; Matt. 18:3)

"Nobody grows old by merely living a number of years. People grow old by deserting their ideals, their faith. There is always the love of wonder, a childlike appetite for what is next, and the joy of your life. You are as young as your faith, as old as your doubt; as young as your self-confidence, as old as your fear or despair. In the center of our heart is a recording chamber, and so long as it receives messages of beauty, hope, cheer, courage, and faith, so long are we young."

David B. Haight (Ensign, Nov. 1983, p. 25)

Mos. 3:15-27   **GOD'S JUSTICE**

"JUSTICE requires that God must be a God of order and that he must be just and impartial. MERCY agrees with justice; however, mercy introduces the possibility of vicarious payment of the laws that have been transgressed (or broken). The Law of mercy paraphrased: Whenever a law is broken a payment (or atonement) must be made; however, the person does not need to make payment if he will repent and if he can find someone who is both able and willing to make payment. Note that the Law of MERCY insists the demands of JUSTICE be met fully."

Daniel H. Ludlow (Companion to Your Study of the Book of Mormon, pp. 176-177)

Mos. 4:2-3   **A REMISSION OF THEIR SINS**
(refer in this text to Mosiah 5:2, 7)

"This process of obtaining a remission of one's sins is further outlined in . . . the aftermath of King Benjamin's mighty discourse about Jesus Christ, his divine sonship and atoning sacrifice. Following this message, we are told how the saints in King Benjamin's time receive a remission of their sins: FIRST: 'They . . . viewed themselves in their own carnal [worldly] state. . . .' NEXT: 'They all cried aloud with one voice, saying: O have mercy, and apply the atoning blood of Christ that we may receive forgiveness of sins, and our hearts may be purified. . . .' FINALLY: 'After they had spoken these words the Spirit of the Lord came upon them, and they were filled with joy, having received a remission of their sins, and having peace of conscience, because of the exceeding faith which they had in Jesus Christ. . . .' This is the manner by which the saints in all ages have come to be converted. . . ."

Ezra Taft Benson (Charge to Religious Educators, 1982, pp. 48-54)

"Often the most difficult part of repentance is to forgive yourself. Discouragement is part of that test. Do not give up. That brilliant morning will come. Then 'the peace of God, which passeth . . . understanding' comes into your life once again. Then you like Him, will remember your sins no more. How will you know? You will know!"

Boyd K. Packer (Ensign, Nov. 1995, p. 20)

Mos. 4:16-23   **ADVICE TO THE AFFLUENT**
(Eccl. 5:13,15; Jacob 2:13-19; D&C 56:16; 104:16-18; Matt. 25:40; *Conference Report*, Apr. 1898, pp. 46-47; refer in this text to Jacob 2:13-17)

"It is better to feed ten impostors than to run the risk of turning away one honest petition."

Joseph Smith (as quoted in the Collected Works of Hugh Nibley, Vol. 9, Ch. 8, p. 226)

"Suppose that in this community there are ten beggars who beg from door to door for something to eat, and that nine of them are imposters who beg to escape work. . . . [What is your choice?] To give food to the ten, . . . or to repulse the ten because you do not know which is the worthy one? You will all say, administer charitable gifts to the ten, rather than turn away the only truly worthy . . . person among them. If you do this, it will make no difference in your blessings, whether you administer to worthy or unworthy persons, inasmuch as you give alms with a single eye to assist the truly needy."

Discourses of Brigham Young, p. 274

Mos. 4:24-25   **ADVICE TO THE POOR**
(D&C 56:17)

"[Those] who have been denied blessings . . . in this life—who say in their heart, 'If I could have done, I would have done, or I would give if I had, but I cannot for I have not'—the Lord will bless you as though you had done, and the world to come will compensate for those who desire in their hearts the righteous blessings that they were not able to have because of no fault of their own."

Harold B. Lee (Ye Are The Light of the World, p. 298)

Mos. 4:27   **ORDER**
(D&C 10:4; 121:7; 132:8; 1 Cor. 14:40; Mark 4:37-39; Heb. 12:1; Psalm 46:10; James 1:3-4; *Kisses At The Window*, Bassett, pp. 73-77; *Just to Illustrate*, Richards, p. 92; *Gospel Ideals*, McKay, p.525; *Spiritual Roots of Human Relations*, Covey, pp. 161-163; *To Whom It May Concern*, Ashton, pp. 234-236; *The Miracle of Personality*, Sill, pp. 49-54; *Ensign*, May 1992, pp. 27, 29; *Ensign*, June 1994, pp. 40-43; refer in this text to Jacob 4:18; 3 Ne. 11:3-5)

"In the fast-paced life that most of us lead, the simple concern of parents finding sufficient time to do the things they want to do is often a big problem. . . . 'The best thing to spend on your children is your time' *(Richard Evans Quote Book*, p. 18)."

Ben B. Banks (Ensign, Nov. 1993, pp. 28,30)

"If you had asked me, 'Can a person accept too many callings in a branch or a ward and get too overloaded in terms of the time left for family, work, community, and so forth,' the answer would be yes, in the sense that you ask. But if we ask ourselves, 'Am I doing quite enough to help further the Lord's work,' then our answer must be no. Most of us can do a better job of managing our time and our talents than we do, but it is important to do as the Lord suggested—to run no faster than we are able. When we run faster than we are able, we get both inefficient and tired. . . . I have on my office wall a wise and useful reminder by Anne Morrow Lindberg concerning one of the realities of life. She wrote, 'My life cannot implement in action the demands of all the people to whom my heart responds.' That's good counsel for us all, not as an excuse to forgo duty, but as a sage point about pace and the need for quality in relationships."

Neal A. Maxwell (Deposition of a Disciple, pp. 57-58)

"A few weeks ago, President McKay related to the Twelve an interesting experience. . . . He said it is a great thing to be responsive to the whisperings of the spirit, and we know that when these whisperings come it is a gift and our privilege to have them. They come when we are relaxed and not under pressure of appointments. (I want you to mark that.) The President then took occasion to relate an experience in the life of Bishop Wells, former member of the Presiding Bishopric. A son of Bishop Wells was killed in Emigration Canyon on a railroad track. . . . His boy was run over by a freight train. Sister Wells was inconsolable. She mourned during the three days prior to the funeral, received no comfort at the funeral, and was in a rather serious state of mind. One day soon after the funeral services while she was lying on her bed relaxed, still mourning, she says that her son appeared to her and said, 'Mother, do not mourn, do not cry. I am alright.' He told her that she did not understand how the accident happened and explained that he had given the signal to the engineer to move on, and then made the usual effort to catch the railing on the freight train, but as he attempted to do so his foot caught on a root and he failed to catch the hand rail, and his body fell under the train. It was clearly an accident. Now listen. He said that as soon as he realized that he was in another environment he tried to see his father, but couldn't reach him. His father was so busy with the duties in his office he could not respond to his call. Therefore, he had come to his mother. He said to her, 'You tell father that all is well with me, and I want you not to mourn anymore.'"

Harold B. Lee (an address given to the Seminary & Institute Faculty, BYU, July 5, 1956)

"Our lives can become cluttered by many things. Some are obvious, such as material things, the stuff we collect. . . . How well I know that we can surround ourselves with the material things to the extent that we have no time for the spiritual. Look around and you will see all the gadgets and toys and the nice and the fun things that cause us to squander and pay, and to wander and play. Other things that clutter our lives and use up our time are not as obvious as the material. They are more subtle and just seem to evolve, taking control of us. . . . Nothing suits the devil better than to become a silent partner with us. . . . He also knows that while in mortality we are subject to time. If by his subtle means he can become our silent partner, he can then influence us to make wrong choices that use up our time unwisely and prevent us from doing that which we should. We give our lives to that which we give our time."

William R. Bradford (Conference Report, Apr. 1992, p. 38)

"Slow me down, Lord! Teach me the art of taking minute vacations . . . of slowing down to look at a flower, to chat with a friend, to pat a dog, to read a few lines from a good book. . . . There is more to life than measuring its speed. Let me look upward into the branches of the towering oak and know that it grew great and strong because it grew slowly and well. Slow me down, Lord, and inspire me to send my roots deep into the soil of life's enduring values. . . ."

-Author Unknown

"[Young People] can have all these blessings if they are in control of themselves and if each one takes the experiences in proper order: first some social get acquainted contacts to develop social skills, then a mission, then courting, then temple marriage and a family, and then schooling and degrees and business. Now the sequence of these things is very serious. If one gets them tipped around topsy-turvy, if some get married first, many of the other dreams fall flat. But if they will take them one at a time in proper order and sequence, they may have all of them. They don't need to choose among them; they merely time them."

Spencer W. Kimball (Charge to Religious Educators, 1982), pp. 43-47)

Mos. 4:30; 5:13   **WATCH YOUR THOUGHTS—WORDS—DEEDS**
(2 Ne. 27:27; 3 Ne. 20:41; Matt. 5:27-28; Job 42:2; Psalm 94:11; D&C 97:15-17; 121:45; refer in this text to Alma 12:14; 3 Ne. 12:27-29; Moro. 7:4-11)

"We cannot indulge in swearing. We cannot be guilty of profanity; we cannot indulge in impure thoughts, words, and acts and have the Spirit of the Lord with us."

Gordon B. Hinckley (Ensign, May 1997, p. 49)

"If men's secret acts shall be revealed it is likely that their secret thoughts will also be revealed. . . . The one who harbors evil thoughts sometimes feels safe in the conviction that these thoughts are unknown to others. . . . Accordingly, men's deeds and thoughts must be recorded in heaven, and recording angels will not fail to make complete recordings of our thoughts and actions. We pay our tithing and the bishop records it in his book and gives us a receipt. But even if the entry fails to get in the ward record, we shall have full credit for the tithes we paid. There will be no omissions in the heavenly records, and they will all be available at the day of judgment."

Spencer W. Kimball (Miracle of Forgiveness, p. 108)

"*Control your thoughts.* No one steps into immorality in an instant. The first seeds of immorality are always sown in the mind. When we allow our thoughts to linger on lewd or immoral things, the first step on the road to immorality has been taken. I especially warn you against the evils of pornography. Again and again we hear from those caught in deep sin that often the first step on their road to transgression began with pornographic materials."

Ezra Taft Benson (BYU Speeches of the Year, 1987-88, pp. 51-52)

"A priesthood holder is *temperate*. This means he is restrained in his emotions and verbal expressions. He does things in moderation and is not given to overindulgence. In a word, he has self-control. He is the master of his emotions, not the other way around. A priesthood holder who would curse his wife, abuse her with words or actions, or do the same to one of his own children is guilty of grievous sin. 'Can ye be angry, and not sin?' asked the Apostle Paul (JST Ephesians 4:26). If a man does not control his temper, it is a sad admission that he is not in control of his thoughts. . . . A priesthood holder is to be patient. Patience is another form of self-control. . . . Patience is composure under stress. . . . A priesthood holder who is patient will be tolerant of the mistakes and failings of his loved ones. Because he loves them, he will not find fault nor criticize nor blame. . . . A priesthood holder is *kind*. Kindness pardons others' weaknesses and faults. Kindness is extended to all—to the aged and the young, to animals, to those low of station as well as the high. These are the true attributes of the divine nature."

Ezra Taft Benson (Ensign, Nov. 1986, p. 47)

"If we entertain temptations, soon they begin entertaining us."

Neal A. Maxwell (Conference Report, Apr. 1987)

"Talking about or looking at immodest pictures of a woman's body can stimulate powerful emotions. It will tempt you to watch improper videocassettes or movies. . . . Work at keeping your thoughts clean by thinking of something good. The mind can think of only one thing at a time. Use that fact to crowd out ugly thoughts. Above all, don't feed thoughts by reading or watching things that are wrong. If you don't control your thoughts, Satan will keep tempting you until you eventually act them out."

Richard G. Scott (Ensign, Nov. 1994, p. 37)

"[Prov. 23:7] Unclean thoughts lead to unclean acts. I remember going to President McKay years ago to plead the cause of a missionary who had become involved in serious sin. I said to President McKay, 'He did it on an impulse.'

The President said to me: 'His mind was dwelling on these things before he transgressed. The thought was father to the deed. There would not have been that impulse if he had previously controlled his thoughts.'"

Gordon B. Hinckley (Ensign, May 1996, p. 48)

"I had read somewhere of a young couple who settled in the wilderness. While the man cleared the land, his wife tended things about the homestead. Occasionally, the cow would get into the garden, and the husband would complain. One day, as he left to get supplies, he said in a sarcastic way, 'Do you think you'll be able to keep the cow in while I am gone?' . . . That night a terrible storm arose. Frightened by thunder, the cow escaped into the woods. Several days later the husband returned to an empty cabin and an apologetic note: 'A storm came up, and the cow got out. I am so sorry, but I think I can find her.' He searched; neither had survived. The author concluded the incident with these words:

> *Boys flying kites haul in their*
> *   white-winged birds;*
> *You can call back your kites, but*
> *   you can't call back you words.*
> *'Careful with fire' is good advice,*
> *   we know;*
> *'Careful with words' is ten times*
> *   doubly so.*
> *Thoughts unexpressed will often*
> *   fall back dead.*
> *But God Himself can't kill them,*
> *   once they are said!'*

Boyd K. Packer (Conference Report, Oct. 1987, p. 18)

"The fundamental reason why the Lord has instructed us to conduct worthiness interviews in His Church is to teach us to keep the commitments we make. In short, we are to be trained during this season of mortal probation to master ourselves (see Alma 34:33-37) to live with integrity and be true to our covenants. Worthiness interviews are conducted in a spirit of loving concern for each son and daughter of a loving God. These interviews represent the rehearsal stage for final judgment. Such interviews are a blessing, a choice opportunity to account to the Lord through His authorized servants for the sacred stewardship we all have to 'watch [ourselves], and [our] thoughts, and [our] words, and [our] deeds.'"

Joseph B. Worthlin (Ensign, May 1997, p. 16)

"We understand that we will live a postmortal life of infinite duration and that we determine the kind of life it will be by our thoughts and actions in mortality. Mortality is very brief but immeasurably important. . . . We can compare our lives with the flight of a spaceship. When its motor is started up, its trajectory is monitored precisely. Any deviation from its decreed course is corrected immediately. Even a fraction of a degree off course would carry it many miles from its destination if not corrected. The longer the correction is delayed, the greater will be the required adjustment. Can you imagine how far off course we can become without course corrections? . . . Our course on earth is . . . determined by the decisions we make each day. We cannot separate our thoughts and actions now from their effects on the future."

Joseph B. Wirthlin (Ensign, May 1998, pp. 14-16)

Mos. 5:2,7

A MIGHTY CHANGE IN OUR HEARTS
(Alma 19:33; Moses 6:59; Alma 5:7, 14, 26; *Conference Report*, Apr. 1898, pp. 65-66; refer in this text to Mosiah 27:24-26; *Ensign*, May 1998, pp. 55-57)

"Being born again, comes by the Spirit of God through ordinances."

Teachings of the Prophet Joseph Smith, p. 162

"Mere compliance with the formality of the ordinance of baptism does not mean that a person has been born again. No one can be born again without baptism, but the immersion of water and the laying on of hands to confer the Holy Ghost do not of themselves guarantee that a person has been or will be born again. The new birth takes place only for those who actually enjoy the Gift or companionship of the Holy Ghost, only for those who are fully converted, who have given themselves without restraint to the Lord."

Bruce R. McConkie (Mormon Doctrine, pp. 100-101)

"In addition to the physical ordinance of baptism and the laying on of hands, one must be spiritually born again to gain exaltation and eternal life."

Ezra Taft Benson (Ensign, July 1989, pp. 2-3)

"(For most of us) this process is usually slow. The unusually quick ones make their way into scripture."

Bruce R. McConkie (1976 BYU Speeches of the Year)

"Let us recognize that to be spiritually born of God and receive the baptism of fire and of the Holy Ghost is, as the scriptures attest, a glorious and wonderful event that prepares us to pursue eternal life. But it does not immediately translate us into perfect beings ready for celestial glory. It does not mean that we will never make a mistake or sin again. Hence, we see the great need to apply the principle of repentance continuously as we strive daily to serve God and keep his commandments."

David W. Hellem (Ensign, June 1992, p. 12)

"That change comes today to every son and daughter of God who repents of his or her sins, who humble themselves before the Lord, and who seek forgiveness and remission of sin by baptism . . . Yet many of us who have received that witness, that new birth, that change of heart, while we may have erred in judgment or have made many mistakes, and often perhaps come short of the true standard in our lives, we have repented of the evil, and we have sought from time to time forgiveness at the hand of the Lord; so that until this day the same desire and purpose which pervaded our souls when we were baptized and received a remission of our sins, still holds possession of our hearts, and is still the ruling sentiment and passion of our souls. Though at times we may be stirred to anger, and our wrath move us to say and do things which are not pleasing in the sight of God, yet instantly on regaining our sober senses and recovering from our lapse into the power of darkness, we feel humble, repentant, and to ask forgiveness for the wrong that we have done to ourselves, and per-chance to others."

Joseph F. Smith (Gospel Doctrine, pp. 96-97)

Mos. 5:10-12   **CHIASMUS**
(Alma 36; *The New Era*, John Welch, Feb. 1972, pp. 6-11)

Mos. 7-8   **HISTORICAL QUESTIONS**
(Book of Mormon 121-122 Student Manual, pp. 59)

Mos. 8:14-17   **A SEER**
(Conference Report, Oct. 1961, pp. 121-122)

"A seer is a prophet selected and appointed to possess and use these holy interpreters [the Urim and Thummim]. . . . The President of the Church holds the office of seership (D&C 107:92; 124:94, 125). Indeed, the apostolic office itself is one of seership, and the members of the Council of the Twelve, together with the Presidency and Patriarch to the Church, are chosen and sustained as prophets, seers, and revelators to the Church. If there are seers among a people, that people is the Lord's. Where there are no seers, apostasy prevails (Isa. 29:10; 2 Ne. 27:5)."

Bruce R. McConkie (Mormon Doctrine, pp. 700-701)

HISTORICAL QUESTIONS
Mosiah 9-24 (Book of Mormon 121-122 Student Manual, pp. 59-61)

Mos. 9:3   **OVERZEALOUS**
(refer in this text to Mosiah 4:27)

"The overzealous tend to judge others by their own standard. True excellence in gospel living—compliance with the established laws and ordinances in a quiet and patient manner—results in humility, in greater reliance upon God, and in broadening love and acceptance of one's fellow man. What I am doing in the name of goodness ought to bring me closer to those I love and serve, ought to turn my heart toward people, rather than causing me to turn my nose up in judgmental scorn and rejection. The greatest man to walk the earth, the only fully perfect human being, looked with tenderness and compassion upon those whose ways and actions were less than perfect."

Robert Millet (CES Symposium, Aug. 1993)

Mos. 10:15   **THE INHERITANCE OF THE ELDEST SON**
(1 Ne. 2:21-22; 16:37; 18:10; 2 Ne. 5:3,19; Alma 54:17-18; Deut. 21:17)

Mos. 11:2   **WALK AFTER THE DESIRES OF HIS OWN HEART (Selfishness)**
(Mosiah 19:8; Hel. 10:4; 3 Ne. 1:29; D&C 56:8)

"Selfishness strikes a deadly blow at the root of true character. Failure in the eternal sense of the word is almost always associated with selfishness. If the youth of the Church are to fulfill their mission properly, they must be taught to overcome selfishness."

Spencer W. Kimball (Charge to Religious Educators, 1982, pp. 43-47)

"The distance between constant self-pleasing and self-worship is shorter than we think. Stubborn selfishness is actually rebellion against God, because, warned Samuel, 'stubbornness is as . . . idolatry' (1 Samuel 15:23). Selfishness is much more than an ordinary problem because it activates all the cardinal sins! . . . The selfish individual has a passion for the vertical pronoun *I*. Significantly, the vertical pronoun *I* has no knees to bend, while the first letter in the pronoun *we* does."

Neal A. Maxwell (Conference Report, Oct. 1990, pp. 15-16)

Mos. 11:19   **BOASTING IN THEIR OWN STRENGTH**
(1 Ne. 2:20; 2 Ne. 1:7; Mosiah 12:15; Morm. 3:9; 4:8,18; D&C 3:4)

"When threatened, we become anti-enemy instead of pro-kingdom of God. . . . We forget that if we are righteous the Lord will either not suffer our enemies to come upon us (and this is the special promise to the inhabitants of the land of the Americas) or he will fight our battles for us. . . ."

Spencer W. Kimball (Ensign, June 1976, p. 6)

"Men of the world are in the world only because they adopt the philosophy of the world which is the philosophy of self sufficiency. It is not a humble philosophy—it is highly egotistical. It makes men themselves the arbiters of all things. They look to no higher source than themselves for the solution of all questions. . . . It requires courage to come out of the world and adopt the philosophy of faith. Sometimes it subjects one to ridicule and the contempt of friends which are harder for most men to endure than physical pain; but because a thing is hard to do or hard to believe is no assurance that it is not right."

Stephen L. Richards (Conference Report, Apr. 1935, p. 30)

Mos. 12:1-2   **HARD TIMES DUE TO NON-REPENTANCE**
(Hel. 13:38; Morm. 2:15)

Mos. 13:3   **I WON'T DIE BEFORE MY TIME**
(Acts 17:26; D&C 42:48; 122:9; Job 14:5; Alma 40:8,10; Eccl. 3:1-2; *History of the Church*, Smith 5:554; *Life Everlasting*, Crowther, pp. 66-67; *Man's Search for Meaning*, Frankl, pp. 82-84; *Ensign*, Dec. 1971, p. 10)

"Stories such as these do not mean that the servants of God are delivered from all hardship or that they are always saved from death. Some believers lose their lives in persecutions, and some suffer great hardships as a result of their faith. But the protection promised to the faithful servants of God is a reality. . . ."

Dallin H. Oaks (Ensign, Nov. 1992, p. 39)

[A blessing given from Joseph Smith Sr. to his son Joseph, as recorded by the Prophet's mother.] "'You shall even live to finish your work.' At this Joseph cried out, weeping, 'Oh! my father, shall I?' 'Yes,' said his father, 'you shall live to lay out the plan of all the work which God has given you to do. This is my dying blessing upon your head in the name of Jesus. . . .'"

History of Joseph Smith by His Mother, Lucy Mack Smith, pp. 309-310

"Many people die before their time because they are careless, abuse their bodies, take unnecessary chances, or expose themselves to hazards, accidents and sickness (Eccl. 7:17)."

Spencer W. Kimball (Faith Precedes the Miracle, p. 103)

Mos. 13:4   APOSTATE ATTITUDE—ANGER AGAINST THE TRUTH
(1 Ne. 16:2-3; 2 Ne. 9:40; Moro.; 1 Tim. 1:8-9; *Ensign*, Maxwell, Nov. 1989, pp. 82-84; refer in this text to Alma 21:3)

"When a corrupt man is chastised he gets angry and will not endure it."

Teachings of the Prophet Joseph Smith, p. 195

Mos. 13:11-26   THE TEN COMMANDMENTS
(Ex. 19:5-6; Deut. 5:2-3)

"Some have mistakenly supposed that the Ten Commandments were a part of the law of Moses. In fact, they are a part of the higher law or the fulness of the gospel. This is illustrated by their reiteration to us as part of the restoration of all things (see D&C 59:5-12). The Ten Commandments were a part of the fulness of the gospel as first given to Moses on Sinai. Though the higher priesthood and its ordinances were taken from Israel because of her transgressions, when Moses returned to Sinai to receive what we know as the law of Moses the Ten Commandments were retained as a part of Israel's covenant with God."

R. Millet and J. F. McConkie (Doctrinal Commentary on the Book of Mormon, 2:216)

Mos. 13:15   **THE NAME OF GOD IN VAIN**
(Ex. 20:7; Morm. 7:7; D&C 58:30)

"Let me tell you of an experience I had when I was a little boy . . . I came home from school one day, threw my books on the table, and took the name of the Lord in vain . . . My mother heard me. She was shocked. She took me by the hand and led me to the bathroom. She . . . then proceeded to wash my mouth out with that terrible soap. She . . . said, 'Don't let me ever hear such words from your lips again.' I hope I have never used the Lord's name in vain since that time. When President Spencer W. Kimball underwent surgery years ago, he was wheeled from the operating room to the intensive care room. The attendant who pushed the gurney which carried him stumbled and let out an oath using the name of the Lord. President Kimball, who was barely conscious, said weakly, 'Please! Please! That is my Lord whose name you revile.' There was a deathly silence; then the young man whispered with a subdued voice, 'I am sorry' (See *Teachings of Spencer W. Kimball*, p. 198)."

Gordon B. Hinckley (Ensign, May 1996, p. 94)

Mos. 13:20   **HONOR THY FATHER & MOTHER**
(refer in this text to 1 Ne. 17:55)

Mos. 13:29-31   **THE LAW OF MOSES**
(Alma 25:15-16; 34:13-14; Jacob 4:5; D&C 84:27)

"In a sense the Law of Moses was given as a type of 'spiritual busywork' a system and pattern that would keep the people constantly involved; with everything pointing toward the coming Savior and Redeemer."

Robert Millet (CES Symposium, Aug. 1986, p. 99)

Mos. 14   **ISAIAH'S TESTIMONY OF THE COMING MESSIAH**
(Isa. 53; *Book of Mormon Symposium*, Millet, Aug. 1986, p. 99-100)

"Now Bible commentators will tell you that this [Isaiah 53] has nothing to do with the life of Jesus Christ. To them this story is one concerning suffering Israel. I want to tell you that it is a story, a synopsis of the life of our Redeemer, revealed to Isaiah 700 years before the Lord was born."

Joseph Fielding Smith (Doctrines of Salvation 1:23)

Mos. 14:2

NO BEAUTY THAT WE SHOULD DESIRE HIM
(Isa. 53:2)

"In appearance he was like men; and so it is expressed here by the prophet that he had no form or comeliness, that is, he was not so distinctive, so different from others that people would recognize him as the Son of God. He appeared as a mortal man."

Joseph Fielding Smith (Doctrines of Salvation 1:23)

Mos. 14:4

BORNE OUR GRIEF AND CARRIED OUR SORROW
(refer in this text to Alma 7:11-12)

"When his body was taken from the cross and hastily placed in a borrowed tomb, he, the sinless Son of God, had already taken upon him not only the sins and temptations of every human soul who will repent, but all of our sickness and grief and pain of every kind. He suffered these afflictions as we suffer them, according to the flesh. He suffered them all. He did this to perfect his mercy and his ability to lift us above every earthly trial."

Howard W. Hunter (Ensign, May 1988, pp. 16-17)

Mos. 14:10

HE SHALL PROLONG HIS DAYS AND THE PLEASURE OF THE LORD SHALL PROSPER IN HIS HAND
(Isa. 53:10; *Book of Mormon Symposium*, BYU, Aug. 1986, p. 100)

"If this prophecy was meant to be fulfilled during his mortal sojourn on earth, we would list it as having failed. He did not prolong his days; a voluntary death overtook him in the prime of life. . . . It is only in the resurrection that the pleasure of the Lord is perfected, for it is only when 'spirit and element' are 'inseparably connected' that either God or man can 'receive a fulness of joy' (D&C 93:33). Thus, having made his soul an offering for sin; having seen his seed—all the righteous dead from the days of Adam to that moment—as they assembled to greet and worship him in the paradise of their Lord; and having thereafter risen in glorious immortality to live and reign forever, our Messiah truly fulfilled the prophetic utterance, for then his days were prolonged forever and the pleasure in his hand was infinite."

Bruce R. McConkie (Promised Messiah, p. 362)

ABINADI'S COMMENTARY ON ISAIAH

Isaiah 53	Abinadi's Commentary
Mosiah 14:2	Mosiah 15:2-4
Mosiah 14:3	Mosiah 15:5
Mosiah 14:4-6	Mosiah 15:9
Mosiah 14:7	Mosiah 15:6
Mosiah 14:8	Mosiah 15:10,12-13
Mosiah 14:10	Mosiah 15:11-12, 23

Mos. 15:1-11;   **CHRIST AS THE FATHER**
17:8   (refer in this text to 1 Ne. 19:10; *Articles of Faith*, Talmage, p. 466-473; *Answers to Gospel Questions*, Smith, 4:177-180; *Book of Mormon Symposium*, Millet, Aug. 1986, pp. 101-102; *Doctrines of Salvation*, Smith, 1:25-27; *Doctrinal New Testament Commentary*, McConkie, 1:74; *Promised Messiah*, McConkie, p. 98; Book of Mormon Preface)

Mos. 15:21-26   **THE FIRST RESURRECTION**
(Articles of Faith, Talmage, p. 385; D&C 76:50-70)

"The righteous dead who lived from the day of Adam to the time when Christ broke the bands of death 'were with Christ in his resurrection' (D&C 133:54-55). . . . All who were with Christ in his resurrection, and all who have so far been resurrected, have come forth with celestial bodies and will have an inheritance in the celestial kingdom (D&C 88:96-102). To those who lived before the resurrection of Christ, the day of his coming forth from the dead was known as the first resurrection. Abinadi and Alma, for instance, so considered it (Mosiah 15:21-25; Alma 40). To those who have lived since that day, the first resurrection is yet future and will take place at the time of the Second Coming (D&C 88:96-102)."

Bruce R. McConkie (Mormon Doctrine, pp. 639-640)

Mos. 15:24   **DIED IN THEIR IGNORANCE**
(refer in this text to Moro. 8:22; 2 Ne. 9:25-27)

"If a person never had the opportunity to know anything about the plan of salvation, then surely he should not be held accountable for his deeds in the flesh on an equality with the man who knew the truth and then refused to obey it. Thousands of these people who lived in this ignorance were devout and faithful to the doctrines which they had been taught. They cannot be held accountable for their actions which were done in faith and obedience to that which they devoutly believed and had been taught."

Joseph Fielding Smith (Answers to Gospel Questions, 4:77)

Mos. 15:25   **LITTLE CHILDREN HAVE ETERNAL LIFE**
(Answers to Gospel Questions, Smith, pp. 56-57; refer in this text to Moro. 8)

". . . I have meditated upon the subject, and asked the question, why it is that infants, innocent children, are taken away from us. . . . The Lord takes many away even in infancy, that they may escape the envy of man, and the sorrows and evils of this present world; they were too pure, too lovely, to live on earth; therefore, if rightly considered, instead of mourning we have reason to rejoice as they are delivered from evil, and we shall soon have them again."

Teachings of the Prophet Joseph Smith, pp. 196-197

Mos. 17   **ABINADI'S DEATH**
(refer in this text to Alma 24:20-24)

"Abinadi may have felt like a failure because he only had one convert. . ."

Joseph Wirthlin (Conference Report, Apr. 1989)

"It is not easy to die, even to die for one's testimony, but the taste of death is so much sweeter to those whose lives bear fervent witness of Him whose servants they are. Occasionally in the overall scheme of things the Lord asks certain of his representatives to shed their own blood in a martyr's death, that their testament might be in full force (See D&C 135:5; Heb. 9:16-17)."

Robert Millet (CES Symposium, Aug. 1986, p. 103)

Mos. 17:11-13   **PEER PRESSURE**
(1 Ne. 8:25; 2 Ne. 8:7,12; D&C 3:6-7; 30:1-2; 60:2; Matt. 14:9; John 12:42-43; *Conference Report*, Apr. 1989, p. 4; *Conference Report*, Apr. 1978, pp. 116-117; *Ensign*, May 1992, pp. 40-42; *Ensign*, May 1993, pp. 53; refer in this text to Alma 39:4)

"I am so grateful that prophets do not crave popularity."

Spencer W. Kimball (Conference Report, Apr. 1978, pp. 116-117)

"My husband said he still remembers going to his first examination at the University of Utah. . . . As the professor passed out the examination and left the room, he said some classmates started to pull out little cheat papers from pockets and from under their books. He said, 'My heart began to pound as I realized how difficult it is to compete with cheaters.' . . . About then a tall, thin student stood up in the back of the room and said, 'I sold my farm and put my wife and three little children in an upstairs apartment to go to medical school, and I'll turn in the first one of you who cheats and YOU BETTER BELIEVE IT!' They believed it. My husband said he looked like Abraham Lincoln. There were many sheepish expressions and those cheat papers started to disappear as fast as they had appeared. . . . That man cared more about character than popularity. When I heard the name of J. Ballard Washburn to be sustained as a member of the Quorum of Seventy, I remembered that he was that medical student."

Janette C. Hales (BYU Devotional, Mar. 16, 1993)

"[To the young women], Choose your friends with caution. In a survey made in selected wards and stakes of the Church, we learned a most significant fact: those persons whose friends married in the temple usually married in the temple, while those persons whose friends did not marry in the temple usually did not marry in the temple. The influence of one's friends appeared to be a highly dominant factor—even more so than parental urging, classroom instruction, or proximity to a temple."

Thomas S. Monson (Ensign, May 1997, pp. 94-95)

"If I now had in my possession one hundred million dollars in cash, I could buy the favor of the publishers of newspapers and control their presses; with that amount I could make this people popular, though I expect that popularity would send us to hell."

Brigham Young (Journal of Discourses 3:160)

"Popularity is never a test of truth. Many a prophet has been killed or cast out. As we come closer to the second coming, you can expect that as the people of the world become more wicked, the prophet will be less popular with them."

Ezra Taft Benson (BYU Speeches of the Year, 1980, pp. 26-30)

"Individuals who do wrong want you to join them because they feel more comfortable in what they are doing when others do it also. They may also want to take advantage of you. It is natural to want to be accepted by peers, to be part of a group—some even join gangs because of that desire to belong, but they lose their freedom, and some lose their lives. . . . You don't need to compromise your standards to be accepted by good friends. . . . No one intends to make serious mistakes. They come when you compromise your standards to be more accepted by others."

Richard G. Scott (Ensign, Nov. 1994, p. 37)

Mos. 18:9   **MOURN WITH THOSE WHO MOURN . . . . BEAR ONE ANOTHER'S BURDENS**
"Someone has said that people would rather be understood than be loved. In truth, the surest way to increase our love for someone is to listen with patience and respect. I believe that our baptismal covenant demands this. How can we 'mourn with those that mourn' and 'bear one another's burdens' (Mosiah 18:8-9) if we don't listen to know what those burdens are? . . . But we must be careful not to listen as Laman and Lemuel listened to each other. They encouraged mutual murmuring. When fellow ward members complain, blame others, and repeat negative tales, it takes self-discipline to stop ourselves from adding more fuel to their fire of disgruntlement. Mutual murmuring is a smoldering fire that can burst into flame and destroy a ward."

Virginia H. Pearce (Ensign, Nov. 1993, p. 80)

Mos. 18:9   **STAND AS A WITNESS**
(Conference Report, Apr. 1951, pp. 32-34)

"I often discuss our theme with young women and ask what it means to them to 'stand as witnesses of God at all time and in all things, and in all places' I believe it means that we show by our behavior what we believe. Surly we are standing as witnesses of God when we sustain his living prophets, especially when we know what it means to sustain. We will abide by the direction and counsel of the prophets. We indeed become witnesses when we make this solemn covenant."

Janette Hales Beckham (Ensign, May 1996, p. 84)

"When we covenant in the waters of baptism to 'stand as witnesses of God at all times and in all things, and in all places,' . . . It may not always be easy, convenient, or politically correct to stand for truth and right, but it is always the right thing to do. Always. . . . Today's young people, just as those 'of the rising generation' (3 Ne. 1:30) in Book of Mormon times, are the most susceptible to the influence of gangs. . . . There is an entire subculture that celebrates contemporary gangs and their criminal conduct with music, clothing styles, language, attitudes, and behaviors. Many of you have watched as trendy friends have embraced the style as something that was 'fashionable' and 'cool,' only to be dragged into the subculture because of their identification with gangs. We've all heard the tragic stories of unsuspecting wannabes who have been victimized by gangs simply because they were wearing the wrong color in the wrong neighborhood. . . . Many of you young men of the Aaronic Priesthood may find yourself on the front line of a battle against those who intend to do things that are morally wrong. I do not believe that you can stand for truth and right while wearing anything that is unbecoming one who holds the priesthood of God. To me, it is impossible to maintain the Spirit of the Lord while listening to music or watching movies or videos that celebrate evil thoughts and use vulgar language."

M. Russell Ballard (Ensign, Nov. 1997, pp. 37-39)

Mos. 18:12-18 **WHERE DID ALMA GET HIS AUTHORITY? WAS ALMA BAPTIZING HIMSELF AT THIS TIME?**
(3 Ne. 19:10-12)

"Alma was baptized and held the priesthood before the coming of Abinadi, but he became involved with other priests under the reign of the wicked King Noah, and when he baptized Helam, he felt he needed a cleansing himself so he buried himself in the water as a token of full repentance."

Joseph Fielding Smith (Doctrines of Salvation, 2:336-337)

"We may conclude that Alma held the priesthood before he, with others, became disturbed with King Noah. . . . If he had authority to baptize that is evidence that he had been baptized. Therefore, when Alma baptized himself with Helam that was not a case of Alma baptizing himself, but merely as a token to the Lord of his humility and full repentance. . . . If I remember correctly, there is no reference to the baptism of Alma the elder or Helaman nor of Nephi and his brother Jacob, but we know they were baptized as were all the faithful members in the Church."

Joseph Fielding Smith (Answers to Gospel Questions, 3:203-204)

Mos. 19:13 **DAUGHTERS PLEAD**
(1 Ne. 7:19; Mosiah 23:33-34; *Lehi in the Desert*, Nibley, p. 80)

Mos. 21:7,
11-12,
14-16

LAMANITES NOT THE REAL ENEMY TO THE NEPHITES
(1 Ne. 2:23-24; 2 Ne. 5:25; Mosiah 11:20-25; refer in this text to Alma 53:8-9)

"I apprehend no danger to our country from a foreign foe. . . . Our destruction, should it come at all, will be from another quarter. From the inattention of the people to the concerns of their government, from their carelessness and negligence. . . ."

Daniel Webster (June 1, 1837; Works 1:403; as quoted in An Enemy Hath Done This, Benson)

"In his book, *Caesar and Christ,* Will Durant, in summarizing the causes of the destruction of the Roman Empire, stated: 'A great civilization is not conquered from without until it has destroyed itself within. The essential causes of Rome's decline lay in her people, her morals, her class struggle, her failing trade, her bureaucratic despotism, her stifling taxes, her consuming wars. . . .'"

Ezra Taft Benson (An Enemy Hath Done This, p. ix)

Mos. 22:14

MORE RECORDS
"The early history contained in the Book of Mormon is obtained from three sets of plates: the brass plates of Laban, the small plates of Nephi, and the large plates of Nephi. However, when Limhi's people join with the people of King Mosiah in the land of Zarahemla they bring with them two additional sets of plates: (1) their own records, which are known as the record of Zeniff, and (2) the 'records which had been found by the people of Limhi,' which are later identified as the records of Ether (see Ether 1:1-2). When Alma and his people come into the land of Zarahemla, they also evidently bring their own records with them (see Mosiah 25:6)."

Daniel H. Ludlow (Companion to Your Study of the Book of Mormon, p. 188)

Mos. 23:21

PATIENCE
(Mosiah 3:19; Heb. 10:36; *Miracle of Forgiveness,* Kimball, p. 98; *Ensign,* Oct. 1980, p. 28; Ashton, *BYU Devotional,* Nov. 10, 1992; refer in this text to Alma 34:40-41)

Mos. 24:14-15

BURDENS EASED—THEY DID SUBMIT CHEERFULLY & WITH PATIENCE
(Hel. 12:1-6; Alma 17:11; D&C 58:2-4; 136:31;1 Cor. 10:13; 2 Cor. 8:2; Mosiah 23:21; Hel. 10:36; John 16:33; Job 23:10; *Teachings of the Prophet Joseph Smith,* p. 185; *Ensign,* May 1992, pp. 25-27; *Lectures on Faith,* 6:3; refer in this text to Alma 14:11; Alma 34:40-41)

"Elder Clinton Cutler said . . . 'The Lord's peace comes not without pain, but in the midst of pain.'"

Rex D. Pinegar (Ensign, May 1993, p. 66)

"Of course the greatest trial I have is that I cannot hear, but I have so many blessings I cannot complain, but if we only will live so that we may receive the instructions of God, there is nothing we are called to pass through but will be for our good."

Rachel Ivins Grant (Russell M. Nelson, Ensign, May 1991, pp. 22-25)

"I do not desire trials. I do not desire affliction. . . . I used to think, if I were the Lord, I would not suffer people to be tried as they are. But I have changed my mind on that subject. Now I think I would, if I were the Lord, because it purges out the meanness and corruption that stick around the Saints, like flies around molasses. . . . I have seen men tempted so sorely that finally they would say, 'I'll be damned if I'll stand it any longer.' Well, you will be damned if you do not. . . . We have learned many things through suffering. We call it suffering. I call it a school of experience."

John Taylor (The Gospel Kingdom, pp. 332-334)

"I rejoice in afflictions, for they are necessary to humble and prove us, that we may comprehend ourselves, become acquainted with our weaknesses and infirmities; and I rejoice when I triumph over them, because God answers my prayers, therefore I feel to rejoice all the day long."

Brigham Young (Journal of Discourses 1:17)

"My theory is that when a man is conscious or a people are conscious that he or they are in the path of duty, doing that which is right in the sight of God, they should always be happy, no matter what the circumstances may be which surround them. I think that God has created us to be happy, and my belief is that he placed happiness within the reach of all, and it is man's own fault if he is not happy and does not enjoy himself every day of his life. This is one of my reasons for liking my religion, . . . because it bestows full happiness and joy upon its believers. They can be happy in the midst of the most adverse circumstances; they can rejoice when their lives are imperilled."

George Q. Cannon (Gospel Truths, p. 125)

[Mary Fielding Smith gave details of her trials at Far West in a letter to her non-member brother in England] "I do not feel in the least discouraged. . . . We have been enabled to rejoice, in the midst of our privations and persecutions, that we were counted worthy to suffer these things, so that we may, with the ancient saints who suffered in like manner, inherit the same glorious reward. If it had not been for this hope, I should have sunk before this; but, blessed be the God and rock of my salvation, here I am, and am perfectly satisfied and happy, having not the smallest desire to go one step backward."

Mary Fielding Smith, wife of Hyrum Smith (Mary Fielding Smith, Corbett, p. 100)

"Concerning his personal suffering, Joseph was promised, 'Thy heart shall be enlarged.' An enlarged Joseph wrote from Liberty Jail, 'It seems to me that my heart will always be more tender after this than ever it was before. . . . I think I never could have felt as I now do if I had not suffered.'"

Neal A Maxwell (Ensign, May 1992, p. 39; quoting from
The Personal Writings of Joseph Smith, Dean C. Jessee, p. 387)

[From Liberty Jail, in a time of anguish and deep suffering for the gospel's sake, the Prophet Joseph Smith wrote the following message to the Saints] "Dear brethren, do not think that our hearts faint, as though some strange thing had happened unto us, for we have seen and been assured of all these things beforehand, and have an assurance of a better hope than that of our persecutors. Therefore God hath made broad our shoulders for the burden. We glory in our tribulation, because we know that God is with us, that He is our friend, and that He will save our souls."

Teachings of the Prophet Joseph Smith, p. 123

"Remember that this work is not yours and mine alone. It is the Lord's work, and when we are on the Lord's errand, we are entitled to the Lord's help. Remember that the Lord will shape the back to bear the burden placed upon it."

Thomas S. Monson (Ensign, May 1992, p. 48)

"Gratitude is a divine principle: 'Thou shalt thank the Lord thy God in all things' (D&C 59:7). This scripture means that we express thankfulness for what happens, not only for the good things in life but also for the opposition and challenges of life that add to our experience and faith. We put our lives in His hands, realizing that all that transpires will be for our experience. When in prayer we say, 'Thy will be done,' we are really expressing faith and gratitude and acknowledging that we will accept whatever happens in our lives."

Robert D. Hales (Ensign, May 1992, p. 65)

"We should seek to be happy and cheerful and not allow Satan to overcome us with discouragement, despair, or depression. As President Benson said, 'Of all people, we as Latter-day Saints should be the most optimistic and the least pessimistic' *(Ensign, Oct. 1986, p. 2)*. . . . We need not feel depressed or discouraged about conditions in the world, for the Lord will help us find the good that will lead us to happiness. . . . Surely we live in troubled times, but we can seek and obtain the good despite Satan's temptations and snares. He cannot tempt us beyond our power to resist. (See 1 Cor. 10:13.)"

Joseph B. Wirthlin (Ensign, May 1990, pp. 87-88)

"Pay attention to what the Lord requires of you and let the balance go. He will take care of that if you will acknowledge His hand in all things. . . . Rejoice evermore, pray without ceasing, and in everything give thanks, even if you have nothing but buttermilk and potatoes."

Brigham Young (Journal of Discourses 3:159)

A CONTRAST IN MAN'S RELIANCE UPON THE LORD
(Jacob 4:10; 2 Ne. 4:34; Prov. 12:15; D&C 103:5-7; Mosiah 15:7; 3 Ne. 11:11; *Conference Report,* Joseph Worthlin, Apr. 1982, p. 33)

"We pit our will against God's. When we direct our pride toward God, it is in the spirit of my will and not thine be done. . . The proud wish God would agree with them."

Ezra Taft Benson (Ensign, May 1989, p. 4)

"If our spirits are inclined to be stiff and refractory, and we desire continually the gratification of our own will to the extent that this feeling prevails in us, the Spirit of the Lord is held at a distance from us; or, in other words, *the Father withholds his Spirit from us in proportion as we desire the gratification of our own will.*"

Erastus Snow (Journal of Discourses 7:352)

"We must learn to pray with meaning, 'Not my will, but Thy will be done.' When you are able to do this, his whisperings to you will be loud and clear. The

Prophet Joseph Smith, after five months of extreme suffering in the dungeon of Liberty Jail, experienced it and he said, 'When the heart is *sufficiently contrite*, then the voice of inspiration steals along and whispers, My son peace be unto thy soul' *(History of the Church*, 3:293; italics added).

Graham W. Doxey (Conference Report, Oct. 1991, p. 34)

"Sadness, disappointment, severe challenges are events in life, not life itself. . . . A pebble held close to the eye appears to be a gigantic obstacle. Cast on the ground, it is seen in perspective. Likewise, problems or trials in our lives need to be viewed in the perspective of scriptural doctrine. . . . Some people are like rocks thrown into a sea of problems. They are drowned by them. Be a cork. When submerged in a problem, fight to be free to bob up to serve again with happiness. . . . Progress is accelerated when you willingly allow Him to lead you through every growth experience you encounter. . . . When you trust in the Lord, when you are willing to let your heart and your mind be centered in His will, when you ask to be led by the Spirit to do His will, you are assured of the greatest happiness along the way . . . If you question everything you are asked to do, or dig in your heels at every unpleasant challenge, you make it harder for the Lord to bless you."

Richard G. Scott (Ensign, May 1996, pp. 24-25)

"Only by aligning our wills with God's is full happiness to be found. Anything less results in a lesser portion. So many of us are kept from eventual consecration because we mistakenly think that, somehow, by letting our will be swallowed up in the will of God, we lose our individuality. It is not a question of one's losing identity but of finding his true identity! As one's will is increasingly submissive to the will of God, he can receive inspiration and revelation so much needed to help meet the trials of life. . . . Consecration, likewise, is not shoulder-shrugging acceptance, but, instead, shoulder-squaring to better bear the yoke. God seeks to have us become more consecrated by giving up everything. Then, when we come home to Him, He will generously give us 'all that He hath' (see D&C 84:38). . . . The submission of one's will is really the only uniquely personal thing we have to place on God's altar. The many other things we 'give,' . . . are actually the things He has already given or loaned to us. However, when you and I finally submit ourselves, by letting our individual wills be swallowed up in God's will, then we are really giving something to Him! It is the only possession which is truly ours to give!"

Neal A. Maxwell (Ensign, Nov. 1995, pp. 23-24)

"Recently I met with a family who had lost a precious son through an unfortunate automobile accident. They wondered when the comforting spirit of the Holy Ghost would envelop them to sustain them. My counsel was that when they were prepared to say to the Lord, 'Thy will be done,' then would come the sweet peace which the Savior promised. This willing submission to the Father is what the Savior exemplified in the Garden of Gethsemane."

James E. Faust (Ensign, Nov. 1996, p. 96)

"Whatever happens in the life of a person, if his attitude is right, the Lord will work that experience for that person's good."

Dennis B. Neuenschwander (Faculty Inservice, Orem Institute of Religion, Dec. 14, 1996)

"It takes great faith and courage to pray to our Heavenly Father, 'Not as I will, but as thou wilt.' The faith to believe in the Lord and endure brings great strength. Some may say if we have enough faith, we can sometimes change the circumstances that are causing our trials and tribulations. Is our faith to change circumstances, or is it to endure them? Faithful prayers may be offered to change or moderate events in our life, but we must always remember that when concluding each prayer, there is an understanding: 'Thy will be done' (Matt. 26:). Faith in the Lord includes trust in the Lord. The faith to endure well is faith based upon accepting the Lord's will and the lessons learned in the events that transpire."

Robert D. Hales (Ensign, May 1998, p. 77)

THE JOURNEY TO LEHI-NEPHI
Zeniff (Mosiah 9:3)   Sons of Mosiah (Mosiah 28:6-7)

"Our capacity to love and our capacity to endure well are inextricably bound together! Real faith in God, therefore, includes not only faith in Him, but in His timing—one of the things most difficult for us to have faith in."

Neal A. Maxwell (BYU Devotional, Dec. 12, 1984)

BATTLE STRATEGY
Noah (Mosiah 11:19; 12:15)   Zeniff (Mosiah 9:17; 10:19)

BURDENS
Limhi (Mosiah 21:7, 11-12,14-16)   Alma (Mosiah 23:27-29; 24:10-15)

DELIVERANCE
Limhi (Mosiah 22:1-13)   Alma (Mosiah 24:16-25)

Mos. 25:12 **CONDUCT OF THEIR FATHERS**
(Jacob 2:35; 3:10; Moses 7:37; D&C 68:25; 93:40-50; Matt. 17:6; Psalm 78:8; refer in this text to 2 Ne. 4:6)

"One of the greatest things a man can do for his children is to love his wife and let them know he loves her. A father has the responsibility to lead his family by desiring to have children, loving them, and by letting virtue garnish his thoughts unceasingly (see D&C 121:45). This is one of the great needs today."

Ezra Taft Benson (God, Family, Country, p. 185)

"Husbands and wives who love each other will find that love and loyalty are reciprocated. This love will provide a nurturing atmosphere for the emotional growth of children. Family life should be a time of happiness and joy that children can look back on with fond memories and associations."

Ezra Taft Benson (Conference Report, Oct. 1982, p. 59)

"We are actively engaged in teaching fathers to be compassionate fathers, and mothers full-time mothers in the home. Fathers are commanded to take the lead in all spiritual matters. We encourage parents to teach their children fundamental spiritual principles that will instill faith in God, faith in their family, and faith in their country. We plead with parents to spend time with their children, both in teaching them and in building positive relationships. These are the things that create and foster strong family units and a stable society."

Ezra Taft Benson (BYU, June 29, 1986)

"In the past twenty years, as homes and families have struggled to stay intact, sociological studies reveal this alarming fact: much of the crime and many of the behavioral disorders in the United States come from homes where the father has abandoned the children. In many societies the world over, child poverty, crime, drug abuse, and family decay can be traced to conditions where the father gives no male nurturing. . . . We need to honor the position of the father as the primary provider for physical and spiritual support. I state this with no reluctance because the Lord has revealed that this obligation is placed upon husbands. . . . (D&C83:2, 4; 84:99; 29:48). No one would doubt that a mother's influence is paramount . . . . Fathers seem best equipped to prepare children to function in the environment outside the family. One authority states, 'Studies show that fathers have a special role to play in building a child's self-respect. They are important, too, in ways we really don't understand, in developing internal limits and controls in children.' He continues, 'Research also shows that fathers are critical in establishment of gender in children. Interestingly, fatherly involvement produces stronger sexual identity and character in both boys and girls. It is well established that the masculinity of sons and the femininity of daughters are each greater when fathers are active in family life' (Karl Zinsmeister, 'Do Children Need Fathers?' *Crises*, Oct. 1992). . . . I urge the husbands and fathers of this church to be the kind of a man your wife would not want to be without."

James E. Faust (Ensign, May 1993, pp. 35-36)

"Fathers, if you wish your children to be taught in the principles of the gospel, . . . if you wish them to be obedient and united with you, love them! and prove to them that you love them by your every word or act to them. . . . However wayward they might be, . . . when you speak or talk to them, do it not in anger; do it not harshly, in a condemning spirit. Speak to them kindly. . . . Use no lash and no violence but . . . approach them with reason, with persuasion and love unfeigned. With this means, if you cannot gain your boys and girls, . . . there will be no means left in the world by which you can win them to yourselves."

Joseph F. Smith (Liahona, The Elders' Journal, Oct. 17, 1911, pp. 260-261)

"You adult brethren, may I suggest an 'I will' for us . . . It is *I will* resolve that the leadership of family will be my most important and sacred responsibility; and *I will* not leave the teaching and governance of my family to society, to the school, or the Church. . . . Perhaps you have heard some say, 'I am so busy with living and providing that I have little time to devote to my family, but I make an effort to see that my limited time is quality time.' Brethren, this type of rationalization is severely flawed. Effective family leadership requires both quantity and quality time. . . . May we never be too busy to do the things that mater most; to preside in righteousness in our homes. . . ."

H. David Burton (Ensign, Nov. 1995, pp. 44-45)

"When my wife and I were first married, my parents lived in another state. . . . We decided to go visit them. . . . After sundown, with two hours of travel still to go, we decided to play a game. . . . We said to the small boy in back, 'Let's play hide-and-seek.' . . . We said, 'Close your eyes and don't open them until we call you.' A front-seat passenger would crouch down in the seat and 10 or 15 seconds later would call, 'Okay.' Our son would bound over the seat and say, 'Aha, I found you!' We would say, . . . 'Close your eyes again.' A minute or more would go by. Then we would call, and again he would energetically climb over the seat to find us. Finally we said, . . . 'Close your eyes and we will call you.' . . . We drove along in silence. . . . We must have traveled 15 miles before we began to whisper quiet congratulations to ourselves on the success of our devious game. Then, from out of the backseat, came the sobbing voice of a heartbroken little boy. 'You didn't call me, and you said you would.' 'You didn't do what you agreed to do.' What a terrible accusation. . . . We knew that we could never play that game again."

F. Burton Howard (Ensign, Nov. 1995, p. 53)

Mos. 25:19   **CHURCHES IN THE LAND**
(refer in this text to 2 Ne. 5:26; *Answers to Gospel Questions*, Smith, 1:124-126; *Mormon Doctrine*, McConkie, pp. 599, 776; *Doctrines of Salvation*, Smith, 3:87; *CES Symposium*, Aug. 1986, pp. 97-98; *Promised Messiah*, McConkie, pp. 412-427; *New Witness for the Articles of Faith*, McConkie, p.348)

Mos. 26:1-3   **RISING GENERATION . . . DID NOT BELIEVE**
(Judges 2:10; Packer, CES Religious Educators Symposium, 8-10-93)

Mos. 26:3   **BELIEF PRECEDES UNDERSTANDING & TESTIMONY**
(Morm. 9:25; Moro. 10:4; D&C 5:16; Ether 4:11,13)

Mos. 26:20   **CALLING AND ELECTION**
(D&C 88:3-4; 131:5; 132:49; 2 Peter 1:10; Enos 1:5,27; 3 Ne. 28:1-3; Ether 12:37; 2 Tim. 4:6-8; *History of the Church*, Smith, 5:388; *Life of Heber C. Kimball*, Whitney, p. 24; *Ensign*, May 1977, pp. 43-45)

"When the Lord has thoroughly proved him, and finds that the man is determined to serve Him at all hazards, then the man will find his calling and his election made sure, then it will be his privilege to receive the other Comforter, which the Lord has promised the Saints. . . . [He then read John 14: 12-27]. Now what is this other Comforter? It is no more nor less than the Lord Jesus Christ Himself; and this is the sum and substance of the whole matter; that when any man obtains this last Comforter, he will have the personage of Jesus Christ to attend him, or appear unto him from time to time. . . ."

Teachings of the Prophet Joseph Smith, pp. 150-151

Mos. 26:29, 35; **CONFESS SINS**
27:31, 35 (D&C 58:43; 61:2; 64:7; 1 John 1:9; *Conference Report*, Oct. 1955, p. 125)

"When the apples in a barrel rot, it is not enough to throw away half of the spoiled apples from the barrel and replace them with fresh apples on top. This would result in all the apples rotting. Instead it would be necessary to empty the barrel and completely clean and scrub—perhaps disinfect—the entire inside. Then the barrel could be safely filled again with apples. Likewise in clearing up problems in our lives it is well also to go to the bottom and *confess* all the transgressions so that repentance begins with no half-truths, no pretense, no unclean residue."

Spencer W. Kimball (Miracle of Forgiveness, p. 180)

"The formula for repentance requires that we *confess*. Our first confession is to the Lord in prayer. When our mistakes are not grievous ones and if they are personal, that may be all that is required. If our transgression includes tampering with the procreative capacities of another of either gender, then there is a necessary confession beyond prayer. The Lord has designated, from his priesthood, the bishop to be the common judge. If your transgression is serious, and your conscience will tell you whether it is or not, seek out the bishop. The bishop represents the Lord in extending forgiveness for the Church. At times he must administer bitter medicine. . . . There is the idea abroad that one can send a postcard of prayer and receive in return full forgiveness and be ready at once for a mission or for marriage in the temple. Not so, there are payments to be made. If a bishop offers comfort only and, in misguided kindness, seeks to relieve you of the painful but healing process in connection with repentance, he will not serve you well."

Boyd K. Packer (BYU Fireside, 3/29/1992)

"You always need to confess your sins to the Lord. If they are serious transgressions, such as immorality, they need to be confessed to a bishop or stake president. Please understand that confession is not repentance. It is an essential step, but is not of itself adequate. . . . Essential to forgiveness is a willingness to fully disclose to the Lord and, where necessary, His priesthood judge all that you have done. Remember, 'He that covereth his sins shall not prosper: but whoso confesseth and forsaketh them shall have mercy.' (Prov. 28:13)."

Richard G. Scott (Ensign, May 1995, p. 76)

Mos. 26:30-31   **FORGIVE OTHERS**
(D&C 64:9-11; Matt. 6:14-15; *Miracle of Forgiveness*, Kimball, p. 332; refer in this text to 1 Ne. 7:20-21)

"Remember that we must forgive even if our offender did not repent and ask forgiveness . . . Do we follow that commandment or do we sulk in our bitterness, waiting for our offender to learn of it and to kneel to us in remorse? . . . this reconciliation suggests also forgetting. Unless you forget, have you forgiven?. . . No bitterness of past frictions can be held in memory if we forgive with all our hearts."

Spencer W. Kimball (Conference Report, Oct. 1949, pp. 132-133)

Mos. 26:36   **BLOTTED OUT**
(Alma 1:24; 5:57; 6:3; Book of Mormon 121-122 Student Manual, p. 73; Ashton, *BYU Devotional*, 11-10-92; refer in this text to Moro. 6:7-8)

"The scriptures speak of Church members being 'cast out' or 'cut off,', or having their names 'blotted out.' This means excommunication."

Teachings of Spencer W. Kimball , p. 100

"In contrast to the punishment that is the intended result of the judgment of a criminal court, the primary purpose of church discipline is to facilitate repentance—to qualify a transgressor for the mercy of God and the salvation made possible through the atonement of Jesus Christ. . . . Church discipline is not an instrument of punishment, but a catalyst for change. . . . The major concern of the laws of God is to perfect the lives of his children."

Dallin H. Oaks (Feb. 7, 1992, Temple Square Assembly Hall, Salt Lake City)

"The Lord is on your side and you must remember that numerous people are saved by excommunication. They are not *lost* by excommunication. They are *saved* through excommunication . . . ."

Teachings of Spencer W. Kimball , p. 98

Mos. 27:1-2   **OPPOSITION FROM WITHIN THE NEPHITE SOCIETY**
(refer in this text to Jacob 5:77)

"Many students who enroll at LDS Church-owned universities and colleges are caught off guard when they discover opposition in what they believed would be a trouble-free environment. . . . But frequently, just when they believe they've left their opposition behind . . . these students discover that opposition has stowed away on board, for it crawls out of the closet when they have hardly unpacked their bags. There may be unstable roommates who have not yet made a genuine break from their habits of the past; there may be disappointments with what appeared to be ideal arrangements for housing or classes; or, surprisingly, there may be new forms of temptation to which the unsuspecting are especially vulnerable when they let down their normal guard. . . . But, if our Church campuses are the Garden of Eden, they unfortunately still have their share of serpents."

Bruce C. Hafen (The Broken Heart, pp. 64-65)

THINK NOT, WHEN YOU GATHER TO ZION   **(Eliza R. Snow)**
Think not when you gather to Zion
Your troubles and trials are through,
That nothing but comfort and pleasure
Are waiting in Zion for you.
Think not when you gather to Zion,
That all will be holy and pure;
That fraud and deception are banished,
And confidence wholly secure.
Think not when you gather to Zion,
The prize and the victory won.
Think not that the warfare is ended,
The work of salvation is done.
No, no; for the great prince of darkness
A tenfold exertion will make,
When he sees you go the fountain,
Where freely the truth you may take.

"There was a time when we were driven by mobs, and our faith was tried in various ways. . . . There are no mobs now, we do not have our houses burnt down now, or our cattle shot down. But shall we be without trials? . . . It is necessary in the providence of God—that there should be liquor saloons, etc., so that Latter-day Saints . . . if they want to drink beer and get drunk, or go in and play billiards and gamble, or go to other places that are worse—can do so. 'But,' says one, 'I thought in coming to Zion I was coming to a place of purity where none of these things existed.' If that had been the case how would you have been tried?"

George Q. Cannon (Journal of Discourses 22:108)

Mos. 27:11   **THE VISIT OF AN ANGEL**
(Companion to Your Study of the Book of Mormon, Ludlow, p. 191; refer in this text to Alma 36:12-16)

Mos. 27:14-16   **THE PRAYER OF THE RIGHTEOUS**
(Alma 10:22; Gen. 18:20-33; James 5:16)

"You remember what Alma did when his son, Alma, didn't walk in the ways of the Lord and went about trying to destroy the church. He just did not give the Lord any rest about it; he took it to the Lord in mighty prayer until an angel of heaven appeared to his son. . . ."

LeGrand Richards (Conference Report, Oct. 1947, p. 75)

[An account of Zion's Camp] "The scourge came as had been foretold, and the Camp of Zion felt its terrible effects. Moanings and lamentations filled the air. . . . Joseph and Hyrum administered assiduously to the sick, and soon they were in the grasp of the cholera. They were together when it seized them; and together they knelt down and prayed for deliverance. Three times they bowed in supplication, the third time with a vow that they would not rise until deliverance from the destroyer was vouchsafed. While they were thus upon their knees a vision of comfort came to Hyrum. He saw their mother afar off in Kirtland praying for her absent sons, and he felt that the Lord was answering her cry. Hyrum told Joseph of the comforting vision and together they arose, made whole every whit."

George Q. Cannon (Life of Joseph Smith, p. 183)

"The stake president asked if I would meet with a distraught mother and father who were grieving over a son's decision to leave his mission . . . We knelt quietly in a private place . . . When we arose, the father said, 'Brother Monson, do you really think our Heavenly Father can alter our son's announced decision to return home before completing his mission? . . . I responded, 'Where is your son serving?' He replied, 'In Dusseldorf, Germany.' I placed my arm around the mother and father and said to them, 'Your prayers have been heard and will be answered. With more than thirty-eight stake conferences being held this day attended by General Authorities, I was assigned to your stake. Of all the Brethren, I am the only one who has the assignment to meet with the missionaries in the Germany Dusseldorf Mission this very Thursday.' Their petition had been honored by the Lord. I was able to meet with their son. He responded to their pleadings. He remained and completed a highly successful mission."

Thomas S. Monson

Mos. 27:24-26   **BORN AGAIN**
(Rom. 6:6; Alma 5:14; *A New Witness for the Articles of Faith*, McConkie, pp. 282-284; refer in this text to Mosiah 5:2, 7)

"The Holy Ghost is a cure and a preventative. While you have the companionship of the Holy Ghost, the cleansing power of the Atonement is operating in your life."

Henry B. Eyring (BYU Devotional, Oct. 29, 1989)

"The experience of each individual who is really born again is similar to this experience of Alma and the sons of Mosiah, although it may not be so dramatic. The effect upon each person's life is likewise similar."

Marion G. Romney (Conference Report, Oct. 1941, pp. 89-91)

"Though they are real and powerful, they are the exception more than the rule. For every Paul, for every Enos, and for every King Lamoni, [and Alma], there are hundreds and thousands of people who find the process of repentance much more subtle, much more imperceptible. Day by day they move closer to the Lord, little realizing they are building a godlike life."

Ezra Taft Benson (Ensign, Oct. 1989, p. 5)

"The very process of being born again spiritually is not a one-time occurrence. Hence, Paul said that he died 'daily' (I Cor. 15:31). Such is the process of putting off the old self as one becomes a woman or a man of God. Quick change artists are rare. I have not seen many put off the old and put on the new very rapidly."

Neal A. Maxwell (BYU Fireside, 12/2/84)

Mos. 28:1-8 **SONS OF MOSIAH DESIRE TO BE MISSIONARIES**
"They pled with their father that they might go and do missionary work among the Lamanites. Now father Mosiah feared for his sons' safety in the land of their enemy. . . . (v. 6). The first part of the Lord's answer might not have been exactly what Mosiah wanted to hear: 'Let them go up' (v. 7). But then follow three marvelous promises: the first, 'For many shall believe on their words,' and the second, 'I will deliver thy sons out of the hands of the Lamanites,' and then the third, 'They shall have eternal life' (ibid.). Now, he did not promise them great wealth, but he did promise the greatest of all the gifts of God, eternal life! The four missionary sons of Mosiah did not choose the easy course. Their choice was neither convenient, nor popular: They gave up the kingship. . . . They were ridiculed even by other members of the Church. . . . (Alma 26:23) Their choice to serve a mission was not one of convenience. . . . (Alma 26:29)."

Harold G. Hillam (Ensign, Nov. 1995, p. 41)

Mos. 28:5-7 **A MY WILL—THY WILL COMPARISON**
(contrast with Zeniff's journey to Lehi-Nephi in Mosiah 9:3)

Mos. 28:6-7 **A BLESSING OF DELIVERANCE**
(Alma 27:12; 56:47-48)

Mos. 28:6-7 **MISSIONARY WORK TO THE LAMANITES**
(Jacob 7:24; Enos 1:20)

Mos. 29:12-40 **NO KINGS UPON THE LAND**
(refer in this text to 2 Ne. 10:11)

Mos. 29:26-27 **THE MAJORITY CHOOSE**
(D&C 98:9-10; 3 Ne. 7:7; 4 Ne. 1:40; *Journal of Discourses* 22:136; *God, Family, Country*, Benson, pp. 277-280, 324; *Speeches at BYU*, May 1965, pp. 9-10; refer in this text to Hel. 5:2; 6:31; 16:10)

"This scripture should make all Americans pause in this day of wickedness to ask themselves whether the 'voice of the people'—that is, the majority—now seeks evil rather than light. . . . The scripture is explicit in saying that if 'the voice of the people doth choose iniquity, then is the time that the judgments of God will come.' . . . But it is a majority which is being reduced each day, as is shown in the rapid increase in crime, immorality, venereal disease, pornography and the other vile blotches upon our land. In a moral way, America is drifting. . . . If we remain adrift, we shall perish, and we shall bring destruction upon our own heads. How safe is America? No safer than its morals and its faith in God! Morals are slipping fast, faith is ebbing. Doesn't it frighten us? It should, especially when we realize what the consequences may be. One might say that other nations are worse than ours. This may be so, but that is no comfort. Let us remember that those other nations are not the 'Promised Land,' which America is. We are in a status far different from all other lands. There is a limit to which the Almighty will allow the inhabitants of this particular continent to submit to pollution. Will we take the necessary steps to save ourselves?"

Church News, Editorial Page, July 4, 1970

"Mr. Frank Stanton, CBS president emeritus, told a Brigham Young University audience that network television standards will continue to decline because they are based on society's standards. He said, 'Standards come from the audience . . . ; the audience determines the programming and program content.' Further, he said, 'I believe there will be more infractions with respect to immorality and violence and it will get a lot worse before it gets better because of the changing standards of our society.' *(The Daily Universe,* Feb 2, 1989, p.1). What a sad commentary on our society! Again we can learn a great principle from the Book of Mormon. When King Mosiah proposed that judges should rule instead of kings, he said: '. . . if the time comes that the voice of the people doth choose iniquity, then is the time that the judgments of God will come upon you (Mosiah 29:26-27).' That time of iniquity came about sixty years later and at several other times. In the book of Helaman we read that 'they who chose evil were more numerous than they who chose good (Hel. 5:2).' If television viewing choices serve as a valid measure of our society, they who choose evil surely are more numerous than they who choose good."

Joseph P. Wirthlin (May 1989, Ensign, p. 9)

"That which is right does not become wrong merely because it may be deserted by the majority, neither does that which is wrong today become right tomorrow by the chance circumstance that it has won the approval or been adopted by overwhelmingly predominant numbers. Principles cannot be changed by, nor accommodate themselves to, the vagaries of popular sentiment."

Albert E. Bowen (Conference Report, Apr. 1941, p. 85)

"The sad part of it is that a lot of us take our civil rights for granted. We were born in a free country. We think freedom could never end. But it could. It is ending today in many countries. We could lose it, too. The only way we can keep our freedom is to work at it. Not some of us. All of us. Not some of the time, but all of the time. So if you value your citizenship and want to keep it for yourself and you children and their children, give it your faith, your belief, and give it your active support in civic affairs."

Teachings of Spencer W. Kimball, p. 405

"I'll tell you how to vote. You read the 134th section of the Doctrine and Covenants and the 29th chapter of Mosiah, and then pray about it and you'll know exactly whom you should vote for at the election. That's how to vote."

Harold B. Lee (address to Seminary & Institute Personnel, BYU, July 8, 1966)

"This land, to God our Father, is a chosen land, dedicated as I have said to the principle of liberty and freedom, not license. Our fathers, under His inspiration, gave us the constitution of our country, the bill of rights which defines our privileges and places limitations beyond which we may not go. . . . there is no power that can wreck the government that God has established in this country unless it be the people themselves, and that I do not expect nor believe can occur."

Anthony W. Ivins (Conference Report, Oct. 1932, pp. 107-108)

Alma 1~4

Alma 1:3-5, 16 **PRIESTCRAFT**
(2 Ne. 26:29; 3 Ne. 16:10; 21:19; 30:2; D&C 124:84; 1 Cor. 2:4; 2 Kings 5:15-16, 26; 1 Peter 5:2; *Journal of Discourses* 13:55; *Conference Report*, Oct. 1954, p. 21; Hunter, CES Symposium, Feb. 10, 1989, p. 3)

"Priesthood and priestcraft are two opposites; one is of God, the other of the devil. When ministers claim but do not possess the priesthood; when they set themselves up as lights to their congregations, but do not preach the pure and full gospel; when their interest is in gaining personal popularity and financial gain, rather than in caring for the poor and ministering to the wants and needs of their fellow men—they are engaged, in a greater or lesser degree, in the practice of priestcrafts."

Bruce R. McConkie (Mormon Doctrine, p. 593)

"The anti-Christs such as Korihor and Sherem, openly rebel against Christ, while the user of priestcraft claims a belief in Christ but perverts his teachings."

Monte Nyman (Book of Mormon Symposium, Aug. 1982, p. 67)

"Persons who write truth for the purpose of gain commit Priestcraft."

Dallin H. Oaks (CES Symposium, 1985)

"The scriptural word for gospel service 'for the sake of riches and honor' is *priestcraft*" (Alma 1:16).

Dallin H. Oaks (Pure in Heart, p. 39)

"With a trained mind and a skillful manner of presentation, a teacher can become unusually popular and effective in teaching. But Satan will try to use that strength to corrupt the teacher by encouraging him or her to gather a following of disciples. A church or church education teacher or L.D.S. university professor who gathers such a following and does this 'for the sake of riches and honor' (Alma 1:16) is guilty of priestcraft. 'Priestcrafts are that men preach and set themselves up for a light unto the world, that they may get gain and praise of the world; but they seek not the welfare of Zion' (2 Nephi 26:29). Teachers who are most popular (and therefore most effective) have a special susceptibility to this form of priestcraft."

Dallin H. Oaks (BYU Fireside, June 7, 1992)

"Such a man or woman might serve in Church positions . . . in an effort to achieve prominence or cultivate contacts that would increase income or aid in acquiring wealth. Others might serve in order to obtain worldly honors."

Dallin H. Oaks (Conference Report, Oct. 1984, p. 14).

"There are some as wolves among us. By that, I mean some who profess membership in this church who are not sparing the flock. And among our own membership, men are arising speaking perverse things. Now perverse means diverting from the right or correct, and being obstinate in the wrong, willfully, in order to draw the weak and unwary members of the Church after them."

Harold B. Lee (Conference Report, Oct. 1972, p. 125)

[Speaking to seminary & institute teachers] "There is a difference between developing and enjoying the needed rapport with our students on the one hand, and developing a following on the other. . . . We cannot always control how people feel toward us or what we teach, but we can strive to be certain that our own motives are pure. I cannot speak for anyone else, but I believe if I have begun to attract people to myself, rather than to the Lord, that I need to undergo some serious introspection. My colleague Joseph McConkie observed to this group some years ago: 'Sometimes we get in our own way. We block the light because we are standing center stage when we should have stepped to the side and just let the [message] speak for itself. We cause what I call a spiritual eclipse.' (CES Symposium, 8-82, p. 1). If I am driven more by ego than by a desire to lead people to Christ; if my desires for acclaim are greater than my desires to love and serve the Lord and his children, then my eye is not single to the glory of God (Matt. 6:22-23; D&C 88:67-68), and I will obstruct the light that might have

been seen and felt. If, on the other hand, I am humbled to be in the presence of
my students, sobered by the sacred assignment to instruct them, and fully cog-
nizant of and willing to trust in Him who [is] the real Teacher and Converter,
then I will have the privilege of witnessing miracles, men and women coming
unto Christ and being perfected in him."

Robert L. Millet (CES Symposium, Aug. 1993, p. 11)

NEHOR'S DOCTRINE OF PRIESTCRAFT
Alma 1:3 (1 Ne. 22:23)
Alma 1:4 (2 Ne. 28:7-8)
Alma 1:5 (Morm. 8:28, 32,37)

Alma 1:6   **COSTLY APPAREL**
(contrast with Alma 1:27, 32 [Alma 4:6; 5:53; Jacob 2:13; Eph. 4:17; James 2:2-
4; 1 Cor. 1:26-29; refer in this text to Alma 31:28 and 32:2])

[Regarding *wealth* among the Nephites during times of *pride*] "Why should we
labor this unpleasant point? Because the Book of Mormon labors it, for our special benefit. Wealth is a jealous master who will not be served half-heartedly and
will suffer no rival—not even God: . . . Along with this, of course, everyone
dresses in the height of fashion, the main point being always that the proper
clothes are expensive—the expression 'costly apparel' occurs 14 times in the
Book of Mormon. The more important wealth is, the less important it is how
one gets it."

Hugh Nibley (Since Cumorah, p. 393)

"When money and possessions become the chief marks of distinction in society
then the pursuit of money becomes the only action worthwhile. And if this pursuit requires the sacrifice of honesty, integrity, compassion and all other virtues,
then so be it for the love of money is indeed the root of all evil. Thus the wearing of costly apparel involves the soul as much as the body."

Mae Blanche (Studies in Scripture, K. Jackson, 7:292)

"Are not many of us materialistic? Do we not find it well-nigh impossible to
raise our sights above the dollar sign? Are not many of us pragmatists—-living
not by principle but by what we can get away with? Are not many of us status-
seekers—measuring the worth of a man by the size of his bank account, his
house, his automobile? . . . surely these are among the many reasons why this is

truly an era of peril. . . . Many of us imagine in the foolishness of pride, that our manifold blessings are due not to God's goodness, but to our own wisdom and virtue. . . . This is a sad commentary of a civilization which has given to mankind the greatest achievements and progress ever known. But it is an even sadder commentary on those of us who call ourselves Christians, who thus betray the ideals given to us by the Son of God himself."

Ezra Taft Benson (Conference Report, Oct.1960, pp. 103,105)

"Fashion is the science of appearances, and it inspires one with the desire to seem rather than to be."

Edwin Hubbell Chapin (quoted in Spiritual Roots of Human Relations, Covey, p. 24)

"I see and admire beauty in people. I am not so concerned with the look that comes of lotions and creams, of pastes and packs as seen in slick-paper magazines and on television. I am not concerned whether the skin be fair or dark. I have seen beautiful people in all of the scores of nations through which I have walked. Little children are beautiful everywhere. And so are the aged, whose wrinkled hands and faces speak of struggle and survival. I believe in the beauty of personal virtue. There is so much of ugliness in the world in which we live. It is expressed in coarse language, in sloppy dress and manners, in immoral behavior which mocks the beauty of virtue and always leaves a scar. Each of us can and must stand above this sordid and destructive evil, this ugly stain of immorality."

Gordon B. Hinckley (Ensign, Aug. 1992, p. 4)

Alma 1:14, 18   **CAPITAL PUNISHMENT**
(Alma 30:10; 46:35; Hel 1:8,12; 3 Ne. 4:28; D&C 42:18-19, 79; Gen. 9:4-6; Deut. 19:11-13; *God, Family, Country*, Benson, p. 288; *Answers to Gospel Questions*, Smith, 1:189-191)

"We solemnly make the following declarations, the Church's position on capital punishment: . . . That this Church views the shedding of human blood with the utmost abhorrence. That we regard the killing of human beings, except in conformity with the civil law, as a capital crime which should be punished by shedding the blood of the criminal, after a public trial before a legally constituted court of the land. . . . The revelations of God to this Church make death the penalty for capital crime, and require that offenders against life and property shall be delivered up to and tried by the laws of the land."

Official Declaration (Millennial Star, Jan. 20, 1890, pp. 33-34)

QUALITIES OF THOSE WHO STAND FAST IN THE FAITH
(Alma 1:25, 26, 27, 29-30)

Alma 2:18, 28, 35

THE LORD'S BATTLE STRATEGY
(refer in this text to 1 Ne. 2:20)

"Safety can't be won by tanks and guns and airplanes and atomic bombs. There is only one place of safety and that is in the realm of the Almighty God that he gives to those who keep his commandments and listen to his voice."

Harold B. Lee (Conference Report, Oct. 1973, p. 169)

Alma 3:6-19

NEPHITE—LAMANITE
(Alma 2:11; refer in this text to 2 Ne. 5:21-23; Jacob 1:13-14; Hel. 11:24)

"Here God places his mark on people as a curse, yet it is an artificial mark which they actually place upon themselves. The mark was not a racial thing but was acquired by 'whosoever suffered himself to be led away by the Lamanites' (Alma 3:10); Alma moreover defines a Nephite as anyone observing 'the traditions of their fathers. . . .' (Alma 3:11). Which makes the difference between Nephite and Lamanite a cultural, not a racial, one. . . . The cultural picture may not be the whole story of the dark skin of the Lamanites, but it is an important part of that story and is given great emphasis by the Book of Mormon itself."

Hugh Nibley (Lehi in the Desert, p. 85)

"Originally, the Lamanites were the children of Laman, Lemuel, and some of the family of Ishmael; but as the centuries passed there were many defections in both nations, when the dissatisfied would join the opposing race and affiliate and intermix with them, so that the two names at last became more an indication of religion and civilization than of birth."

George Reynolds (A Complete Concordance of the Book of Mormon, p. 395)

"It should be noted that the Lamanites were often absorbed by, and were called Nephites when they were righteous, and it is true also that the Nephites when they rebelled and became wicked, were often times called Lamanites, and there was undoubtedly a considerable mixture among them."

Spencer W. Kimball (Conference Report, Apr. 1949, p. 107)

Alma 3:26-27

RECEIVE WAGES FROM THE SPIRIT WE OBEY
(Hel. 13:37; Mosiah 2:32-33, 37; D&C 84:88; Alma 5:40-42; Rom. 6:23)

"If our eyes were open to see the spirit world around us, . . . we would not be so unguarded and careless and so indifferent whether we had the spirit and power of God with us or not but we would be continually watchful and prayerful to our Heavenly Father for His Holy Spirit and His holy angels to be around about us to strengthen us to overcome every evil influence."

George Q. Cannon (Gospel Truths, 1:82)

"Let me read you what Parley P. Pratt said about this matter. 'In all ages and dispensations God has revealed many important instructions and warnings to men by means of dreams. When the outward organs of thought and perception are released from their activity, the nerves unstrung, the whole of mortal humanity lies hushed in quiet slumbers in order to renew its strength and vigor, it is then that the spiritual organs are at liberty in a certain degree to assume their wanted functions . . . Their kindred spirits, their guardian angels, then hover about them with the fondest affection, the most anxious solicitude. Spirit communes with spirit, thought meets thought, soul blends with soul, in all the raptures of mutual pure and eternal love. In this situation the spiritual organs, . . . our spirit body has eyes to see, ears to hear, tongue to speak, and so on . . . the spiritual organs are susceptible of converse with Deity, or of communion with angels, and the spirits of just men made perfect. In this situation we frequently hold communion with our departed father, mother, brother, sister, son or daughter, or with the former husband or wife of our bosom whose affections for us, being rooted and grounded in the eternal elements, issuing from under the sanctuary of love's eternal fountain, can never be lessened or diminished by death, distance of space, or length of years.' When we begin to understand that, beyond sight, as Brigham Young said, is the spirit world right here round about us. If our spiritual eyes could be open, we could see others visiting with us, directing us. And if we will learn not to be so sophisticated that we rule out that possibility of impressions from those who are beyond sight, then we too may have a dream that may direct us as a revelation."

Harold B. Lee (BYU Devotional, Oct. 15, 1952)

"I am convinced that one of the profound themes of the Book of Mormon, one which may not yet have been developed enough in our teaching of young people, is the role and prevalence and central participation of angels in the gospel story. . . . Obviously I speak here not alone of the angel Moroni but also of those more personal ministering angels who are with us and around us, empowered to help us and who do exactly that. . . . Perhaps more of us . . . could literally, or at least figuratively, behold the angels around us if we would but awaken from our stupor and hear the words God is trying to tell us. . . . I believe we need to speak of and believe in and bear testimony to, the ministry of angels more than we sometimes do. They constitute one of God's great methods of witnessing through the veil, and no document in all this world teaches that principle so clearly and so powerfully as does the Book of Mormon."

Jeffrey R. Holland (CES Symposium, BYU, Aug. 9, 1994, pp. 16-17, 19)

"We forget that God and angels are looking upon us; we forget that the spirits of just men made perfect and our ancient fathers . . . are gazing upon us, and that our acts are open to the inspection of all the authorized agencies of the invisible world. And, forgetting these things sometimes, we act the part of fools, and the Spirit of God is grieved; it withdraws from us, and we are then left to grope our way in the dark."

John Taylor (The Gospel Kingdom, p. 179)

"[A missionary testimony meeting while David O. McKay was serving in Scotland in 1899] During the progress of the meeting, an elder on his own initiative arose and said, 'Brethren, there are angels in this room.' . . . President James L. McMurrin arose and confirmed that statement by pointing to one brother sitting just in front of me saying, 'Yes, brethren, there are angels in this room, and one of them is the guardian angel of that young man sitting there.' And he designated one who today is a patriarch of the Church. Pointing to another elder, he said, 'And one is the guardian angel of that young man there,' And singled out one whom I had known from childhood. . . . He turned to me and . . . said: 'Let me say to you Brother David, . . . if you will keep the faith, you will yet sit in the leading councils of the Church.'"

David O. McKay (Cherished Experiences from the writings
of President David O. McKay, Middlemiss, pp. 13-14)

"The spirits of the just are . . . blessed in their departure to the world of spirits. . . . They are not far from us, and know and understand our thoughts, feelings, and motions, and are often pained therewith."

Teachings of the Prophet Joseph Smith, p. 326

"Every person who desires and strives to be a Saint is closely watched by fallen spirits that came here when Lucifer fell, and by the spirits of wicked persons

who have been here in tabernacles and departed from them. . . . Those spirits
are never idle, they are watching every person who wishes to do right and are
continually prompting them to do wrong."

Brigham Young (Journal of Discourses 7:239)

"There is a vast number of fallen spirits, cast out with him here on the earth.
They do not die and disappear; they have not bodies only as they enter the
tabernacles of men. They . . . are not to be seen with the sight of the eye. But
there are many evil spirits amongst us, and they labor to overthrow the Church
and kingdom of God. There never was a prophet in any age of the world but
what the devil was continually at his elbow."

Wilford Woodruff (Journal of Discourses 13:163)

"If you live up to your privileges, the angels cannot be restrained from being
your associates."

Teachings of the Prophet Joseph Smith, pp. 226-227

Alma 4:6-12	**PEOPLE OF THE CHURCH WAX PROUD** (Alma 1:22; refer in this text to 2 Ne. 9:28-51; Jacob 2:13-17; 3 Ne. 6:10-16)

"Pride is the great stumbling block of Zion. Pride is ugly, it says if you succeed,
I am a failure. Pride is basically competitive in nature. When competition ends,
pride ends."

Ezra Taft Benson (Conference Report, Apr. 1989)

Alma 4:9	**PRIDE OF MEMBERS EXCEED THAT OF NONMEMBERS** (refer in this text to Mosiah 29:26-27)

Alma 4:10-11	**EXAMPLE OF THE CHURCH** Example sheds a genial ray Which men are apt to borrow; So first improve yourself today, And then your friends tomorrow.

"One of our best missionary tools is the sterling examples of members who live the gospel. This is what the Lord meant when He said to the Church, 'Zion must increase in beauty, and in holiness. . . . Zion must put on her beautiful garments' (D&C 82:14)."

Ezra Taft Benson (Ensign, May 1985, p. 7)

". . . how much easier it is to understand and accept if the seeker after truth can also see the principles of the gospel at work in the lives of other believers. No greater service can be given to the missionary calling of this Church than to be exemplary in positive Christian virtues in our lives."

Teachings of Spencer W. Kimball, p. 555

". . . the time is coming when we will be mixed up in these now peaceful valleys to that extent that it will be difficult to tell the face of a Saint from the face of an enemy to the people of God. Then, brethren, look out for the great sieve, for there will be a great sifting time, and many will fall; for I say unto you there is a test, a TEST, A TEST coming, and who will be able to stand? . . . To meet the difficulties that are coming, it will be necessary for you to have a knowledge of the truth of this work for yourselves. The difficulties will be of such a character that the man or woman who does not possess this personal knowledge or witness will fall. If you have not got the testimony, live right and call upon the Lord and cease not till you obtain it. If you do not you will not stand. . . . The time will come when no man nor woman will be able to endure on borrowed light. Each will have to be guided by the light within himself. If you do not have it, how can you stand?"

Heber C. Kimball (Whitney, Life of Heber C. Kimball, pp. 446, 449-450)

Alma 4:15   **THE SPIRIT DID NOT FAIL HIM**
(contrast with Alma 30:60)

Alma 4:19   **PURE TESTIMONY**
"Those who have prepared carefully for the fast and testimony meeting won't . . . give sermons nor exhortations nor travel reports nor try to entertain as they bear witness. Because they will have already expressed appreciation to people privately, they will have less need to do it publicly. Neither will they feel a need to use eloquent language or to go on at length. A testimony is a simple expression of what we feel . . . . Even a child can feel such things, . . . and our preparation of fasting

and prayer produces in us child-like feelings. That preparation for the fast and testimony meeting is a covenant obligation for members of the Church."

Henry B. Eyring (Ensign, Nov. 1996, p. 32)

"The fundamental principles of our religion are the testimony of the Apostles and prophets, concerning Jesus Christ, that He died, was buried, and rose again the third day, and ascended into heaven; and all other things which pertain to our religion are only appendages to it."

Teachings of the Prophet Joseph Smith, p. 12

Alma 5~8

Alma 5:7,12-14, CHANGE OF HEART
26; 7:14 (Alma 19:33; Moses 6:59; *Teachings of the Prophet Joseph Smith*, p. 162; *Ensign*, Jun1992, pp. 10-13; *Ensign*, Nov. 1988, pp. 15-17; *Ensign*, May 1975, pp. 41-45; refer in this text to Mosiah 5:2, 7; Mosiah 27:24-26)

"Would not the progress of the Church increase dramatically today with an increasing number of those who are spiritually reborn? Can you imagine what would happen in our homes? Can you imagine what would happen with an increasing number of copies of the Book of Mormon in the hands of an increasing number of missionaries who know how to use it and who have been born of God? . . . The Lord works from the inside out. The world works from the outside in. The world would take people out of the slums. Christ takes the slums out of people, and then they take themselves out of the slums. The world would mold men by changing their environment. Christ changes men, who then change their environment. The world would shape human behavior, but Christ can change human nature."

Ezra Taft Benson (Conference Report, Oct. 1985, p.5)

Alma 5:14, 19 **THE IMAGE OF GOD ENGRAVEN UPON YOUR COUNTENANCE**
(Studies in Scripture, ed. by Jackson, 7:301)

"We are called upon to purify our inner feelings, to change our hearts, to make our outward actions and appearance conform to what we say we believe and feel inside."

Howard W. Hunter (Ensign, May 1992, p. 62)

Alma 5:15 **EYE OF FAITH**
(Alma 32:40; Ether 12:18-19; D&C 121:34-36)

"The 'eye of faith' means the ability and capacity to keep your eyes on the power source (see Matt. 14:23-32)."

Ross Cole (address to CES Educators, Ricks College, June 30, 1995)

Alma 5:26   **CAN YE FEEL SO NOW**

"I was building a shed next to my home. . . . I asked my son to go over to the neighbors and borrow a power drill so that 'turning the screws in' would not be such a tedious job. He returned with a rechargeable power drill. . . . I found that as I tried to put in the screws the drill would take them in about half-way and then the power would give out. The battery-powered drill did not have sufficient power for the difficult task. I told my son to take the drill back and ask the neighbor for his other drill because the rechargeable one did not have enough power for the job I was doing. When he returned with the other drill, we plugged it into the outlet in our home. I found that I now had more than enough power to drive the screws all the way into the wood. Both power drills were instruments in my hands; however, only one was able to perform the task that I needed done. As [returned] missionaries and servants of the Lord we might ask ourselves, Am I like the rechargeable drill trying to get by on spirituality stored up from past experiences, or am I striving to be in tune continually so I am like a power drill that is plugged into the source of all power?"

Clyde J. Williams (Alma - Testimony of the Word, ed. by Nyman and Tate, p. 91)

Alma 5:27   **HUMILITY**

(D&C 1:28; Ether 12:27; refer in this text to Mosiah 2:25-26; *The Screwtape Letters*, C.S. Lewis)

"It's hard to feel sufficiently humble. If you can, you may not be."

Henry B. Eyring

"The Prophet Joseph Smith, in our own dispensation, said this: 'When the Twelve or any other witnesses stand, before the congregations of the earth, and they preach in the power and demonstration of the Spirit of God, and the people are astonished and confounded at the doctrine, and say, "That man has preached a powerful discourse, a great sermon," Then let that man or those men take care that they do not ascribe the glory unto themselves, but be careful that they are humble, and ascribe the praise and glory to God and the Lamb; for it is by the power of the Holy Priesthood and the Holy Ghost that they have power thus to speak. What art thou, O man, but dust? And from whom receivest thou thy power and blessings, but from God?'

Who has the right to be smug and conceited in his own powers or accomplishments or talents? God gave us our breath, our life, our talents, our brains, our capacities."

Spencer W. Kimball (BYU Speeches, Jan. 1963, pp. 10-11)

"Humility! That does not mean weakness; that does not mean lack of courage, lack of faith, lack of self-confidence; but it means the recognition of a higher power upon which we are dependent . . ."

Ezra Taft Benson (So Shall Ye Reap, pp. 33-34)

"When one becomes conscious of his great humility, he has already lost it. When one begins boasting of his humility, it has already become pride—the antithesis of humility. . . . Somebody asked me this morning, 'How do you keep humble? Sometimes I am humble and sometimes I am unhumble.' I think there is a formula that will never fail. First, you evaluate yourself. . . . I would be nothing without the Lord. My breath, my brains, my hearing, my sight, my locomotion, my everything depends upon the Lord. That is the first step and then we pray, and pray often, and we will not get up from our knees until we have communicated. The line may be down; we may have let it fall to pieces, but I will not get up from my knees until I have established communication—if it is twenty minutes, if it is all night like Enos. . . If it takes all day long, you stay on your knees until your unhumbleness has dissipated, until you feel the humble spirit and realize, 'I could die this minute if it were not for the Lord's good grace. I am dependent upon him—totally dependent upon him,' and then you read the scriptures."

Teachings of Spencer W. Kimball, pp. 233-234

ALMA'S SPIRITUAL CHECKLIST
(Alma 5:14, 26, 27, 28, 29, 30 [Ether 12:26; D&C 45:44, 49-50])

Alma 5:37-39, 57, 60

WHO IS YOUR SHEPHERD?
[Speaking of some members of the Church] "They have refused to live the gospel, when they knew it to be true; or have been blinded by tradition; or for other causes have been not willing to walk in the light. In this class we could properly place those who refuse to take upon them the name of Christ, even though they belong to the Church; and those who are not willing when called to go forth and preach to a perverse world 'Jesus Christ, and him crucified.' They may live clean lives; they may be honest, industrious, good citizens, and all that;

but they are not willing to assume any portion of the labor which devolves upon members of the Church, in carrying on the great work of redemption of mankind. We have known members of the Church who have gone out in the world and have mingled with those not of our faith, and these members were ashamed to have it known that they were Latter-day Saints. Such persons certainly are not valiant in the testimony of Jesus."

Joseph Fielding Smith (Doctrines of Salvation, 2:28-29)

Alma 5:45-47   **I KNOW . . . BY THE HOLY SPIRIT OF GOD**
(refer in this text to Moro. 10:3-5; Alma 17:3)

Alma 6:1; 5:44   **PRIESTS & ELDERS**
(Mormon Doctrine, McConkie, p. 598-599; refer in this text to 2 Ne. 5:26)

Alma 6:6   **GATHER TOGETHER OFT**
(refer in this text to Moro. 6:5-6)

Alma 7:10   **CHRIST BORN AT JERUSALEM**
(Alma 21:1-2; *Answers to Gospel Questions*, Smith, 1:173-175; refer in this text to 1 Ne. 1:4)

"It was the rule in Palestine and Syria from ancient times, . . . for a large area around a city and all the inhabitants of that area to bear the name of the city. . . . But this was quite unknown at the time the Book of Mormon was written. . . . One of the favorite points of attack on the Book of Mormon has been the statement in Alma 7:10 that the Saviour would be born 'at Jerusalem which is the land of our forefathers.' Here Jerusalem is not the city 'in the land of our forefathers,' it is the land. Christ was born in a village some six miles from the city of Jerusalem; it was not in the city, but it was in what we now know the ancients themselves designated as 'the land of Jerusalem.'"

Hugh Nibley (An Approach to the Book of Mormon, 1957 edition, pp. 85-86)

Alma 7:10   **CONCEIVED BY THE POWER OF THE HOLY GHOST**
(John 3:16; D&C 76:23; *Doctrinal New Testament Commentary*, McConkie, 1:82-83; *Jesus the Christ*, Talmage, p. 81; *Messages of the First President* 4:327-332; *The Mortal Messiah*, McConkie, p. 314-315; *Doctrines of Salvation*, Smith, 1:18; *Sermons and Missionary Services of Melvin J. Ballard*, Hinckley, pp. 116-117)

Alma 7:11-12   **HE WILL TAKE UPON HIM THEIR INFIRMITIES**
(Ether 12:27; 2 Ne. 9:20-22; D&C 88:6; 122:7-8; Hel. 2:18; 4:15-16; refer in
this text to Mosiah 3:7; Mosiah 14:4)

"The Savior knows what it's like to die from cancer."

Neal A. Maxwell (Even As I Am, pp. 116-117)

"He [Christ] showed condescension when he chose to suffer, not only for our
sins, but for the infirmities, sicknesses, and illnesses of mankind. But the agonies of the Atonement were infinite and first-hand! *Since not all human sorrow
and pain is connected to sin, the full intensiveness of the Atonement involved bearing our pains, infirmities, and sicknesses, as well as our sins.*"

Neal A. Maxwell (Doctrines of the Book of Mormon, 1991 Sperry Symposium, p. 87)

"Whatever the source of pain, Jesus understands and can heal the spirit as well
as the body. The Savior, as a member of the Godhead, knows each of us personally. . . . In the garden and on the cross, Jesus saw each of us and not only
bore our sins, but also experienced our deepest feelings so that he would know
how to comfort and strengthen us."

Merrill J. Bateman (Ensign, May 1995, p. 14)

"Jesus knows and understands when we are stressed and perplexed. The complete
consecration which effected the Atonement insured Jesus' perfect empathy; He felt
our very pains and afflictions before we did and knows how to succor us."

Neal A. Maxwell (Ensign, Nov. 1995, p. 24)

"To succor means to 'run to.' I testify that in my fears and in my infirmities the
Savior has surely run to me. I will never be able to thank Him enough for such
personal kindness and such loving care."

Jeffrey R. Holland (Ensign, Nov. 1997, p. 66)

Alma 7:20   **HIS COURSE IS ONE ETERNAL ROUND**
(Morm. 9-10; D&C 20:11-12; James 1:17; 1 Ne. 10:18; Moro. 10:19; *The
Promised Messiah*, McConkie, pp. 197-198)

"The divine delight in what seems to us to be mere repetition is one clue to the sublime character of God. Since we must, at times, accept what appears to us to be routine, repeated experiences, we too, if we try, can find fresh meaning and fresh joy in the repeated experiences. God's course is one eternal round but it is not one monotonous round. God is never bored, for one who has perfect love is never bored. There is always so much to notice, so much to do, so many ways to help, so many possibilities to pursue."

Neal A. Maxwell (A More Excellent Way, pp. 84-85)

Alma 8:1   **REST**
"We must not be too busy sawing to take time to sharpen the saw."

Stephen R. Covey

Alma 8:10-15   **DISCOURAGEMENT IN THE MISSION FIELD**
(1 Ne. 2:1; Alma 17:5-11; 26:27; John 16:33; refer to the quote by Joseph F. Smith under 1 Ne. 8:2, 36)

"In June 1830, Samuel Harrison Smith trudged down a country road in New York State on the first official missionary journey of the restored Church. He had been set apart by his brother, the Prophet Joseph. This first missionary traveled twenty-five miles that first day without disposing of a single copy of the new and strange book that he carried on his back. Seeking lodging for the night, faint and hungry, he was turned away, after briefly explaining his mission, with the words: 'You liar, get out of my house. You shan't stay one minute with your books.' Continuing his journey, discouraged and with heavy heart, he slept that first night under an apple tree. So began, in the most inauspicious way, the missionary work of this dispensation through the restored Church, The Church of Jesus Christ of Latter-day Saints."

Ezra Taft Benson (God, Family, Country, p. 188)

"One of the greatest secrets of missionary work is *work*. If a missionary works, he will get the Spirit; if he gets the Spirit, he will touch the hearts of the people, and he will be happy. Then there will be no homesickness nor worrying about families, for all time and talents and interests are centered on the work of the ministry. Work, work, work—there is no satisfactory substitute, especially in missionary work. We must not allow ourselves to become discouraged. Missionary work brings joy, optimism, and happiness. We must not give Satan an opportunity to discourage us. Here again, work is the answer. The Lord has given us a key by which we can overcome discouragement (Matt. 11:28-30)."

Ezra Taft Benson (Come Unto Christ, p. 96-97)

[To missionaries] . . . "you must know that Lucifer will oppose you, and be prepared for his opposition. Do not be surprised. He wants you to fail. Discouragement is one of the devil's tools. Have courage and go forward. Recognize that the gospel has been preached with some pain and sorrow from the very beginning of time. Do not expect that your experience will be otherwise."

James E. Faust (Ensign, May 1996, p. 42)

"I received a mission when I embraced this work; it has never been taken from me yet. . . . We [John Taylor and I] have been over a great many rough roads, [and] traveled hard. . . . For over thirty years we have labored to preach the gospel. . . . In my early missions . . . I have waded swamps and rivers and have walked seventy miles or more without eating. In those days we counted it a blessing to go into a place where there was a Latter-day Saint. I went once 150 miles to see one; and when I got there he had apostatized, and tried to kill me. Then, after travelling seventy-two miles without food, I sat down to eat my meal with a Missouri mobocrat, and he damning and cursing me all the time."

Wilford Woodruff (Journal of Discourse, 12:11-12)

Alma 8:14   **ANGUISH BECAUSE OF WICKEDNESS OF THE PEOPLE**
(Hel. 19:3; 1 Ne. 15:4-5; 17:19; Morm. 6:17-20)

"It is interesting to note that, other than in the book of Job and a few other places, there are very few scriptural references to physical or mortal pain. The pain most frequently spoken of in the scriptures is the pain and anguish of the Lord and His prophets for the disobedient souls."

Robert D. Hales (Ensign, Nov. 1998, p. 15)

Alma 8:20   **NEPHITE**
(refer in this text to Hel. 11:24; Jacob 1:13-14; 2 Ne. 5:21-23; Alma 3:6-19)

Alma 8:30-31   **THE POWER GIVEN UNTO THEM**

Alma 9:12-13, 24 **REPENT OR BE DESTROYED**
(refer in this text to Ether 14:25; Hel. 13:6)

Alma 9:16-17 **LAMANITES WON'T BE DESTROYED**
(Jacob 3:5-7; 2 Ne. 3:3; 4:5; 30:3-6; Hel. 6:36; 7:24; 15:7-11; *Book of Mormon Prophecies*, Warner, pp. 116-117)

"At the time that the Prophet Joseph Smith translated this Book of Mormon, I suppose the impression was general, as it is today, [1884] that the Indians were a perishing race, that they would soon disappear from the face of the land. . . . Joseph found . . . that we as a race and the nation to which we belong, should not have power to destroy the Indians. This was a most remarkable statement to make when we consider where Joseph was brought up, and the circumstances surrounding him."

George Q. Cannon (Journal of Discourses 25:123)

Alma 9:15-24 **WHERE MUCH IS GIVEN MUCH IS REQUIRED**
(refer in this text to 2 Ne. 9:25-27)

Alma 10:3 **THE GENEALOGY OF LEHI**
(1 Ne. 5:14; 2 Ne. 3:4; 30:4; Omni 1:15; *Companion to Your Study of the Book of Mormon*, Ludlow, pp. 198-199, 245; *Journal of Discourses* 23:184-185; *Answers to Gospel Questions*, Smith, 1:142-143)

Alma 10:4-6 **RICHES BY THE HAND OF MY INDUSTRY**
(refer in this text to Jacob 2:13-17; 3 Ne. 13:19-24)

"A friend . . . proudly boasted that his climb toward wealth had come from tireless work and lessons learned in the 'school of hard knocks.' But his fortune had come at the expense of his spiritual development. When it was too late, he regretfully discovered that his ladder of success had been leaning against the wrong wall."

Russell M. Nelson (Ensign, Nov. 1992, p. 7)

Alma 10:22-23   THE PRAYER OF THE RIGHTEOUS MINORITY
(Alma 62:40; Hel. 13:12-14; 1 Sam. 7:9; Gen. 18:23-33; James 5:16)

"Our world is now much the same as it was in the days of the Nephite prophet who said: '. . . if it were not for the prayers of the righteous . . . ye would even now be visited with utter destruction' (Alma 10:22). Of course, there are many upright and faithful who live all the commandments and whose lives and prayers keep the world from destruction."

Spencer W. Kimball (Ensign, June 1971, p. 6)

"What can we do to keep the light of freedom alive? Keep the commandments of God. . . . Pay our tithes and fast offerings. Attend our temples. Stay morally clean. Participate in local elections . . . Be honest in all our dealings. Faithfully hold our family home evenings. Pray—pray to the God of heaven that He will intervene to preserve our precious freedoms that His gospel may go to every nation and people."

Ezra Taft Benson (This Nation Shall Endure, pp. 9-10)

"The Lord has made it plain to us that if we are not a prayerful people, if we fail to remember the king of this land, Jesus Christ, we can lose all of these blessings. . . . [Alma 10:22-23]. And so it seems to me that what we need in this fair land of ours is a shining example of prayerfulness, and the Latter-day Saints are the people who are chosen to exemplify to the world the power of prayer."

Joseph B. Wirthlin (Conference Report, Apr. 1949, p. 159)

Alma 11:1-19   NEPHITE MONEY
(*Since Cumorah*, Nibley, pp. 255-256; *Companion to Your Study of the Book of Mormon*, Ludlow, pp. 199-200)

Alma 11:23-24   THE RIGHTEOUS YIELDETH NOT TO THE LOVE OF LUCRE
(3 Ne. 13:24; Jacob 2:18-19)

Alma 11:38-39   SON OF GOD—THE ETERNAL FATHER
(refer in this text to 1 Ne. 19:10)

Alma 11:43   **A BRIGHT RECOLLECTION OF ALL OUR GUILT**
(refer in this text to 2 Ne. 9:14, 33)

"In reality a man cannot forget anything. He may have a lapse of memory; he may not be able to recall at the moment a thing that he knows or words that he has spoken; he may not have the power of his will to call up these events and words; but let God Almighty touch the mainspring of the memory and awaken recollection, and you will find then that you have not even forgotten a single idle word you have spoken."

Joseph F. Smith (Man, His Origin and Destiny, pp. 358-360)

"Man himself is a self-registering machine, his eyes, his ears, his nose, the touch, the taste, and all the various senses of the body, are so many media whereby man lays up for himself a record which perhaps nobody else is acquainted with but himself; and when the time comes for that record to be unfolded all men that have eyes to see, and ears to hear will be able to read all things as God himself reads them and comprehends them, and all things, we are told, are naked and open before him with whom we have to do."

John Taylor (Journal of Discourses 26:31)

Alma 11:43-44   **RESURRECTION**
(1 Cor. 15:22; *Gospel Doctrine*, Smith, p. 449; *Doctrines of Salvation*, Smith, 2:293-294; *Teachings of the Prophet Joseph Smith*, pp. 199-200; *Kisses at the Window*, Bassett, pp. 58-59; *Ensign*, May 1992, p. 11; refer in this text to Alma 40:23)

Alma 12:3, 7;   **DISCERNMENT**
10:17;   (Heb. 4:12; Acts 5:1-10; Hel. 9:41; Jacob 2:5; Luke 9:47; D&C 6:16)
18:16, 18,
20, 32   [an experience of Heber C. Kimball] "Being in charge of the Endowment House, while the Temple was in the process of construction, Heber C. Kimball met with a group who were planning to enter the temple for ordinance work. He felt impressed that some were not worthy to go into the temple, and he suggested first that if any present were not worthy, they might retire. No one responding, he said that there were some present who should not proceed through the temple because of unworthiness and he wished they would leave so the company could proceed. It was quiet as death and no one moved nor responded. A third time he spoke, saying that there were two people present who were in adultery, and if they did not leave he would call out their names. Two people walked out and the company continued on through the temple."

Spencer W. Kimball (Miracle of Forgiveness, p. 112)

"Often blessed with the power to know and understand beyond their experience, women draw on this strength as they visit monthly to teach in the homes or to assess needs as directed by the bishop. We use it as we nurture our children and teach them the gospel. . . . Discernment is critical for our times. President Boyd K. Packer has said, 'We need women with the gift of discernment who can view the trends in the world and detect those that, however popular, are shallow' (*Ensign*, Nov. 1978, p. 8). That is exactly what we need."

Elaine Jack (Ensign, Nov. 1996, p. 77)

Alma 12:6, 11; 13:30

SATAN'S CHAINS
(refer in this text to 2 Ne. 1:13,23)

Alma 12:9

NOT IMPART ONLY . . . WHICH HE DOTH GRANT
(Luke 2:19; refer in this text to Alma 37:28; 2 Ne. 32:7)

"It is not wise to continually talk of unusual spiritual experiences. They are to be guarded with care and shared only when the Spirit itself prompts you to use them to the blessing of others. I am ever mindful of Alma's words (Alma 12:9). I heard President Marion G. Romney once counsel mission presidents and their wives . . . , 'I do not tell all I know, . . . for I found out that if I talked too lightly of sacred things, thereafter the Lord would not trust me.'"

Boyd K. Packer (Ensign, Jan. 1983, p. 53)

Alma 12:9-11

HARD HEARTS GIVEN LESSER PORTION OF THE WORD
(Matt. 7:6; 13:11-12)

"The best educated man in the world may not be able to comprehend the simple truths of the gospel because his soul is not in tune; he has not been enlightened by the Spirit of the Lord. He, therefore, fails to see and feel the significance of these principles. They cannot be seen except through the touch of the Holy Ghost. For this reason Alma explained to Zeezrom how gospel light may be known." [Alma 12:9-11].

Joseph Fielding Smith (Doctrines of Salvation, 1:296-297)

Alma 12:14

OUR THOUGHTS WILL CONDEMN US
(3 Ne. 12:27-28; D&C 6:16; Matt. 5:27-28; Job 42:2; Psalm 94:11; *Miracle of Forgiveness*, Kimball, pp. 107-109; refer in this text to Mosiah 4:30)

"In the armory of thought man forges the weapons by which he destroys himself; he also fashions the tools with which he builds himself heavenly mansions of joy and strength and peace. . . . Between these two extremes are all grades of character, and man is the maker and master . . . and shaper of condition, environment and destiny. . . . All that a man achieves and all that he fails to achieve is the direct result of his own thoughts."

James Allen (As a Man Thinketh)

"All evils to which so many become addicted begin in the mind and in the way one thinks. Experience teaches that when the will and imagination are in conflict, the imagination usually wins. What we imagine may defeat our reason and make us slaves to what we taste, see, hear, smell, and feel in the mind's eye. The body is indeed the servant of the mind."

Joseph B. Wirthlin (Ensign, May 1982, pp. 23-25)

Alma 12:16 **SPIRITUAL DEATH**
(Companion to Your Study of the Book of Mormon, Ludlow, pp. 136-137; *Doctrines of Salvation*, Smith, 2:222-224)

Alma 12:34, 36, **THE REST OF THE LORD**
37; 13:6, (D&C 84:19-25; Moro. 7:3-4; *Teachings of the Prophet Joseph Smith*, pp.150-151)
12, 13, 16,
29; 16:17 "The ancient prophets speak of 'entering into God's rest'; what does it mean? To my mind, it means entering into the knowledge and love of God, having faith in his purpose and in his plan, to such an extent that we know we are right, and that we are not hunting for something else, we are not disturbed by every wind of doctrine, or by the cunning and craftiness of men who lie in wait to deceive. . . . The man who has reached that degree of faith in God that all doubt and fear have been cast from him, he has entered into 'God's rest,' . . . The rest here referred to is not physical rest, for there is no such thing as physical rest in the Church of Jesus Christ. . . . We may thus enter into the rest of the Lord today, by coming to an understanding of the truths of the gospel. . . . But there are many [Saints] who, not having reached this point of determined conviction, are driven about by every wind of doctrine, thus being ill at ease, unsettled, restless. These are they who are discouraged over incidents that occur in the Church, and in the nation, and in the turmoils of men and associations. They harbor a feeling of suspicion, unrest, uncertainty. Their thoughts are disturbed, and they become excited with the least change, like one at sea who has lost his bearings. . . . Let them seek for it in the written word of God; let them pray to him in

their secret chambers, where no human ear can hear, Jesus, and they will immediately begin to grow in the knowledge of the truth. . . . Let them seek for strength from the Source of all strength, and he will provide spiritual contentment, a rest which is incomparable with the physical rest that cometh after toil. All who seek have a right to, and may enter into, the rest of God, here upon the earth, from this time forth, now, today; and when earth-life is finished, they shall also enjoy his rest in heaven."

Joseph F. Smith (Gospel Doctrine, pp. 58, 126)

Alma 13:3-5

FOREORDINATION
(Abr. 3:22-23; Rom. 2:29-30; *Mormon Doctrine*, McConkie, p. 477; *The Mortal Messiah*, McConkie, pp. 22-26; *Decisions for Successful Living*, Lee, pp. 168-169; *Conference Report*, Harold B. Lee, Oct 1973, p. 7; *Conference Report*, Romney, Apr. 1944, p. 141)

"Every . . .[person] who has a calling to minister to the inhabitants of the world was ordained to that very purpose in the Grand Council of heaven before this world was. I suppose I was ordained to this very office in that Grand Council."

Teachings of the Prophet Joseph Smith, p. 365

"Remember, in the world before we came here, faithful women were given certain assignments while faithful men were foreordained to certain priesthood tasks. While we do not now remember the particulars, this does not alter the glorious reality of what we once agreed to."

Teachings of Spencer W. Kimball, p. 316

"Our young people are among the most blessed and favored of our Father's children. They are the nobility of heaven, a choice and chosen generation who have a divine destiny. Their spirits have been reserved to come forth in this day when the gospel is on earth, and when the Lord needs valiant servants to carry on his great latter-day work."

Joseph Fielding Smith (Improvement Era, June 1970, p. 3)

"For nearly six thousand years, God has held you in reserve to make your appearance in the final days before the Second Coming of the Lord. . . . God has saved for the final inning some of His strongest and most valiant children, who will help bear off the kingdom triumphantly. That is where you come in, for you are the generation that must be prepared to meet your God. . . . Make no mistake

about it—you are a marked generation. There has never been more expected of
the faithful in such a short period of time than there is of us. Never before on the
face of this earth have the forces of evil and the forces of good been so well
organized. . . . The final outcome is certain—the forces of righteousness will
finally win. But what remains to be seen is where each of us personally, now and
in the future, will stand in this battle—and how tall we will stand. Will we be
true to our last days and fulfill our foreordained mission?"

Ezra Taft Benson (Dedication of the Boise Institute of Religion, Nov. 20, 1983)

"We are quite well aware that Joseph Smith and Jeremiah and the apostles and
prophets . . . were foreordained to particular ministries. But that is only a part
of the doctrine of foreordination. The whole House of Israel was foreordained,
. . . millions upon millions—comparatively few compared to the total preexis-
tent host—but millions of people were foreordained."

Bruce R. McConkie (1969 BYU Speeches of the Year, p. 6)

Alma 13:28 **TEMPTATION—ABOVE THAT WHICH WE CAN BEAR**
(1 Cor. 10:13; 1 Ne. 15:24; Alma 34:39; refer in this text to 2 Ne.1:13, 23;
2 Ne. 28:19-22)

"Some transgressions are so powerful that it is unlikely that you will begin to overcome them without another's help. Seek that help. In time, with the strength that
comes from continued use of agency to live truth, you will be healed through the
Savior."

Richard G. Scott (Ensign, Nov. 1992, p.62)

[A letter to Gordon B. Hinckley which he shared in General Conference] "I am
a 35-year-old male and am a convert to the Church of more than ten years. For
most of my adult life I have been addicted to pornography. I am ashamed to
admit this. My addiction is as real as that of an alcoholic or a drug addict. . . .
I think it is ironic that those who support the business of pornography say that
it is a matter of freedom of expression. I have no freedom. I have lost my free
agency because I have been unable to overcome this. It is a trap for me, and I
can't seem to get out of it. Please, please, please, plead with the brethren of the
Church to not only avoid but eliminate the sources of pornographic material in
their lives. . . . Pray for me and others in the Church who may be like me to
have the courage and strength to overcome this terrible affliction."

Gordon B. Hinckley (Ensign, Nov. 1992, p. 51)

"Often 1 Cor. 10:13 is quoted to suggest that God will somehow snatch us from any and all circumstances and not permit us to be tempted beyond our ability to withstand. Alma seems to be saying that we have a responsibility in this matter - a responsibility to earnestly strive through prayer and humility to avoid circumstances that may bring overpowering temptations."

Larry E. Dahl (Studies in Scripture, ed. by K. Jackson, 7:320)

". . . sin is intensely habit-forming and sometimes moves men to the tragic point of no return . . . . As the transgressor moves deeper and deeper in his sin, and the error is entrenched more deeply and the will to change is weakened, it becomes increasingly near-hopeless, and he skids down and down until either he does not want to climb back or he has lost the power to do so."

Spencer W. Kimball (Miracle of Forgiveness, p. 117)

"All beings who have bodies have power over those who have not. The devil has no power over us only as we permit him. The moment we revolt at anything which comes from God the devil takes power."

Teachings of the Prophet Joseph Smith, pp. 181, 187, 189

"Satan is still trying to take away our free agency by persuading us to voluntarily surrender our will to his. . . . Some people are more susceptible to some addictions than other people. . . . One person has a taste for nicotine and is easily addicted to smoking. Another person cannot take an occasional drink without being propelled into alcoholism. Another person samples gambling and becomes a compulsive gambler. . . . We all seem to have susceptibilities to one disorder or another, but whatever our susceptibilities, we have the will and the power to control our thoughts and our actions. . . . A person who insists that he is not responsible for the exercise of his free agency because he was 'born that way' is trying to ignore the outcome of the War in Heaven. We are responsible, and if we argue otherwise, our efforts become part of the propaganda effort of the adversary."

Dallin H. Oaks (BYU Devotional & Fireside Speeches, pp. 44-46)

Alma 14:11   **WHY DOES GOD ALLOW TRAGEDY?**
(Hel. 12:1-6; *Faith Precedes the Miracle*, Kimball, pp. 95-106; *Ensign*, May 1993, pp. 67-68; *Ensign*, May 1994, pp. 7-9; refer in this text to Mosiah 24:14-15; Alma 17:11)

"The right question to ask is not why good people have trials, but how shall good people respond when they are tried? . . . God does not deny us the experience we came here to have. He does not insulate us from tribulation or guarantee immunity from trouble. Much of the pain we suffer and inevitably impose upon others is self-induced through our own bad judgment, through poor choices. . . . But much that happens to us in this life we cannot control; we only respond. Knowing what God has promised can provide the courage and faith we need. We are assured in the scriptures that we may know of a surety that the Lord does visit his people in their afflictions. . . . Thus the promise is that in times of sorrow and affliction, if we endure and remain faithful and put our trust in him and are courageous, the Lord will visit us in our afflictions, strengthen us to carry our burdens and support us in our trials. He'll be with us to the end of our days, lift us at the last day to greater opportunities for service, and exalt us at last with him and reunited loved ones, and he will consecrate our afflictions to our gain."

Marion D. Hanks (Ensign, Nov 1992, p. 64)

"Now, we find many people critical when a righteous person is killed, a young father or mother is taken from a family, or when violent deaths occur. Some become bitter when oft-repeated prayers seem unanswered. Some lose faith and turn sour when solemn administrations by holy men seem to be ignored and no restoration seems to come from repeated prayer circles. But if all the sick were healed, if all the righteous were protected and the wicked destroyed, the whole program of the Father would be annulled and the basic principle of the Gospel, free agency, would be ended. If pain and sorrow and total punishment immediately followed the doing of evil, no soul would do a misdeed. If joy and peace and rewards were instantaneously given the doer of good, there could be no evil—all would do good and not because of the rightness of doing good. . . . Should all prayers be immediately answered according to our selfish desires and our limited understanding, then there would be little or no suffering, sorrow, disappointment or even death, and if these were not there would also be an absence of joy, success, resurrection, eternal life and Godhood. . . . Being human we would expel from our lives, sorrow, distress, physical pain and mental anguish and assure ourselves of continual ease and comfort, but if we closed the doors upon such, we might be evicting our greatest friends and benefactors. Suffering can make saints of people as they learn patience, long suffering and self-mastery. The sufferings of our Savior were part of his education."

Spencer W. Kimball (Tragedy or Destiny, pp. 4-5)

"Yes, each of us will walk the path of disappointment, perhaps due to an opportunity lost, a power misused, or a loved one not taught. The path of temptation, too, will be the path of each. . . . Likewise shall we walk the path of pain. We cannot go to heaven in a feather bed. The Savior of the world entered after great pain and suffering. We, as servants, can expect no more than the Master. Before Easter there must be a cross."

Thomas S. Monson (Ensign, Sept 1992, p. 4)

"We have reviewed from scriptures and from living prophets four major reasons for suffering: (1) experience, (2) our good, (3) our own sins, and (4) accidents. It is important for our spiritual growth that [we] recognize the validity of these reasons."

Keith W. Perkins (Sperry Symposium on the D&C and Church History, 1992, p. 287)

"I can understand why someone who lacks an eternal perspective might see the horrifying news footage of starving children and man's inhumanity to man and shake a fist at the heavens and cry, 'If there is a God, how could he allow such things to happen' . . . God has put his plan in motion. It proceeds through natural laws that are, in fact, God's laws. Since they are his, he is bound by them, as are we. . . . The Lord can control the elements. For the most part, however, he does not cause but he allows nature to run its course. In this imperfect world, bad things sometimes happen. . . . [However], much adversity is man-made. . . . Much adversity has its origin in the principle of agency. . . . Often overlooked is the fact that choices have consequences. . . . At times we will be affected adversely by the way other people choose to exercise their agency. Our Heavenly Father feels so strongly about protecting our agency that he allows his children to exercise it, either for good or for evil. . . . But if we know and understand Heavenly Father's plan, we realize that dealing with adversity is one of the chief ways we are tested."

M. Russell Ballard (Ensign, May 1995, p. 23)

"Trials, disappointments, sadness, and heartache come to us from two basically different sources. Those who transgress the laws of God will always have those challenges. The other reason for adversity is to accomplish the Lord's own purposes in our life that we may receive the refinement that comes from testing. . . . If you are suffering the disheartening effects of transgression, please recognize that the only path to permanent relief from sadness is sincere repentance with a broken heart and a contrite spirit. . . . When those trials are not consequences of your disobedience, they are evidence that the Lord feels you are prepared to grow more (see Prov. 3:11-12). . . . When you face adversity, you can be led to ask many questions. Some serve a useful purpose; others do not. To ask, Why does this have to happen to me? Why do I have to suffer this, now? What have I done to cause this? will lead you into blind alleys. . . . Rather ask, What am I to do? What am I to learn from this experience? What am I to change? Whom am I to help? How can I remember my many blessings in times of trial? Willing sacrifice of deeply held personal desires in favor of the will of God is very hard to do. Yet, when you pray with real conviction, 'Please let me know Thy will' and 'May Thy will be done,' you are in the strongest position to receive the maximum help from your loving Father."

Richard G. Scott (Ensign, Nov. 1995, p. 16)

"Since we assembled in general conference last April, . . . I experienced my third heart attack. . . . While I was lying in my hospital bed and for several weeks at home, my physical activity was severely restricted by intense pain which disabled my weakened body, but I learned the joy of freeing my mind to ponder the meaning of life and the eternities. . . . I discovered that if I dwelt only upon my pain, it inhibited the healing process. I found that pondering was a very important element in the healing process for both soul and body. Pain brings you to a humility that allows you to ponder. It is an experience I am grateful to have endured. . . . I have come to understand how useless it is to dwell on the *whys*, *what ifs*, and *if onlys* for which there likely will be given no answers in mortality. To receive the Lord's comfort, we must exercise faith. The questions Why me? Why our family? Why now? are usually unanswerable questions. These questions detract from our spirituality and can destroy our faith. We need to spend our time and energy building our faith by turning to the Lord and asking for strength to overcome the pains and trials of this world and to endure to the end for greater understanding. . . . We must surrender ourselves to the Lord. In doing so, we give up whatever is causing our pain and turn everything over to Him. 'Cast thy burden upon the Lord, and he shall sustain thee (Psalms 55:22).' . . . Healing comes in the Lord's time and the Lord's way; be patient. Our Savior waits for us to come to Him through our scripture study, pondering, and prayer to our Heavenly Father."

Robert D. Hales (Ensign, Nov. 1998, pp. 14-17)

Alma 15:16, 18; 10:4

REJECTED BY FAMILY

"The Gospel of Salvation is perfectly calculated to cause division."

Brigham Young (Journal of Discourses 1:235)

Alma 16:2-3, 9;   **ALMA 10:22-23 FULFILLED**
    25:2

Alma 16:5-8   **PRO-KINGDOM vs. ANTI-ENEMY**
(refer in this text to Mosiah 11:19)

Alma 17~20

Alma 17:2-5,   **MISSIONARY WORK**
9, 11-12   (Alma 31:36-38; 3 Ne. 13:25-34; Matt. 6:25-34; D&C 18:15; 84:80-81,85; refer in this text to Alma 29:1-2; *Teachings of Spencer W. Kimball*, p. 24; *Ensign*, Backman, Oct. 1992, pp. 13-15)

[To the young men of the Church] "You have missions to perform. Each of you should plan for missionary service. You may have some doubts. You may have some fears. Face your doubts and your fears with faith. Prepare yourselves to go. You have not only the opportunity; you have the responsibility. . . . Is it too much to ask that you give two years totally immersed in His service? . . . You know what is right. You know what is wrong. You know when and how to make the choice. you know that there is a power in heaven on which you can call in your time of extremity and need. . . . Stand up and walk as becomes the sons of God.

[Speaking of the Sister Missionaries] They perform a remarkable work. They can get in homes where the elders cannot. . . . Now having made that confession, I wish to say that the First Presidency and the Council of the Twelve are united in saying to our young sisters that they are not under obligation to go on missions. . . . Some of them will very much wish to go. If the idea persists, the bishop will know what to do. . . . missionary work is essentially a priesthood responsibility. As such, our young men must carry the major burden. This is their responsibility and their obligation. We do not ask the young women to consider a mission as an essential part of their life's program. Over a period of many years, we have held the age level higher for them in an effort to keep the number going relatively small. Again to the sisters I say that you will be as highly respected, you will be considered as being as much in the line of duty, your efforts will be as acceptable to the Lord and to the Church whether you go on a mission or do not go on a mission. . . . I certainly do not wish to say or imply that their services are not wanted. I simply say that a mission is not necessary as a part of their lives."

Gordon B. Hinckley (Ensign, Nov. 1997, p. 52)

"The question is frequently asked, Should every young man fill a mission? The answer to this inquiry has been given by the Lord. It is yes. Every young man should fill a mission. While every young man should serve a mission, we realize that every young man is not physically, emotionally, nor morally prepared. As a consequence, some may be deprived of missionary opportunities. But all should prepare to go—to be worthy to serve the Lord. . . . Some young men, because of transgression, say they are not interested in serving a mission. The real reason, of course, is feelings of unworthiness. If such young men would go to their bishop, confide to him their problem, and sincerely repent, they may yet fill honorable missions."

Teachings of Ezra Taft Benson, pp. 182-183

"And I say to you . . . Elders, Awaken up! God has placed the priesthood upon you, and he expects you to magnify it. . . . We want some manhood, and some priesthood and power of God to be manifested in Israel. . . . And I pray God, the Eternal Father, to waken up these Elders, that the spirit of their mission may rest upon them, and that they may comprehend their true position before God."

Brigham Young (Journal of Discourses 20:23)

"The Lord wants every young man to serve a full-time mission. Presently only a third of the eligible young men in the Church are serving missions. This is not pleasing to the Lord. We can do better. We must do better. Not only should a mission be regarded as a priesthood duty, but every young man should look forward to this experience with great joy and anticipation. A young man can do nothing more important. School can wait. Scholarships can be deferred. Occupational goals can be postponed. Yes, even temple marriage should wait until after a young man has served an honorable full-time mission for the Lord. . . . Remember, young women, you may also have the opportunity to serve a full-time mission. I am grateful my own eternal companion served a mission in Hawaii before we were married in the Salt Lake Temple, and I am pleased that I have had three grand-daughters serve full-time missions. Some of our finest missionaries are young sisters."

Teachings of Ezra Taft Benson, pp. 190,194

"Now you young unmarried sisters from twenty-one to sixty-nine with good health, there is no obligation to serve, but you are certainly welcome and wanted if the Spirit encourages you to volunteer. . . . Now you young men, unmarried, nineteen to twenty-six (eighteen outside the United States), . . . a mission has been emphasized as a priesthood responsibility of such priority that again today we stress, *your mission comes before marriage, education, professional opportunities, scholarships, sports, cars, or girls.* . . . You will have twenty-four years' worth of spiritual adventures. You will see people change; soften; become more humble, more obedient; have their prayers answered; and come to a knowledge that our message is true."

Robert E. Wells (Conference Report, Oct. 1985, p. 36)

"A mother and father were in my office accompanied by a 265-pound BYU sophomore All-WAC tackle. They had asked for an appointment to help resolve a confusing family situation. After we greeted the mother and the father and their son, Lance Reynolds, we had a few words of friendly conversation. I knew why they had come. The trying decision was does Lance go on a mission or does he stay and play football? I looked at the mother and said, 'What do you think your son should do?' She said, 'I think he can render a special service and example to the Church if he maintains his standards and continues to play football and hopefully help in bringing football fame to BYU and the Church. I think his football playing can be his mission.' I looked at the father, and I said, 'What do you think Lance should do?' He was smart enough not to disagree in that setting with his wife, so he merely said, 'I'm not quite certain.' I looked at Lance and I said, 'Lance, what do you want to do?' He said, 'I want to go on a mission.' I responded with, 'Why don't you?' He said, 'I will.' Our interview was over. Lance went on his mission, was an outstanding missionary, came back and reaped all-conference honors, and is now on the BYU's football coaching staff. He is a special friend of mine today."

Marvin J. Ashton (BYU Devotional, Aug. 24, 1992)

"An acquaintance of mine grew up not far from here. . . . Many universities offered him scholarships to play basketball. After his first year playing at a university, he told his coach that he would like to be excused for two years to go on a mission. The coach said, 'If you leave, you can be sure of one thing: you will never again wear one of our basketball uniforms!' Many thought that his 'mission' ought to be playing basketball. Even some family members, including his parents, tried to convince him not to serve a mission. But he was totally committed. . . . He was called, and he served an honorable mission. When he returned, . . . his coach decided to repent. . . . In his senior year, his team not only won the conference championship but went on to the finals in national competition. . . . Modern prophets have taught that every young man who is physically and mentally able should prepare himself to serve an honorable mission. The Lord did not say, 'Go on a mission if it fits your schedule, or if you happen to feel like it, or if it doesn't interfere with your scholarship, your romance, or your educational plans.' Preaching the gospel is a commandment and not merely a suggestion. . . . Even though for some of you there may be very tempting reasons for you not to serve a full-time mission, the Lord and his prophets are counting on you."

Joe J. Christensen (Ensign, Nov. 1996, pp. 40-41)

"One young man, when called on a mission, replied that he didn't have much talent for that kind of thing. What he was good at was keeping his powerful new automobile in top condition. He enjoyed the sense of power and acceleration, and when he was driving, the continual motion gave him the illusion that he was really getting somewhere. All along, his father had been content with saying, 'He likes to do things with his hands. That's good enough for him.' Good enough for a son of God? This young man didn't realize that the power of his automobile is infinitesimally small in comparison with the . . . priesthood power that he could have been developing in the service of the Lord. He settled for a pitiful god, a composite of steel and rubber and shiny chrome.

An older couple retired from the world of work and purchased a pickup truck and camper and, separating themselves from all obligations, set out to see the world and simply enjoy what little they had accumulated the rest of their days. They had not time . . . for missionary service. . . . Their experience and leadership were sorely needed . . . but, unable to 'endure to the end,' they were not available."

Spencer W. Kimball (Ensign, June 1976, p. 5)

"I have a vision of thousands of missionaries going into the mission field with hundreds of passages memorized from the Book of Mormon so that they might feed the needs of a spiritually famished world. I have a vision of the whole Church getting nearer to God by abiding by the precepts of the Book of Mormon. Indeed, I have a vision of flooding the earth with the Book of Mormon."

Ezra Taft Benson (Ensign, Nov. 1988, pp. 4-6)

"I throw out a challenge to every young man within this vast congregation tonight. Prepare yourself now to be worthy to serve the Lord as a full-time missionary. . . . Prepare to consecrate two years of your lives to this sacred service. That will in effect constitute a tithe on the first twenty years of your lives. . . . I promise you that the time you spend in the mission field, if those years are spent in dedicated service, will yield a greater return on investment than any other two years of your lives. . . . You will develop powers of persuasion which will bless your entire life. Your timidity, your fears, your shyness will gradually disappear as you go forth with boldness and conviction. You will learn to work with others. . . . The cankering evil of selfishness will be supplanted by a sense of service to others. You will draw nearer to the Lord than you likely will in any other set of circumstances. You will come to know that without His help you are indeed weak and simple, but that with His help you can accomplish miracles. You will establish habits of industry. You will develop a talent for the establishment of goals of effort. You will learn to work with singleness of purpose. . . . If you serve a mission faithfully and well, you will be a better husband, you will be a better father, you will be a better student, a better worker in your chosen vocation."

Gordon B. Hinckley (Ensign, Nov. 1995, pp. 51-52)

"Prepare now to go on a mission. It will not be a burden. It will not be a waste of time. It will be a great opportunity and a great challenge. It will do something for you that nothing else will do for you. It will sharpen your skills. It will train you in leadership. It will bring testimony and conviction into your heart. You will bless the lives of others as you bless your own. It will bring you nearer to God and to His Divine Son as you bear witness and testimony of Him. Your knowledge of the gospel will strengthen and deepen. Your love for your fellowman will increase. Your fears will fade as you stand boldly in testimony of the truth."

Gordon B. Hinckley (Ensign, May 1997, p. 50)

"Now, my dear young friends, I hope all of you are pointed in the direction of missionary service. I cannot promise you fun. I cannot promise you ease and comfort. I cannot promise you freedom from discouragement, from fear, from downright misery at times. But I can promise you that you will grow as you have never grown in a similar period during your entire lives. I can promise you a happiness that will be unique and wonderful and lasting. I can promise you that you will reevaluate your lives, that you will establish new priorities, that you will live closer to the Lord, that prayer will become a real and wonderful experience, that you will walk with faith in the outcome of the good things you do."

Gordon B. Hinckley (Ensign, Nov. 1998, p. 52)

"We must be willing to release the death grip which we have on things, which have become as a security blanket in our lives. Count the many hundreds of needed missionary couples who would be serving in the field if that firm grip on the familiarities of home and of children and grandchildren could be loosened. The

Lord is prepared to perform the miracle that will follow, which miracle is that both they and you will survive, even grow, with an eighteen-month separation."

Graham W. Doxey (Conference Report, Oct. 1991, p. 34)

"In addition to the need for more young men and women to serve, there is an urgent need for couples. Each time we visit a mission, the universal request is for more couples. The need is great for mature couples who are financially able, possessing strong testimonies, and with reasonably good health. Their entry into the mission field adds strength and maturity to our missionary effort. . . . Is this not the special time of decision for all of you . . . special mature older couples? Have you ever sat down and contemplated what kind of entries you will prepare for your life's history? Will yours be one comprised of slides and videos of worldly acquisitions of boats and motor homes, of travel and entertainment for personal gratification and amusement? Or will your history express the joy you have experienced in preaching and teaching the message of our Lord and Savior to all who would hear your voice?"

Angel Abrea (Ensign, May 1992, pp. 24-25)

"The cause to which I speak is of missionary work as couples. . . . There is a need, not to leave homes forever, but for a time—then return and reap the rich harvest of the faithful labor. Your children and grandchildren will be blessed. . . . President Harold B. Lee taught the principle that only as we make ourselves totally available are we worthy disciples of Christ and obtain another promise that reaches beyond us. We worry and ache and pain over family members who have erred. The thirty-first section of the Doctrine and Covenants provides a great key in verse five: 'Therefore, thrust in your sickle with all your soul, and your sins are forgiven you, and you shall be laden with sheaves upon your back, for the laborer is worthy of his hire. Wherefore, your family shall live.' . . . The promise is sure, 'Wherefore, your family shall live.' Blessings will come to our wayward or wandering children, even those who are married and have children of their own. . . . As we come to the latter years of life, we come to a mature spiritual understanding. What better way have we to prepare to meet our God than to serve a mission when the autumn and winter of life is upon us?"

Vaughn J. Featherstone (Ensign, May 1992, pp. 42-44)

"There is an urgent need in the Church today for missionary couples, not to go first-contacting or teaching the discussions, unless you want to do so, but for meaningful missionary service in all of the activities of the Church throughout the world. There is far greater flexibility in the service opportunities of couples than for single elders or sisters. In consultation with your bishop, you can indicate your own preferences for missionary service. We must train a growing number of fathers and mothers and priesthood and auxiliary leaders throughout the world who want very much to serve the Lord but simply do not know how to do it. You can help them as a leadership missionary couple. You can serve in temples, family history, educational and medical activities, welfare service projects, public affairs, and visitors' centers. . . . Your children and grandchildren will be positively influenced for good as witnessed by many couples who have honorably served, some on their third, fourth, or fifth mission. Don't wait to be asked. I invite each of you to come forth to participate some way in the glorious and varied opportunities for missionary service. . . ."

Richard G. Scott (Ensign, Nov. 1997, pp. 36-37)

Alma 17:2 **THEY HAD SEARCHED THE SCRIPTURES DILIGENTLY**
(1 Ne. 5:10; D&C 11:22; refer in this text to 1 Ne. 19:23; 1 Ne. 8:19, 24, 30; 2 Ne. 4:15-16)

"May I suggest . . . a formula [in missionary work] that will insure your success: Search the scriptures with diligence! . . . Your confidence will be directly related to your knowledge of God's word. Oh, I am sure you have heard of some missionaries who were lazy, less than effective, and anxious for their missions to conclude. A careful examination of such instances will reveal that the actual culprit is not laziness, nor disinterest, but is the foe known as fear. Our Father chastised such: '. . . with some I am not well pleased, for they will not open their mouths, but they hide the talent which I have given unto them, because of the fear of man (D&C 60:2).' Had not this same loving Heavenly Father provided a prescription to overcome this malady. . . . In a revelation given through Joseph Smith the Prophet, January 2, 1831, the Lord declared: ". . . if ye are prepared ye shall not fear" (D&C 38:30). This is the key. Will you use it? Let me provide but one reference that has immediate application to our lives. In the Book of Mormon, the seventeenth chapter of Alma, we read the account of Alma's joy as he once more saw the sons of Mosiah and noted their steadfastness in the cause of truth. . . . [Alma 17:2-3]."

Thomas S. Monson (Conference Report, Oct. 1969, pp. 93-94)

"To understand requires more than casual reading or perusal—there must be concentrated study. . . . Not only should we study each day, but there should be a regular time set aside when we can concentrate without interference. . . . The important thing is to allow nothing else to ever interfere with our study. . . . There are some who read to a schedule of a number of pages or a set number of chapters each day or week. . . . It is better to have a set amount of time to give scriptural study each day than to have a set amount of chapters to read. Sometimes we find that the study of a single verse will occupy the whole time."

Howard W. Hunter (Ensign, Nov. 1979, pp. 64-65)

"I find that when I get casual in my relationships with divinity and when it seems that no divine ear is listening and no divine voice is speaking, that I am far, far away. If I immerse myself in the scriptures the distance narrows and the spirituality returns. I find myself loving more intensely those whom I must love with all my heart and mind and strength, and loving them more, I find it easier to abide their counsel."

Teachings of Spencer W. Kimball, p. 135

"It is not enough to read the scriptures. Random reading results in reduced retention. . . . Our spirits should never be deprived of the much-needed spiritual nourishment which comes from scripture study. Without this spiritual food our spirits become starved and weakened to temptation. President Kimball taught the principle that 'no father, no son, no mother, no daughter should get so busy that he or she does not have time to study the scriptures and the words of modern prophets.' *(Ensign,* May 1976, p. 47)."

L. Lionel Kendrick (Ensign, May 1993, p. 14)

"When individual members and families immerse themselves in the scriptures regularly and consistently, . . . other areas of activity will automatically come. Testimonies will increase. Commitment will be strengthened. Families will be fortified. Personal revelation will flow."

Ezra Taft Benson (Ensign, May 1986, p. 81)

"We should make daily study of the scriptures a lifetime pursuit. . . . The most important [thing] you can do . . . is to immerse yourselves in the scriptures. Search them diligently. . . . Learn the doctrine. Master the principles. . . . You must . . . see that . . . searching the scriptures is not a burden laid upon [us] by the Lord, but a marvelous blessing and opportunity."

Ezra Taft Benson (Ensign, Nov. 1986, p. 47)

"True doctrine, understood, changes attitudes and behavior. The study of the doctrines of the gospel will improve behavior quicker than a study of behavior will improve behavior. Preoccupation with unworthy behavior can lead to unworthy behavior. That is why we stress so forcefully the study of the doctrines of the gospel."

Boyd K. Packer (Ensign, Nov. 1986, p. 17)

"Some may think that the language of the scriptures is too difficult for children, but . . . [w]e need to remember that the Lord has given children faculties for learning language even greater than those of adults. . . . It is good for children to hear their favorite passages of scripture, and their other favorite stories, too, over and over. . . . We should not bring up our children to respond to the exciting, the thrilling. . . . They are a titillation of the nerves. To be moved is one thing; to be excited or titillated, a very different thing. If we bring up our children always to be wanting something new, . . . they will have to have a stronger [and stronger] stimulus each time until they finally [burst]. But if we inure our children to stability, to repetition, to normal life . . . , then they will live decent lives."

Arthur Henry King (as quoted by Janette Hales Beckham, Ensign, Nov. 1997, p. 76)

Alma 17:3   **FASTING AND PRAYER**
(Acts 10:3-4; 13:2-3; Mark 9:14-29; 3 Ne. 27:1; Alma 5:45-47; Psalm 35:13)

"The Saints by fasting and praying can sanctify the soul and elevate the spirit to Christlike perfection, and thus the body would be brought into subjection to the spirit, promote communion with the Holy Ghost, and insure spiritual strength and power to the individual. By observing fasting and prayer in its true spirit, the Latter-day Saints cannot be overpowered by Satan tempting them to evil. . . . Recently it was my privilege to tour the Northern California Mission, and as I listened to the missionaries, your sons and daughters, make their reports and bear testimony, I was so pleased when they referred time and again to fasting and prayer, and this they resorted to often to obtain God's blessings for themselves in their work. They fasted and prayed for those who were sick among them and when they found it difficult to impress people with the gospel message of the restored Church, they fasted and prayed about it and received great blessings from such fasting and prayer."

Delbert L. Stapley (Conference Report, Oct. 1951, pp. 122-125)

". . . according to Alma, they gave themselves to much fasting and prayer. You see there are certain blessings that can only be fulfilled as we conform to a particular law. . . . Too many Latter-day Saint parents today are depriving themselves and their children of one of the sweetest spiritual experiences that the Father has made available to them."

Robert L. Simpson (Conference Report, Oct. 1967, pp. 17-18)

"Failing to fast is a sin. In the 58th chapter of Isaiah, rich promises are made by the Lord to those who fast and assist the needy. Freedom from frustrations, freedom from thralldom, and the blessing of peace are promised. Inspiration and spiritual guidance will come with righteousness and closeness to our Heavenly Father. To omit to do this righteous act of fasting would deprive us of these blessings."

Spencer W. Kimball (The Miracle of Forgiveness, p. 98)

Alma 17:10-11   **BE PATIENT IN AFFLICTION**
(D&C 24:8; 67:13; 1 Peter 2:20; refer in this text to Mosiah 24:14-15; Alma 34:40-41)

"It is easy enough to be pleasant,
When life flows by like a song,
But the man worth while is the one who will smile,
When everything goes dead wrong.
For the test of the heart is trouble,
And it always comes with the years,
And the smile that is worth the praises of earth
Is the smile that shines through tears." (Ella Wheeler Wilcox)

"Suffering can make Saints of people as they learn patience, long suffering and self-mastery. The sufferings of our Savior were part of his education."

Spencer W. Kimball (1955 BYU Speeches of the Year, p. 9)

Alma 17:18,
25; 18:17   **LEADER—SERVANT**
(Alma 18:10-11; 21:19; 22:3; Matt. 23:11; *Discourses of Wilford Woodruff*, pp. 123-124; refer in this text to Mosiah 2:16-17)

(In a letter to Brother Edward Hunter, under date of January 5, 1842, the Prophet shows his humility and the love of his heart in these words): "The store has been filled to overflowing and I have stood behind the counter all day, distributing goods as steadily as any clerk you ever saw, to oblige those who were compelled to go without their Christmas and New Year's dinners for the want of a little sugar, molasses, raisins, etc.; and to please myself also, for I love to wait upon the Saints and to be a servant to all, hoping that I may be exalted in the due time of the Lord."

Joseph Smith (Life of Joseph Smith, Cannon, p. 386)

Alma 17:27-38   **GOD'S ARMY OF ONE**
(Ex. 14:12-14; 2 Kings 6:16-17; 1 Ne. 4:1-3; Mosiah 28:7; Alma 19:22-23; refer in this text to Hel. 10:1-4, 16)

"What are we to fear when the Lord is with us? Can we not take the Lord at his word and exercise a particle of faith in him? Our assignment is affirmative . . . to carry the Gospel to our enemies, that they might no longer be our enemies."

Spencer W. Kimball (Ensign, June 1976, p. 6)

[A vision of the Prophet Joseph Smith] "Also, I saw Elder Brigham Young standing in a strange land, in the far south and west, in a desert place, upon a rock in the midst of about a dozen men . . . who appeared hostile. He was preaching to them in their own tongue, and the angel of God standing above his head, with a drawn sword in his hand, protecting him, but he did not see it."

Joseph Smith (History of the Church 2:381)

"What did Ammon say? 'Be of good cheer . . .' (Alma 17:31). Now, we may read this as a story about some shepherds trying to round up some missing sheep, but the message is much more powerful and significant than that. Ammon was a missionary with noble intentions to bring the king and his kingdom back to the fold of righteousness, to the well of living water. The challenge looked daunting to those who could see only, in everyday terms, sheep strung out on hillsides and not enough manpower to round them up. They were discouraged and fearful that the king would discover their loss. Ammon not only led the force to recapture the sheep, he drove away the evil men who caused the problems; and his heroic efforts persuaded the king to follow him and to follow the Savior. Ammon teaches us that no matter our circumstances, we can be an example to others, we can lift them, we can inspire them to seek righteousness, and we can bear testimony to all of the power of Jesus Christ."

Robert D. Hales (Ensign, May 1997, p. 82)

Alma 17:39	**MERCENARY CUSTOM**
(1 Sam. 18:25)

Alma 18:14	**SILENCE**

Alma 18:24-28	**MILK vs. MEAT**
(refer in this text to Alma 22:7-10)

Alma 18:16,	**DISCERNMENT**
18:20, 32	(refer in this text to Alma 12:3, 7)

Alma 18:42;	**SPIRITUAL EXHAUSTION**
19:6, 13-	(JS-H. 1:20; 1 Ne. 1:7; 17:47; 19:20; Mosiah 27:19; Moses 1:9-10; Dan. 10:8;
17; 22:18;	D&C 324-325 Student Manual, pp.158-159)
27:17-19

"It appears that a trance is a state in which the body and its functions become quiescent in order that the full powers of the Spirit may be centered on the revelations of heaven. Freed from the fetters of a mortal body, a man's spirit can be ushered into the divine presence; it can hear what otherwise could not be heard and see what otherwise could not be seen—even the visions of eternity and even the Almighty himself. . . . It is of interest that the false prophet Shemaiah wrote to the priest Zephaniah, charging him to keep the temple a house of order by putting the mad prophets in prison and in stocks. His reference to mad prophets is understood to have been directed to those prophets who claimed authority through some ecstasy or trance. His purpose in so doing was to have the prophet Jeremiah imprisoned, it being well-known that Jeremiah made claim to such experiences. (See Jeremiah 29:26-27). The story of Ammon and Lamoni affirms religious trances as a legitimate revelatory device. Lamoni, as already noted, came forth from his trance testifying that he had seen the Redeemer and then prophesied relative to the Savior's birth and the necessity of all mankind believing on his name. The testimony of his servants was that while they were in this state of physical insensibility, angels instructed them in the principles of salvation and their obligation to live righteously. Indeed, they experienced a change of heart and no longer had a desire to do evil. Such is the state in which the power of God overcomes the 'natural frame' and one is 'carried away in God.'"

R. Millet and J. F. McConkie (Doctrinal Commentary on the Book of Mormon, 3:140-141)

Alma 19:22-23	**DIVINE PROTECTION**
(*Life of Joseph Smith*, Cannon; *Instructor*, 15:110-111; *Autobiography of Parley P. Pratt*, p. 477; *Millennial Star* 64:411-414; refer in this text to 1 Ne. 22:16-17, 19; Hel. 5:20-52)

Alma 20:10, 13   **THE BIRTHRIGHT**
(Deut. 21:17; 1 Ne. 2:22; 18:10; 2 Ne. 1:25; 5:3,19; Alma 54:17; refer in this text to Mosiah 10:15)

Alma 20:29   **PATIENT IN THEIR SUFFERING**
(refer in this text to Mosiah 24:14-15; Alma 14:11; Alma 31:31, 33, 38; Alma 34:40-41)

Alma 21:3 **APOSTATE ATTITUDES—HARD HEARTS**
(Alma 23:13-14; 24:29-30; refer in this text to Mosiah 13:4)

"When the Prophet [Joseph Smith] had ended telling how he had been treated [by apostates], Brother Behunnin remarked: 'If I should leave this Church I would not do as those men have done: I would go to some remote place where Mormonism had never been heard of, settle down, and no one would ever learn that I knew anything about it.' The great Seer immediately replied: 'Brother Behunnin, you don't know what you would do. No doubt these men once thought as you do. Before you joined this Church you stood on neutral ground. When the gospel was preached good and evil were set before you. You could choose either or neither. There were two opposite masters inviting you to serve them. When you joined this Church you enlisted to serve God. When you did that you left the neutral ground, and you never can get back on to it. Should you forsake the Master you enlisted to serve it will be by the instigation of the evil one, and you will follow his dictation and be his servant.' He [further] emphasized the fact that a man or woman who had not taken sides either with Christ or Belial could maintain a neutral position, but when they enlisted under either the one or the other they left the neutral ground forever."

Daniel Tyler (Recollections of the Prophet Joseph Smith, Juvenile Instructor, Aug. 15,1892, p. 492)

Alma 21:16; **LED BY THE SPIRIT IN MISSIONARY WORK**
22:1, 4 (1 Ne. 4:6; Moses 6:32; D&C 28:15-16; 84:85; 100:6; 124:97)

Alma 22:9-10 **IS GOD THE GREAT SPIRIT?**
(Alma 18:24-28)

"According to Lamanite traditions, God is the Great Spirit. It is obvious that by this designation the Lamanites had in mind a personal being, for King Lamoni mistakenly supposed that Ammon was the Great Spirit. (Alma 18:2-28; 19:25-27). Both Ammon and Aaron, using the same principle of salesmanship applied by Paul on Mars Hill (Acts 17:22-31), taught that the Great Spirit was the God who created the heavens and the earth (Alma 18:8-29; 22:8-11). This same Lamanite concept that God is the Great Spirit has existed among the American Indians in modern times."

Bruce R. McConkie (Mormon Doctrine, p. 340)

Alma 22:15-16   **BORN OF GOD**
(refer in this text to Alma 5:7, 12; Mosiah 5:2, 7; Mosiah 27:24-26)

Alma 22:18   **WILL GIVE AWAY ALL MY SINS TO KNOW THEE**
(contrast Alma 20:21-23)

"We may not always succeed as quickly as we would want, but as we make repentance a constant part of our lives, miracles occur. This is what happens as we see that we really can overcome our sins: Our 'confidence [waxes] strong in the presence of God' (D&C 121:45). We kneel in humility before our Father. We tell him openly of our progress, and also of our fears and doubts. As we draw near to him, he draws near to us. He gives us peace and encouragement. He heals our souls. As we continue inch by inch to repent, we determine that nothing will hold us back: we will do our part. We come to feel like that great Lamanite king who cried, 'Oh God, . . . wilt thou make thyself known unto me, and I will give away all my sins to know thee' (Alma 22:18). With this commitment to who we can become, the spiritual doors swing open. There is a new freedom to feel and to know, a freedom to become."

Neil L. Anderson (Ensign, Apr. 1995, p. 52)

Alma 23:5-13   **CONVERSION OF THE LAMANITES**
"In the twenty-third and twenty-fourth chapters of Alma we have a dramatic account of the power of the gospel changing almost a whole nation from a bloodthirsty, indolent, warlike people into industrious, peace-loving people. Of these people the record says that thousands were brought to a knowledge of the Lord, and that as many as were brought to a knowledge of the truth never did fall away. . . . That is the great message I want to leave here. It is the softening of the hearts that this gospel does to the people who receive it. . . . Now this remarkable transformation wrought in the hearts of these thousands of people was done in a very short period of time under the influence and power of the

gospel of Jesus Christ. It would do the same thing today for all the peoples of the earth if they would but receive it. . . ."

Marion G. Romney (Conference Report, Oct. 1948, p. 75)

Alma 23:17   **ANTI-NEPHI-LEHIES**
(Hel. 5:51; 15:7-9; *Book of Mormon Study Guide*, Ricks, p. 63; *Book of Mormon Compendium*, Sperry, p. 343)

"However, Dr. Hugh Nibley has found a Semitic and common Indo-European root corresponding to anti that means in the face of or facing, as of one facing a mirror, and by extension either one who opposes or one who imitates."

Daniel H. Ludlow (Companion to Your Study of the Book of Mormon, pp. 209-210)

Alma 24   **WAR—THE LORD'S RULES**
(refer in this text Alma 43-51; Alma 52-63)

Alma 24:9-13;   **WERE THE ANTI-NEPHI-LEHIES GUILTY OF MURDER?**
27:23   (Alma 29:5; 3 Ne. 30:2; Alma 54:7; refer in this text to Alma 39:5-6)

"We do know that there are murders committed by Gentiles for which they at least can repent, be baptized, and receive a remission of their sins."

Bruce R. McConkie (New Witness for the Articles of Faith, p. 231)

"Even among willful murderers there are grades and categories. There are . . . [those] who kill for sadistic pleasure. There are those who kill in drunkenness, in rage, in anger, in jealousy. There are those who kill for gain, for power, for fear. There are those who kill for lust. They certainly will suffer different degrees of punishment hereafter."

Spencer W. Kimball (Miracle of Forgiveness, pp. 130-131)

Alma 24:16-18;   **BURY WEAPONS**
25:13-14;   *(God's Chosen People of America,* Brinkerhoff, pp. 57,70)
26:32

     THE PROBLEM OF WRITING ON PLATES

Alma 24:20-24   **WILLINGNESS TO DIE (Anti-Nephi-Lehies)**
(refer in this text to Mosiah 17)

"In 1979, . . . I was serving as president in the Mexico City North Mission. . . . A (community) meeting was called . . . at which Church members were given the following options : denounce the Church, leave the village, or be killed (not an idle threat). The members, particularly the women, said they knew the Church to be true and would not denounce it. They also indicated they had worked just as hard as the rest of the community to secure their homesteads, and they would not leave. Boldly stepping forward, they told their taunters if they were going to kill them, to get on with it. The moment grew tense as machetes were raised, then finally lowered while the Latter-day Saints stood up for that which the Spirit had testified to them to be true. These Saints eventually learned, as most of us do, that it is harder to live the gospel day by day than to die for it in an instant, but their early commitment came because the Spirit had touched their hearts and changed their lives."

John B. Dickson (Ensign, Feb. 1995, p. 7)

Alma 24:19   (Mosiah 7:8; Alma 50:32; Hel. 3:33; 3 Ne. 16:4)

Alma 24:21-26   **A SILVER LINING**
"I have seen, at close range, the manner in which the Lord has turned disasters—war, occupation, and revolution—into blessings."

Teachings of Ezra Taft Benson, p. 168

"How extensive the present European war will be we do not know. . . . The wars that are now taking place will have a tendency, in some measure, to open the way for the Elders of the Church of Jesus Christ to go and establish the Church and kingdom of God among those nations."

Masterful Discourses of Orson Pratt, p. 141

[referring to the Vietnam War] "Notwithstanding the evil and the tragedy, I see a silver thread shining through the dark and bloody tapestry of conflict. I see the finger of the Lord plucking some good from the evil designs of the adversary. I see coming out of this conflict, as I have witnessed in other conflicts in Asia, an enlargement of the Lord's program."

Gordon B. Hinckley (Conference Report, Apr. 1968, p.21)

Alma 24:30   **THEIR STATE BECOMES WORSE THAN THOUGH THEY HAD NEVER KNOWN**
(Book of Mormon 121-122 Student Manual, p. 84; 2 Ne. 31:14; Alma 9:19)

Alma 25:2   **PEOPLE OF AMMONIHAH DESTROYED**
(refer in this text to Alma 16:2-3)

Alma 25:15-16   **LAW OF MOSES**
(Alma 34:13-14; Mosiah 13:29-30; Jacob 4:5; refer in this text under Mosiah 13:29-31)

Alma 26:10-12,   **BOASTING**
16, 35-36   (Hel. 4:13; 5:8; 2 Cor. 10:17-18; D&C 84;73; 1 Cor. 1:31; refer in this text to Alma 39:2; Morm. 3:9)

"I would rather hear an Elder speak only five words accompanied by the power of God, and they would do more good than to hear long sermons without the Spirit."

Discourses of Brigham Young, p. 330

Alma 26:23, 25   **THE WORD OR THE SWORD**
(refer in this text to Alma 31:5)

Alma 26:27   **DEPRESSED AND ABOUT TO TURN BACK**
(Moro. 10:22; Joshua 1:9; Prov. 17:22; refer in this text to Alma 8:10-15; Hel. 10:1, 4, 16; refer to the Joseph F. Smith quote under 1 Ne. 8:2, 36; *My Father David O. McKay*, David Lawrence McKay, pp. 17-25; *Hugh B. Brown: His Life & Thought*, Campbell and Poll, pp. 30-33)

"There are times when you simply have to righteously hang on and outlast the devil until his depressive spirit leaves you. As the Lord told the Prophet Joseph Smith: 'Thine adversity and thine afflictions, shall be but a small moment: And then, if thou endure it well, God shall exalt thee on high' (D&C121:7-8). To press on in noble endeavors, even while surrounded by a cloud of depression, will eventually bring you out on top into the sunshine."

Ezra Taft Benson (Ensign, Nov. 1974)

[An experience of Gordon B. Hinckley on his mission to England] "Elder Hinckley found some of that discouragement common to missionaries facing new circumstances in a new land. He was not well physically, and as he went to his first street meeting . . . he recalls: 'I was terrified. I stepped up on that little stand and looked at that crowd of people that had gathered. . . . They looked rather menacing and mean, but I somehow stumbled through whatever I had to say.' Down in spirit and facing no success in missionary endeavors, Gordon wrote a letter to his father, saying: 'I am wasting my time and your money. I don't see any point in my staying here.' In due course a gentle but terse reply came from his father. That letter read: 'Dear Gordon. I have your letter [of such and such a date]. I have only one suggestion. Forget yourself and go to work, With love, Your Father.' President Hinckley says of that moment, 'I pondered his response and then the next morning in our scripture class we read that great statement of the Lord: "For whosoever will save his life shall lose it; but whosoever shall lose his life for my sake and the gospel's, the same shall save it" (Mark 8:35). That simple statement, that promise, touched me. I got on my knees and made a covenant with the Lord that I would try to forget myself and go to work.'"

Jeffrey R. Holland (Ensign, June 1995, p. 8)

"As you nurture the seedlings of faith in others, you will find yourself saying, 'Is it already the end of the day?' rather than 'Will this day ever end?' Pioneer women did not have time to wallow in discouragement. They were too busy working their way toward Zion."

Mary Ellen Smoot (Ensign, Nov. 1997, p. 13)

Alma 27:9   **SLAVERY**
(Mosiah 2:13; Alma 48:11)

"He who would be no slave must consent to have no slave. Those who deny freedom to others deserve it not for themselves."

Abraham Lincoln (Lincoln's Life Stories and Speeches, Selby, p. 258)

Alma 27:12   **A BLESSING OF DELIVERANCE**
(Mosiah 28:6-7; Alma 56:47-48)

Alma 27:28;   **MOURNING DEATH**
28:11-12;   (D&C 42:46-47; 101:36; John 14:27; Morm. 6:7; *Mormon Doctrine*, McConkie,
30:2   pp. 518-519)

"To those who mourn we speak comfort. Know that your Savior is well acquainted with grief. He who notes the sparrow's fall is aware of you and desires to comfort and bless you. Turn to Him and lay your burden at His feet."

Ezra Taft Benson (First Presidency Christmas Message, Church News, Dec. 15, 1985, p.3)

"The only way to take sorrow out of death is to take love out of life. . . . As seedlings of God, we barely blossom on earth; we fully flower in heaven. . . . Think of the alternative [to death]. If all sixty-nine billion people who have ever lived on earth were still here, imagine the traffic jam! . . . Scriptures teach that death is essential to happiness: [Alma 42:8; 2 Ne. 9:6]. Our limited perspective would be enlarged if we could witness the reunion on the other side of the veil, when doors of death open to those returning home. . . . We need not look upon death as an enemy. . . . I know by experiences too sacred to relate that those who have gone before are not strangers to leaders of this Church. To us and to you, our loved ones may be just as close as the next room—separated only by the doors of death."

Russell M. Nelson (Ensign, May 1992, pp. 72-74)

"More painful to me are the thoughts of annihilation than death. If I have no expectation of seeing my father, mother, brothers, sisters and friends again, my heart would burst in a moment, and I should go down to my grave. The expectation of seeing my friends in the morning of the resurrection cheers my soul and makes me bear up against the evils of life. It is like they're taking a long journey, and on their return we meet them with increased joy."

Teachings of the Prophet Joseph Smith, p. 296

"I once attended a funeral service with Elder M. Russell Ballard. A statement he made there has remained with me to this day. He said, 'Life isn't over for a Latter-day Saint until he or she is safely dead, with their testimony still burning brightly.' 'Safely dead'—what a challenging concept. Brothers and sisters, we will not be safe until we have given our hearts to the Lord—until we have learned to do what we have promised."

F. Burton Howard (Ensign, May 1996, p. 28)

"I have thought about the lessons taught by death—particularly the death of a loved one. The first lesson is that life is short whether one dies at seventeen or at eighty. . . . Second, death reminds us that there is a spirit in man. . . . Another lesson taught by death concerns the importance of eternal families. Just as there are parents to greet a newborn on earth, the scriptures teach that caring family members greet the spirits in paradise and assist them in the adjustments to a new life (see Gen. 25:8; 35:29; 49:33). . . . A fourth lesson, and perhaps the most important, concerns the purpose of life. . . . Death, even if accidental, must be part of the plan. . . . Death teaches that we do not experience a fulness of joy in mortality and that everlasting joy can be achieved only with the assistance of the Master (see D&C 93:33-34)."

Merrill J. Bateman (Ensign, May 1995, p. 13)

Alma 29:1-2   **MISSIONARY WORK**
(refer in this text to Alma 17:2-5; *Ensign*, May 1992, pp. 11-12)

"There is no living soul in all the Church of Jesus Christ of Latter-day Saints, who has gone forth to proclaim this gospel, . . . who like Alma of old has had that same joy and that same happiness, when he or she has been an instrument in the hands of God of bringing some soul to a knowledge of the divinity of the work in which you and I are engaged. . . . I know of no joy on earth that can compare with that which comes to the heart of the . . . [person] who is an instrument in the hands of God of saving some soul and turning it from that broad way that leadeth to destruction, into that straight and narrow path that leadeth to life eternal."

Heber J. Grant (Conference Report, Oct. 1922, pp. 187-188)

"There is no other labor in all the world that brings to a human heart, judging from my own personal experience, more joy, peace and serenity than proclaiming the gospel of the Lord Jesus Christ. I remember that while I was laboring in Japan, [after two years] . . . I received a cable: 'Come home on the first vessel.' When I arrived home President Smith told me that they had decided to send me to Europe [for at least one year] to succeed Brother Lyman. When I went into his office and bade him goodbye, and said, 'I will see you in a year,' he said, 'We have decided to make it a year and a half.' I said, 'Multiply it by two and say nothing about it, and it will please me,' and that is exactly what he did. I was there a little over three years, and never have I had sweeter joy, more genuine satisfaction in my life than during those three years, when I had no thought except the spreading of the gospel of the Lord Jesus Christ."

Heber J. Grant (Conference Report, Oct. 1926, p. 4)

"I recall my own mission call to Argentina. After sharing the excitement of my call with my parents, I sought out my mentor, who was not a member of the Church, a former U.S. senator, to share the news of my call with him. He was not impressed, let me know in no uncertain terms that if I insisted on serving a mission, upon my return all the good jobs would be taken and I would never amount to anything. I was disappointed, but realized that he saw my future only as the world perceives. Years later I realized that my mission had prioritized my life toward family, service, and gospel principles. As an added bonus, I was far ahead of most of my former classmates in worldly achievements. . . . The call to missionary service rarely comes when it is convenient or easy to serve."

Gardner H. Russell (Ensign, Nov. 1991, p. 82)

"I am grateful to bishops who helped me as a young man prepare to receive the Melchizedek Priesthood. One patient, loving bishop helped me understand that missionary service was far more important than perfecting my golf game, which had been the chief ambition of my teen years."

H. David Burton (Ensign, May 1993, p.47)

"Truly effective missionaries have many talents, varied and beautiful, but one quality they all seem to have is the ability to stick with their commitments—that is, the power to do what they agree to do. They tell themselves to get up in the morning, on time, and do it. They don't depend on companions, district leaders, or anyone else. They commit to the mission president that they will follow the gospel study program every morning and not run out of steam in a few days. They understand that the Lord has called them to teach and testify, baptize and build the kingdom in His name, and they are happily at their work."

L. Aldin Porter (Ensign, May 1992, p. 45)

Alma 29:4　　**GRANTED MEN ACCORDING TO THEIR DESIRE**
(D&C 137:8-9)

"We are free to choose, but we are not free to alter the consequences of those choices."

Ezra Taft Benson (Come Unto Christ, p. 40)

"*Desire* denotes a real longing or craving. Hence righteous desires are much more than passive preferences or fleeting feelings. Of course our genes, circumstances, and environments matter very much, and they shape us significantly. Yet there remains an inner zone in which we are sovereign, unless we abdicate. In this zone lies the essence of our individuality and our personal accountability. . . . Mostly, brothers and sisters, we become the victims of our own wrong desires. . . . Like it or not, therefore, reality requires that we acknowledge our responsibility for our desires. . . . Righteous desires need to be relentless, therefore, because , said President Brigham Young, 'the men and women, who desire to obtain seats in the celestial kingdom will find that they must battle every day' (*Journal of Discourses* 11:14). Therefore, true Christian soldiers are more than weekend warriors. . . . Some of our present desires, therefore, need to be diminished and then finally dissolved."

Neal A. Maxwell (Ensign, Nov. 1996, pp. 21-22)

Alma 29:3, 6-8   OUR ALLOTMENT

". . . we had our own free agency in our pre-mortal existence, and whatever we are today is likely the result of that which we willed to be heretofore. We unquestionably knew before we elected to come to this earth the conditions under which we would here exist. . . . I have a conviction deep down in my heart that we are exactly what we should be, each one of us, except as we may have altered that pattern by deviating from the laws of God here in mortality."

Henry D. Moyle (Conference Report, Oct. 1952, pp. 71-72)

Alma 29:8   ALL NATIONS TAUGHT OF THEIR OWN NATION
(Cowley & Whitney on Doctrine, pp. 292-293; *Conference Report*, Apr. 1921, pp. 32-33)*

"Since about 92% of all missionaries in the field are Americans, we must call to the attention of all members in other lands that we need far more local missionaries. Through Alma the Lord said, [Alma 29:8]. This scripture indicates, brethren, that every nation is to furnish its own missionaries and we expect that to follow. . . . It is all nations of their nation and tongue. We need far more, thousands—more Brazilians to preach in Brazil in Portuguese; thousands more Mexicans to preach in Spanish—Chileans, Peruvians, Bolivians, Colombians, Argentines, Venezuelans—Spanish to proselyte in Spanish—hundreds more of local men to preach in Scandinavian, German, French, Filipino, Indian and all nationalities in all tongues and nations. . . . Since the local men can better represent their own people without problems of language, visas, and other rights and services, we need soon hundreds of more young men of every race and nation."

Spencer W. Kimball (Regional Representatives Seminar, Sept. 1977, p. 17)

"We believe that Joseph Smith was called by God as the prophet to inaugurate this present era, known as 'the dispensation of the fulness of times' (see Eph. 1:10; D&C 112:30; 121:31; 124:41; 128:18, 20; 138:48). . . . This modern dispensation of which I speak fulfills the biblical promise of a 'restitution of all things' (Acts 3:21; see also Rev. 14:6-7). It also fulfills another scriptural promise that 'the Lord doth grant unto all nations, of their own nation and tongue, to teach his word' (Alma 29:8)."

Russell M. Nelson (Ensign, Nov. 1993, p. 104)

Alma 30

"... the Book of Mormon exposes the enemies of Christ. ... It fortifies the humble followers of Christ against the evil designs, strategies, and doctrines of the devil in our day. The type of apostates in the Book of Mormon is similar to the type we have today. *God, with his infinite foreknowledge, so molded the Book of Mormon that we might see the error and know how to combat false educational, political, religious, and philosophical concepts of our time.*"

Ezra Taft Benson (A Witness and a Warning, p. 3)

ALMA 30:6 **ANTI-CHRIST**
(1 John 2:18,22; 4:3; 2 John 7; Jacob 7; *Doctrinal Commentary on the Book of Mormon*, McConkie and Millet, 3:201)

"An antichrist is an opponent of Christ. He is one who offers salvation to men on some other terms than those laid down by Christ."

Bruce R. McConkie (Mormon Doctrine, p. 39)

"I bless you with increased discernment to judge between Christ and anti-Christ. I bless you with increased power to do good and to resist evil. I bless you with increased understanding of the Book of Mormon. I promise you that from this moment forward, if we will daily sup from its pages and abide by its precepts, God will pour out upon each child of Zion and the Church a blessing hitherto unknown. ..."

Ezra Taft Benson (Ensign, May 1986, p. 78)

ALMA 30:10   **CAPITAL PUNISHMENT**
(D&C 42:18-19,79; Gen. 9:6, 12-13; Deut. 19:11-13; 2 Ne. 9:35; Alma 34:12; 46:35; refer in this text to Alma 1:14)

ALMA 30:12-28   **THE NINE DOCTRINES OF KORIHOR AN ANTI-CHRIST**
(Studies in Scripture, Jackson, 8:1-13; *Ensign,* Sept. 1977, pp. 18-21; *Ensign,* July 1992, pp.16-22; *Alma, The Testimony of the Word*, ed. by Nyman & Tate, pp. 107-128; *Sustaining and Defending the Faith*, Millet and McConkie, pp. 87-97)

(1) Alma 30:12; (2) Alma 30:13-14; (3) Alma 30:15 [see also Jacob 7:7]; (4) Alma 30:16-17; (5) Alma 30:17; (6) Alma 30:17; (7) Alma 30:18; (8) Alma 30:24 [see also Moses 5:33]; (9) Alma 30:28

"One of Satan's frequently used deceptions is the notion that the commandments of God are meant to restrict freedom and limit happiness. Young people especially sometimes feel that the standards of the Lord are like fences and chains, blocking them from those activities that seem most enjoyable in life. But exactly the opposite is true. The gospel plan is the plan by which men are brought to a fulness of joy. The gospel principles are the steps and guidelines which will help us find true happiness and joy."

Teachings of Ezra Taft Benson, p. 357

"Societies structured by situational ethics—the belief that all truths are relative—create a moral environment defined by undistinguished shades of gray."

Richard B. Wirthlin (Ensign, Nov. 1997, p. 9)

"Korihor was arguing, as men and women have falsely argued from the beginning of time, that to take counsel from the servants of God is to surrender God-given rights of independence. But the argument is false because it misrepresents reality. When we reject the counsel which comes from God, we do not choose to be independent of outside influence. We choose another influence. We reject the protection of a perfectly loving, all-powerful, all-knowing Father in Heaven, whose whole purpose, as that of His Beloved Son, is to give us eternal life, to give us all that He has, and to bring us home again in families to the arms of His love. In rejecting His counsel, we choose the influence of another power, whose purpose is to make us miserable and whose motive is hatred. We have moral agency as a gift of God. Rather than the right to choose to be free of influence, it is the inalienable right to submit ourselves to whichever of those powers we choose."

Henry B. Eyring (Ensign, May 1997, p. 25)

"It is a real travesty today when we hear the voices of the atheist, the godless, and the anti-Christ who would deny us the right of public expression of our worship of the Master. First they moved against the long-established institution of prayer in our public schools. They would remove any vestige of Christianity or worship of the Savior of mankind in our public gatherings; they would remove the 'In God We Trust' insignia from our nation's emblems and seals and from our national coins. The latest move of these anti-Christs would prohibit our own children from singing the beautiful and inspiring Christmas carols, relating to the Savior's birth or divinity, or 'the heavenly angels singing' from our public schools."

Teachings of Spencer W. Kimball, pp. 411-412

"Isn't it interesting that these groups consider it 'freedom of expression' to profane the Lord's name and use obscenities, but oppose prayer in public places. These groups combat public faith and prayer yet uphold the right of anyone to have an abortion."

Joseph B. Wirthlin (Ensign, Mar. 1993, p. 72)

Alma 30:25   **A CHILD IS NOT GUILTY BECAUSE OF ITS PARENT**
(*Sustaining and Defending the Faith*, Millet and McConkie, pp. 89-91)

Alma 30:43   **SHOW ME A SIGN**
(D&C 46:8: 63:7-12; 3 Ne. 2:1-2; Jacob 7:13-20; Ether 12:5; *Doctrinal Commentary on the Book of Mormon*, McConkie and Millet, 2:87-89; Matt. 12:38-39; 16:4; *Teachings of the Prophet Joseph Smith*, pp.156-159; *History of the Church*, Smith, 1:226; 5:268; D&C 63:7-16; 66:3, 10; *New Era*, Toscano, June 1973, p. 44; *Ensign*, Dec. 1994, pp. 60-61)

Sign seeking may be an attempt to gain faith and knowledge without humility, obedience and paying the price.
"In a world filled with skepticism and doubt, the expression 'seeing is believing' promotes the attitude, 'You show me, and I will believe.' We want all of the proof and all of the evidence first. It seems hard to take things on faith. When will we learn that in spiritual things it works the other way about—that believing is seeing? Spiritual belief precedes spiritual knowledge. When we believe in things that are not seen but are nevertheless true, then we have faith."

Boyd K. Packer (Faith, p. 43)

"Show me Latter-day Saints who have to feed upon miracles, signs and visions in order to keep them steadfast in the Church, and I will show you members of the Church who are not in good standing before God, and who are walking in slippery paths. It is not by marvelous manifestations unto us that we shall be established in truth, but it is by humility and faithful obedience to the commandments and laws of God. When I as a boy first started out in the ministry, I would frequently go out and ask the Lord to show me some marvelous thing, in order that I might receive a testimony. But the Lord withheld marvels from me, and showed me the truth, line upon line, precept upon precept, here a little and there a little, until he made me to know the truth from the crown of my head to the soles of my feet, and until doubt and fear had been absolutely purged from me. He did not have to send an angel from the heavens to do this, nor did he have to speak with the trump of an archangel. *By the whisperings of the still small voice of the Spirit of the living God, he gave to me the testimony I possess. And by this principle and power he will give to all the children of men a knowledge of the truth. . . . And no amount of marvelous manifestations will ever accomplish this.*"

Joseph F. Smith (Gospel Doctrine, p. 7)

"Some great examples of this can be found in Church history. Ezra Booth, in company with others (including Mrs. John Johnson), visited Joseph Smith at his home in Kirtland in 1831. While there Ezra Booth witnessed a miracle. Mrs. Johnson, who had had a lame arm for a number of years, was healed by the Prophet Joseph. Booth was so awe-struck by this that he joined the Church. It was not long, however, until his faith waned and he finally apostatized and wrote a series of letters against the Church. (See History of the Church, 1:215-217.) Another example is that of Simonds Ryder, who joined the Church after what he felt was a supernatural experience. A short time later, he left after his name was misspelled in an inspired mission call. 'He thought if the Spirit through which he had been called to preach could err in the matter of spelling his name, it might have erred in calling him to the ministry as well' *(History of the Church,* 1:261). Having lost whatever faith he had, and encouraged by Booth's letters, Simonds Ryder led a mob against the Prophet Joseph at Father Johnson's home where Joseph and Sidney Rigdon were tarred and feathered. This incident also caused the death of one of Joseph and Emma's adopted children. (See *History of the Church*, 1:261-265.) Whenever we base our belief on miracles, we must constantly be fed by miracles or our belief grows weak. . . . Perhaps some members of the Church today are troubled with a less dramatic form of sign seeking. In section 121 of the Doctrine and Covenants the Lord refers to members aspiring to the honors of men. One of the reasons we aspire to position is that we somehow feel that being called to a high position is a 'sign' that the Lord approves of our efforts and that if we are not called, we have failed to measure up."

Michael K. Parson (Book of Mormon Symposium, Aug. 1982, pp. 73-75)

"A Campbellite preacher . . . came to Joseph Smith, I think his name was Hayden. He came in and made himself known to Joseph, and said that he had come a considerable distance to be convinced of the truth. 'Why,' said he, 'Mr. Smith, I want to know the truth, and when I am convinced, I will spend all my talents and time in defending and spreading the doctrines of your religion, and I will give you to understand that to convince me is equivalent to convincing all my society, amounting to several hundreds.' Well, Joseph commenced laying before him the coming forth of the work, and the first principles of the Gospel, when Mr. Hayden exclaimed, 'O this is not the evidence I want, the evidence that I wish to have is a notable miracle; I want to see some powerful manifestation of the power of God, I want to see a notable miracle performed; and if you perform such a one, then I will believe with all my heart and soul, and will exert all my power and all my extensive influence to convince others; and if you will not perform a miracle of this kind, then I am your worst and bitterest enemy.' 'Well,' said Joseph, 'what will you have done? Will you be struck blind, or dumb? Will you be paralyzed, or will you have one hand withered? Take your choice, choose which you please, and in the name of the Lord Jesus Christ it shall be done.' 'That is not the kind of miracle I want,' said the preacher. 'Then, sir,' replied Joseph, 'I can perform none; I am not going to bring any trouble upon any body else, sir, to convince you.'"

George A. Smith (Journal of Discourses 2:326)

Alma 30:44   **ALL THINGS DENOTE GOD**
(Hel. 8:2; Moses 6:63; Psalm 19:1-2: D&C 88:7-13,42-47; *Articles of Faith*, Talmage, p.30; *Teachings of the Prophet Joseph Smith*, pp.197-198; *Ensign*, Aug. 1992, p. 2)

"All of beauty in the Earth bears the fingerprint of the Master Creator."

Gordon B. Hinckley (Ensign, May 1978, p.59)

"Just a bit nearer to the sun, and Planet Earth's seas would soon be boiling; just a little farther out, and the whole world would become a frozen wilderness. . . . 'If our orbit happened to be the wrong shape . . . then we should alternately freeze like Mars and fry like Venus once a year. Fortunately for us, our planet's orbit is very nearly a circle. The 21 percent of oxygen is another critical figure. Animals would have difficulty breathing if the oxygen content fell very far below that value. But an oxygen level much higher than this would also be disastrous, since the extra oxygen would act as a fire-raising material. Forests and grasslands would flare up every time lightning struck during a dry spell, and life on earth would become extremely hazardous.'"

Neal A. Maxwell (quoting the British scientist Alan Hayward in First Nephi, The Doctrinal Foundation, BYU Religious Studies Center, p. 7)

Alma 30:52-53   WHAT WAS KORIHOR'S MOTIVE?
(1 Ne. 22:23)

". . . The most powerful opposition to the work of the Savior on this earth comes from those who know the truth and then deliberately turn from it and seek to destroy others."

Chauncey C. Riddle (Ensign, Sept. 1977, p. 18)

"Remember that the very worst enemies that we've had are those that are within the Church. It was Judas that betrayed the Master. . . . Today it's the same. The greatest and worst enemies we have in the Church today are those within our ranks. . ."

Harold B. Lee (CES address, BYU, July 8, 1966)

"Korihor is described in the heading as an Antichrist, but I'm not sure that he started out that way. Have you ever thought that possibly Korihor started out as a college student with lots of questions? Although his questioning may have begun honestly, he made two really bad mistakes. First, he denied his faith. He denied the Light of Christ that had been given to him. Second, he started to preach false doctrine to others. Alma, his leader, bore his testimony to Korihor and then Korihor made another mistake. Rather than listening to his leader and listening and relying on the Spirit, he defended his position . . . and became more argumentative. He demanded that he be given a sign. . . . He perhaps didn't intend for the sign to have such an affect on him personally, but often the consequences of our mistakes do affect us personally. Verses 52 and 53 of chapter 30 I believe are most important when Korihor acknowledges, 'I always knew that there was a God, but Satan hath deceived me.' Isn't that interesting? 'I always knew.' He had the Light of Christ in him, but Satan deceived him."

Janette C. Hales (BYU Devotional, Mar. 16, 1993)

Alma 30:54-56 **WHY DIDN'T ALMA HEAL KORIHOR?**
(Ensign, Maxwell, Nov. 1991, p. 31, *Doctrinal Commentary on the Book of Mormon,* McConkie and Millet, 3:213)

Alma 30:60 **WHY WON'T THE THE DEVIL SUPPORT HIS CHILDREN?**
(1 Ne. 8:26; 3 Nephi 27:11; Alma 34:39)

"Satan does not support those who follow him. He can't! It's the Lord who sustains; the Spirit sustains; righteousness sustains. That sustenance is not Satan's to give."

Janette C. Hales (BYU Devotional, Mar. 16, 1993)

Alma 31~35

ALMA 31:5   **MORE POWERFUL THAN THE SWORD**
(1 Ne. 21:2; Hel. 3:29; 5:50-52; Alma 26:23, 25, 31-32; D&C 6:2; *Ensign*, Sept. 1976, pp. 20-21)

"The gospel is the only answer to the problems of the world. We may cry peace. We may hold peace conferences. And I have nothing but commendation for those who work for peace. But it is my conviction that peace must come from within. It cannot be imposed by state mandate. It can come only by following the teachings and the example of the Prince of Peace."

Ezra Taft Benson (Title of Liberty, pp. 213-214)

"There are no armaments, no governmental schemes, no international organizations, and no mechanisms for the control of weapons which can preserve an unrighteous people. . . . Alma has given us compelling evidence of his conviction that repentance is more effectual than arms in maintaining peace. You will recall that he was the elected chief judge of the Nephite nation. As such he was the governor of the people of Nephi and commander-in-chief of their armies. Seeing many of them dissenting and conniving with the enemy, he, notwithstanding his power to strengthen and command his armies, placed the affairs of state in other hands that he himself might cry repentance unto the dissenters. . . ."

Marion G. Romney (Conference Report, Apr. 1950, pp. 87-88)

"True doctrine, understood, changes attitudes and behavior. The study of the doctrines of the gospel will improve behavior quicker than a study of behavior will improve behavior."

Boyd K. Packer (Conference Report, Oct. 1986, p. 20)

"Decaying cities are simply a delayed reflection of decaying individuals. . . . The commandments of God give emphasis to improvement of the individual as the only real way to bring about the real improvement in society."

Ezra Taft Benson (A Plea for America, p. 18)

"The Lord works from the inside out. The world works from the outside in. The world would take people out of the slums. Christ takes the slums out of the people, and then they take themselves out of the slums. The world would mold men by changing their environment. Christ changes men, who then change their environment. The world would shape human behavior, but Christ can change human nature."

Ezra Taft Benson (Ensign, Nov. 1985, p. 6)

Alma 31:21   RAMEUMPTOM
(Companion to Your Study of the Book of Mormon, Ludlow, p. 213; *Since Cumorah*, Nibley, pp. 275-276)

"Doing home teaching, earning a scout merit badge, or doing other assigned acts of service can become little more than offerings on the Rameumptom, if our hearts are not earnest and our daily nature not Christian."

Elaine Shaw Sorensen (Alma, The Testimony of the Word, ed. by Nyman and Tate, p. 131)

Alma 31:28; 32:2 COSTLY APPAREL
(contrast this with Matt. 22:9-14; Alma 5:14,19; refer in this text to Alma 1:6)

"Our society may well be as guilty as the wealthy Zoramites of using fashion as 'the science of appearances, inspiring us with the desire to seem rather than to be' (Edwin Hubbell Chapin). In our day the costly apparel syndrome may be identified as one aspect of the modern-day term 'conspicuous consumption.' The word *conspicuous* alludes to the visual side of vanity—the need to be seen, to be recognized. *Consumption* refers to that which we take in or that which we consume. Conspicuous consumption may be defined as that which we take to ourselves in order to be recognized and approved by others. By its very definition, the person trapped in conspicuous consumption, especially as it applies to 'costly apparel,' must be focused on the opinions of others, because what is 'in' today may be 'out' tomorrow. Vanity then becomes its own punishment, because there is never time to be satisfied—the eyes and opinions of others can turn so quickly to embrace someone else. For us, the disease that afflicted the

Zoramites encompasses more than clothing. It can include cars, houses, boats, diplomas, and anything else that has a foundation where the need for the approval of man carries more weight than the need to be accepted by God."

K. Douglas Bassett (Doctrines of the Book of Mormon, 1991 Sperry Symposium, pp. 18-19)

Alma 31:31, 33, 38; 32:6; 33:23

AFFLICTION, SWALLOWED UP IN THE JOY OF CHRIST

(Alma 58:10-11; Matt. 11:28; refer in this text to Mosiah 24: 14-15; Alma 14:11; Alma 34:40-41)

"God never bestows upon His people, or upon an individual, superior blessings without a severe trial to prove them, to prove that individual, or that people, to see whether they will keep their covenants with Him, and keep in remembrance what He has shown them. . . . So when individuals are blessed with visions, revelations, and great manifestations, look out, then the devil is nigh you, and you will be tempted in proportion to the vision, revelation, or manifestation you have received."

Brigham Young (Journal of Discourses 3:205-206)

"It has been wisely observed that a blessing is anything that brings us nearer to God. Thus our afflictions often become our greatest blessings. It is in our extremities that most often we meet God, not in our comfort. Thus any time conditions come to pass—even what at the time might be construed as tragic or unfortunate conditions—that lead us toward the truth or contribute to our eventual well-being, we have indeed been blessed."

Robert Millet and Joseph McConkie (Doctrinal Commentary on the Book of Mormon, 3:224)

"Why is non-endurance a denial of the Lord? Because giving up is a denial of the Lord's loving capacity to see us through 'all these things'! Giving up suggests that God is less than He really is. . . . So much of life's curriculum consists of efforts by the Lord to get and keep our attention. Ironically, the stimuli He uses are often that which is seen by us as something to endure. Sometimes what we are being asked to endure is His 'help'—help to draw us away from the cares of the world; help to draw us away from self-centeredness; attention-getting help when the still, small voice has been ignored by us; help in the shaping of our souls; and help to keep the promises we made so long ago to Him and to ourselves. . . . Whether the afflictions are self-induced, as most of them are, or whether they are of the divine-tutorial type, it matters not. Either way, the Lord can help us so that our afflictions, said Alma, can be 'swallowed up in the joy of

Christ' (Alma 31:38). Thus, afflictions are endured and are overcome by joy. The sour notes are lost amid a symphony of salvational sounds. Our afflictions, brothers and sisters, may not be extinguished. Instead, they can be dwarfed and swallowed up in the joy of Christ. This is how we overcome most of the time—not the elimination of affliction, but the placing of these in that larger context."

Neal A. Maxwell (BYU Fireside, December 2, 1984)

Alma 32

FAITH
(Mosiah 26:3; Morm. 9:25; Ether 4:11; 12:6-22, 29-30; Heb. 4:2; 11:1, 6; Mark 9:23; Heb. 11:6; D&C 5:16; *Lectures on Faith,* 1:10,24; 6;7; *A New Witness For the Articles of Faith*, McConkie, pp. 209-210; *Ensign*, May 1994, pp. 96-97)

Faith is not a substitute for truth but a pathway to it.

"Belief in a sense is passive, an agreement or acceptance only; faith is active and positive embracing such reliance and confidence as will lead to works."

James E. Talmage (Articles of Faith, pp. 96-97)

"Faith, then, is the first great governing principle which has power, dominion, and authority over all things; by it they exist, by it they are upheld, by it they are changed, or by it they remain, agreeable to the will of God. Without it there is no power, and without power there could be no creation nor existence."

Joseph Smith (Lectures on Faith, 1:24)

"So the combination of faith in Christ plus *faith unto repentance* is vitally important. That concept is one of the greatest insights we have into the importance of simple, clear faith—faith sufficient to repent. Apparently faith great enough to move mountains is not required; faith enough to speak in tongues or to heal the sick is not needed; all that we need is just enough faith to recognize that we have sinned and to repent of our sins, to feel remorse for them, and to desire to sin no more but to please Christ the Lord."

Robert E. Wells (Doctrines of the Book of Mormon, 1991 Sperry Symposium, pp. 6-7)

"Of all our needs, I think the greatest is an increase in faith."

Gordon B. Hinckley (Ensign, Nov. 1987, p. 54)

"Could faith be the answer? We all know that more faith won't make our problems disappear. But I believe as our faith increases, we become more able to not only survive the hard times but become better because of them. . . . faith means that I really believe that: (1) Heavenly Father and Jesus Christ live, and they are in charge of this world. (2) They know me. (3) They love me. (4) They have a plan for my future. (5) I will obey the commandments, work hard, and trust in their plan. Sooner or later, everything will be okay."

Virginia H. Pearce (Ensign, May 1994, p. 92)

[A lesson learned as a missionary on a sailboat in Tonga] "Once I asked the Lord to bless us with a good tail wind so we could get to Foa quickly. As we got under way, one of the older men said, 'Elder Groberg, you need to modify your prayers a little.' 'How's that?' I replied. 'You asked the Lord for a tail wind to take us rapidly to Foa. If you pray for a tail wind to Foa, what about the people who are trying to come from Foa to Pangai? They are good people, and you are praying against them. Just pray for a good wind, not a tail wind.' . . . We may pray for a particular type of weather, or to preserve someone's life, when that answer to our prayer may hurt someone else. That's why we must always pray in faith, because we can't have true, God-given faith in something that is not according to His will. If it's according to His will, all parties will benefit. I learned to pray for a good wind and the ability to get there safely, not necessarily a tail wind."

John H. Groberg (In the Eye of the Storm, p. 175)

Alma 32:19   **HE THAT KNOWETH THE WILL OF GOD & DOETH IT NOT**
(D&C 82:3; 2 Ne. 9:27; *Journal of Discourses* 3:206)

Alma 32:21, 32   **REAL FAITH MUST BE BASED ON TRUTH**
(*Man's Search for Meaning*, Frankl, pp.117-121; *Teachings of the Prophet Joseph Smith*, p. 58; *Conference Report*, Apr. 1978, p.20; refer in this text to 3 Ne. 18:20)

"By way of illustration I borrow the following from the works of Orson Pratt: 'When Europeans first began their explorations in the New World, the Indians whom they met were much amazed at the power and explosive properties of gunpowder and asked many questions respecting the manner in which it was produced. The Europeans, taking advantage of the ignorance of the . . . [Indians], and seeing an opportunity to increase their wealth by the deception, told the Indians that it was the seed of a plant which grew in the lands they had come from, and doubtless it would thrive in their land also. The Indians, of course, believed this statement, and purchased the supposed seed, giving in exchange for it large quantities of gold. In implicit faith they carefully planted the supposed seed, and anxiously watched for its sprouting and the appearance of the plant; but it never came. They had faith in the statements made to them by the Europeans, but as these statements were false, and therefore the evidence on which the Indians based their belief untrue, their faith was vain.' Thus must it ever be. Only correct evidence, only truthful testimony can produce fruitful, profitable, true faith. *No matter how sincere one's belief may be in an error, that will not transform the error into truth. The sincere faith of the Indians in what the Europeans had said about the gunpowder seed did not make that substance produce a plant yielding gunpowder.* And so faith in false doctrines, founded upon false testimony, cannot savor of salvation."

B. H. Roberts (The Gospel and Man's Relationship to Deity, pp. 46-47)

Alma 32:28

PLANT THE SEED IN YOUR HEART
(refer to Virginia H. Pearce quote under DEVELOPING FAITH at the conclusion of Alma 32)

"To soundly plant good seeds in your heart requires prolonged, intense, unremitting pondering. It is a deep, ongoing, regenerating process which refines the soul."

Joseph B. Wirthlin (Ensign, May 1982, pp. 23-25)

"Just as soil needs preparation for a seed, so does a human heart for the word of God to take root. Before he told the people to plant the seed, Alma told them that their hearts were prepared. They had been persecuted and cast out of their churches. Alma with his love and the circumstances of their lives, which led them to be humble, had prepared them. They were then ready to hear the word of God. If they chose to plant it in their hearts, the growth in their souls would surely follow, and that would increase their faith. . . . First of all that to plant the seed, they have to try it by keeping commandments. . . . That feeling of surrender is not likely to come unless they experience some feeling of being loved and lowly of heart."

Henry B. Eyring (Ensign, Nov. 1995, p. 38)

Alma 32:34-35

SWELLETH SOULS & ENLIGHTEN UNDERSTANDING
"A few weeks ago our four-year-old grandson, Michael, reported to his parents, 'When I pray, my heart feels like a roasted marshmallow.' . . . The prophet Alma described these feelings . . . [in Alma 32:34-35]. Learning to discern the teachings of the Spirit is an important part of helping faith become a reality. My daughter

Karen shared her experience. She said, 'When I was just a little girl, I started read-ing the Book of Mormon for the first time. After many days of reading, I came one night to 1 Nephi 3:7: . . . I felt strongly impressed. . . . but the deep impression was really more of a feeling. I had seen my parents mark verses in their scriptures with red pencils. So I got up and searched through the house until I found a red pencil, and with a great sense of solemnity and importance, I marked that verse in my own Book of Mormon.' Karen continued, 'Over the years as I read the scriptures, that experience was repeated time and time again. . . In time I came to recognize that feeling as the Holy Ghost.'"

Janette Hales Beckham (Ensign, Nov. 1997, p. 75)

DEVELOPING FAITH
(Book of Mormon 121-122 Student Manual, p. 89)

Hypothesis	*Experiment*	*Conclusions*
v. 21, 27, 33-34	v. 23-32	v. 37-43

"Alma used a seed to stand for the word. He taught the discouraged Zoramites that if they would 'give place, that a seed may be planted in [their] heart[s]' (Alma 32:28), and then notice if good feelings went with it, they would begin to understand and life would be different for them. Could that be a way of say-ing: 'Decide, just for yourself, that you will make a place for scripture reading. And then, as you begin to do that notice what feelings go with it'? Alma then taught that 'as the tree beginneth to grow' (Alma 32:37), it would need to be nourished with great care. Could that be a way of saying: 'Nourish the desire to read. Do some things that will keep you reading and help you to understand in new ways. Let others keep you excited and help you learn more from the scrip-tures so that the word will continue to grow'? Alma taught that if this nourish-ing continued for a long time, there would be wonderful fruit. Please turn to Alma, chapter 32, verse 42: . . .'ye shall pluck the fruit, . . . and ye shall feast upon this fruit . . . that ye hunger not, neither shall ye thirst.' Could that be a way of saying: 'When you continue reading, and doing the things that you read about, eventually life will change in a way that is difficult to even imagine. Your daily discouragements will be replaced with a knowledge of how much God loves you. You will feast and be filled'"?

Virginia H. Pearce (Ensign, May 1995, p. 89)

Alma 33   **ZENOS**
(Since Cumorah, Nibley, pp. 136, 313-327; Jacob 5; Hel. 8:19)

Alma 34:10-12   INFINITE ATONEMENT
(refer in this text to 2 Ne. 9:7-9)

Alma 34:13-15   THE LAW OF MOSES FULFILLED
(Alma 25:15-16; Mosiah 13:29-30; Jacob 4:5)

Alma 34:15   FAITH UNTO REPENTANCE
(Converted to Christ through the Book of Mormon, England, pp. 1-2)

Alma 34:18-27   CRY UNTO HIM IN YOUR HOUSES
(D&C 19:38; Ether 1:43; 2 Ne. 9:52; 32:9; Mosiah 18:23; 3 Ne. 20:1; Alma 26:22; *Teachings of Spencer W. Kimball*, p. 233; *Mormon Doctrine*, McConkie, p. 586; refer in this text to Alma 37:37; 3 Ne. 18:15-23)

". . . May I ask this important question: How many families in the Church of Jesus Christ of Latter-day Saints have regular nightly and morning family prayer? Those who neglect to do so are displeasing the Lord and are entitled to the same rebuke which the Lord gave some of the leading elders of the Church in the early days. No parent should depend solely on the organizations of the Church for the training of the children. They should be taught to pray regularly, secretly as well as in the family circle. The counsel that Alma and Amulek gave to the straying Zoramites is just as essential to the Latter-day Saints today as it was two thousand years ago."

Joseph Fielding Smith (Answers to Gospel Questions, 5:48)

"No man can retain the Spirit of the Lord, unless he prays. No man can have the inspiration of the Holy Spirit, unless in his heart is found this spirit of prayer. . . . And if a man will pray as he is commanded to do in this passage of scripture which I have read [Alma 34:18-27], then he more than likely will be found in all things righteously keeping the commandments of the Lord. He will not be found scheming to take advantage of his neighbor in some trade of bargain, but in all things dealing justly, because he has prayed in the morning and has in his heart the spirit of prayer throughout the day, that the Lord will bless him in the increase of his goods, of his fields, of his flocks, or whatever it may be he is engaged in."

Joseph Fielding Smith (Conference Report, Oct. 1919, pp. 142-143)

"It is not such a difficult thing to learn how to pray. It is not the words we use particularly that constitute prayer. Prayer does not consist of words, altogether.

True, faithful, earnest prayer consists more in the feeling that rises from the heart and from the inward desire of our spirits to supplicate the Lord in humility and in faith, that we may receive His blessings. It matters not how simple the words may be, if our desires are genuine and we come before the Lord with a broken heart and a contrite spirit to ask Him for that which we need."

Joseph F. Smith (Conference Report, Oct. 1899, p. 69)

"Prayer should be direct and simple as if spoken to our earthly father. Routine forms of prayer should be avoided. The words spoken are less important than the humble faith in which they are uttered. 'Prayer is the soul's sincere desire, uttered or unexpressed.' It is the spirit of prayer that gives life to our desires. The direct simplicity of the Lords prayer should be kept in mind."

John A. Widtsoe (Evidences and Reconciliations, p. 316)

"In the summer of my thirteenth year, . . . I eagerly joined some neighborhood friends to light fireworks. . . . Not all of our fireworks worked as they should have. . . . We set the duds aside until we had tried to light all of the fireworks. We had so many defective ones remaining, we wondered what to do. We couldn't just throw them away. What if we emptied the powder from all of them into the cardboard box? We could toss in a match and have one gigantic blast! . . . The match was tossed; we quickly ran away and waited. Nothing happened. . . . We tried a second time, using a makeshift fuse of rolled-up newspaper. . . . Again, to our good, nothing happened. . . . Foolishly, we gave it one more try. . . . Then it happened! The 'gigantic blast' we thought we wanted exploded with fury into our faces. The force of the explosion knocked us off our feet, and flames from the ignited powder burned us severely. . . . Our friend's mother gathered us into her home. 'First we will pray,' she said, 'and then we will call the doctor.' That was the first of many prayers I remember being offered for us. Soon after, I felt my face, hands, and arms being wrapped in bandages. I heard the voices of my father and my doctor administering a priesthood blessing to me. I heard my mother's voice many times, pleading with Heavenly Father to please let her son see again. . . . I had felt with a surety that I would be healed. From the moment that first prayer was offered in my friend's home, I felt a comforting peace. . . . Each day when the doctor changed my bandages, my mother would ask, 'Can he see?' For many days the answer was the same: 'No, not yet.' Finally, when all the bandages were permanently removed, my eyesight began to return. . . . The peace and comfort I had earlier felt gave me assurance that all would be well. However, when my vision cleared enough for me to see my hands and face, I was shocked, unprepared for what I saw. . . . Seeing my scarred and disfigured skin brought great fear and doubt into my mind. I can remember thinking, nothing can help this skin to be healed—not even the Lord. Gratefully, as my prayers and the prayers of others continued, I felt the gifts of faith and of peace restored, and then, in time, my eyesight and my skin were healed. . . . May we always seek to obtain the Lord's miraculous gift of peace through prayer."

Rex E. Pinegar (Ensign, May 1993, pp. 65-68)

Alma 34:28-29   **THE ROYAL LAW**
(James 2:8; Matt. 23:11; 25:31-46; Gal. 5:14; refer in this text to Mosiah 2:16-17)

"We must have this law in mind in all that we do in our welfare work. We must love our neighbor as ourselves. The Savior put this law second only to the love of God. . . ."

Marion G. Romney (Conference Report, Apr. 1978, p.142)

"One cannot ask God to help a neighbor in distress without feeling motivated to do something oneself toward helping that neighbor."

Gordon B. Hinckley (Ensign, Feb. 1991, pp. 2-5)

"To worthy causes and needy people, we can give time if we don't have money, and we can give love when our time runs out. . . . Sister Drusilla Hendricks and her invalid husband, James, who had been shot by enemies of the Church in the Battle of Crooked River, arrived with their children at a hastily shaped dugout in Quincy, Illinois, to live out the spring of that harrowing year. Within two weeks the Hendrickses were on the verge of starvation, having only one spoonful of sugar and a saucerful of cornmeal remaining in their possession. In the great tradition of LDS women, Drusilla made mush out of it for James and the children, thus stretching its contents as far as she could make it go. When that small offering was consumed by her famished family, she washed everything, cleaned their little dugout as thoroughly as she could, and quietly waited to die. Not long thereafter the sound of a wagon brought Drusilla to her feet. It was their neighbor Reuben Allred. He said he had a feeling they were out of food, so on his way into town he'd had a sack of grain ground into meal for them. Shortly thereafter Alexander Williams arrived with two bushels of meal on his shoulder. He told Drusilla that he'd been extremely busy but the Spirit had whispered to him that 'Brother Hendricks' family is suffering, so I dropped everything and came [running].' . . . May [we] hear the

whispering of the Holy Spirit when any neighbor anywhere 'is suffering,' and
. . . 'drop everything and come running.'"

Jeffrey R. Holland (Ensign, May 1996, pp. 30-31)

Alma 34:32-33   **CAN YOU REPENT AFTER DEATH?**
(Mosiah 2:33, 38-40; 15:26; Alma 42:4; Hel. 13:38; 2 Ne. 9:27, 38; D&C 84:41;
Teachings of the Prophet Joseph Smith, p. 197; *Doctrines of Salvation*, Smith, 2:97-
98. Contrast with D&C 138:58; Moses 7:38-39)

"We know not fully on what terms repentance will be obtainable in the hereafter; but to suppose that the soul who has willfully rejected the opportunity of
repentance in this life will find it easy to repent there is contrary to reason. To
procrastinate the day of repentance is to deliberately place ourselves in the
power of the adversary. . . ."

James E. Talmage (Articles of Faith, p. 115)

"Now I have read to you the scripture. (Alma 34:30-35). I believe it is the word
of God 'with the bark on it,' where the prophet of the Lord declared unto apostates and those who have heard the gospel that if they did not repent and come
into the Church now, in this day of repentance, but continued to procrastinate
their repentance unto the end, that the night would come when no work could
be done for them, and their souls would be lost. I think that is pretty good scripture. I do not know how the Lord could do otherwise in justice."

Joseph Fielding Smith (Doctrines of Salvation, 2:189)

"You can progress much more rapidly here on earth with your mortal body in
this environment of good and evil than you will as a spirit in the spirit world."

Richard G. Scott (Ensign, May 1997, p. 54)

Alma 34:33   **DON'T PROCRASTINATE REPENTANCE**
(refer in this text to Hel. 13:38; 1 Ne. 18:20; Morm. 2:13; John 9:4; *Miracle of
Forgiveness*, Kimball, pp. 7-10)

"We should take warning and not wait for the death-bed to repent, as we see the
infant taken away by death, so may the youth and middle-aged, as well as the
infant be suddenly called into eternity. Let this, then, prove as a warning to all
not to procrastinate repentance, or wait till a death-bed, for it is the will of God

that man should repent and serve Him in health, and in the strength and power of his mind, in order to secure his blessing, and not wait until he is called to die."

Teachings of the Prophet Joseph Smith, p. 197

"We are concerned that some young people who are anticipating serving a mission or being married in the temple have a very lax attitude toward sin. 'I'll just have a few free ones,' they say, 'and then I'll repent quickly, and go on my mission (or get married in the temple), and everything will be alright.'. . . Such persons want the present convenience or enjoyment of sin and the future effects of righteousness, in that order. They want to experience the sin, but avoid its effects. . . . There is something very peculiar about the state of mind or heart of the person who deliberately commits sin in the expectation that he or she will speedily and comfortably repent and continue as a servant of God, preaching repentance and asking others to come unto Christ. . . . Am I suggesting that the benefits of the atonement are not available for the person who heedlessly sins? Of course not. But, I am suggesting that there is a relationship between sin and suffering, that is not understood by people who knowingly sin in the expectation that all the burden of suffering will be borne by another, that the sin is all theirs, but the suffering is all His. That is not the way. Repentance, which is an assured passage to an eternal destination, is nevertheless not a free ride."

Dallin H. Oaks (BYU Fireside, Aug.5, 1990)

"Yes, one can repent of . . . transgression. The miracle of forgiveness is real, and true repentance is accepted of the Lord. But, it is not pleasing to the Lord to sow one's wild oats, to engage in . . . transgression of any nature and then expect that *planned* confession and quick repentance will satisfy the Lord."

Teachings of Ezra Taft Benson, p. 70

"It is my judgment that some of our youth *do not believe* that repentance for serious transgression 'is difficult and painful and may take a long time.' Where has this grave misunderstanding come from? To you young people, if any of us who are older have given you the impression that it isn't too serious to disobey the commandments of God, forgive us. . . . Priesthood leaders, let us be careful that we do not permit young missionaries to go into the mission field with unresolved transgression. It is literally like going into battle without helmet, sword, or shield. Let us remember that it takes time to develop the power to resist the fires of temptation. It takes time to receive the sweet comfort that always comes to the heart of the truly penitent. Allow them sufficient time."

L. Aldin Porter (Ensign, May 1992, p. 46)

"As the time of repentance is procrastinated, the ability to repent grows weaker; neglect of opportunity in holy things develops inability."

James E. Talmage (Articles of Faith, p. 114)

"The thought of intentionally committing serious sin now and repenting later is perilously wrong. Never do that. Many start that journey of intentional transgression and never make it back. Premeditated sin has greater penalties and is harder to overcome. If there is sin, repent now—while you can."

Richard G. Scott (Ensign, Nov. 1994, p. 38)

"I believe, to use an insurance phrase, we must pay the deductible. We must experience sorrow enough, suffering enough, guilt enough so we are conscious and appreciative of the heavier burden borne by the Savior. My soul pains when His atonement is treated lightly, when the blessing of repentance is reduced to simply 'taking care of it with the bishop,' when there is brief confession without humility or godly sorrow. This attitude of entitlement rather than privilege was recently expressed by a young Church member who wrote: 'I have done bad things that I knew were bad because I've been taught that ever since I can remember. . . . I know repentance is a great gift. Without it I would be lost. I am not ready to repent of my sins; but I know that when I am ready, I can.' Such indulgence in premeditated sin shows pitiful misunderstanding of repentance."

J. Richard Clarke (Ensign, May 1993, p.10)

Alma 34:34-35   ATTITUDES AND HABITS IN THE SPIRIT WORLD
(2 Ne. 9;16; *The Miracle of Forgiveness*, Kimball, p.168; *Discourses of Brigham Young*, p. 70, 379; *Journal of Discourses* 7:333)

"Do not let any of us imagine that we can go down to the grave not having overcome the corruptions of the flesh and then lose in the grave all our sins and evil tendencies. They will be with us. They will be with the spirit when separated from the body."

Gordon B. Hinckley (Sermons and Missionary Services of Melvin J. Ballard, pp. 240-242)

Alma 34:40-41   BE PATIENT IN AFFLICTION
(D&C 67:13; 101:16; 121:7-8; 122:5-8; 1 Peter 2:20; *Mary Fielding Smith*, Corbett, p.100; Alma 31:31, 38; 33:23; 36:27; 2 Cor. 4:8-17; Mosiah 23:21; refer in this text to Mosiah 24:14-15)

"Religious faith gives confidence that human tragedy is not a meaningless sport of physical forces. Life is not what Voltaire called it, 'A bad joke,' it is really a school of discipline whose author and teacher is God."

Hugh B. Brown (Conference Report, Oct. 1969, p. 105-107)

"The great challenge in this earthly life is not to determine how to escape the afflictions and problems, but rather to carefully prepare ourselves to meet them. I say prepare ourselves because it demands persistent effort to develop patience as a personal attribute. In practicing patience, one comes to understand it and to acquire it. . . . We must have patience in order to withstand pain and grief without complaint or discouragement, which detract from the Spirit. . . . We are not talking here about a passive patience which waits only for the passing of time to heal or resolve things which *happen to us,* but rather a patience that is active, which *makes things happen.* . . . (Rom. 2:7; 1 Peter 2:20). Patience in affliction and adversity means to persist firmly and never forsake that which we know to be true, standing firm with the hope that in the Lord's due time we will gain an understanding of that which we do not understand now and which causes us suffering. . . . The faithful Latter-day Saint—instead of despairing because a goal on his or her agenda was not realized, because his or her timetable does not bring a solution to the problems, or because comfort does not come to calm the troubles of today—waits patiently for fulfillment of promises, according to the Lord's timetable."

Angel Abrea (Conference Report, Apr. 1992, pp. 34-37)

"Mormon surely knew that no pain we suffer, no trial that we experience is wasted. It ministers to our education, to the development of such qualities as patience, faith, fortitude and humility. All that we suffer and all that we endure, especially when we endure it patiently, builds up our characters, purifies our hearts, expands our souls, and makes us more tender and charitable, more worthy to be called the children of God."

Howard W. Hunter (Ensign, Nov. 1987, p. 60)

"Sometimes we pray for the strength to endure yet resist the very things that would give us that strength. Too often we seek the easy way, forgetting that strength comes from overcoming things that require us to put forth more effort than we normally would be inclined to do."

John H. Groberg (Ensign, Nov. 1993, p. 26)

It is easy enough to be pleasant,
When life flows by like a song,
But the man worth while is one who will smile,
When everything goes dead wrong.
For the test of the heart is trouble,
And it always comes with the years,
And the smile that is worth the praises of earth
Is the smile that shines through tears.

Ella Wheeler Wilcox (as quoted by Thomas S. Monson, Ensign, Nov. 1993, p. 71)

"I am grateful for the things which I have suffered in the flesh, which have been blessings in my life that have taught me patience, long-suffering, faith, and a sensitivity to those who are less fortunate. . . . I have learned in my life that trials are blessings in disguise if we accept them with humility, faith, and fortitude. All that we suffer and endure with patience will build within us a more charitable and tender person, having acquired the education we came on earth to receive."

Lloyd P. George (Ensign, May 1994, p. 28)

"When we are pushed, stung, defeated, embarrassed, hurt, rejected, tormented, forgotten—when we are in agony of spirit crying out 'why me?' we are in a position to learn something. Inner resources can be stirred under such stress. Hidden strengths awaken that can be a blessing to others."

Elaine Cannon (Adversity, p. 20)

"No pain that we suffer, no trial that we experience is wasted. It ministers to our education, to the development of such qualities as patience, faith, fortitude and humility. All that we suffer and all that we endure, especially when we endure it patiently, builds up our characters, purifies our hearts, expands our souls, and makes us more tender and charitable, more worthy to be called the children of God, . . . and it is through sorrow and suffering, toil and tribulation, that we gain the education that we come here to acquire."

Orson F. Whitney (Improvement Era, Mar. 1966, p. 211)

Alma 35:15   **OFFENDED BY THE WORD**
(1 Ne. 16:2-3; 2 Ne. 9:40; Mosiah 13:4; Moro. 9:4-5; refer in this text to 1 Ne. 8:20)

"We may get angry with parents, or a teacher, or the Bishop, and dwarf ourselves into nameless anonymity as we shrivel and shrink under the venom and poison of bitterness, little realizing the suffering of the hater, the latter cheats himself. . . . To terminate activity in the Church just to spite leaders or to give vent to wounded feelings is to cheat ourselves."

Teachings of Spencer W. Kimball, p. 242-243

Alma 36 ~ 38

Alma 36 **CHIASMUS**
(Book of Mormon Authorship, ed. by Reynolds, pp. 33-52; *The New Era*, Feb. 1972, pp. 6-11; *Ensign*, Sept. 1977, pp. 45-48)

Alma 36:1, 30; **NEPHI'S FREEDOM THESIS**
37:13; (1 Ne. 1:20; 2:20; 4:4; Jarom 1:9-12; Omni 1:6; Mosiah 1:7; 2:22; refer in this
38:1 text to 1 Ne.1:20; Alma 48:15; 2 Ne. 1:7, 20, 30-32; Ether 2:7-9, 12, 15)

Alma 36:12-16 **OPENING THE DOOR TO REPENTANCE**
(Conference Report, Apr. 1975, p. 116; refer in this text to Alma 38:8)

"When we come to recognize our sin sincerely and without reservations, we are ready to follow such processes as will rid us of sin's effects. . . . Young Alma was so deep in his sin that it was most difficult for him to humble himself toward repentance, but when his experience broke down his resistance, softened his rebellion and overcame his stubbornness, he began to see himself in his true light and appraise his situation as it really was. His heart was softened. His repentance was being born."

Spencer W. Kimball (The Miracle of Forgiveness, pp. 157-159)

Alma 36:17-19 **I WAS HARROWED UP BY THE MEMORY OF MY SINS NO MORE**
(Ensign, June 1992, pp. 30-31; refer in this text to Alma 42:29)

Alma 36:17-21 **I REMEMBERED ALSO TO HAVE HEARD MY FATHER**
(1 Ne. 2:16; 11:1-5; 14:29; Enos 1:1-5; Hel. 5:5)

Alma 36:27   **SUPPORTED UNDER TRIALS**
(Mosiah 27:32; refer in this text to Mosiah 24:14-15; Alma 14:11; Alma 34:40-41)

"If we do our best to keep the commandments of God, come what may, we will be all right. Of course, that does not necessarily mean that we will be spared personal suffering and heartache. Righteousness has never precluded adversity. But faith in the Lord Jesus Christ—real faith, whole-souled and unshakable—is a power to be reckoned with in the universe. . . . It can be a source of inner strength, through which we find peace, comfort, and the courage to cope."

M. Russell Ballard (Ensign, Nov. 1992, p. 32)

Alma 37:6-7   **SMALL AND SIMPLE THINGS**
(Kisses at the Window, Bassett, pp. 47-50)

Alma 37:23,38   **GAZELEM AND LIAHONA**
"*Gazelem* is a name given to a servant of God. The word appears to have its roots in Gaz—a stone, and Aleim, a name of God as a revelator, or the interposer in the affairs of men. If this suggestion is correct, its roots admirably agree with its apparent meaning—a seer.

Liahona. This interesting word is Hebrew with an Egyptian ending. It is the name which Lehi gave to the ball or director he found outside his tent. . . . *L* is a Hebrew preposition meaning 'to,' and sometimes used to express the possessive case. *Iah* is a Hebrew abbreviated form of 'Jehovah,' common in Hebrew names. *On* is the Hebrew name of the Egyptian 'City of the sun.' . . . *L-iah-on* means, therefore, literally, 'To God is Light'; or, 'of God is Light.' That is to say, God gives light, as does the Sun. The final *a* reminds us that the Egyptian form of the Hebrew name *On* is *Annu,* and this seems to be the form Lehi used."

G. Reynolds and J. Sjodahl (Commentary on the Book of Mormon, 4:162, 178.)

Alma 37:25, 28, 31   **A CURSE UPON THE LAND**
(Ether 2:6-12; 2 Ne. 1:7; Enos 10; refer in this text to under Hel. 1:11-12; Ether 8:18-25)

Alma 37:27, 29, 32   **DO NOT TEACH DARKNESS**
(Alma 63:12; Hel. 6:25; 2 Ne. 25:2; 26:23; *BYU Speeches of the Year,* Packer, Oct. 4, 1966, p. 7)

"It is not necessary that our young people should know of the wickedness carried on in anyplace. Such knowledge is not elevating and it is quite likely that more than one young man can trace the first step of his downfall to a curiosity which led him into questionable places."

Joseph F. Smith (Gospel Doctrine, pp. 373-374)

"As I have met with many groups of missionaries throughout the mission, I find a tendency for missionaries to tell their faults to their companions, their friends, and sometimes in public. There is not place in the mission field to publicize your weaknesses. . . . There is no reason why you should tell every companion the fact that you might have smoked a few cigarettes in your life before you came, or that you had taken the name of the Lord vain, or any other of your weaknesses. We go forward on the assumption that you are worthy to do this work. If there is something of major importance in your life that had not been adjusted before your coming into the mission field, then certainly you should make those adjustments through your president. Don't tell the saints. That does not do anyone any good. It does not mean you are being hypocritical. You had some weaknesses, you repented, and those weaknesses are no longer a part of your life. . . ."

Teachings of Spencer W. Kimball, p. 96

Alma 37:34   **REST TO THEIR SOULS**
(John 14:27; Matt. 11;28-30; Moro. 7:3-4; Jacob 1:7)

"In the midst of a very unsettled world one can be at peace. That peace is made possible through the Savior and his gospel that we call the plan of salvation. If we are not at peace then either our perceptions or our behavior (or both) needs adjusting."

Larry E. Dahl (BYU Religious Education Faculty Pre-School Meeting, Aug. 27, 1992

"The man or woman who enjoys the spirit of our religion has no trials; but the man or woman who tries to live according to the Gospel of the Son of God, and at the same time clings to the spirit of the world, has trials and sorrows acute and keen, and that, too, continually. This is the deciding point, the dividing line. They who love and serve God with all their hearts rejoice evermore, pray without ceasing, and in everything give thanks; but they who try to serve God and still cling to the spirit of the world, have got on two yokes—the yoke of Jesus and the yoke of the devil . . . They will have a warfare inside and outside, and the labor will be very galling, for they are directly in opposition one to the other. Cast off the yoke of the enemy, and put on the yoke of Christ, and you will say that his yoke is easy and his burden is light. This I know by experience."

Brigham Young (Journal of Discourses 16:123)

"The ancient prophets speak of 'entering into God's rest'; what does it mean? To my mind, it means entering into the knowledge and love of God, having faith in his purpose and in his plan, to such an extent that we know we are right, and that we are not hunting for something else, we are not disturbed by every wind of doctrine, or by the cunning and craftiness of men who lie in wait to deceive. . . . The man who has reached that degree of faith in God that all doubt and fear have been cast from him, he has entered into 'God's rest,' . . . The rest here referred to is not physical rest, for there is no such thing as physical rest in the Church of Jesus Christ. Reference is made to the spiritual rest and peace which are born from a settled conviction of the truth in the minds of men. We may thus enter into the rest of the Lord today, by coming to an understanding of the truths of the gospel. . . . But there are many [members] who, not having reached this point of determined conviction, are driven about by every wind of doctrine, thus being ill at ease, unsettled, restless. These are they who are discouraged over incidents that occur in the Church, and in the nation, and in the turmoils of men and associations. They harbor a feeling of suspicion, unrest, uncertainty. Their thoughts are disturbed, and they become excited with the least change, like one at sea who has lost his bearings. . . . Let them seek for it in the written word of God; let them pray to him in their secret chambers, where no human ear can hear, and in their closets petition for light; let them obey the doctrines of Jesus, and they will immediately begin to grow in the knowledge of the truth. . . . Let them seek for strength from the Source of all strength, and he will provide spiritual contentment, a rest which is incomparable with the physical rest that cometh after toil. All who seek have a right to, and may enter into, the rest of God, here upon the earth, from this time forth, now, today; and when earth-life is finished, they shall also enjoy his rest in heaven."

Joseph F. Smith (Gospel Doctrine, pp. 58, 126-127)

Alma 37:35; 38:2 YOUTHFUL OBEDIENCE
(Eccl. 12:1; refer in this text to 1 Ne. 3:7)

"I have said again and again that I believe this is the best generation [in the Church] we have ever had. . . . You live in a world of terrible temptations. Pornography, with its sleazy filth, sweeps over the earth like a horrible, engulfing tide. It is poison. Do not watch it or read it. It will destroy you if you do. It will take from you your self-respect. It will rob you of a sense of the beauties of life. It will tear you down and pull you into a slough of evil thoughts and possibly of evil actions. Stay away from it. Shun it as you would a foul disease, for it is just as deadly. Be virtuous in thought and in deed. God has planted in you, for a purpose, a divine urge which may be easily subverted to evil and destructive ends.

When you are young, do not get involved in steady dating. When you reach an age where you think of marriage, then is the time to become so involved. But you boys who are in high school don't need this, and neither do the girls. We receive letters, we constantly deal with people who, under the pressures of life, marry while very young. . . . Have a wonderful time . . . but do not get too serious too soon. You [young men] have missions ahead of you. . . . Stay away from alcohol. Graduation from high school is no reason for a beer bust. Better stay away and be thought a prude than go through life regretting it ever afterwards. Stay away from drugs. You cannot afford to touch them. They will utterly destroy you. The euphoria will quickly pass, and the deadly, strangling clutches of this evil thing will embrace you in its power. You will become a slave, a debauched slave. You will lose control of your life and your actions. Do not experiment with them. Stay free of them! Walk in the sunlight, strength, and virtue of self-control and of absolute integrity. Get all the schooling you can. Education is the key that unlocks the door of opportunity."

Gordon B. Hinckley (Ensign, Nov. 1997, pp. 51-52)

". . . Charting the course prevents one from living an unplanned, haphazard life—a tumbleweed existence."

Spencer W. Kimball (The Miracle of Forgiveness, pp. 233-234)

"The decisions we make, individually and personally, become the fabric of our lives. That fabric will be beautiful or ugly according to the threads of which it is woven. I wish to say particularly to the young men who are here that you cannot indulge in any unbecoming behavior without injury to the beauty of the fabric of your lives. Immoral acts of any kind will introduce an ugly thread. Dishonesty of any kind will create a blemish. Foul and profane language will rob the pattern of its beauty. 'Choose the right when a choice is placed before you' is the call to each of us *(Hymns, 1985, no. 239)."*

Gordon B. Hinckley (Ensign, May 1995, p. 53)

"How glorious and near to the angels is youth that is clean. This youth will have joy unspeakable here and eternal happiness hereafter."

First Presidency Message (Improvement Era, May 1942, p. 273)

"Give me a young man who has kept himself morally clean and has faithfully attended his Church meetings. Give me a young man who has magnified his priesthood and has earned his Duty to God Award and is an Eagle Scout. Give me a young man who is a seminary graduate and has a burning testimony of the Book of Mormon. Give me such a young man and I will give you a young man who can perform miracles for the Lord in the mission field and throughout his life."

Teachings of Ezra Taft Benson, p. 197

"Young [people], the family unit is forever, and you should do everything in your power to strengthen that unit. In your own family, encourage family home evenings and be an active participant. Encourage family prayer. Be on your knees with your family in that sacred circle. Do your part to develop real family unity and solidarity. In such homes there is no generation gap. That is another tool of the devil. Your most important friendships should be with your own brothers and sisters and with your father and mother. Love your family. Be loyal to them. Have a genuine concern for your brothers and sisters. Help carry their load."

Ezra Taft Benson (Ensign, Nov. 1986, p. 81)

"Never feed the foxes! What does that mean? Breaking commandments is like feeding foxes. In England where we live, my wife and I had heard that foxes were right in town. We wanted to see a fox. A neighbor told us that if we left food for the foxes we probably would see one. Our butcher gave us some bones. Each night we would place some bones out in the backyard. Soon a fox came to eat. Then a few more. Now we have at least five foxes racing through our flower garden, digging up the lawn, and leaving a shamble every night, sort of like a furry Jurassic Park. What started out as a curiosity is now a problem, and sin is much the same. An indiscretion can begin a process that can make a mess of a whole life. Remember, if you don't start feeding the foxes, they will never tear up your yard. If you avoid making the seemingly small and harmless mistakes, your life will be free of many larger problems later on."

Hugh W. Pinnock (Ensign, Nov. 1993, p. 41)

"Commandments are loving instructions provided by God our Father for our physical and spiritual well-being and happiness while in mortality. Commandments allow us to know the mind and will of God regarding our eternal progression. And they test our willingness to be obedient to His will. . . . Every commandment of the Lord is given for our development, progress, and growth. The Prophet Joseph Smith taught: 'God has designed our happiness. . . . He never will institute an ordinance or give a commandment to His people that is not calculated in its nature to promote that happiness which He has designed'

(Teachings of the Prophet Joseph Smith, p. 256). . . . They guide and protect us and allow us to return back into the presence of our Heavenly Father. If we faithfully obey the commandments, we are promised the blessings of eternal life."

Robert D. Hales (Ensign, May 1996, p. 36)

Alma 37:37   **COUNSEL WITH THE LORD**
                   (refer in this text to 3 Ne. 18:15-23; Alma 34:18-27)

"Successful people need counsel. Unsuccessful people need counsel. The hasty impulse, the know-it-all attitude, the pride that keeps us from asking—these are the dangerous approaches to any problem from the youngest in years to the oldest of age, there is no one who can be always sure he is right, no one who has learned so much of life that he doesn't need the counsel of others and a prayerful approach to all problems. 'Counsel with the Lord in all thy doings,' said Alma, 'and he will direct thee for good. . . .' (Alma 37:37). There is safety in counsel, no safety without it. They that will not be counselled, cannot be helped."

Richard L. Evans (Conference Report, Apr. 1968, p. 86)

Alma 37:46   **THE EASINESS OF THE WAY**
                   (Matt. 11:30)

"Several years ago while my husband, Ed, and I were serving in the England London South Mission, there was an unexpected storm. All night the winds raged. . . . Many trees throughout . . . all of southern England had been uprooted. It was amazing to see the fallen trees with their gigantic root systems, still intact, jutting into the air. I came to the conclusion that because of the 'easiness of the way' (Alma 37:46)—rain is plentiful in England—the trees had no need to sink their roots deep into the earth to get the nourishment they needed. Their roots were not strong enough or deep enough to withstand the hurricane-force winds. On the other hand, the giant redwood trees that grow in northern California also have a very shallow root system. But when they are surrounded by other redwood trees, the strongest, fiercest wind cannot blow them over. The roots of the giant redwood trees intertwine and strengthen each other. When a storm comes, they actually hold each other up."

Patricia P. Pinegar (Ensign, Nov. 1994, p. 78)

Alma 37:47   **LOOK TO GOD AND LIVE**
                   "Please know that we are not without understanding of some of your problems. We are aware that many of you carry very heavy burdens. We plead with the

Lord in your behalf. We add our prayers to your prayers that you may find solutions to your problems. We leave a blessing upon you, even an apostolic blessing. We bless you that the Lord may smile with favor upon you, that there may be happiness and peace in your homes and in your lives, that an atmosphere of love and respect and appreciation may be felt among husbands and wives, children and parents. May you 'look to God and live' (Alma 37:47) with happiness, with security, with peace, with faith."

Gordon B. Hinckley (Ensign, May 1995, p. 88)

Alma 38:8

RECOGNITION OF THE SAVIOR
(refer in this text to Alma 36:12-16)

"Of all the necessary steps to repentance, I testify that the most critically important is for you to have a conviction that forgiveness comes because of the Redeemer. It is essential to know that only on His terms can you be forgiven. Witness Alma's declaration: [Alma 38:8]. That means you trust Him and you trust His teachings. Satan would have you believe that serious transgression cannot be entirely overcome. The Savior gave His life so that the effects of all transgression can be put behind us, save the shedding of innocent blood and the denial of the Holy Ghost."

Richard G. Scott (Ensign, May 1995, pp. 76-77)

Alma 38:12

BRIDLE YOUR PASSIONS
(James 3; refer in this text to Alma 39:5-6)

"What is a bridle for? To kill, to diminish, or even to limit the spirit and power of the steed? Never. Once you have trained your pony you can direct him with the merest nudge. Eventually you can 'give him his head' and ride free, bareback like the wind. We are given our bodies and our emotions not to destroy but to ride. The bridle warns you that to get excited without listening to the voice of the Spirit (the rider) will bring a complaint, "Hey wait for me!" When the body is susceptible to the Spirit, it can always catch up to the Spirit. But I defy anyone to get the Spirit in harmony with the runaway body."

Truman G. Madsen (Four Essays on Love, p. 36)

"It is the habit of self denial which gives the advantage to men we call self-made . . . If he is successful in any way in life he has learned to resist. He has learned to say no at the right time and then to stand by it. Life is such that he cannot escape temptation but as he faces it and masters it, he learns the true way to righteousness."

Alvin R. Dyer (The Challenge, pp. 159-160)

"The world needs self-discipline. You can find it in fasting and prayer. Our generation is sick for lack of self-control. Fasting and prayer help to instill this virtue."

Robert L. Simpson (Conference Report, Oct. 1967, pp. 18-19)

"The notion that you can endanger your physical and mental health by letting strong passions go unsatisfied is a vicious falsehood. Self-control is one mark of a mature person; it applies to control of language, physical treatment of others, and the appetites of the body."

Joseph B. Wirthlin (Ensign, Mar. 1993, p. 71)

"Patience is another form of self-control. It is the ability to postpone gratification and to bridle one's passions. In his relationships with loved ones, a patient man does not engage in impetuous behavior that he will later regret. Patience is composure under stress. A patient man is understanding of others' faults. A patient man also waits on the Lord. We sometimes read or hear of people who seek a blessing from the Lord, then grow impatient when it does not come swiftly. Part of the divine nature is to trust in the Lord enough to 'be still and know that [He is] God' (D&C 101:16). A priesthood holder who is patient will be tolerant of the mistakes and failings of his loved ones. Because he loves them, he will not find fault nor criticize nor blame."

Ezra Taft Benson (Ensign, Nov. 1986, p. 47)

Alma 39

Alma 39:2;
38:11-14

BOASTING
(2 Cor. 10:7-18; Alma 31:25; 26:8-16, 35; Mosiah 2:17-26; 3 Ne. 6:10; D&C 50:32-33; refer in this text to Morm. 3:9; Mosiah 11:19)

"Boasting in the arm of flesh, one of the commonest of all sins among worldly people is a gross evil; it is a sin born of pride, a sin that creates a frame of mind which keeps men from turning to the Lord and accepting his saving grace. When a man engages in self exultation because of his riches, his political power, his worldly learning, his physical prowess, his business acumen, or even his works of righteousness, he is not in tune with the Spirit of the Lord."

Bruce R. McConkie (Mormon Doctrine, pp. 93-94)

"The hen is the wisest of all animal creation because she never cackles until after the egg is laid."

Abraham Lincoln (quoted in The Civil War, Burns, Burns, and Ward, p. 203)

Alma 39:3-4

FORSAKE THE MINISTRY
(Luke 9:62; 2 Sam. 11:1; LDS *Hymns,* no. 270)

"I wish that every Latter-day Saint could say and mean it with all his heart: 'I'll go where you want me to go. I'll say what you want me to say. I'll be what you want me to be.' (Hymns, 1985, p. 270). If we could all do that, we would be assured of the maximum of happiness here and exaltation in the celestial kingdom of God hereafter."

Teachings of Ezra Taft Benson, p. 344

"As we see the hideous dress standards among the men and women, as we learn of the terrifying portrayal of filth and rot in entertainment places, we say, as we said to the brethren last night: Never go to any place that you wouldn't take your priesthood with you. Stay out of such places. Someone said, when you find a place that is labeled 'adults only; no children or youth allowed,' no adults should be allowed either, if you will be safe from the pitfalls of the devil. We are members whom the Lord expects to be a light unto the world, and to set a standard for people to seek to it."

Harold B. Lee (Ensign, Nov. 1971, p. 14)

Alma 39:4   **THE MANY IS NO EXCUSE FOR THEE**
(refer in this text to 1 Ne. 8:25; Mosiah 17:11-13)

"He had begun to associate with the wrong kinds of people; he eventually surrendered to the allurements and pressures to conform to the ways of the worldly. But, Alma scolded, because others gave in to sin was no reason for him to do the same: This was no excuse for thee, my son. Thou shouldst have tended to the ministry where with thou wast entrusted (Alma 39:3-4)."

Robert Millet (Studies in Scripture, ed. by K. Jackson, 8:49)

"Oh, if our young people could learn this basic lesson to always keep good company, never to be found with those who tend to lower their standards! Let every youth select associates who will keep him on tiptoe, trying to reach the heights. Let him never choose associates who encourage him to relax in carelessness."

Teachings of Spencer W. Kimball, p. 287

"Genuine friends often can provide spiritual shepherding. Note that I refer to genuine friends in the category of spiritual shepherds. Notice also that I did not include peers in that group. I readily acknowledge that peers in some cases can be and are an influence for good. . . . Unfortunately, so many times there are situations where peer influence has a definite negative effect. We read and hear of so many surveys and interviews where youth disclose that it was the influence and pressure of peers that led them to immoral and foolish behavior. Satan knows this. . . . He is aware of the tremendous influence a group of peers can have on an individual. There is a compelling desire to belong—to be one of the group. . . . Often the easiest and simplest nudging is that 'everyone is doing it' or 'it's the cool thing' or 'how do you know it's bad if you haven't tried it?' Don't be deceived. Don't be influenced with this kind of enticement. Keep your eyes above the crowd."

W. Eugene Hansen (Ensign, May 1996, pp. 38-39)

"We know that we are often judged by the company we keep. We know how influential classmates, friends, and other peer groups can be. If any of our companions are prone to be unrighteous in their living, we are better off seeking new associations immediately. Our friends should be companions who inspire us, who help us rise to our best."

Joseph B. Wirthlin (Ensign, Nov. 1997, p. 34)

Alma 39:4-6   **ADULTERY (Sexual Immorality)**
(Jacob 2:22; Prov. 6:32; D&C 42:24-26; 59:6; *Doctrines of Salvation*, Smith, 2:94; *Miracle of Forgiveness*, Kimball, pp. 347-352; 1 Cor. 6:9-11; *Faith Precedes the Miracle*, Kimball, pp. 151-159; Prov. 30:20; Moro. 9:7-10; *Teachings of the Prophet Joseph Smith*, pp. 188-189, 339; 1965 *BYU Speeches of the Year*, Kimball, pp. 20-21; *Conference Report*, Oct. 1942, pp. 10-12; *Conference Report*, Oct. 1962, p. 57; *Doctrinal New Testament Commentary* 3:256; *History of the Church*, Smith 6:81; *Gospel Doctrine*, Smith, p. 273; refer in this text to Moro. 9:9)

"There are at least three dangers that threaten the Church within. . . . They are flattery of prominent men in the world, false educational ideas, and sexual impurity. But the third subject mentioned—personal purity, is perhaps of greater importance than either of the other two. We believe in one standard of morality for men and women. If purity of life is neglected, all other dangers set in upon us like the rivers of waters when the flood gates are opened."

Joseph F. Smith (Gospel Doctrine, p. 313)

"Do not be misled by Satan's lies. There is no lasting happiness in immorality. There is no joy to be found in breaking the law of chastity. Just the opposite is true. There may be momentary pleasure. For a time it may seem like everything is wonderful. But quickly the relationship will sour. . . . Love begins to die. Bitterness, jealousy, anger, and even hate begin to grow. All of these are the natural results of sin and transgression. On the other hand, when we obey the law of chastity and keep ourselves morally clean, we will experience the blessings of increased love and peace, greater trust and respect for our marital partners, [and] deeper commitment to each other. . . ."

Ezra Taft Benson (1987-88 BYU Devotional & Fireside Speeches, p. 51)

"The power of procreation is not an incidental part of the plan of happiness, it is the key—the very key. . . . True love requires respect and reserving until after marriage the sharing of that affection which unlocks those sacred powers in that fountain of life. It means avoiding situations where physical desire might take control. Courtship is a time to measure integrity, moral strength, and worthiness. The invitation, 'If you love me, you will let me,' exposes a major flaw in character. It deserves the reply, 'If you really loved me, you would never ask me to transgress. If you understood the gospel, you couldn't!' . . . In the universal battle for human souls, the adversary takes enormous numbers of prisoners. . . . Every soul confined in a concentration camp of sin and guilt has a key to the gate. The key is labeled **Repentance**. . . . The world being what it is, if you have already made a mistake, it can certainly be understood. It cannot, under the law, be condoned, but it can be understood. You must stop conduct that is immoral. You must stop it now! I know of no sin connected with transgression of the moral law which cannot be forgiven, assuming, of course, full and complete repentance."

Boyd K. Packer (BYU Fireside, Mar. 29, 1992)

"Every soul is entitled to the right to come into this world in a legitimate way—in the way the Father has willed that souls should come. Whosoever takes a course contrary to this is guilty of an almost irreparable crime. Is there any wonder, then, that the Lord places the violation of this covenant of marriage and the loss of virtue as second only to the shedding of innocent blood?"

Joseph F. Smith (Doctrines of Salvation, 2:92-93)

"One may bathe hourly, perfume oneself often, have hair shampooed frequently, have fingernails manicured daily, and be a master at soft-spoken utterances, and still be as filthy as hell's cesspools. What defiles is sin, and especially sexual sin. . . . This area of conduct presents a tremendous temptation, especially to the youth of this age of loose talk and loose action on college campuses and elsewhere which favor premarital sex and experience."

Spencer W. Kimball (The Miracle of Forgiveness, pp. 62-63)

"Clearly God's greatest concern regarding mortality are how one gets into this world and how one gets out of it. . . . As for the taking of life, we are generally quite responsible. Most people, it seems to me, readily sense the sanctity of life and as a rule do not run up to friends, put a loaded revolver to their heads, and cavalierly pull the trigger. Furthermore, when there is a click of the hammer rather than an explosion of lead, and a possible tragedy seems to have been averted, no one in such a circumstance would be so stupid as to sigh, 'Oh, good. I didn't go all the way'. . . . But in the significance and sanctity of giving life, some of us are not so responsible, and in the larger world swirling around us we find near-criminal irresponsibility."

Jeffrey R. Holland (On Earth As It Is in Heaven, pp. 182-191)

"A quarter of a century ago historian John Lukacs perceptively warned that sexual immorality was not merely a marginal development but, instead, was at the center of the moral crisis of our time. Some thought Lukacs was overstating it, but consider the subsequent and sobering tragedy of children having children, of unwed mothers, of children without parents, of hundreds of thousands of fatherless children, and of rampant spousal infidelity. These and related consequences threaten to abort society's future even before the future arrives! Yet carnalists are unwilling to deny themselves, even though all of society suffers from an awful avalanche of consequences!"

Neal A. Maxwell (Ensign, May 1995, p. 67)

"Whenever you step over the line in an immoral act or in doing any other evil thing, the Church is that much weaker. . . . When you stand true and faithful, it is that much stronger. Each one of you counts. . . . If any of you has stepped over the line, please do not think all is lost. The Lord reaches out to help you, and there are many willing hands in the Church also who will help. Put evil behind you. Pray about the situation, talk with your parents if you can, and talk with your bishop. You will find that he will listen and do so with confidentiality. . . . There is hope for you. Your lives are ahead, and they can be filled with happiness, even though the past may have been marred by sin. . . . This is the time, this is the very hour, to repent of any evil in the past, to ask for forgiveness, to stand a little taller and then to go forward with confidence and faith."

Gordon B. Hinckley (Ensign, May 1996, p. 94)

Alma 39:5   **MURDER**
(2 Ne. 9:35; Alma 54:7; D&C 42:18, 79; 1 John 3:15; 5:16-17; *Teachings of the Prophet Joseph Smith*, pp. 188-189, 339; *Mormon Doctrine*, McConkie, p. 520; *Alma, Testimony of the Word*, ed. by Nyman & Tate, pp. 161-163; *Doctrinal New Testament Commentary*, McConkie, 3:584; *Encyclopedia of Mormonism*, 4:1443; *New Witness for the Articles of Faith*, McConkie, p. 231; refer in this text to Alma 24:9-13)

". . .if a member of our Church, having received the light of the Holy Spirit, commits this capital crime [murder], he will not receive forgiveness in this world nor in the world to come. The revelations of God to the Church abound in commandments forbidding us to shed blood."

Wilford Woodruff

[The Church defines murder as] "The deliberate and unjustified taking of human life."

General Handbook 10-13

Alma 39:5-6   **DENY HOLY GHOST**
(Jacob 7: 19; D&C 76:31-37; Matt. 12:31-32; *Answers to Gospel Questions*, Smith, 1:62-64; 4:92; *The Holy Ghost*, McConkie & Millet, pp. 143-148)

"What must a man do to commit the unpardonable sin? He must receive the Holy Ghost, have the heavens opened unto him, and know God, and then sin against Him. After a man has sinned against the Holy Ghost, there is no repentance for him. He has got to say that the sun does not shine while he sees it; he has got to deny Jesus Christ when the heavens have been opened unto him, and to deny the plan of salvation with his eyes open to the truth of it; and from that time he begins to be an enemy."

Teachings of the Prophet Joseph Smith, p. 358

"The eyes can be deceived, as can the other physical senses, but the testimony of the Holy Ghost is certain. The sin against the Holy Ghost requires such knowledge that it is manifestly impossible for the rank and file to commit such a sin. Comparatively few Church members will . . . deny the Holy Ghost."

Teachings of Spencer W. Kimball, p. 23

"A sin that is unpardonable cannot be paid for either by the atoning blood of Christ or by the personal suffering of the sinner. The only sin that falls into this category is denying the Holy Ghost. . . . Alma identified denying the Holy Ghost as the most abominable sin. According to the Lord, individuals committing this sin do five things: (1) They 'know my power, and (2) have been made partakers thereof, and (3) suffered themselves through the power of the devil to be overcome and (4) to deny the truth and (5) defy my power' (D&C 76:31). The key to these requirements appears to be the power of the priesthood. An individual must bear and be a partaker of the priesthood and then defy that power. . . . A person must have made priesthood covenants with God and then have received knowledge and power beyond what the vast majority of us have received. . . . If they have lived on this earth and have received a mortal body, they shall come forth in the last resurrection with an immortal body; but that body will not be glorified. Instead they 'go away into the lake of fire and brimstone, with the devil and his angels' (D&C 76:36)."

Dean Garrett (Alma, Testimony of the Word, ed. Nyman and Tate, pp.157-160)

Alma 39:8   **YE CANNOT HIDE YOUR CRIMES**
(D&C 88:109; 2 Ne. 9:14; Alma 11:43; *Companion to Your Study of the Book of Mormon*, Ludlow, pp. 203-204; *Psycho-Cybernetics*, Maltz, pp. 19-20)

"Do not take comfort in the fact that your transgressions are not known by others. That is like an ostrich with his head buried in the sand. He sees only darkness and feels comfortably hidden. In reality he is ridiculously conspicuous. Likewise our every act is seen by our Father in Heaven and His Beloved Son. They know everything about us. . . . I invite each one of you to thoughtfully review your life. . . . Is there a dark corner that needs to be cleaned out? . . . When it is quiet and you can think clearly, does your conscience tell you to repent?"

Richard G. Scott (Ensign, May 1995, p. 77)

Alma 39:9   **LUST OF YOUR EYES**
(2 Ne. 27:31; 1 Tim. 5:22; *Ensign*, May 1997, p. 49)

"The lust of your eyes. In our day, what does that mean? Movies, television programs, and video recordings that are both suggestive and lewd. Magazines and books that are obscene and pornographic. We counsel you young men, not to pollute your minds with such degrading matter, for the mind through which this filth passes is never the same afterwards. Don't see R-rated movies or vulgar videos or participate in any entertainment that is immoral, suggestive, or pornographic."

Ezra Taft Benson (Ensign, May 1986, p.45)

"Turn it off, walk away from it, burn it, erase it, destroy it. I know it is hard counsel we give when we say movies that are R-rated, and many with PG-13 ratings, are produced by satanic influences. Our standards should not be dictated by the rating system. I repeat, because of what they really represent, these types of movies, music, tapes, etc. serve the purposes of the author of all darkness."

H. Burke Peterson (Ensign, Nov. 1993, p. 43)

"There is neither happiness nor peace to be gained from surrendering to the weakness of indulging in these things which degrade and destroy. When such material is on television, turn off the set. Stop being a boob in front of the tube. Avoid titillating videotapes as you would a foul disease. They are in the same category. Stay away from pornographic magazines and other destructive literature. There is too much of good to see, there is too much of wonderful reading to be experienced to waste time and destroy character and willpower in submitting to such destructive rot."

Gordon B. Hinckley (Ensign, Nov. 1992, pp. 51-52)

"Each person must keep himself clean and free from lusts. . . . He must shun ugly, polluted thoughts and acts as he would an enemy. Pornographic and erotic stories and pictures are worse than polluted food. Shun them. The body has power to rid itself of sickening food. The person who entertains filthy stories or pornographic pictures and literature records them in his marvelous human computer, the brain, which can't forget such filth. Once recorded, it will always remain there, subject to recall."

Spencer W. Kimball (Ensign, July 1978, pp. 3-7)

"We must be very careful of the entertainment we allow into our homes. Parents sometimes allow their children to see and hear things that are objectionable because they have more and more difficulty finding a movie, videotape, or television program that does not contain offensive elements. Rather than ban entertainment, parents tend to permit their children to watch a movie with violence or profanity or sexual content, hoping their children will realize that Hollywood's standards do not reflect those of the parents. The difference between Hollywood's standards and those of most Americans is appalling, as shown in a 1991 study. 'More than one hundred top television writers and executives were asked questions that paralleled a poll taken of average American viewers. The results:
- A whopping 85 percent of the country believes adultery to be wrong. But in Hollywood, it's 49 percent.
- . . . 4 percent of the nation says it has no religious affiliation, compared to 45 percent in Hollywood.
- Some 76 percent of Americans feel [homosexuality is] wrong. In Hollywood, it's 20 percent.
- Abortion rights are supported by 59 percent of the country [which is appalling] compared to Hollywood's 97 percent.' (Chris Hicks, Deseret News, 6/19/92)
Truly, parents and children will need to be diligent and cautious in choosing what type of entertainment to take into their homes."

Joseph B. Wirthlin (Ensign, Mar. 1993, p. 71)

"We are surrounded by the promotional literature of illicit sexual relations, on the printed page and on the screen. For your own good, avoid it. Pornographic or erotic stories and pictures are worse than filthy or polluted food. The body has defenses to rid itself of unwholesome food. With a few fatal exceptions bad food will only make you sick but do no permanent harm. In contrast, a person who feasts upon filthy stories and pornographic or erotic pictures and literature records them in this marvelous retrieval system we call a brain. The brain won't vomit back filth. Once recorded, it will always remain subject to recall, flashing its perverted images across your mind and drawing you away from the wholesome things in life."

Dallin H. Oaks (New Era, Feb. 1974, p. 18)

"Be clean. I cannot emphasize that enough. Be clean. It is so very very important and you at your age are in such temptation all the time. It is thrown at you on television. It is thrown at you in books and magazines and videos. You do not have to rent them. Don't do it. Just don't do it. Don't look at them. If somebody proposes that you sit around all night watching some of that sleazy stuff, you say, 'It's not for me.' Stay away from it."

Gordon B. Hinckley (Denver, Colorado, Youth Meeting, Apr. 14, 1996)

"A bishop reported that he had observed that the spiritual level of the young priesthood bearers in his ward was declining. Through his personal interviews with them, he discovered that many of them were watching R-rated movies. When he asked them where they went to see such trash, they said, '. . . We watch them at home. We have cable television, and when our parents are gone we watch anything we want to.' . . . The Lord and his living prophets are counting on you to avoid the trash that surrounds you in the media. . . . Temptations are all around us, and today with the advent of the Internet, they are increasing. There is much that is positive in the world of the media, but here is so much that is negative. If we permit ourselves to become involved with the negative, there will be much more cause for the devil to laugh and his angels to rejoice."

Joe J. Christensen (Ensign, Nov. 1996, p. 40)

"The girl you marry can expect you to come to the marriage altar absolutely clean. She can expect you to be a young man of virtue in thought and word and deed. I plead with you boys tonight to keep yourselves free from the stains of the world. . . . You must not fool around with the Internet to find pornographic material. . . . You must not rent videos with pornography of any kind. . . . Stay away from pornography as you would avoid a serious disease. It is as destructive. It can become habitual, and those who indulge in it get so they cannot leave it alone. It is addictive. . . . It seduces and destroys its victims. . . . I plead with you young men not to get involved in its use. You simply cannot afford to. The girl you marry is worthy of a husband whose life has not been tainted by this ugly and corrosive material."

Gordon B. Hinckley (Ensign, May 1998, p. 49)

Alma 39:9   **CROSS YOURSELF**
(JST Matt. 16:26; 3 Ne. 12:30; refer in this text to Moro. 10:32)

Alma 39:11   **EXAMPLE**
(Mosiah 25:12; 27:8-9; Matt. 17:6; 1 Tim. 4:12; *Conference Report,* Vandenberg, Apr. 1965, p. 49)

"The Lord says if we labor all our days and save but one soul, how great will be our joy with him; on the other hand how great will be our sorrow and our condemnation if through our acts we have led one soul away from this truth. . . . For the destruction of a soul is the destruction of the greatest thing that has ever been created."

Joseph Fielding Smith (Doctrines of Salvation, 1:313-314)

"Never before has the Church had a better reputation than it has now. This is because of you, my brethren and sisters. The opinions of people concerning us for the most part arise out of personal and individual experiences. It is your friendliness, your concern for others, and the good examples of your lives that result in the opinions held by others concerning the Latter-day Saints."

Gordon B. Hinckley (Ensign, Nov. 1997, p. 4)

Alma 39:13   **CONFESS**
(D&C 59:12; 61:2; 2 Ne. 27:27; *Miracle of Forgiveness,* Kimball, pp. 177-189; refer in this text to Mosiah 26:29)

Alma 40:8

TIME MEASURED UNTO MEN
(Abr. 3:4, 5:13; D&C 38:2; 130:7; *Teachings of the Prophet Joseph Smith*, p. 220; *The Book of Mormon: Jacob Through Words of Mormon*, Packer, BYU Religious Studies Center, p. 24)

"Abraham was told that one revolution (or day) on Kolob equals a thousand of our years (Abraham 3:4). If one were to carry the ratio down to smaller units of time we see some interesting implications.

Kolob Time	Earth Time
1 day	1,000 years
1 hour	41.67 years
1 minute	253 days
1 second	4.22 days
.25 second	1.1 days
.01 second	1 hour

Think of the implications of that. While a person on Kolob takes a two-hour nap, a person on Earth is born, lives to the age of eighty, and dies before the other awakens. One blink on the part of a Kolobian and he misses one whole day of ours."

Gerald Lund (First Nephi, The Doctrinal Foundation, pp. 158-159)

Alma 40:11

TAKEN HOME TO GOD
(*Journal of Discourses* 3:112-113, 368; 16:365; Eccl. 12:7; *Gospel Truths*, Cannon, p. 73)

"These words of Alma as I understand them, do not intend to convey the thought that all spirits go back into the presence of God for an assignment to a place of peace or a place of punishment and before him receive their individual sentence. 'Taken home to God,' simply means that their mortal existence has come to an end, and they have returned to the world of spirits, where they are assigned to a place according to their works with the just or with the unjust, there to await the resurrection. 'Back to God' is a phrase which finds an equivalent in many other well-known conditions. For instance: a man spends a stated time in some foreign mission field. When he is released and returns to the United States, he may say, 'It is wonderful to be back home' ; yet his home may be somewhere in Utah or Idaho or some other part of the West."

Joseph Fielding Smith (Answers to Gospel Questions, 2:84-86)

Alma 40:12   **PARADISE - REST - PEACE**
(2 Ne. 9:13; *Life Beyond*, Millet and McConkie p. 18)

"The spirits of all men, as soon as they depart from this mortal body, whether they are good or evil, we are told in the Book of Mormon, are taken home to that God who gave them life, where there is a separation, a partial judgement, and the spirits of those who are righteous are received into a state of happiness which is called paradise, a state of rest, a state of peace, where they expand in wisdom, where they have respite from all their troubles and where care and sorrow do not annoy. The wicked, on the contrary, have no part nor portion in the Spirit of the Lord, and they are cast into outer darkness, being led captive, because of their iniquity, by the evil one. And in this space between death and the resurrection of the body, the two classes of souls remain, in happiness or in misery, until the time which is appointed of God that the dead shall come forth and be reunited both spirit and body, and be brought to stand before God, and be judged according to their works."

Joseph F. Smith (Gospel Doctrine, p. 448)

Alma 40:13-14   **OUTER DARKNESS**
(D&C 38:5; 138:22, 30, 57; 2 Ne. 9:12; *Mormon Doctrine*, McConkie pp. 551-552; *Gospel Doctrine*, Smith, p. 448)

Alma 40:15   **PARTIAL JUDGEMENT**
(*Gospel Doctrine,* Smith, pp. 448-449; *Mormon Doctrine,* McConkie, p. 402)

Alma 40:23   **RESURRECTION - A HAIR WON'T BE LOST**
(2 Ne. 9:12; Mosiah 16:6-11; Alma 11:43-44; D&C 88:15; 1 Cor. 3:16; *Teachings of the Prophet Joseph Smith*, pp. 62, 199-200; *Gospel Doctrine*, Smith, p. 449; refer in this text to Alma 11:43-44)

". . . A man who has lost a leg in childhood will have his leg restored. . . . Deformities and the like will be corrected, if not immediately at the time of the uniting of the spirit and body, so soon thereafter [almost instantly] that it will make no difference. . . . Infants and children do not grow in the grave, but when they come forth, they will come forth with the same body and in the same size in which the body was when it was laid away. After the resurrection the body will grow until it has reached the full stature of manhood or womanhood."

Joseph Fielding Smith (Doctrines of Salvation, 2:293-294)

"The question frequently arises as to whether a child that died in infancy will remain a child in the hereafter, and whether in the resurrection the spirit will take up the same body that it tabernacled in the flesh. . . . . The late President Joseph F. Smith in an editorial in the *Improvement Era*, June 1904, . . . stated, 'The body will come forth as it is laid to rest, for there is no growth or development in the grave. As it is laid down, so will it arise, and changes to perfection will come by the law of restitution. But the spirit will continue to expand and develop, to the full stature of man.' Parents, therefore, who have been parted from their children by death may rest assured that, if worthy through obedience to the principles of the gospel, they will not only meet their children in the spirit world, but will also recognize them and know them as they knew them in this life. Parents too, have even a greater comfort in the fact that their little ones whose lives on earth were cut short will continue to grow and develop, and receive every blessing to which their inheritance and faithfulness will entitle them."

David O. McKay (Gospel Ideals, p. 75)

"Man is a dual being, a spirit within a mortal body. It is difficult to teach about the intangible, spiritual part. But there are ways to do it. . . . A personal computer made of metal, plastic, glass and a dozen other materials will hold an astonishing amount of information. All of the standard works can be stored there, and in addition, sets of encyclopedias, dictionaries, books on a whole library of subjects, even illustrations and mathematical formulas. With the press of a few keys one can select any part of what is stored and see it instantly on a screen. One may, by pressing a few more keys, rearrange, add to, or subtract from what is stored in the computer. Press another key or two and you can print a copy of whatever you desire, even in full color. You then can hold in your hand tangible, absolute proof of what is inside there and how it is arranged. However, if you should take the computer completely apart, you could not find one word of it, not one illustration, not one tangible evidence that there are volumes, verses, poems, and illustrations inside the computer. You could dissolve the computer with acids or burn it and you would not find one tangible word of evidence. You could no more find words in the ashes of a computer than you can find the spirit in the ashes of a cremated human body. No one doubts that this great base of information is actually stored in the computer. It should not be too difficult to teach each youngster that there is within the human body a spirit."

Boyd K. Packer (CES Symposium, Aug. 10, 1993)

Alma 40:26

SECOND DEATH
(D&C 64:7; 76:31-37; Rev. 20:12-15; Hel. 14:15-18; 2 Ne. 9:15-16; *Doctrines of Salvation*, Smith, 2:224-225)

"Thus, eventually, all are redeemed from spiritual death except those who have 'sinned unto death' (D&C 64:7), that is, those who are destined to be sons of perdition."

Bruce R. McConkie (Mormon Doctrine, p.758)

"Where is the spirit world? It is right here. . . . Can you see it with your natural eyes? No. Can you see spirits in this room? No. Suppose the Lord should touch your eyes that you might see, could you then see the spirits? Yes, as plainly as you now see bodies. . . ."

Discourses of Brigham Young, pp. 376-377

[Following death] "The spirits of the just are . . . blessed in their departure to the world of spirits. . . . They are not far from us, and know and understand our thoughts, feelings, and motions, and are often pained therewith. . . ."

Teachings of the Prophet Joseph Smith, p. 326

"Many spirits of the departed, who are unhappy, linger in lonely wretchedness about the earth, and in the air, and especially about their ancient homesteads, and the places rendered dear to them by the memory of the former scenes."

Parley P. Pratt (Key to the Science of Theology, p. 117)

"We have more friends behind the veil than on this side, and they will hail us more joyfully than you were ever welcomed by your parents and friends in this world; and you will rejoice more when you meet them than you ever rejoiced to see a friend in this life; and then we shall go on from step to step, from rejoicing to rejoicing, and from one intelligence and power to another, our happiness becomes more and more exquisite and sensible as we proceed. . . ."

Discourses of Brigham Young, pp. 379-380

"Brother Joseph Smith gave an explanation of [evil influences]. There are places in the Mississippi Valley where the influence or the presence of invisible spirits are very perceptibly felt. He said that numbers had been slain there in war and that there were evil influences or spirits which affect the spirits of those who have tabernacles on the earth. I myself have felt those influences in other places besides the continent of America; I have felt them on the old battle grounds on the Sandwich Islands. I have come to the conclusion that if our eyes were open to see the spirit world around us, we should feel differently on this subject than we do; we would not be so unguarded and careless and so indifferent whether we had the spirit and power of God with us or not; but we would be continually watchful and prayerful to our Heavenly Father for His Holy Spirit and His holy angels to be around about us to strengthen us to overcome every evil influence."

George Q. Cannon (Gospel Truths, 1:82)

"I know it is a startling idea to say that the Prophet and the persecutor of the Prophet, all go to prison together. What is the condition of the righteous? They are in possession of the spirit of Jesus—the power of God. . . . Jesus will administer to them; angels will administer to them; and they have a privilege of seeing and understanding more than you or I have, in the flesh; but they have not got their bodies yet, consequently they are in prison. . . . What is the condition of the wicked? They are in prison. Are they happy? No. . . ."

Brigham Young (Journal of Discourses 3:95)

"When our spirits leave these bodies, will they be happy? Not perfectly so. Why? Because the spirit is absent from the body; it cannot be perfectly happy while a part of the man is lying in the earth."

Orson Pratt (Journal of Discourses 1:289-290)

"Every man that has been baptized and belongs to the kingdom has a right to be baptized for those who have gone before; and as soon as the law of the Gospel is obeyed here by their friends who act as proxy for them, the Lord has administrators there to set them free."

Teachings of the Prophet Joseph Smith, p. 367

". . . many other great truths not known before, have been declared to the people, and one of the greatest is that to hell there is an exit as well as an entrance. Hell is no place to which a vindictive judge sends prisoners to suffer and to be punished principally for his glory; But it is a place prepared for the teaching, the disciplining of those who failed to learn here upon the earth what they should have learned. . . . No man will be kept in hell longer than is necessary to bring him to a fitness for something better. When he reaches that stage the prison doors will open and there will be rejoicing among the hosts who welcome him into a better state."

James E. Talmage (Conference Report, Apr. 1930, p. 97)

"The work of the righteous is to preach the gospel to as many as will receive it, so that whosoever receives it unto repentance may leave the spirit prison and enter into paradise when the ordinances have been done vicariously for them on earth. Through the institution of baptism for the dead, the Church is able to open the gate of baptism, which allows the repentant spirits to exit the spirit prison of hell, the state of the wicked in the spirit world."

Richard O. Cowan (Alma, The Testimony of the Word, ed. by Nyman and Tate, p. 184)

Alma 41:1-15;   **RESTORATION**
42:27-28   (Hel. 12:24; 14:31)

"When we hear the term *restoration* we typically think of the latter-day return of the Church and the revelation of the gospel in its fulness. Book of Mormon prophets, however, use this term in a rather different sense. They teach that every individual will receive a temporal as well as a spiritual restoration, good for good, evil for evil."

Richard O. Cowan (Alma, Testimony of the Word, ed. by Nyman and Tate, p. 198)

Alma 41:7   **THEY ARE THEIR OWN JUDGES**
                     (refer in this text to Alma 11:43)

"The great misery of departed spirits in the world of spirits, where they go after death, is to know that they come short of the glory that others enjoy and that they might have enjoyed themselves, and they are their own accusers."

Teachings of the Prophet Joseph Smith, pp. 310-311

"The reality is that there will be a whole hierarchy of judges who, under Christ, shall judge the righteous. He alone shall issue the decrees of damnation for the wicked."

Bruce R. McConkie (The Millennial Messiah, p. 520)

Alma 41:10   **WICKEDNESS NEVER WAS HAPPINESS**
(Alma 34:34; Morm. 2:13; Hel. 13:38; *Psycho-Cybernetics*, Maltz, pp. 87-100; *Articles of Faith* 1:13; *Improvement Era*, 17 [no. 2]:172-173; *For the Strength of Youth pamphlet*, p. 4)

"When I do good I feel good, when I do bad I feel bad."

Abraham Lincoln

"You can never get enough of what you don't need, because what you don't need will never satisfy you."

Dallin H. Oaks (Conference Report, Oct. 1991, p. 104)

"You cannot do wrong and feel right. It is impossible."

Ezra Taft Benson (New Era, June 1986, p. 5)

"Happiness is the object and design of our existence; and will be the end thereof, if we pursue the path that leads to it; and this path is virtue, uprightness, faithfulness, holiness, and keeping all the commandments of God."

Joseph Smith (History of the Church 5: 134-135)

"So many of us are fearful of what our peers will say, that we will be looked upon with disdain and criticized if we stand for what is right. But I remind you that 'wickedness never was happiness' (Alma 41:10). Evil never was happiness. Sin never was happiness. Happiness lies in the power and the love and the sweet simplicity of the gospel of Jesus Christ. We need not be prudish. We need not slink off in a corner, as it were. We need not be ashamed. We have the greatest thing in the world, the gospel of the risen Lord."

Gordon B. Hinckley (Ensign, May 1997, p. 49)

"Laws do not change. A law, like truth, 'abideth and hath no end' (D&C 88:66). A theory is tentative, subject to change, and may or may not be true. A theory is a means to an end, not the end in itself. . . . Laws governing spiritual things were irrevocably decreed in heaven before the foundation of the earth (D&C 130:20). Often young people fail to accept moral and spiritual laws because the laws are not measured by methods they have been accustomed to using. Physical or natural laws are much easier to demonstrate, and can be useful in teaching about spiritual things. Let me illustrate. At 32 degrees Fahrenheit, water freezes and changes from a liquid to a solid. At 212 degrees Fahrenheit it turns into a gas. Your students know that and there isn't anything they can do about it—they can't change it. It can be described accurately or inaccurately, in complicated measurements in Fahrenheit or centigrade or anything else, and nothing that is said about it is going to change it because it operates according to law. It will freeze or evaporate according to the law. It should not be difficult to understand that there are basic spiritual laws that have always existed, that never change, that beget consequences, and we can't change them. The wonder is that we can depend on these spiritual laws. 'Wickedness never was happiness,' and anybody that has tried to find out, has found out. It is a law."

Boyd K. Packer (CES Symposium, Aug. 10, 1993)

Alma 42:8   **THE GREAT PLAN OF HAPPINESS**
(Moses 1:39; Alma 12:32; John 13:17; *The Book of Mormon: Jacob Through Words of Mormon*, BYU Religious Studies Center, p. 14)

"The prophet Alma called the plan the 'great plan of happiness.' It is known more commonly as the plan of salvation. . . . The plan teaches that all who have or will live on earth are the spirit children of heavenly parents. We lived with them before coming to this earth to receive our bodies of flesh and bone. . . . Our Father's plan provides for redemption from the Fall through the atonement of Jesus Christ. . . . All shall rise from the dead with immortal bodies as a result of the Atonement. However, the Atonement is conditional as it pertains to each person's individual sins. It touches everyone to the degree that he or she has faith in Jesus Christ, repents, and obeys the gospel. Exaltation and eternal life with God are reserved for those who keep the commandments. Mortality, then, is the time to test our ability to understand our Heavenly Father's plan and, of course, our willingness to be obedient."

M. Russell Ballard (Ensign, May 1995, pp. 22-23)

"In obedience there is joy and peace unspotted, . . . and as God has designed our happiness—and the happiness of all His creatures, he never has—He never will institute an ordinance or give a commandment to His people that is not calculated in its nature to promote that happiness which He has designed, and which will not end in the greatest amount of good and glory to those who become the recipients of his laws and ordinances."

Teachings of the Prophet Joseph Smith, pp. 256-257

Alma 42:13-31   **JUSTICE - MERCY AND THE ATONEMENT**
(Alma 34:16-18; Mosiah 15:27; D&C 19:16-19; *Lectures on Faith*, 4:17; *Conference Report*, Packer, Apr. 1977, pp. 79-80; *Miracle of Forgiveness,* Kimball, pp. 358-359)

"Justice requires that God must be a God of order and that he must be just and impartial. Mercy agrees with justice; however, mercy introduces the possibility of vicarious payment of the laws that have been transgressed. The law of mercy paraphrased as follows: Whenever a law is broken, a payment (or atonement) must be made; however the person does not need to make payment if he will repent and if he can find someone who is both able and willing to make payment. Note the law of mercy insists the demands of justice be met fully."

Daniel H. Ludlow (Companion to Your Study of the Book of Mormon, pp. 176-177)

"Justice has many meanings. One is balance. A popular symbol of justice is scales in balance. Thus, when the laws of man have been violated, justice usually requires that a punishment be imposed, a penalty that will restore the balance. . . . Punishments prescribed by the laws of man only follow the judge's action, but under the laws of God the consequences and penalties of sin are inherent in the act. . . . By itself, justice is uncompromising. The justice of God holds each of us responsible for our own transgressions and automatically imposes the penalty. . . . If we are to return to the presence of our Heavenly Father, we need the intervention of some powerful influence that transcends justice. That powerful intervention is the atonement of Jesus Christ. The good news of the gospel is that because of the atonement of Jesus Christ there is something called *mercy. Mercy* signifies an advantage greater than is deserved. . . . If justice is balance, then mercy is counterbalance. If justice is exactly what one deserves, then mercy is *more* benefit than one deserves. In its relationship to justice and mercy, *the Atonement* is the means by which justice is served and mercy is extended."

Dallin H. Oaks (Address given to CES Religious Educators, Temple Square Assembly Hall, Feb. 7, 1992)

"I once wondered if those who refuse to repent but who then satisfy the law of justice by paying for their own sins are then worthy to enter the celestial kingdom. The answer is no. The entrance requirements for celestial life are simply higher than merely satisfying the law of justice. For that reason, paying for our sins will not bear the same fruit as repenting of our sins. Justice is a law of balance and order and it must be satisfied, either through our payment or his. But if we decline the Savior's invitation to let him carry our sins, and then satisfy justice by ourselves, we will not yet have experienced the complete rehabilitation that can occur through a combination of divine assistance and genuine repentance. Working together, those forces have the power permanently to change our hearts and our lives, preparing us for celestial life."

Bruce C. Hafen (The Broken Heart, pp. 7-8)

"I believe that our Heavenly Father wants to save every one of his children. I do not think he intends to shut any of us off because of some slight transgression, some slight failure to observe some rule or regulation. . . . I believe that in his justice and mercy, he will give us the maximum reward for our acts, give us all that he can give, and in the reverse, I believe that he will impose upon us the minimum penalty which it is possible for him to impose."

J. Reuben Clark Jr. (Conference Report, Sept. 30, 1955, p. 24)

"All of us have made wrong turns along the way. I believe the kind and merciful God, whose children we are, will judge us as lightly as He can for the wrongs that we have done and give us the maximum blessing for the good that we do."

James E. Faust (Ensign, Nov. 1996, p. 53)

Alma 42:16   **REPENTANCE & PUNISHMENT**
"Alma bluntly told his wayward son that 'repentance could not come unto men except there were a punishment.' The punishment may, for the most part, consist of the torment we inflict upon ourselves. It may be the loss of privilege or progress. . . . We are punished by our sins, if not for them."

Boyd K. Packer (Ensign, Nov. 1995, p. 19)

Alma 42:29   **TROUBLE YOU DOWN UNTO REPENTANCE**
(Enos 1:6; Alma 36:17-19; 2 Cor. 7:9-10; D&C 58:42; Morm. 2:13; *Psycho-Cybernetics*, Maltz, pp. 60-62, 112; *Conference Report*, Apr. 1973, pp. 177-178; *Ensign*, June 1992, pp. 30-31)

"Alma desired that his son experience appropriate guilt—no more than was requisite, but surely no less than is needful to bring about change."

Robert Millet (Studies in Scripture, ed. by K. Jackson, 8:51)

"Alma didn't promise that Corianton would forget. He taught him how to live with his memories, productively, humbly, continually appreciative for the mercy and long-suffering and forgiveness of God. 'You'll remember your sins' we can almost hear Alma saying. 'You probably won't ever forget. But remember in the right way for the right reasons.'"

Marion D. Hanks (Improvement Era, Mar. 1966, p. 246}

"Sometimes even after confession and penalties the most difficult part of repentance is to forgive oneself. President Joseph Fielding Smith, a man whom I love—great friend, told of a woman who had repented of immoral conduct and was struggling to find her way. She asked him what she should do now. In turn, he asked her to read to him from the Old Testament the account of Sodom and Gomorrah, of Lot and of Lot's wife who was turned to a pillar of salt (see Gen. 19:26). Then he asked her what lesson did those verses hold for her. She answered, 'The Lord will destroy those who are wicked.' 'Not so,' President Smith told this repentant woman, 'The lesson for *you* is *'Don't look back!'*"

Boyd K. Packer (BYU Fireside, Mar. 29, 1992)

"At times the statement is made, 'I never can forgive [this person or that person].' Such an attitude is destructive to an individual's well-being. It can canker the soul and ruin one's life. In other instances, an individual can forgive another but cannot forgive himself. Such a situation is even more destructive. Early in my ministry as a member of the Council of the Twelve, I took to President Hugh B. Brown the experience of a fine person who . . . could not show mercy to himself. He could forgive others but not himself. . . . President Brown suggested that I visit with that individual and counsel him along these lines: . . . 'Tell that man that he should not persist in remembering that which the Lord has said He is willing to forget' (D&C 64:10). Such counsel will help to cleanse the soul and renew the spirit of any who applies it."

Thomas S. Monson (Ensign, May 1995, pp. 59-60)

Alma 42:30   **DO NOT ENDEAVOR TO EXCUSE YOURSELF**
(The Miracle of Forgiveness, Kimball, pp. 150-151)
"The most famous maxim of the nineteenth century military theorist Karl von Clausewitz defined war as the continuation of politics by other means."

(Burns, Burns, and Ward, The Civil War, p. 350)

"We recognize the battle-field as a reality, but it stands as a remote one. It is like a funeral next door. It attracts your attention, but it does not enlist your sympathy. But it is very different when the hearse stops at your own door and the corpse is carried over your own threshold."

A New York Times reporter, 1862 (The Civil War, Burns, Burns, and Ward, p.161)

"Latter-day Saints know this earth will never again during its Telestial existence, be free from civil disturbance and war."

Marion G. Romney (Improvement Era, June 1967, p.77)

"If men of good will can bring themselves to do so, they may save the world from a holocaust, the depth and breadth of which can scarcely be imagined. We are confident that when there is enough of a desire for peace and a will to bring it about, it is not beyond the possibility of attainment."

First Presidency Statement (Church News, Dec. 20, 1980, p.3)

"War doesn't solve a single human problem, and yet the one place where our generation excels most is in its ability to make war. . . . Our failure has been that while we have perfected weapons, we have failed to perfect the men who may be asked to use them."

Sterling W. Sill (Conference Report, Apr. 1966, pp. 20-21)

"In our society today, we find that we are very well prepared for war. However, in that preparation for war we have lost the spiritual strength necessary to prevent it."

Dean Garrett (CES Book of Mormon Symposium, 1986, p.52)

Alma 43:23   **BASIC STRATEGY IN WAR**
(Alma 16:5-6; 48:16; D&C 98:33; *Since Cumorah*, Nibley, pp. 273-274)

"When threatened, we become anti-enemy instead of pro-kingdom of God. . . . We forget that if we are righteous the Lord will either not suffer our enemies to come upon us—and this is the special promise to the inhabitants of the land of the Americas (2 Ne. 1:7)—or he will fight our battles for us."

Spencer W. Kimball (Ensign, June 1976, p. 6)

"There are, however, two conditions which may justify a truly Christian man to enter—mind you, I say enter, not begin—a war: (1) An attempt to dominate and to deprive another of his free agency, and (2) Loyalty to his country. Possibly there is a third, viz., Defense of a weak nation that is being unjustly crushed by a strong, ruthless one."

David O. McKay (Conference Report, Apr., 1942, p. 72)

"We love peace, but not peace at any price. There is a peace more destructive of the manhood of living man than war is destructive of the body. Chains are worse than bayonets."

David O. McKay (Conference Report, Apr., 1955, p. 24)

Alma 44:8, 11,   **OATH TAKING**
14-15,19-   (refer in this text to 1 Ne. 4:32, 37)
20; 46:35;
48:13; 49:
13, 17, 27;

Alma 50:36,   **OATH TAKING, Continued**
39; 51:6

Alma 45:15-16   **CONDITIONAL FREEDOM OF THIS LAND**
(refer in this text to 2 Ne. 1:7)

"I know, too, that if we will keep the commandments of God—live as he has directed and does now direct, through his prophets—we will continue to have His protecting hand over us. But we must be true to the eternal verities, the great Christian virtues that God has revealed. Then, and only then, will we be safe as a nation and as individuals. God grant that the faithfulness of the Latter-day Saints will provide the balance of power to save this nation in time of crisis."

Ezra Taft Benson (This Nation Shall Endure, p.145)

Alma 46:12,   **THE TITLE OF LIBERTY**
13, 21,   *(Ancient Israel,* DeVaux, 1: 227; 1 Sam. 17:29; *Approach to the Book of Mormon,*
36; 62:4-5 1959 ed., Nibley, pp. 178-189; *A Nation Asleep,* Benson, pp. 22, 46-47)

"We as a people have never known bondage. Liberty has always been our blessed lot. Few of us have ever seen people who have lost their freedom—their liberty. And when reminded of the danger of losing our liberty and independence our attitude has usually been: 'It cannot happen here.' We must never forget that nations may, and usually do, sow the seeds of their own destruction while enjoying unprecedented prosperity. . . . This is our need today—to plant the standard of liberty among our people throughout the Americas."

Ezra Taft Benson (Conference Report, Oct. 1962, pp. 14-15)

"Of course, the war in heaven over free agency is now being waged here on earth, and there are those today who are saying, 'Look, don't get involved in the fight for freedom. Just live the gospel.' That counsel is dangerous, self-contradictory, unsound. . . . Now part of the reason we may not have sufficient priesthood bearers to save the Constitution, let alone to shake the powers of hell, is because unlike Moroni, I fear, our souls do not joy in keeping our country free, and we are not firm in the faith of Christ, nor have we sworn with an oath to defend our rights and the liberty of our country. Moroni raised a title of liberty and wrote upon it these words: 'In memory of our God, our religion, and freedom, and our peace, our wives, and our children.' Why didn't he write upon it: 'Just live your religion; there's no need to concern yourselves about your freedom, your peace, your wives, or your children'? The reason he didn't do this was because all these things were a part of his religion, as they are of our religion today. Should we counsel people, 'Just live your religion. There's no need to get involved in the fight for freedom'? No, we should not, because our stand for freedom is a most basic part of our religion; this stand helped get us to this earth, and our reaction to freedom in this life will have eternal consequences. Man has many duties, but he has no excuse that can compensate for his loss of liberty."

Ezra Taft Benson (Conference Report, Oct. 1966, p. 122)

"Young women, you are like titles of liberty as you strive to protect your families from such intruders as selfishness, harshness, anger, and strife. Your banner stands for peace and love and service to your families."

Sharon G. Larson (Ensign, May 1998, p. 93)

Alma 46:39, 41 **DIED IN THE FAITH OF CHRIST**
(Alma 56:11; D&C 42:46-47; *Kisses at the Window*, Bassett, pp. 65-66)

Alma 48:11-13, 17; 50:22-23 **IS IT POSSIBLE TO BE RIGHTEOUS IN WAR?**
(Alma 53:20-21; 58:40; Jacob 1:9-10)

Alma 48:12 **HIS HEART DID SWELL WITH THANKSGIVING**
(Alma 19:14; 34:38; 3 Ne. 10:10; Moro. 10:3; Luke 17:11-19; Psalm 30:12; 2 Cor. 9:15; 1 Thes. 5:18; *Conference Report*, Apr. 1992, pp. 79-84)

". . . 'thank you' frequently expressed will cheer your spirit, broaden your friendships, and lift your lives to a higher pathway as you journey toward perfection."

Thomas S. Monson (Ensign, Nov. 1998, p. 17)

Alma 48:14-16 **NEPHITES FIGHT DEFENSIVELY**
(refer in this text to 3 Ne. 3:20-21; Mormon 3:10)

Alma 48:15, 25; 50:19-22 **NEPHI'S FREEDOM THESIS**
(Alma 44:4; 46:18; 49:3, 28-30; D&C 71:7-11; refer to Alma 36:1; 1 Ne. 1:20)

"I do not believe the greatest threat to our future is from bombs or guided missiles. I do not think our civilization will die that way. I think it will die when we no longer care—when the spiritual forces that make us wish to be right and noble die in the hearts of men."

Ezra Taft Benson (Annual Boy Scouts Banquet, Commerce, Texas, May 13, 1968)

"Despite the world's crises . . . the greater crisis by far is that we might forget the Lord. How much protection would our missiles and nuclear weapons prove to be if we did not take at face value the Lord's injunction: 'Thou shalt love the Lord thy God with all thy heart, and with all thy soul, and with all thy strength, and with all thy mind; and thy neighbor as thyself' (Luke 10:27)?

Ezra Taft Benson (Crossfire: The Eight Years with Eisenhower, p. 441)

"We are a warlike people easily distracted from our assignment of preparing for the coming of the Lord. When enemies rise up, we commit vast resources to the fabrication of gods of stone and steel—ships, planes, missiles, fortifications—and depend on them for protection and deliverance. When threatened, we become anti-enemy instead of pro-kingdom of God; we train a man in the art of war and call him a patriot, thus, in the manner of Satan's counterfeit of true patriotism, perverting the Savior's teaching: 'Love your enemies, bless them that curse you, do good to them that hate you, and pray for them which despitefully use you, and persecute you; That ye may be the children of your father which is in heaven' (Matt. 5:44-45). We forget that if we are righteous the Lord will either not suffer our enemies to come upon us—and this is the special promise to the inhabitants of the land of the Americas (see 2 Ne. 1:7)—or he will fight our battles for us (Exodus 14:14; D&C 98:37, to name only two references of many)."

Spencer W. Kimball (Ensign, 1976, p. 6)

Alma 51:13-20   **ANSWERING THE CALL TO SERVE IN THE MILITARY**
(Alma 27:24; 46:35; 53:13-17; 62:9-11; D&C 58:21-22; 98:4-7; 134:4-5; 1 Peter 2:13-17; Articles of Faith 1:12; Book of Mormon 121-122 Student Manual, p. 102; *Articles of Faith*, Talmage, pp. 422-423; *Gospel Doctrine*, Smith, p. 512; *A New Witness for the Articles of Faith*, pp. 687-688)

"Even though we sense the hellish origin of war, even though we feel confident that war will never end war, yet, under existing conditions, we find ourselves as a body committed to combat this evil thing. With other loyal citizens we serve our country as bearers of arms, rather than to stand aloof to enjoy a freedom for which others have fought and died."

David O. McKay (Man May Know for Himself, ed. by Middlemiss, pp. 365-368)

"We have been asked today [1942] to be patriotic. This Church, as has been read by President McKay, has a record of accomplishment that is a . . . testimony to the world of the patriotism of this people. We have been sending our boys into the army, and will continue to do so. We will buy war bonds and stamps. We will pay inordinate taxes, for the carrying on of the work for the buying of planes and munitions of war. We will produce and conserve foodstuffs, that there may be sufficient of the necessities to carry on, as we have been requested by our government. But beyond all that, the Latter-day Saints have a responsibility, that may be better understood when we recall the prophecy of Joseph Smith who declared that 'the time would come when (the destiny and) the Constitution of these United States would hang as it were by a thread, and that this people, the sons of Zion, would rise up and save it from threatened destruction' *(Journal of Discourses* 7:15). I want to ask you to consider the meaning of that prophecy, in the light of the declaration of the prophets of the Book of Mormon times, who declared that this land was a choice land above all other lands, and would be free from bondage and from captivity, and from all other nations under heaven, if they will but serve the God of this land, even our Savior, Jesus Christ (Ether 2:12). This is a people whom the Lord has chosen to preach the gospel of righteousness. We talk of security in this day, and yet we fail to understand that here on this Temple Block we have standing the holy temple wherein we may find the symbols by which power might be generated that will save this nation from destruction. Therein may be found the fulness of the blessings of the Priesthood."

Harold B. Lee (Conference Report, Apr. 1942, p. 87)

"A Latter-day Saint must give allegiance to (his) sovereign and render it loyal service when called thereto. This includes military service. The attitude of a Latter-day Saint should be fully to render loyalty to (his) country and to free institutions which the loftiest patriotism calls for. . . . The Church is and must be against war. . . . It cannot regard war as a righteous means of settling international disputes; these should and could be settled—the nations agreeing—by peaceful negotiation and adjustment. But the Church membership are citizens or subjects of sovereignties over which the Church has no control. . . . When, therefore, constitutional law, obedient to these principles, calls the manhood of the Church into the armed service of any country to which they owe allegiance, their highest civic duty requires that they meet that call."

Heber J. Grant, J. Reuben Clark Jr., David O. McKay (Conference Report, Apr. 1942, pp. 92-95)

"The Church is opposed to war because it causes the blood of brothers and sisters to be shed. It opposes war because wars destroy spirituality. . . . But notwithstanding the horrors and evils of war and the beauty of peace, there is a greater purpose in life than merely remaining peaceful. Life calls for growth of the soul. The opportunities for growth requires that man shall retain his freedom, his free agency, his right to live and work and worship according to the dictates of his own conscience. . . . The right to a world where the individual is recognized, the right to protect our loved ones, our liberties and our religion is more important than the keeping of peace."

William E. Berrett (Teachings of the Book of Mormon, p. 177-178)

"Certainly a true American cannot have too much patriotism. Surely Americans who have respect for our traditions, who support our freedoms and are willing to fight to preserve them have been called patriots from the very beginning of our nation. I am proud to be called a patriot, for it correctly denotes one who loves his country. I love America's traditions and its freedoms and I believe they are well worth fighting for, against all that which threatens from within as well as from without."

Ezra Taft Benson (The Red Carpet, p. 199)

"The only real peace—the one most of us think about when we use the term—is a peace with freedom. A nation that is not willing, if necessary, to face the rigors of war to defend its real peace-in-freedom is doomed to lose both its freedom and its peace! These are the hard facts of life. We may not like them, but until we live in a far better world than exists today, we must face up to them squarely and courageously."

Ezra Taft Benson (An Enemy Hath Done This, pp. 161-162)

"A man does not necessarily have to volunteer. In fact, it would be hoped that young members of the Church would have the strengthening stabilizing development of missionary service, and perhaps some schooling, before they enter the service, if indeed they are required to do so at all. And sometimes they are required to serve. If so, the brethren have said: '. . . the members of the Church have always felt under obligation to come to the defense of their country when a call to arms was made . . .' (*Improvement Era*, May 1942, pp. 346, 348-49). Though all the issues of the conflict are anything but clear, the matter of citizenship responsibility is perfectly clear."

Boyd K. Packer (Improvement Era, June 1968, pp. 58, 60-61)

"Someone asked me once how I felt about amnesty for the draft card burner and the deserter. I told him that I thought every one of them should be taken before General Moroni to be judged."

Vaughn J. Featherstone (Ensign, Nov. 1975, pp. 7-10)

"There are many persons who are engaged in wars who are devout Christians. They are innocent instrumentalities—war instrumentalities, for the most part—of their warring sovereignties. On each side, people believe that they are fighting for a just cause, for defense of home and country and freedom. On each side they pray . . . for victory. Both sides cannot be wholly right; perhaps neither is without wrong. God will work out in his own due time and in his own sovereign way, the justice and right of the conflict. But he will not hold the innocent instrumentalities of the war—our brethren in arms—responsible for the conflict."

Harold B. Lee (From the Valley of Despair to the Mountain Peaks of Hope, p. 3)

"If, hearkening to that call [to serve one's country] and obeying those in command over them, they shall take the lives of those who fight against them, that will not make them murderers, nor subject them to the penalty that God has prescribed for those who kill. . . . For it would be a cruel God that would punish His children as moral sinners for acts done by them as the innocent instrumentalities of a sovereign whom He had told them to obey and whose will they were powerless to resist. . . . In this terrible war now waging, thousands of our righteous young men in all parts of the world and in many countries are subject to a call into the military service of their own countries. . . . That in their work of destruction they will be striking at their brethren will not be held against them. That sin, as Moroni of old said, is to the condemnation of those who 'sit in their places of power in a state of thoughtless stupor,' those rulers in the world who in a frenzy of hate and lust for unrighteous power and dominion over their fellow men, have put into motion eternal forces they do not comprehend and cannot control. God, in His own due time, will pass sentence upon them."

Heber J. Grant, J. Reuben Clark Jr., David O. McKay (Conference Report, Apr. 1942, pp. 92-96)

Alma 52-63

"We have grasped the mystery of the atom and rejected the Sermon on the Mount . . . Ours is a world of nuclear giants and ethical infants. We know more about war than we know about peace, more about killing than we know about living."

General Omar Bradley (quoted in Studies in Scriptures, ed. by K. Jackson, 8:78)

"Every gun made, every warship launched, every rocket fired signifies, in the final sense, a theft from those who hunger and are not fed, those who are cold and are not clothed. This world in arms is not spending money alone. It is spending the sweat of its laborers, the genius of its scientists, the hopes of its children."

Pres. Dwight D. Eisenhower (quoted in Studies in Scriptures, ed. by K. Jackson, 8:78)

"Victory and defeat alike leave countries devastated and the conqueror and the conquered reduced. Wickedness brings war, and war vomits destruction and suffering, hate and bloodshed upon the guilty and the innocent. This impressive book [the Book of Mormon] should convince all living souls of the futility of war and the hazards of unrighteousness."

Teachings of Spencer W. Kimball, p. 414

"I would like to share an incident which took place during the Vietnam War. . . . President Harold B. Lee was the President of the Church at the time. While at an area conference in another country he was interviewed by reporters from the international news services. One reporter asked President Lee, 'What is your church's position on the Vietnam War?' Some recognized the question as a trap—one which could not be answered without a very real risk of being misunderstood or misinterpreted. If the prophet answered, 'We are against the war, the inter-national media could state, 'How strange—a religious leader who is against the position of the country he is obliged to sustain in his own church's Articles of Faith' (Article of Faith 1:12). On the other hand, if President Lee answered, 'We are in favor of the war,' the media could question, 'How strange—a religious leader in favor of war?' Either way, the answer could result in serious problems regarding public opinion both inside and outside the Church. President Lee, with great inspiration and wisdom, answered as would a man who knows the Savior: 'We, together with the whole Christian world, abhor war. But the Savior said, 'In me ye might have peace. In the world ye shall have tribulation' (John 16:33). And then the prophet quoted that other comforting scripture from John: 'Peace I leave with you, my peace I give unto you: not as the world giveth, give I unto you' (John 14:27). President Lee then explained: 'The Savior was not talking about the peace that can be achieved between nations, by military force or by negotiation in the halls of parliaments. Rather, he was speaking of the peace we can each have in our own lives when we live the commandments and come unto Christ with broken hearts and contrite spirits.'"

Robert Wells (Ensign, May 1991, p. 86)

Alma 53:8,9; 54:6, 9, 10; 55:28, 31; 56:8, 19, 46; 57: 35; 58:9-11, 33, 37; 59:11-12; 17, 20-21, 60:11, 14-28; 61:13, 21

LAMANITES NOT A THREAT WHEN NEPHITES ARE RIGHTEOUS
(1 Ne. 2:23-24; 2 Ne. 5:25; refer in this text to handout Mosiah 21:7)

"So it was a blessing to the Nephites after all to have the Lamanites on their doorstep to stir them up to remembrance. . . . No matter how wicked and ferocious and depraved the Lamanites might be (and they were that!), no matter by how much they outnumbered the Nephites, . . . they were not the Nephite problem. They were merely kept there to remind the Nephites of their real problem, which was to walk uprightly before the Lord."

Hugh Nibley (Since Cumorah, p. 376)

Alma 53:16-21; 56:45-48, 55-56; 57:21, 25-27; 58:40

THE STRIPLING WARRIORS - THE SONS OF HELAMAN
(Romans 8:31; *Conference Report*, Apr. 1942, p. 96; *Conference Report*, 1952, pp. 89-90; *Conference Report*, Oct. 1927, pp. 11-12)

"Before the final triumphal return of the Lord, the question as to whether we may save our constitutional republic is simply based on two factors—the number of patriots and the extent of their obedience."

Teachings of Ezra Taft Benson, p. 344

"In the spiritual battles you are waging, I see you as today's sons of Helaman."

Teachings of Ezra Taft Benson, p. 520

"What does it mean to be true to the faith? That word *true* implies *commitment, integrity, endurance,* and *courage.* It reminds us of the Book of Mormon's description of the 2,000 young warriors: [in Alma 53:20-21]. In the spirit of that description I say to our returned missionaries—men and women who have made covenants to serve the Lord and who have already served Him in the great work of proclaiming the gospel and perfecting the Saints—are you being true to the faith? Do you have the faith and continuing commitment to demonstrate the principles of the gospel in your own lives, consistently? You have served well, but do you, like the pioneers, have the courage and the consistency to be true to the faith and to endure to the end?"

Dallin H. Oaks (Ensign, Nov. 1997, p. 73)

Alma 54:17, 18, 24   **THE BIRTHRIGHT**
(1 Ne. 2:22; 2 Ne. 5:3; Mosiah 10:12-17; *Companion to Your Study of the Book of Mormon,* Ludlow, p.182)

Alma 55:28, 31   **VICTORY AND REMEMBERING THE LORD**
(contrast with Mosiah 9:3)

Alma 56:11   **DEATH - THEY ARE HAPPY**
(Alma 46:39, 41; Morm. 6:7; D&C 42:46-47; refer in this text to Alma 27:28)

Alma 56:47-48   **RIGHTEOUS MOTHERS**
(*"To the Mothers of Zion,"* Ezra Taft Benson, Feb. 22, 1987; *Journal of Discourses* 1:67; Prov. 29:15)

"All that I am, or hope to be I owe to my angel mother."

Abraham Lincoln (Lincoln's Life - Stories & Speeches, Selby, p. 221)

[Referring to the stripling warriors and their mothers] "I think that is one of the greatest tributes that has ever been paid to motherhood—that in circumstances such as they were experiencing, when they were surrounded by enemies, they could train their children to have that faith in God that would carry them through and would bring them home without losing their lives. . . . I realize that there is a force in the Latter-day Saint homes where our wives and mothers and daughters are, and when it comes to faith in God and prayer it is equal to anything that the men may be able to muster. I fear that sometimes we neglect them. . . . [Speaking to the Priesthood] I am asking myself the question, 'How many of you who are here tonight, before you came here to wait upon the Lord, put your arms around the woman who stood by your side, the mother of your children, and told her that you were grateful that she would keep the home-fires burning when you couldn't be there?' I wonder if we appreciate the daughters of God as He appreciates them. Do we treasure their virtues and their faith and their devotion and their motherhood as our Heavenly Father does?"

George Albert Smith (Conference Report, Apr. 1943, pp. 89-90)

"Your mother is your best friend. Never forget that. She gave you life. She cared for you, nurtured you, nursed you when you were sick, and looked after your every need. Listen to her now. Talk with her candidly and confidentially. You will find that she will keep your confidence and that her wisdom will prove to be wonderful."

Gordon B. Hinckley (Ensign, May 1996, p. 93)

"It is the mothers of young children I would like to address first. . . . These are years when you will probably do the most important work of your lives. Don't wish away your years of caring for small children. Life is what happens to you while you are making other plans. This is a time of great opportunity for you to build the Kingdom. When you teach children to love their Heavenly Father, you have done one of the greatest things you will ever do. If you can be a full-time homemaker, be grateful. If not, you must do what is best. . . . I for one have never felt a need to apologize for my role as a full-time homemaker."

Marjorie Hinckley (as quoted in Ensign, May 1995, p. 74)

"Suggestions for mothers as they guide their precious children:
1. Take time to always be at the crossroads in the lives of your children, whether they be six or sixteen.
2. Take time to be a real friend to your children.
3. Take time to read to your children. Remember what the poet wrote:
    You may have tangible wealth untold:
    Caskets of jewels and coffers of gold.
    Richer than I you can never be—
    I had a mother who read to me.
4. Take time to pray with your children.
5. Take time to have a meaningful weekly home evening. Make this one of your great family traditions.

6. Take time to be together at mealtimes as often as possible.

7. Take time daily to read the scriptures together as a family.

8. Take time to do things together as a family.

9. Take time to teach your children.

10. Take time to truly love your children. A mother's unqualified love approaches Christlike love."

Ezra Taft Benson (Come Listen to a Prophet's Voice, pp. 32-36)

"If I were asked to name the world's greatest need, I should say unhesitatingly *wise mothers*; and the second greatest, *exemplary fathers*. . . . The noblest calling in the world is that of mother. True motherhood is the most beautiful of all arts, the greatest of all professions. She who can paint a masterpiece or who can write a book that will influence millions deserves the plaudits and admiration of mankind; but she who rears successfully a family of . . . sons and daughters whose immortal souls will be exerting an influence throughout the ages long after painting[s] shall have faded, and books and statues shall have been destroyed, deserves the highest honor that man can give."

David O. McKay (Secrets of a Happy Life, pp. 2-4)

"Recently I reviewed the history of many missionaries and found a powerful correlation between exceptional missionaries and mothers who chose to remain home, often at great financial and personal sacrifice. . . . President Benson has taught that a mother with children should be in the home. He also said, 'We realize . . . that some of our choice sisters are widowed and divorced and that others find themselves in unusual circumstances where, out of necessity, they are required to work for a period of time. But these instances are the exception, not the rule' (Ezra Taft Benson, *To the Mothers in Zion*, pamphlet, 1987, pp. 5-6). You in these unusual circumstances qualify for additional inspiration and strength from the Lord. Those who leave the home for lesser reasons will not."

Richard G. Scott (Ensign, May 1993, pp. 33-34)

"In ten years, one-half of all children born in America will be illegitimate. More and more children have no functioning fathers. Already 70% of our juvenile criminals come from fatherless homes. Less than half of the children born today will live continuously with their own mother and father throughout childhood. One-fourth of all adolescents contract a sexually transmitted disease before they graduate from high school. Fifty-five percent of American children under the age of six have both parents or their only parent working in the labor force. . . .

Annually in America there are four million reports of domestic violence, rivaling the number of births in America! Violence in America now kills 'the equivalent of a classroomful' of children 'every two days.' In the face of such challenges, we need more mothers who know the truth, whose children do not doubt their mothers know it (see Alma 56:48)."

Neal A. Maxwell (Ensign, May 1994, pp. 88-90)

"A man who holds the priesthood does not have an advantage over a woman in qualifying for exaltation. The woman, by her very nature, is also co-creator with God and the primary nurturer of the children. Virtues and attributes upon which perfection and exaltation depend come naturally to a woman and are refined through marriage and motherhood. . . . During World War II, men were called away to fight. In the emergency, wives and mothers worldwide were drawn into the work force as never before. The most devastating effect of the war was on the family. It lingers to this generation. In the October 1942 general conference, the First Presidency delivered a message to the Saints in every land.

'. . . This divine service of motherhood can be rendered only by mothers. It may not be passed to others. Nurses cannot do it; public nurseries cannot do it; hired help cannot do it—only mother, aided as much as may be by the loving hands of father, brothers, and sisters, can give the full needed measure of watchful care. . . . The mother who entrusts her child to the care of others, that she may do non-motherly work, whether for gold, for fame, or for civic service, should remember that *a child left to himself bringeth his mother to shame* (Prov. 29:15). In our day the Lord has said that unless parents teach their children the doctrines of the Church *the sin be upon the heads of the parents* (D&C 68:25). Motherhood is near to divinity. It is the highest, holiest service to be assumed by mankind. It places her who honors its holy calling and service next to the angels.'

That message and warning from the First Presidency is needed more, not less, today than when it was given. Any soul who . . . must act alone in rearing children, working to support them will not be denied in the eternities any blessing—provided they keep the commandments."

Boyd K. Packer (Ensign, Nov. 1993, pp. 22-23)

"As I visit the missions in the world, I hear the young men bear their testimonies. They say, 'My mother told me this. . . . my mother is prime, she's first.' She really is first, and if all women could understand this, they would want to have families instead of following the present fad. . . It has been said that 'When you educate a man, you educate an individual; but when you educate a woman, you educate a whole family' (Dr. Charles D. McIver). We want our women to be well educated, for children may not recover from the ignorance of their mothers. After marriage young wives should be happily occupied in bearing and rearing children. . . . You sometimes read things quite different from that. But it is still true, and it will be true when the last trumpet is sounded. I know of no scriptures nor authorities which authorize young wives to forego families purposely. Young married couples can make their way and reach their educational heights if they are truly determined."

Spencer W. Kimball (Charge to Religious Educators, 1982, pp. 43-47)

"Government and social plans will not effectively correct [violence], . . . nor can the best efforts of schools and churches fully compensate for the absence of the tender care of a compassionate mother and wife in the home. . . . As a mother guided by the Lord, you weave a fabric of character in your children from threads of truth through careful instruction and worthy example. . . . No day-care center can do that. It is your sacred right and privilege. Of course, as a woman you can do exceptionally well in the work-place, but is that the best use of your divinely appointed talents and feminine traits? As a husband, don't encourage your wife to go to work to help in your divinely appointed responsibility of providing resources for the family, if you can possibly avoid it. . . . Don't be lured away from the plan of our God to the ways of the world, where motherhood is belittled, femininity is decried, and the divinely established role of wife and mother is mocked. Let the world go its way. You follow the plan of the Lord. . . ."

Richard G. Scott (Ensign, Nov. 1996, pp. 74-75)

"Some years ago President Benson delivered a message to the women of the Church. He encouraged them to leave their employment and give their individual time to their children. I sustain the position which he took. Nevertheless, I recognize, as he recognized, that there are some women (it has become very many in fact) who have to work to provide for the needs of their families. To you I say, do the very best you can. I hope that if you are employed full-time you are doing it to ensure that basic needs are met and not simply to indulge a taste for an elaborate home, fancy cars, and other luxuries. . . . It is well-nigh impossible to be a full-time homemaker and a full-time employee. I know how some of you struggle with decisions concerning this matter. I repeat, do the very best you can. You know your circumstances, and I know that you are deeply concerned for the welfare of your children."

Gordon B. Hinckley (Ensign, Nov. 1996, p. 69)

[To the young women] "Becoming like men is not the answer. Rather, the answer lies in being who you are and living up to your divine potential by fulfilling eternal commitments. You cannot trust the many conflicting voices that clamor about what women should or should not do in today's society. Some of the loudest voices are echoes of those others who are out of harmony with themselves and out of tune with life in general rather than being unhappy with their role as women. . . . Entreating voices may tell you that what you have seen your mothers and grandmothers do is old-fashioned, unchallenging, boring, and drudgery. . . . Homemaking is whatever you make of it. Every day brings satisfaction along with some work which may be frustrating, routine, and unchallenging. But it is the same in the law office, the dispensary, the laboratory, or the store. There is, however, no more important job than homemaking. As C.S. Lewis said, 'A housewife's work . . . is the one for which all others exist.' . . . Women today are encouraged by some to have it all: money, travel, marriage, motherhood, and separate careers in the world. For women, the important ingredients for happiness are to forge an identity, serve the Lord, get an education, develop your talents, serve your family, and if possible to have a family of your own. However, you cannot do all these things well at the same time. . . . You cannot be a 100-percent wife, a 100-percent mother, a 100-percent Church worker, a 100-percent career person, and a 100-percent public-service person at the same time. How can all of these roles be coordinated? I suggest that you can have it sequentially. *Sequentially* is a big word meaning to do things one at a time at different times. The book of Ecclesiastes [3:1] says: 'To every thing there is a season, and a time to every purpose under . . . heaven.'"

James E. Faust (Ensign, May 1998, p. 96)

Alma 56:47-48   A BLESSING OF DIVINE PROTECTION
(Mosiah 28:6-7; Alma 27:11-12)

Alma 57:20-21   OBEY WITH EXACTNESS
(D&C 82:10; *Ensign*, July 1994, pp. 22-23; refer in this text to 1 Ne. 3:7)

"Who wants the family unit to end at death? Our happiness and joy is in our families. But how do we get this major blessing? Obedience—obedience to the requirements of the restored Church of Jesus Christ. In the Brazil Sao Paulo South Mission there was an Elder Malheiros who entered into the field not being able to read or write very proficiently. He was even a little fearful of giving a prayer in public. But this young man, according to his mission president, Wilford Cardon, became one of the very greatest missionaries imaginable. The president asked him toward the end of his mission how he had turned into such a dynamic, very successful missionary. (He had baptized more than two hundred people and had baptized every week for fifty-two consecutive weeks). In a very humble manner Elder Malheiros answered, 'Well, president, I never doubted you. You said one could baptize every week, so I knew I could baptize every week. I never doubted. It was not always easy, *but I tried to obey.'* . . . In Alma 57 we read about the 2,060 sons of Helaman who fought valiantly in many wars. . . . Yet not one lost his life because they knew 'that if they did not doubt, God would deliver them.' (Alma 56:47). In Alma 57:21 we read: 'Yea, and they did *obey and observe to perform every word of command with exactness.' They were totally obedient.* Hence, they had unbelievable protection and success."

Teddy E. Brewerton (Ensign, May 1981, p. 69)

Alma 58:9-11, 34-35, 37   **WE DO NOT DESIRE TO MURMUR**
(1 Ne. 3:6; Eph. 4:15, 22, 29, 31-32; 5:4, 6, 12; refer in this text to 1 Ne. 18:16)

"If our lips are closed to murmuring, then our eyes will be open."

Neal A. Maxwell (Ensign, Nov. 1989, pp. 82-84)

"Your criticism may be worse than the conduct you are trying to correct."

James E. Faust (Ensign, Nov. 1987, p. 35)

"The primary reason we are commanded to avoid criticism is to preserve our own spiritual well-being, not to protect the person whom we would criticize. . . . Does this counsel to avoid faultfinding and personal criticism apply only to statements that are false? Doesn't it also apply to statements that are true? The fact that something is true is not always a justification for communicating it. . . . For example, it is wrong to make statements of fact out of an evil motive, even if the statements are true. One who focuses on faults, though they be true, tears down a brother or a sister. . . . Even though something is true, we are not necessarily justified in communicating it to any and all persons at any and all times. . . . One who focuses on faults, though they be true, fosters dissensions and divisions among fellow Church members in the body of Christ."

Dallin H. Oaks (Ensign, Feb. 1987, pp. 68-69)

Alma 60:13   **THE LORD SUFFERETH THE RIGHTEOUS TO BE SLAIN IN BATTLE**
(D&C 42:46; 136:39; Book of Mormon 121-122 Student Manual, p. 103; *Companion to Your Study of the Book of Mormon*, Ludlow, pp. 205-206; refer in this text to Hel. 12:1-6)

"Recently I received a letter from parents in California whose son had written home just before last Christmas and then shortly thereafter his life was taken in the war in Vietnam. This is part of what he wrote: 'War is an ugly thing, a vicious thing. It makes men do things they would not normally do. It breaks up families, causes immorality, cheating, and much hatred. It is not the glorious John Wayne type thing you see in the movies. It is going a month without a shower and a change of clothing. It is fear creeping up your spine when you hear a mortar tube in the jungle. It is not being able to get close enough to the ground when coming under enemy fire; hearing your buddy cry out because of being ripped with a hot piece of shrapnel. You . . . be proud of your American citizenship, because many brave and valiant men are here preserving your freedom. God has given you the gift of a free nation, and it is the duty of each of you to help in whatever way you can to preserve it. America is the protector of our Church, which is dearer to me than life itself.' And then this young man said this very significant thing: 'I realize now that I have already received the greatest gift of all, and that is the opportunity to gain exaltation and eternal life. If you have this gift, nothing else really matters.'"

Harold B. Lee (From the Valley of Despair to the Mountain Peaks of Hope, pp. 5-6)

"It is my conviction that the present devastating scourge of war in which hundreds of thousands are being slain, many of whom are no more responsible for the causes of the war than are our own boys, is making necessary an increase of missionary activity in the spirit world and that many of our boys who bear the Holy Priesthood and are worthy to do so will be called to that missionary service after they have departed this life."

Harold B. Lee (Conference Report, Oct. 1942, pp. 72-73)

Alma 61:9,19   **SUPPORTING EACH OTHER DURING TOUGH TIMES**
(1 Ne. 5:2-7; 7:19-21; 16:18-25; Acts 23:5,10-11; refer in this text to 1 Ne. 16:23)

"So why should a Sunday School teacher who seems to us weak and simple and less experienced be called by inspiration to teach us? One reason is that it requires humility on our part. It requires a humble heart to believe that you can be taught by someone who apparently knows a good deal less than you do, and perhaps seems less likely to get revelation."

Henry B. Eyring (BYU Devotional, Sept. 1988)

"The men under you will never be loyal to you if they see that you are disloyal to those who preside in authority over you."

Harold B. Lee (BYU speech to CES, July 8, 1966)

"It is better to carry out a plan that is not so wise, if you are united on it. Speaking generally, a plan or a policy that may be inferior in some respects is more effective if men are united upon it than a better plan would be upon which they were divided. . . . When they carry that counsel out unitedly and in the same spirit, they will be blessed, and the Church will be blessed, and, as I have said, God will supplement our weakness by His strength and our want of knowledge by His infinite knowledge and His great power."

George Q. Cannon (Gospel Truths, pp. 163-164)

"God will not ennoble a person, man or woman, who refuses to uphold by faith, prayer, and works those whom God has called and ordained to preside over them."

James E. Faust (Ensign, May 1998, p. 97)

"I have worked with seven Presidents of this Church. I have recognized that all have been human. But I have never been concerned over this. They may have had some weaknesses. But this has never troubled me. I know that the God of heaven has used mortal men throughout history to accomplish His divine purposes. They were the very best available to Him, and they were wonderful."

Gordon B. Hinckley (Ensign, May 1992, p. 53)

"What is meant by sustaining a person? . . . For instance, if a man be a teacher, and I vote that I will sustain him in his position. . . . I will do everything I can to sustain him. . . . I would not say anything derogatory to his character. . . . And then if anybody in my presence were to whisper something about him disparaging to his reputation, I would say, Look here! are you a Saint? Yes. Did you not hold up your hand to sustain him? Yes. Then why do you not do it? . . . If any man make an attack upon his reputation—for all men's reputations are of importance to them—I would defend him in some such way. When we vote for men in the solemn way in which we do, shall we abide by our covenants? or shall we violate them? If we violate them we become covenant-breakers."

John Taylor (Journal of Discourses 21:207-208)

"Our critics at home and abroad are watching us. In an effort to find fault, they listen to every word we say, hoping to entrap us. We may stumble now and again. But the work will not be materially hindered. We will stand up where we fell and go forward. We have nothing to fear and everything to gain. God is at the helm. We [the leaders] will seek His direction. We will listen to the still, small voice of revelation. And we will go forward as He directs. His Church will not be misled. Never fear that. If there were any disposition on the part of its leaders to do so, he could remove them."

Gordon B. Hinckley (Ensign, May 1997, p. 83)

"In my lifetime, there have been very few occasions when I questioned the wisdom and inspiration given by key priesthood leaders. I have always tried to follow their counsel, whether I agreed with it or not. I have come to know that most of the time they were in tune with the Spirit and I was not. The safe course is to sustain our priesthood leaders and let God judge their actions. In the early days of the Church, many fell away because they would not sustain Joseph Smith as the Lord's anointed. In fact, the Prophet Joseph said of some of the leaders in Kirtland that 'there have been but two but what have lifted their heel against me—namely Brigham Young and Heber C. Kimball' (History of the Church, 5:412). Because of their faithful loyalty, the Lord called Brigham Young to lead the Church west, and when the First Presidency was reorganized, Heber C. Kimball was called as First Counselor to Brigham Young. I do not speak of blind obedience, but rather the obedience of faith, which supports and sustains decisions with confidence that they are inspired. I advocate being more in tune with the Spirit so we may feel a confirming witness of the truthfulness of the direction we receive from our priesthood leaders. There is great safety and peace in supporting our priesthood leaders in their decisions."

James E. Faust (Ensign, May 1997, p.42-43)

"People are not necessarily called to positions of responsibility because they are the most qualified, the most talented, or the best informed. Our challenge is to sustain, that is, give our full loyalty and support, to people who are often less than perfect, even people that we might feel to be less capable than ourselves."

Robert L. Millet (CES Symposium, BYU, Aug. 1993)

"A few do's and don'ts may be helpful: • **Do** learn to take counsel. Seek direction from file leaders and receive it willingly. • **Don't** speak ill of Church leaders. • **Don't** covet a calling or position. • **Don't** second-guess who should or should not have been called. • **Don't** refuse any opportunity to serve. • **Don't** resign from a call. • **Do** inform leaders of changing circumstances in your life, knowing that leaders will weigh all factors when prayerfully considering the proper timing of your release."

Russell M. Nelson (Ensign, May 1993, p. 39)

"One who rationalizes that he or she has a testimony of Jesus Christ but cannot accept direction and counsel from the leadership of His church is in a fundamentally unsound position and is in jeopardy of losing exaltation."

Ezra Taft Benson (Ensign, May 1982, p. 64)

"I remember years ago when I was a Bishop I had President [Heber J.] Grant talk to our ward. After the meeting I drove him home. . . . Standing by me, he put his arm over my shoulder and said: 'My boy, you always keep your eye on the President of the Church, and if he ever tells you to do anything, and it is wrong, and you do it, the Lord will bless you for it.' Then with a twinkle in his eye, he said, 'But you don't need to worry. The Lord will never let his mouth-piece lead the people astray.'"

Marion G. Romney (Conference Report, Oct. 1960, p. 78)

"Rejection of or murmuring against the counsel of the Lord's servants amounts to actions against the Lord himself. How could it be otherwise? The Lord acts through his servants. . . . His servants are not perfect. . . . But if we murmur against the Lord's servants, we are working against the Lord and his cause and will soon find ourselves without the companionship of his Spirit. So what do we do when we feel that our Relief Society president or our bishop or another authority is transgressing or pursuing a policy of which we disapprove? . . . The question is not whether we have such differences, but how we manage them. . . . We should conduct ourselves in such a way that our thoughts and actions do not cause us to lose the companionship of the Spirit of the Lord. The first principle in the gospel procedure for managing differences is to keep our personal differences private. . . . We know that such differences are discussed, but not in public. . . . All of this is done quietly and loyally. . . . Why aren't these differences discussed in public? Public debate—the means of resolving differences in a democratic government—is not appropriate in our Church government. We are all subject to the authority of the called and sustained servants of the Lord. They and we are all governed by the direction of the Spirit of the Lord, and that Spirit only functions in an atmosphere of unity. That is why personal differences about Church doctrine or procedure need to be worked out privately. There is nothing inappropriate about private communications concerning such differences, provided they are carried on in a spirit of love."

Dallin H. Oaks (Ensign, Feb. 1987, p. 71)

"We have a stewardship for a season, then move on to other things and sustain someone else in his or her stewardship, with perhaps a different style for another season. It seems that is as it should be. In all of this shifting we should be loyal to one another and to ourselves. If we do not understand, or if we disagree with those who currently administer a program, let us do as the Lord directs and go to them privately and discuss the matter. To do otherwise seems out of harmony with gospel teachings, does not resolve the issues at hand, and does not bring peace. What I am asking for is that we help one another move individually and collectively to a higher level than we are now—that we strive for more meekness."

Larry E. Dahl (address given to BYU Religious Educators, Aug. 27, 1992)

Alma 62:40   **THE PRAYERS OF THE RIGHTEOUS MINORITY**
(Alma 10:19-22; Hel. 13:12-13; James 5:16)

"There are many upright and faithful who live all the commandments and whose lives and prayers keep the world from destruction."

Spencer W. Kimball (Ensign, June 1971, p. 16)

Alma 63:5-10   **NEPHITE MIGRATIONS BY SEA**
(Matthew Cowley Speaks, pp. 114-115; *Conference Report*, Apr. 1947, pp. 145-146; Book of Mormon 121-122 Student Manual, p. 104; *New Zealand Area Conference*, Feb. 1976, p. 15)

Helaman 1~6

Hel. 1:11-12;
2:7,13
6:22-24;
7:4-5

SECRET COMBINATIONS
(Moses 5:18, 28-31; 3 Ne. 9:9; 4 Ne. 42, 46; Alma 37:27-31; *Mormon Doctrine*, McConkie, p. 698; *Since Cumorah*, Nibley, p. 399-409; *Improvement Era*, Feb. 1903, p. 305; *Improvement Era*, Aug. 1936, p. 488; refer in this text to Ether 8:18-25)

"Our nation will continue to degenerate unless we read and heed the words of the God of this land, Jesus Christ, and quit building up and upholding the secret combinations which the Book of Mormon tells us proved the downfall of both previous American civilizations."

Ezra Taft Benson (A Witness and a Warning, p. 6)

Hel. 3:4-11

ANCIENT CEMENT
(*Conference Report*, Apr. 1929, p. 129; *Archaeology and the Book of Mormon*, Hunter, pp. 104-105; *Toward a Better Life*, Peterson, pp. 189-190; *Since Cumorah*, Nibley, p. 254)

Hel. 3:24-25

PROSPERITY
(Jer. 32:5; Prov. 28:13; 2 Chron. 20:15, 17, 20; 1 Kings 2:1-3; D&C 71:9; 97:18; 109:25; refer in this text to 1 Ne. 1:20; 2:20; refer also to the quote by Harold B. Lee in this text under Hel. 12:2-5)

General Use	Temporal/Riches	Spiritual	Deliverance from Enemies
1 Ne. 2:20	2 Ne. 5:11,13	Mosiah 2:36	2 Ne. 1:9, 31-32
1 Ne. 4:14	Mosiah 9:9	Mosiah 25:23-24	Jarom 1:9
1 Ne. 13:15, 20	Mosiah 10:5	Mosiah 26:37	Omni 1:6-7
1 Ne. 20:15	Mosiah 21:16	Mosiah 27:9	Mosiah 1:7,13-14
2 Ne. 1:20	Mosiah 27:7	Alma 37:43	Mosiah 2:4, 31

General Use	Temporal/Riches	Spiritual	Deliverance from Enemies
2 Ne. 4:4	Alma 1:30-31	Alma 49:30	Mosiah 7:29, 33
Mosiah 1:7	Alma 9:22	Hel. 3:24-26	Mosiah 10:5
Mosiah 1:17	Alma 34:24		Mosiah 12:15
Mosiah 2:22	Alma 37:43		Alma 9:10-13
Mosiah 14:10	Alma 50:17-18		Alma 48:14-16, 25
Mosiah 23:19-20	Alma 62:48-49		Alma 50:20-22
Alma 30:17	Hel. 3:36		Alma 59:3
Alma 36:1, 30	Hel. 12:1-2		Alma 62:50-51
Alma 37:13	4 Ne. 1:7, 23		Hel. 4:13,15
Alma 38:1	Ether 6:28		Hel. 12:1-2
Alma 45:8	Ether 9:16		3 Ne. 22:17
Hel. 3:20			
Hel. 11:20			
3 Ne. 5:22			
3 Ne. 6:4-5			
4 Ne. 1:18			
Ether 7:19, 26			
Ether 10:16, 28			

"Since 1960, the U.S. population has increased 41%. . . . But during the same . . . period there has been a 560% increase in violent crime; a 419% increase in illegitimate births; a quadrupling in divorce rates; a tripling of the percentage of children living in single-parent homes, more than a 200% [increase] . . . The health of any society, the happiness of its people, their prosperity, and their peace all find their roots in the teaching of children by fathers and mothers."

Gordon B. Hinckley (Ensign, Nov. 1993, pp. 54 ,59-60)

"The scriptures contain many evidences of the Lord's willingness to prosper his people with the riches of the earth when they demonstrate that they will use this abundance prudently, with humility and charity, always acknowledging the source of their blessings."

Dean L. Larsen (Conference Report, Oct. 1992, p. 57)

"In the time of prosperity, which we are now enjoying, it is highly proper for the Latter-day Saints to get out of debt. . . . Our experience in the years that have passed must have led us to the conclusion that we have periods of prosperity, followed by periods of depression. . . . I can pay more of my debts to my neighbors . . . after I have met my honest obligations with the Lord, than I can by neglecting the latter; and you can do the same. If you desire to prosper, and to be free men and women and a free people, first meet your just obligations to God, and then meet your obligations to your fellow men."

Joseph F. Smith (Gospel Doctrine, pp. 259-260)

"It was revealed to me in the commencement of this Church, that the Church would spread, prosper, grow and extend, and that in proportion to the spread of the Gospel among the nations of the earth, so would the power of Satan rise."

Brigham Young (Journal of Discourses 13:280)

"This land is a land choice above all other lands, and God has blessed the people upon this land. He has fulfilled the words recorded in this book time and time again, that those who should come up to fight against the people of this land should not prosper."

Heber J. Grant (Conference Report, Oct. 1899, p. 18)

Hel. 3:35   **FAST AND PRAY OFT**
(Alma 17:3: Matt. 6:16-18)

"The world needs self-discipline. You can find it in fasting and prayer. Our generation is sick for lack of self-control. Fasting and prayer help to instill this virtue. . . . In addition to the occasional fasting experience for a special purpose, each member of the Church is expected to miss two meals on the fast and testimony Sunday. To skip two consecutive meals and partake of the third normally constitutes approximately a 24-hour period. Such is the counsel. Competent medical authorities tell us that our bodies benefit by an occasional fasting period. That is blessing number one and perhaps the least important. Second, we contribute the money saved from missing the meals as a fast offering to the bishop for the poor and the needy. And third, we reap a particular spiritual benefit that can come to us in no other way. It is a sanctification of the soul for us today just as it was for some choice people who lived 2,000 years ago" [Helaman 3:35].

Robert L. Simpson (Conference Report, Oct. 1967, p. 18)

Hel. 4:12   **DENYING THE SPIRIT OF PROPHECY & REVELATION**
(Morm. 1:14; Alma 30:13-15)

Hel. 4:11-13, 24-26	**LAMANITES BECOME A THREAT TO UNRIGHTEOUS NEPHITES**
	(refer in this text to Mosiah 21:7,11-12,14-16; Alma 53:8-9)

Hel. 5:2; 6:31; 16:10

THE MAJORITY CHOOSE EVIL
(3 Ne. 7:7; 4 Ne. 40-45; refer in this text to Mosiah 29:26-27)

Hel. 5:5-14; 11:7, 34; 12:13

REMEMBER
(F.A.R.M.S. UPDATE, #67; Conference Report, 1958, pp. 10-12; *Helaman Through 3 Nephi 8, According to Thy Word,* BYU Religion Studies Center, ed. by Tate & Nyman, pp. 241-250, Mar. 1990; Rev. 3:3; Alma 37:8; 3 Ne. 15:1)

"'Remember' is the most important word in the English language."

Spencer W. Kimball (Charge to Religious Ed., June 28, 1968)

"If you love the truth you can remember it."

Discourses of Brigham Young, p. 10

"God gave us memories that we might have June roses in the December of our lives."

James Barrie (as quoted by Thomas Monson, Ensign, May 1995, p. 98)

"That is the real purpose of the sacrament, to keep us from forgetting, to help us to remember. I suppose there would never be an apostate, there would never be a crime, if people remembered, really remembered, the things they had covenanted at the water's edge or at the sacrament table and in the temple. . . . I guess we as humans are prone to forget. It is easy to forget. Our sorrows, our joys, our concerns, our great problems seem to wane to some extent as time goes on, and there are many lessons that we learn which have a tendency to slip from us. The Nephites forgot. They forgot the days when they felt good. I remember a young Navaho boy returning from his mission. . . . I happened to be present the day he made his report and as tears rolled down his face, he said, 'Oh, if I could only remember always just how I feel now.'"

Teachings of Spencer W. Kimball, pp. 112-113

"Satan wants us to be slow to remember what we have received and heard. He wants us to minimize and even forget the quiet witnesses of the Spirit that have told us who we really are."

Susan L. Warner (Ensign, May 1996, pp. 78-79)

Hel. 5:6   **YOUR NAME**
                     (refer in this text to Mosiah 1:11-12)

"A number of years ago I was seriously ill. In fact, I think everyone gave me up but my wife. With my family I went to St. George, Utah, to see if it would improve my health. We went as far as we could by train, and then continued the journey in a wagon, in the bottom of which a bed had been made for me. In St. George we arranged for a tent for my health and comfort, with a built-in floor raised about a foot above the ground, and we could roll up the south side of the tent to make the sunshine and fresh air available. I became so weak as to be scarcely able to move. It was a slow and exhausting effort for me even to turn over in bed. One day, under these conditions, I lost consciousness of my surroundings and thought I had passed to the Other Side. I found myself standing with my back to a large and beautiful lake, facing a great forest of trees. There was no one in sight, and there was no boat upon the lake or any other visible means to indicate how I might have arrived there. I realized, or seemed to realize, that I had finished my work in mortality and had gone home. I began to look around, to see if I could not find someone. There was no evidence of anyone living there, just those great, beautiful trees in front of me and the wonderful lake behind me. I began to explore, and soon I found a trail through the woods which seemed to have been used very little, and which was almost obscured by grass. I followed this trail, and after I had walked for some time and had traveled a considerable distance through the forest, I saw a man coming towards me. I became aware that he was a very large man, and I hurried my steps to reach him, because I recognized him as my grandfather. In mortality he weighed over three hundred pounds, so you may know he was a large man. I remember how happy I was to see him coming. I had been given his name and had always been proud of it. When Grandfather came within a few feet of me, he stopped. His stopping was an invitation for me to stop. Then—and this I would like the boys and girls and young people never to forget—he looked at me very earnestly and said: 'I would like to know what you have done with my name.' Everything I had ever done passed before me as though it were a flying picture on a screen—everything I had done. Quickly this vivid retrospect came down to the very time I was standing there. My whole life had passed before me, I smiled and looked at my grandfather and said: 'I have never done anything with your name of which you need be ashamed.' He stepped forward and took me in his arms, and as he did so, I became conscious again of my earthly surroundings. My pillow was as wet as though water had been poured on it—wet with tears of gratitude that I could answer unashamed. I have thought of this many times, and I want to tell you that I have been trying, more than ever since that time, to take care of that name. So I want to say to the boys and girls, to the young men and women, to the youth of the Church and of all the world: Honor your fathers and your mothers. Honor the names that you bear, because some day you will have the privilege and the obligation of reporting to them (and to your Father in heaven) what you have done with their name."

George Albert Smith (Improvement Era, Mar. 1947, p. 139)

"You got it from your father, its all he had to give.
It's yours to use and cherish for as long as you may live.
You may lose the watch he gave you; it can always be replaced.
But, a black mark on your name son can never be erased.
It was clean the day you took it, a worthy name to bear.
When he got it from his father there was no dishonor there.
So always guard it wisely after all is said and done;
So there will be no dishonor when you give it to your son."

(Shane Harrison, a former student of mine had this on a plaque in his room, from his father)

"Those who know him understand that President [James E.] Faust will not yield to mere pressure. . . . [His] son Robert . . . relates his father's integrity to the motto 'To thine own self be true,' citing how his father regularly counseled, 'The most important thing is your name and reputation.'"

Neal A. Maxwell (Ensign, Aug. 1995, p. 12)

Hel. 5:12   **BUILD UPON THE ROCK OF CHRIST**
(2 Ne. 25:20; 28:28; *Answers to Gospel Questions*, Smith, 1:98-99)

"The place to cure most of the ills of society is in the homes of the people. Building our homes as fortresses of righteousness for protection from the world takes constant labor and diligence. Membership in the Church is no guarantee of a strong, happy family. Often parents feel overwhelmed. . . . The righteous molding of an immortal soul is the highest work we can do, and the home is the place to do it. To accomplish this eternal work, we should make our homes gospel centered. When peace and harmony abound, the Holy Spirit will ever be present. The storms of the evil one can be stopped at the very entrance of our homes. Let us be sure the spiritual foundation of each home is the rock of our Redeemer, as Helaman taught his sons: [Hel. 5:12]. The Lord's standards for building a temple apply also to building spiritual strength in our homes: 'Organize yourselves; prepare every needful thing; and establish a house, even a house of prayer, a house of fasting, a house of faith, a house of learning, a house of glory, a house of order, a house of God' (D&C 88:119). Do we heed this counsel from the Lord? Do we do what He asks? We would do well to build our homes according to this plan or they are destined to fail."

Joseph B. Wirthlin (Ensign, May 1993, p. 69)

"Anchor your life in Jesus Christ, your Redeemer. Make your Eternal Father and his Beloved Son the most important priority in your life—more important than life itself, more important than a beloved companion or children or anyone on earth. Make their will your central desire. Then all that you need for happiness will come to you."

Richard G. Scott (Ensign, May 1993, pp. 32-34)

Hel. 5:20-52   **FIRE FROM HEAVEN**
(3 Ne. 17:23-25; 19:13-15; refer in this text to 1 Ne. 22:16-17)

"Now God will not permit America, His base of operations, to be destroyed. He has promised protection to this land if we will but serve the God of the land. He has also promised protection to the righteous even, if necessary, to send fire from heaven to destroy their enemies. No, God's base of operations will not be destroyed. But it may be weakened and made less effective."

Ezra Taft Benson (A Nation Asleep, p. 11)

Hel. 5:30-31, 46   **THE STILL SMALL VOICE WHISPERS**
(D&C 85:6; refer in this text to 3 Ne. 11:3-5)

"A few years ago I met with a prospective mission president and his wife to discuss their availability for service. I asked whether their responsibilities to aged parents would preclude their service at the time. This sister was the only daughter of a wonderful mother, then about 80, whom she visited and helped each week. Though somewhat dependent physically, this mother was strong spiritually. She had served four missions and fifteen years as a temple worker. Because she was in tune with the Spirit, she had a remarkable experience. Several months before this interview she told her daughter that the Spirit had whispered that her daughter's husband would be called as a mission president. So advised, the mother had prepared herself for the needed separation and assured her daughter, long in advance of my assignment for the exploratory interview, that she would 'not be a hindrance' to their service."

Dallin H. Oaks (Ensign, Nov. 1996, p. 61)

Hel. 5:52

MISSIONARY WORK BRINGS PEACE TO THE LAND
(Hel. 6:37; 11:23; Alma 31:5; refer in this text to 4 Ne. 1:6)

"The gospel is the only answer to the problems of the world. We may cry peace. We may hold peace conferences. And I have nothing but commendation for those who work for peace. But it is my conviction that peace must come only by following the teachings and the example of the Prince of Peace."

Ezra Taft Benson (Title of Liberty, pp. 213-214)

"We do not favor war. We do not like the blood of war, the stench of war, the suffering of war, the deprivations of war, the cruelty of war, the degradation of war. We hate war but there are considerations that must be kept in mind. How can war be eliminated from the earth? The answer is simple but hard to realize. Let the people of this world live the gospel. Before peace can come to the world around us, it must come into our hearts."

Teachings of Spencer W. Kimball p. 414

"In these days of uncertainty and unrest, liberty-loving people's greatest responsibility and paramount duty is to preserve and proclaim the freedom of the individual, his relationship to Deity, and the necessity of obedience to the principles of the gospel of Jesus Christ. Only thus will mankind find peace and happiness."

David O. McKay (Conference Report, Oct. 1962, pp. 7-8)

Hel. 6:1,4-5, 34-36

NEPHITES AND LAMANITES CHANGE HATS
(Hel. 15:4-16)

Hel. 6:36

THE LAMANITES' WILLINGNESS TO BELIEVE
(refer in this text to Hel 13:7)

[Speaking of the latter-day Lamanites] "They do suffer from an inferiority complex that is well-nigh annihilating. Prisoners of war, slaves, and downtrodden people usually develop such a complex. But give them comparable education and opportunity with their non-Indian brother, acceptance and brotherly love by him, and they will emerge a rejuvenated people. . . . The chasm between what he is and what he will be is *opportunity* It is ours to give. . . . The Lamanites have believing blood, as evidenced by the words from the sixth chapter of Helaman" [verse 36].

Spencer W. Kimball (Conference Report, Apr. 1949, pp. 105-106)

"I have asked for increased effort in the missionary work among the Lamanites, and I have been most gratified by the response. The missions in the Lamanite areas are the most active and most productive of all, with many more converts per missionary than in any of the other missions. It is as in days of old: [Hel. 6:36]. We have many Lamanite missionaries in the field now, and there will be many, many more, I am sure."

Spencer W. Kimball (Ensign, Dec. 1975, p. 7)

"The converted Lamanite is devout. Few ever apostatize. Some lose their way as they partake of the worldliness about them, but generally the children of Lehi of the twentieth century have inherited that grace and ability to believe like their ancestors of the long ago (Hel. 6:36)."

Teachings of Spencer W. Kimball , p. 178

Helaman 7~12

Hel. 7:16, 20-21 **HOW COULD YOU?**
(1 Ne. 22:23; 3 Ne. 13:24)

Temporary success may be nothing more than postponed failure.

Hel. 7:22-23, 28; **NEPHI'S FREEDOM THESIS**
11:34 (refer in this text to 1 Ne. 1:20; Alma 48:15; 36:1)

Hel. 8:5-6 **ANTI-ENEMY vs PRO-KINGDOM OF GOD**
(refer to quote by Spencer W. Kimball in this text under Alma 43:23)

Hel. 10:1-4 **YOU'RE NOT ALONE**
(Alma 8:13-15; Psalm 27:1; 2 Kings 6:16; Joshua 1:9; *Kisses at the Window*, Bassett, pp. 37-42; refer in this text to Alma 8:10-15; Alma 26:27)

"One on God's side is a majority."

Wendell Philips (quoted in Civil War, Burns, Burns, & Ward, p. 399)

"I solemnly testify that Jesus Christ guides this, His church. He knows and loves you personally."

Richard G. Scott (Ensign, Nov. 1993, p. 88)

"Be sure you understand that God will not allow you to be tempted beyond your ability to resist. (See 1 Cor. 10:13). He does not give you challenges that you cannot surmount. He will not ask more than you can do, but may ask right up to your limits so you can prove yourselves. The Lord will never forsake or abandon anyone. You may abandon him, but he will not abandon you. You never need to feel that you are alone."

Joseph B. Wirthlin (Ensign, Nov. 1989, p. 75)

"There are times when we are growing up when we feel alone or left out. . . . I believe that there are some things that help in these growing-up times so we don't feel so alone. Spend more time talking to Heavenly Father and reading the scriptures. Listen to the still, small voice. In the words of a young woman of Beehive age: 'At first when I would say my prayers and read scriptures, I would never get a good feeling about it. But after about two months of my scriptures and prayer, I began to feel very happy, and I loved my family, and I felt like being nice to everyone.'"

Janette C. Hales (Ensign, May 1992, pp. 79-80)

"Man does not stand alone, or at least, he need not stand alone. Prayer will open doors; prayer will remove barriers; prayer will ease pressures; prayer will give inner peace and comfort during times of strain and stress and difficulty. Thank God for prayer."

Ezra Taft Benson (Conference Report, Oct. 1956, p. 104)

"While President [James E.] Faust has spent so much of his life serving others . . . he has also known what it is like to be alone. . . . Though the only Church member on a transport ship in the South Pacific in World War II, . . . he nevertheless worshipped alone on Sundays. Searching out places where he could sing alone from a pocket-sized hymnal, he would read the scriptures, meditate, and pray in private. Often this meant going up to the front of the ship, where the waves would drown out his singing."

Neal A. Maxwell (Ensign, Aug. 1995, p. 14)

"If it were not for the assurance that I have that the Lord is near to us, guiding, directing, the burden would be almost beyond my strength, but because I know that he is there, and that he can be appealed to, and if we have ears to hear attuned to him, we will never be left alone."

Harold B. Lee (Ensign, Jan. 1974, p. 129)

"One young mother wrote: 'When I was 13 I knew my life was not worth living. I was living in an abusive home where there never seemed to be lasting happiness. My two best friends told me they didn't want to be friends with me anymore because I thought I was too good for them, which made no sense but left me feeling completely alone. As the battles in my house continued to rage, I went to my bedroom. I was so scared. I knelt down and called to the one person I still knew I had. I pleaded to my Father in Heaven to somehow take me home. I said, 'Father, I need to be with you. I need to feel your arms around me.' As I sat crying and quietly waiting in that desperate moment for Heavenly Father's arms to reach down, I heard a voice, 'Put your arms around yourself, and I will be with you.' As I followed that prompting, I felt Heavenly Father's love assure me that I could go on, and I would go on and I was not alone.'"

Janette Hales Beckham (Ensign, Nov. 1997, p. 76)

"Valiant servants of the Lord [are] . . . not entirely alone, . . . if [they] . . . are worthy of His companionship and the companionship of the Holy Spirit. . . . Sarah Ann Meeks . . . stood alone on the doorstep of her home in far-off England nearly a century and a half ago. Her father met her there with a small bundle containing a few of her belongings and with these words, 'You join that church and you must never set foot in my home again.' Unfortunately that was the last she saw of her family. Alone? Very much alone! But . . . she loved the Lord. She had been touched by the Spirit and knew that the gospel of Jesus Christ had been restored to the earth in its fulness. . . . From that one stalwart woman has sprung a progeny of faithful Latter-day Saints difficult to number. . . . One of those descendants now stands here as an especial witness of the Savior Jesus Christ. . . . "

Wm. Rolfe Kerr (Ensign, Nov. 1996, pp. 80-81)

"When the pathway of life takes a cruel turn, there is the temptation to ask the question 'Why me?' . . . At times there appears to be no light at the tunnel's end, no dawn to break the night's darkness. We feel surrounded by the pain of broken hearts, the disappointment of shattered dreams, and the despair of vanished hopes. . . . We feel abandoned, heartbroken, alone. . . . Our problem is that we often expect instantaneous solutions, forgetting that frequently the heavenly virtue of patience is required. Do any of the following challenges sound familiar to you?
  • Handicapped children
  • The passing of a loved one
  • Employment downsizing
  • Obsolescence of one's skills

- A wayward son or daughter
- Mental and emotional illness
- Accidents
- Divorce
- Abuse
- Excessive debt

". . . In the world of today there is at times a tendency to feel detached—even isolated—from the Giver of every good gift. We worry that we walk alone. . . . Rarely is the assurance [from God] communicated by a flashing sign or a loud voice. Rather, the language of the Spirit is gentle, quiet, uplifting to the heart, and soothing to the soul."

Thomas S. Monson (Ensign, May 1998, pp. 52-53)

Hel. 10:5

ANSWERS TO PRAYER
(3 Ne. 18:20; D&C 46:30; 50:29-30; *Conference Report*, Oct. 1944, pp. 55-56)

Hel. 10:6-10; 11:4,13

SEALING POWER
(D&C 128:8; 132:46; Matt. 16:19; *Ensign*, DeHaan, Nov. 1980, pp. 87-88)

Hel. 11:24

NEPHITE—LAMANITE
(Rom. 9:6; *Since Cumorah*, Nibley, p. 246; *Firm Foundation of Mormonism*, Vestal & Wallace, pp. 101-102; *Book of Mormon Prophecies*, Warner, p. 115; *Lehi in the Desert*, Nibley, p. 85; *A Complete Concordance of the Book of Mormon*, Reynolds, p. 395; refer in this text to Jacob 1:13-14)

Nephites	*Lamanites*
2 Ne. 5:6	Jacob 1:14
Alma 2:11	Alma 3:10, 16, 18
Alma 3:11	Alma 31:8-11; 43:4, 13
Alma 8:20	Alma 44:2
Alma 27:27	Alma 45:13-14
Alma 48:9-10	Hel. 3:16
Alma 53:10, 16	4 Ne. 1:17, 20, 38-39
Hel. 9:16	
3 Ne. 2:12-16	
4 Ne. 1:36-37	

Hel. 12:1-6   **WHY DO BAD THINGS HAPPEN TO GOOD PEOPLE?**
(Rom. 5:3; 1 Cor. 10:13; D&C 136:31; Mosiah 23:21-22; Ether 12:6, 27; Alma 34:40-41; refer in this text to Mosiah 24:14-15; Alma 14:11)

"If all the sick for whom we pray were healed, if all the righteous were protected and the wicked destroyed, the whole program of the Father would be annulled and the basic principle of the gospel, free agency, would be ended. No man would have to live by faith. . . . Should all prayers be immediately answered according to our selfish desires and our limited understanding, then there would be little or no suffering, sorrow, disappointment, or even death, and if these were not, there would also be no joy, success, resurrection, nor eternal life and Godhood."

Spencer W. Kimball (Faith Precedes the Miracle, p. 97)

"Prosperity, abundance, honor, and praise lead some men to the false security of haughty self-assurance and the abandonment of the inclination to pray. Conversely, turmoil, tribulation, sickness, and death crumble the castles of men's pride and bring them to their knees to plead for power from on High."

Thomas S. Monson (Ensign, Aug. 1995, pp. 4-5)

"When I held my little son in my arms, knowing that he may be sentenced to life in a defective body, I suffered anguish of soul. We had not prepared ourselves to deal with this. . . . Our pain was founded in a deep concern for the welfare of our son. I felt confident with the Lord's help my son would be healed. I fasted and prayed for the Lord's direction in giving Boyd a blessing. As I laid my hands on his head, everything I desired made me anxious for his body to be made whole. But, even in my overzealous state, I had to admit I could feel no spiritual promptings in blessing him to recover from Cystic Fibrosis. . . . This caused me more pain than when I had first discovered his illness! I felt personally responsible for Boyd's disease. As I searched for an explanation I read these words of Brigham Young, 'In many instances our anxiety is so great that we do not pause to know the spirit of revelation. . . . We have anxiety instead of faith. He lays his hands upon the sick, but they are not healed. It is in consequence of not being completely molded to the will of God' *(Journal of Discourses* 12:125). I had prayed for a miracle and . . . in God's own time the miracles came, but not in the way that I had expected. There is a God in Heaven who understands the destiny of each of his children. He also understands the pathway of challenges each will be confronted with in order to reach their destiny. (See Acts 17:26; Ether 12:27). Without this insight

I could not hope to see the reason for this particular challenge in Boyd's life. As his life unfolded, I grew to understand it better."

K. Douglas Bassett (Kisses at the Window, pp. 15-16)

Hel. 12:2-5   **FORGET THE LORD THEIR GOD**
(refer in this text to Hel. 5:5-14)

"It is frightening to observe that in places where there is the greater prosperity, there is the unmistakable evidence that, like the peoples of other dispensations, when the people prosper they forget God. They are seemingly rich in things that money can buy, but they are devoid of most of the precious things money cannot buy."

Harold B. Lee (Stand Ye in Holy Places, p. 82)

Hel. 12:7-17   **LESS THAN THE DUST OF THE EARTH**
(1 Ne. 20:13; Jacob 2:21; Moses 1:10; refer in this text to Mosiah 2:25-26)

"The point he is making is that the dust of the earth is obedient. . . . Everything in the universe obeys the law given unto it, so far as I know, except man. Everywhere you look you find law and order, the elements obeying the law given to them, true to their calling. But man rebels, and in this thing man is less than the dust of the earth because he rejects the counsels of the Lord. . . ."

Joseph Fielding Smith (Conference Report, Apr. 1929, pp. 54-55)

Hel. 12:18-19;   **SLIPPERY TREASURE**
13:18-23,   (Psalm 73:18; refer in this text to Morm. 1:18)
30-36

"When we consider the condition of the Latter-day Saints, and see how many there are who seem to have their eyes fixed upon the things of this world, things that are not lasting, but that perish in the handling, and how anxious they are to obtain them, how do you think I feel about it? We see many of the Elders of Israel desirous of becoming wealthy, and they adopt any course that they think will bring them riches, which to me is as unwise as anything can be—to see men of wisdom, men that seem to have an understanding of the world and of the things of God, searching after minerals throughout these mountains. . . . These treasures that are in the earth are carefully watched, they can be removed from place to place according to the good pleasure of Him who made them and owns them. He has his messengers at his service, and it is just as easy for an angel to remove the minerals from any part of one of these mountains to another, as it is for you and me to walk up and down this hall. . . . People do not know it, but I know there is a seal set upon the treasures of earth; men are allowed to go so far and no farther. I have known places where there were treasures in abundance; but could men get them? No. You can read in the Book of Mormon of the ancient Nephites holding their treasures, and of their becoming slippery; so that after they had privately hid their money, on going to the place again, lo and behold it was not there, but was somewhere else, but they knew not where. The people do not understand this; I wish they did, for they would then do as I do, pay attention to the legitimate business that God has given them to perform."

Brigham Young (Journal of Discourses 19:36-39)

Hel. 13:6

ONLY REPENTANCE CAN SAVE THIS PEOPLE

"I fully realize that the Lord has predicted wars and rumors of wars (D&C 45:26). I recognize that only true repentance can stay the destructive forces of war and calamity."

Teachings of Ezra Taft Benson, p.706

Hel. 13:7; 14:10

PREJUDICE

(Prov. 11:12; Philip. 2:3; Jacob 3:5, 9; *Conference Report*, Apr. 1949, pp. 110-113; refer in this text to Hel. 6:36)

"If the Indians had all that was rightfully theirs they would not be where they are and we would not be where we are. Remember that. We are here through the grace of God, and do not forget it. The Lord gave us to share an inheritance with the Indians in this glorious land which is choice above all other lands in all the world. But it is ours only on the condition, as I see it, that we do our part in seeing that these people come into the Church. What the Lamanite needs is opportunity. The only difference between us and the Indian is opportunity. Give them an opportunity, . . . so that they, too, can enjoy the blessings that you do. And take this message back to your people in the stakes, that they leave off their racial prejudice. Racial prejudice is of the devil. Racial prejudice is of ignorance. There is no place for it in the gospel of Jesus Christ."

Teachings of Spencer W. Kimball, p. 237

Hel. 13:8; 4:24; 6:35

WITHDRAWAL OF HOLY GHOST

(Moro. 9:4-5; 2 Cor. 3:17; *Teachings of the Prophet Joseph Smith*, p.328; *Journal of Discourses* 21:317-318; refer in this text to 2 Ne. 26:11; Morm. 1:14-17)

The Prophet Joseph Smith appeared to Brigham Young following Joseph's death and instructed his successor as follows: "Tell the people to be humble and faithful, and be sure to keep the Spirit of the Lord and it will lead them right. . . . They can tell the Spirit of the Lord from all other spirits; it will whisper peace and joy to their souls; it will take malice, hatred, strife and all evil from their hearts; and their whole desire will be to do good. . . ."

Brigham Young (Journal History, 23 Feb. 1847)

"Joseph Smith visited me a great deal after his death, and taught me many important principles. . . . Among other things, he told me to get the Spirit of God; that all of us needed it. . . . He said, 'I want you to teach the people to get the Spirit of God. You cannot build up the Kingdom of God without that.' . . . But how is it with the Holy Ghost? The Holy Ghost does not leave me if I do my duty. It does not leave any man who does his duty."

Wilford Woodruff (Deseret News [Weekly], 7 Nov. 1896)

"The gift of the Holy Ghost is as important to man as sunshine and water are to the plants. You take them away, and the plants would die. You take the Holy Ghost out of this Church, and this Church would not be any different than any other church."

LeGrand Richards (Ensign, 1979, p. 76)

Hel. 13:12-14   THE RIGHTEOUS MINORITY
(Alma 10:19-23; 62:40; Gen. 18:23-33; refer in this text to the quote by Spencer W. Kimball under Alma 62:40)

Hel. 13:37   ENCIRCLED ABOUT BY ANGELS OF THE DEVIL
(Mosiah 2:32-33, 37; 3 Ne. 7:22; D&C 35:9; 50:32-33; refer in this text to Alma 3:26-27)

"Any person that he can find that will yield to him, he will bind him, and take possession of the body and reign there, glorying in it mightily, not caring that he had got merely a stolen body; and by and by some one having authority will come along and cast him out and restore the tabernacle to its rightful owner. The devil steals a tabernacle because he has not one of his own: but if he steals one, he is always liable to be turned out of doors."

Teachings of the Prophet Joseph Smith, p. 298

"When those have come into this world and received tabernacles, then died and again have risen and received glorified bodies, they will have an ascendency over the spirits who have received no bodies, or kept not their first estate, like the devil. The punishment of the devil was that he should not have a habitation like men. The devil's retaliation is, he comes into this world, binds up men's bodies, and occupies them himself."

Teachings of the Prophet Joseph Smith, pp. 305-306

"When I saw devils possessing the bodies of the children of men I knew that God . . . permitted them to be on the earth, and wherein would this be a state of probation, without those devils?"

Brigham Young (Journal of Discourses 3:321)

"Brother Joseph Smith gave an explanation of [evil influences]. There are places in the Mississippi Valley where the influence or the presence of invisible spirits are very perceptibly felt. He said that numbers had been slain there in war and that there were evil influences or spirits which affect the spirits of those who have tabernacles on the earth. I myself have felt those influences in other places besides the continent of America; I have felt them on the old battle grounds on the Sandwich Islands. I have come to the conclusion that if our eyes were open to see the spirit world around us, we should feel differently on this subject than we do; we would not be so unguarded and careless and so indifferent whether we had the spirit and power of God with us or not; but we would be continually watchful and prayerful to our Heavenly Father for His Holy Spirit and His holy angels to be around about us to strengthen us to overcome every evil influence."

George Q. Cannon (Gospel Truths, 1:82)

Hel. 13:38   **YOUR DAYS OF PROBATION ARE PAST**
(refer in this text to Alma 34:33; Morm. 2:13; *Miracle of Forgiveness*, Kimball, pp. 145-146; *Answers to Gospel Questions*, Smith, 1:72,79)

Hel. 14   **THE PROPHECIES OF SAMUEL THE LAMANITE**
(Book of Mormon 121-122 Student Manual, pp. 110-111)

Hel. 14:30-31   **YE ARE FREE TO CHOOSE**
(refer in this text to 2 Ne. 2:11, 27)

"Parents, don't make the mistake of purposefully intervening to soften or eliminate the natural consequences of your child's deliberate decisions to violate the commandments. Such acts reinforce false principles, open the door for more serious sin, and lessen the likelihood of repentance."

Richard G. Scott (Ensign, May 1993, pp. 32-34)

Hel. 15:3		**THE LORD CHASTENS HIS PEOPLE**
			(D&C 95:1, Mosiah 23:21-22; *Journal of Discourses* 5:206-207)

Hel. 16:2;		**REJECTING A PROPHET**
13:26-28		(D&C 21:4-5; refer in this text to 2 Ne. 27:32; Ether 13:13-15)

"Whether or not we have modern prophets and revelation really depends on whether the Book of Mormon is true. Therefore, the only problem the objector has to resolve for himself is whether the Book of Mormon is true. For if the Book of Mormon is true, then Jesus is the Christ, Joseph Smith was his prophet, the Church of Jesus Christ of Latter-day Saints is true, and it is being led today by a prophet receiving revelation."

Ezra Taft Benson (A Witness and a Warning, p. 5)

". . . many are prone to garnish the sepulchers of yesterday's prophets and mentally stone the living ones."

Spencer W. Kimball (Conference Report, 1949, p. 121)

"Now the only safety we have as members of this church is to do exactly what the Lord said. . . . We must learn to give heed to the words and commandments that the Lord shall give through his prophet. . . . There will be some things that take patience and faith. You may not like what comes from the authority of the Church. It may contradict your political views. It may contradict your social views. It may interfere with some of your social life. But if you listen to these things, as if from the mouth of the Lord himself, . . . 'the gates of hell shall not prevail against you; yea, and the Lord God will disperse the powers of darkness from before you, and cause the heavens to shake for your good, and his name's glory' (D&C 21:6)."

Harold B. Lee (Conference Report, 1970, p.152)

"Many men will say I will never forsake you, but will stand by you at all times. But the moment you teach them some of the mysteries of the kingdom of God that are retained in the heavens, and are to be revealed to the children of men when they are prepared for them, they will be the first to stone you and put you to death. It was this same principle that crucified the Lord Jesus Christ, and will cause the people to kill the prophets in this generation. . . . If the Church knew all the commandments, one-half they would reject through prejudice and ignorance."

Joseph Smith (quoted in Life of Heber C. Kimball, Whitney, p. 322)

"The story is told in the early days of the Church—particularly, I think, at Kirtland—where some of the leading brethren in the presiding councils of the Church met secretly and tried to scheme as to how they could get rid of the Prophet Joseph's leadership. They made the mistake of inviting Brigham Young to one of these secret meetings. He rebuked them, after he had heard the purpose of their meeting. This is part of what he said: 'You cannot destroy the appointment of a prophet of God, but you can cut the thread that binds you to the prophet of God and sink yourselves to hell.'"

Harold B. Lee (Conference Report, Apr. 1963, p. 81)

"How we respond to the words of a living prophet when he tells us what we need to know, but would rather not hear, is a test of our faithfulness."

Ezra Taft Benson (BYU Speeches of the Year, 1980, p. 28)

Hel. 16:2, 6-7   **THE LORD'S ARMOR**
(Alma 17:34-38; Hel. 5:23-25; *Autobiography of Parley P. Pratt*, pp. 210-211)

Hel. 16:10   **THE MAJORITY CHOOSE EVIL**
(refer in this text to Hel. 5:2; Mosiah 29:26-27)

Hel. 16:22   **SATAN DID STIR THEM UP TO DO INIQUITY CONTINUALLY**
"This account of wickedness and contentions among the Nephites prior to the Lord's birth in the meridian of time is duplicated in the wickedness, contentions, and deceptions of our day as we approach the second coming of our Lord. . . . Here is a partial list of areas where, in my judgment, the warning applies. . . . In the field of politics the party is so often first, regardless of candidate qualifications or record or party platform and legislative program. Decisions frequently based upon political expediency and not what is best for the people. Selfish ambitions of men in departments of government who also

seek to perpetuate themselves in office. Harassing investigations, many of which are either publicity stunts or smoke screens to deceive the public from the underlying motives and purposes. Pressure groups seeking preferential treatment at the expense of the people as reflected in increased tax burdens. . . . The theatre and cinema which so frequently portray and encourage the indecent, immoral, lustful, and worldly imaginations and desires of mankind. Glamorizing the movie star, the entertainer, or the athlete and placing him or her upon a publicity pedestal when his or her personal life may not measure up. . . . Newspapers and other periodicals . . . frequently accept advertising which is false and misleading. Radio and television portray crime, sex, and the sensational. . . . Organizations with deceptive aims and purposes which operate under the cloak if humanitarian, social, or political guise to gain personal goals or preferred group benefits. . . . The narcotic racket which includes the promotion and use of harmful drugs is a constant menace to this and other countries. . . . The disgraceful abortion racket draws into its net young women pregnant out of wedlock who wish to cover up their sin. Married couples are also guilty of this heinous sin. . . . Scientists are human, and many channel their knowledge developing commercial products to realize increased personal wealth. . . . Although good ethics exist in the profession of law, nevertheless the profession is not without the unscrupulous, cunning, and designing fellow members. In the practice of medicine and surgery, quacks and non-professional practitioners are found. . . . Teachers in educational fields promoting wrong ideas and theories, also personal views which undermine the ethical, moral, and spiritual values which youth should freely receive in the classroom. In the field of philosophy are found the deceptive sophistries of men. Also the modern intellectual and free thinker who attempts to modify, change, or improve upon the glorious truths, principles, and standards revealed of God to his chosen prophets who speak authoritatively by his divine power and wisdom. Then there are always the insincere and unethical, as well as the deceiver and anti-Christ to deal with. . . . Will we heed the warning and not yield to Satan's powers and stratagems to deceive and to destroy us? Our peace, our safety, our happiness is in listening to and following the teachings and instructions of the Lord's anointed."

Delbert L. Stapley (Conference Report, Apr. 1967, p. 69)

3 CYCLES OF THE NEPHITE DISEASE IN THE BOOK OF HELAMAN

FIRST CYCLE

Reign of Judges		Stages	Repeated During Wickedness
49th year	3:22, 24-25	Peace & Prosperity	
51st year	3:33-34, 36	Pride	

54th year	4:1-10	War		
61st year	4:10-13	Wickedness		
		(postscript to the war)	3:23	Secret Combinations
			4:24	Spirit Withdrawal
			5:2	Most Choose Evil
61st &				
62nd year	6:1,			
	45; 4:15-17	Repentance (Nephites & Lamanites)		

SECOND CYCLE

Reign of Judges		Stages	Repeated During Wickedness	
63rd year	6:1, 6-14	Peace & Riches (prosperity)		
67th year	6:16	Wickedness	6:18-30;7:2	Secret Combinations
			6:31	Most Choose Evil
			6:35	Spirit Withdrawal
67th year	6:16-17	Hearts Set on Riches (pride)		
72nd year	11:1-5	War & Famine		
75th year	11:6-9	Repentance		

THIRD CYCLE

Reign of Judges		Stages	Repeated During Wickedness	
76th year	11:20-21	Peace & Prosperity		
80th year	11:24	War		
85th year	11:37	Pride & Wickedness		
86th year	13:1	Wickedness		
		continues	11:26	Secret Combinations
			13:8	Spirit Withdrawal (prophecy of Samuel the Lamanite)
			16:10	Majority Choose Evil

Helaman 12	Mormon's Commentary on the Nephite Disease

"In 1787 Edward Gibbon completed his noble work *The Decline and Fall of the Roman Empire*. Here is the way he accounted for the fall.

1. The undermining of the dignity and sanctity of the home, which is the basis of human society.

2. Higher and higher taxes and the spending of public monies for free bread and circuses for the populace.

3. The mad craze for pleasure, sports becoming every year more and more exciting and brutal.

4. The building of gigantic armaments when the real enemy was within the decadence of the people.

5. The decay of religion—faith fading into mere form, losing touch with life, and becoming impotent to warn and guide the people.

Is there a parallel for us in America today? Could the same reasons that destroyed Rome destroy America? . . . The lessons of history, many of them very sobering, ought to be turned to during this hour of our great achievements, because during the hour of our success is our greatest danger. Even during the hour of our great prosperity, a nation may sow the seeds of its own destruction. History reveals that rarely is a great civilization conquered from without unless it has weakened or destroyed itself within."

Ezra Taft Benson (God, Family, Country, pp. 363-364)

"Great nations rise and fall—the people go from bondage to spiritual faith, from spiritual faith to great courage, from courage to liberty, from liberty to abundance, from abundance to selfishness, from selfishness to complacency, from complacency to apathy, from apathy to dependency, from dependency back to bondage."

Robert Muntzel (Manage Magazine, Jan. 1961)

3 Ne. 1:8 **THEY DID WATCH STEADFASTLY**

"In the Book of Mormon we find a pattern for preparing for the Second Coming. A major portion of the book centers on the few decades just prior to Christ's coming to America. By careful study of that time period, we can determine why some were destroyed in the terrible judgments that preceded His coming and what brought others to stand at the temple in the land of Bountiful and thrust their hands into the wounds of His hands and feet."

Ezra Taft Benson (Conference Report, Oct. 1986, p. 5)

3 Ne. 1:12-14 **DIVINE INVESTITURE OF AUTHORITY**

(refer in this text to 1 Ne. 19:10)

"The Book of Mormon account of Christ speaking to Nephi the grandson of Helaman and saying, 'On the morrow come I into the world' (3 Ne. 1:13), is not intended to infer that the spirit does not enter the body until the moment of the actual birth. Rather this revelation to the Nephites was itself being conveyed in a miraculous and unusual way. Quite probably the one uttering the words was speaking in the first person as though he were Christ, in accordance with the law enabling others to act and speak for Deity on the principle of divine investiture of authority."

Bruce R. McConkie (Doctrinal New Testament Commentary, 1:85)

3 Ne. 1:14 **THE FATHER BECAUSE OF ME AND THE SON BECAUSE OF MY FLESH**

(refer in this text to 1 Ne. 19:10)

It sounds as though the Lord is stating that he will come into the world to fulfill two wills—the will of Jehovah, the premortal God of the ancients (perhaps referred to here as 'me'), and the will of the mortal Messiah (the person of 'flesh'). Of course we know that they, Jehovah and Jesus, are one and the same being. At the same time, this statement dramatizes the separate and severable roles that would be played by the Master, that of the Holy One of Israel (premortal) and that of Jesus of Nazareth (mortal). There is a sense, then, in which we might speak of the Lord Jehovah, acting always under the direction of Elohim, our Heavenly Father, as the one who sent Jesus Christ into the world. Note the following language from the Psalmist: 'The LORD [Jehovah] said unto my Lord [Jesus], Sit thou at my right hand, until I make thine enemies thy footstool' (Psalm 110:1; compare Matthew 22:41-45). A similar pattern emerges in the greatest of all messianic prophecies. In speaking of the suffering Savior, Isaiah wrote that 'the LORD [Jehovah] hath laid on him [Jesus] the iniquity of us all.' Further, 'it pleased the LORD [Jehovah] to bruise him [Jesus]; he Jehovah hath put him [Jesus] to grief' (Isaiah 53:6,10; Mosiah 14:6,10). In the same vein the Lord Jehovah spoke to the brother of Jared: 'And whatsoever thing persuadeth men to do good is of me; for good cometh of none save it be of me. I am the same that leadeth men to all good; he that will not believe my words will not believe me—that I am; and *he that will not believe me will not believe the Father who sent me. For behold, I am the Father,* I am the light, and the life, and the truth of the world' (Ether 4:12, italics added)."

R. Millet & J. F. McConkie (Doctrinal Commentary on the Book of Mormon, 4:7)

3 Ne. 1:24   **CONTENTION IN PREACHING**
(Hel. 3:1, 33; 4:1, 11, 23-24; refer in this text to 3 Ne. 11:28-30)

"There are some of other faiths who do not regard us as Christians. . . . I hope we do not argue over this matter. There is no reason to debate it. . . . We must not become disagreeable as we talk of doctrinal differences. . . . We can respect other religions, and must do so. . . . We must teach our children to be tolerant and friendly toward those not of our faith. . . . A holier-than-thou attitude is not becoming to us."

Gordon B. Hinckley (Ensign, May 1998, pp. 4-5)

3 Ne. 2:5-8   **THE NEPHITE CALENDAR SYSTEMS**
(Companion to Your Study of the Book of Mormon, Ludlow, p. 254)

Event	Date	Scriptural Reference
Lehi left Jerusalem	600 BC	1 Ne. 1
The Reign of the Judges	92 BC	Mosiah 29
The Sign of Christ's Birth	AD 9	3 Ne. 2:7-8

3 Ne. 2:12, 14-16

WHAT WERE THE ELEMENTS OF THE CURSE UPON THE LAMANITES?

"The dark skin was a sign of the curse. The curse was the withdrawal of the Spirit of the Lord. The dark skin . . . is no longer considered a sign of the curse. Many of these converts are delightsome and have the Spirit of the Lord."

Joseph Fielding Smith (Answers to Gospel Questions 3:123-124)

IS GOD PREJUDICED?

(1 Sam. 16:7; 1 Ne. 17:35, 40; refer in this text to Hel. 13:7; 14:10; 2 Ne. 26:24-28, 33)

3 Ne. 3:10

GADIANTON ROBBERS—LAMANITES

(refer in this text to Alma 54:17-18, 24)

3 Ne. 3:20-21

NEPHITES FIGHT DEFENSIVELY

(Companion to Your Study of the Book of Mormon, Ludlow, pp. 254-256; *Mormon Doctrine*, McConkie, p. 826; Alma 48:14-16; Morm. 3:10, 14-15; 4:4,18; Omni 1:10; Jacob 1:10; refer in this text to Alma 43:45-47)

"We as Latter-day Saints . . . [should not] manifest a bloodthirsty disposition. We should be a peaceful people, seeking peace, and endeavoring to escape all the horrors of war, and to avert them from the nations of the earth. . . ."

George Q. Cannon (Conference Report, Apr. 1898, p. 85)

3 Ne. 4:4,16, 18-20

FOOD STORAGE

(Teachings of Ezra Taft Benson, pp. 263-266)

"For years we have been counseled to have on hand a year's supply of food. Yet there are some today who will not start storing until the Church comes out with a detailed monthly home storage program. Now, suppose that never happens. We still cannot say we have not been warned. Should the Lord decide at this time to cleanse the Church—and the need for that cleansing seems to be increasing—a famine in this land of one year's duration could wipe out a large percentage of slothful members, including some ward and stake officers. Yet we cannot say we have not been warned. You do not need to go into debt to obtain a year's supply. Plan to build up your food supply just as you would a savings account. Save a little for storage each paycheck. . . . We urge you to do this prayerfully and do it now. I speak with a feeling of great urgency. . . . The revelation to produce and store food may be as essential to our temporal welfare today as boarding the ark was to the people in the days of Noah."

Teachings of Ezra Taft Benson, pp. 265-266

3 Ne. 4:28   **A PROPER HANGING**
(*F.A.R.M.S.*, Nov. 1984; *Studies in Scripture*, Jackson, 8:132-133,138)

3 Ne. 5:22   **NEPHI'S FREEDOM THESIS**
(2:18; 3:12, 15, 25; 4:8-10, 29-33; 6:5)

3 Ne. 5:25-26   **GATHERING IS FIRST TO CHRIST**
(refer in this text to 2 Ne. 30:7; 3 Ne. 20:13, 29-33)

THE NEPHITE DISEASE (cont).

Reign of Judges		*Stages*
92nd year	3 Ne. 1:4, 23	Repentance
92nd year	3 Ne. 1:23	Peace
95th year	3 Ne. 2:1	Hard Hearts (pride)
95th year	3 Ne. 2:1, 3, 10	Wickedness

Repeated During Wickedness
3 Ne. 1:27-30; 2:11
Secret Combinations

Since the Sign		*Stages*
13th year	3 Ne. 2:11, 13, 17	War
16th year	3 Ne. 3:15-16, 25	Repentance

3 Nephi 6 ~ 10

3 Ne. 6:10-16   **A CLASS SOCIETY**
(Prov. 16:18; 2 Tim. 3:7; refer in this text to 2 Ne. 9:28-30, 42, 50-51; Jacob 2:13-17; 4 Ne. 1:24-26)

"Pride gets no pleasure out of possessing something but, possessing more of it than the next man. . . . It is the comparison that makes you proud: the pleasure of being above the rest. Once the element of competition has gone, pride has gone."

C.S. Lewis (Mere Christianity, pp. 109-110)

"Pride is the great stumbling block of Zion. . . . Pride is ugly; it says if you succeed I am a failure. . . . Pride is basically competitive in nature, when competition ends, pride ends."

Ezra Taft Benson (Conference Report, Apr. 1989, pp. 3-7)

"The best educated man in the world may not be able to comprehend the simple truths of the Gospel because his soul is not in tune; he has not been enlightened by the Spirit of the Lord."

Joseph Fielding Smith (Doctrines of Salvation 1:296-297)

"You who find schooling easily available must remember this: 'God is no respecter of persons: But in every nation he that feareth him, and worketh righteousness, is accepted with him.' (Acts 10:34-35; see also Moro. 8:12; D&C 1:35; 38:16). The Lord does not, and the Church cannot, admit to favoritism toward those who are able to obtain professional degrees as compared to those who seek training in a practical field or those who have little or no schooling at all."

Boyd K. Packer (Ensign, Nov. 1992, p. 72)

"The two groups who seem to have the greatest difficulty with pride are the learned and the rich."

Ezra Taft Benson (Conference Report, Apr. 1986, p.6)

"Social commentators almost unanimously refer to the 1980's as 'America's Age of Greed.' . . . The Census Bureau reports that the richest one-fifth of American households now receive almost 10 times the average income of the poorest one-fifth, which is the highest ratio of inequality since they began keeping records following World War II. . . . How can anyone in a position to help simply sit back and enjoy a life of ease? Is not the lack of social action in this regard an indictment of American society? . . . It is not impossible for the recipient of a high income to live a modest lifestyle and use the money to benefit others. But as the scriptures repeatedly remind us, a high income represents a temptation that very few can withstand. . . . How long will Church members join mainstream America in not only condoning, but promoting and admiring materialistic self-aggrandizement."

Richard E. Johnson (BYU Today, Sept. 1990, pp. 47-58)

"And what has this to do with the environment? That whole economy was based on seizing and selling the treasures of the earth beyond one's own personal needs—the land itself, the minerals, water, soil, forests, grass; all are converted into means of making or purchasing the long list of unnecessary wares. . . . In the process, their beauty and value are destroyed, the short-lived finished product soon joining the earlier industrial wastes to cumber the earth with refuse. Why are we so foolish? For the same reason the Nephites were, because 'Satan had great power, . . . tempting them to seek for power, and authority, and riches, and the vain things of the world' (3 Nephi 6:15). The 'love of this world' is not an appreciation of the wonderful things that are in it but the desire to possess it here and now, before we have shown that we can deal lovingly and wisely. The voice of Brother Brigham [Young, Journal of Discourses 8:125] still pleads: 'Do not obey the lusts of the flesh, the lusts of the eye, and the grovelling grasping after property.'"

Hugh Nibley (Brother Brigham Challenges the Saints, p. 48)

"How did education enter into this negative scenario? Education to the Nephites brought wealth, and wealth was needed to obtain an education. This process created an inner circle that allowed the upper class to serve itself while at the same time separating it by a wall of pride from those who had little hope of obtaining 'the good life.' Mormon described that wall well: 'Some were ignorant because of their poverty, and others did receive great learning because of their riches' (3 Nephi 6:12). Wealth was the key to education, and education was the key to wealth. The lower classes never held either of the keys. It is amazing to think that education could have proven so destructive to their society."

K. Douglas Bassett (Doctrines of the Book of Mormon, 1991 Sperry Symposium, p. 20)

"Material abundance without character is the surest way to destruction."

Thomas Jefferson (quoted by Ezra Taft Benson, A Nation Asleep, p. 45)

3 Ne. 6:18

WILLFULLY REBEL AGAINST GOD
(Alma 10:4-6; 4 Ne. 1:38; Morm. 1:16)

"There is a big difference between an honest mistake made in a moment of spiritual weakness and a willful decision to disobey persistently the commandments of God. Those who deliberately choose to violate God's commandments or ignore the standards of the Church, even when promising themselves and others that someday they will be strong enough to repent, are stepping onto a dangerously slippery slope upon which many have lost their spiritual footing."

M. Russell Ballard (Ensign, Nov. 1997, p. 40)

3 Ne. 6:18, 21; 7:18-20

ANGER TOWARDS THE TRUTH
(2 Ne. 28;19-20; Prov. 16:32)

"Most of us recognize a fool when we see one but, few of us recognize a fool when we are one. Often it is anger which blurs our vision."

"Letting off steam produces more heat than light."

Neal A Maxwell (Ensign, Nov. 1989, pp. 82-84)

3 Ne. 6:30; 7:6

GOVERNMENT DESTROYED
"Now I tell you it is time the people of the United States were waking up with the understanding that if they don't save the Constitution from the dangers that threaten it, we will have a change of government."

"Even this nation will be on the very verge of crumbling to pieces and tumbling to the ground, and when the Constitution is upon the brink of ruin, this people will be the staff upon which the nation shall lean, and they shall bear the Constitution away from the very verge of destruction."

Joseph Smith (quoted in Journal of Discourses 7:15)

"But whatever may be our fate, be assured that this [Constitution] will stand. We . . . face difficult days in this beloved land. . . . It may cost us blood before we are through. It is my conviction, however, that when the Lord comes, the Stars and Stripes will be floating on the breeze over this people."

Ezra Taft Benson (The Constitution, A Heavenly Banner, Sept. 17, 1987)

3 Ne. 7:2-4, 14   TRIBES TAKE THE PLACE OF GOVERNMENT
(Companion to Your Study of the Book of Mormon, Ludlow, p. 258)

3 Ne. 7:15-8:1   NEPHI - A SERVANT WITH POWER
(Acts 6:10)

"I would be happier to have my sons effective missionaries that to have them honored in high secular places. . . . For there is no greater work in which to be engaged, and the proselyting work does not end with death, but carries over into the life beyond."

Teachings of Spencer W. Kimball, p. 548

3 Ne. 7:18;   ANGELS
17:24;   (Alma 13:21-25; Moro. 7:30-31; 2 Ne. 32:3; Heb. 13:1-2; *Teachings of the*
19:14   *Prophet Joseph Smith*, p. 191; refer in this text to Alma 3:26-27)

"It is contrary to the law of God for the heavens to be opened and messengers to come to do anything for man that man can do for himself. . . . You cannot point to anywhere in the scriptures where a messenger has come from the heavens and bestowed upon man something man could do for himself, but angels have come and told men what to do and sent men to do it."

Joseph Fielding Smith (Doctrines of Salvation, 1:196)

"The Lord is here with us, not in person, but his angels are around us, and he takes cognizance of every act of the children of men, as individuals and as nations. He is here ready by his agents, the angels, . . . to bring most perfect and absolute deliverance unto all who put their trust in him, when they are ready to receive it. . . . What is the difference between Saints of God and an angel of God? One is clothed upon with mortality, the other has passed through mortality and has received the celestial glory of our Heavenly Father, and is free from the contaminating influences of sin that we have to contend with. . . . When the Lord commands those invisible beings, shall I say, those who have had their resurrection? yes, millions and millions more than the inhabitants of this earth, they can fight your battles."

Discourses of Brigham Young, pp. 41-42

3 Ne. 8:5-23   **TEMPESTS, EARTHQUAKES, FIRES, WHIRLWINDS, PHYSICAL UPHEAVALS**
(D&C 88:89-90; *Since Cumorah*, Nibley, pp. 262-268; Book of Mormon 121-122 Student Manual, p. 114; *Mormon Doctrine*, McConkie, pp. 211-212; *Conference Report*, Kimball, Apr. 1977, pp. 4-5; *The Messiah in Ancient America*, Ferguson, Chapter 2; *Doctrines of Salvation*; Smith, 3:41-43; *Conference Report*, Kimball, Apr. 1963, pp. 64-65; *Journal of Discourses* 21:195)

"Just as surely as Jesus was born in Bethlehem, just so surely will he come again, a resurrected, glorified being, and with him will come hosts, and there will be many spectacular changes. It will not be the end of the world in the sense of annihilation, but the end of its present relationships, and there will be many, many changes. Beginning with the bridegroom's coming will come the celestializing of this earth and tremendous changes which we can hardly think of or believe. . . . At any rate, not anyone in this building knows when the end is coming or when the Christ will come. . . . And so the time is coming, I do not know when it will be. I only hope when the examination is put on the blackboard, we will all be . . . able to answer the questions satisfactorily."

Teachings of Spencer W. Kimball, pp. 440-441

3 Ne. 9:2   **THE DEVIL LAUGHETH AND HIS ANGELS REJOICE**
(Moses 7:26, 1 Ne. 8:26-27; 3 Ne. 27:11; Alma 30:60)

"Never should a bearer of the Aaronic Priesthood be guilty of saying anything discourteous or disrespectful to his mother. The scriptures teach us that whenever we are abusive, thoughtless, or unkind to others, 'the devil laugheth, and his angels rejoice' (3 Ne. 9:2); also, that 'the heavens withdraw themselves; the Spirit of the Lord is grieved; and when it is withdrawn, Amen [or the end] to the priesthood or the authority of that man' (D&C 121:37)."

Joe J. Christensen (Ensign, Nov. 1996, pp. 39-40)

3 Ne. 9:13;
10:12

YE WERE MORE RIGHTEOUS THAN THEY
(2 Ne. 26:3-8; refer in this text to 3 Ne. 10:6-7)

"Too many of our wives and mothers prefer the added luxuries of two incomes to the satisfactions of seeing children grow up in the fear and love of God. We golf and boat and hunt and fish and watch sports rather than solemnize the Sabbath. Total morality is found neither among the people nor among the leaders of the state and nation. Personal interests and ulterior motives block the way. Old Man 'Rationalization' with his long beard is ever present to tell us that we are justified in these deviations, and because we are not vicious enough to be confined in penitentiaries we rationalize that we are not failing to measure up. The masses of the people are perhaps much like those who escaped destruction in the ancient days of this continent. The Lord said to them: 'O all ye that are spared because ye were more righteous than they [the slain ones], will ye not now return unto me, and repent of your sins, and be converted, that I may heal you?' (3 Ne. 9:13)."

Spencer W. Kimball (The Miracle of Forgiveness, p. 317)

"This account of wickedness and contentions among the Nephites prior to the Lord's birth in the meridian of time is duplicated in the wickedness, contentions, and deceptions of our day as we approach the Second Coming of our Lord. . . ."

Delbert L. Stapley (Conference Report, Apr. 1967, p. 69)

"When we say that only the righteous shall abide the day, . . . we must take into account the fact that there are no perfect men. . . . Even the most faithful saints commit sin and live in some degree after the manner of the world. But such worldly works as remain with the righteous shall be burned so that the saints themselves may be saved. . . . The burning that destroys every corruptible thing is the same burning that cleanses the righteous. . . . If only perfect people were saved, there would be only one saved soul—the Lord Jesus."

Bruce R. McConkie (The Millennial Messiah, pp. 543-544)

3 Ne. 9:19-20

SACRIFICES & BURNT OFFERINGS DONE AWAY
"It is difficult for us today to realize the tremendous revolution involved in altering the ritualism of the Law of Moses into the humble and lowly concept of

worship, not with the sacrificial blood of animals, but with this broken heart and contrite spirit of the worshipper. . . . [Animal sacrifice] was always a vicarious sacrifice, apparently with little actual sacrifice except for the value of the animal sacrificed, by the individuals themselves, to cancel the debit, so to speak, against their lives and living in the eyes of the Almighty One. The sinner seemingly, in general, took on no obligation and considered himself under no obligation to abandon his sins, but took on only the obligation to offer sacrifice therefore. But under the new covenant that came in with Christ, the sinner must offer the sacrifice out of his own life, not by offering the blood of some other creature; he must give up his sins, he must repent, he himself must make the sacrifice. . . ."

J. Reuben Clark, Jr. (Behold the Lamb of God, pp. 107-109)

3 Ne. 10:6-7   **REPENT AND TURN UNTO ME**

"Let us not be so self-righteous that we think that we have no need for repentance, for the Savior himself preached repentance to the more righteous who were spared from the great destruction at the time of the crucifixion (3 Nephi 10:6-7)."

Eldred G. Smith (Conference Report, Apr. 1954, p. 88)

THE NEPHITE DISEASE (cont).

Since the Sign		Stages
26th year	3 Ne. 6:1, 3-4	Peace & Prosperity
29th year	3 Ne. 6:10-16	Pride
30th year	3 Ne. 6:17	Wickedness

Repeated During Wickedness
3 Ne. 6:28-30; 7:9-10
Secret Combinations
3 Ne. 7:7-8
Majority Choose Evil

34th year	3 Ne. 8:5-19	Destruction of Wicked

3 Nephi 11~14

"What a blessing it would be if every family would frequently read together 3 Nephi, discuss its sacred contents, and then determine how they can liken it unto themselves and apply its teachings in their lives! Third Nephi is a book that should be read and read again. Its testimony of the resurrected Christ in America is given in purity and beauty. . . . I testify that 3 Nephi is a true account of the resurrected Christ's visit to ancient America and contains His teachings in their pristine truth. I testify that Jesus is the Christ and that he stands at the head of His Church today, even the Church of Jesus Christ of Latter-day Saints. I testify that He will come again in power and great glory and that He will leave nothing undone for our eternal welfare."

Ezra Taft Benson (A Witness and a Warning, pp. 43-45)

"In the Book of Mormon we find a pattern for preparing for the Second Coming. A major portion of the book centers on the few decades just prior to Christ's coming to America. By careful study of that time period, we can determine why some were destroyed in the terrible judgments that preceded His coming and what brought others to stand at the temple in the land of Bountiful and thrust their hands into the wounds of His hands and feet."

Ezra Taft Benson (Ensign, Nov. 1986, pp. 6-7)

3 Ne. 11:1   **GATHERING AT THE TEMPLE**
(2 Ne. 5:16; 12:2; Jacob 1:17; Mosiah 1:18)

"No member of the Church has received the ultimate which this Church has to give until he or she has received his or her temple blessings in the house of the Lord."

Gordon B. Hinckley (Ensign, Nov. 1997, p. 49)

"I remember . . . as a . . . boy, coming in from the field and approaching the old farm home. . . . I could hear my mother singing, 'Have I Done Any Good in the World Today' (Hymns, 1950, no. 58). I can . . . see her in my mind's eye bending over the ironing board . . . with beads of perspiration on her forehead. She was ironing long strips of white cloth, with newspapers on the floor to keep them clean. When I asked her what she was doing, she said, 'These are temple robes, my son. Your father and I are going to the Logan Temple.' Then she put the old flatiron on the stove, drew a chair close to mine, and told me about temple work—how important it [was] to be able to go to the temple and participate in the sacred ordinances performed there. She also expressed her fervent hope that some day her children . . . grandchildren and great-grandchildren would have the opportunity to enjoy those priceless blessings.' I am happy to say that her fondest hopes in large measure have been realized."

Ezra Taft Benson (Ensign, Aug. 1985, p. 8)

"Sometimes in the peace of lovely temples, the serious problems of life find their solutions. [At times] pure knowledge flows to us there under the influence of the Spirit. I am grateful to the Lord for temples. The blessings of the House of the Lord are eternal. They are of the highest importance to us because it is in the temples that we obtain God's greatest blessings pertaining to eternal life. Temples really are the gateways to heaven. May we remember always, as we [visit and work in these temples], that the veil may become very thin between this world and the spirit world. I know this is true. It is well also that we keep in mind that it is all one great program on both sides of the veil and it is not too important whether we serve here or over there, as long as we serve with all our heart, might, mind, and strength."

Ezra Taft Benson (Address given at dedication of Denver Colorado Temple, Oct. 25, 1986)

"I promise you that, with increased attendance in the temples of our God, you shall receive increased personal revelation to bless your life as you bless those who have died."

Ezra Taft Benson (Ensign, May 1987, p. 85)

"Regular temple attendance is one of the simplest ways you can bless those who are waiting in the spirit world. . . . Elder John A. Widtsoe made this remarkable statement: 'When the history of human thought shall be written from the point of view of temple worship, it may well be found that temples and the work done in them have been the dominating influence in shaping human thought from the beginning of the race' *(Temple Worship*, p. 52). Our joy—or our disappointment—in the eternities may hinge on our willing participation in this great latter-day work."

David B. Haight (Ensign, May 1993, p. 25)

"Look to the temple of the Lord as the great symbol of your membership. It is the deepest desire of my heart to have every member of the Church worthy to enter the temple. . . . The things that we must do and not do to be worthy of a temple recommend are the very things that ensure we will be happy as individuals and as families. Let us be a temple-attending people. Attend the temple as frequently as personal circumstances allow. Keep a picture of a temple in your home that your children may see it. Teach them about the purposes of the house of the Lord. Have them plan from their earliest years to go there and to remain worthy of that blessing."

Howard W. Hunter (Ensign, Nov. 1994, p. 8)

"Let us truly be a temple-attending and a temple-loving people. . . . We should go not only for our kindred dead but also for the personal blessing of temple worship, for the sanctity and safety that are within those hallowed and consecrated walls. As we attend the temple, we learn more richly and deeply the purpose of life and the significance of the atoning sacrifice of the Lord Jesus Christ. Let us make the temple, with temple worship and temple covenants and temple marriage, our ultimate earthly goal and the supreme mortal experience."

Howard W. Hunter (Ensign, Feb. 1995, p. 5)

3 Ne. 11:3-5   A SMALL VOICE WHICH PIERCED TO THE CENTER
(Hel. 5:30-31; D&C 85:6; 1 Kings 19:12; *Kisses at the Window*, Bassett, pp. 73-77; *Spiritual Roots of Human Relations*, Covey, pp. 161-163; *Conference Report*, Apr. 1929, pp. 129-130; refer in this text to Hel. 5:30-31, 46)

"The still small voice is so quiet you won't hear it when you're noisy inside."

Henry B. Eyring (BYU Devotional, Oct. 29, 1989)

"Now, I testify it is a small voice. It whispers, not shouts. And so you must be very quiet inside. That is why you may wisely fast when you want to listen. And that is why you will listen best when you feel, 'Father, thy will, not mine, be done.' You will have a feeling of 'I want what you want.' Then, the still small voice will seem as if it pierces you. It may make your bones to quake. More often it will make your heart burn within which will lift and reassure."

Henry B. Eyring (Ensign, May 1991, p. 67)

"Dramatic and miraculous answers to prayer may come, but they are the exceptions. Even at the highest levels of responsibility in this kingdom of God which is being built up upon the earth, *the voice is still small*. . . . My testimony is that the Lord is speaking to you! But with the deafening decibels of today's environment, all too often we fail to hear him. . . . I was interested in someone's observation: 'With TV and radio and tapes, what young person has time to listen. . . ?' Listening is a challenge for us all today."

Graham W. Doxey (Conference Report, Oct. 1991, p. 33)

"The burning bushes, the smoking mountains, . . . the Cumorahs, and the Kirtlands were realities; but they were the exceptions. The great volume of revelation came to Moses and to Joseph and comes to today's prophet in the less spectacular way—that of deep impressions, without spectacle or glamour or dramatic events. Always expecting the spectacular, many will miss entirely the constant flow of revealed communication."

Spencer W. Kimball (Conference Report, Munich Germany Area Conference 1973, p. 77)

"The Spirit does not get our attention by shouting or shaking us with a heavy hand. Rather it whispers. It caresses so gently that if we are preoccupied we may not feel it at all. (No wonder that the Word of Wisdom was revealed to us, for how could the drunkard or the addict feel such a voice?) Occasionally it will press just firmly enough for us to pay heed. But most of the time, if we do not heed the gentle feeling, the Spirit will withdraw and wait until we come seeking and listening. . . ."

Boyd K. Packer (Ensign, Jan. 1983, p. 53)

3 Ne. 11:15   **THEY WENT FORTH ONE BY ONE**
(3 Ne. 17:21, 25; 28:1; Moses 7:28-31; Luke 15:4-7,10; *Conference Report*, Oct. 1975, p. 29; *This Is My Gospel*, BYU Religious Studies Center, p. 173)

"Faithful servants nourish by focusing on the individual. *God loves us one by one*."

Alexander B. Morrison (Ensign, May 1992, p. 14)

"Despite trials, worldly confusion, and caustic voices, we can trust in the Lord and go forward with happy hearts, knowing that with every challenge or problem, there's the strength to go on. Why? Because we know His promises are real, that *He does know us by name and has a plan for each of us*. He will help us learn what it is and give us joy in doing it."

Elaine L. Jack (Ensign, May 1992, p. 91)

3 Ne. 11:28-30;
18:34

CONTENTION

(3 Ne. 1:24; Hel. 16:22; D&C 10:62-63; 38:39; 136:23; 2 Ne. 26:32; 4 Ne. 1:2, 15; Mosiah 2:32-33, 37; 18:18, 21; Phil. 2:3; *Gospel Doctrine*, Smith, p. 373; *Conference Report*, Oct. 1945, pp. 90-91; *Conference Report*, Oct. 1969, p. 35; *Doctrines of the Book of Mormon*, ed. by Van Oren & Top, pp. 21-23)

"Quarrel not at all. No man resolved to make the most of himself can spare time for personal contention. Better give your path to a dog than be bitten by him."

Abraham Lincoln (A letter to J. M. Cutts, Oct. 26, 1863)

"He [Satan] damages and often destroys families within the walls of their own homes. His strategy is to stir up *anger* between family members. . . . The verb *stir* sounds like a recipe for disaster: Put tempers on medium heat, stir in a few choice words, and bring to a boil; serve cold; lots of leftovers. . . . This doctrine or command from the Lord presupposes agency and is an appeal to the conscious mind to make a decision. The Lord expects us to make the choice *not* to become angry."

Lynn G. Robbins (Ensign, May 1998, p. 80)

"Another face of pride is contention. Arguments, fights, unrighteous dominion, generation gaps, divorces, spouse abuse, riots, and disturbances all fall into this category of pride. Contention in our families drives the Spirit of the Lord away. It also drives many of our family members away. Contention ranges from hostile spoken words to worldwide conflicts. The scriptures tell us that 'only by pride cometh contention' (Proverbs 13:10; 28:25)."

Ezra Taft Benson (Conference Report, Apr. 1989, p. 5)

"As we dread any disease that undermines the health of the body, so should we deplore contention, which is a corroding canker of the spirit. . . . My concern is that contention is becoming accepted as a way of life. From what we see and hear in the media, the classroom, and the workplace, all are now infected to some degree with contention. . . . Well do I remember a friend who would routinely sow seeds of contention in church classes. His assaults would invariably be preceded by this predictable comment: 'Let me play the role of devil's advocate.' Recently he passed away. One day he will stand before the Lord in judgment. Then, I wonder, will my friend's predictable comment again be repeated?"

Russell M. Nelson (Conference Report, Apr. 1989, p. 85)

"Contention and division are of the devil. . . . Hence, there is no occasion to debate, to argue, to contend, to champion one cause as against another. Those who have the Spirit do not hang doggedly to a point of doctrine or philosophy for no other reason than to come off victorious in a disagreement."

Bruce R. McConkie (Doctrinal New Testament Commentary, 3:105)

"Whenever factions exist among us, whenever disunion prevails, whenever there is opposition in views concerning points of doctrine or concerning counsel, it may be set down as indisputable that the Spirit of God is not in our midst and that there is something wrong. Whenever two men in this Church differ upon points of doctrine, they may know and others who may be acquainted with the fact may know also that there is something wrong; for the Spirit of God will not teach two men different ideas. . . . Men may differ in their views, but after they have expressed these differences then contention should cease; in fact, it should never exist. . . . I do not care what we may claim or what our pretensions may be, we are not the people of God when we are not united. Union is one of the fruits of the Spirit. . . . [The devil] seeks for division, for contention and for strife. . . . He tries to persuade the people that it is true independence to divide up and every man go for himself and to refuse to do as the servants of God say."

George Q. Cannon (Gospel Truths, pp. 159-160, 165)

"Be one who nurtures and who builds. Be one who has an understanding and a forgiving heart, who looks for the best in people. Leave people better than you found them. Be fair with your competitors, whether in business, athletics, or elsewhere. Don't get drawn into some of the parlance of our day and try to 'win' by intimidation or by undermining someone's character. . . . The Spirit of the Lord cannot dwell where there is bickering, judging, contention, or any kind of bashing."

Marvin J. Ashton (Ensign, May 1992, p. 20)

"Should there be any quarrelling or fault-finding? No; because where the Spirit of God exists there is no disposition of this character. There is a manifestation to suffer wrong rather than to do wrong; not to revile, not to prosecute, not to assail back when we are assailed. If a brother comes up to me, he is in a bad temper, he says something that is annoying, and I lose my temper and reply in the same spirit, do I do right? Certainly not. However much the provocation may be, it is not my duty as a Latter-day Saint . . . to indulge in any such feeling or expression. . . . If a man forgets himself so far as to call his brother a liar, or any other offensive name, there should be enough of the Spirit of God and the spirit of patience and the spirit of self-respect left in the brother to bear the insult without resenting in the same spirit. . . . It is the duty of every man and woman in this Church to live at peace with him and herself, and then to live at peace with everybody else, husbands with wives, wives with husbands, parents with children, children with parents, brothers with sisters and sisters with brothers. . . ."

George Q. Cannon (Journal of Discourses 22:102-103)

3 Ne. 12:2-12   BEATITUDES
(Life and Teachings of Jesus and His Apostles, p. 60-63)

3 Ne. 12:6   HUNGER AND THIRST AFTER RIGHTEOUSNESS
(Alma 32:42; 2 Ne. 9:51)

"A new convert to the Church recently shared this story. 'I was in and out of enforced confinement most of my teen years. It wasn't so bad being there . . . But it did get boring, so when anyone had any reading material, funny books, magazines, or anything, we would trade our food for a chance to borrow those items. One day I saw a fellow with a nice, thick book. I knew it would take a long time to read, so I offered him my main course food items for a week. He accepted my offer and loaned me the book. As I read it, I knew I was reading something very special and very true. The book for which I had sacrificed my food was titled the Book of Mormon. When I had a chance, I found the missionaries, changed my habits, and am now finding a new way of life. I love that book for which I traded my food.'"

Marvin J. Ashton (Conference Report, Apr. 1981, p. 30)

3 Ne. 12:8   PURE IN HEART
(Autobiography of Parley P. Pratt, p. 123)

"We have the power so to live, that becoming pure in heart, we shall see the face of God while we yet dwell as mortals."

Bruce R. McConkie (Conference Report, Oct. 1977, p. 52)

"If you would see God, you must be pure. There is in Jewish writings the story of a man who saw an object in the distance, an object that he thought was a beast. As it drew nearer he could perceive it was a man and as it came still closer he saw it was his friend. You can see only that which you have eyes to see. Some of the associates of Jesus saw him only as a son of Joseph the carpenter. Others thought him to be a winebibber or a drunkard because of his words. Still others thought he was possessed of devils. Only the righteous saw him as the Son of God. Only if you are the pure in heart will you see God, and also in a lesser degree will you be able to see the 'God' or good in man and love him because of the goodness you see in him. Mark well that person who criticizes and maligns the man of God or the Lord's anointed leaders in his Church. Such a one speaks from an impure heart."

Harold B. Lee (Decisions for Successful Living, p. 59)

3 Ne. 12:13-16   SALT AND LIGHT
(Manners and Customs of the Bible, Freeman, pp. 335-336; *Jesus the Christ*, Talmage, pp. 388-389)

3 Ne. 12:18   JOT-TITTLE
(Manners and Customs of the Bible, Freeman, pp. 335-336)

3 Ne. 12:22   RACA-FOOL
(John 8:7; Morm. 8:17; D&C 42:27; 1 Peter 2:1; Eph. 4:31)

"Look for the good in those about you, and emphasize that good. Never go around gossiping about your associates or speaking unkind words concerning them. Such words will only backfire to hurt you. Jehovah has commanded, 'Thou shalt not bear false witness' (Ex. 20:16)."

Gordon B. Hinckley (Ensign, May 1996, p. 92)

"If we will go forward, never losing sight of our goal, speaking ill of no one, living the great principles we know to be true, this cause will roll on in majesty and power to fill the earth."

Gordon B. Hinckley (Ensign, Nov. 1997, p. 68)

3 Ne. 12:22 **WITHOUT A CAUSE**
(compare to Matt. 5:24; refer in this text to 3 Ne. 11:28-30; Moro. 9:3-4)

[Comparing Matt. 5:22] "How interesting that the phrase 'without a cause' is not found in the inspired Joseph Smith Translation (see Matt. 5:24), nor in the 3 Nephi 12:22 version. When the Lord eliminates the phrase 'without a cause,' He leaves us without an excuse. . . . Understanding the connection between agency and anger is the first step in eliminating it from our lives. We can choose not to become angry. And we can make that choice today, right now: 'I will never become angry again.' Ponder this resolution."

Lynn Robbins (Ensign, May 1998, pp. 80-81)

3 Ne. 12:27-30 **ADULTERY IN YOUR HEART**
(D&C 42:22-23; 63:16; 66:3,10; Prov. 23:7; *Spiritual Roots of Human Relations*, Covey, pp. 65-73; *Miracle of Forgiveness*, Kimball, p. 70; *The Jerusalem Bible*, pp. 1252-1253; refer in this text to Mosiah 4:30; Alma 12:14)

"The greatest battles in life are fought within the silent chambers of the soul."

David O. McKay

"Sometimes we limit our own progress by thinking of minimum expectations as maximum goals. 'Thou shalt not commit adultery' is the minimum expectation the Lord has of our conduct towards each other. The higher, celestial law is: 'Thou shalt love thy wife with all thy heart, and shalt cleave unto her and none else. And he that looketh upon a woman to lust after her shall not have the Spirit; and if he repents not he shall be cast out' (D&C 42:22-23; 63:16)."

W. Jeffrey Marsh (Ensign, July 1994, p. 47)

3 Ne. 12:31-32 **WRITING OF DIVORCEMENT**
(Matt. 19:3-9; Eph. 5:25; Titus 2:4; *Companion to Your Study of the Book of Mormon Companion*, Ludlow, pp. 266-267; *Jesus the Christ*, Talmage, p. 474; *Mormon Doctrine*, McConkie, p. 203-4; *Ensign*, Nov. 1993, p. 17; *Doctrines of Salvation*, Smith, 2:84; refer in this text to 2 Ne. 7:1)

"There may be now and again a legitimate cause for divorce. I am not one to say that it is never justified. But I say without hesitation that this plague among us, which seems to be growing everywhere, is not of God, but rather is the work of the adversary of righteousness and peace and truth."

Gordon B. Hinckley (Ensign, May 1991, p. 74)

"There are too many broken homes among our own. The love that led to marriage somehow evaporates, and hatred fills its place. Hearts are broken, children weep. Can we not do better? Of course, we can. It is selfishness that brings about most of these tragedies. If there is forbearance, if there is forgiveness, if there is an anxious looking after the happiness of one's companion, then love will flourish and blossom. . . . There are good families everywhere. But there are too many who are in trouble. This is a malady with a cure. The prescription is simple and wonderfully effective. It is love. It is plain, simple, everyday love and respect. It is a tender plant that needs nurturing. But it is worth all of the effort we can put into it."

Gordon B. Hinckley (Ensign, Nov. 1997, p. 69)

"Those marriages performed in our temples, meant to be eternal relationships, then, become the most sacred covenants we can make. . . . What, then, might be 'just cause' for breaking the covenants of marriage? . . . In my opinion, 'just cause' should be nothing less serious than a prolonged and apparently irredeemable relationship which is destructive of a person's dignity as a human being. At the same time, I have strong feelings about what is not provocation for breaking the sacred covenants of marriage. Surely it is not simply 'mental distress,' nor 'having grown apart,' nor having 'fallen out of love.' This is especially so where there are children."

James E. Faust (Ensign, May 1993, p. 36)

"Divorce is not part of the gospel plan no matter what kind of marriage is involved. But because men in practice do not always live in harmony with gospel standards, the Lord permits divorce for one reason or another, depending upon the spiritual stability of the people involved. In ancient Israel man had power to divorce their wives for relatively insignificant reasons. (Deut. 24:1-4). Under the most perfect conditions there would be no divorce permitted except where sexual sin was involved. In this day divorces are permitted in accordance with civil statutes, and the divorced persons are permitted by the Church to marry again without the stain of immorality which under a higher system would attend such a course."

Bruce R. McConkie (Doctrinal New Testament Commentary, 1:547)

"With divorce rates escalating throughout the world today, it is apparent that many spouses are failing to endure to the end of their commitments to each other. . . . An enduring [temple] marriage results when both husband and wife regard their union as one of the two most important commitments they will ever make. [The other commitment is membership in the Lord's Church].

Without a strong commitment to the Lord, an individual is more prone to have a low level of commitment to a spouse. . . . If Satan can get you to love anything—fun, flirtation, fame, or fortune—more than a spouse or the Lord with whom you have made sacred covenants to endure, the adversary begins to triumph. . . . When priorities are proper, . . . they will protect you from cheating—in marriage, in the Church, and in life."

Russell M. Nelson (Ensign, May 1997, pp. 71-72)

3 Ne. 12:33-37   OATHS
(refer in this text to 1 Ne. 4:32, 37; *Companion to Your Study of the Book of Mormon*, Ludlow, pp. 96-97)

3 Ne. 12:43-45   LOVE THY NEIGHBOR & THINE ENEMY
(Matt. 22:37-40; 1 John 4:20-21; Luke 10:25-37; D&C 42:27-28; 52:40)

"The true greatness of a person, in my view, is evident in the way he or she treats those where courtesy and kindness are not required. . . . When we subordinate personal interests out of love and give of ourselves with no thought of receiving in return, we are moving toward becoming true disciples."

Joseph B. Wirthlin (Ensign, May 1992, pp. 86-87)

"For Relief Society, the *charity* of our motto is not an abstraction. It is a love beyond the emotion we might feel for or from others. It isn't a 'what's in it for me?' kind of love. Being friendly, generous, and respectful of others moves us along the way from self-concern, but the selflessness of the kind of love that Christ commanded us to learn is a high step indeed. 'Bless them that curse you, do good to them that hate you, and pray for them who despitefully use you' (3 Ne. 12:44)."

Aileen H. Clyde (Ensign, Nov. 1993, p. 93)

"Love your enemies, bless them that curse you, do good to them that hate you, and pray for them which despitefully use you, and persecute you' (3 Ne. 12:44). Think what this admonition alone would do in your neighborhood and mine, the communities in which you and your children live, in the nations which make up our great global family. I realize this doctrine poses a significant challenge, but surely it is a more agreeable challenge than the terrible tasks posed for us by the war and poverty and pain the world continues to face. How are we supposed to act when we are offended, misunderstood, unfairly or unkindly treated, or sinned against? What are we supposed to do if we are hurt by those we love, or passed over for promotion, or are falsely accused, or have our motives unfairly assailed? Do we fight back? Do we send in an ever-larger battalion? Do we revert to an eye for an eye and a tooth for a tooth, or, as Tevye says in *Fiddler on the Roof,* do we come to the realization that this finally leaves us blind and toothless? . . . We can all be a little more forgiving."

Howard W. Hunter (Ensign, Nov. 1992, p. 18)

"Besides loving God, we are commanded to do what to many is a more difficult commandment—to love all, even enemies, and to go beyond the barriers of race or class or family relationships. It is easier, of course, to be kind to those who are kind to us—the usual standard of friendly reciprocity. . . . Whom would you bar from your circle? We might deny ourselves a nearness to our Savior because of our prejudices . . . , attitudes that Christ would surely condemn. Love has no boundary, no limitation of good will."

David B. Haight (Ensign, Nov. 1982, pp. 10-12)

"Let us also love our neighbors. Let us banish from our lives any elements of self-righteousness. . . . Let us be friendly. Let us be helpful. Let us live the Golden Rule. Let us be neighbors of whom it might be said, 'He or she was the best neighbor I ever had.'"

Gordon B. Hinckley (Ensign, Nov. 1997, p. 69)

3 Ne. 12:48   **BE YE THEREFORE PERFECT**
(D&C 93:11-14, 20, 26-28; *Teachings of the Prophet Joseph Smith*, pp. 345-346; *History of the Church*, Smith, 6:306-307; *Doctrines of Salvation*, Smith 2:36; *Miracle of Forgiveness*, Kimball, pp. 208-209; *Companion to Your Study of the Book of Mormon*, Ludlow, p. 267; *Conference Report*, Apr. 1953, pp. 110-111; *Journal of Discourses* 2:129-130; refer in this text to 3 Ne. 27:27)

"C. S. Lewis . . . had this to say . . . 'The command Be ye perfect is not idealistic gas. Nor is it a command to do the impossible. He [Christ] is going to make us creatures that can obey that command. He said (in the Bible) that we were 'Gods' and He is going to make good His words. If we let Him—for we can prevent Him, if we choose—He will make the feeblest and filthiest of us into a god or goddess, a dazzling, radiant, immortal creature, pulsating all through with such energy and joy and wisdom and love as we cannot now imagine, a bright stainless mirror which reflects back to God perfectly (though, of course, on a smaller scale) His own boundless power and delight and goodness. The process will be long and in parts very painful; but that is what we are in for. Nothing less. He meant what He said' *(Mere Christianity*, p. 172). The command 'Be ye . . . perfect' (Matt. 5:48) is not one that can be executed overnight, or even by the end of mortality. It takes much, much longer to overcome all our mortal weaknesses. . . . Even if we subscribed to the possibility of becoming perfect in mortality, . . . the pathway to perfection is just too long, the time to walk it exceeding whatever our allotted years in mortality may be."

Alexander B. Morrison (Ensign, Apr. 1995, p. 42)

3 Ne. 13:1-4   **ALMS**

(Mormon Doctrine, McConkie, p. 82; Alma 34:28; *Ensign*, June 1992, pp. 2-5; refer in this text to Mosiah 2:16-17)

"In every gospel dispensation the Lord has required his saints to care for the temporal well-being of the poor among them. Organized almsgathering was one of the accepted features of Jewish life in the days of Jesus. Much of the giving, however, was done in a spirit of ostentatious display, with the expectancy of gaining popularity and honor from men. Modern almsgivers often follow the same pattern, trumpeting their donations and contributions through the columns of the press, no doubt expecting to gain business or political rewards which will outweigh the cost of the contribution. Verily, they have their reward."

Bruce R. McConkie (Doctrinal New Testament Commentary, 1:232-233)

3 Ne. 13:7   **VAIN REPETITIONS**

(Bible Manners and Customs, Freeman, p. 340)

"How often do we hear people who wax eloquent in their prayers to the extent of preaching a complete sermon? The hearers tire and the effect is lost, and I sometimes wonder if perhaps the dial of the heavenly radio is not turned off when long and wordy prayers are sent heavenward."

Teachings of Spencer W. Kimball, p. 119-120

"Do not learn a prayer by heart, and say it every morning and evening. That is something I dislike very much. It is true that a great many people fall into the rut of saying over a ceremonious prayer. They begin at a certain point, and they touch at all the points along the road until they get to the winding-up scene;

and when they have done, I do not know whether the prayer has ascended beyond the ceiling of the room or not."

Joseph F. Smith (Conference Report, Oct. 1899, pp. 71-72)

"Don't worry about your clumsily expressed feelings. Just talk to your Father. He hears every prayer and answers in His way."

Richard G. Scott (Ensign, Nov. 1989, pp. 30-32)

3 Ne. 13:9-13 **THE LORD'S PRAYER**
(Companion to Your Study of the Book of Mormon, Ludlow, p. 267)

WHAT IS THE LANGUAGE OF PRAYER?
(Faith Precedes the Miracle, Kimball, p. 201; Conference Report, Oct 1951, p. 175; Ensign, Jan. 1976, pp. 12, 44-47; Ensign, Nov. 1983, p. 13)

"When we go to worship in a temple or a church, we put aside our working clothes and dress ourselves in something better. This change of clothing is a mark of respect. Similarly, when we address our Heavenly Father, we should put aside our working words and clothe our prayers in special language of reverence and respect. . . . In our day the English words *thee, thou, thy,* and *thine* are suitable for the language of prayer, not because of how they were used anciently but because they are currently obsolete in common English discourse. Being unused in everyday communications, they are now available as a distinctive form of address in English, appropriate to symbolize respect, closeness, and reverence for the one being addressed. I hope this renewal of counsel that we use special language in our prayers will not be misunderstood. Literary excellence is not our desire. We do not advocate flowery and wordy prayers. We do not wish to be among those who 'pray to be heard of men, and to be praised for their wisdom' (Alma 38:13). We wish to follow the Savior's teaching, 'When ye pray, use not vain repetitions, as the heathen do: for they think that they shall be heard for their much speaking' (3 Ne. 13:7). Our prayers should be simple, direct, and sincere. . . . I am sure that our Heavenly Father, who loves all of his children, hears and answers all prayers, however phrased. If he is offended in connection with prayers, it is likely to be by their absence, not their phraseology."

Dallin H. Oaks (Ensign, May 1993, p. 17)

3 Ne. 13:34   **SUFFICIENT IS THE DAY UNTO THE EVIL**
"The men and women who desire to obtain seats in the Celestial Kingdom will find that they must battle with the enemy of all righteousness every day."

Brigham Young (Journal of Discourses 11:14)

3 Ne. 13:14-15   **FORGIVE OTHERS**
(3 Ne. 12:23-24, 43-44; D&C 19:30; 64:9-11; John 8:1-11; Luke 6:26-38; Matt. 18:21-22; *Companion to Your Study of the Book of Mormon*, Ludlow, p. 269; *Psycho-Cybernetics*, Maltz, pp. 60-63; *The Civil War*, Burns-Burns & Ward, pp. 381-382, 410-412; *Doctrinal New Testament Commentary*, McConkie 1:222-223; *Journal of Discourses* 23:283-285; *Ensign*, May 1992, pp. 31-33, 62; refer in this text to 1 Ne. 7:20-21; Mosiah 26:30-31)

"(Forgiving others) relieves the offended of the destructive burden that resentment and anger can cause."

Marion D. Hanks (Conference Report, Oct. 1973, pp. 15-16)

"The nearer we get to our heavenly Father, the more we are disposed to look with compassion on perishing souls. . . . If you would have God have mercy on you, have mercy on one another."

Teachings of the Prophet Joseph Smith, p. 241

"Recently there came over my desk the poignant words of a father who had erred years ago and who was repentant. He agonized as he related that his sons and daughters refused to forgive him, even to the point of refusing to talk to him or see him in person after more than five years. The Lord tells us in D&C 64:9: 'Wherefore, I say unto you, that ye ought to forgive one another; for he that forgiveth not his brother his trespasses standeth condemned before the Lord; for there remaineth in him the greater sin.' I've seen many examples . . . of those who just don't seem to be able to forgive another. . . . This surely is one of the more important ingredients in spiritual healing."

Malcolm S. Jeppsen (Ensign, May 1994, p.18)

"Remember that we must forgive even if our offender did not repent and ask forgiveness. . . . It frequently happens that offenses are committed when the offender is not aware of it. Something has been said or done [which] is misconstrued or misunderstood. The offended one treasures in his heart the offense, adding to it such other things as might give fuel to the fire and justify his con-clusions. . . . Do we [forgive] or do we sulk in our bitterness, waiting for our offender to learn of it and to kneel to us in remorse? And this reconciliation sug-gests also forgetting. Unless you forget, have you forgiven? . . . No bitterness of past frictions can be held in memory if we forgive with all our hearts."

Spencer W. Kimball (Conference Report, Oct. 1949, pp. 132-133)

"Consider this lesson taught to me many years ago by a patriarch. . . . He mar-ried his sweetheart. . . . They were deeply in love, and she was expecting their first child. The night the baby was to be born, there were complications. . . . After many hours of labor, the condition of the mother-to-be became desper-ate. Finally the doctor was located. In the emergency, he acted quickly and soon had things in order. The baby was born and the crisis, it appeared, was over. Some days later, the young mother died from the very infection that the doctor had been treating at another home that night. John's world was shat-tered. . . . As the weeks wore on, his grief festered. 'That doctor should not be allowed to practice,' he would say. 'He brought that infection to my wife. If he had been careful, she would be alive today.' He thought of little else, and in his bitterness, he became threatening. Today, no doubt, he would have been pressed by many others to file a malpractice suit. And there are lawyers who would see in his pitiable condition only one ingredient—money! . . . One night a knock came at his door. A little girl said simply, 'Daddy wants you to come over. He wants to talk to you.' 'Daddy' was the stake president. A griev-ing, heartbroken young man went to see his spiritual leader. . . . The counsel from that wise servant was simply, 'John, leave it alone. Nothing you do about it will bring her back. Anything you do will make it worse. John, leave it alone.' My friend told me then that this had been his trial—his Gethsemane. How could he leave it alone? Right was right! A terrible wrong had been com-mitted and somebody must pay for it. . . . He determined to follow the counsel of that wise spiritual leader. He would leave it alone. Then he told me, . . . 'It was not until I was an old man that I could finally see a poor country doc-tor—overworked, underpaid, run ragged from patient to patient, with little medicine, no hospital, few instruments, struggling to save lives, and succeed-ing for the most part. He had come in a moment of crisis, when two lives hung in the balance, and had acted without delay.' . . . And that is the coun-sel I bring again to you. If you have a festering grudge, if you are involved in an acrimonious dispute, [Mormon 8:20]. I say, therefore, John, leave it alone. Mary, leave it alone."

Boyd K. Packer (Conference Report, Oct. 1987, p. 19)

"'Blame keeps wounds open. Only forgiveness heals!' *(O Pioneers!* by Willa Cather). Recently I read where an elderly man disclosed at the funeral of his brother, with whom he had shared, from early manhood, a small, one room cabin near Canisteo, New York, that following a quarrel, they had divided the room in half with a chalk line and neither had crossed the line nor spoken a word to the other since that day—sixty-two years before! What a human tragedy—all for the want of mercy and forgiveness. . . . 'He [who] cannot forgive others breaks the bridge over which he himself must pass if he would ever reach heaven; for everyone has need to be forgiven.'"

Thomas S. Monson (Ensign, May 1995, pp. 59-60)

"Life is too short to be spent nursing animosities or in keeping a box score of offenses against us. . . . We don't want God to remember our sins, so there is something fundamentally wrong in our relentlessly trying to remember those of others. When we have been hurt, undoubtedly God takes into account what wrongs were done to us and what provocations there are for our resentments, but clearly the more provocation there is and the more excuse we can find for our hurt, all the more reason for us to forgive and be delivered from the destructive hell of such poisonous venom and anger. It is one of those ironies of godhood that in order to find peace, the offended as well as the offender must engage the principle of forgiveness."

Jeffrey R. Holland (Ensign, Nov. 1996, p. 83)

3 Ne. 13:19-24,   TWO MASTERS
33   (Jacob 2:18-19; Morm. 8: 38; Mosiah 5:13; James 1:6-8; *Lectures on Faith* 6:7)

"Our affections are often too highly placed upon the paltry perishable objects. Material treasures of earth are merely to provide us, as it were, room and board while we are here at school. It is for us to place gold, silver, houses, stocks, lands, cattle, and other earthly possessions in their proper place. Yes, this is but a place of temporary duration. We are here to learn the first lesson toward exaltation— obedience to the Lord's gospel plan."

Teachings of Ezra Taft Benson, p. 26

"We each have exactly 24 hours in a day and 168 hours in a week. If we use the bulk of those hours in the pursuit . . . of material things, there is little time left for relationships, ideas, service, observation, peaceful rest, true religion, and for other non-material things. . . . The only way we know to fight [materialism] is to try to understand it and to realize what it can do to you. You must then adopt an attitude that is opposite of materialism, an attitude that you actually own nothing, that everything belongs to God and that you are only a steward over anything that you might have, even over your children and over your own talents and potential. You will be judged by your stewardship, by how well you take care of and use the things that are loaned to you."

Linda and Richard Eyre (Home Base, Nov. 1984, pp. 16-17)

"Some would never *sell* Jesus for thirty pieces, but they would not *give* Him their all either! Unfortunately, we tend to think of consecration only in terms of property and money. But there are so many ways of keeping back part. One might be giving of money and time and yet hold back a significant portion of himself. . . . One might accept a Church calling but have his heart more set on maintaining a certain role in the world. . . . Each of us is an innkeeper who decides if there is room for Jesus! Consecration is the only surrender which is also a victory. It brings release from . . . selfishness and emancipation from the dark prison of pride. . . . But is being consecrated and 'swallowed up' a threat to our individuality? No! Heavenly Father is only asking us to lose the old self in order to find the new and the real self. It is not a question of losing our identity, but of finding our true identity! . . . Consecration may not require giving up worldly possessions so much as being less possessed by them. . . . Brothers and sisters, whatever we embrace instead of Jesus and His work will keep us from qualifying to enter His kingdom and therefore from being embraced by Him."

Neal A. Maxwell (Ensign, Nov. 1992, pp. 66-67)

"Every step in the direction of increasing one's personal holdings is a step away from Zion, which is another way of saying, as the Lord has proclaimed in various ways, that one cannot serve two masters: to the degree in which he loves the one he will hate the other, and so it is with God and business, mammon is simply the standard Hebrew word for any kind of financial dealing."

Hugh Nibley (Approaching Zion, p. 37)

"When one puts business or pleasure above his home, he that moment starts on the downgrade to soul-weakness. When the club becomes more attractive to any man than his home, it is time for him to confess in bitter shame that he has failed to measure up to the supreme opportunity of his life and flunked in the final test of true manhood. No other success can compensate for failure in the home. The poorest shack in which love prevails over a united family is of greater value to God and future humanity than any other riches. In such a home God can work miracles and will work miracles."

David O. McKay (Conference Report, Apr. 1964, p. 5)

"They who love and serve God with all their hearts rejoice evermore. . . . But they who try to serve God and still cling to the spirit of the world, have got on two yokes—the yoke of Jesus and the yoke of the devil. . . . They will have a warfare inside and outside, and the labor will be very galling, for they are directly in opposition one to the other. Cast off the yoke of the enemy, and put on the yoke of Christ, and you will say that his yoke is easy and his burden is light. This I know by experience."

Brigham Young (Journal of Discourses 16:123)

"One man I know of was called to a position of service in the Church, but he felt that he couldn't accept because his investments required more attention and more of his time than he could spare for the Lord's work. He left the service of the Lord in search of Mammon, and he is a millionaire today. But I recently learned an interesting fact: If a man owns a million dollars worth of gold at today's prices, he possesses approximately one 27-billionth of all the gold that is present in the earth's thin crust . . . The Lord who created and has power over all the earth created many other earths as well, even 'worlds without number' (Moses 1:33); and when this man received the oath and covenant of the priesthood (D&C 84:33-44), he received a promise from the Lord of 'all that my Father hath' (v. 38). To set aside all these great promises in favor of a chest of gold and a sense of carnal security is a mistake in perspective of colossal proportions. To think that he has settled for so little is a saddening and pitiful prospect indeed. . . ."

Spencer W. Kimball (Ensign, June 1976, p. 5)

"[One] reason for increase in debt . . . is the rise of materialism, as contrasted with commitment to spiritual values. Many a family, in order to make a 'proper showing,' will commit itself for a larger and more expensive house than is needed, in an expensive neighborhood. Almost everyone would, it seems, like to keep up with the Joneses. . . . As a result, there is a growing feeling, unfortunately, that material things should be had now, without waiting, without saving, without self-denial."

Ezra Taft Benson (Ensign, June 1987, pp. 3-4)

"In quiet moments when you think about it, you recognize what is critically important in life and what isn't Be wise and don't let good things crowd out those that are essential. . . . Whether you intend to or not, when you live as though the Savior and His teachings are only one of many other important priorities in your life, you are clearly on the road to disappointment and likely on the path to tragedy. . . . If you have been enticed by the things of the world to forget the things of God, correct your priorities."

Richard G. Scott (Ensign, May 1997, pp. 54,59)

3 Ne. 14:1-5   **JUDGING OTHERS**
(Rom. 2:1; John 7:24; D&C 121:16-17; Mosiah 29:12; Morm. 8:19-20; *Spiritual Roots of Human Relations*, Covey, pp. 134-136: *Teachings of Spencer W. Kimball*, p. 262; *Journal of Discourses* 5:206-207)

"When you do not worry or concern yourself too much with what other people do and believe and say, there will come to you a new freedom."

Teachings of Spencer W. Kimball, p. 236

"Aren't we rather prone to see the limitations and the weaknesses of our neighbors? Yet that is contrary to the teachings of the gospel of Jesus Christ. . . . If we have the spirit of fault finding, of pointing out the weaknesses and failings of others in a destructive manner, that never comes as the result of the companionship of the Spirit of our Heavenly Father and is always harmful."

George Albert Smith (Conference Report, Oct. 1934, p. 50)

"What I am suggesting is that each of us turn from the negativism that so permeates our society and look for the remarkable good among those with whom we associate, that we speak of one another's virtues more than we speak of one another's faults."

Gordon B. Hinckley (Ensign, Apr. 1986, pp. 3-4)

"Most of us think we see the world as it is, but I believe this is not the case. We each see not with the eye but with the soul. Each person sees the world not as it is but as he or she is. When he opens his mouth to describe what he sees, he in effect describes himself, that is, his perception."

Stephen R. Covey (The Divine Center, p. 3)

"Don't have Religious Hobbies. . . . They are dangerous because they give undue prominence to certain principles or ideas to the detriment and dwarfing of others just as important. . . . We have noticed this difficulty: that Saints with hobbies are prone to judge and condemn their brethren and sisters who are not so zealous in the one particular direction of their pet theory as they are. The man with the Word of Wisdom only in his brain, is apt to find unmeasured fault with every other member of the Church who entertains liberal ideas as to the importance of other doctrines of the gospel. . . . The man with a hobby is apt to assume an 'I am holier than thou' position, to feel puffed up and conceited, and to look with distrust . . . on his brethren and sisters who do not so perfectly live that one particular law. This feeling hurts his fellow-servants and offends the Lord."

Joseph F. Smith (Gospel Doctrine, pp. 116-117)

"The art of being wise is the art of knowing what to overlook."

William James

3 Ne. 14:13-14   STRAIT GATE
(refer in this text to 1 Ne. 8:20)

3 Ne. 15:5-6,10   **THE LAW AND THE PROPHETS**
(Unger's Bible Dictionary, p.144)

"At the time of Jesus the Jewish scriptures (our Old Testament) were divided into three major sections. The *Law*, or the Torah, included the five books of Moses (Genesis, Exodus, Leviticus, Numbers, and Deuteronomy). The *Prophets* included the writings of the various prophets (such as Isaiah, Jeremiah, Ezekiel and Daniel). The third section, the *Writings*, included the historical books (such as Joshua, Judges, Samuel, Kings) and the poetic books (such as Psalms and Proverbs)."

Book of Mormon 121-122 Student Manual, p. 120

3 Ne. 15:8   **THE LAW OF MOSES HATH AN END IN CHRIST**
(2 Ne. 25:23-25; Mosiah 13:27-32; Gal. 3:24; *Mormon Doctrine*, McConkie, pp. 434-436)

Sacrifice *under the Law of Moses was done away with and replaced with* Sacrament *under the Law of Christ*

"The law that was done away with in Christ was the strict ceremonies, observances and offerings peculiar to the law of Moses."

Book of Mormon121-122 Student Manual, p. 120

3 Ne. 15:13;   **THE LAND OF INHERITANCE FOR THE LAMANITES**
16:16;   (refer in this text to 2 Ne. 1:5)
20:14,
22; 21:22   "The Lord gave this land upon which we dwell, America, as an everlasting possess-

ion to Joseph, the son of Jacob. His posterity, when cleansed from sin, and when they come forth in the resurrection, shall inherit this part of the earth. This land shall be theirs forever. The Lord gave this land also to others at an earlier date, the Jaredites, and they, too, who are righteous among them, shall possess it forever."

Joseph Fielding Smith (Doctrines of Salvation, 1:88)

"By it, [the Book of Mormon] we learn that our western tribes of Indians are descendants from that Joseph who was sold into Egypt, and that the land of America is a promised land unto them. . . ."

Teachings of the Prophet Joseph Smith, p. 17

3 Ne. 15:15-24   DID CHRIST TELL THE JEWS ABOUT THE NEPHITES?
(John 7:35; 10:16; *Jesus the Christ*, Talmage, p. 728; *Doctrines of Salvation*, Smith, 3:214)

3 Ne. 16:1-3   CHRIST VISITS OTHER TRIBES OF ISRAEL
(refer in this text to 2 Ne. 29:12-14; 3 Ne. 21:28-29)

"Did not Jesus visit them, [other tribes of Israel] after he ministered among the Nephites? Answer: Of course he did, in one or many places as suited his purposes. He assembled them together then in exactly the same way he gathered the Nephites in the land Bountiful so that they too could hear his voice and feel the prints of the nails in his hands and in his feet. Of this there can be no question. And we suppose that he also called twelve apostles and established his kingdom among them even as he did in Jerusalem and in the Americas. Why should he deal any differently with one branch of Israel than with another?"

Bruce R. McConkie (The Millennial Messiah, pp. 216-217)

3 Ne. 16:8-9   LAMANITES TRODDEN UNDER FEET OF GENTILES
(1 Ne. 22:7, 8; 2 Ne.1:10-11; 26:15, 19; 3 Ne. 20:27-28; Morm. 5:9, 20; *Treasures of the Book of Mormon*, Skousen, pp. 1186-1187; *Book of Mormon Prophecies*, Warner, pp. 121-126; refer in this text to 1 Ne. 13:14-15)

Indian Population

Year	North America	Year	Haiti and Santo Domingo
1492	10,000,000	1492	2-300,000 (estimate)
1900	235,000	1548	500

"The Indians as described by Columbus were 'gentle beings, souls of hospitality, curious and merry, truthful and faithful, walking in beauty and possessors of spiritual religion.'"

John Collier (The Indians of the Americas, pp. 97-98)

[Concerning the invasion of the Gentiles] "The situation was as if a mysterious stranger, announcing himself with words of love, welcomed with delight as a guest, embraced as a friend, given the run of the house and taken into the family's bosom, had suddenly revealed himself as no man at all but a devouring werewolf."

John Collier (The Indians of the Americas, p. 97)

"Unfortunately, these benighted descendants of Lehi had lost the records which we are now reading [Book of Mormon], so they did not know that before their Fair God returned to earth, the Gentiles would come and scatter them to the four winds. They also did not know that after they were conquered it would be another group of Gentiles who would bring them the Gospel and prepare them for the return of the Fair God, Jesus Christ. All the descendants of Lehi were going to have to find out the hard way."

Cleon Skousen (Treasures of the Book of Mormon, 1:1187)

3 Ne. 16: 10-16   GOSPEL REMOVED FROM WICKED GENTILES & THEIR DESTRUCTION
(2 Ne. 27:1-2; 3 Ne. 21; 12; Morm. 5:22-24; *The Mortal Messiah*, McConkie, 4:334-335; *The Millennial Messiah*, McConkie, pp. 242, 248: *Since Cumorah*, Nibley, pp. 420-421; *Companion to Your Study of the Book of Mormon*, Ludlow, pp. 277-278; *Doctrines of Salvation,* Smith, 2:249-250; *History of the Church*, Smith, 2:261; refer in this text to 3 Ne. 20:15-16, 20)

WHAT IS MEANT BY THE TERMS ISRAEL & GENTILE & JEWS?
(Answers to Gospel Questions, Smith, 1:138-141; refer in this text to 3 Ne. 21:5-6)

"Israel meant the literal descendants of Jacob and the twelve sons of Jacob, or house of Israel. The Gentiles, as the word literally means, were 'The other people.' . . . Eventually both of these words were enlarged in their scope to include land designation—the land where the Israelites lived, and the land where the Gentiles lived. Still a third meaning eventually developed, so that 'Israel' designated those who by covenant accept the true religion, and 'Gentiles' meant those who did not."

Robert J. Matthews (Studies in Scripture, ed. by K. Jackson, 8: 168-171)

"After the Kingdom of Israel was destroyed and the Ten Tribes were led away into Assyrian captivity, those of the Kingdom of Judah called themselves Jews and designated all others as Gentiles. It is this concept that would have been taught to Lehi, Mulek and the other Jews who came to the Western Hemisphere to found the great Nephite and Lamanite civilizations. It is not surprising, therefore, to find the Book of Mormon repeatedly speaking of Jew and Gentile as though this phrase marked a division between all men; to find the United States described as a Gentile Nation (1 Ne. 13; 3 Ne. 21); and to find the promise that the Book of Mormon would come forth 'by way of the Gentile' (Title page of Book of Mormon; D&C 20:9)."

Bruce R. McConkie (Mormon Doctrine, p. 311)

"The literal descendants of Abraham (Hebrews) include [among others] the descendants of Jacob (Israelites), [and] Judah, (Jews), [Judah was the fourth born son of Jacob]. . . . The basic meaning of the word *Gentile* is 'foreign,' 'other,' or 'non.' Thus, to a Hebrew, a Gentile is a non-Hebrew; to an Israelite, a Gentile is a non-Israelite; and to a Jew, a Gentile is a non-Jew. In this sense, some Latter-day Saints have referred to those who are not members of the Church as Gentiles, even though the non-members might be Jews! The word *Gentile* might also be used in several different ways to refer to family, religious, political, or even geographical relationships. For example, a person might be considered an Israelite in a family or blood sense, but might be called a Gentile in a political or geographical sense because he lives in a land or nation that is primarily Gentile, or non-Israelitish."

Daniel H. Ludlow (Ensign, Jan. 1991, pp. 51-52)

3 Nephi 17 ~ 19

3 Ne. 17:3

PONDER

(Moro. 10:3; 2 Ne.4:16: 1 Ne.11:1; D&C 138:1; *Conference Report*, Apr. 1980, p. 5)

"To ponder is to meditate, to think, to feast, and to treasure. It is more than a mental method, it is a spiritual striving to obtain and to understand truth. We should follow the process taught by the Savior to the Nephites as he taught them sacred principles. He then instructed them to 'Go ye unto your homes, and ponder upon the things which I have said, and ask of the Father, in my name, that ye may understand, and prepare your minds for the morrow' (3 Ne. 17:3)."

L. Lionel Kendrick (Ensign, May 1993, pp. 14-15)

"When our children were young, . . . we decided to read the Book of Mormon with the goal to complete the book by the end of the school year. Each morning we read a chapter before breakfast, and we reached our goal. While I would not wish to take anything away from the good things that came from that experience for all of us, we reflected in the end that perhaps our focus was more on our goal than on what we were learning in the process. In the early-morning rush hour that ended at the breakfast table, we had little time to share ideas or ponder on the meaning of God's word in our lives. [3 Nephi 17:3]. . . . The Savior has given us a pattern to follow as we study the scriptures We hear the word, we ponder upon its meaning, we ask our Heavenly Father to help us understand, and then our minds and hearts are prepared to receive the promised blessings. Pondering is more than reading words; it is searching for meanings that will help us as we relate to one another and as we make choices in our lives. It is allowing the word to move from our minds to our hearts. The Spirit bears witness to our hearts as we prayerfully seek to know the things of our Heavenly Father. . . . By so doing, we help . . . [our children] keep the eternal perspective always in focus so they never forget who they are and where they are and where they are going."

Anne G. Wirthlin (Ensign, May 1998, p. 10)

3 Ne. 17:4   **THE LOST TRIBES**
(3 Ne.16:1-3; 2 Ne.29:12; *Companion to Your Study of the Book of Mormon*, Ludlow, p. 271; *Signs of the Times*, Smith, p.159)

3 Ne. 17:5-9   **HE DID HEAL THEM EVERY ONE**
(Ensign, Nov. 1992, pp. 60-62)

3 Ne. 17:11-24   **BEHOLD YOUR LITTLE ONES**
(Psalm 127:3; Mark 10:14; Matt. 18:1-6; refer in this text to 3 Ne. 26:14, 16)

"His invitation in verse 11 was neither casual nor inconsequential. 'He *commanded* that their little children should be brought.' And notice what verse 11 *doesn't* say. It doesn't say never mind the little ones because they aren't accountable yet. It doesn't say the children were to be taken elsewhere so they wouldn't disrupt the proceedings. And it doesn't imply that the children won't understand. . . . 'So they brought their little children and set them down upon the ground round about him, and Jesus stood in the midst.' (v. 12). Do any of us ever consider serving children to be beneath us? Clearly the Savior felt that the Nephite children were worthy not only to be in his presence, but they were also worthy of his time and his attention. The children needed *him,* and he stood right in their midst. Verse 12 also indicates that Jesus waited 'till they had *all* been brought to him.' He wasn't looking for a representative sample, and he wasn't content with just some of the children. He wanted them *all* to be there, and he ministered to them *all.* Then Jesus prayed unto the Father so powerfully that 'no tongue can speak, neither can there be written by any man, neither can the hearts of men conceive so great and marvelous thing.' (v. 17). And the children were there! They heard that prayer; they saw that event, and they were affected by it. Children can understand and should witness marvelous events— events like priesthood blessings, special ward and family fasts, the testimonies and prayers of their parents and leaders, and gospel discussions with people they love. 'He took their little children, one by one, and blessed them, and prayed unto the Father for them.' (v. 21). Jesus was ministering to a group of about 2,500 men, women, and children. Consider how much time it must have taken for him to bless and pray over each child, 'one by one.' He must have held many of them in his arms or on his lap. And he wept because he was overcome with joy. 'He spake unto the multitude, and said unto them: Behold your little ones.'

(v. 23). Jesus specifically directed the attention of the multitude to the children. To me, the word *behold* is significant. It implies more than just 'look and see.' When the Lord instructed the Nephites to *behold* their little ones, I believe he told them to give attention to their children, to contemplate them, to look beyond the present and see their eternal possibilities. . . . It's significant to me that later the Savior gave the most sacred teachings only to the children, then loosed their tongues so they could teach the multitude. (See 3 Ne. 26:14). Is it any wonder that following the Savior's visit to the Nephites, they lived in peace and righteousness for two hundred years? Because of miraculous instructions, blessings, and attention they and their children received, righteousness was perpetuated by their children's children for many generations. Let us not underestimate the capacity and potential power of today's children to perpetuate righteousness. No group of people in the Church is as receptive to the truth. . . ."

Michaelene P. Grassli (Ensign, Nov. 1992, pp. 92-94)

"When the Savior invited the multitude to behold their little ones, was He speaking in the collective sense of a group of little children? Or was He drawing their attention, and ours, to the individual nature and importance of each of those little *ones*—each of those little individuals? I believe that by His example the Savior was teaching us of the individual and tender care we should give to each one of our little children—indeed to each of our Heavenly Father's children. It may be the loveable toddler or the wayward teen, the grieving widow. . . . It may even be your own son or daughter or your own husband or wife. . . ."

Wm. Rolfe Kerr (Ensign, Nov. 1996, p. 80)

3 Ne. 17:21-22 **JESUS WEPT**
(Jacob 5:41; D&C 76:26; Moses 7:28-29)

"A choice bishop share[d] with others in a meeting . . . concerning the loss of his wife to cancer. . . . Twenty years earlier he had watched his mother pass through severe suffering before she died, and he had carried with him through the years a sense of resentment for the anguish she had endured. With his wife's ordeal, however, harsh as it was for her . . . his anger sublimated into a closer spiritual relationship with the Lord, and he was able more gracefully to share her burden. Shortly before she died, his wife asked him to give her a blessing for relief from the intense pain. They both wept as he laid his hands on her head and talked with the Lord, 'and,' he said, 'I felt the spiritual presence of our Father in Heaven. I had the strongest sensation that someone else was there weeping with us!' Near the end, severely physically debilitated, she said, 'Never have I been more whole!' The strong sensation that He was there, 'weeping with us.' Of course; why not? Jesus wept at the grave of Lazarus; he wept over Jerusalem's portending afflictions; and he wept when he came to the American continent and knelt with his people, and especially when 'he took their little children, one by one, and blessed them, and prayed unto the Father for them.' (3 Ne. 17:21; see also v. 22; John 11:35; Luke 19:41)."

Marion D. Hanks (Ensign, Nov. 1992, pp. 64-65)

3 Ne. 17:23-25;   ENCIRCLED AS IF BY FIRE
19:13-15   (refer in this text to Hel. 5:20-52)

3 Ne. 18   **SACRAMENT**
(refer in this text to Moro. 4:3; 5:2)

"We eat food to stimulate our physical bodies. Without the partaking of food we would become weak and sickly, and fail physically. It is just as necessary, for our spiritual body, that we should partake of this sacrament and by it obtain spiritual food for our souls. . . We must come, however, to the sacrament table hungry. If we should repair to a banquet where the finest of earth's providing may be had, without hunger, without appetite, the food would not be tempting, nor do us any good. If we repair to the sacrament table, we must come hungering and thirsting for righteousness, for spiritual growth. . . . The method to obtain forgiveness is not through re-baptism; . . . it is to repent of our sins, to go to those against whom we have sinned or transgressed and obtain their forgiveness and then repair to the sacrament table where, if we have sincerely repented and put ourselves in proper condition, we shall be forgiven, and spiritual healing will come to our souls. It will really enter into our being. . . . Comfort and happiness come to the soul that is worthy and truly desirous of partaking of this spiritual food. Why do we not all come? Why do we not come regularly to the sacrament service and partake of these emblems and perform this highest worship we can give to our Father in the name of His Beloved Son? It is because we do not appreciate it. It is because we do not feel the necessity for this blessing, or it is because, perhaps, we feel ourselves unworthy to partake of these emblems."

Melvin J. Ballard, Crusader for Righteousness, pp. 132-133

"The sacrament is so sacred that it is recommended during the sacramental services, that no music be played, nor should there be any distractions whatsoever during the service. It is a time for meditation, a time for resolve, not a time for visiting, nor the chewing of gum, as so many people do, nor permitting our minds to dwell upon other things foreign to the sacred ordinance of the sacrament itself."

Delbert L. Stapley (BYU Speeches of the Year, May 8 1956, p. 5)

"Next, *partake* of the sacrament. Don't merely *take* the sacrament. Think of the covenants you are remaking. Truly witness unto the Father that you will take upon yourself the name of his Son, even Jesus Christ. Recommit yourself to always remember him, to keep the commandments which he has given you. Your obedience will entitle you to have his Spirit to be with you. If this sacred ordinance has become commonplace in your worship, if you let your mind wander elsewhere during this weekly opportunity for spiritual renewal, if you just *take* the bread and water as it passes with no thought or recommitment in your life, then you have turned off a significant aid to your hearing [of the Spirit]."

Graham W. Doxey (Conference Report, Oct. 1991, p. 34)

3 Ne. 18:3 **SACRAMENT (WINE)**
(D&C 27:1-3)

3 Ne. 18:4-5, 9 **AND THEY WERE FILLED**
(3 Ne.12:6; 20:9)

3 Ne. 18:7, 13 **MORE OR LESS THAN THESE**
(Companion to Your Study of the Book of Mormon, Ludlow, p. 272; *Outlines in Ecclesiastical History*, Roberts, pp. 144-149)

3 Ne. 18:15-23 **PRAYER**
(History of the Church 5:31; refer in this text to Mosiah 27:14-16)

"I was in Idaho Falls and was the guest in a home of a typical Church family. There were a dedicated set of parents and many children. The oldest was in military duty in the dreaded South Pacific, and the hearts of the family followed him from place to place. They handed me his latest letter from the war zone. I read this: 'There have been times when we were so scared, we would tremble, but the fear was out of our minds with prayer and the knowledge that we were being guided by the Lord. Dad, I live my religion and I am proud that I had someone like you and mother to teach me to pray. Then I also know that you are praying for me each morning and night. . . .'"

Spencer W. Kimball (Conference Report, Apr. 1973, pp. 152-153)

"Christ taught the Nephites that prayer is more than just a means to receive our Father in Heaven's generosity; rather, prayer itself is an act of faith as well as an act of righteousness. . . . This is because the act of prayer itself can change and purify us, both individually and as a group. As our Bible Dictionary states, 'The object of prayer is not to change the will of God, but to secure for ourselves and for others blessings that God is already willing to grant, but that are made conditional on our asking for them' (p. 753). In other words, prayers bring our desires and the desires of our Father into harmony, thus bringing us both the blessing we are seeking and also the blessing of greater unity with the Father. . . . The greatest blessing and benefit is not the physical or spiritual blessings that may come as answers to our prayers but in the changes to our soul that come as we learn to be dependent on our Heavenly Father for strength. . . . The very act of praying will improve us. . . . Surely, as our creator, He knows our cares, our worries, our joys, our struggles without our informing Him. The reason our Heavenly Father asks us to pray cannot be that we are able to tell Him something He does not already know. Rather, the reason He asks us to pray is that the process of learning to communicate effectively with Him will shape and change our lives . . ."

David E. Sorensen (Ensign, May, 1993, pp. 30-31)

"Do you have prayers in your family? . . . And when you do, do you go through the operation like the [grinding] of a piece of machinery, or do you bow in meekness and with . . . sincere desire to seek the blessing of God upon you and your household? That is the way . . . we ought to do, and cultivate a spirit of devotion and trust in God, dedicating ourselves to him, and seeking his blessings."

John Taylor (Journal of Discourses 21:118)

"Never let a day go by without holding family prayer and family scripture study. Put this, the Lord's program, to the test; and see if it does not bless your home with greater peace, hope, love, and faith. I promise you that daily family prayer and scripture study will build within the walls of your home a security and bonding that will enrich your lives and prepare your families to meet the challenges of today and the eternities to come."

L. Tom Perry (Ensign, May 1993, p. 92)

3 Ne. 18:20   **ASK . . . WHICH IS RIGHT**
(*Heber J. Grant: Highlights in the Life of a Great Leader*, Hinckley, pp. 243-244; refer in this text to Alma 32:21, 32)

"[3 Ne. 18:20]. Here the Savior reminds us that faith, no matter how strong it is, cannot produce a result contrary to the will of him whose power it is. The exercise of faith in the Lord Jesus Christ is always subject to the order of heaven, to the goodness and will and wisdom and timing of the Lord. That is why we cannot have true faith in the Lord without also having complete trust in the Lord's will and in the Lord's timing. When we have that kind of faith and trust in the Lord, we have true security in our lives."

Dallin H. Oaks (Ensign, May 1994, p. 100)

"The praying Christ. That is the example to which we are to point others. . . . The Christ who is one with the Father in at least one way that we may be united with him as well—through prayer. . . . Give your students this promise as Christ gave it to the Nephite multitude—'And whatsoever ye shall ask the Father in my name, which is right, believing that ye shall receive, behold it shall be given unto you' (3 Nephi 18:20). They need to believe that. And they will if you believe it."

Jeffrey R. Holland (CES Symposium, BYU, Aug. 9, 1994, p. 21)

3 Ne. 18:28-29   **PARTAKING OF THE SACRAMENT UNWORTHILY**
(D&C 46:4; *The Articles of Faith*, Talmage, p. 175; *Answers to Gospel Questions*, Smith, 2:88-90; *Doctrines of Salvation*, Smith, 2:343-344)

"The sacrament is a sacred ordinance and should be participated in only when a person is striving sincerely to keep the covenants thereof. However, if a person waits until he is totally free from sin, he will never partake of the sacrament. The sacrament is a source of spiritual power, and compounds the problem of becoming more worthy. However, sins of a serious nature may cause us to lose the privilege of partaking of the sacrament through probation, disfellowshipment, or excommunication. Generally, if a sin is serious enough to warrant not partaking of the sacrament for any length of time, it is probably serious enough to warrant a discussion of that transgression with priesthood leaders."

Book of Mormon 121-122 Student Manual, pp. 121-122

"If any of the members are not in good standing; if they have in their hearts any feeling of hatred, envy, or sin of any kind, they should not partake of these emblems. If there are any differences or feelings existing between brethren, these differences should be adjusted before the guilty parties partake. . . . We should all see that our hearts and hands are clean and pure."

Joseph Fielding Smith (Doctrines of Salvation, 2:343)

OUR PROMISE IN THE SACRAMENT
(Moro. 4:3; *Ensign*, Mar. 1995, pp. 66-67)

"I have wondered how members of the Church can go to the sacrament service and partake of these emblems, and make these solemn covenants, and then immediately after the close of the meeting go out to some place of amusement, to attend a picture show, a baseball game, or some resort, or to gather at some home to play cards. When any of these things is done, the guilty person violates this sacred covenant so recently made or renewed. . . . The fact remains, however, that when we indulge in habits of this kind we are covenant breakers . . . If a man fully realized what it means when he partakes of the sacrament, that he covenants to take upon him the name of Jesus Christ and to always remember him and keep his commandments, and this vow is renewed week by week—do you think such a man will fail to pay his tithing? Do you think such a man will break the Sabbath day or disregard the Word of Wisdom? Do you think he will fail to be prayerful, and that he will not attend his quorum duties and other duties in the Church? It seems to me that such a thing as a violation of these sacred principles and duties is impossible when a man knows what it means to make such vows week by week unto the Lord and before the saints."

Joseph Fielding Smith (Doctrines of Salvation, 2:345-346)

THE LORD'S PROMISE IN THE SACRAMENT
(Moro. 4:3)

"All of us face different family circumstances and home situations. All of us need strength in dealing with them. This strength comes from faith in the Savior's love and in the power of his atonement. If we trustingly put our hand in the Savior's, we can claim the promise of the sacramental prayer to always have his Spirit with us. All problems are manageable with that strength, and all other problems are secondary in urgency to maintaining a strong spiritual life."

Chieko N. Okazaki (Ensign, Nov. 1993, p. 94)

"Do we always stop to think, on that sacred Sabbath day when we meet together to partake of the sacrament, that we witness, promise, obligate ourselves, in the presence of one another, and in the presence of God, that we will do certain things? . . . The first: We are willing to take upon ourselves the name of the Son. In so doing we choose him as our leader and our ideal: and he is the one perfect character in all the world. Second: That we will always remember him. Not just on Sunday, but on Monday, in our daily acts, in our self-control. When our brother hurts us, we are going to try to master our feelings and not retaliate in the same spirit of anger. . . . That's the spirit of the Christ, and that's what we have promised—that we will do our best to achieve these high standards of Christianity, true Christian principles. The third: We promise to '. . . keep his commandments which he has given . . .' —tithing, fast offerings, the Word of Wisdom, kindness, forgiveness, love. The obligation of a member of the Church of Jesus Christ is great, but it is as glorious as it is great, because obedience to these principles gives life, eternal life."

David O. McKay (Gospel Ideals, p. 146)

3 Ne. 18:36   **HE TOUCHED THEM**
(3 Ne. 28:12; Moro. 2)

3 Ne. 19:10-13   **WHY REBAPTIZED?**
(3 Ne.11:21; *Answers to Gospel Questions*, Smith, 3:205-206; 4:95-97)

"When Christ appeared to the Nephites on this continent, he commanded them to be baptized, although they had been baptized previously for the remission of their sins. . . . We read that the Savior commanded Nephi and the people to be baptized again, because he had organized anew the Church under the gospel. Before that it had been organized under the law."

Joseph Fielding Smith (Doctrines of Salvation 2:336)

3 Ne. 19:23, 29 **HOW CHRIST & THE FATHER ARE ONE**
(Matt. 3:17; 17:5; Luke 22:42; 23:34, 46; Mark 15:34; John 12:28; Acts 7:55-56)

"The Father and the Son are the two personages of the Deity, with the Holy Ghost as their ministering Spirit or agent. . . . While they are two Personages, they are but one—one in feeling, one in thought, one in mind, one in everything, in fact, in every direction in which their power is or can be exercised."

George Q. Cannon (Gospel Truths, p. 161)

3 Ne. 19:24   **GIVEN TO THEM WHAT THEY SHOULD PRAY**
(D&C 50:30; Romans 8:26; *Mormon Doctrine,* McConkie, p.586)

3 Ne. 19:25, 30 **HIS COUNTENANCE DID SHINE UPON THEM**
(3 Ne. 28:15; Moses 1:1, 5, 11, 14; D&C 76:118)

3 Ne. 19:32   **TONGUE CANNOT SPEAK . . . NEITHER CAN BE WRITTEN**
(3 Ne.17:16-17; 28:13-14)

[An experience similar to the one in 3 Nephi 19 was described by Elder Bruce R. McConkie. He, with the other Apostles, had been with President Spencer W. Kimball when the great revelation on the priesthood being made available to all worthy men was given.]

"On the first day of June in this year, 1978, the First Presidency and the Twelve, after full discussion of the proposition and all the premises and principles that are involved, importuned the Lord for a revelation. President Kimball was mouth, and he prayed with great faith and great fervor; this was one of those occasions when an inspired prayer was offered. . . . He prayed by the power of the Spirit, and there was perfect unity, and complete harmony, between the Presidency and the Twelve on the issue involved. . . . The Lord in his providences poured out the Holy Ghost upon the First Presidency and the Twelve in a miraculous and marvelous manner, beyond anything that any then present had ever experienced. The revelation came to the President of the Church; it also came to each individual present. . . . The result was that President Kimball knew, and each one of us knew, independent of any other person, by direct and personal revelation to us, that the time had now come to extend the gospel and all its blessings and all its obligations, including the priesthood and the blessings of the house of the Lord, to those of every nation, culture, and race, including the black race. There was no question whatsoever as to the word and message that came. . . . There is no way to describe in language what is involved. This cannot be done. You are familiar with Book of Mormon references where the account says that no tongue could tell and no pen would write what was involved in the experience and that it had to be felt by the power of the Spirit. This was one of those occasions. . . . I cannot describe in words what happened; I can only say that it happened and that it can be known and understood only by the feeling that can come into the heart of man."

Bruce R. McConkie (A Symposium on the Book of Mormon, 1979, pp. 4-5)

3 Ne. 20:13,
29-33

GATHERING OF ISRAEL
(1 Ne. 10:14; 19:15-17; 2 Ne. 9:2; 25:16-17; 30:7; 3 Ne. 5:26; 16:4-5; *Mormon Doctrine,* McConkie, pp. 722-723; *Journal of Discourses* 18:166; *Millennial Messiah,* p. 229; *Doctrines of Salvation,* Smith, 3:9; *Conference Report,* Oct. 1918, pp. 45-47; *Conference Report,* Apr. 1927, pp. 36-37; refer in this text to 2 Ne. 6:10-11; 2 Ne. 25:16-17)

3 Ne. 20:29 was spoken by the Savior in 34 A.D.; the Book of Mormon was published in 1830; the modern state of Israel was established in 1948.

"Until June 5, 1967, the dominant theme of Jewish theology was the same as it had been for the last 1,897 years—wandering and exile. Since June 5, 1967, the dominant theme has been HOMECOMING." [June 5 was the date when the war broke out between Israel and the Arab states.]

Rabbi Richard L. Rubenstein (as quoted in the Church News, Mar. 9, 1968)

"This latter-day gathering, Christ testified, would be first spiritual and then temporal. Israel, he said, must return first to their covenants and then to their covenant lands."

Joseph McConkie (Studies in Scripture, ed. by K. Jackson, 8:184)

3 Ne. 20:15-20,
22

REMNANT OF JACOB & THE DESTRUCTION OF THE GENTILE NATIONS
(3 Ne. 21:12-21; JST Matt. 21:47-56; refer in this text to 3 Ne.16:10-16)

"When the Lord is speaking of his covenants, he is not confining them to the descendants of Lehi, but applies them to all the house of Israel. . . . [3 Ne. 20:15-16.]

Are we justified in applying this merely to the Lamanites and saying that they are to go forth as a young lion pouring out vengeance upon the gentiles? Also does the phrase, 'Ye who are a remnant of the house of Jacob,' in verse 16, have reference just to the Lamanites? The verses which follow indicate that it has reference to the remnants of Israel, which had been scattered in all lands. To apply it to the Lamanites in face of the entire theme of this discourse, in my judgment, narrows it too greatly. Then again, this prophecy was also given to Micah and has reference to 'many people,' not merely to the gentiles on this land."

Joseph Fielding Smith (Doctrines of Salvation, 2:249-250)

"If the gentiles on this land reject the word of God and conspire to overthrow liberty and the Constitution, then their doom is fixed, and they 'shall be cut off from among my people who are of the covenant.' (1 Nephi 14:6; 3 Nephi 21:11; 14,21; D&C 84:114-115, 117)."

Ezra Taft Benson (God - Family - Country, p. 345)

3 Ne. 20:27-28   GENTILES SCOURGE LAMANITES
(Refer in this text to 3 Ne. 16:8-9)

3 Ne. 20:27-28   MIGHTY ABOVE ALL
(1 Ne. 2:20; 2 Ne. 1:5; Ether 1:42-43; 2:7)

"But in 1830, they were still calling the United States 'that great and foolish American experiment.' Europe didn't even give us the status of a nation. . . . Chicago was known as little Ft. Dearborn, way out on the western frontier, with sixty-five inhabitants, most of them military men who slept with their rifles within reach for fear the savage Indians would scalp them in their sleep. We had only three miles of steam railway. We were so poor as a nation that the president and his cabinet had to borrow on their personal finances to pay the cost of government in the year of 1830. . . . [It was not until] 1917 before we stepped into first place as [the wealthiest] nation of the earth. The statement that this was 'a land and choice above all other lands' sounded fantastic in 1830. Today we know it is absolutely true."

Jack West (as quoted in Book of Mormon Prophecies, Warner, pp.87-88)

3 Ne. 20:32-45   OFTEN QUOTED ISAIAH 52
(Rev. 18:4; 2 Cor. 6:17; 1 Ne. 22:10-11; 2 Ne. 8:24-25; Mosiah 12:21-24; 15:29-31; Moro. 10:31; 3 Ne. 16, 21; D&C 38:42; 82:14; 84:98-99)

3 Ne. 21:3-5   **THE DESTINY OF AMERICA - THE GENTILES TO SPREAD THE WORD**
(1 Ne. 22:7-8; 26:8; Morm. 5:15, 19-20; Ether 12:22; *Companion to Your Study of the Book of Mormon*, Ludlow, pp. 280-281; Title Page of the Book of Mormon; *A Marvelous Work and a Wonder*, Richards, p. 179; refer in this text to 1 Ne. 13:34-38)

"And one of the most important of all the requirements of the Church is that they should establish the Lord's word among the Lamanites."

Spencer W. Kimball (BYU Speeches of the Year, Apr. 1965, p. 7)

"That is the reason there is an America. That is the destiny of America. . . . Old Glory was raised up because there was to be a restoration of the gospel."

Mark E. Petersen (BYU Speeches of the Year, 1968)

"This nation will endure. It may cost blood, but it is God-ordained for a glorious purpose. We must never forget that the gospel message we bear to the world is to go forth to the world from this nation, and that gospel message can prosper only in an atmosphere of freedom. We must maintain and strengthen our freedom in this blessed land."

Ezra Taft Benson (This Nation Shall Endure)

"The establishment of this great Christian nation with a spiritual foundation was all in preparation for the restoration of the gospel following the long night of apostasy. . . .

This then becomes the Lord's base of operations in these latter days. And this base will not be shifted out of its place—the land of America. This nation will, in a measure at least, fulfill its mission even though it may face serious and troublesome days. The degree to which it achieves its full mission depends upon the righteousness of its people."

Ezra Taft Benson (A Nation Asleep, pp. 8,10)

"There is not another nation under heaven but this, in whose midst the Book of Mormon could have been brought forth. The Lord has been operating for centuries to prepare the way for the coming forth of the contents of that Book from the bowels of the earth. . . . It was the Lord who directed the discovery of this land to the nations of the Old World and its settlement, and the war for independence, and the final victory of the colonies, and the unprecedented prosperity of the American nation, up to the calling of Joseph the Prophet. The

Lord has dictated and directed the whole of this, for the bringing forth and establishing of His kingdom in the last days."

Brigham Young (Journal of Discourses 11:17)

3 Ne. 21:5-6   THE GENTILES NUMBERED AMONG ISRAEL
(3 Ne. 30:2; Abr. 2:10; D&C 86:8-10; *Mormon Doctrine*, McConkie, p. 23; *Teachings of the Prophet Joseph Smith*, pp. 149-150; Mormon 5:19; *Ensign*, Jan. 1991, pp. 51-55; *Answers to Gospel Questions*, Smith, 3:63; *Improvement Era*, Oct. 1923, p. 1149; *Journal of Discourses* 2:269)

"Every person who embraces the gospel becomes of the house of Israel. In other words, they become members of the chosen lineage, or Abraham's children through Isaac and Jacob unto whom the promises were made. The great majority of those who become members of the Church are literal descendants of Abraham through Ephraim, son of Joseph. Those who are not literal descendants of Abraham and Israel must become such, and when they are baptized and confirmed they are grafted into the tree and are entitled to all the rights and privileges as heirs."

Joseph Fielding Smith (Doctrines of Salvation, 3:246)

3 Ne. 21:10   THE LIFE OF MY SERVANT
(3 Ne. 20:43-44; *Studies in Scripture*, Jackson, 8:191)

3 Ne. 21:22-24   WHO SHALL BUILD NEW JERUSALEM?
(3 Ne.20:14, 22; *Doctrines of Salvation*, Smith, 2:247-248, 250-251; *Companion to Your Study of the Book of Mormon*, Ludlow, p. 282; *History of the Church*, Smith, 2:261-262; refer in this text to Ether 13:2-11; *Teachings of the Prophet Joseph Smith*, p. 17)

"The Latter-day Saints in these [Rocky] mountains never can have the privilege of going back to Jackson County and building that city which is to be called the New Jerusalem, until quite a large portion of the remnants of Joseph [Lamanites] go back with us. Now then, here is a work for us, and we have no need to pray to the Father to return us to Jackson County until the work is done."

Orson Pratt (as quoted by Paul E. Felt, The Book of Mormon, the Lamanite, and His Prophetic Destiny, pp. 32-33)

"How I wish you could go with me through the Indian reservations and particularly Navajo lands and see the poverty, want, and wretchedness, and realize again that these are sons and daughters of God; that their miserable state is the result, not only of their centuries of wars and sins and godlessness, but is also attributable to us, their conquerors, who placed them on reservations with such limited resources and facilities, to starve and die of malnutrition and unsanitary conditions, while we become fat in the prosperity from the assets we took from them. Think of these things, my people, and then weep for the Indian, and with your tears, pray; then work for him. Only through us, the 'nursing fathers and mothers,' may they eventually enjoy a fulfillment of the many promises made to them. . . . They shall prosper in the land and will, with our help, build up a holy city, even the New Jerusalem, unto their God. Only in our doing all in our power to restore these people to their heritage, can we even approach a justification for having taken their promised land."

Teachings of Spencer W. Kimball, pp. 605-606

3 Ne. 21:24   **GATHERING TO NEW JERUSALEM**
(D&C 45:66-71; *Doctrines of Salvation*, Smith, 3:68-69)

"The Zion of God, or the place where the city of the New Jerusalem shall be built, which shall be the first of the cities of Zion, shall, therefore, be established in Jackson County, Missouri."

Alvin R. Dyer (BYU Speeches of the Year, Feb. 7, 1967, p. 7)

"What then is the power of the Book of Mormon? It will build the New Jerusalem; it will prepare a people for the Second Coming; it will usher in the Millennium—at least it will play such an important part in all of these that its value and power can be scarcely overstated."

Bruce R. McConkie (The Millennial Messiah, p. 171)

3 Ne. 21:28-29   **ISRAEL GATHERED FROM ALL NATIONS**
(1 Ne. 22:3-4; 19:16; 3 Ne. 5:23-24; D&C 110:11; 133:26-32; Deut. 4:27; 28:29; Jer. 16:14-15; 31:8; Ezek. 11:15-17; Hosea 9:16-17; Dan. 9:7; *History of the Church*, Smith, 1:176; Old Testament 302 Student Manual, p. 115; refer in this text to 2 Ne. 29:12-14; 2 Ne. 25:16-17)

"Through this scattering the Lord has caused Israel to mix with the nations and bring the Gentiles within the blessings of the seed of Abraham. We are preaching the gospel now in all parts of the world, and for what purpose? To gather out from the Gentile nations the lost sheep of the house of Israel. It is by this scattering that the Gentile nations have been blessed, and if they will truly repent they are entitled to all the blessings promised to Israel. . . ."

Joseph Fielding Smith (Answers to Gospel Questions, 2:57)

"But, says one, are they [the lost tribes of Israel] not in a body somewhere in the land of the north? Answer: They are not; they are scattered in all nations. The north countries of their habitation are all the countries north of their Palestinian home, north of Assyria from whence they escaped. . . . Query: What happened to the Ten Tribes after the visit of the Savior to them . . . ? Answer: The same thing that happened to the Nephites. There was righteousness for a season, and then there was apostasy and wickedness. . . . In this day when the head of the Church can communicate with all men on earth, there is no longer any need for one kingdom in Jerusalem and another in Bountiful and others in whatever place or places the Ten Tribes were when Jesus visited them. This is the promised day when there shall be one God, one Shepherd, one prophet, one gospel, one church, and one kingdom for all the earth. This is the day when one man shall direct all of the Lord's work in all the earth; the day when he shall bring all Israel into one fold. . . ."

Bruce R. McConkie (The Millennial Messiah, pp. 216-217)

3 Ne. 22:1
AND THEN SHALL THAT WHICH IS WRITTEN COME TO PASS
(Isa. 54)

"The fulfillment of this beautiful poem—Isaiah 54 is all poetry—is to be found in this dispensation. Part of it has probably already been fulfilled since the restoration of the gospel; the remainder will be in a time yet future."

Sidney Sperry (Book of Mormon Compendium, p. 412)

3 Ne. 22:2
LENGTHEN THY CORDS
(Isa. 54:1-2; D&C 101:21; 109:59; 133:9; *Teachings of Spencer W. Kimball,* p.175)

"The tent . . . represents the gospel of Christ. He states that in the last days the cords of the tent would be stretched across the earth and stakes would be planted in every land. We literally are seeing that fulfilled today."

Merrill J. Bateman (Ensign, May 1994, p. 65)

3 Ne. 22:7, 10, 13
GREAT SHALL BE THE PEACE OF THY CHILDREN
(D&C 45:58; refer in this text to Enos 1:1-3)

[Sister Wirthlin quoted 3 Ne. 22:7,10,13, and then said] "These words of the Savior are the theme for Primary . . . to teach children the gospel of Jesus Christ and help them learn to live it. As we witness the unfolding events of the last days, we cannot doubt that in this scripture the Lord is speaking directly to us. We are Israel of the latter days. . . . Peace that endures is not dependent upon outside forces that are beyond our control. . . . The Lord's words . . . give comfort to righteous parents who teach their children of Him. They speak to us at a time when peace in the hearts of children can seem but an elusive dream. But the Savior has assured us that it can be a reality if we teach our children. Primary supports parents in this important responsibility."

Anne G. Wirthlin (Ensign, May 1998, p. 9)

3 Ne. 22:8 **WRATH**
(Isa. 54:8)

"A distinction should be made between the appropriate anger of God, which is a righteous application of the law of justice, and the unbridled anger of a fallible mortal. The Lord had consistently counseled his children against anger (Matt. 5:21-22; 3 Ne. 11:21-22); furthermore, we have been instructed that the devil 'is the father of contention . . .' (3 Ne. 11:29). One who is angry loses the Spirit and his love of his fellowman (Moroni 9:3-5). In contrast, properly understood, God's anger is a divine display of his love. It is a manifestation to truth (see 2 Ne. 1:24-27)."

Hoyt W. Brewster, Jr. (Isaiah Plain and Simple, p. 266)

3 Ne. 22:11 **LAY THE FOUNDATIONS WITH SAPPHIRES**
(Isa. 54:11)

"In the midst of a troubling world, the foundations I rely on come by my covenants with the Lord. They are indeed like sapphires and are treasures beyond price. . . . They are the restored principles and ordinances of the gospel of Jesus Christ which are available to righteous women and men alike through the power of the holy priesthood of God. They include baptism, the gift of the Holy Ghost, the sacrament, and temple covenants."

Aileen H. Clyde (Ensign, May 1995, p. 28)

3 Ne. 22:13 **GREAT SHALL BE THE PEACE OF THY CHILDREN**
(Isa. 54:13; D&C 45:58)

"Surely every good parent would like this peace for his offspring. It comes from the simple life of the true Latter-day Saint as he makes his home and family supreme."

Spencer W. Kimball (Ensign, July 1973, p. 16)

3 Ne. 22:17   **NO WEAPON FORMED AGAINST THEE SHALL PROSPER**
(1 Ne. 14:3; D&C 71:7-10; 109:24-25; refer in this text to 1 Ne. 22:16-17; Hel. 5:20-52)

"He [Ezra Taft Benson] always kept this verse from the Book of Mormon in his wallet: [3 Ne. 22:17]. And always this statement was kept on his desk or in his study: 'Be right, and then be easy to live with, if possible, but in that order.'"

Boyd K. Packer (remarks made at the funeral of Pres. Benson, Ensign, July 1994, p. 32)

"Now, I think we all understand that this great latter-day kingdom has been set up for the last time, never again to be destroyed, and that never again will the necessity arise for another and future restoration. . . . But there is one great thing about this dispensation which differs from all the dispensations of the past. It is that this time, with the opening of the heavens and the revealing of the gospel in our day, there came the positive, unqualified assurance that the gospel was to remain on earth; that the kingdom was to be secure; that the Church of Jesus Christ of Latter-day Saints was to remain among men to prepare a people for the second coming of the Son of man."

Bruce R. McConkie (Conference Report, Oct. 1958, pp. 114-115)

[A portion of the dedicatory prayer of the Kirtland Temple] "We ask thee, Holy Father, to establish the people that shall worship, and honorably hold a name and standing in this thy house, to all generations and for eternity; That no weapon formed against them shall prosper; that he who diggeth a pit for them shall fall into the same himself."

Joseph Smith (as quoted in Isaiah Plain and Simple, Brewster, p. 271)

"No unhallowed hand can stop the work from progressing; persecutions may rage, mobs may combine, armies may assemble, calumny may defame, but the truth of God will go forth boldly, nobly, and independent, till it has penetrated every clime, swept every country, and sounded in every ear, till the purposes of God shall be accomplished, and the Great Jehovah shall say the work is done."

Joseph Smith (History of the Church, 4:540)

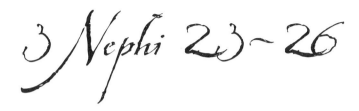

3 Ne. 23:1   **GREAT ARE THE WORDS OF ISAIAH**
(3 Ne.16:17-20; 20:11-12; Morm. 8:23)

3 Ne. 23:11   **HOW BE IT THAT YE HAVE NOT WRITTEN?**
(Moses 6:5; D&C 76:28; *Conference Report*, Oct. 1979, p. 6)

"Your own private journal should record the way you face up to challenges that
beset you. Do not suppose life changes so much that your experiences will not be
interesting to your posterity. . . . Your journal should contain your true self rather
than a picture of you when you are 'made up' for a public performance. There is
a temptation to paint one's virtues in rich color and whitewash the vices, but
there is also the opposite pitfall of accentuating the negative. Personally I have little respect for anyone who delves into the ugly phases of the life he is portraying,
whether it be his own or another's. The truth should be told, but we should not
emphasize the negative. Even a long life full of inspiring experiences can be
brought to the dust by one ugly story. . . . What could you do better for your
children and your children's children than to record the story of your life, your
triumphs over adversity, your recovery after a fall, your progress when all seemed
black, your rejoicing when you had finally achieved? . . . Get a notebook, my
young folks, a journal that will last through all time, and maybe the angels may
quote from it for eternity. Begin today and write in it your goings and comings,
your deepest thoughts, your achievements and your failures, your associations
and your triumphs, your impressions and your testimonies. Remember, the
Savior chastised those who failed to record important events."

Teachings of Spencer W. Kimball, pp. 350-351

3 Ne. 24:3   **SONS OF LEVI**
(D&C 84:31; 128:24; *Studies in Scripture*, Jackson, 8:199-200; *History of the*

Church 1:357-359; *Messenger and Advocate* 1:14-16; *The Mortal Messiah*, McConkie, 1:128; *Doctrinal Commentary on the Book of Mormon*, Millet & McConkie, 3:249-250)

"It should be remembered that the great temple, which is yet to be built in the City Zion, will not be one edifice, but twelve. Some of these temples will be for the lesser priesthood. When these temples are built, it is very likely that provision will be made for some ceremonies and ordinances which may be performed by the Aaronic Priesthood and a place provided where the sons of Levi may offer their offering in righteousness. This will have to be the case because all things are to be restored. . . . The sacrifice of animals will be done to complete the restoration when the temple spoken of is built; at the beginning of the millennium, or in the restoration, blood sacrifices will be performed long enough to complete the fulness of the restoration in this dispensation. Afterwards sacrifice will be of some other character."

Joseph Fielding Smith (Doctrines of Salvation, 3:93-94)

"These sacrifices, as well as every ordinance belonging to the Priesthood, will, when the Temple of the Lord shall be built, and the sons of Levi be purified, be fully restored and attended to in all their powers, ramifications, and blessings . . . . Else how can the restitution of all things spoken of by the Holy Prophets be brought to pass. It is not to be understood that the law of Moses will be established again with all its rites and variety of ceremonies; this has never been spoken of by the prophets; but those things which existed prior to Moses' day, namely, sacrifice, will be continued. It may be asked by some, what necessity for sacrifice, since the Great Sacrifice was offered? In answer to which, if repentance, baptism, and faith existed prior to the days of Christ, what necessity for them since that time?"

Teachings of the Prophet Joseph Smith, p. 173

"We have asked the members of the Church to further the work of turning the hearts of the children to the fathers by getting their sacred family records in order. These records, including especially the 'book containing the records of our dead' (D&C 128:24), are a portion of the 'offering in righteousness' referred to by Malachi (3:3), which we are to present in His holy temple, and without which we shall not abide the day of His coming."

Teachings of Spencer W. Kimball, pp. 542-543

3 Ne. 24:5   **OPPRESS THE HIRELING IN HIS WAGES**
(refer in this text to 2 Ne. 15:8)

3 Ne. 24:8-12   **TITHING**
(Mal. 3:10-12; D&C 119:4; Gen. 14:20; 28:22; Lev. 27:30-34; *Improvement Era*, June 1928, pp. 633-645; *Ensign*, May 1995, p. 40; *Improvement Era*, Apr. 1968, p. 38; *Improvement Era*, Nov. 1948, p. 757)

"By this principle the loyalty of the people of this Church shall be put to the test. By this principle it shall be known who is for the kingdom of God and who is against it. By this principle it shall be seen whose hearts are set on doing the will of God and keeping His commandments, thereby sanctifying the land of Zion unto God, and who are opposed to this principle and have cut themselves off from the blessings of Zion. There is a great deal of importance connected with this principle, for by it it shall be known whether we are faithful or unfaithful. In this respect it is as essential as faith in God, as repentance of sin, as baptism for the remission of sin, or as the laying on of hands for the gift of the Holy Ghost."

Joseph F. Smith (Conference Report, Apr. 1900, p. 47)

[Speaking of the question 'will a man rob God?'] "I picture . . . in my mind . . . a masked burglar, sneaking about under the cover of darkness, taking that which was not his. To represent the theory of embezzlement I thought of a non-tithe payer. The Lord's share came into his hands lawfully, but he misappropriated it to his own use. This seems to be the accusation. . . ."

Howard W. Hunter (Conference Report, Apr. 1964, p. 34)

"Tithing is not a donation. It is not optional for members. It is a commandment from God, with great blessings and promises given to those who obey. The Lord's promises to those who faithfully comply with this commandment are that spiritual and temporal blessing will be poured out on them; bounteous harvest (that is, hunger will not stalk the door of that home); and a blessing to an entire nation.

Teachings of Ezra Taft Benson, pp. 470-474

"Tithing is a commandment with a promise. . . . The promised blessings are temporal and spiritual. . . . (3 Ne. 24:10-12; Mal. 3:10-12). I believe these are promises to the nations in which we reside. When the people of God withheld their tithes and offerings, Malachi condemned 'this whole nation' (Mal. 3:9). Similarly, I believe that when many citizens of a nation are faithful in the payment of tithes, they summon the blessings of heaven upon their entire nation. The Bible teaches that 'righteousness exalteth a nation' (Prov. 14:34), and 'a little leaven leaveneth the whole lump' (Gal. 5:9; see Matt. 13:33). The payment of tithing also brings the individual tithe payer unique spiritual blessings. Tithe paying is evidence that we accept the law of sacrifice. It also prepares us for the law of consecration and the other higher laws of the celestial kingdom."

Dallin H. Oaks (Ensign, May 1994, p. 34)

"The Lord has promised that he will rebuke the devourer for our sakes. . . . May not that rebuke of the devourer apply to various of our personal efforts and concerns? There is the great blessing of wisdom, of knowledge, even hidden treasures of knowledge. We are promised that ours shall be a delightsome *land* if we will walk in obedience to this law. I can interpret the word land as people, that those who walk in obedience shall be a delightsome people. What a marvelous condition to be a delightsome people whom others would describe as blessed!"

Gordon B. Hinckley (Ensign, May 1982, p. 40)

"The promise following obedience to . . . [tithing] is that the windows of heaven would be open and blessings would be poured out that we would hardly be able to contain. The opening of the windows of heaven, of course, means revelations from God to him who is willing thus to sacrifice."

Harold B. Lee (Ensign, Nov. 1971, p. 16)

"God has commanded the Latter-day Saints to keep His commandments. Ever since I can remember we have had preached unto us what our duties and obligations are. Well do I remember, when a boy, hearing President Brigham Young, in the conferences that were held in the old bowery, teach the Latter-day Saints their duties and obligations. I say as Nephi of old said, that God has required nothing at our hands save He will prepare a way whereby we can accomplish it. What does God require at our hands? He requires that we shall overcome our selfishness; that we shall be honest in our dealings with Him, and that we shall pay an honest tithing."

Heber J. Grant (Conference Report, Oct. 1900, p. 34)

"Only a small percentage of the Church members worldwide are tithe payers today. For many who live in conditions of material poverty, there may be no other way to escape their impoverishment than to give obedience to this law. As I visit among the stakes of the Church, I find it is not uncommon to discover that fewer than 50 percent of the households are contributing to the fast offerings of the Church, and the trends are not improving."

Dean L. Larsen (Ensign Nov. 1992, p. 42)

"My mother was a widow, with a large family to provide for. One spring when we opened our potato pits she had her boys get a load of the best potatoes, and she took them to the tithing office; potatoes were scarce that season. . . . When we drove up to the steps of the tithing office, ready to unload the potatoes, one of the clerks came out and said to my mother, 'Widow Smith, it's a shame that you should have to pay tithing.' . . . He chided my mother for paying her tithing, called her anything but wise or prudent. . . . My mother turned upon him and said: 'William, you ought to be ashamed of yourself. Would you deny me a blessing? If I did not pay my tithing, I should expect the Lord to withhold His blessings from me. I pay my tithing, not only because it is a law of God, but because I expect a blessing by doing it. By keeping this and other laws, I expect to prosper and to be able to provide for my family.'"

Joseph F. Smith (Conference Report, Apr. 1900, p. 48)

"During World War II, my widowed mother supported her three young children on a schoolteacher's salary that was meager. When I became conscious that we went without some desirable things because we didn't have enough money, I asked my mother why she paid so much of her salary as tithing. I have never forgotten her explanation: 'Dallin, there might be some people who can get along without paying tithing, but we can't. The Lord has chosen to take your father and leave me to raise you children. I cannot do that without the blessings of the Lord, and I obtain those blessings by paying an honest tithing. When I pay my tithing, I have the Lord's promise that he will bless us, and we must have those blessings if we are to get along."

Dallin H. Oaks (Ensign, May 1994, p. 33)

"I bear witness—and I know that the witness I bear is true—that the men and the women who have been absolutely honest with God, who have paid their tithing. . . . God has given them wisdom whereby they have been able to utilize the remaining nine-tenths, and it has been of greater value to them, and they have accomplished more with it than they would if they had not been honest with the Lord."

Heber J. Grant (Conference Report, Apr. 1912, p. 30)

"During the Great Depression, . . . some of our bishops observed that members who paid their tithing were able to support their families more effectively than those who did not. The tithe payers tended to keep their employment, enjoy good health, and be free from the most devastating effects of economic and spiritual depression (see *Church News*, Dec. 1961, p. 16). Countless tithe-paying Latter-day Saints can testify to similar blessings today. . . . Some people say, 'I can't afford to pay tithing.' Those who place their faith in the Lord's promises say, 'I can't afford not to pay tithing.'"

Dallin H. Oaks (Ensign, May 1994, pp. 33-34)

3 Ne. 24:16   **BOOK OF REMEMBRANCE**
(D&C 88:2)

"We receive the gospel, not that we may have our names written in the Lamb's book of life, but that our names may not be blotted out of that book. 'For,' saith the Lord, 'He that overcometh, the same shall be clothed in white raiment, and I will not blot out his name out of the book of life.' Why? Because he had overcome through his faithfulness. My doctrine is—that there never was a son and daughter of Adam and Eve born on this earth whose names were not already written in the Lamb's book of life, and there they will remain until their conduct is such that the angel who keeps the record is authorized to blot them out and record them elsewhere."

Brigham Young (Journal of Discourses 12:101)

3 Ne. 25:5-6   **ELIJAH**
(3 Ne. 24:1; D&C 110:13-16; 138:47-48; Mal. 4:6; *Teachings of the Prophet Joseph Smith*, p. 172; *Doctrines of Salvation*, Smith, 3:129-130; *Studies in Scripture*, Jackson, 8:202-203; *Answers to Gospel Questions*, Smith, 5:130)

"Some members of the Church have been confused in thinking that Elijah came with the keys of baptism for the dead or of salvation for the dead. Elijah's keys were greater than that. They were the keys of sealing, and those keys of sealing pertain to the living and embrace the dead who are willing to repent."

Joseph Fielding Smith (Doctrines of Salvation, p. 130)

"Now, the word *turn* here should be translated *bind*, or seal."

Teachings of the Prophet Joseph Smith, p. 330

"Now keep in mind this: that when the full measure of Elijah's mission is understood, that the hearts of the children will be turned to the fathers and the fathers to the children. It applies just as much on this side of the veil as it does on the other side of the veil. If we neglect our families here in having home night and we fail in our responsibility here, how could we feel we are doing our full duty in turning the hearts of our children to their fathers? . . . So, the hearts of you fathers and mothers must be turned to your children right now, if you have the true spirit of Elijah, and not think it applies merely to those who are beyond the veil. Let your hearts be turned to your children, and teach your children; but you must do it when they are young enough to be properly schooled. If you are neglecting your family home evening, you are neglecting the beginning of the mission of Elijah just as certainly as if you were neglecting your genealogy research work."

Harold B. Lee (1973 Annual Priesthood Genealogical Research Seminar)

"This sealing power bestowed upon Elijah, is the power which binds husbands and wives, and children to parents for time and eternity. It is the binding power existing in every Gospel ordinance. . . . It was the mission of Elijah to come, and restore it so that the curse of confusion and disorder would not exist in the kingdom of God."

Joseph Fielding Smith (Elijah the Prophet and His Mission, p. 5)

"Men, women, and children . . . honor and respect the divine roles of both fathers and mothers in the home. . . . In this way, the great sealing keys restored by Elijah, spoken of by Malachi, might operate 'to turn the hearts of the fathers to the children, and the children to the fathers, lest the whole earth be smitten with a curse' (Mal. 4:6). . . . Perhaps we regard the power bestowed by Elijah as something associated only with formal ordinances performed in sacred places. But these ordinances become dynamic and productive of good only as they reveal themselves in our daily lives. Malachi said that the power of Elijah would turn the *hearts* of the fathers and the children to each other. The heart is the seat of the emotions and a conduit for revelation. This sealing power thus reveals itself in family relationships, in attributes and virtues developed in a nurturing environment, and in loving service. These are the cords that bind families together, and the priesthood advances their development."

James E. Faust (Ensign, May 1993, p. 37)

3 Ne. 26:9-10   **THE LESSER PORTION OF THE WORD**
(Book of Mormon 121-122 Student Manual, p. 126; Ether 4:4-6; refer in this text to 2 Ne. 27:6-7, 11)

"There is another truth regarding the relationship of doing (being obedient or keeping the commandments) and knowing (having the truth of the gospel made known to us through our application of it). This additional truth concerns the Lord's practice of testing our hearts and minds relative to our new knowledge. He does this so that through our overcoming a trial, we will, in a sense, have the truth of the gospel indelibly stamped upon our souls. Our understanding and our heart become further purified, almost as gold—and our inner surety after having our trials will be rich. For example, the Lord instructs Mormon to not put certain information on the plates that we were to receive in the last days because it 'is expedient . . . to try their faith, and if it so be that they shall believe these things then shall the greater things be made manifest unto them' (3 Ne. 26:9)."

Kenneth Johnson (Ensign, Mar. 1995, pp. 10-11)

3 Ne. 26:14, 16   **LOOSEN THE TONGUE OF THE CHILDREN**
(Alma 32:23; *Proven Paths*, Simpson, p.150; refer in this text to 3 Ne. 17:11-24)

"Some time ago, Nate, then just over three, said: 'Mommy, there is another little girl who is supposed to come to our family. She has dark hair and dark eyes and lives a long way from here.'
    The wise mother asked, 'How do you know this?'
    'Jesus told me, upstairs.'
    The mother noted, 'We don't have an upstairs,' but quickly sensed the significance of what had been communicated. After much travail and many prayers, the Barker family were in a sealing room in the Salt Lake Temple in the fall of 1995—where a little girl with dark hair and dark eyes, from Kazakhstan, was sealed to them for time and eternity. Inspired children still tell parents 'great and marvelous things.'"

Neal A. Maxwell (Ensign, May 1996, pp. 69-70)

3 Ne. 26:19   **EVERY MAN DEALING JUSTLY**
(Article of Faith 1:3; refer in this text to 4 Ne. 1:2-3)

"When you get what you want in your struggle for gain,
    and the world makes you king for a day,
Just go to the mirror and look at yourself

and see what the man has to say.
It isn't your father or mother or wife,
    whose judgment upon you must pass,
The one whose verdict counts most in your life
    is the one staring back in the glass.
He's the one you must satisfy beyond all the rest,
    for he's with you right up to the end;
And you have passed your most difficult test
    if the man in the glass is your friend!
You may be one who got a good break —
    then say I'm a wonderful guy;
But the man in the glass says you're only a fake;
    if you can't look him straight in the eye.
You may fool the world down your pathway of years,
    and get pats on the back as you pass;
But your final reward will be heartaches and
    tears if you've cheated the man in the glass."

David Horton Elton

"One day in the middle of an important examination in high school, the point of my lead pencil broke. In those days we used pocketknives to sharpen our pencils. I had forgotten my penknife, and turned to ask a neighbor for his. The teacher saw this; he accused me of cheating. When I tried to explain, he gave me a tongue-lashing for lying; worse, he forbade me to play on the basketball team in the upcoming game. I could see that the more I protested the angrier he seemed to become. But again and again I stubbornly told what had happened. Even when the coach pleaded my cause, the teacher refused to budge. The disgrace was almost more than I could bear. Then, just 5 minutes before the game, he had a change of heart and I was permitted to play. But there was no joy in it. We lost the game; and though that hurt, by far the deeper pain was being branded a cheat and a liar. Looking back, I know that lesson was God-sent. Character is shaped in just such crucibles. My parents believed me; they were understanding and encouraging. Supported by them and a clear conscience, I began to realize that when you are at peace with your Maker you can, if not ignore human criticism, at least rise above it."

Teachings of Ezra Taft Benson, pp. 367-368

3 Ne. 27:3-9   **THE NAME OF THE CHURCH**
(D&C 115:4; *Conference Report*, Nelson, Apr. 1990, pp. 17-21; *Ensign*, Hinckley, Nov. 1990, pp. 51-54; *Answers to Gospel Questions*, Smith, 1:96; *Teachings of the Prophet Joseph Smith*, pp. 299-300; *Ensign*, Nov. 1993, p. 6)

"There is no valid reason why Latter-Day Saints should speak of themselves as Mormons. Missionaries should not be engaged in selling Mormonism, but in the mission of persuading people to believe in Christ . . . and becoming members of his Church. . . . We belong to the Church of Jesus Christ of Latter-day Saints. . . . "

Joseph Fielding Smith (Answers to Gospel Questions, 4:174-175)

"The matter of the name his Church should bear was of great importance to the Savior. . . . Thus the name of the Church was not obtained through study or research, but by revelation direct from the Lord. Does it not seem incredible that of all the churches in the world, there was not one that bore his name when the Lord restored his Church in this dispensation?"

LeGrand Richards (A Marvelous Work and a Wonder, pp. 135-136)

"[The Savior] gave it his name, and he advised us that it should be so called. Again I want to mention that fact to some of our brethren. Don't let the Lord down by calling this the Mormon Church. He didn't call it the Mormon Church. It is all right for us to believe in the Book of Mormon. He expects us to do that, but he told us what to call this Church. The Lord has said: [3 Ne. 27:8]."

George Albert Smith (Conference Report, Apr. 1948, p. 160)

"Rather than using 'Mormon Church,' we should call the Church by its name—The Church of Jesus Christ of Latter-day Saints, 'for thus,' the Lord told us in a revelation, 'shall my church be called in the last days' (D&C 115:3-4)."

Boyd K. Packer (Ensign, Feb. 1993, p. 13)

"When he revealed the name by which the Church was to be called, he used some interesting expressions. He said, 'For thus shall my church be called in the last days, even The Church of Jesus Christ of Latter-day Saints' (D&C 115:4). The word *the* is significant: not just Church of Jesus Christ of Latter-day Saints, because to say '*The* Church' distinguishes this as the only true church on the face of the earth. He didn't say Mormon Church; he didn't say LDS Church, but the clear, firm, unequivocal statement, 'even The Church of Jesus Christ of Latter-day Saints.'"

Harold B. Lee (Ensign, Nov. 1971, p. 13)

"The First Presidency has requested that we not refer to ourselves as 'the Mormon Church' but by the name the Lord gave his church by revelation: 'The Church of Jesus Christ of Latter-day Saints' (D&C 115:4)."

Dallin H. Oaks (Ensign, Mar. 1994, p. 66)

3 Ne. 27:11   FOR A SEASON
(refer in this text to Alma 30:60)

3 Ne. 27:13-15   THE GOSPEL IN A SENTENCE
"In this short statement the Master named four eternal verities upon which all else in his gospel is founded: first, the relationship between himself and his father; second, the fact of his atonement; third, the universal resurrection; and fourth, the judgment. As to the relationship between himself and his father, he said: 'I came into the world to do the will of my father; because my father sent me.' This verity, so simply put, is the cornerstone of his gospel. . . . That the atonement was a fact is as essential to the gospel of Jesus Christ as is the Sonship of Jesus. We have the sacrament to remind us every week of his atonement. The only purpose, or at least the main purpose, for which Jesus came into the world was to make the atonement. . . . The resurrection is inherent in the atonement. . . . The purpose for which he was to be lifted up upon the cross was that he might draw all men to him. That he does through the resurrection. The purpose for which men are to come before him after the resurrection is that they may be judged of the works which they have done in the flesh. . . . All men who believe in Jesus and want to be his followers will have to accept those our verities."

Marion G. Romney (Conference Report, Apr. 1955, pp. 13-14)

3 Ne. 27:16-19   NO UNCLEAN THING CAN ENTER
(Conference Report, Oct. 1953, pp. 35-36; *Answers to Gospel Questions*, Smith, 3:26-27; *Conference Report*, Apr. 1959, pp. 11-12)

"One of my great sorrows is that so many members of the Church fail to recognize this truth which I have read. We are not going to be saved in the kingdom of God just because our names are on the records of the Church. It will require more than that. We will have to have our names written in the Lamb's Book of Life and if they are written in the Lamb's Book of Life then it is an evidence we have kept the commandments. Every soul who will not keep these commandments shall have his name blotted out of that book."

Joseph Fielding Smith (Conference Report, Oct. 1950, pp. 9-10)

3 Ne. 27:20   SANCTIFICATION
(2 Ne. 31:17; Alma 13:12; 3 Ne. 11:31-40; Moses 6:59-60; Moro. 10:32-33; Ether 4:7; Hel. 3:35; refer in this text to 2 Ne. 31:17)

"Two things work together to bring about this cleansing—the scriptural word is sanctification. First, sanctification is made possible because of Christ's atoning sacrifice. He paid the price with his own life to meet the demands of justice. . . . Second, a person is actually cleansed or purified of the terrible effects of sin by the sanctifying, cleansing, purging influence of the Holy Ghost. We are sanctified by the reception of the Holy Ghost."

Book of Mormon 121-122 Student Manual, p. 127

"Take it individually or take it collectively, we have suffered and we shall have to suffer again; and why? Because the Lord requires it at our hands for our sanctification."

Lorenzo Snow (Journal of Discourses 5:323)

"The most important of all the commandments of God is that one that you're having the most difficulty keeping. . . . Today is the day for you to work . . . until you've been able to conquer that weakness. Then you start on the next one that's most difficult for you to keep. That's the way to sanctify yourselves by keeping the commandments of God."

Harold B. Lee (Church News, May 5, 1973, p. 3)

3 Ne. 27:24-26; **JUDGED OUT OF THE BOOKS**
  28:34-35 (2 Ne. 29:11; 33:14-15; refer in this text to 2 Ne. 25:22)

"No member of this Church can stand approved in the presence of God who has not seriously and carefully read the Book of Mormon."

Joseph Fielding Smith (Conference Report, Oct 1961, p. 18)

"I recalled the solidarity of the homes of long past—when family prayer—daily devotion—the reading of the scriptures and the singing of hymns was a common practice in American homes. A practice which, I am sorry to say, has all but disappeared today."

Ezra Taft Benson (A Nation Asleep, p. 44)

3 Ne. 27:27; **EVEN AS I AM**
  28:10 (refer in this text to 3 Ne. 12:48)

"Hard to do? Of course. The Lord never promised an easy road, nor a simple gospel, nor low standards, nor a low norm. The price is high, but the goods attained are worth all they cost. The Lord himself turned the other cheek; he suffered himself to be buffeted and beaten without remonstrance; he suffered every indignity and yet spoke no word of condemnation. And his question to all of us is: 'Therefore, what manner of men ought ye to be?' And his answer to us is: 'Even as I am.'"

Spencer W. Kimball (Conference Report, Oct. 1977, p.71)

"The expression 'follow the Brethren' has a broader meaning than some would apply to it. It means not only to agree with the counsel given to the Church by the Brethren, but also to follow their example in appearance and deportment. . . . You need constantly to ask, 'How would the Savior have me appear before others? How would He have me act?' You should not imitate worldly fashions in your dress or . . . in your language. Your hair style should be in conformity with the standards of the Church . . . in impressing our young men to serve missions. . . . Live by the covenants you took in the temple; do not live on the fringes. You will be judged by the kinds of movies you attend, by the way you dress, and by the music to which you listen. Some years ago one of our teachers told his students that he used cola drinks and that it did not prevent him from holding a temple recommend. This was an indication of poor judgment on his part. . . . 'What manner of men ought ye to be?' asked the Savior. And His answer to us: 'Verily I say unto you, even as I am!'"

Ezra Taft Benson (Charge to Religious Educators, 1982, pp. 48-54)

3 Ne. 27:29   ASK AND YE SHALL RECEIVE

"'Ask, and ye shall receive' does not assure that you will get what you want. It does guarantee that, if worthy, you will get what you need, as judged by a Father that loves perfectly, who wants your eternal happiness even more than do you."

Richard G. Scott (Ensign, Nov. 1995, p. 17)

3 Ne. 27:33   FEW THERE BE THAT FIND IT

3 Ne. 28   THE THREE NEPHITES AND TRANSLATED BEINGS
(Morm. 1:16; 8:10-11; 3 Ne.19:25,30; *Mormon Doctrine*, McConkie, p.803-807; *Companion to Your Study of the Book of Mormon*, Ludlow, p. 292-294; *Answers to Gospel Questions*, Smith, 1:165; 2:46; *Teachings of the Prophet Joseph Smith*, pp. 170-171; *History of the Church* 4:425)

"In a little while you will find another prophecy will be fulfilled, and that is the prophecy that Jesus made to the three Nephites who, having power over death, are still living upon this continent. He spoke to them of a time when they would perform a great and mighty work among the Gentiles; and that has not yet been fulfilled, but it will be. You will find that many districts where the Elders of Israel cannot reach will be penetrated by these men who have power over death. . . . My testimony is that these men are going abroad in the nations of the earth before the face of your sons, and they are preparing the hearts of the children of men to receive the Gospel. They are administering to those who are heirs of salvation, and preparing their hearts to receive the truth, just as the farmer prepares the soil to receive the seed. The Lord has promised that He would send His angels before the face of His servants, and He does so."

John W. Taylor (Conference Report, Oct. 1902, p. 75)

3 Ne. 28:13-15,   TRANSFIGURED & TRANSLATED
36-40   (Mosiah 13:5; Acts 6:15; D&C 67:11-12; Moses 1:2,5, 11, 15, 31; 6:36; *Conference Report*, Apr., 1964, pp. 94-95; *Doctrines of Salvation*, Smith, 2:300-301; *Answers to Gospel Questions*, Smith, 1:163-165; 2:46; *History of the Church*, Smith, 4:210; *Journal of Discourses* 2:245)

"The difference, then, between transfiguration and translation is that transfiguration is more temporary. The Three Nephites were transfigured for a time so that they could view the visions of eternity. They were also translated, which condition is of a longer duration, until the Judgment Day."

Book of Mormon 121-122 Student Manual, p. 127

"All translated beings [eventually] receive what amounts to an instantaneous death and resurrection. Those who were translated before the resurrection of our Lord 'were with Christ in his resurrection' (D&C 133:55). Those who have been translated since the resurrection of Christ shall continue to live as mortals until the Second Coming when they shall receive their immortal glory."

Bruce R. McConkie (Mormon Doctrine, pp. 807-808)

"We are telestial mortals, translated beings are terrestrial mortals, while exalted resurrected beings are celestial immortals."

Richard Cowan (Alma, The Testimony of the Word, ed. by Nyman and Tate, pp. 201-202)

3 Ne. 29:1-2   A SIGN OF THE GATHERING OF ISRAEL

3 Ne. 29:8   MAKE GAME OF ISRAEL
(Ether 12:26)

"At no time should we do anything that can be avoided which would chagrin, inconvenience or pain our fellow men, and no word or sentence should ever pass our lips, even in a joke, which will not bear the strictest scrutiny under the searchlight of truth. If our surplus energy must find vent in some way, let it be utilized in providing surprises in the shape of blessings for the widows and the fatherless or in doing something that will contribute to the happiness and well being of our fellow men."

George Q. Cannon (Gospel Truths, p. 452)

3 Ne. 30:2   MORMON'S COUNSEL TO THE GENTILES

4 Nephi ~ Mormon 2

4 Nephi covers 285 years, which is almost one-third of all the years covered in the entire Book of Mormon.

A ZION SOCIETY
(Conference Report, Lee, Oct. 1972, pp. 63-64: Moses 7:18; D&C 82:19; 38:24, 27; *Mormon Doctrine,* McConkie, p. 852)

"Surely there could not be a happier people among all the people who had been created by the hand of God" (4 Nephi 1:16).

"What a glorious time that must have been when everybody was happy, when everybody was at peace, when everyone loved his neighbor as himself, and above all he loved God, because we are informed here that the thing which brought about this condition of happiness was the fact that the love of God was in the hearts of the people. There never will be a time of peace, happiness, justice tempered by mercy, when all men will receive that which is their right and privilege to receive, until they get in their hearts the love of God."

Joseph Fielding Smith (Doctrines of Salvation, 3:319-320)

"However, when the Lord appeared, he established one unified society in which there was no sin, no crime, and no wars. . . . [4 Nephi 1:15-16]. What would one not give to live in a society like that? . . . But how are those races able to live as a celestial society for so long? We might also ask, 'How will it be possible during the Millennium for the people to remain righteous for almost a thousand years?' The answer seems to be the same in both cases, and I believe that it consists in this: Parents teaching their children the gospel, and doing so especially during that early period of their lives when they cannot be tempted."

H. Verlan Andersen (Conference Report, Oct. 1991, pp. 110-111)

"When we are swallowed up in the will of Him who has called us; when we enjoy the peace and the smiles of our Father in Heaven, the things of His Spirit, and all the blessings we are capacitated to receive and improve upon, then are we in Zion, *that is Zion*."

Brigham Young (Journal of Discourses 1:3)

"In one context, Zion is geographic, having a center, while enlarging its boundaries to eventually fill the earth. . . . Another context shows Zion as an organization wherein we work to strengthen its stakes through our callings. . . .The scriptures suggest that Zion has a third context, an intensely personal one. It is the perfecting process within us. Those willing to serve are invited to labor in the vineyard of the Lord, steadily transforming themselves to become the pure in heart."

Dale E. Miller (Ensign, May 1998, pp. 29-30)

[As a guide to becoming a Zion Society] "First, we must eliminate the individual tendency to selfishness that snares the soul, shrinks the heart, and darkens the mind. . . . Second, we must cooperate completely and work in harmony one with the other. There must be unanimity in our decisions and unity in our actions. . . . Third, we must lay on the altar and sacrifice whatever is required by the Lord. We begin by offering a 'broken heart and contrite spirit.' We follow this by giving our best effort in our assigned fields of labor and callings. We learn our duty and execute it fully. Finally we consecrate our time, talents, and means as called upon by our file leaders and as prompted by the whisperings of the Spirit."

Spencer W. Kimball (Conference Report, Apr. 1978, p. 123)

4 Ne. 1:2 **EVERY MAN DID DEAL JUSTLY**
(refer in this text to 2 Ne. 9:41)

"A young man came to me not long ago and said, 'I made an agreement with a man that requires me to make certain payments each year. I am in arrears, and I can't make those payments, for if I do, it is going to cause me to lose my home. What shall I do?' I looked at him and said, 'Keep your agreement.' [The young man replied], 'Even if it costs me my home?' I said, 'I am not talking about your home. I am talking about your agreement; and I think your wife would rather have a husband who would keep his word, . . . and have to rent a home than to have a home with a husband who will not keep his covenants and his pledges.'"

N. Eldon Tanner (Ensign, May 1997, p. 29-30)

"We need to learn, practice, study, know and understand how angels live with each other. When this community comes to the point to be perfectly honest and upright, you will never find a poor person; none will lack, all will have sufficient. Every man, woman, and child will have all they need just as soon as they all become honest. When the majority of the community are dishonest, it maketh the honest portion poor, for the dishonest serve and enrich themselves at their expense."

Discourses of Brigham Young, p. 232

"Honesty is a very important part of character. We have all seen men who think they are not accountable to the laws of men or of God. They seem to feel that the rules of human conduct do not apply to them. A popular philosophy is 'What can I get away with?' As someone once said, 'The difference between a moral man and a man of honor is that the latter regrets a discreditable act even when it has worked.' Honesty begins when we are young. When I was 11 years old, I looked forward eagerly to my magical 12th birthday when I could become a deacon and a Scout. My mother helped me learn the Articles of Faith, the Scout Law and Motto. . . . One day Mother left me to wash the dishes and clean the kitchen while she attended to a sick neighbor. I agreed to do these duties but put off doing the dishes. Time ran out and they didn't get done. In fact, they didn't even get started. When Mother came home and saw the kitchen, she put on her apron and went to the sink. She spoke only three words, which stung worse than the sting of a dozen hornets. They were the first three words of the Scout Law: 'On my honor.' That day I resolved that I would never give my mother cause to repeat those words to me again."

James E. Faust (Ensign, May 1998, p.44)

4 Ne. 1:3   **ALL THINGS COMMON**
(3 Ne. 26:19; D&C 42:30-32; 51:3; 82:17-19; Acts 4:33-35; *Studies in Scripture*, ed. by Jackson, 8:223; *Improvement Era*, Aug. 1936, 39:488)

[In regard to the United Order, D&C 42] ". . . there were two cardinal principles: (1) consecration and (2) stewardship . . . one consecrated all his possessions to the Church. . . . Having thus voluntarily divested himself of title to all his property, the consecrator received from the Church a stewardship by a like conveyance. This stewardship could be more or less than his original consecration, the object being to make 'every man equal according to his family, according to his circumstances and his wants and needs' (D&C 51:3). This procedure preserved in every man the right to private ownership and management of his property. At his own option he could alienate it or keep and operate it and pass it on to his heirs . . . He consecrated to the Church the surplus he produced above the needs and wants of his family. This surplus went into a storehouse from which stewardships were given to others and from which the needs of the poor were supplied."

Marion G. Romney (Conference Report, Apr. 1966, pp. 96-98)

"The fundamental principle of this system was the private ownership of property. Each man owned his portion, or inheritance, or stewardship, with an absolute title, which he could alienate, or hypothecate, or otherwise treat as his own. The Church did not own all of the property, and the life under the United Order was not a communal life, as the Prophet Joseph, himself, said. *(History of the Church*, 3:28). The United Order is an individualistic system, not a communal system. . . . The Church never was, and under existing commandments never will be, a communal society. . . . The United Order was not communal or communistic."

J. Reuben Clark, Jr. (quoted by Ezra Taft Benson, Charge to Religious Educators, 1982, pp. 48-54)

4 Ne. 1:6   **PEACE**
(Words of Mormon 1:18; Mosiah 15:18; 27:37; Alma 4:5; 24:20; *Church News*, Oct. 11, 1990, p. 72; *Gospel Ideals*, McKay, p. 280; refer in this text to Hel. 5:52)

"Opposition to war cannot ensure peace, because peace is more than the absence of war. . . . Peace can only come through the gospel of Jesus Christ. . . . The peace the gospel brings is not just the *absence* of war. It is the *opposite* of war. Gospel peace is the opposite of any conflict, armed or unarmed. . . . We cannot have peace among nations without achieving general righteousness among the people who comprise them."

Dallin H. Oaks (Conference Report, 1990, p. 91, 93)

4 Ne. 1:17   **NOR ANY MANNER OF -ITES**
(Gal 3:28; Col. 3:11; Acts 17:24, 26; refer in this text to 2 Ne. 26:24-28, 33)

"Throughout the world, however, strident voices are engaged in divisive disputation and name-calling. Often demeaning nicknames are added to—or even substituted for—given names. Unfortunately, terms of derision obscure the true identity of children of the covenant. . . . When the Nephites were truly righteous, they avoided divisive nicknames. . . . 'There were no . . . Lamanites, nor any manner of -ites; but they were in one, the children of Christ, and heirs to the kingdom of God' (4 Ne. 1:17). That lesson from history suggests that we also delete from our personal vocabularies names that segregate. . . ."

Russell M. Nelson (Ensign, May 1995, p. 34)

[Regarding 4 Ne. 1:15, 17] "That is worth keeping in mind as we open a discussion on the origin of man, a subject which often leads defenders of opposing views to controversy and to label one another. In the Spirit of the Book of Mormon, please may we drop all labels, all of the 'ites,' and 'isms,' and 'ists'? Let there be no 'evolution*ists*' nor 'creation*ists*' nor any manner of 'ists'; just seekers after truth."

Boyd K. Packer (The Book of Mormon: Jacob Through Words of Mormon, To Learn with Joy, p. 2)

4 Ne. 1:17, 20, 38-39   **LAMANITES (defined)**
(Jacob 1:14; refer in this text to Hel.11:24)

"It is significant that the name 'Lamanite' here appears to become a generic term. That is, it refers to a general classification of people—those who revolted from the Church. These people may or may not have been the direct descendants of Laman and Lemuel."

Dean L. Larsen (You and the Destiny of the Indian, pp. 21-22)

4 Ne. 1:24-26   **DIVIDED INTO CLASSES**
(refer in this text to 3 Ne. 6:10-16)

"When the principles of the Gospel were practised among the . . . [Nephites] they were equal to a very great extent; but when they began to violate the principles of the Gospel, their inequality manifested itself. Some were lifted up in pride, some looked with scorn upon their poor brethren and sisters. Classifications arose in society which had their origin not in virtue, not in holiness, not in purity, not in any superiority arising from intelligence, but because some were richer than others, some could dress better than others, some could have better surroundings than others, doubtless dwelt in finer houses, better furnished, and they were better clad, and had probably finer and nicer food. Distinctions of this kind grew up not out of the Gospel, but out of the violation of the principles of the Gospel. Wherever the Gospel of the Lord Jesus Christ is taught, . . . it makes the man who may know and understand the things of God feel that he is no better than his fellow man, and the woman who understands the things of God feel that she is no better than her sister. . . . There is something in the human heart of that character that when human beings are prospering they are apt to be lifted up in pride and to forget the cause or the source of their prosperity; they are apt to forget God, who is the fountain of all their blessings, and to give glory to themselves. . . . God has sent us here and given unto us a mission on the earth not to accumulate riches, not to become worldly-minded, not to pile up the things of this world. . . . The happiness of a people does not consist in the abundance of worldly things. . . ."

George Q. Cannon (Journal of Discourses 22:99-101)

4 Ne. 1:36-37 **NEPHITES (defined)**
(Alma 3:11; refer in this text to Hel. 11:24)

Morm. 1:14-17 **ABSENCE OF THE SPIRIT**
(contrast with 3 Ne. 19:9, 13-15 [1 Ne. 7:14; Morm. 2:26; 5:16; Ether 2:15; 15:19; Hel. 4:24; 6:35; 13:8; Moses 8:17; D&C 1:33; 19:20; 63:32; Alma 24:30; Gen. 6:3; Moro. 8:27-28; 9:4-5; *Teachings of the Prophet Joseph Smith*, p. 328; refer in this text to 2 Ne. 26:11; Hel. 13:8])

"Young men, you must live righteously for many reasons. One of them is that you must be accompanied by the Spirit of the Lord as you labor in the mission field. The association of the Spirit of the Lord is dependent upon personal righteousness. If you do not strive diligently for the assistance of the Spirit, you will find your missionary work extremely difficult and your results very disappointing."

L. Aldin Porter (Ensign, May 1992, p. 46)

"The healing of the sick among us has become so common that it is apparently but little thought of. We have also seen the lame made to walk, and the blind to receive their sight, the deaf to hear, and the dumb to speak. These things we have seen done by the power of God and not by the cunning or wisdom of men; we know that these signs do follow the preaching of the gospel. Yet these testimonies of its truth are but poor and weak when compared with the whisperings of the still small voice of the Spirit of God."

Joseph F. Smith (Gospel Doctrine, pp. 83-84)

"Our preaching and our teaching must be by the power of the Holy Ghost. We must ever remember that in this glorious work, the most essential element is the Spirit."

Teachings of Ezra Taft Benson, p. 313

"The gift of the Holy Ghost adapts itself to all these organs or attributes. It quickens all the intellectual faculties, increases, enlarges, expands and purifies all the natural passions and affections. . . . It develops beauty of person, form and features. It tends to health, vigor, animation and social feeling. It invigorates all the faculties of the physical and intellectual man. It strengthens and gives tone to the nerves. In short, it is, as it were, marrow to the bone, joy to the heart, light to the eyes, music to the ears, and life to the whole thing. In the presence of such persons one feels to enjoy the light of their countenances, as the genial rays of a sunbeam. Their very atmosphere diffuses a thrill, a warm glow of pure gladness and sympathy to the heart and nerves of others who have kindred feelings, or sympathy of spirit. No matter if the parties are strangers, entirely unknown to each other in person or character; no matter if they have never spoken to each other, each will be apt to remark in his own mind, and perhaps exclaim when referring to the interview, 'O what an atmosphere encircles that stranger! How my heart thrilled with pure and holy feelings in his presence! What confidence and sympathy he inspired! His countenance and spirit gave me more assurance than a thousand written recommendations or introductory letters.' Such is the gift of the Holy Ghost, and such are its operations when received through the lawful channel, the divine, eternal Priesthood."

Parley P. Pratt (Key to Theology, pp. 99-101)

"I sat in the office of the first Presidency and President Monson took President Benson by the arm to lead him toward my chair to give me a blessing. . . . Following that beautiful blessing as I stood and turned to face President Benson . . . and spoke with him briefly, I was quite unprepared for the magnificence of his spirit, and I realized that as our bodies age and grow old and wear out, our spirits continue to grow."

Janette C. Hales (BYU Devotional, Mar. 16, 1993)

"If our spirits are inclined to be stiff and refractory, and we desire continually the gratification of our own will to the extent that this feeling prevails in us, the Spirit of the Lord is held at a distance from us; or, in other words, *the Father withholds his Spirit from us in proportion as we desire the gratification of our own will.*"

Erastus Snow (Journal of Discourses 7:352)

"But during my travels in the southern country last winter I had many interviews with President Young, and with Heber C. Kimball, and Geo. A. Smith, and Jedediah M. Grant, and many others who are dead. They attended our conference, they attended our meetings. And on one occasion, I saw Brother

Brigham and Brother Heber . . . when I was on my way to attend conference; and they were dressed in the most priestly robes. . . . I asked Prest. Young if he would preach to us. He said, 'No, I have finished my testimony in the flesh I shall not talk to this people any more, But (said he) I have come to see you; I have come to watch over you, and to see what the people are doing. Then (said he) I want you to teach the people—and I want you to follow this counsel your-self—that they must labor and so live as to obtain the Holy Spirit, for without this you cannot build up the kingdom; without the spirit of God you are in dan-ger of walking in the dark. . . ."

Wilford Woodruff (Journal of Discourses 21:318)

"The Lord declared to His servants . . . that He was . . . withdrawing His Spirit from the earth; and we can see that such is the fact, for not only the churches are dwindling away, . . . the governments of the earth are thrown into confusion and division; and *Destruction*, to the eye of the spiritual beholder, seems to be written by the finger of an invisible hand, in large capitals, upon almost every thing we behold."

Joseph Smith (History of the Church, 1:314)

Morm. 1:18; 2:10 SLIPPERY TREASURES
(Ether 14:1-2; Hel. 12:18; 13:18-23, 30-38; *Journal of Discourses* 19:36-39)

"I am wondering if the time has come to realize that we are . . . suffering from a subsidence of our foundation. . . . No part of the country, rural or urban, is immune. Life and property are relatively more unsafe than in any other civilized country in the world."

Herbert Hoover, Apr. 22, 1929 (quoted in Book of Mormon Prophecies, Warner, p. 98)

Morm. 2:13   WORLDLY SORROW vs GODLY SORROW
(1 Ne. 18:20; 2 Ne. 2:7; 4:17; Alma 36:12-17; 42:29; Hel. 13:38; 2 Cor. 7:9-10; *Teachings of Spencer W. Kimball*, pp. 86-89; refer in this text to Alma 34:33; 1 Ne. 18:20; Alma 42:29)

"Repentance, which is an assured passage to an eternal destination, is nev-ertheless not a free ride. . . . Why is it necessary for us to suffer on the way to repentance for serious transgressions? We often think of the results of repen-tance as simply cleansing us from sin. But that is an incomplete view of the mat-ter. A person who sins is like a tree that bends easily in the wind. On a windy and rainy day the tree bent so deeply against the ground that the leaves became soiled with mud, like sin. If we only focus on cleaning the leaves, the weakness in the tree that allowed it to bend and soil its leaves may remain. Merely cleaning the leaves does not strengthen the tree in the next high wind. The susceptibility to repetition continues until the tree has been strengthened."

Dallin H. Oaks (BYU Fireside, Aug. 5, 1990)

"Repentance means more than simply a reformation of behavior. Many men and women in the world demonstrate great willpower and self-discipline in overcoming bad habits and the weaknesses of the flesh. Yet at the same time they give no thought to the Master, sometimes even openly rejecting Him. Such changes of behavior, even if in a positive direction, do not constitute true repentance. . . . It is not uncommon to find men and women in the world who feel remorse for the things they do wrong. Sometimes this is because their actions cause them or loved ones great sorrow and misery. Sometimes their sorrow is caused because they are caught and punished for their actions. Such worldly feelings do not constitute 'godly sorrow.'. . . . Godly sorrow is a gift of the Spirit. It is a deep realization that our actions have offended our Father and our God. It is the sharp and keen awareness that our behavior caused the Savior, He who knew no sin, even the greatest of all, to endure agony and suffering. Our sins caused Him to bleed at every pore. This very real mental and spiritual anguish is what the scriptures refer to as having a broken heart and a contrite spirit.' Such a spirit is the absolute prerequisite for true repentance."

Ezra Taft Benson (Ensign, Oct. 1989, pp. 2,4)

"Often people indicate that they have repented when all they have done is to express regret for a wrong act. But true repentance is marked by that godly sorrow that changes, transforms, and saves. To be sorry is not enough. Perhaps the felon in the penitentiary, coming to realize the high price he must pay for his folly, may wish he had not committed the crime. That is not repentance. The vicious man who is serving a stiff sentence for rape may be very sorry he did the deed, but he is not repentant if his heavy sentence is the only reason for his sorrow. That is the sorrow of the world. The truly repentant man is sorry before he is apprehended. He is sorry even if his secret is never known. He desires to make voluntary amends. . . . Repentance of the godly type means that one comes to recognize the sin and voluntarily and without pressure from outside sources begins his transformation."

Spencer W. Kimball (The Miracle of Forgiveness, p. 153)

THE NEPHITE DISEASE (cont.)

		Stages
1. 34th year	4 Ne.1:4, 7	Peace & Prosperity
2. 201st year	4 Ne.1:24	Pride
3. 201st year	4 Ne.1:24, 34	Wickedness

Repeated During Wickedness

4 Ne.1:40
  Majority Choose Evil
4 Ne.1:42, 46
  Secret Combinations
Morm. 1:14;
2:26; 5:16
  Spirit Withdrawal

4. 322nd year	Morm. 1:8	War

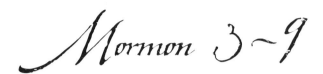

Mormon 3~9

Morm. 3:9; 4:8   **BOASTING**
(Alma 26:10-12; Hel. 4:13; 5:8; *Discourses of Wilford Woodruff,* pp. 123-124; refer in this text to Alma 39:2; Mosiah 11:19)

"Boasting is to speak with pride and take pride in, to brag about or to be proud to possess. It is glorifying oneself, talking in a vain manner or specifically emphasizing one's own deeds."

Marvin J. Ashton (Conference Report, Apr. 1990)

Morm. 3:10, 14, **OFFENSIVE WAR**
16; 4:1, 4, (Mosiah 21:7-15; Alma 44:4; 48:14-16; Hel. 4:11; D&C 71:9-11)
15, 18

"Safety can't be won by tanks and guns and the airplanes and atomic bombs. There is only one place of safety and that is within the realm of the power of Almighty God that he gives to those who keep his commandments and listen to his voice, as he speaks through the channels that he has ordained for that purpose."

Harold B. Lee (Conference Report, Oct. 1973, p. 169)

"When threatened, we become anti-enemy instead of pro-kingdom of God. . . . We forget that if we are righteous the Lord will either not suffer our enemies to come upon us—and this is the special promise to the inhabitants of the land of the Americas (2 Ne. 1:7)—or he will fight our battles for us."

Spencer W. Kimball (Ensign, June 1976, p. 6)

Morm. 3:18-19   **APOSTLES AND THE JUDGMENT**
(1 Ne. 12:9-10; 3 Ne. 27:27)

"The reality is that there will be a whole hierarchy of judges who, under Christ, shall judge the righteous. He alone shall issue the decrees of damnation for the wicked."

Bruce R. McConkie (The Millennial Messiah, p. 520)

Morm. 4:5   **BY THE WICKED ARE THE WICKED PUNISHED**
(Matt. 26:52; *Conference Report*, Apr., 1942, p. 95)

Morm. 4:11   **DELIGHT IN SHEDDING OF BLOOD**
(Moro. 9:5, 20; Mosiah 11:19; Gen. 6:11-12; Moses 8:28)

"In 1985 hand guns killed eight people in Great Britain, 48 people in Japan, 34 in Switzerland, 52 in Canada, 58 in Israel, 21 in Sweden, 42 in West Germany, and 10,728 in the United States. There are more murders each year on Manhattan Island which is 3 miles by 12 miles than in the United Kingdom including Ireland."

Victor Cline (American Fork High School, 1990)

Morm. 5:10   **REALIZE & KNOW FROM WHENCE BLESSINGS COME**

"In the outer office of the Council of Twelve hangs a painting by Utah artist Arnold Friberg, depicting George Washington, the father of our country, on his knees at Valley Forge. That painting symbolizes the faith of our forebears. I wish it could be in every American home. In the 1940's, while serving as the executive officer of the National Council of Farmer Cooperatives in Washington, D.C., I saw in a Hilton Hotel a placard depicting Uncle Sam, representing America, on his knees in humility and prayer. Beneath the placard was the inscription 'Not beaten there by the hammer and sickle, but freely, responsibly, confidently . . . We need fear nothing or no one save God.' That picture has stayed in my memory ever since. America on her knees—in recognition that all our blessings come from God! America on her knees—out of a desire to serve the God of this land by keeping His commandments! This is the sovereign remedy to all of our problems and the preservation of our liberties."

Ezra Taft Benson (This Nation Shall Endure, pp. 45-46)

Morm. 5:9, 15,20   **LATTER-DAY GENTILES PRESENT GOSPEL TO THE LAMANITES**
(refer in this text to 3 Ne. 21:3-5)

Morm. 5:22-24   **LATTER-DAY UNREPENTANT GENTILES**
(refer in this text to 3 Ne. 16:10-16)

Morm. 6:1-6   **HILL CUMORAH**
(Ether 15:11; *History of the Church*, Smith, 2:79-80; *Doctrines of Salvation*, Smith, 3:232-234; *Journal of Discourses* 19:38; *Conference Report*, Apr. 1928, pp. 12-14)

Morm. 6:16-22   **NEPHITE LAMENTATION**
(*Relief Society Magazine*, VI, No. 6, June 1919, pp. 369-370; *Companion to Your Study of the Book of Mormon*, Ludlow, p. 303; *Journal of Discourses* 10:287)

"The tragedy of the Book of Mormon is not what became of the Nephites but what the Nephites became."

Hugh Nibley (Since Cumorah)

"A story is told about the great Lincoln in the dark days of the Civil War. As the president paced the floor wondering who would be the victor, North or South, his secretary said, 'Mr. Lincoln, I hope the Lord is on our side.' To this, the president answered, 'I hope we are on the Lord's side.' What a difference in point of view. When the whole world is in turmoil, we can all ask are we on the Lord's side?"

Gilbert Charles Orme (The Four Estates of Man, p. 121)

"If destruction be our lot, we must ourselves be its author and finisher. As a nation of freemen, we must live through all time, or die by suicide."

Abraham Lincoln, 1838 (as quoted in the preface of Civil War, Ward)

"Great nations do not fall because of external aggression; they first erode and decay inwardly, so that, like rotten fruit, they fall of themselves. The strength of a country is the sum total of the moral strength of the individuals in that country."

Ezra Taft Benson (This Nation Shall Endure, p. 95)

"The gospel is the only answer to the problems of the world. We may cry peace. We may hold peace conferences. And I have nothing but commendation for those who work for peace. But it is my conviction that peace must come from within. It cannot be imposed by state mandate. It can come only by following the teachings and the example of the Prince of Peace."

Teachings of Ezra Taft Benson, p.705

Morm. 8

MORONI TAKES OVER THE WRITING

"Moroni becomes something of three witnesses in one. . . . His first witness is his conclusion to his father's book, comprising chapters eight and nine of that test. . . . His second witness comes with the book of Ether—his own comments in that book. . . . Those twenty-eight verses in the third chapter of Ether may well be the single most remarkable encounter with Christ ever experienced by mortal man, and we are indebted to Moroni for preserving it. . . . Moroni's third and final testimony comes in his own concluding book, emphasizing faith in Christ, hope in Christ, the charity of Christ with the prayer that these three great Christian virtues, these consummate Christian principles, will lead us to—purity."

Jeffrey R. Holland (CES Symposium, BYU, Aug. 9, 1994)

Morm. 8:12, 17-20

JUDGE NOT

(Ether 12:35; refer in this text to 3 Ne. 14:1-5)

Morm. 8:26-41

THE NEPHITES SAW OUR DAY

(2 Ne. 26:14-22; 28:2-32; *Journal of Discourses* 19:38; *Gospel Standards*, Grant, pp. 290-291; *Conference Report*, Oct. 1963, p. 107; *Conference Report*, Apr., 1971, p. 90)

"The Book of Mormon was written for us today. . . . God who knows the end from the beginning, told (Mormon) what to include in his abridgement that we would need for our day. . . ."

Ezra Taft Benson (Conference Report, Apr. 1975, pp. 96-97)

"The Nephites never had the book; neither did the Lamanites of ancient times. It was meant for us. Mormon wrote near the end of the Nephite civilization. Under the inspiration of God, who sees all things from the beginning, he abridged centuries of records, choosing the stories, speeches, and events that would be most helpful to us. Each of the major writers of the Book of Mormon testified that he wrote for future generations [see 2 Ne. 25:21; Jacob 1:3; Enos 1:15-16; Jarom 1:2; Mormon 7:1; Mormon 8:34-35; 9:30] . . . . If they saw our day and chose those things which would be of greatest worth to us, is not that how we should study the Book of Mormon? We should constantly ask ourselves, 'Why did the Lord inspire Mormon (or Moroni or Alma) to include that in his record? What lesson can I learn from that to help me live in this day and age?'"

Ezra Taft Benson (Conference Report, Oct. 1986, p.5)

"The type of apostates in the Book of Mormon are similar to the type we have today. God, with his infinite foreknowledge, so molded the Book of Mormon that we might see the error and know how to combat false educational, political, religious and philosophical concepts of our time."

Ezra Taft Benson (Ensign, May 1975, p. 64)

"Political unrest, warfare, and economic chaos prevail in many parts of the world, and the plagues of pornography, drug misuse, immorality, AIDS, and child abuse become more oppressive with each passing day. The media busily satisfies an apparently insatiable appetite of audiences to witness murder, violence, nudity, sex, and profanity. Is not this the day of which Moroni spoke when he recorded: 'Behold, I speak unto you as if ye were present, and yet ye are not. But behold, Jesus Christ hath shown you unto me, and I know your doing.' (Morm. 8:35). And then he prophesied of conditions of the world as they are today."

M. Russell Ballard (Ensign, Nov. 1992, p. 31)

[Morm. 8:34-38] "I guess one of the greatest mysteries of mortality is why mankind fails to learn from history. Why do those who profess to be true followers of Christ so often become victims of the enticements of the world? . . . We see so many members seeking worldly pursuits contrary to the words of the Lord's prophets through the ages. Many of us are more concerned about our fine apparel, the size of our homes, and our cars and their gadgets than we are about the needs of the poor and the needy. . . . We need to heed Moroni's warning to avoid the fate which destroyed his people. . . . Who would not want to heed the voice of warning of one who has witnessed such heartache and misery? Moroni's words are not just a voice of warning, but also a voice of hope, as he lets us know that every one of God's children are precious to Him."

L. Tom Perry (Ensign, Nov. 1992, pp. 16-17)

"Speaking of the last days, the Prophet Moroni declared, 'Yea, it shall come in a day when there shall be great pollutions upon the face of the earth' (Morm. 8:31). Sadly, the effects of this great pollution are perhaps most evident in the mass media, films, television, and popular music. . . . In most areas of the mass media there seems to be a declaration of war against almost everything the majority treasures most: the family, religion, and patriotism. Marriage is degraded, while premarital and extramarital relations are encouraged and glamorized. Profanity and the foulest of vulgar gutter language bombard the ears of all who listen. . . . Human life itself is trivialized by the constant barrage of violence and killings. . . . Parents who really want to receive assistance must return to the basics—the fundamentals of the gospel. Among all that could be said, here are four specific suggestions that, if applied, can make a positive difference: First, *do not be afraid to set clear moral standards and guidelines. . . .* Second, *teach your children to work and to take responsibility. . . .* Third, *create an environment in your family in which spiritual experiences can occur. . . .* Fourth, *follow the counsel of the prophets.*"

Joe J. Christensen (Ensign, Nov. 1993, pp. 11-13)

Morm. 8:29, **O YE POLLUTIONS**
31, 38 (Moses 2:26-28; Ezek. 34:18; Num. 35:33-34; D&C 49:19-21; 59:18-20; 84:59; 103:13-14; *Journal of Discourses* 15:227)

"The soil, the air, the water are all pure and healthy. Do not suffer them to become polluted with wickedness. Strive to preserve the elements from being contaminated by . . . those who pervert the intelligence God has bestowed upon the human family. . . . Keep your valley pure, keep your towns as pure as you possibly can, keep your hearts pure. . . ."

Brigham Young (Journal of Discourses 8:79-80)

"We will . . . build up Zion on the earth and purify it and cleanse it from all pollutions. Let there be an hallowed influence go from us over all things over which we have any power; over the soil we cultivate, over the houses we build, and over everything we possess. . . . We are the lords of the earth."

Discourses of Brigham Young, p. 443

"A sex saturated society cannot feel the needs of its suffering members because instead of developing the love that looks outward, it turns man selfishly inward. Imperviousness to the promptings of the still small voice of God will also mean that we have ears, but cannot hear, not only the promptings of God but also the pleas of men . . . we shut out people, nature, and God." Neal A. Maxwell *(A Time to Choose*, p. 59-60, 71) [Continuing that same reasoning in General Conference Bro. Maxwell stated] "Without hope, [in this world] why forego now in order to preserve precious resources for future generations? The loss of hope sends self-ishness surging, as many turn, even more intensively, to pleasing themselves."

(Ensign, Nov. 1994, p. 34)

"The people are striving with all their might to learn the things of God; but if I could only get them to understand the work and the worth of their present life, I should feel well satisfied. . . . The time we now occupy is in eternity; it is a portion of eternity. Our present life is just as much a life in eternity as the life of any being can possibly be. Could we all live so as to honour the life that we now possess . . . ? The very object of our existence here is to handle the tempo-ral elements of this world and subdue the earth, multiplying those organisms of plants and animals God has designed shall dwell upon it. When we have learned to live according to the full value of the life we now possess, we are prepared for further advancement in the scale of eternal progression—for a more glorious and exalted sphere. . . . Our Father in heaven wishes us to preserve that which he gives to us. . . . If we could only learn enough . . . we should then have learned what the Gods have learned before us, and what we must eventually learn before we can be exalted. . . . We have also been greatly blessed, but we have treated lightly our blessings in neglecting to properly and frugally use them. . . . The Lord has poured out his blessings on the atmosphere, on the water, and on the soil of this country. . . . If we abuse these choice blessings, the Lord will blast the . . . elements with his withering touch, and leave us desolate. . . . We have often heard it said by our Elders that all the heaven we shall ever have is the one we make for ourselves."

Brigham Young (Journal of Discourses 9:168-170)

"In the name of 'progress' and growth,' we have plundered our planet and despoiled our environment. . . . Many of our environmental problems arise from the fact that our society has become obsessed with materialism. Paul spoke an eternal truth when he said that 'the love of money is the root of all evil.' . . . Yet a never-ending search for more material prosperity cannot be the major fac-tor in our lives. The society that looks no further than its gross national prod-uct is doomed to ultimate decay and destruction. Man's true purposes are spir-itual, not material. . . . The reason we are in trouble ecologically is because of our inability to see ourselves as a part of nature. . . . We have behaved as though we have some sort of divinely provided right to despoil the physical world. In a very real sense I believe this reflects a misinterpretation . . . of God's injunction to Adam about subduing the earth." [Moses 2:28]

A. B. Morrison (Ensign, Aug. 1971, pp. 64, 69)

"When I . . . fly over the vast and beautiful expanses of our globe, . . . I have the feeling that the good earth can hardly bear our presence upon it. . . . The Brethren constantly cry out against that which is intolerable in the sight of the Lord: against pollution of mind, body, and our surroundings. . . ."

Spencer W. Kimball (Ensign, June 1976, p. 4)

"One of the best-known teachings of the Jews is that when man (Israel in particular) falls away from God, all nature becomes his enemy. . . . In the end, as the wise rabbis saw, it is pollution that makes the earth uninhabitable: 'When you completely defile the land,' Israel is told, 'then I will no longer dwell in it; and then before long you can no longer dwell in it!'"

Hugh Nibley (Brigham Young Challenges the Saints, pp. 16, 50)

"The world is after riches. Riches is the god they worship. . . . What constitutes health, wealth, joy, and peace? In the first place, good pure air is the greatest sustainer of . . . life."

Brigham Young (Millennial Star, 22:738)

"The air is precious to the red man, for all things share the same breath - the beast, the tree, the man, they all share the same breath. The white man does not seem to notice the air he breathes. Like a man dying for many days, he is numb to the stench. But if we sell you our land, you must remember that the air is precious to us, that the air shares its spirit with all the life it supports. The wind that gave our grandfather his first breath also receives his last sigh. And if we sell you our land, you must keep it apart and sacred, as a place where even the white man can go to taste the wind that is sweetened by the meadow's flowers. . . . For we do not understand when the buffalo are all slaughtered, the wild horses are tamed, the secret corners of the forest heavy with scent of many men, and the view of the ripe hills blotted by talking wires. Where is the thicket? Gone. Where is the eagle? Gone. The end of living and the beginning of survival."

A letter from Chief Seattle to the President of the United States in 1854

"America from first to last had been frontier! . . . In record time the face of the continent was completely changed. But the finished product was not 'America the Beautiful.' . . . [In second-grade] we sang a lot about the alabaster cities where nobody ever cries, but that is not what came out of the frontier."

Hugh Nibley (Approaching Zion, p. 413)

"The worst thing about the 'filthy air' is that it turns out to be a smoke-screen. . . . It is a smooth, white-collar scam . . . oftentimes, to win us to our harm. . . . Such pleasant bits as those pacifying public relations assurances, 'We are not monsters or ogres, we are people just like you. We love our families just like you, we go to church too!' Or to quote the scriptures, 'I am no devil' (2 Nephi 28:22). . . . When getting gain entails the destruction and degrading of life, what should we do? The great fortunes that made America a world-class power were paid for by mill towns in which life was very near to hell. But the owners lived far away, and starving immigrants desperately competing for jobs were willing to submit to anything. No more vivid description of that world can be found than one written in 1855 by a prominent Latter-day Saint living in England. I thought of his essay last fall. Looking toward Provo, . . . I paused to behold the dense, murky, brown fog jammed against the mountains right behind the Brigham Young University by the prevailing winds, and I remembered the opening lines of the composition,

'. . . *Over the valley before you rests an awful, impenetrable, dark, black cloud. . . . You walk down the hillside, and, as you enter the thick, dark cloud. . . . A sense of oppressiveness falls upon you, and you realize, to your unmistakable discomfort, that the darkness around [you] can not only be seen, but felt and tasted. Suddenly, to your great astonishment, you discover that this dreary spot is inhabited by human beings!'" (Millennial Star, 17:337)*

Our Latter-day Saint philosopher of the 1850s tells us what he found when he entered the factory town: . . . Who would ever have thought 135 years ago that this would be an accurate description of our inner cities today?"

Hugh Nibley (Brigham Young Challenges the Saints, pp. 61-63)

Morm. 8:34   **SHORTLY**
(2 Ne. 26:10)

Morm. 8:37-39   **ADORN YOURSELVES WITH THAT WHICH HATH NO LIFE**
(refer to student handout Jacob 2:13-17; Alma 1:6; 3 Ne. 6:10-16)

"Few men have ever knowingly and deliberately chosen to reject God and his blessings. Rather, we learn from the scriptures that because the exercise of faith has always appeared to be more difficult than relying on things more immediately at hand, carnal man has tended to transfer his trust in God to material things. Therefore, in all ages when men have fallen under the power of Satan and lost the faith, they have put in its place a hope in the 'arm of flesh' and in 'gods of silver, and gold, of brass, iron, wood, and stone, which see not, nor hear, nor know' (Dan. 5:23) . . . I am afraid that many of us have been surfeited with flocks and herds and acres and barns and wealth and have begun to worship them as false gods, and they have power over us. Do we have more of these good things than our faith can stand? Many people spend most of their time working in the service of a self-image that includes sufficient money, stocks, bonds, investment portfolios, property, credit cards, furnishings, automobiles, and the like to *guarantee*, . . . it is hoped, a long and happy life. Forgotten is the fact that our assignment is to use these many resources in our families and quorums to build up the kingdom of God. . . . Instead, we expend these blessings on our own desires, and as Moroni said, 'Ye adorn yourselves with that which hath no life, and yet suffer the hungry, and the needy, and the naked, and the sick and the afflicted to pass by you, and notice them not' (Morm. 8:39)."

Spencer W. Kimball (Ensign, June 1976, pp. 4-5)

"Moroni was troubled by what he saw. Are we troubled enough to set aside our love of substance and hear the cry of the hungry, the needy, the naked, and the sick?"

H. David Burton (Ensign, May 1997, p. 76)

"I guess one of the greatest mysteries of mortality is why mankind fails to learn from history. Why do those who profess to be true followers of Christ so often become victims of the enticements of the world? . . . We see so many members seeking worldly pursuits contrary to the words of the Lord's prophets. . . . Many of us are more concerned about our fine apparel, the size of our homes, and our cars and their gadgets than we are about the needs of the poor and the needy."

L. Tom Perry (Conference Report, Oct. 1992, pp. 19-20)

Morm. 9:31   **CONDEMN ME NOT BECAUSE OF MINE IMPERFECTION**
(Morm. 8:17; Ether 12:23-27; Title Page of Book of Mormon; *Cowley & Whitney on Doctrine*, pp. 185-186; refer in this text to Alma 61:9,19)

Morm. 9:32-34 **REFORMED EGYPTIAN**
(Book of Mormon 121-122 Student Manual, p. 4; refer in this text to 1 Ne. 1:2)

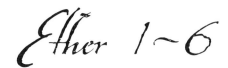

Ether 1~6

Ether 1:6-32 **JAREDITE GENEALOGY**
(Lehi in the Desert, Nibley, pp. 148-149; *Companion to Your Study of the Book of Mormon*, Ludlow, p. 309)

"Incidentally, the genealogy in Ether, chapter one, explains why neither the brother of Jared nor his children are ever named. . . . It is, of course, because 'he that wrote this' is a direct descendant of Jared (1:2, 32), and not of Jared's brother, and is giving the history of his own line only."

Hugh Nibley (Lehi in the Desert, pp. 149-150)

"While residing in Kirtland, Elder Reynolds Cahoon had a son born to him. One day, while the Prophet Joseph Smith was passing by his door, he called the Prophet in and asked him to bless and name the baby. Joseph did so and gave the baby the name of Mahonri Moriancumer. When he had finished the blessing he laid the child upon the bed, and turning to the father, Elder Cahoon, he said, 'The name I have given your son is the name of the Brother of Jared; the Lord has just shown (or revealed) it to me.' Elder William F. Cahoon, who was standing nearby, heard the Prophet make this statement to his father; and this was the first time the name of the Brother of Jared was known in the Church in this dispensation."

George Reynolds (Commentary on the Book of Mormon, 6:69)

Ether 1:33 **THE TOWER**
(Lehi in Desert, Nibley, p. 154-160; *Messiah in Ancient America*, Warren and Ferguson, p. 120)

"The people being of one language, gathered together to build a tower to reach, as they supposed the crystalized heavens. They thought that the City of Enoch was caught up a little ways from the earth, and that the city was within the first sphere above the earth; and that if they could get a tower high enough, they might get to heaven, where the City of Enoch and the inhabitants thereof were located."

Orson Pratt (Journal of Discourses 16:50)

"The people who built the Tower of Babel are said to have done so in order that its top might 'reach unto heaven.' It was to prevent them from accomplishing this purpose, that the Lord confounded their language. (Gen. 11:1-9.) Tradition credits Joseph Smith with the statement that the 'heaven' they had in view was the translated city."

Cowley & Whitney on Doctrine, p. 307

Ether 1:34-35   **THE LANGUAGE OF THE JAREDITES**
(Lehi in the Desert, Nibley, p. 165; *Companion to Your Study of the Book of Mormon*, Ludlow, p. 309; Moses 6:5-6; *Journal of Discourses* 2:342)*

"It is stated in the Book of Ether that Jared and his brother made the request of the Lord that their language be not changed at the time of the confusion of tongues at the Tower of Babel. Their request was granted, and they carried with them the speech of their fathers, the Adamic language, which was powerful even in its written form, so that the things Mahonri wrote 'were mighty even . . . unto the overpowering of man to read them.' That was the kind of language Adam had and this was the language with which Enoch was able to accomplish his mighty work."

Joseph Fielding Smith (The Way to Perfection, p. 69)

Ether 1:33-35, 38; 2:23-25; 6:5, 8   **THE DRIVING OUT vs THE CONFOUNDING**
(Lehi in the Desert, Nibley, pp. 167-174)*

Ether 1:41; 2:6-7   **THE JAREDITE MIGRATION vs THE NEPHITE MIGRATION**
(contrast 1 Ne. 2:4-6 *[Lehi in the Desert*, Nibley, pp. 179, 181-182])

Ether 2:3   **DESERET**
(Lehi in the Desert, Nibley, pp. 184-189)*

Ether 2:5   **WHERE THERE NEVER HAD MAN BEEN**
(Since Cumorah, Nibley, p. 238)

Ether 2:6-7   **BARGES**
(Lehi in the Desert, Nibley, pp. 177-178)

Ether 2:7-9,   **CONDITIONAL FREEDOM OF THE PROMISED LAND**
12,15   (Ether 9:20; Prov. 14:34; Heb. 11:16; *This Nation Shall Endure*, Benson, p. 145; *Doctrines of Salvation*, Smith, 3:321-322; *Conference Report*, Oct. 1916, pp. 69-70; *The Way of the Master*, Peterson, p. 172, refer in this text to 2 Ne. 1:7, 20, 30-32; 1 Ne. 1:20)

"The Lord's law for this land is declared in the Book of Mormon, where we read that this land is a 'land of promise' that 'the Lord God had reserved for a righteous people. . . . And whatsoever nation shall possess it shall serve God, or they shall be swept off.' The only power strong enough to withstand a fulness of iniquity is the fulness of the gospel of Jesus Christ."

Joseph B. Wirthlin (Ensign, Nov. 1994, p. 77)

"Our Constitution was made only for a moral and religious people. It is wholly inadequate to govern any other."

John Adams

"It is the duty of nations as well as men to own their dependence upon the overruling power of God, to confess their sins and transgressions in humble sorrow, yet with assured hope that genuine repentance will lead to mercy and pardon, and to recognize the sublime truth, announced in the Holy Scriptures and proven by all history, that those nations only are blessed whose God is the Lord."

Abraham Lincoln (quoted by Ezra Taft Benson, Righteousness Exalteth a Nation, p. 5)

"Our government rests upon religion. It is from that source that we derive our reverence for truth and justice, for equality and liberality, and for the rights of mankind. Unless the people believe in these principles they cannot believe in our government. There are only two main theories of government in the world. One rests on righteousness and the other on force. One appeals to reason, and the other appeals to the sword. One is exemplified in the republic, the other is represented by a despotism. The government of a country never gets ahead of the religion of a country. There is no way by which we can substitute the authority of law for the virtue of man. Of course we endeavor to restrain the vicious, and furnish a fair degree of security and protection by legislation and police control, but the real reform which society in these days is seeking will come as a result of our religious convictions, or they will not come at all. Peace, justice, humility, charity—these cannot be legislated into being. They are the result of divine grace."

Calvin Coolidge (as quoted in Doctrines of Salvation, Smith, 3:317-318)

"The success, which has hitherto attended our united efforts, we owe to the gracious interposition of Heaven; and to that interposition let us gratefully ascribe the praise of victory, and the blessings of peace."

George Washington (To the Executive of New Hampshire, Nov. 3, 1789, Writings, 12:175)

[Pres. Benson adds this to aforementioned quote by G. Washington] "Yes, it was this faith in God that sustained them in their hours of extremity. We too will need this same faith to sustain us in the critical days ahead."

Ezra Taft Benson (This Nation Shall Endure, p. 44)

"We must protect the soul of America—we must return to a love and respect for the basic spiritual concepts upon which this nation has been established. . . . God rules this world—It is the duty of nations as well as men to own their dependence upon the overruling power of God, to confess their sins and transgressions in humble sorrow . . . and to recognize the sublime truth that those nations only are blessed whose God is the Lord."

Ezra Taft Benson (A Nation Asleep, pp. 15, 43)

"We must study and learn for ourselves the principles laid down in the Constitution which have preserved our freedoms for the last two hundred years. If we do not understand the role of government and how our rights are protected by the Constitution, we may accept programs or organizations that help erode our freedoms. An informed citizenry is the first line of defense against anarchy and tyranny. We must teach our children about the spiritual roots of this great nation. We must become actively involved in supporting programs and textbooks in the public schools that teach the greatness of the early patriots who helped forge our liberties. We must teach our children that it is part of our faith that the Constitution of the United States was inspired by God. We reverence it akin to the revelations that have come from His hand. The great heritage of freedom bequeathed to us by our forbears must be handed on to each succeeding generation with great care."

Ezra Taft Benson (Righteousness Exalteth a Nation, pp. 5-6)

"This is a Christian nation. Before the Revolution it was so in accord with law; since the Revolution it has remained so in fact. We, the people of the United States, guarantee full religious freedom to all within our jurisdiction, whether they be non-Christian or Pagan. But the nation itself is a Christian nation. Our standards and principles are Christian. Thus we of America can stand for no cause which would dethrone Christianity here and put in its place any other creed, whether non-Christian or Pagan. . . ."

J. Reuben Clark, Jr. (Conference Report, Oct. 1939, p.10)

Ether 2:14   **PRAYER**
(contrast with Ether 1:43)

Ether 2:15   **MY SPIRIT WILL NOT ALWAYS STRIVE WITH MAN**
(contrast with Ether 15:19 [refer in this text to Morm. 1:14-17])

Ether 2:16; 6:13 **GO TO WORK**
(contrast with 2 Ne. 5:17, 24; Alma 23:18)

Ether 2:16-20 **CONSTRUCTION OF THE BARGES**
(*Since Cumorah*, Nibley, p. 7; *Book of Mormon Treasury*, pp. 136-137; *Companion to Your Study of the Book of Mormon*, Ludlow, pp. 313-315)

Ether 2:23; 3:1 **WINDOWS—GLASS**
"[Ether 2:23; 3:1] This would make the invention of glass far older than anyone dreamed it was until the recent finding of such objects as Egyptian glass beads from the end of the third millennium B.C. . . . We need not be surprised if the occurrences of glass objects before the sixteenth century B.C. are few and far between, for glass rots, like wood, and it is a wonder that any of it at all survives from remote antiquity. There is all the difference in the world, moreover, between few glass objects and none at all."

Hugh Nibley (Lehi in the Desert, pp. 213-215)

Ether 2:24-25; 6:5 **WINDS**
(*Firm Foundation of Mormonism*, Vestal & Wallace, p. 87; *Lehi in the Desert*, Nibley, pp. 167-174; *An Approach to the Book of Mormon*, 1957 edition, Nibley, pp. 290-295)

Ether 3:1   **SHINING STONES**
(*Book of Mormon Treasury*, p. 133-151; *An Approach to the Book of Mormon*, 1957 edition, Nibley, pp. 295-297)

Ether 3:14   **CHRIST - THE FATHER AND THE SON**
(refer in this text to 1 Ne. 19:10)

Ether 3:15   **NEVER HAVE I SHOWN MYSELF UNTO MAN**
(Answers to Book of Mormon Questions, Sperry, pp. 47-51; *Companion to Your Study of the Book of Mormon*, Ludlow, pp. 317-319; *Answers to Gospel Questions*, Smith, 2:123-125; *BYU Studies*, V. 30, No. 3; *Autobiography of Parley P. Pratt*, pp. 122-123)*

"We would assume all of the major prophets living prior to the brother of Jared had seen God. . . . Adam's face-to-face conversations with God in the Garden of Eden can be exempted because of the paradisical, pre-fallen state of that setting and relationship. Furthermore, other prophets' visions of God, such as Moses and Isaiah in the Bible, or Nephi and Jacob in the Book of Mormon, came after this 'never before' experience of the Brother of Jared. But before the era of the Tower of Babel, the Lord did appear unto Adam and 'the residue of his posterity who were righteous' in the valley of Adam-ondi-Ahman three years before Adam's death (see D&C 107:53-55). And we are left with Enoch, who said very explicitly, 'I saw the Lord; and he stood before my face, and he talked with me, even as a man talketh one with another, face to face' (Moses 7:4). We assume there would have been other prophets living in the period between Adam's leaving the Garden of Eden and the building of the Tower of Babel who also saw God in a similar manner, including Noah who 'found grace in the eyes of the Lord' and 'walked with God' (Genesis 6:8-9), the same scriptural phrase used to describe Enoch's relationship with the Lord (see Genesis 5:24). . . . Surely the most persuasive—explanation for me is that Christ is saying to the brother of Jared, 'Never have I showed myself unto man *in this manner, without my volition, driven solely by the faith of the beholder.*' As a rule, prophets are *invited* into the presence of the Lord, are bidden to enter his presence by him and only with his sanction. The brother of Jared, on the other hand stands alone then (and we assume now) in having thrust himself through the veil, not as an unwelcome guest but perhaps technically an uninvited one. . . . (Ether 3:9,15) . . . Indeed it would appear that this is Moroni's own understanding of the circumstance, for he later writes, 'Because of the knowledge [which has come as a result of faith] of this man *he could not be kept from beholding within the veil. . . . Wherefore, having this perfect knowledge of God, he could not be kept from within the veil*; therefore he saw Jesus' (Ether 3:19-20; emphasis added). . . . This may be an absolutely unprecedented case of a prophet's will and faith and purity so closely approaching that of heaven's that the man moves from understanding God to being actually like him, with his same thrust of will and faith, at least in this one instance."

Jeffrey R. Holland (Nurturing Faith Through the Book of Mormon; 24th Annual Sperry Symposium, pp. 15-18)

"I have always considered Ether 3:15 to mean that the Savior stood before the Brother of Jared plainly, distinctly, and showed him his whole body and explained to him that he was a spirit. In his appearance to Adam and Enoch, he had not made himself manifest in such a familiar way. His appearances to earlier prophets had not been with that same fulness. The scriptural accounts of talking face to face and of walking with God should not be interpreted in the sense that the Savior stood before those prophets and revealed his whole person. That he may have done so at later periods in the cases of Abraham and Moses is possible, but he had not done so in that fulness in the antediluvian days. For the Brother of Jared he removed the veil completely. He had never showed himself to man before in the manner and way he did to that prophet."

Joseph Fielding Smith (Doctrines of Salvation, 1:37)

"Why would Jehovah say: 'Never have I showed myself into man'? First, perhaps the Lord was speaking of the total and complete manner in which he revealed himself to the brother of Jared. (*Doctrines of Salvation* 1:37; *The Promised Messiah*, pp. 47, 599-600). Second, Sidney B. Sperry suggested that the Lord's statement may have to do with the principle that he does not reveal himself to men, (meaning 'sons of men,' unbelieving men); he only reveals himself to believers, to those who trust in and rely on him, who like Moriancumer, become redeemed from the Fall (*Answers to Book of Mormon Questions*, p. 49). Third, Daniel H. Ludlow has written: 'Another possible interpretation is that Jesus Christ . . . is essentially saying in Ether 3:15 that he has never *had* to show himself unto man before' (A *Companion to Your Study of the Book of Mormon*, p. 318). Fourth, President Harold B. Lee suggested that the uniqueness of Moriancumer's experience lay in the fact that he saw the Lord Jesus as he would be, that is, he saw a vision of Christ as his body would be, that is during his mortal ministry in some two thousand years. (*To Be on Speaking Terms with God*, pp. 8-9). Fifth, . . . it may be that this is the first occasion in history . . . when Jehovah manifested himself as Jesus Christ, *the Son*. Before this time he had made himself known by speaking to such persons as Adam (Moses 6), Enoch (Moses 6-7), and Noah (Moses 8) in the language and person of the Father, by divine investiture of authority. . . . Finally, perhaps the matter is simpler than we had supposed. Could it be that the pronouncement is a relative statement, that it pertains only to the Jaredites? That is, it may be that Jehovah was explaining, in essence, 'Never before have I showed myself to anyone in your dispensation, the Jaredite dispensation.'"

R. Millet, J. F. McConkie, and B. Top (Doctrinal Commentary on the Book of Mormon, 4:276-278)

Ether 3:15 **MAN CREATED IN THE IMAGE OF GOD**
(Abr. 4:26-27; Moses 6:8)

"It is held by some that Adam was not the first man upon this earth, and that the original human being was a development from lower orders of the animal creation. These, however, are the theories of men. The word of the Lord declares that Adam was 'the first man of all men' (Moses 1:34), and we are therefore in duty bound to regard him as the primal parent of our race. It was shown to the brother of Jared that all men were created in the beginning after the image of God; and whether we take this to mean the spirit or the body, or both, it commits us to the same conclusion: Man began life as a human being, in the likeness of our heavenly Father."

Joseph F. Smith, John R. Winder, & Anthon H. Lund (Improvement Era, Nov. 1909; 13:75-81)

Ether 3:23-24 **TWO STONES**
(Companion to Your Study of the Book of Mormon, Ludlow, pp. 319-320)

Ether 4:1-7 **SEALED PORTION OF THE PLATES**
(3 Ne. 26:9-10; refer in this text to 2 Ne. 27:6-7, 11; *Companion to Your Study of the Book of Mormon*, Ludlow, pp. 320-321; *Conference Report*, Smith, Oct. 1961, pp. 19-20)

Ether 4:13-15 **REND THE VEIL OF UNBELIEF**
"The Book of Mormon is predicated on the willingness of men and women to 'rend the veil of unbelief' in order to behold the revelations—and the Revelation—of God (Ether 4:15). It would seem that the humbling experience of the brother of Jared in his failure to pray and his consternation over the sixteen stones were included in this account to show just how mortal and just how normal he was . . . at least in some ways so much like ourselves. His belief in himself and his view of himself may have been limited—much like our view of ourselves. But his belief in God was unprecedented. It was without doubt or limit. . . . Ordinary individuals with ordinary challenges could rend the veil of unbelief and enter the realms of eternity. And Christ . . . would be standing at the edge of that veil to usher the believer through."

Jeffrey R. Holland (Nurturing Faith Through the Book of Mormon; The 24th Annual Sperry Symposium, pp. 23-24)

Ether 5 **MORONI'S NOTES TO FUTURE TRANSLATOR**
(2 Ne. 27:21; Ether 1:4; 5:1; *Answers to Gospel Questions*, Smith, 1:203-204)

"Did you know that a portion of the record from which the *Book of Mormon* is taken is sealed? The Prophet was not permitted to break the seals, and we will not receive the sealed record until the time comes when the people will show by their faith their willingness to accept it."

Joseph Fielding Smith (Doctrines of Salvation, pp. 201-202)

"It was returned by Joseph Smith to Moroni, its divinely appointed custodian. Nor did even Joseph Smith either read or translate it. [The sealed portion of the plates.] We know of no one among mortals since Mormon and Moroni who have known its contents. It was known among the Nephites during the nearly two hundred years of their Golden Era. [Fourth Nephi.] But for the present, the book is kept from us; only the portion upon which no seal was placed has been translated."

Bruce R. McConkie (A New Witness for the Articles of Faith, p. 443)

Ether 6:9   **MUSIC**
(D&C 25:11-12; 136:28; Alma 26:8; refer in this text to 1 Ne. 18:9)

"A missionary should never permit himself to see a movie or cheap literature, or hear music that tends to interfere with or which dampens the spirit of missionary work. There is ample evidence that rock music is offensive to the Spirit and affects adversely the spirituality of the missionaries and thus the success of the proselyting work."

Teachings of Ezra Taft Benson, p. 202

"Don't listen to music that is degrading. Music can, by its tempo, by its beat, by its intensity (and I would add by its lyrics) dull the spiritual sensitivity of men (and women). Young people, you cannot afford to fill your minds with this unworthy, hard music of our day."

Teachings of Ezra Taft Benson, p. 326

"I have spoken before of the experience I had as a twelve-year-old boy, a newly ordained deacon. With my father I went to our stake priesthood meeting. He sat on the stand as a member of the stake presidency, and I sat on the back row of the chapel. The men of that large congregation stood and sang,

Praise to the man who communed with Jehovah!
Jesus anointed that Prophet and Seer.

Blessed to open the last dispensation,
Kings shall extol him, and nations revere.
(Hymns, 1985, no. 27)

As I heard them sing that hymn with power and conviction, there came into my heart a witness of the divine calling of the boy Joseph, and I am grateful that the Lord has sustained it seventy years since then."

Gordon B. Hinckley (Ensign, Nov. 1993, p. 51)

"I stopped at a . . . ward meetinghouse and slipped unnoticed into the overflow area just as the congregation was beginning to sing. . . . As we sang, . . . I glanced around at members of the congregation and was stunned to observe that about a third of them were not singing. How could this be? . . . What are we saying, what are we thinking, when we fail to join in singing in our worship services? I believe some of us . . . are getting neglectful in our worship, including the singing of hymns."

Dallin H. Oaks (Ensign, Nov. 1994, p. 11)

"On a beautiful Sunday morning in the fall of 1841, my great-grandfather, William Minshall Evans, then sixteen years of age, was walking down the streets of Liverpool, England, on his way to church. Suddenly he heard singing that thrilled him beyond anything he had ever heard before. He followed the sound down an alley and up some rickety stairs into a room where a few people were holding a meeting. John Taylor, who later became president of the Church and who had a beautiful tenor voice was the singer. The song he sang was so beautiful that William remained to hear the sermon. Upon returning home, William was reprimanded by his elder brother, David, for being absent from his accustomed place in the choir. Asked to give an account of himself, William replied, 'I have been where you should have been, and I shall not be satisfied until you all hear the wonderful truth I have heard this morning.' . . .William and David were converted to the gospel, and then helped convert other members of their family. . . . I never sing the hymns of the Church without remembering that it was the singing of a hymn that opened the door to the gospel for my family and made it possible for me to enjoy all the blessings that have followed."

Marjorie Hinckley (Ensign, July 1981, p. 48)

Ether 6:22-23   KING - LEADETH INTO CAPTIVITY
(Mosiah 29:16-24)

Ether 7~12

Ether 7:5, 7;   **SERVE IN CAPTIVITY**
8:3,4;
10:14-15,   "Such is the practice . . . of keeping a king prisoner throughout his entire lifetime,
30-32;   allowing him to beget and raise a family in captivity, even though the sons thus
11:9,   brought up would be almost sure to seek vengeance for their parent and power for
18-19, 23 themselves upon coming of age. . . . It seems to us a perfectly ridiculous system,
yet it is in accordance with the immemorial Asiatic usage. . . . Benjamin of Tudela
tells how the khalif, the spiritual ruler of all western Asia, arranged for 'the brothers and other members of the khalif's family' to live lives of ease, luxury, and
security: 'every one of them possesses a palace within that of the khalif, but they are
all fettered by chains of iron, and a special officer is appointed over every household to prevent their rising in rebellion against the great king.' . . . It was the custom
of Turkish kings, as was long doubted by scholars but has recently been
proved, to allow their defeated rivals to sit upon their thrones by day, but lock
them up in iron cages for the night! . . . Moving back to the earliest records of
all, we find a large class of legends all over the ancient world telling how a victorious god in the beginning bound and imprisoned his rebellious relatives—not
killing them, since they partook of his own divine nature. . . ."

Hugh Nibley (Lehi in the Desert, pp. 201-203)

Ether 8:18-25   **SECRET COMBINATIONS**
(refer in this text to Hel. 1:11-12; *Gospel Ideals*, McKay, p. 306; *Conference
Report*, Oct. 1961, pp. 70-72)

". . . traffickers in illegal drugs represent a modern-day example of the Gadianton
robbers. The demand for these drugs must be cut off just as the Nephites cut off
the food supply of the army of the robbers [3 Ne. 4:18, 20]. . . .
    "Recent articles in *Time* (March 14, 1988) document the seriousness of the
problems caused by drug traffickers. According to the article, among other

things '70% of all local crimes (in Detroit) are drug related and 67% of a rising number of murders in Washington, D.C., are due to local drug wars.' . . . Attorney General Edwin Meese said about the efforts by some countries in helping the U.S. stop the supply of drugs, 'They are less than fully successful because of intimidation, bribery and corruption.' And finally, Sterling Johnson, a special narcotics prosecutor in New York City, suggests, 'Every American better just pray each night that we don't lose [the war on drugs].'"

Terrence L. Szink (Studies in Scriptures, ed. by K. Jackson, 8:133,137)

"Among today's secret combinations are gangs. . . . There are some simple things that we can do in our day to prevent others from drifting toward gangs and crime. We can avoid the temptation of being cliquish at school or at church. All of us can refrain from finding fault or alienating anyone by our words or actions. Nothing is more hurtful than to feel left out or made fun of. Therefore, we must never do anything that may drive others toward being accepted by a gang because they feel rejected by us. . . . Guard against spreading rumors or saying unkind things or allowing anything to occur that may hurt another. Make friends with your neighbors, watch out for each other, and help build a spirit of unity, peace, and love among them. These may seem like small things, but I assure you, . . . they . . . [will] be . . . effective in keeping people away from evil and crime. . . ."

M. Russell Ballard (Ensign, Nov. 1997, pp. 38-39)

"But the greatest handbook for freedom in this fight against evil is the Book of Mormon. . . . This most correct book on earth states that the downfall of two great American civilizations came as a result of secret conspiracies whose desire was to overthrow the freedom of the people. (Ether 8:21). Now undoubtedly Moroni could have pointed out many factors that led to the destruction of the people, but notice how he singled out the secret combinations, just as the Church today could point out many threats to peace, prosperity, and the spread of God's work, but it has singled out as the greatest threat the Godless conspiracy. There is no conspiracy theory in the Book of Mormon—it is a conspiracy fact. This scripture [Ether 8:22] should alert us to what is ahead unless we repent, because there is no question but that as people of the free world, we are increasingly upholding many of the evils of the adversary today. . . . Moroni seemed greatly exercised lest in our day we might not be able to recognize the startling fact that the same secret societies which destroyed the Jaredites and decimated numerous kingdoms of both Nephites and Lamanites would be precisely the same form of criminal conspiracy which would rise up among the gentile nations in this day."

Ezra Taft Benson (God, Family, Country, pp. 321-322)

"We have not been using the Book of Mormon as we should. Our homes are not as strong unless we are using it to bring our children to Christ. Our families may be corrupted by worldly trends and teachings unless we know how to use the book to expose and combat the falsehoods in socialism, organic evolution, rationalism, humanism, and so forth. . . . And our nation will continue to degenerate unless we read and heed the words of the God of this land, Jesus Christ, and quit building up and upholding the secret combinations which the Book of Mormon tells us proved the downfall of both previous American civilizations."

Teachings of Ezra Taft Benson, pp. 60-61

Ether 8:22   **BLOOD CRY FROM THE GROUND**
(New Witness for God, Roberts, 3:251-253; Journal of Discourses 17:276)

Ether 12:6-22   **NO WITNESS UNTIL AFTER THE TRIAL OF FAITH**
(Heb. 6:15; 10:36; *Lectures on Faith* 7:18)

"Being human, we would expel from our lives physical pain and mental anguish and assure ourselves of continual ease and comfort, but if we were to close the doors upon sorrow and distress, we might be excluding our greatest friends and benefactors. Suffering can make saints of people as they learn patience, long-suffering, and self-mastery."

Spencer W. Kimball (Faith Precedes the Miracle, pp. 95-106)

Adversity can increase faith or instead can cause the troubling roots of bitterness to spring up. . . . One's life, therefore, cannot be both faith-filled and stress-free. . . . Therefore, how can you and I really expect to glide naively through life, as if to say, 'Lord, give me experience, but not grief, not sorrow, not pain, not opposition, not betrayal, and certainly not to be forsaken. Keep from me, Lord, all those experiences which made Thee what Thou art! Then, let me come and dwell with Thee and fully share Thy joy!'"

Neal A. Maxwell (Ensign, May 1991, pp. 88-90)

"It is not unusual to have a missionary say, 'How can I bear testimony until I get one? How can I testify that God lives, that Jesus is the Christ, and that the gospel is true? If I do not have such a testimony, would that not be dishonest?' Oh, if I could teach you this one principle. A testimony is to be found in the bearing of it! Somewhere in your quest for spiritual knowledge, there is that 'leap of faith,' as the philosophers call it. It is the moment when you have gone to the edge of the light and stepped into the darkness to discover that the way is lighted ahead for just a footstep or two. . . . It is one thing to receive a witness from what you have read or what another has said; and that is a necessary beginning. It is quite another to have the Spirit confirm to you in your bosom that what you have testified is true. Can you not see that it will be supplied as you share it? As you give that which you have, there is a replacement, with increase! . . . 'Ye receive no witness until after the trial of your faith' (Ether 12:5-6). To speak out is the test of your faith. . . . The skeptic will say that to bear testimony when you may not know you possess one is to condition yourself; that the response is manufactured. Well, one thing for sure, the skeptic will never know. . . . The Spirit and testimony of Christ will come to you for the most part when, and remain with you only if, you share it. In that process is the very essence of the gospel. Is not this a perfect demonstration of Christianity? You cannot find it, nor keep it, nor enlarge it unless and until you are willing to share it. It is by giving it away freely that it becomes yours."

Boyd K. Packer (Ensign, Jan. 1983, pp. 54-55)

Ether 12:26-27   **I GIVE UNTO MEN WEAKNESS**
(Jacob 4:6-7; Acts 17:26; Deut. 32:7-9; D&C 1:19, 23, 28; 122:9; Job 14:5; 2 Cor. 12:9-10; 2 Ne. 3:13; Moses 6:31; 7:3; Num. 12:3; Psalm 84:5, 7; Isa. 41:10; Ex. 15:2; 2 Sam 2:33; Luke 1:37; Philip. 4:13; *Kisses at the Window*, Bassett, pp. 15-16, 33-41)

"Where do you suppose we get these weaknesses? If you pose this question to a group of Saints, it will astound you how many different answers you get to this particular question. Some will say that they are responsible for their own weaknesses; well, if you keep your weaknesses, that's true, but that is not where they come from. Another will say weaknesses come from heredity or environment; in either instance, we are passing the responsibility to someone else, either our parents or our neighborhood. Both of these sources have great influence upon us, but they do not give us our weaknesses. Still another may blame Lucifer, the devil, for their weaknesses; surely he is always on the job, but this is not where we get our weaknesses, either. Where do they really come from? The Lord tells us the answer to this question very plainly in the Book of Mormon. (Ether 12:27). So where do we get our weaknesses? We get them from the Lord; the Lord gives us weaknesses so we will be humble. This makes us teachable. Now don't misunderstand me—the Lord is not responsible for the sin; he is only responsible for the weakness. It seems that all men have weaknesses in one form or another, character traits that make one more subject to a particular temptation than another. . . . Giving us weakness, however, is one of the Lord's ways of getting our attention. He says this is the means he uses to make us humble, but he also says that if we will come unto him and have faith in him, he will make us strong wherein we are weak. I know this is the truth."

Hartman Rector, Jr. (Conference Report, Apr. 1970, pp. 139-140)

"As some of you have noticed, I only have one arm. . . . I want you to know that having one arm for nearly thirty years has been one of the greatest blessings of my life. It hasn't been my greatest challenge, but it has been a great teacher to me, teaching me to be more patient and tolerant with others as I have had to learn to be more patient with myself. It has helped me to understand the necessity of our having challenges in life to help develop our character and stamina, helping us to become what the Lord ultimately wants us to become. Our challenges may be physical, spiritual, economic, or emotional, but if we will treat them as opportunities and stepping-stones in our progress, rather than barriers and stumbling blocks, our lives and growth will be wonderful. I have learned that between challenges it is very restful but that any real growth that I have ever enjoyed has always come with a challenge."

John B. Dickson (Ensign, Nov. 1992, p. 45)

"God does nothing by chance but always by design as a loving Father. The manner of our coming into the world, our parents, the time, and other circumstances of our birth and condition, are all according to eternal purposes, direction, and appointment of divine providence."

Spencer W. Kimball (Ensign, Dec. 1974, p. 5)

"I believe that our Savior possessed a foreknowledge of all the vicissitudes through which He would have to pass in the mortal tabernacle. If Christ knew beforehand, so did we. But in coming here, we forgot all, that our agency might be free indeed, to choose good or evil."

Joseph F. Smith (Gospel Doctrine, p. 13)

". . . we had our own free agency in our pre-mortal existence, and whatever we are today is likely the result of that which we willed to be heretofore. We unquestionably knew before we elected to come to this earth the conditions under which we would here exist. . . . I have a conviction deep down in my heart that we are exactly what we should be, each one of us, except as we may have altered that pattern by deviating from the laws of God here in mortality."

Henry D. Moyle (Conference Report, Oct. 1952, pp. 71-72)

"Obviously, the personal burdens of life vary from person to person, but every one of us has them. Furthermore, each trial in life is tailored to the individual's capacities and needs as known by a loving Father in Heaven."

Howard W. Hunter (Conference Report, Oct. 1990, p. 20)

"Our Eternal Father knows all of his spirit children, and in his infinite wisdom, he chooses the very time that each comes to earth to gain a mortal body and undergo a probationary experience. Everything the Lord does is for the benefit and blessing of his children. And each of these children is subjected to the very trials and experiences that Omniscient Wisdom knows he should have. . . ."

Bruce R. McConkie (Millennial Messiah, p. 660)

"Some are tested by poor health, some by a body that is deformed or homely. Others are tested by handsome and healthy bodies; some by the passion of youth; others by the erosions of old age. Some suffer disappointment in marriage, family problems; others live in poverty and obscurity. Some (perhaps this is the hardest test) find ease and luxury. All are part of the test. *And there is more equality in this testing than sometimes we suspect.*"

Boyd K. Packer (Ensign, Nov. 1980, p. 21)

"On one occasion Theodore Roosevelt was decorating one of his generals for bravery. He said, 'This is the bravest man that I have ever seen.' He said, 'He walked right behind me all the way up San Juan Hill.' Theodore Roosevelt was a sickly child. He began life as a weakling, not expected to live; but he trained himself to think courage, strength, health, and vitality, and that is what he got. One of the things that frightens me most as I go about a little bit is to hear so many people talking weakness, failure, and sin. The most widespread disease in the world is the inferiority complex. And when we think inferiority, that is what we get. Another missionary described his problem by saying, 'I can't concentrate.' One of our most unfortunate weaknesses is that we sometimes think we are under sentence to remain forever as we presently are. Yet one of the most exciting ideas in life is the possibility of changing ourselves for the better."

Sterling W. Sill (Conference Report, Oct. 1963, p. 80)

"Strengthen yourselves by seeking the source of true strength—the Savior. Come unto him. He loves you. He desires your happiness and exults in your desires for righteousness. Make him your strength, your daily companion, your rod and your staff. Let him comfort you. There is no burden we need bear alone. His grace compensates for our deficiencies."

Chieko N. Okazaki (Ensign, Nov. 1994, p. 94)

"If you go to the Lord with a broken heart and a contrite spirit, he will show to you all your faults, and all your weaknesses, he will bring plainly before you wherein you have come short in doing his will, and when you see yourself in the light of that spirit instead of being filled with pride, you will feel to abase yourselves and bring yourselves down in the very dust of humility; your own unworthiness will be so plain before you, that if pride should come into your heart at any time, you will almost be shocked at it, and you will feel to put it away from you. It is in this way that we as Latter-day Saints should live."

George Q. Cannon (Journal of Discourses 22:101-102)

"In order to recognize our personal problems or weaknesses which hinder us from being better marriage partners, we should come to the Lord in prayer and reap the benefits of this powerful Book of Mormon promise: [Ether 12:27]. And so the need to pray. Many church leaders and marriage counselors indicate that they have not seen one marriage in serious trouble where the couple was still praying together daily. When problems arise and marriages are threatened, praying together as a couple may be the most important remedy."

Joe J. Christensen (Ensign, May 1995, p. 64)

"Each of us who have made covenants with God face challenges unique to us. . . . Our Heavenly Father knows us and our circumstances and even what faces us in the future. . . . [Jesus Christ] . . . has perfect understanding of the feelings, the suffering, the trials, and the needs of every individual. Because of that, a way will be prepared for us to keep our covenants, however difficult that may now appear, if we go forward in faith."

Henry B. Eyring (Ensign, Nov. 1996, p. 33)

"Indeed, when we are unduly impatient with an omniscient God's timing, we really are suggesting that we know what is best. Strange, isn't it—we who wear wristwatches seek to counsel Him who oversees cosmic clocks and calendars. Because God wants us to come home after having become more like Him and His Son, part of this developmental process, of necessity, consists of showing unto us our weaknesses. Hence, if we have ultimate hope we will be submissive, because, with His help, those weaknesses can even become strengths (see Ether 12:27). It is not an easy thing, however, to be shown one's weaknesses. . . . Nevertheless, this is part of coming unto Christ, and it is a vital, if painful, part of God's plan of happiness. Besides, as Elder Henry B. Eyring has wisely observed, 'If you want praise more than instruction, you may get neither' (1993 Annual University Conference, BYU, p. 42)."

Neal A. Maxwell (Ensign, Nov. 1998, p. 63)

Ether 12:36-38 COMFORT TO MORONI & JOSEPH SMITH
(contrast with D&C 135:4-5)

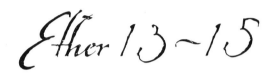

Ether 13:2-11

NEW JERUSALEM
(Rev. 21:1-2; Moses 7:62-64; 3 Ne. 20:21; *Doctrines of Salvation*, Smith, 3:68-71; *Mormon Doctrine*, McConkie, pp. 532-533; *History of the Church*, Smith, 2:262; refer in this text to 3 Ne. 21:22-24)

"In the day of regeneration, when all things are made new, . . . there will be the Jerusalem of old which shall be rebuilt according to the prophecy of Ezekiel. One will be the city of Zion, or of Enoch, which was taken from the earth when Enoch was translated and which will be restored; and the city Zion, or New Jerusalem, which is to be built by the seed of Joseph on this the American continent. . . . After the close of the millennial reign we are informed that Satan, who was bound during the millennium, shall be loosed and go forth to deceive the nations. Then will come the end. The earth will die and be purified and receive its resurrection. During this cleansing period the City Zion, or New Jerusalem, will be taken from the earth; and when the earth is prepared for the celestial glory, the city will come down according to the prediction in the Book of Revelation."

Joseph Fielding Smith (Answers to Gospel Questions, 2:105-106)

Ether 13:13-15, 20-22

REJECT THE LIVING PROPHET
(1 Ne. 14:6-7; 3 Ne. 16:10; refer in this text to Hel. 16:2; 1 Ne. 3:7; 1 Ne. 17:50)

"If we complain against the Lord's servants, the heavens are offended, the Spirit is withdrawn, and amen to that individual's faith. President David O. McKay once wrote: 'Murmuring against priesthood and auxiliary leadership is one of the most poisonous things that can be introduced into the home of a Latter-day Saint.'"

Ezra Taft Benson (Improvement Era, Mar. 1969, p. 3)

"If you want to be close to the Lord, if you want to have His favor and Spirit to be with you, follow the counsel of those who have been called to preside over you."

Ezra Taft Benson (London England Area Conference, June 1976)

"A man said to me, 'You know, there are people in our state who believe in following the Prophet in everything they think is right, but when it is something they think isn't right, and it doesn't appeal to them, then that's different.' He said, 'then they become their own prophet. They decide what the Lord wants and what the Lord doesn't want.' I thought, how true! We will be led astray, because we are false prophets to ourselves when we do not follow the prophet of God. No, we should never discriminate between these commandments, as to those we should and should not keep."

N. Eldon Tanner (Conference Report, Oct. 1966, p. 98)

"It is too much to suppose that all the priesthood at this juncture will unite behind the prophet in the fight for freedom. Yet we can pray for that day, and in the meantime the faithful should strive to be in harmony with the inspired counsel given by the Lord's mouthpiece—the prophet—and thus in unity with the Lord—and hence receive peace to their souls. The more we are united with the Lord and His prophet, the greater will be our chances to preserve our families and to live in freedom."

Ezra Taft Benson (An Enemy Hath Done This, p. 311)

"If we want to know how well we stand with the Lord, let us ask ourselves how well we stand with His mortal captain. How closely do our lives harmonize with the Lord's anointed—the living prophet, the President of the Church, and with the Quorum of the First Presidency? May God bless us all to look to the prophet and the presidency in the critical and crucial days ahead is my prayer."

Ezra Taft Benson (1980 BYU Devotional Speeches of the Year, p. 30)

"If you will not be loyal in the small things you will not be loyal in the large things. . . . A man who says he will sustain the President of the Church or the General Authorities, but cannot sustain his own bishop is deceiving himself. The man who will not sustain the bishop of his ward and the president of his stake will not sustain the President of the Church. . . . Some of us are very jealous of our prerogatives and feel that obedience to priesthood authority is to forfeit one's agency. If we only knew, my brethren and sisters, that it is through obedience that we gain freedom."

Boyd K. Packer (BYU Devotional, Mar. 23, 1965)

"Is not our attitude toward these prophets an unerring reflection of our innermost feeling toward God? I mean our real, basic allegiance when it is divested of all outward show and stripped of all pretensions. Can we truly love the Lord and at the same time reject his servants? If we really do love God, then indeed we must and we will love and revere his anointed ones."

Mark E. Petersen (Conference Report, Oct. 1981, pp. 90-91)

"The Lord and his prophets are one, and no one can believe in Christ and reject his prophets."

Bruce R. McConkie (The Mortal Messiah, 2:79)

"One day when President Grant was living, I sat in my office across the street following a general conference. A man came over to see me, an elderly man. He was very upset about what had been said in this conference by some of the Brethren, including myself. I could tell from his speech that he came from a foreign land. After I had quieted him enough so he would listen, I said, 'Why did you come to America?'
'I am here because a prophet of God told me to come.'
'Who was the prophet?' I continued.
'Wilford Woodruff.'
'Do you believe Wilford Woodruff was a prophet of God?'
'Yes,' said he.
'Do you believe that President Joseph F. Smith was a prophet of God?'
'Yes, sir.'
Then came the sixty-four dollar question. 'Do you believe that Heber J. Grant is a prophet of God?'
His answer: 'I think he ought to keep his mouth shut about old age assistance.'
Now I tell you that a man in his position is on the way to apostasy. He is forfeiting his chances for eternal life. So is everyone who cannot follow the living prophet of God."

Marion G. Romney (Conference Report, Apr. 1953, p. 125)

Ether 14:1-2   **SLIPPERY TREASURES**
(refer in this text to Morm. 1:18)

Ether 14:21-23   **THE SCENT OF THE DEAD**
(Alma 2:34; Morm. 6:7-22)

"On June 27, [1864] thirteen thousand Union men stormed the Confederates on Kennesaw Mountain—and failed. . . . Three days after the battle, an armistice was granted for burying the fallen—'Not for any respect either army had for the dead,' a Confederate remembered, 'but to get rid of the sickening stench.'"

Geoffrey C. Ward, Ric Burns, & Ken Burns (The Civil War, p. 324)

Ether 14:25   **DESTRUCTION OF A NATION**
(3 Ne. 16:10; D&C 1:35)

"We have been warned that we are ripening in iniquity and that we will be destroyed if we do not repent. Now my beloved brothers and sisters, I realize that these predictions are not pleasing, but nevertheless they speak the truth. . . . There is but one way these impending calamities can be avoided, and that way is repentance . . . the foreboding calamities can be averted if the inhabitants of the earth will repent, believe, and have faith in God as our Heavenly Father, in His Son Jesus Christ as our Redeemer, and will conform to their teachings."

Marion G. Romney (The Tragic Cycle, pp. 15-16)

"Other great civilizations have died by suicide. The first free people, the Greeks, died thus. And why did Greece fall? A slackness and softness finally came over them to their ruin. In the end more than they wanted freedom they wanted security, a comfortable life, and they lost all—security, comfort and freedom. We as a people have never known bondage. LIBERTY has always been our blessed lot. Few of us have ever seen people who have lost their freedom—their LIBERTY. And when reminded of the danger of losing our LIBERTY and independence our attitude has usually been—IT CANNOT HAPPEN HERE. We must never forget that nations may—and they usually do—sow the seeds of their own destruction while enjoying unprecedented prosperity."

Ezra Taft Benson (A Nation Asleep, pp. 13, 20)

Ether 15:19   **SPIRIT WITHDRAWS - HARD HEARTS**
(refer in this text to Morm. 1:14-17)

Ether 15:29-30   **KING vs. KING**

"The insane wars of the Jaredite chiefs ended in the complete annihilation of both sides, with the kings the last to go. . . . This all seems improbable to us, but two circumstances peculiar to Asiatic warfare explain why the phenomenon is by no means without parallel: (1) Since every war is strictly a personal contest between kings, the battle must continue until one of the kings falls or is taken. (2) And yet things are so arranged that the king must be the very last to fall, the whole army existing for the sole purpose of defending his person. This is clearly seen in the game of chess, in which all pieces are expendable except the king, who can never be taken. 'The shah in chess,' writes M. E. Moghadam, 'is not killed and does not die. The game is terminated when the shah is pressed into a position from which he cannot escape. This is in line with all good traditions of chess playing, and back of it the tradition of capturing the king in war rather than slaying him whenever that could be accomplished.' . . . In the code of medieval chivalry, taken over from central Asia, the person of the king is sacred, and all others must perish in his defense. After the battle the victor may do what he will with his rival—and infinitely ingenious tortures were sometimes devised for the final reckoning—but as long as the war went on, the king could not die, for whenever he did die, the war was over, no matter how strong his surviving forces. . . . The circle of warriors, 'large and mighty men as to the strength of men' (Ether 15:26) that fought around their kings to the last man, represent that same ancient institution, the sacred 'shieldwall,' which our own Norse ancestors took over from Asia and which meets us again and again in the wars of the tribes, in which on more than one occasion the king actually was the last to perish. So let no one think the final chapter of Ether is at all fanciful or overdrawn. Wars of extermination are a standard institution in the history of Asia."

Hugh Nibley (Lehi in the Desert, pp. 235-236)

THE NEPHITE DISEASE AND THE JAREDITES

"We are not given the step-by-step backsliding of this Jareditic civilization till it reached the social and governmental chaos the record sets out, but those steps seem wholly clear from the results. Put into modern terms, we can understand them. First there was a forsaking of the righteous life, and the working of wickedness; then must have come the extortion and oppression of the poor by the rich; then retaliation and reprisal by the poor against the rich; then would come a cry to share the wealth which should belong to all; then the easy belief that society owed every man a living whether he worked or not; then the keeping of a great body of idlers; then when community revenues failed to do this, as they always failed and always will fail, a self-helping by one to the goods of his neighbor; and finally when the neighbor resisted, as resist he must, or starve with his family, then death to the neighbor and all that belonged to him. This was the decreed 'fulness of iniquity.'"

Heber J. Grant, J. Reuben Clark, David O. McKay (Messages of the First Presidency, 6:99)

6 CYCLES OF THE NEPHITE DISEASE IN THE BOOK OF ETHER
FIRST CYCLE

Ether	Stages	Repeated During Wickedness	
6:28-30	Humble, Prosper, Rich		
7:5, 9, 16-21	War		
7:23	Wickedness	7:23-24	Prophet Rejected
		7:23	Curse Upon the Land
7:25-26	Repentance		

SECOND CYCLE

Ether	Stages	Repeated During Wickedness	
7:26-27	Prosper, No Wars, Righteous		
8:5; 9:12	War (Near Destruction)	8:9-25;	
		9:5-6	Secret Combinations

THIRD CYCLE

Ether	Stages	Repeated During Wickedness	
9:15-16, 21-22	Peace, Prosperity, Rich, Righteous		
9:26	Wickedness	9:26	Secret Combinations
		9:28-29	Prophet Rejected
9:30	Famine	9:28, 30	Curse Upon the Land
9:34	Repentance		

FOURTH CYCLE

Ether	Stages
10:2-3	Righteousness, Peace
10:5-7	(Wickedness) Unauthorized Plural Marriage, Heavy Taxes
10:8-9, 14-15	War

FIFTH CYCLE

Ether	Stages	Repeated During Wickedness	
10:16, 28	Prosper, Lived Right in the Sight of God		
		10:33	Secret Combinations
		11:1-2, 5	Prophets Rejected
		11:6	Curse Upon the Land
11:4, 7	Wars, Contentions, Famine, Pestilence		
11:8	Repentance		

SIXTH CYCLE

Ether	Stages	Repeated During Wickedness	
11:11, 13-14	Wickedness, Hardened Hearts		
		11:12	
		13:22	Prophets Rejected
		11:15	
		14:10	Secret Combinations
		14:1	Curse Upon the Land (Slippery Treasures)
13:15-15:32	War		
15:19	Spirit Is Withdrawn		
15:19-32	TOTAL DESTRUCTION OF THE NATION		

Moroni

(Written fifteen to thirty-five years after the battle at Cumorah)

Moro. 2-6   (D&C 52:15-16; 84:20-22; *Studies in Scripture*, ed. by Jackson, 8:287-288)

"Being born again comes by the Spirit of God through ordinances."

Teachings of the Prophet Joseph Smith, p. 162

"Good conduct without the ordinances of the gospel will neither redeem nor exalt mankind; covenants and ordinances are essential."

Boyd K. Packer (Conference Report, Oct. 1984, p. 105)

Moro. 2:1   (1 Ne. 12:8-10; *Doctrines of Salvation*, Smith, 3:158)

"[The Book of Mormon] . . .also tells us that our Savior made His appearance upon this continent after His resurrection; that He planted the Gospel here in all its fulness, and richness, and power, and blessing; that they had Apostles, Prophets, Pastors, Teachers, and Evangelists; the same priesthood, the same ordinances, gifts, powers, and blessings, as were enjoyed on the eastern continent. . . ."

Joseph Smith (History of the Church, 4:538)

"While in every instance the Nephite twelve are spoken of as disciples, the fact remains that they had been endowed with divine authority to be special witnesses for Christ among their own people. Therefore, they were virtually apostles to the Nephite race, although their jurisdiction was, as revealed to Nephi, eventually to be subject to the authority and jurisdiction of Peter and the twelve chosen in Palestine. (see 1 Nephi 12:8-10). According to the definition prevailing in the world an apostle is a witness for Christ, or one who evangelizes a certain nation or people. 'A zealous advocate of a doctrine or cause.' Therefore the Nephite twelve became apostles, as special witnesses, just as did Joseph Smith and Oliver Cowdery in the Dispensation of the Fulness of Times."

Joseph Fielding Smith (Answers to Gospel Questions, 1:121-122)

Moro. 4:3; 5:2   **ALWAYS REMEMBER HIM**
(D&C 20:77, 79; refer in this text to Hel. 5:5-14; 3 Ne. 18)

"How we treat our family members, our neighbors, business associates, and all we meet will reveal if we have taken His name upon us and do always remember Him. How we conduct our lives, all we do and all we say, reflects on how we remember Him."

Robert D. Hales (Ensign, Nov. 1997, p. 25)

[Regarding a conversation with two missionaries] ". . . I climbed into the front seat of the car. . . . After we had become acquainted, I leaned back over the seat and asked, 'What would you like to know about?' Both of them, eagerly and almost in chorus, said, 'Tell us how we can become more humble.' You might have struggled with that as I did. . . . They already had the first lesson in their hearts. The fact that they even asked meant that they had gone beyond being overwhelmed by their doubts about themselves to hope that if they would just submit, if they could just learn what to do, they could be better. If I had the chance again, I would have . . . given them just this one bit of counsel, counsel about what to do. I would have said just this: 'Always remember him' (Moro. 4:3; 5:2)."

Henry B. Eyring (Ensign, May 1995, p. 25)

OUR PROMISE IN THE SACRAMENT
(Moro. 4:3; *Ensign*, Mar. 1995, pp. 66-67)

"I have wondered how members of the Church can go to the sacrament service and partake of these emblems, and make these solemn covenants, and then immediately after the close of the meeting go out to some place of amusement, to attend a picture show, a baseball game, or some resort, or to gather at some home to play cards. When any of these things is done, the guilty person violates this sacred covenant so recently made or renewed. . . . The fact remains, however, that when we indulge in habits of this kind we are covenant breakers . . . If a man fully realized what it means when he partakes of the sacrament, that he covenants to take upon him the name of Jesus Christ and to always remember him and keep his commandments, and this vow is renewed week by week—do you think such a man will fail to pay his tithing? Do you think such a man will break the Sabbath day or disregard the Word of Wisdom? Do you think he will fail to be prayerful, and that he will not attend his quorum duties and other duties in the Church? It seems to me that such a thing as a violation of these sacred principles and duties is impossible when a man knows what it means to make such vows week by week unto the Lord and before the saints."

Joseph Fielding Smith (Doctrines of Salvation, 2:345-346)

THE LORD'S PROMISE IN THE SACRAMENT
(Moro. 4:3)

"All of us face different family circumstances and home situations. All of us need strength in dealing with them. This strength comes from faith in the Savior's love and in the power of his atonement. If we trustingly put our hand in the Savior's, we can claim the promise of the sacramental prayer to always have his Spirit with us. All problems are manageable with that strength, and all other problems are secondary in urgency to maintaining a strong spiritual life."

Chieko N. Okazaki (Ensign, Nov. 1993, p. 94)

"Do we always stop to think, on that sacred Sabbath day when we meet together to partake of the sacrament, that we witness, promise, obligate ourselves, in the presence of one another, and in the presence of God, that we will do certain things? . . . The first: We are willing to take upon ourselves the name of the Son. In so doing we choose him as our leader and our ideal: and he is the one perfect character in all the world. Second: That we will always remember him. Not just on Sunday, but on Monday, in our daily acts, in our self-control. When our brother hurts us, we are going to try to master our feelings and not retaliate in the same spirit of anger. . . . That's the spirit of the Christ, and that's what we have promised—that we will do our best to achieve these high standards of Christianity, true Christian principles. The third: We promise to '. . . keep his commandments which he has given . . .' — tithing, fast offerings, the Word of Wisdom, kindness, forgiveness, love. The obligation of a member of the Church of Jesus Christ is great, but it is as glorious as it is great, because obedience to these principles gives life, eternal life."

David O. McKay (Gospel Ideals, p. 146)

"In partaking of the sacrament, we can renew the effects of our baptism. . . . The renewal of our covenants by partaking of the sacrament should also be preceded by repentance, so we come to that sacred ordinance with a broken heart and a contrite spirit (see 2 Ne. 2:7; 3 Ne. 12:19; D&C 59:8). Then, as we renew our baptismal covenants and affirm that we will 'always remember him' (D&C 59:8), the Lord will renew the promised remission of our sins, under the conditions and at the time he chooses. . . . Out of the seemingly small act of consciously and reverently renewing our baptismal covenants comes a renewal of the blessings of baptism by water and by the Spirit, that we may always have his Spirit to be with us. In this way all of us will be guided, and in this way all of us can be cleansed."

Dallin H. Oaks (Ensign, Nov. 1996, p. 61)

"Even a child can understand what to do to have the Holy Ghost as a companion. The sacramental prayer tells us. . . . First, we promise to take His name upon us. That means we must see ourselves as His. We will put Him first in our lives. We will want what He wants rather than what we want or what the world teaches us to want. As long as we love the things of the world first, there will be no peace in us. Holding an ideal for a family or a nation of comfort through material goods will, at last, divide them. . . . Second, we promise always to remember Him. We do that every time we pray in His name. Especially when we ask for His forgiveness, as we must do often, we remember Him. . . . We also keep our promise to remember Him when as families we pray together and when we read the scriptures. . . . Third, we promise as we take the sacrament to keep His commandments, all of them. President J. Reuben Clark, Jr., . . . warned us against being selective in what we will obey. He put it this way: 'The Lord has given us nothing that is useless or unnecessary. . . . When we partake of the Sacrament we covenant to obey and keep his commandments. There are no exceptions' *(Conference Report, Apr. 1955, pp. 10-11)."*

Henry B. Eyring (Ensign, May 1998, p. 67)

Moro. 6:4   **NOURISHED**
(Luke 15:3-7; Hel. 6:3; *Studies in Scripture*, ed. by Jackson, 8:288-291; *Ensign*, Nov. 1997, pp. 82-84)

"The greatest tragedy in the Church . . . is the loss of those who join the Church and then fall away. With very few exceptions it need not happen."

Gordon B. Hinckley (Regional Representatives' Seminar, Apr. 3, 1987)

"We are becoming a great global society. But our interest and concern must always be with the individual. Every member of this church is an individual . . . Our great responsibility is to see that each is 'remembered and nourished by the good word of God' (Moro. 6:4), that each has opportunity for growth and expression and training in the work and ways of the Lord, that none lacks the necessities of life, that the needs of the poor are met, that each member shall have encouragement, training, and opportunity to move forward on the road of immortality and eternal life. This, I submit, is the inspired genius of this the Lord's work."

Gordon B. Hinckley (Ensign, May 1995, p. 52)

"It is not an easy thing to become a member of this Church. In most cases it involves setting aside old habits, leaving old friends and associations, and stepping into a new society which is different and somewhat demanding. With the ever-increasing number of converts, we must make an increasingly substantial effort to assist them as they find their way. Every one of them needs three things: a friend, a responsibility, and nurturing with 'the good word of God' (Moro. 6:4). It is our duty and opportunity to provide these things. . . . The Savior of all mankind left the ninety and nine to find the one lost. That one who was lost need not have become lost. But if he is out there somewhere in the shadows, and if it means leaving the ninety and nine, we must do so to find him. (See Luke 15:3-7). . . . In my view nothing is of greater importance."

Gordon B. Hinckley (Ensign, May 1997, pp. 47-48)

"Unfortunately, with this acceleration in conversions, we are neglecting some of these new members. . . . There is no point in doing missionary work unless we hold on to the fruits of that effort. The two must be inseparable. I should like to read you a letter. . . . A man writes:

'. . . I earnestly studied the Church and felt as if I had found a home. I decided to be baptized on October 8, 1994. It was one of the greatest days of my life.

'However, after my baptism, things with the Church changed. I suddenly was thrown into an environment where I was supposed to know what was going on. I now was not the focus of attention but just another member. I was treated as if I was in the Church for years. . . .

'At this same time, I was feeling intense pressure from my fiancée to not be in the Church. She was extremely anti-Mormon [in her] beliefs and didn't want me to be a part of it. We fought often about the Church. . . .

'I used the missionaries for a lot of support. . . . That worked until the missionaries were transferred. . . . I looked to the members for support, but there was none. The bishop helped, but he could only do so much. I gradually lost my 'warm, fuzzy feeling' about the Church. I felt like a stranger. I began to doubt the Church and its message. Eventually, I started to listen more to my fiancée. Then I made a decision that maybe I had rushed into the Church too quickly. I wrote my bishop and asked that my name be removed from the Church records. . . . That was a low point in my life. . . .

'I regret that I left the Church and had my name removed from the records, but at the time I felt that there was no other option. The experience left a bad impression with me, and it would be difficult to overcome.

'I wanted you to know . . . that I think a lot of new converts may have similar experiences to mine. . . . I know from my past that had the support been there, I would not be writing this letter to you. . . .'

Someone has failed, failed miserably. . . . You cannot disregard the converts. . . . They need nurturing with the good word of God. They come into the Church with enthusiasm for what they have found. We must immediately build on that enthusiasm. . . . I am satisfied the Lord is not pleased with us. . . . I invite every member to reach out in friendship and love for those who come into the Church as converts."

Gordon B. Hinckley (Ensign, Nov. 1997, pp. 50-51)

"It [has been] . . . our privilege to attend various wards in several different states. . . . We began to notice differences in the spirits of the various wards. Some wards our children loved to visit because they quickly found friends among the youth, and we all received a warm and hearty welcome. But there were other wards to which our children returned with less enthusiasm, and there was noticeable absence of the warm and hearty welcome. We then began to observe that in some wards . . . if we had been investigators or new members, we would not have felt very welcome. . . . On occasion we felt like 'strangers and foreigners' in the very Church of Jesus Christ to which we belonged. . . . [As members], we do pretty well at fulfilling callings, at going to meetings, at paying our tithing; but have we learned to truly live the second great commandment: 'Thou shalt love thy neighbour as thyself?' (Matt. 22:39). . . . It is my prayer that we may be open and outgoing, friendly, and helpful to all who come among us."

Carl B. Pratt (Ensign, Nov. 1997, pp. 11-12)

"Church members did not become inactive while crossing the plains, when the sense of belonging and being needed was so profound."

Neal A. Maxwell (Ensign, May 1982, p. 37)

"Long years ago, Joseph Lyon of Salt Lake City shared with me the lesson of a lecture which a minister from another faith observed as he spoke to the Associated Credit Men of Salt Lake. The minister boldly proclaimed, 'Mormonism is the greatest philosophy in the world today. The biggest test for the Church will come with the advent of television and radio, which tend to keep people away from the Church.' He then proceeded to relate what I've called the 'hot coals' story. He described a warm fireplace where the pieces of wood had burned brightly, with the embers still glowing and giving off heat. He then observed that by taking in hand brass tongs, he could remove one of the hot embers. That ember would then slowly pale in light and turn black. No longer would it glow. No longer would it warm. He then pointed out that by returning the black, cold ember to the bed of living coals, the dark ember would begin to glow and brighten and warm. He concluded, 'People are somewhat like the coals of a fire. Should they absent themselves from the warmth and spirit of the active church membership, they will not contribute to the whole, but in their isolation will be changed. As with the embers removed from the heat of the fire, as they distance themselves from the intensity of the spirit generated by the active membership, they will lose that warmth and spirit.' The reverend closed his comments by observing, 'People are more important than the embers of a fire.' As years come and then go and life's challenges become more difficult, the visits of home teachers to those who have absented themselves from Church activity can be the key which will eventually open the doors to their return."

Thomas S. Monson (Ensign, Nov. 1997, pp. 47-48)

"There are still too many . . . [converts] who do not feel warmly welcomed. Recently a new member wrote to me: 'Sometimes I . . . feel like it was a mistake for me to be baptized. I know this Church is true, and I have a strong testimony, but I still question. . . . When I was investigating, everyone from my ward were always there for me and . . . always wanted to help me out. . . . Since I was baptized it's like they don't even notice when I go to church or when I don't. I hardly hear from anybody. . . . I can't understand why the people in my ward have just forgotten me. I feel so lonely and confused. . . . I can't talk to my bishop because . . . we aren't close at all. He didn't even remember me when I went back to church. Please help me if you can.' . . . Every soul is very precious to our Heavenly Father. We must never forget that through the Atonement, the Lord Jesus Christ paid a great price for the redemption of each one of us. His suffering must not be in vain because we fail to nurture and teach those who are striving to be active in the Church."

M. Russell Ballard (Ensign, Nov. 1998, pp. 7-8)

Moro. 6:5-6   **MEET TOGETHER OFT**
(Alma 5:6; D&C 20:75)

"Unless the Saints attend their meetings it will be hard for them to keep alive in the Gospel."

Anthon H. Lund (Conference Report, Oct. 1907, p. 9)

"Those members of the Church who habitually absent themselves from the sacrament meeting and who do not enter into the covenants which the sacrament requires of them, are guilty of grievous sin and are under grave condemnation. The Spirit of the Lord cannot dwell in them, and they deny to themselves the guidance of that Spirit. Willful and protracted absence is a sign of apostasy, and if persisted in will lead to faultfinding, disagreement with authorities, and misunderstanding and criticism of the doctrines of the Church. If such a course is continued, it will lead those who are guilty out of the Church, for the Spirit of the Lord cannot be their companion when they show indifference to this sacred commandment."

Joseph Fielding Smith (Doctrines of Salvation, 2:344)

"A man of my acquaintance remained home each Sabbath and justified himself by saying that he could benefit more by reading a good book at home than by attending the sacrament meeting and listening to a poor sermon. But the home, sacred as it should be, is not the house of prayer. In it no sacrament is administered; in it is not found the fellowship with members, nor the confession of sins to the brethren. The mountains may be termed the temples of God and forests and streams his handiwork, but only in the meetinghouse, or house of prayer, can be fulfilled all the requirements of the Lord. And so he has impressed upon us that: [D&C 20:75]. But we do not go to Sabbath meetings to be entertained or even simply to be instructed. We go to worship the Lord. It is an individual responsibility, and regardless of what is said from the pulpit, if one wishes to worship the Lord in spirit and in truth, he may do so by attending his meetings, partaking of the sacrament, and contemplating the beauties of the gospel. If the service is a failure to you, you have failed. No one can worship for you; you must do your own waiting upon the Lord."

Teachings of Spencer W. Kimball, p. 220

Moro. 6:7-8 **CHURCH COURTS**
(Book of Mormon 121-122 Student Manual, p. 144; refer in this text to Mosiah 26:36)

"Church discipline . . . is not for the purpose of punishment only, but is intended to heal and renew."

Ronald E. Poelman (Ensign, Nov. 1993, p. 85)

"Church discipline is not limited to sexual sins but includes other acts such as murder, abortions, burglary, theft, fraud, and other dishonesty, deliberate disobedience to the rules and regulations of the Church, advocating or practicing polygamy, apostasy, or any other unchristianlike conduct, including defiance or ridicule of the Lord's anointed, contrary to the law of the Lord and the order of the Church. . . . Among the activities considered apostate to the Church include when members '(1) repeatedly act in clear, open, and deliberate public opposition to the Church or its leaders; (2) persist in teaching as Church doctrine information that is not Church doctrine after being corrected by their bishops or higher authority; or (3) continue to follow the teachings of apostate cults (such as those that advocate plural marriage) after being corrected by their bishops or higher authority' *(General Handbook of Instructions*, 1989, p. 10-3)"

James E. Faust (Ensign, Nov. 1993, p. 36)

Moro. 7-9

MORMON'S WORDS
"Mormon's sermon ranks as one of the greatest, surpassed only by those of the Savior."

Monte Nyman (Studies in Scripture, ed. by K. Jackson, 8:293)

Moro. 7:3-4

PEACEABLE FOLLOWERS OF CHRIST
(Jacob 1:7; D&C 84:24; refer in this text to Alma 37:34)

"[These people] depend completely upon the saving power of His Gospel, and are therefore at rest in all the tumult of mind and public agitation which beset the way."

Joseph F. Smith (Improvement Era, July 1904, 7:714)

Moro. 7:4-11

MOTIVES
(D&C 58:26-29; 88:33; 137:9; Heb. 4:12-13; Psalm 24:3-4; Alma 5:19; 29:4-5; 41:3, 6; Rom. 2: 2; Cor. 8:12; *Ye Are the Light of the World*, Lee, p. 292; refer in this text to Alma 12:14; Mosiah 4:30; 3 Ne. 12:27-29)

"Sister Romney and I moved into a ward in which they were just beginning to build a meetinghouse. The size of the contribution the bishop thought I ought to contribute rather staggered me. I thought it was at least twice as much as he should have asked. However, I had just been called to a rather high Church position, so I couldn't very well tell him where to go. Therefore, I said, 'Well, I will pay it, Bishop, but I will have to pay it in installments because I don't have the money.' And so I began to pay. And I paid and paid until I was down to about the last three payments, when, as is my habit, I was reading The Book of Mormon, and came to the scripture which said: '. . . if a man . . . giveth a gift . . . grudgingly; wherefore it is counted unto him the same as if he had retained the gift; wherefore he is counted evil before God' (Moroni 7:8). This shocked me because I was out about a thousand dollars. Well, I went on and paid the three installments I had promised to pay, and then I paid several more installments to convince the Lord that I had done it with the right attitude."

Marion G. Romney (Relief Society Magazine, Feb. 1968, pp. 84-85)

"Have you ever found yourself doing something you thought was right, but doing it because you 'had' to? Did you ever keep a commandment of God with an attitude of resentment. . . . Do you think such feelings will be ignored by a Father in Heaven who gave us the willpower we call agency? . . . We are accountable for our feelings and desires as well as our acts. Evil thoughts and desires will be punished. Acts that seem to be good bring blessings only when they are done with real and righteous intent. On the positive side, we will be blessed for the righteous desires of our hearts even though some outside circumstance has made it impossible for us to carry those desires into action."

Dallin H. Oaks (BYU 1985-86 Devotional & Fireside Speeches, pp. 29, 31)

Moro. 7:12-17   **KNOWING GOOD FROM EVIL**
(D&C 46:8, 27; Omni 1:25; Ether 4:12; Moses 6:56; Isa. 5:20; *Teachings of the Prophet Joseph Smith*, pp. 202-215; *Improvement Era*, Apr. 1947, p. 201)

"We must realize that all things, including information disseminated by our schools, churches, and government, should be judged according to the words of the prophets, especially the living Prophet. This procedure coupled with the understanding which will come through the Spirit of the Lord, if we are living in compliance with the scriptures, is the only sure foundation and basis of judgment. Any other course of action leaves us muddled, despondent, wandering in shades of gray, easy targets for Satan."

Ezra Taft Benson (A Nation Asleep, p. 16)

"With the Lord there are no 'gray areas.' We are for Him or we are not. He asks us to serve Him with ALL our hearts, might and minds, and no one can give his all and still hold something back. But many nevertheless try to create 'gray areas' to justify their compromises."

Church News, Editorial Page, Feb. 25, 1967

"We can help yielding to wrong influences and being quarrelsome and selfish. We can help giving way to the spirit of theft, and we can resist the spirit of lust. God has given us power to resist these things, that our hearts may be kept free from them and also from doubt. . . . Whenever darkness fills our minds, we may know that we are not possessed of the Spirit of God, and we must get rid of it. When we are filled with the Spirit of God, we are filled with joy, with peace and with happiness no matter what our circumstances may be; for it is a spirit of cheerfulness and of happiness."

George Q. Cannon (Gospel Truths, pp. 16-17)

Moro. 7:16   **THE LIGHT OF CHRIST**
(D&C 84:45-46; 88:7-13; *Companion to Your Study of the Book of Mormon*, Ludlow, p. 335; *Gospel Doctrine*, Smith, pp. 66-68; *Journal of Discourses* 13:157; *Teachings of the Prophet Joseph Smith*, p. 199)

"The Lord has not left men (when they are born into this world) helpless, groping to find the light and truth, but every man that is born into the world is born with the right to receive the guidance, the instruction, the counsel of the Spirit of Christ, or Light of Truth. . . . If a man who has never heard the gospel will hearken to the teachings and manifestations of the Spirit of Christ, or the Light of Truth, which come to him, often spoken of as conscience—every man has a conscience and knows more or less when he does wrong, and the Spirit guides him if he will hearken to its whisperings—it will lead him eventually to the fulness of the gospel. . . . This light of Christ is not a personage. It has no body. I do not know what it is as far as substance is concerned; but it fills the immensity of space and emanates from God. It is the light by which the worlds are controlled, by which they are made. It is the light of the sun and all other bodies. It is the light which gives life to vegetation. It quickens the understanding of men. . . . We have often heard of guardian angels attending us and many patriarchs have spoken of such protection. There are times no doubt when some unseen power directs us and leads us from harm. However, the true guardian angel given to every man who comes into the world is the Light of Truth or Spirit of Christ. The Holy Ghost is given to faithful members of the Church to guard and direct them; theirs is the privilege, through their faithfulness, to have such guidance and protection."

Joseph Fielding Smith (Doctrines of Salvation, 1:51-55)

"God's light, [the Light of Christ] includes the physical light we see, which makes us feel so warm and comfortable. God's light is also the power to understand and comprehend all things. In other words, all kinds of light are related to intelligence and truth."

Theodore M. Burton (Conference Report, Apr. 1981, p. 38)

"We are separated from animals by more than upright posture, an articulated thumb, and the size of our brain. We are separated by a conscience. . . . Our conscience might be described as a memory, a residual awareness of who we really are, of our true identity. It is perhaps the best example of the fact that we can become aware of truths because we *feel* them. . . . This knowledge of right and wrong, is called the light of Christ, moral sense, or conscience, it moderates our actions unless, that is, we subdue it or destroy it. . . . It affirms . . . the reality of good and evil, justice, mercy, honor, courage, faith, love, and virtue, as well as their necessary opposites, hatred, greed, brutality, and jealousy."

Boyd K. Packer (The Book of Mormon: Jacob Through Words of Mormon, To Learn with Joy, BYU Religious Studies Center, ed. by Nyman and Tate, pp. 3-4)

"The Light of Christ, which is sometimes called the Spirit of Christ or the Spirit of God, 'giveth light to every man that cometh into the world' (D&C 84:46). This is the light 'which is in all things, which giveth life to all things' (D&C 88:13). . . . The Light of Christ enlightens and gives understanding to all men (see D&C 88:11). In contrast, a manifestation of the Holy Ghost is more focused. . . . These manifestations are available to everyone. The Book of Mormon declares that the Savior 'manifesteth himself unto all those who believe in him, by the power of the Holy Ghost; yea, unto every nation, kindred, tongue, and people' (2 Ne. 26:13). The gift of the Holy Ghost is more comprehensive. . . . The gift of the Holy Ghost includes the right to constant companionship, that we may 'always have his Spirit to be with [us]' (D&C 20:77)."

Dallin H. Oaks (Ensign, Nov. 1996, p. 60)

Moro. 7:27, 29, 37-38 **MIRACLES CEASE THROUGH UNBELIEF**
(Moro. 10:19, 24; Morm. 1:13-14)

"The Lord will not force himself upon people; and if they do not believe, they will receive no visitation. If they are content to depend upon their own limited calculations and interpretations, then, of course, the Lord will leave them to their chosen fate. (Moroni 7:38)."

Spencer W. Kimball (Conference Report, Oct. 1966, p. 22)

Moro. 7:29-31 **ANGELS**
(*Mormon Doctrine*, McConkie, p. 639; *History of the Church*, Smith, 4:425)

"One hot afternoon in the tropics, I stood before a zone conference of missionaries. I was telling them that missionaries should so conduct themselves and be so spiritually prepared in their way of teaching and be such perfect gentlemen and ladies that the investigators and members would actually see them as 'angels.' . . . In fact, *angel* means 'messenger' in Hebrew (malak). I quoted from Moroni 7:29. . . . My eyes darted across the column to verse 31 and it glowed—it jumped out at me. So I read it as well and, while I was reading it out loud to the missionaries, I saw it as a new writing with a new meaning. . . . It says: 'The office of their ministry [the ministry of angels] is to call men unto repentance, and to fulfill and to do the work of the covenants of the Father, . . . to prepare the way among the children of men, by declaring the word of Christ unto the chosen vessels of the Lord.' It was made clear to me at that moment that angels and missionaries do the very same work—the very same things. . . . In other words, no wonder some special, elect people are so in tune with the Spirit that they see the missionaries as angels. They see only the missionaries, but they feel angels present, so they believe the missionaries to be angels, too."

Robert E. Wells (Doctrines of the Book of Mormon, 1991 Sperry Symposium, pp. 14-15)

Moro. 7:33

POWER TO DO WHAT IS EXPEDIENT IN ME

"Because of my learning disability, it was hard to read the words and even more difficult to understand them. I often felt embarrassed and frustrated. I didn't like to go to Young Women because I felt inadequate. I was afraid I might be called on to read. I felt more comfortable with my family, but I continued to feel frustrated. I prayed for help and I found this scripture. Please turn with me to Moroni 7:33 . . . 'And Christ hath said: If ye will have faith in me ye shall have power to do whatsoever thing is expedient in me.' What a wonderful promise! If I would put my faith in the Lord, he would help me. He would help me to understand the scriptures. This was the key for me. One verse at a time, one day at a time, I began to understand. Even my schoolwork improved. The Book of Mormon got me through high school. I still have my learning disability and face challenges every day, but daily scripture study reminds me to have faith in my Heavenly Father."

Hilarie Cole (Ensign, May 1995, p. 95)

Moro. 7:40-44

HOPE

(2 Ne. 31:20; Rom. 5:3-4; Psalm 146:24; 1 Peter 3:15; Articles of Faith 1:13; *BYU Devotional*, Groberg, June 3, 1984; *Ensign*, Maxwell, Nov. 1994, pp. 34-36; refer in this text to Moro. 10:20)

"Hope is the desire of faithful people to gain eternal salvation in the Kingdom of God hereafter."

Bruce R. McConkie (Mormon Doctrine, p. 365)

"We must not lose hope. Hope is an anchor to the souls of men. Satan would have us cast away that anchor. In this way he can bring discouragement and surrender. But we must not lose hope. The Lord is pleased with every effort, even the tiny, daily ones in which we strive to be more like Him. Though we may see that we have far to go on the road to perfection, we must not give up hope."

Teachings of Ezra Taft Benson, p. 398

Moro. 7:40-44   FAITH
(refer in this text to Alma 31-35; Ether 12:6; *Lectures on Faith*, 1:7-13, 24)

Moro. 7:43-44   MEEK AND LOWLY IN HEART
(3 Ne. 12:5; Matt. 11:29; 2 Cor. 10:1)

"Meekness, however, is more than self-restraint; it is the presentation of self in a posture of kindness and gentleness, reflecting certitude, strength, serenity, and a healthy self-esteem and self-control. Without meekness, the conversational points we insist on making often take the form of 'I' . . . We even make nervous jokes about meekness, such as, 'If the meek intend to inherit the earth, they are going to have to be more aggressive about it!' We even tend to think of a meek individual as being used and abused—as being a doormat for others. However, Moses was once described as being the most meek man on the face of the earth (see Num. 12:3), yet we recall his impressive boldness in the courts of Pharaoh and his scalding indignation following his descent from Sinai. . . . Not only are the meek less easily offended, but they are less likely to give offense to others. In contrast, there are some in life who seem, perpetually, to be waiting to be offended. Their pride covers them like boils which will inevitably be bumped. . . . Meekness does not mean tentativeness. But thoughtfulness. Meekness makes room for others. . . . Meekness is not display humility; it is the real thing. True meekness is never proud of itself, never conscious of itself. Among the meek there is usually more listening and less talking. . . . Besides, even if our being meek results in our being abused in this world, we need to remember that we are being fitted for chores in another and better world—one which will be everlasting, not fleeting."

Neal A. Maxwell (Ensign, Mar. 1983, p. 73)

"And what of the meek? In a world too preoccupied with winning through intimidation and seeking to be number one, no large crowd of folk is standing in line to buy books that call for mere meekness. But the meek shall inherit the earth, a pretty impressive corporate takeover—and done *without* intimidation!

. . . Every knee shall bow and every tongue will confess that gentleness is better than brutality, that kindness is greater than coercion, that the soft voice turneth away wrath."

Howard W. Hunter (Ensign, May 1993, pp. 64-65)

Moro. 7:45-47 **CHARITY**
(2 Ne. 26:30; *Mere Christianity*, C.S. Lewis, pp. 164-165)

"Charity gives to those who don't deserve and expects nothing in return: It is the love God has for us, and the love we have for little children, of whom we expect nothing but for whom we would give everything."

Hugh Nibley

"Real charity is not something you give away; it is something that you acquire and make a part of yourself. And when the virtue of charity becomes implanted in your heart, you are never the same again. It makes the thought of being a basher [speaking ill of someone] repulsive. Perhaps the greatest charity comes when we are kind to each other, when we don't judge or categorize someone else, when we simply give each other the benefit of the doubt or remain quiet. Charity is accepting someone's differences, weaknesses, and shortcomings; having patience with someone who has let us down; or resisting the impulse to become offended when someone doesn't handle something the way we might have hoped. Charity is refusing to take advantage of another's weakness and being willing to forgive someone who has hurt us. Charity is expecting the best of each other."

Marvin J. Ashton (Ensign, May 1992, p. 19)

[Charity] "The phrase 'love of Christ' might have meaning in three dimensions: . . . First, love *for* Christ. This concept proclaims Jesus as the object of our love, and our lives should be an external expression of our gratitude for him. . . . A second dimension of the meaning of charity is love *from* Christ. (Ether 12:33-34.) The Savior's act of redemption for our sins is of no effect without our willingness to comply with the conditions of his atonement. . . . A third perception of charity is to possess a love that is *like* Christ. (2 Ne. 33:7-9; John 13:34). Charity is not just . . . a word to describe actions or attitudes. Rather, it is an internal condition that must be developed and experienced in order to be understood. . . . People who have charity have a love for the Savior, have received of his love, and love others as he does."

C. Max Caldwell (Ensign, Nov. 1992, pp. 29-30)

Moro. 8 **INFANT BAPTISM**
(Matt 18:6-10; 19:13-15; Mark 10:13-16; Mosiah 15:24-25; *Answers to Gospel Questions*, Smith, 1:51-52, 56-57; 3:113; *The Great Apostasy*, Talmage, pp. 119, 126-127; *Outlines in Ecclesiastical History*, Roberts, pp. 142, 148; *The Gospel Through the Ages*, Hunter, pp. 204-205).

"The doctrine of baptizing children, or sprinkling them, or they must welter in hell, is a doctrine not true, not supported in Holy Writ, and is not consistent with the character of God. All children are redeemed by the blood of Jesus Christ, and the moment that children leave this world, they are taken to the bosom of Abraham."

Joseph Smith (History of the Church, 4:5)

"During these formative, innocent years, [prior to age eight] a child may learn wrong behavior; but such is not the result of Satan's temptations, but comes from the wrong teachings and the bad example of others."

Merlin R. Lybbert (Ensign, May 1994, p. 32)

Moro. 8:16 **FEAR**
(1 Ne. 22:17, 22; 2 Ne. 8:7; Psalm 27:1; 2 Tim. 1:1-7; D&C 6:32, 34, 36; 29:4-7; 32:3; 38:30; 68:5-6; 84:87-88; John 14:27)

"We see individuals and families facing heightened anxiety and fear. It would seem that discouragement, depression, and despair are our contemporary 'Black Plague.' Ours is, as Jesus said it would be, a time of distress with perplexity (see Luke 21:25). . . . If I may be so bold this morning, may I suggest 'direction for deliverance'? . . . We need to turn to God. We need to reaffirm our faith, and we need to reassert our hope. . . . Without religious faith, without recognizing the reality and necessity of spiritual life, the world makes no sense, and a non-sense world is a place of horror."

Jeffrey R. Holland (Ensign, Nov. 1993, pp. 13-14)

"A large part of conquering daily fear is simply doing things that we don't know how to do—yet. . . . I've just finished reading Eleanor Roosevelt's biography. . . . This was a woman whose early life was ruled by fear and self-doubt. She described herself as an awkward adolescent, unattractively tall, with protruding teeth, dressed inappropriately, and so ill at ease with others her own age that parties and dances were dreaded occasions. How did she move from that to the kind of confidence that allowed her to contribute so widely? She said, 'You gain strength, courage, and confidence by every experience in which you really stop to look fear in the face. You must do the thing which you think you cannot do' (Karen McAuley, *Eleanor Roosevelt,* New York: Chelsea House Publishers, 1987, p. 105). As we concentrate on pleasing the Lord rather than others and continue to work hard, doing the things we don't know how to do yet, we will experience personal growth. . . . Are you remembering that you have had hands laid on your head—that you have been given a gift? Use that gift to conquer your fears!"

Virginia H. Pearce (Ensign, Nov. 1992, pp. 91-92)

"Action is inhibited by fear. . . . You rightly have concerns about measuring up and finding your place in life. You more often recognize your inadequacies rather than your strengths. . . . We can overcome all of our fears, not all at once, but one at a time. As we do so we will grow in confidence. The following is the story of a young man who encountered a fear that each one of us has faced or will face at some time in our lives: It was a hot July afternoon, and the chapel was filled for stake priesthood meeting. There was a young priest sitting on the stand in 'contained nervousness,' and after the hymn the stake president announced him as the next speaker. He spread out his notes, and as he did so his quivering hands betrayed his fear. He began to speak, but soon his speech quickened to a gabble, his words wild and repetitive. Worse followed as he began to stammer and then stopped speaking altogether. A heavy silence settled on the room. Who has not felt the terror of standing before an awesome audience? Everyone thought he would sit down, but no, he stayed on his feet, his head down. A few ominous seconds ticked by, and then he squared his shoulders and blurted out: 'Brethren I ask for an interest in your faith and prayers, that I might have sureness of speech.' Then he went back to where he had left off, speaking quietly but clearly. Soon his voice rose to its natural resonance, and he delivered his message to its full conclusion. It was not so much his message that thrilled those who were there. It was the image of that young man, unflinching even though he felt himself teetering on a precipice of fear, taking up the banner of courage and rallying himself for the cause of truth."

James E. Faust (Ensign, Nov. 1997, pp. 43-44)

Moro. 8:22   **WITHOUT THE LAW**
(Alma 24:9; 29:5; *Journal of Discourses* 16:42; refer in this text to Mosiah 15:24; 2 Ne. 9:25-27)

"The Lord has made it known by revelation that children born with retarded minds shall receive blessings just like little children who die in infancy. They are free from sin, because their minds are not capable of a correct understanding of right and wrong. . . . Therefore the Church of Jesus Christ of Latter-day Saints considers all deficient children with retarded capacity to understand, just the same as little children under the age of accountability. They are redeemed without baptism and will go to the celestial kingdom of God, there, we believe, to have their faculties or other deficiencies restored according to the Father's mercy and justice."

Joseph Fielding Smith (Answers to Gospel Questions, 3:20-21)

Moro. 8:25-26   A PROCESS OF CHANGE
(refer in this text to Mosiah 2:16-17; Mosiah 5:2, 7; Mosiah 27:24-26; Alma 5:7)

"Just think about what you must do . . . to touch lives with faith for him. You will need to love the people you serve. You will need to be humble and full of hope. You will need to have the Holy Ghost as your companion to know when to speak and what to say and how to testify. But all of that will come naturally, in time, from the covenants you make and keep as you follow him. Here is the description of how that will happen, from the eighth chapter of Moroni, the twenty-fifth and twenty-sixth verses: . . . You may not have seen that mighty change in yourself yet. But it will come as you continue to follow him. You can trust that he will qualify you as his servant, to assist him in touching lives with faith to bring to pass the eternal life of man. And you will find satisfaction in that service beyond your fondest dreams."

Henry B. Eyring (Ensign, Nov. 1995, p. 40)

"A testimony comes when the Holy Ghost gives the earnest seeker a witness of the truth. A moving testimony vitalizes faith; that is, it induces repentance and obedience to the commandments. Conversion, on the other hand, is the fruit of, or the reward for, repentance and obedience. (Of course one's testimony continues to increase as he is converted). Conversion is effected by divine forgiveness, which remits sins. The sequence is something like this. An honest seeker hears the message. He asks the Lord in prayer if it is true. The Holy Spirit gives him a witness. This is a testimony. If one's testimony is strong enough, he repents and obeys the commandments. By such obedience he receives divine forgiveness which remits sin. Thus he is converted to a newness of life. His spirit is healed."

Marion G. Romney (Conference Report, Oct. 1963, pp. 23-26)

Moro. 8:27-28;   HARD HEARTS & THE HOLY GHOST
9:4-5
(Ether 3:15; 15:19; *Journal of Discourses* 21:317-318; *Conference Report*, Apr. 1989, pp. 3-7; refer in this text to 2 Ne. 26:11; Hel. 13:8; Morm. 1:14-17)

". . . only the spreading of the Gospel can save the World."

L. Tom Perry (Conference Report, Apr. 1989, pp. 15-18)

"I prophesy, in the name of the Lord God of Israel, anguish and wrath and tribulation and the withdrawing of the Spirit of God from the earth await this generation, until they are visited with utter desolation."

Teachings of the Prophet Joseph Smith, p. 328

Moro. 9:3-4 **ANGER**
(3 Ne. 11:29; Ether 15:23; Abr. 3:28; Psalm 37:8; Prov. 14:17; 15:18; 16:32; 22:24; 27:4; Eccl. 7:9; Col. 3:19, 21; refer in this text to 3 Ne. 11:28-30; 3 Ne. 12:22)

"It is tragic what a lack of courtesy can bring. We see it every day as we move in the traffic of the cities in which we live. A moment spent in letting someone else get into the line does good for the one who is helped, and it also does good for the one who helps. Something happens inside of us when we are courteous and deferential toward others. It is all part of a refining process, which if persisted in, will change our very natures. On the other hand, anger over a little traffic problem, with swearing and filthy gestures, demeans those who make them and offends those at whom they are aimed. To practice the kind of self-discipline which can control one's temper in the little things that happen almost every day is an expression of emotional cleanliness."

Gordon B. Hinckley (Ensign, May 1996, p. 49)

"Unfortunately a few of you [sisters] may be married to men who are abusive. Some of them put on a fine face before the world during the day, and come home in the evening, set aside their self-discipline, and on the slightest provocation fly into outbursts of anger. No man who engages in such evil and unbecoming behavior is worthy of the priesthood of God. No man who so conducts himself is worthy of the privileges of the House of the Lord. I regret that there are some men undeserving of the love of their wives and children. There are children who fear their fathers and wives who fear their husbands. If there be any such within the hearing of my voice, as a servant of the Lord I rebuke you and call you to repentance. Discipline yourselves. Master your temper. Most of the things that make you angry are of very small consequence. And what a terrible price you are paying for your anger. Ask the Lord to forgive you. Ask your wife to forgive you. Apologize to your children."

Gordon B. Hinckley (Ensign, Nov. 1996, p. 68)

"[Anger] . . . is another serious thing to which many young men become addicted. . . . With the least provocation they explode into tantrums of uncontrolled rage. . . . But even worse, they are prone to lose all sense of reason and do things which later bring regret. We hear much these days of the phenomenon called road rage. Drivers become provoked over some small irritation. They fly into a rage, even resulting in murder. A life of regret follows. As the writer of Proverbs has said, 'He that is slow to anger is better than the mighty; and he that ruleth his spirit than he that taketh a city' (Prov. 16:32). If you have a temper, now is the time to learn to control it. . . . Let no member of this Church ever lose control of himself in such an unnecessary and vicious manner. . . . I constantly deal with those cases of members of the Church who have . . . appl[ied] . . . for a cancellation of their temple sealing. When first married, they are full of great expectations. . . . But the flower of love fades in an atmosphere of criticism and carping, of mean words and uncontrolled anger. Love flies out the window as contention enters. I repeat, my brethren, if any of you young men have trouble controlling your temper, I plead with you to begin the work of making that correction now. Otherwise you will bring only tears and sorrow into the homes which you will someday establish."

Gordon B. Hinckley (Ensign, May 1998, p. 50)

Moro. 9:5   **FEAR OF DEATH**

Moro. 9:7-11,   **A FALLEN PEOPLE**
18-19, 23   "The tragedy of the Book of Mormon is not what became of the Nephites but what the Nephites became."

Hugh Nibley

"We stand in danger of losing our liberties, and that once lost, only blood will bring them back; and once lost, we of this Church will, in order to keep the Church going forward, have more sacrifices to make and more persecutions."

J. Reuben Clark (Conference Report, Apr. 1944, p. 116)

Moro. 9:9   **PRECIOUS ABOVE ALL THINGS . . . VIRTUE**
(Prov. 31:10; refer in this text to Alma 39:4-6)

"If we look at love between two who are preparing for temple marriage, we see the elements of sacrifice and of serving each other's best interests, not a short-sighted 'me' interest. True love and happiness in courtship and marriage are based upon honesty, self-respect, sacrifice, consideration, courtesy, kindness, and placing 'we' ahead of 'me.' Those who would have us forfeit virtue and chastity to prove our love in sexual participation out of wedlock are neither friends nor eternally family-oriented. To classify them as selfish and unwise is not too severe. Those who serve the flesh will never know the love and fruits of purity."

Marvin J. Ashton (Conference Report, Apr. 1981, p. 30)

"Virtue has many definitions, such as moral excellence, right action and thinking, goodness of character, or chastity. . . . The First Presidency has said: 'How glorious and near to the angels is youth that is clean; this youth has joy unspeakable here and eternal happiness hereafter. Sexual purity is youth's most precious possession; it is the foundation of all righteousness' *(Improvement Era*, May 1942, p. 273). This implies that the virtue of [our youth] . . . should be equal to the angels (see *Collected Discourses of George Q. Cannon*, Oct. 5, 1890)."

James E. Faust (Ensign, May 1998, p. 95)

Moro. 9:20   **PAST FEELING**
(Eph. 4:19; 1 Ne. 17:45)

"A sex saturated society cannot feel the needs of its suffering members because instead of developing the love that looks outward, it turns man selfishly inward. Imperviousness to the promptings of the still small voice of God will also mean that we have ears, but cannot hear, not only the promptings of God but also the pleas of men. . . . We shut out people, nature, and God."

Neal A. Maxwell (A Time to Choose, pp. 59-60, 71)

"People who wrongly celebrate their capacity to feel finally reach a point where they lose much of their capacity to feel! . . . Such individuals become 'past feeling.' When people proceed 'without principle,' erelong they will be 'without civilization,' 'without mercy,' and 'past feeling' (see Moro. 9:11-20). Such individuals do not experience real joy, such as being quietly and deeply grateful to a generous God, or of helping to restore those who 'droop in sin' (2 Ne. 4:28), or of gladly forgoing praise and recognition so that it might flow, instead, to parched souls."

Neal A. Maxwell (Ensign, May 1995, pp. 67-68)

Moro. 10:3-5   **A WITNESS TO THE TRUTHFULNESS OF THE BOOK OF MORMON**
(1 Ne. 10:17-19; 15:24; 2 Ne. 25:22; 29:11; Morm. 8:12; D&C 8:2-3; 17:6; *Ensign*, Apr. 1994, pp. 12-16; refer in this text to 2 Ne. 33:4, 14)

"May I test your unity as Latter-day Saints? Have ye received a witness of the Spirit to your souls testifying that this is the truth?"

Harold B. Lee (Conference Report, Apr. 1950, pp. 99-100)

"Search the scriptures . . . and ask your Heavenly Father, in the name of His Son Jesus Christ, to manifest the truth unto you, and if you do it with an eye single to His glory nothing doubting, He will answer you by the power of His Holy Spirit. You will then know for yourselves and not for another. You will not then be dependent on man for the knowledge of God; nor will there be any room for speculation."

Teachings of the Prophet Joseph Smith, pp. 11-12

"We have a great many members of this Church who have never reached a manifestation through the Holy Ghost. Why? Because they have not made their lives conform to the truth."

Joseph Fielding Smith (Church News, Nov. 4, 1961, p. 14)

"I believe that no man can open that book and read it with a prayerful heart and ask God, in the name of Jesus Christ for a testimony regarding its divinity, but what the Lord will manifest unto him by His Spirit the truth of the book. Now that is the promise made in the book itself, and God has performed it; He has done it in thousands of cases. There is a mark of divinity on this book; and I maintain that no man could read [it] . . . without receiving an impression of this kind."

Heber J. Grant (Conference Report, Apr. 1908, p. 57)

"To meet the difficulties that are coming, it will be necessary for you to have a knowledge of the truth of this work for yourselves. The difficulties will be of such a character that the man or woman who does not possess this personal knowledge or witness will fall. If you have not got the testimony, live right and call upon the Lord and cease not till you obtain it. If you do not you will not stand. . . . The time will come when no man nor woman will be able to endure on borrowed light. Each will have to be guided by the light within himself. If you do not have it, how can you stand?"

Heber C. Kimball (Life of Heber C. Kimball, Whitney, p. 450)

"Social, ethical, cultural, or educational converts will not survive under the heat of the day unless their taproots go down to the fulness of the gospel which the Book of Mormon contains."

Ezra Taft Benson (Ensign, May 1975, p. 65)

"No man had yet so much as heard the Book of Mormon but what the Spirit of the Lord whispered quietly to his soul that the book was true."

Brigham Young (quoted by B. H. Roberts, Conference Report, Oct. 1905, pp. 44, 45)

"Take away the Book of Mormon and the revelations, and where is our religion?"

Teachings of the Prophet Joseph Smith, p. 71

Moro. 10:4 **REAL INTENT**
(refer in this text to Enos 1:4)

Moro. 10:5 **BY THE POWER OF THE HOLY GHOST YE MAY KNOW**
(refer in this text to Mosiah 5:2, 7; Mosiah 27:24-26; Alma 5:7, 12-14; Moro. 7:16)
"[The Holy Ghost] has a more powerful effect upon the soul than anything else received in any other way. A millennium of experience through sight, sound, touch, taste, smell, and all the powers of the universe combined cannot approach the sublime and complete experience of one brief moment under the influence of the Holy Ghost."

Keith B. McMullin (Ensign, May 1996, p. 9)

Moro. 10:8-18 **GIFTS OF THE SPIRIT**
"The receipt is always predicated upon obedience to the law, but because they are available to all the obedient they are called gifts. They are . . . reserved for the faithful and none else."

Bruce R. McConkie (Mormon Doctrine, pp. 314-315)

Moro. 10:20 **HOPE**
(refer in this text to Moro. 7:40-44)

"Admittedly, we have ample reason to be deeply concerned because we see no immediate answers to the seemingly unsolvable problems confronting the human family. But regardless of this dark picture, which will ultimately get worse, we must never allow ourselves to give up hope! Moroni, having seen our day, counseled, 'Wherefore, there must be faith; and if there must be faith there must also be hope' (Moro. 10:20)."

M. Russell Ballard (Ensign, Nov. 1992, p. 31)

"Let me compare [hope] . . . to this ingenious fan-hat that was given to me in Tonga. . . . If it's hot and muggy, you can use this fan to provide a cooling breeze, and its curved ribs provide an even greater current of air than a flat fan. But if it should start to rain, the fan can quickly become a hat and provide shelter from the storm. In much the same way, hope is a virtue for all seasons and all adversities, whether the problem is a storm or too much pleasant weather. What is the opposite of hope? Despair, of course, but despair comes when we feel powerless to influence events and when the sources of meaning in our life disappear. Despair is a kind of disorientation so profound that we lose contact with the sources of life itself. . . . Hope does not calculate odds. It is a double-sided virtue. Like this fan-hat, it is prepared for either sunny or stormy weather. To choose hope is to choose life. To choose hope is to choose love. . . . We literally cannot despair—unless we choose to. . . . We can choose to feed the darkness and death in our lives, or we can choose to feed the brightness of hope in our lives. We can worry. We can deny the light. We can refuse to ally ourselves with Jesus Christ, the already triumphant master of life. . . . We can cooperate with the killing of our spirits and the strangling of our hopes until meaninglessness and despair overcome us. . . . If we choose, if we even desire to choose, if we even hope for the desire to choose, we set in motion powerful forces for life that are led by Jesus Christ himself. He responds to those tender tendrils of crippled life with the force and energy that will bring them to flowering. . . . Choose hope even though despair seems close! Choose to grow even though circumstances oppress you! Choose to love, even though ours are days of violence and vengeance. Choose to forgive, to pray, to bless another's life with simple kindness."

Chieko N. Okazaki (Ensign, Nov. 1996, pp. 89-91)

"Real hope keeps us 'anxiously engaged' in good causes even when there appear to be losing causes on the mortal scoreboard (see D&C 58:27). Likewise, real hope is much more than wishful musing. It stiffens, not slackens, the spiritual spine. Hope is serene, not giddy, eager without being naive, and pleasantly steady without being smug. Hope is realistic anticipation which takes the form of a determination—not only to survive adversity but, moreover, to 'endure . . . well' to the end (D&C 121:8). . . . Genuine, ultimate hope helps us to be more loving even while the love of many waxes cold (see Matt. 24:12). We are to be more holy, even as the world ripens in iniquity; more courteous and patient in a coarsening and curt world, and to be of strong hearts even when the hearts of others fail them (see Moro. 10:22)."

Neal A. Maxwell (Ensign, Nov. 1998, pp. 62-63)

Moro. 10:22 **DESPAIR COMETH BECAUSE OF INIQUITY**
(contrast with Alma 8:10-15; Alma 26:27; *Ensign,* Oct. 1974, pp. 65-67)

"Moroni taught that 'despair cometh because of iniquity' (Moroni 10:22). Those who are caught in immorality may be experiencing the devastating effects of despair. But there is an alternative. For those who pay the price required by true repentance, the promise is sure. You can be clean again. The despair can be lifted. The sweet peace of forgiveness will flow into your lives."

Ezra Taft Benson (1987-88 BYU Devotional & Fireside Speeches, p. 54)

"Satan, the great deceiver, would have us believe that there is joy in sin, and much of the world has gone along with his lies. A medical or psychological counselor who tells a person to overcome his guilt feelings for what he does wrong and to feel free to do whatever he wishes doesn't understand this basic principle. Though there may be temporary pleasure in evil, there is no real joy. If a person is in a state of deep despair (which is more than sorrow over death and suffering) it is because he is in the bonds of iniquity."

Book of Mormon 121-122 Student Manual, p. 527 (out of print)

"A grumpy cynicism pervades politics in so many places on this planet. Holocausts, famine, pestilence, and tides of refugees have taken a terrible toll on human hope, with much of that toll coming from man-made, avoidable disasters. Causality can be assigned to one or another form of iniquity. No wonder, as the scriptures say, despair comes of iniquity! (Moro. 10:22). . . . Henry David Thoreau correctly observed that 'unconscious despair is concealed even under what are called the games and amusement of mankind' (*Walden Pond*, New York: Harper and Row, 1965, p. 7). No wonder so much hollow laughter emanates from the 'lonely crowd.' . . . Doubt, despair, and desensitization go together. . . . Despair, like dandelions, needs so little encouragement to sprout and spread. Despair comes so naturally to the natural man!"

Neal A. Maxwell (Ensign, Nov. 1994, pp. 34-35)

Moro. 10:31 **BEAUTIFUL GARMENTS—STRENGTHEN STAKES—ENLARGE BORDERS**
(3 Ne. 22:2)

"Verse 31 says: 'Awake, and arise from the dust, O Jerusalem; yea, and put on thy *beautiful garments*.' Then, '*strengthen they stakes*' follows, and, lastly, '*enlarge thy borders forever.*' I could clearly see that 'enlarge thy borders' meant to enlarge the Church through missionary work and to *proclaim* the gospel to all the world. It seemed that I could also see clearly that 'strengthen they stakes' meant to *perfect* the Saints through the priesthood organizations and the auxiliaries. And, it seemed to me that 'put on thy beautiful garments' referred to the temple robes and going to the temples of the Lord to *redeem* our beloved ancestors."

Robert E. Wells (Doctrines of the Book of Mormon, 1991 Sperry Symposium, p. 14)

Moro. 10:32 **COME UNTO CHRIST, AND BE PERFECTED IN HIM, AND DENY YOURSELVES OF ALL UNGODLINESS**
(Alma 39:9; Luke 9:23)

"I know another good man who was reared in a family without the blessings of the gospel. Through a series of unfortunate events in his early youth, he was introduced to homosexuality, and gradually he became a prisoner of this addictive behavior. One day two young missionaries knocked on his door and asked if he would be interested in learning of the restored gospel of Jesus Christ. In his heart of hearts he wanted to be freed from his prison of uncleanness, but feeling unable to change the direction his life had taken, he terminated the missionary discussions. Before leaving his apartment, the two elders left a copy of the Book of Mormon with him, and testified of its truthfulness. My friend placed the book on his bookshelf and forgot about it for several years. He continued acting out his homosexual tendencies, assuming that such relationships would bring him happiness. But alas, with each passing year, his misery increased. One day in the depths of despair, he scanned his bookshelf for something to read which might edify and uplift him and restore his self-worth. His eye caught hold of the book with a dark-blue cover, which the missionaries had given him several years before. He began to read. . . . And as my good friend continued reading, he too was filled with the Spirit of the Lord. . . . By the time he reached the final page of the Book of Mormon, he was prepared to accept Moroni's loving invitation to 'come unto Christ, and be perfected in him, and deny yourselves of all ungodliness' (Moro. 10:32). My friend contacted the Church and was taught the gospel and was baptized. Within a relatively short time, he married a lovely young woman, and they are the parents of several beautiful children. He and his wife are very dynamic and committed servants of the Lord, influencing many others for good."

Spencer J. Condie (Ensign, Nov. 1993, pp. 16-17)

"Moroni declared the need for us to deny ourselves 'all ungodliness,' thus including both large and small sins. While boulders surely block our way, loose gravel slows discipleship, too. Even a small stone can become a stumbling block. . . . Putting off the views and appetites of the natural man is such a large part of denying oneself, a process sometimes accompanied by scalding shame and the reflux of regret (see JST, Luke 14:28). Even so, in today's world, individual appetites, far from being denied, are actually celebrated! As one writer noted, this mantra has its own incessant 'beat,' and it goes 'Me . . . Me . . . Me!' (David Frum)."

Neal A. Maxwell (Ensign, May 1995, pp. 66-67)

HE WILL MANIFEST THE TRUTH OF IT UNTO YOU
(*Testimonies of the Book of Mormon*)

"The Book of Mormon (is) the most correct of any book on earth, and the keystone of our religion, and a man would get nearer to God by abiding by its precepts, than by any other book."

Joseph Smith (History of the Church 4:461)

"I am just as firmly convinced that this Book of Mormon from which I have read is the word of God and was revealed, as Joseph Smith declared it was revealed, as I am that I stand here looking into your faces. Every soul on the face of the earth who has intelligence enough to understand may know that truth. . . . My witness to all the world is that this book is true. I have read it many, many times, I have not read it enough. It still contains truths that I still may seek and find, for I have not mastered it, but I know it is true. . . . There is not a soul who cannot receive that testimony if he desires to receive it, by reading this book prayerfully and faithfully, with a desire to know the truth as Moroni has declared by revelation."

Joseph Fielding Smith (Conference Report, Oct. 1949, pp. 89-90)

"I started to read the Book of Mormon before I was old enough to be a deacon, and I have been reading it ever sense, and I know that it is true. Every member of the Church ought to know that it is true, and we ought to be prepared with an answer to all of these critics who condemn it."

Joseph Fielding Smith (Conference Report, Oct. 1961, p. 18)

[Wilford Woodruff's first meeting with the Elders] "Upon my arrival home my sister-in-law informed me of the meeting. I immediately turned out my horses and started for the schoolhouse without waiting for supper. On my way I prayed most sincerely that the Lord would give me his Spirit, and that if these men were the servants of God I might know it, and that my heart might be prepared to receive the divine message they had to deliver. When I reached the place of meeting, I found the house already packed. My brother Azmon was there before I arrived. He was equally eager to hear what these men had to say. I crowded my way through the assembly and seated myself upon one of the writing desks where I could see and hear everything that took place. Elder Pulsipher opened with prayer. He knelt down and asked the Lord in the name of Jesus Christ for what he wanted. His manner of prayer and the influence which went with it impressed me greatly. The Spirit of the Lord rested upon me and bore witness that he was a servant of God. After singing, he preached to the people for an hour and a half. The Spirit of God rested mightily upon him, and he bore a strong testimony of the divine authenticity of the Book of Mormon and of the mission of the Prophet Joseph Smith. I believed all that he said. The Spirit bore witness of its truth. Elder Cheney then arose and added his testimony to the truth of the words of Elder Pulsipher. Liberty was then given by the elders to anyone in the congregation to arise and speak for or against what they had heard as they might choose. Almost instantly I found myself upon my feet. The Spirit of the Lord urged me to bear testimony to the truth of the message delivered by these elders. I exhorted my neighbors and friends not to oppose these men; for they were the servants of God. They had preached to us that night the pure gospel of Jesus Christ. When I sat down, my brother Azmon arose and bore similar testimony. He was followed by several others."

Wilford Woodruff (Improvement Era, Nov. 1960, p. 814)

[Willard Richards' first contact with the Book of Mormon] "He opened the book, without regard to place, and totally ignorant of its design or contents, and before reading half a page, declared that, 'God or the devil has had a hand in that book, for man never wrote it.' He read it twice through in about ten days; and so firm was his conviction of the truth, that he immediately commenced settling his accounts, selling his medicine, and freeing himself from every encumbrance, that he might go to Kirtland, Ohio, seven hundred miles west, the nearest point he could hear a Saint, and give the work a thorough investigation; firmly believing, that if the doctrine was true, God had some greater work for him to do than peddle pills."

Andrew Jenson (LDS Biographical Encyclopedia, 1:53-54)

[Parley P. Pratt's experience of reading the Book of Mormon] "We visited an old Baptist deacon by the name of Hamlin. . . . He began to tell of a book, a strange book, *a very strange book!* . . . I felt a strange interest in the book. . . . Next morning I called at his house, where, for the first time, my eyes beheld the 'Book of Mormon'—that book of books. . . . I opened it with eagerness and read its title page. I then read the testimony of several witnesses in relation to the manner of its being found and translated. After this I commenced its contents by course. I read all day; eating was a burden, I had no desire for food; sleep was a burden when the night came, for I preferred reading to sleep. As I read, the Spirit of the Lord was upon me, and I know and comprehended that the book was true, as plainly and manifestly as a man comprehends and knows that he exists. My joy was full, as it were, and I rejoiced sufficiently more than to pay me for all the sorrows, sacrifices, and toils of my life."

Parley P. Pratt (Autobiography of Parley P. Pratt, pp. 36-37)

"What did Oliver Cowdery (one of the three witnesses to the Book of Mormon) say, after he had been away from the Church years and years? He saw and conversed with the angel, who showed him the plates, and he handled them. He left the Church because he lost the love of the truth; and after he had traveled alone for years, a gentleman walked into his law office and said to him, 'Mr. Cowdery, what do you think of the Book of Mormon now? Do you believe that it is true?' He replied, 'No, sir, I do not.' 'Well,' said the gentleman, 'I thought as much; for I concluded that you had seen the folly of your ways and had resolved to renounce what you once declared to be true.' 'Sir, you mistake me: I do not believe that the Book of Mormon is true; I am past belief on that point, for I know that it is true, as well as I know that you now sit before me.' 'Do you still testify that you saw an angel?' 'Yes, as much as I see you now; and I know the Book of Mormon to be true.'"

Brigham Young (Journal of Discourses 7:55)

"I remember an incident with my own sons. They called me one day to ask if I wouldn't come up to their bedroom. When I got there, I found they had several books on the bed. One of them said to me, 'You know, we have a job with our uncle herding turkeys this summer. I once heard you say that the turkey is the dumbest animal on the farm, so I assume we're going to have time on our hands.' Then they asked me to pick out the books I would recommend. I picked up a little military edition of the Book of Mormon. I said, 'This will fit in your hip pocket.' They said, 'You mean to tell us we're to take only one book?' I said, 'Yes, and you'll learn to love it, and you'll learn to love missionary work'—and they did."

Ezra Taft Benson (Ensign, May 1984, p. 45)

"President Brigham Young received a testimony of the truth of the Book of Mormon after two years of studious consideration. President John Taylor required only three weeks . . . President Wilford Woodruff searched diligently for six years before finding the truth. He finally found it in the teachings and testimony of two Mormon missionaries. President Lorenzo Snow . . . met the Prophet Joseph Smith in 1831. He wrote, 'A light arose in my understanding which has never been extinguished.' . . . [David O. McKay] in his boyhood . . . desired to know. . . . One day, while herding cattle in the foothills near his home, he sought a testimony through prayer. He said: 'I dismounted, threw my reins over my horse's head, and there under a serviceberry bush I prayed that God would declare to me the truth of his revelation to Joseph Smith.' He prayed fervently and sincerely with as much faith as he could find within him. When he finished his prayer, he waited for an answer. Nothing seemed to happen. Disappointed, he rode slowly on, saying to himself at the time, 'No spiritual manifestation has come to me. If I am true to myself, I must say I am just the same 'old boy' that I was before I prayed.' A direct answer to this prayer was many years in coming. While serving a mission in Scotland, Elder McKay received a powerful spiritual manifestation. He later commented, 'Never before had I experienced such an emotion. . . . It was a manifestation for which as a doubting youth I had secretly prayed most earnestly on hillside and in meadow. It was an assurance to me that sincere prayer is answered.' . . . We cannot merely ask in prayer for a testimony and expect it to be given immediately to us. Generally, testimony emerges over time and through life's experiences. . . . Testimonies often come when there is willingness to serve where we are called. They come when a decision is made to strive to be obedient. Testimonies come during efforts to help, lift, and strengthen others. They come from prayer and from studying the scriptures and applying them in our lives. . . . There is no greater search in life that we can embark upon than the quest to gain a testimony of the truth."

Robert D. Hales (Ensign, Nov. 1994, pp. 21-22)

"Sister Celia Cruz Ayala of the Puerto Rico San Juan Mission decided to give the Book of Mormon to a friend. She wrapped it in attractive paper and set out to deliver her present. On the way, she was attacked by a bandit who stole her purse and with it the wrapped copy of the Book of Mormon. A few days later she received this letter:

Mrs. Cruz,

Forgive me, forgive me. You will never know how sorry I am for attacking you. But because of it, my life has changed and will continue to change. That book [the Book of Mormon] has helped me in my life. . . . I am returning your five pesos for I can't spend them. I want you to know that you seemed to have a radiance about you. That light seemed to stop me [from harming you, so] I ran away instead. I want you to know that you will see me again, but when you do, you won't recognize me, for I will be your brother. . . . Here, where I live, I have to find the Lord and go to the church you belong to. The message you wrote in that book brought tears to my eyes. Since Wednesday night I have not been able to stop reading it. I have prayed and asked God to forgive me, [and] I ask you to forgive me. . . . I thought your wrapped gift was something I could sell. [Instead,] it has made me want to make my life over. Forgive me, forgive me, I beg you.

Your absent friend.

Such is the conversion power of the Book of Mormon."

James E. Faust (Ensign, May 1996, pp. 41-42)

"Consider the experience of an early convert, Luman Andros Shurtliff, who went to Kirtland to see if the Church was true and ended up getting baptized. Following baptism, he nearly faltered until the converting power of the Spirit entered his life. 'In the morning I went to the office and bought a Book of Mormon and started [home], intending to get onto the stage road as soon as I could. . . . Soon my thoughts ran thus. I had [been] to Kirtland and was on my return. I knew that some of the neighbors had partially known my feeling and were watching me, and as soon as I got [home] would ask me questions relative to my discoveries, and what I had learned about the [Latter-day Saints]. What could I tell them? I could tell them I had been [baptized] and confirmed a member of the . . . Church, and what evidence have I obtained more than I had years ago? Not any. Have I received the Holy Ghost since I was [baptized]? No more [than] when I was [baptized] before. Did I believe the Book of Mormon? No more [than] I did four years ago. Do I believe that Joseph Smith Jun. is a Prophet of God? No, I do not. At this I was shocked at my situation and began to call on the Lord in earnest. And while I was praying, something came on my head . . . and passed gradually down through my whole system, removing all pain and made me a sound man from the top of my head to the soles of my feet. As soon as this was past, I heard a . . . voice above me say, 'Joseph Smith, Jun. is a Prophet of the Most High God, raised up for the restoration of Israel in these last days, and the Book of Mormon which you hold under your arm is true and brought forth for the restitution of the scattered remnants of Jacob.'. . . I was in the road a sound man praising God.'"

Loren C. Dunn (Ensign, June 1995, p. 25)

LATTER-DAY
Commentary

ON THE BOOK OF MORMON

PROPHETIC INSIGHTS TO AID YOUR STUDY OF THE BOOK OF MORMON

Over many years of painstaking research and collection, Brother Douglas Bassett has compiled and abridged thousands of statements by prophets, General Authorities, scriptural scholars, and others who have unique insights into the marvelous principles and promises contained in the Book of Mormon. They relate to virtually every aspect of this extraordinary book, from historical contexts to doctrinal issues to inspiring stories. Brother Bassett presents this fascinating material by topic within a chronological overview, making the Book of Mormon's pages come to life with the hopes, admonitions, and promises of the gospel of Jesus Christ. This volume, with its wealth of information and inspiration, is the perfect accompaniment for individual, classroom, or family study of the Book of Mormon.

ABOUT THE AUTHOR

K. Douglas Bassett is a graduate of Brigham Young University and received his doctoral degree from the University of New Mexico. He has taught seminary, religion classes at BYU, and is currently an instructor at the Orem Institute of Religion. Brother Bassett and his family enjoy a variety of activities including basketball, racquetball, weightlifting, motorcycles, and horses. He and his wife, the former Arlene Chapman, live in Mona, Utah, where he is currently the instructor for the high priests group in his ward. They are the parents of eight children.